AFRICAN AMERICAN HISTORY DAY BY DAY

AFRICAN AMERICAN HISTORY DAY BY DAY

A REFERENCE GUIDE TO EVENTS

Karen Juanita Carrillo

GREENWOOD

AN IMPRINT OF ABC-CLIO, LLC
Santa Barbara, California • Denver, Colorado • Oxford, England

Library of Congress Cataloging-in-Publication Data

Carrillo, Karen Juanita.
    African American history day by day : a reference guide to events / Karen Juanita Carrillo.
        p. cm.
    Includes bibliographical references and index.
    ISBN 978–1–59884–360–6 (hard copy : alk. paper) — ISBN 978–1–59884–361–3 (ebook)
1. African Americans—History—Chronology. I. Title.
E185.C34   2012
973′.0496073—dc23   2012006083

ISBN: 978–1–59884–360–6
EISBN: 978–1–59884–361–3

16 15 14 13 12   1 2 3 4 5

This book is also available on the World Wide Web as an eBook.
Visit www.abc-clio.com for details.

Greenwood
An Imprint of ABC-CLIO, LLC

ABC-CLIO, LLC
130 Cremona Drive, P.O. Box 1911
Santa Barbara, California 93116-1911

This book is printed on acid-free paper ∞

Manufactured in the United States of America

Contents

Acknowledgments

I want to thank some of the most important people in my life for the love and support they have shown me while writing this book—and during the course of my life.

First, I need to give praises to my partner and very best friend for life, Lisa J. Scott. Lisa has been my biggest cheerleader and we first met while I was in the design stages of this project. I thank God for Lisa every day of my life.

My mother, Dr. Juanita Carrillo, has always been my bastion of support and she was truly the first person I ever remember idolizing—she has always been my model of what it is to be a Black woman. And both my mother and my father, Manuel R. Carrillo, Sr., taught me to always believe in myself and in my abilities, as well as to *always. . . . question. . . . everything*! My brother, Manuel R. Carrillo, Jr., and I were both raised by two awesome individuals who have always pointed to the importance of our heritage in our everyday lives. The more I learn in life, the more I understand how truly great our parents are.

My editor on this project, Kim Kennedy White, has been remarkable. I am indebted to her for her long-standing patience and the kind words of support she sent while I ploughed through finishing this book.

I want to also express my appreciation to my best friends, Alesia C. LoPiano and Manon R. Louiseau, and to my aunts, Joanne Morgan and Lori Garrison. My extended family and friends have been instrumental in making me curious about life, and particularly about Black life.

My fondest childhood memories are of my Uncle Barry Fortney sitting me and my cousins down at family get-togethers and making us answer pop quiz questions about African American history. If you knew the answer, you were golden; but if you didn't, well, it was understood that you had a long road ahead of you and a lot to learn along the way! Since my childhood, I have wanted to know enough to make Uncle Barry, and everybody else, proud. This book is part of my effort to do so.

Introduction

Up until the early twentieth century, most people in the United States had little knowledge about the people of African descent who lived here. If they knew anything, it was limited to the idea that African Americans were the survivors of slavery.

But there has been a long tradition among Black people of knowing our own story.

Among ourselves, we comment on the local, national, and even international people of African descent who have discovered countries, founded schools, won wars, and created movements. If only among ourselves, we have interpreted this information and passed it down at family gatherings and spoken about it in local stores and in friends' living rooms.

Those who have been able to publish and promote facts about our history are widely celebrated. We recognize them for having gone out of their way, taken on an extraordinary risk, and stood up to speak out about a subject that seems to be taboo.

The long list of people who have made Black history a priority includes Ida B. Wells, Arturo Alfonso Schomburg, Malcolm X, Martin Robison Delany, Carter G. Woodson, J. A. Rogers, Edward Wilmot Blyden, Bishop Henry McNeil Turner, Marcus Mosiah Garvey, George Wells Parker, W. E. B. DuBois, John Henrik Clarke, Yosef ben-Jochannan, and Ivan Van Sertima, to name just a few. These are all leaders whose concern about Black history made them overly conscious of the present. Every opportunity to better the prospects for the Black community was taken by each one of them, because they each understood the struggles African Americans have already overcome.

Taking the time to remember and record information about the Black past allows us to understand the complex progress of African Americans—the advancement of a community of people who arrived with next to nothing but their skin color, and made their lives anew. African Americans have been able to recall their African traditions and reinvent who they are.

With *African American History Day by Day: A Reference Guide to Events*, I am trying to add to the tradition of promoting Black culture. This book looks at all of the diasporic Africans who have contributed to Black life in the United States. There is information about us out there—we are a vital part of the creation and maintenance of the United States of America, and this book is meant to give proof of that fact for every single day of the year.

January

January 1

1808

The trans-Atlantic slave trade, begun in 1441, is officially banned within the United States. President Thomas Jefferson signed the Act to Prohibit the Importation of Slaves into any Port or Place Within the Jurisdiction of the United States, From and After the First Day of January, in the Year of our Lord One Thousand Eight Hundred and Eight on March 2, 1807, but the law did not go into effect until New Year's Day of 1808. The law prohibited further importation of enslaved Africans to U.S. territory, but it did not end ownership of Blacks within the United States or put an end to the involvement of U.S. citizens in the trans-Atlantic slave trade. The slave trade (also known by the African Kiswahili words, the Maafa or Maangamizi "the disastrous trade" and as the Middle Passage or "way of death")—which essentially sent goods, such as guns and textiles, from Europe and traded those products for enslaved Africans—continued on illegally to 1888, and some 50 to 75 million Africans were shipped to the Western Hemisphere to be enslaved.

> Excerpt from "An Act to Prohibit the Importation of Slaves into any Port or Place Within the Jurisdiction of the United States . . . ":
>
> *Be it enacted by the Senate and House of Representatives of the United States of America in Congress assembled, That from and after the first day of January, one thousand eight hundred and eight, it shall not be lawful to import or bring into the United States or the territories thereof from any foreign kingdom, place, or country, any negro, mulatto, or person of color, with intent to hold, sell, or dispose of such negro, mulatto, or person of color, as a slave, or to be held to service or labor.*
>
> *Source*: From Blaustein, Albert P., and Robert L. Zangrando. *Civil Rights and African Americans: A*
> *Documentary History*. Evanston, IL: Northwestern University Press, 1991, p. 54.

Books

Davidson, Basil. *The African Slave Trade*. Boston: Little, Brown/Back Bay Books, 1988. Provides insights on how slavery was practiced on the Continent prior its use in the Americas.

Thomas, Hugh. *The Slave Trade: The Story of the Atlantic Slave Trade, 1440–1870*. New York: Simon & Schuster, 1999. Author traces the financing and support systems that created and sustained the trans-Atlantic slave trade.

Websites

African Holocaust Society. Features scholarly articles that try to present a balanced study of the African experience, past and present. http://www.africanholocaust.net/.

Breaking the Silence—Learning about the Transatlantic Slave Trade. UNESCO and Anti-Slavery International—supported site that promotes the teaching and learning about the dangers of slavery and how it can be abolished. http://www.antislavery.org/breakingthesilence/index.shtml.

1831

Abolitionist/journalist William Lloyd Garrison publishes the first issue of his weekly antislavery newspaper, *The Liberator*. It is published consistently in Boston, Massachusetts, until January 1, 1866, after the end of the Civil War and passage of the Thirteenth Amendment abolishing slavery.

> Excerpt from Garrison's first editorial, "To the Public":
>
> *I determined, at every hazard, to lift up the standard of emancipation in the eyes of the nation, within sight of Bunker Hill and in the birthplace of liberty. That standard is now unfurled; and long may it float, unhurt by the spoliation of*

> *time or the missiles of a desperate foe—yea, till every chain be broken, and every bondman set free! Let Southern oppressors tremble—let their secret abettors tremble—let their Northern apologists tremble—let all the enemies of the persecuted blacks tremble.*
>
> *Source: The Liberator, January 1, 1831.*

Books

Garrison, William Lloyd, edited by William E. Cain. *William Lloyd Garrison and the Fight against Slavery: Selections from the Liberator.* New York: Bedford Books of St. Martin's Press, 1994. Looks at U.S. society leading up to the Civil War and how that time period affected William Lloyd Garrison and his aggressive efforts to end African slavery.

Mayer, Henry. *All on Fire: William Lloyd Garrison and the Abolition of American Slavery.* New York: W.W. Norton, 2008. This biography of Garrison shows him as a strident abolitionist who was regularly at odds with more moderate antislavery advocates.

Websites

Biography.com. William Lloyd Garrison biography. http://www.biography.com/search/article.do?id=9307251.

Spartacus Educational. William Lloyd Garrison biography. http://www.spartacus.schoolnet.co.uk/USASgarrison.htm.

1863

President Abraham Lincoln issues the Emancipation Proclamation, which declares freedom for those enslaved Africans still held in any of the rebel Confederate States of America.

> **Excerpt from the Emancipation Proclamation:**
> *That on the first day of January, in the year of our Lord one thousand eight hundred and sixty-three, all persons held as slaves within any State or designated part of a State, the people whereof shall then be in rebellion against the United*

> *States, shall be then, thenceforward, and forever free; and the Executive Government of the United States, including the military and naval authority thereof, will recognize and maintain the freedom of such persons, and will do no act or acts to repress such persons, or any of them, in any efforts they may make for their actual freedom.*
>
> *Source: The Emancipation Proclamation. http://www.archives.gov/exhibits/featured_documents/emancipation_proclamation/transcript.html.*

Books

Guelzo, Allen C. *Lincoln's Emancipation Proclamation: The End of Slavery in America.* Author examines the importance of the Emancipation Proclamation and shows how and why it was written.

January, Brendan. *The Emancipation Proclamation.* Danbury, CT: Scholastic Inc.: Children's Press, 1998. Tells the story of the Emancipation Proclamation, which led to the passage of the Thirteenth Amendment and discusses the role of President Abraham Lincoln in freeing enslaved Africans.

Websites

The National Endowment for the Humanities looks at why the Emancipation Proclamation is so important. http://edsitement.neh.gov/view_lesson_plan.asp?id=290.

The National Archives has a digitized version of the original Emancipation Proclamation. http://www.archives.gov/exhibits/featured_documents/emancipation_proclamation/transcript.html.

1915

John Henrik Clarke, Pan-African historian, is born in Union Springs, Alabama, to poor sharecroppers. As a young boy, Clarke recognized that many of the Bible stories he had heard seemed to take place in Africa yet never mentioned the involvement of Black people. This led him to search for a true understanding of African history. He founded the African Heritage Studies Association in 1968, and in 1969 he became founding chairman of the

Department of Africana and Puerto Rican/ Latino Studies at New York City's Hunter College. In 1996, actor Wesley Snipes executive-produced a documentary about the life of Clarke, entitled *John Henrik Clarke: A Great and Mighty Walk*. Clarke died on July 16, 1998.

> Clarke wrote often about the importance of education and its power:
>
> *If the oppressed understood how power is maintained they would know that powerful people cannot afford to educate powerless people for fear that they will ultimately take their power away from them.*
>
> Source: Clarke, John Henrik. *Africans at the Crossroads: Notes for an African World Revolution.* Lawrenceville, NJ: Africa World Press, Inc., & The Red Sea Press, Inc., 1992, p. 331.

Books

Clarke, John Henrik. *Harlem Voices from the Soul of Black America,* 2nd edition. Brooklyn, NY: A & B Book. Distributors Inc., September 1993. Author looks at the work of some of Harlem's most famous writers.

Clarke, John Henrik. *My Life in Search of Africa.* Lawrenceville, NJ: Third World Press, February 1, 1999. In this biographical work, Clarke talks about how he became a scholar of Black history and African traditions.

Multimedia

John Henrik Clarke: A Great and Mighty Walk. DVD produced by Amen-Ra Films/Black Dot Media, directed by St. Claire Bourne, 1996. 90 minutes. This historical film portrays Dr. Clarke's life and work and features many of the scholars' own recollections.

Websites

The National Black United Front maintains the John Henrik Clarke Virtual Museum Website. Provides biographical information and examines many of Clarke's writings. http://www.nbufront.org/MastersMuseums/JHClarke/JHCvmuseum.html.

The Schomburg Center for Research in Black Culture has a Legacy Exhibition: John Henrik Clarke section available online. Showcases John Henrik Clarke's collection of important African and African descendant manuscripts and memorabilia. http://www.nypl.org/research/sc/WEBEXHIB/legacy/imgins15.htm.

Cornell University sponsors the John Henrik Clarke Africana Library that features research in Africana studies and is named in honor of Clarke, who taught Black History at Cornell. http://www.library.cornell.edu/africana/clarke/.

Also Noteworthy

1854

Lincoln University (http://www.lincoln.edu) is chartered in Oxford, Pennsylvania. Originally known as Ashmun Institute, the school's name was changed to Lincoln University in 1866, in honor of the assassinated president. Lincoln University is one of the oldest Black colleges in the nation; some of its famous alumni include Harlem Renaissance poet Langston Hughes, Supreme Court Justice Thurgood Marshall, and Kwame Nkrumah, the first president of Ghana.

1916

Historian Carter G. Woodson founds the *Journal of Negro History* as a quarterly research journal published by the Association for the Study of African American Life and History. In 2002, the *Journal of Negro History* became the *Journal of African American History* (http://jaah.asalh.net/jaah.htm).

1923

White-led riot leads to the murders of seven and the displacement of an entire community of nearly 1,000 African Americans in Rosewood, Florida. After a white woman from Sumner, Florida, claimed to have been assaulted by a Black man, whites rioted in this Central Florida town from January 1 through 8; Rosewood's African Americans were forced to hide in the nearby swamps to save their lives.

1963

Centennial of the signing of the Emancipation Proclamation.

January 2

1893

Abolitionist Frederick Douglass speaks at the Chicago World's Fair—the "World's Columbian Exposition"—to commemorate the 400th anniversary of Christopher Columbus's arrival in the Americas. Since Columbus had visited the island shared by Haiti and the Dominican Republic, the opening of the Fair's Haitian Pavilion was a symbolic kickoff to the Fair. Douglass had served as U.S. Minister to Haiti from 1889 to 1891 and spoke during the dedication of the Haitian Pavilion.

> Douglass's speech urged his audience to applaud Haiti for having fought for its freedom and to understand why Black people find the island republic an inspiration:
>
> *In just vindication of Haiti . . . I can speak of her, not only words of admiration, but words of gratitude as well. She has grandly served the cause of universal human liberty. We should not forget that the freedom you and I enjoy to-day; that the freedom that eight hundred thousand colored people enjoy in the British West Indies; the freedom that has come to the colored race the world over, is largely due to the brave stand taken by the black sons of Haiti ninety years ago. When they struck for freedom, they built better than they knew. Their swords were not drawn and could not be drawn simply for themselves alone. They were linked and interlinked with their race, and striking for their freedom, they struck for the freedom of every black man in the world.*
>
> *Source*: Lecture on Haiti: The Haitian Pavilion Dedication Ceremonies. http://haitiforever.com/ windowsonhaiti/fdouglass1.shtml or http://the louvertureproject.org/index.php?title=Frederick _Douglass_lecture_on_Haiti_%281893%29.

Books

McFeely, William S. *Frederick Douglass.* New York: W. W. Norton & Company, 1995. Biography shows how Douglass worked alongside activists like Ida B. Wells to insist on acknowledgment of Black progress at the 1893 World's Fair.

Sweeney, Fionnghuala. *Frederick Douglass and the Atlantic World.* Chicago: University of Chicago Press, 2007. Examines how traveling and living abroad affected the political and intellectual understanding Frederick Douglass had of himself as a person of African descent in the Americas.

Websites

The Electronic Encyclopedia of Chicago. Entry on Haiti notes the importance of Douglass's speech at the 1893 World's Fair. http:// encyclopedia.chicagohistory.org/pages/ 1495.html.

Library of Congress. Facsimile of Douglass's handwritten speech at the Haitian Pavilion dedication ceremonies. http://memory.loc .gov/cgi-bin/query/P?mfd:8:./temp/~ammem _3RrF.

1915

Historian John Hope Franklin is born in Rentiesville, Oklahoma. After attending Booker T. Washington High School in Tulsa, Oklahoma, Franklin went to college at Fisk University and earned a doctorate in history in 1941 from Harvard University. Franklin focused on the history of the southern United States and on the contributions African Americans have made to the development of the United States in works such as *From Slavery to Freedom* (1947), *The Militant South: 1800–1860* (1956), *Reconstruction after the Civil War* (1961), *Color and Race* (1968), *Racial Equality in America* (1976), *Race and History* (1989), and *The Color Line* (1993). Franklin served as president of the Organization of American Historians, the American Historical Association, and the Southern Historical Association, and was awarded the Presidential Medal of Freedom. He was appointed as President Bill Clinton's adviser on race in 1997.

> **Excerpt from the autobiography of John Hope Franklin:**
>
> With the appearance of each new institution or industry, racism would rear its ugly head again. When the age of the automobile made its debut, there was the question of whether African Americans should be given the opportunity to acquire the skills necessary to find work within that industry. It was the same with the advent of the computer age. More than one company dragged its feet when it came to making certain that young people on "both sides of the track" had an opportunity to acquire the skills necessary to be successful participants in the new scientific revolution. Indeed, the expansion of numerous American industries caused debates or at least discussions regarding the abilities of African Americans to cope with new developments, whatever they were. Even at the end of the twentieth century, many Americans continued to debate nineteenth-century racial theories regarding the abilities of blacks to see at night, to make accurate calculations, and to learn foreign languages. These debates ranged from discussions having to do with the effect of African Americans on the growth of the gross national product to their ability to resist new diseases or their capacity to adjust to new educational or cultural developments. Throughout a life spent at the intersection of scholarship and public service, I have been painfully aware that superstitions and quaint notions of biological and even moral differences between blacks and whites continue to affect race relations in the United States—even into the twenty-first century.
>
> Source: From John Hope Franklin. *Mirror to America: The Autobiography of John Hope Franklin.* New York: Farrar, Straus and Giroux, 2006, p. 5.

Books

Franklin, Buck Colbert, John Hope Franklin, and John Whittington Franklin. *My Life and an Era: The Autobiography of Buck Colbert Franklin.* Baton Rouge: Louisiana State University Press, 1997. John Hope Franklin and John Whittington Franklin use the edited notes from a book first written by Buck Colbert Franklin, John Hope's father, to tell the story of what life was like for an African American in the Western Indian Territory (Oklahoma) at the dawn of the twentieth century.

Franklin, John Hope. *Mirror to America: The Autobiography of John Hope Franklin.* New York: Farrar, Straus and Giroux, 2005. Franklin recalls some of the major events of the twentieth century that pushed for Civil Rights for African Americans.

Websites

John Hope Franklin helped establish the John Hope Franklin Research Center at Duke University, which is a repository of documentation and promotes education about African diaspora history. http://library.duke.edu/special collections/franklin/.

C-Span's "Book-TV" featured a three-hour interview with Franklin, available at http://www.c-spanvideo.org/program/194400-1.

1969

The play *To Be Young, Gifted and Black* premiers at New York City's off-Broadway Cherry Lane Theater. Produced by the actor/activist Harry Belafonte, the work featured Cicely Tyson and was an adaptation of the writings of playwright/journalist Lorraine Hansberry, who died of cancer at age 34 on January 12, 1965. *To Be Young, Gifted and Black: An Informal Autobiography* was released as a book in 1970. The play's title also inspired Nina Simone to write a song, "To Be Young, Gifted and Black," which became a rhythm and blues hit in the 1970s and both a Civil Rights and Black Consciousness Movement anthem.

> **Excerpt from Hansberry's autobiography:**
>
> . . . I wish to live because life has within it that which is good, that which is beautiful, and that which is love. Therefore, since I have known all of

these things, I have found them to be reason enough and—I wish to live. Moreover, because this is so, I wish others to live for generations and generations and generations and generations.

Source: From Robert Nemiroff. *To Be Young, Gifted and Black: An Informal Autobiography.* New York: Signet, 1970, p. 11.

Books

Brown-Guillory, Elizabeth. *Their Place on the Stage: Black Women Playwrights in America.* Westport, CT: Praeger, 1990. Describing her as an "artist/activist," the author notes that Hansberry grew up in a world of intellectual and political activism, and the progressive ideas she was reared with came through in her work.

hooks, bell. *Remembered Rapture: The Writer at Work.* New York: Henry Holt, 1999. Feminist writer, bell hooks, recalls the strength of Hansberry's writings and how plays like *To Be Young, Gifted and Black* helped hooks to choose her own road as a writer and intellectual.

Websites

Playwrights' database lists all of the details of Hansberry's plays. http://www.doollee.com/ PlaywrightsH/hansberry-lorraine.html.

Women of Color/Women of Words features a biography of Hansberry. http://www.scils .rutgers.edu/~cybers/hansberry2.html.

Also Noteworthy

1624

William Tucker, the first recorded child of African descent in what is now the United States, is born to Antoney and Isabella Tucker in Jamestown, Virginia.

January 3

1927

Jamaican American Harold George Belafonete (later, Belafonte), Jr., is born in Harlem, New York, but raised partly in Jamaica and partly in the United States. As an adult Harry Belafonte won world renown for his calypso singing and social activism. With the release of his 1956 album *Calypso*—which featured "Day-O (Banana Boat Song)"—Belafonte became the first U.S. recording artist to sell over 1 million albums. Belafonte's celebrity led him to work closely with Martin Luther King, Jr., during the 1950s and 1960s. Belafonte provided financial support to King and his family, who struggled in living solely on King's salary; bailed King out of the Birmingham City Jail; raised thousands of dollars to support the 1964 Freedom Rides; and was crucial in organizing the 1963 March on Washington.

In 1993, Belafonte talked about how difficult it had been to work as an artist-activist:

...Harry Belafonte...shared anecdotes about their relationship. Belafonte commented about the days when he and [Sidney] Poitier struggled to make it during "bleak, hard, difficult" times. ... "There were not too many things there for us to grab on to," Belafonte said, making reference to the role models that novices need for guidance. However, he continued, "We were fortunate to have Paul Robeson. We were very fortunate to have W.E.B. DuBois. We were very fortunate to have Marian Anderson ... We were very fortunate that we had each other."

Source: From Felecia Piggott McMillan. *The North Carolina Black Repertory Company: 25 Marvtastic Years.* Greensboro, NC: Open Hand Publishing, LLC, 2005, pp. 88–89.

Book

Fogelson, Genia. *Harry Belafonte: Singer & Actor.* New York: African American Book Company, 2008. Biography depicts Belafonte's work as a recording artist and a movie actor.

Multimedia

Richardson, Julieanna L. *An Evening with Harry Belafonte & Danny Glover.* New York: Carousel Film & Video, 2003. 2001 interview conducted by Belafonte's friend and fellow actor/activist, Danny Glover, that examines Belafonte's life and film career.

Websites

Harry Belafonte Official Myspace page. http://www.myspace.com/harrybelafonte.

"We Have Got to Bring Corporate America To Its Knees" is Belafonte's acceptance speech in San Francisco for the 2004 Human Rights Award from the group Global Exchange, where he spoke of his life in the struggle to end racism and poverty. http://www.democracynow.org/2004/6/15/we_have_got_to_bring_corporate.

1971

African American House of Representative members of the 77th Congress founded the Congressional Black Caucus (CBC). After originally forming in 1969 and calling themselves the "Democratic Select Committee," in 1971 the group took its present name and began with 13 founding members, including Shirley Chisholm (New York), Louis Stokes (Ohio), William L. Clay (Missouri), George Collins (Illinois), John Conyers Jr. (Michigan), Ronald Dellums (California), Charles Diggs (Michigan), Augustus Hawkins (California), Ralph Metcalfe (Illinois), Parren Mitchell (Maryland), Robert Nix (Pennsylvania), and Charles Rangel (New York). Walter Fauntroy served as a delegate from the District of Columbia.

The Congressional Black Caucus was formed in 1969 when the 13 black members of the U.S. House of Representatives joined together to strengthen their efforts to address the legislative concerns of black and minority citizens. African-American representatives had increased in number from six in 1966 to nine, following the 1969 elections. Those members believed that a black caucus in Congress, speaking with a single voice, would provide political influence and visibility far beyond their numbers.

Source: From Congressional Black Caucus— History & Agenda. http://thecongressionalblack caucus.lee.house.gov/history_details.html.

Books

Copson, Raymond W. *The Congressional Black Caucus and Foreign Policy.* Hauppauge, NY: Nova Publishers, 2003. Looks at CBC's influence on foreign policy toward countries with large Black populations, particularly South Africa and Haiti.

Swain, Carol M. *Black Faces, Black Interests: The Representation of African Americans in Congress.* Lanham, MD: Rowman & Littlefield, 2006. Examines the work of African American politicians to see how they affect the lives of Black and white constituents.

Websites

The Congressional Black Caucus. Gives information about the history and agenda of the organization. http://www.thecongressional blackcaucus.com/.

The Congressional Black Caucus Foundation. The Congressional Black Caucus Foundation works to implement the programs and policies of the CBC. http://www.cbcfinc.org.

January 4

1943

William Levi Dawson is elected United States Representative of the state of Illinois. Born on April 26, 1886, to Levi and Rebecca Kendrick Dawson in Albany, Georgia, Dawson was raised in Georgia but moved to Illinois after finding he had little opportunity in the South. After marrying and becoming a lawyer, Dawson ran for Congress as a Democrat and was elected to represent Chicago's South Side on his third attempt. He served from January 3, 1943, until his death on November 9, 1970.

Dawson was reelected to the House 13 times. During his tenure he was the senior black member of that body, and until Edward Brooke took his seat in the U.S. Senate in 1967, he was the highest elected black official in the nation. In 1949 he became, by virtue of seniority, the chairman of the committee on government operations, thus making him the first black chairman of a permanent congressional committee. Despite these high-level positions, he was not a flamboyant leader, preferring instead to work behind the scenes for small victories that eventually added up to something large. As committee chairman, he worked to end racial discrimination among defense contractors. He also opposed regressive income taxes, which hurt poor African Americans, and the poll tax, which kept African Americans from voting.

Source: From Charles W. Carey. *African-American Political Leaders*. New York, NY: Infobase Publishing, 2004, p. 72.

Books

Clay, William L. and Malaika Adero. *Just Permanent Interests: Black Americans in Congress, 1870–1992.* Former Congressman William L. Clay demonstrates how African American politicians have kept the interests of their Black constituents in the forefront.

Manning, Christopher. *William L. Dawson and the Limits of Black Electoral Leadership.* DeKalb, IL: Northern Illinois University Press, 2009. Author looks at Dawson's political career. Although he was not part of the Civil Rights era, Dawson was instrumental in progressing Black politics in the decades before the 1960s.

Websites

The Biographical Directory of the United States Congress Website has a biography of Dawson's political life. http://bioguide.congress.gov/scripts/biodisplay.pl?index=d000158.

Dawson is profiled on Black Americans in Congress. http://baic.house.gov/member-profiles/profile.html?intID=27.

January 5

1911

Ten African American students at Indiana University's predominately white campus in Bloomington, Indiana, founded the first Black Greek–letter fraternity in the United States: Kappa Alpha Psi Fraternity, Inc. The fraternity's founders are Elder Watson Diggs, Bryan K. Armstrong, John M. Lee, Henry T. Asher, Marcus P. Blakemore, Guy Levis

Grant, Paul W. Caine, George Edmonds, Ezra D. Alexander, and Edward G. Irvin. Initially adopted and incorporated as Kappa Alpha Nu, the name was later changed to Kappa Alpha Psi (ΚΑΨ).

Achievement. That is the foundation of Kappa Alpha Psi Fraternity, Inc. When Founders Elder Diggs and Byron Kenneth Armstrong ventured to the Indiana University campus, after having become friends at Howard University in 1910, they realized that life on a predominately white campus would not be easy. . . .

Elder Diggs gathered nine African American men, and soon Alpha Omega was formed. This organization was formed to hold the men together as research began on forming a permanent African American Fraternity. An interesting thing began as the students worked to form a Fraternity. The sense of isolation left, and friendships were created. This was very important as weeks could pass without African American students seeing another African American student on the Indiana University campus.

Source: From Lawrence C. Ross, Jr. *The Divine Nine: The History of African American Fraternities and Sororities.* New York: Kensington Publishing Corporation, 2002, pp. 46–47.

Books

Anderson, Walter "Big Walt." *Sweet Nupe: An Unauthorized History of Kappa Alpha Psi.* Arlington, TX: Milk & Honey Pub., 2002. Anderson examines the history of the famed Black fraternity and writes about some of the secrets the organization holds dear.

Crump, William L. *The Story of Kappa Alpha Psi: A History of the Beginning and Development of a College Greek Letter Organization, 1911–1991,* 4th edition. Philadelphia, PA: Kappa Alpha Psi Fraternity, 1991. Author depicts the founding and growth of Kappa Alpha Psi Fraternity.

Websites

The official Website of Kappa Alpha Psi Fraternity, Inc., provides information about the fraternity's past and present. http://www.KappaAlphaPsi1911.com.

The Alpha Chapter of Kappa Alpha Psi Fraternity, Inc., is the founding chapter of the

Greek-letter organization. http://www
.alphachapter1911.com/.

1975

The Wiz, an African American adaptation of
L. Frank Baum's *The Wonderful Wizard of
Oz*, opens on Broadway, featuring the
singer/actress Stephanie Mills. The musical
won seven Tony Awards and had a four-
year run of more than 1,600 performances.

> By the mid-1970s Blacks themselves were adapt-
> ing white musicals. It had been assumed that
> The Wizard of Oz (1939 film) could not be remade
> because the American psyche had canonized Judy
> Garland in the role of Dorothy. On 5 January 1975,
> the black version opened to mixed reviews, includ-
> ing a negative one from the New York Times; it
> seemed a self-fulfilling prophecy that "somewhere
> over the rainbow" was reserved for white people.
> Many assumed The Wiz to be doomed; however,
> the producer, Twentieth Century-Fox, wooed black
> suburban and church audiences with television
> and radio ads, designating The Wiz as a satire
> that white critics did not understand. Bus loads
> of African Americans arrived at Broadway's Majes-
> tic Theatre. The musical was not a remake of the
> Garland version, but a genuine black cultural
> event with music by Charlie Smalls, choreography
> by George Faison, and costumes and direction by
> Geoffrey Holder. The Wiz ran for 1,672 perfor-
> mances, winning seven Tony Awards (including
> best musical) and five Drama Desk Awards.
>
> Source: From Errol Hill and James Vernon Hatch.
> A History of African American Theatre. New
> York, NY: Cambridge University Press, 2003,
> pp. 379–380.

Book

Smalls, Charlie, Lyman Frank Baum, and William Ferdinand Brown. *The Wiz: Adapted from
The Wonderful Wizard of Oz by L. Frank Baum.*
New York: Samuel French, Inc., 1979. The
original script and score for the musical are
available in this book.

Multimedia

Anobile, Richard J. *The Wiz—The Super Soul
Musical: Original Cast Album (1975 Broadway
Cast) [Cast Recording].* New York, NY: Atlantic Records Group/WEA International Inc.,
1975. Audio CD.

Websites

The official site for the musical, *The Wiz*, features the initial newspaper reviews of the
musical and links to the song recordings used
in the play. http://thewiztheatrecompany.com.
The Guide to Musical Theatre has a synopsis
of the musical and shows how it was intended
to be performed. http://www.guidetomusical
theatre.com/shows_w/wiz.htm.

January 6

1869

Classes begin at the Howard University Law
Department—which soon became the
Howard University Law School—the first
African American law school in the nation.
Professor John Mercer Langston, a former
activist in the antislavery movement,
founded the school.

> [Thurgood] Marshall wanted to attend the Uni-
> versity of Maryland Law School, which was only
> ten minutes from his home, but did not even
> bother to apply, because of its segregationist poli-
> cies—Maryland had graduated only two black
> students in its entire history. A disappointed
> Marshall was forced to commute forty miles to
> Howard University Law School, in Washington,
> D.C. This was, nonetheless, a fortunate turn of
> events that would alter the course of race relations
> in America. It was at Howard that Marshall met
> his future mentor Charles Hamilton Houston.
> Marshall graduated at the top of his law school
> class in 1933.
>
> Source: From Charles J. Ogletree. All Deliberate
> Speed: Reflections on the First Half-Century of
> Brown v. Board of Education. New York: W. W.
> Norton & Company, 2004, p. 136.

Books

McNeil, Genna Rae. *Groundwork: Charles Hamilton Houston and the Struggle for Civil Rights.* Philadelphia, PA: University of Pennsylvania Press, 1984. Author looks at the influence Charles Hamilton Houston had on his law students, among them the future Supreme Court Justice Thurgood Marshall. Houston served as the dean of the Howard University Law School.

Schmoke, Kurt L., Seth M. Kronemer, and Jacqueline C. Young. *A Legacy of Defending the Constitution: Howard University School of Law: 1869–2009.* Washington, DC: Howard University School of Law, 2009. Details the founding and teachings of the school and looks at its alumni's nationwide influence.

Websites

Howard University School of Law programs and contact are on its Website. http://www.law.howard.edu.

In his online article, *Brown Fifty Years Later: A Brief History of Brown, HUSL's Role in It, and Its Impact,* Professor Steven D. Jamar examines the role Howard University's School of Law and its alumni played in the most famous school desegregation case, *Brown v. Board of Education.* http://www.brownat50.org/brownChrono/BrownHistory.html.

Also Noteworthy

1966

Harold R. Perry is named auxiliary bishop of New Orleans, making him the nation's first Roman Catholic bishop of African descent in the twentieth century.

January 7

1890

William B. Purvis receives U.S. Patent No. 419,065 for his improvements to the fountain pen. Purvis's patent helped reduce ink spills from the fountain pen and allowed the pen to retain its ink for a longer time. Purvis also invented a self-inking hand stamp, several devices for electric railroads, machines to make paper bags, and a bag fastener.

> A study of the list disclosed the fact that the African American inventor has very often, like his white brother, caught the spirit of invention, and not being contented with a single success, has frequently been led to exert his energies along many different lines of inventions.
>
> Elijah McCoy, of Detroit, Mich., headed the list with twenty-eight patents, relating particularly to lubricating appliances for engines both stationary and locomotive, but covering also a large variety of other subjects. The next was Granville T. Woods, of Cincinnati, whose inventions were confined almost exclusively to electricity and force. Mr. W. B. Purvis, of Philadelphia, came next with sixteen patents relating especially to paper bag machinery, but including a few other subjects as well. Mr. F. J. Ferrell, of New York, had ten patents on valves adapted for a variety of uses. Then came ex-Congressman Geo. W. Murray of South Carolina, with eight patents on agricultural implements. Mr. Henry Creamer had seven patents on steam traps, and more than a dozen among the number had patented as many as five different inventions.
>
> Source: From Donald Wilson and Jane Wilson. *The Pride of African American History.* Bloomington, IN: 1st Books Library, 2003, p. 14.

Books

McKissack, Pat and Fredrick McKissack. *African-American Inventors: A Proud Heritage.* Brookfield, CT: Millbrook Press, 1994. Authors look at the inventions and discoveries made by African Americans.

Sluby, Patricia Carter. *The Inventive Spirit of African Americans: Patented Ingenuity.* Westport, CT: Greenwood Publishing Group, 2004. The author looks at the patented products created by African Americans throughout history.

Websites

The Black Inventor Online Museum provides brief descriptions of inventions made by people of African descent. http://www.blackinventor.com.

Black Inventors . . . Extraordinary Inventions! Features a list of Black inventors and their inventions. http://www.littleafrica.com/resources/inventors.htm.

1891

The novelist Zora Neale Hurston is born in Notasulga, Alabama, and raised in Eatonville, Florida, the nation's first town incorporated by people of African descent. Hurston had some renown during her lifetime, but after her death she was truly appreciated for her writings like the novel *Their Eyes Were Watching God* (1937), her autobiographical *Dust Tracks on a Road* (1942), and her book of African American folklore, *Mules and Men* (1935).

*Hurston's peak had been extraordinarily productive, however. She wrote and published six of her seven books between 1933 and 1945—a span of less than ten years. All three of the novels she wrote during this time—*Jonah's Gourd Vine, Their Eyes Were Watching God, and Moses, Man of the Mountain—were remarkable. If Hurston had done nothing except publish these three novels over the course of her life—let alone in one decade—she would have earned bragging rights for a distinguished career. But Zora had done so much more and still felt she had even more to do.*

Source: From Valerie Boyd. *Wrapped in Rainbows: the Life of Zora Neale Hurston.* New York, NY: Simon & Schuster, 2003, p. 419.

Books

Hurston, Zora Neale. *Their Eyes Were Watching God.* Saint Paul, MN: EMC/Paradigm Pub., 2004. Hurston's novel tells the story of Janie Crawford, an African American woman finding her cultural, spiritual, and sexual identity in the 1930s.

Patterson, Tiffany Ruby. *Zora Neale Hurston and a History of Southern Life.* Philadelphia, PA: Temple University Press, 2005. Book looks at the culture and traditions of the early twentieth-century southern African American communities that influenced Hurston's writing.

Websites

The official Zora Neale Hurston Website gives information about her life and work and provides material for teachers who want to teach Hurston's books. http://zoranealehurston.com/.

The Library of Congress has four of Zora Neale Hurston's plays online. http://www.memory.loc.gov/ammem/znhhtml/znhhome.html.

1974

Maynard Holbrook Jackson, Jr., takes office as the first African American mayor of Atlanta, Georgia. Jackson's great-grandparents had been enslaved yet he became the first Black to be elected mayor of any U.S. southern city since the Reconstruction era. Born in Dallas, Texas, Maynard attended and graduated from Morehouse College with a Bachelor of Arts degree in political science and history when he was just 18 years old. After receiving his law degree cum laude from North Carolina Central University Law School, he became Atlanta's first African American vice mayor in 1959 and served as mayor of Atlanta for three terms, beginning in 1974. After leaving office in 1982, Maynard was reelected in 1989 and remained in office until 1994.

Atlanta mayor Maynard Jackson exemplified the priorities of Black political leadership. . . . The Voting Rights Act energized the Atlanta black community and heightened its political consciousness. In addition, by the late 1960s blacks comprised 41 percent of the city's population. In the 1969 mayoral campaign, an outsider, Jewish businessman Sam Masssell, won the election with a coalition of blacks and white liberals. Maynard Jackson became vice mayor. By 1973, Massell had managed to alienate both of these constituencies and Jackson won the office, carrying 95 percent of the black vote and 17.5 percent of the white electorate. Though Jackson supported the economic development objectives of his predecessors, particularly the expansion of Hartsfield International Airport, he was determined to enlist a greater role for blacks. Accordingly he set aside 20 percent of the city contracts on the airport expansion for minority firms. In addition Jackson informed bank presidents that evidence of dis-crimination in loans and promotions to minorities would result in the removal of city funds to banks in Birmingham (an event that would have left Atlanta's bankers perpetually red-faced). Jackson also improved service levels in black neighbor-hoods and removed the white chief of police who had been a source of friction between blacks and city hall. Although business leaders chafed under what they considered the mayor's arrogance, voters of both races generally approved his administration. Blacks appreciated his forthright-ness and the substantive gains in jobs and serv-ices, and whites, especially those in the revitalized inner-city neighborhoods such as Inman Park and Ansley Park, liked his emphasis on services rather than on the architectural aggrandizement and highway construction that marked previous administrations. Jackson won a landslide re-election victory in 1977.

Source: From David R. Goldfield. *Black, White, and Southern: Race Relations and Southern Cul-ture, 1940 to the Present.* Baton Rouge, LA: LSU Press, 1991, pp. 176–177.

Books

Burman, Stephen. *The Black Progress Question: Explaining the African-American Predicament.* Thousand Oaks, CA: Sage Publications, 1995. Book features a segment on the rise of Maynard Jackson and what his political posi-tion meant in terms of African American progress.

Grady-Willis, Winston A. *Challenging U.S. Apartheid: Atlanta and Black Struggles for Human Rights, 1960–1977.* Durham, NC: Duke University Press, 2006. Book examines the methods African American activists and poli-ticians used to gain political power in Atlanta. This work particularly looks at the initial 1977 term of Maynard Jackson, Atlanta's first Black mayor.

Websites

Racematters.org has posted the June 24, 2003, obituary of Maynard Jackson. http://www.racematters.org/maynardjacksonjr.htm.

Atlantalife.com looks at Maynard Jackson's life before, during, and after his service as Atlanta's first Black mayor. http://www.atlantalife.com/main.asp?urh=js_MaynardJackson.

January 8

1811

Charles Deslondes, a free person of color who had taken work as a laborer on the Andry plantation in St. Charles and St. James, Louisiana, leads an uprising against African slavery. Deslondes' revolt began in St. John the Baptist Parish, and he led an estimated 200 to 500 rebels on a march down the coast of the Mississippi river, toward New Orleans. The rebels got as far as St. Charles Parish before being turned back. As the group traveled, they killed two white people and burned down crops and five plantations. By January 11, the rebellion was put down: many rebel slaves were killed in battle; others were tried and later exe-cuted. Charles Deslondes was tortured: his hands were chopped off and he was later burned to death. Although the rebellion was quickly ended, the Deslondes rebellion is known as the largest slave rebellion in U.S. history.

...In 1811, the biggest revolt in the history of slavery in the United States took place on the German Coast in the parishes along the Missis-sippi River north of New Orleans. Historians have long tried to portray Louisiana slaves as incompe-tent, content, and passive, attributing all unrest among them to "outside influences." Charles Gayarrée, a white Creole historian of the nine-teenth century, claimed that Charles Deslondes, the main leader of the 1811 Revolt, was a free man of color from Haiti. But he was actually a mulatto Louisiana Creole slave. On October 15, 1795, he was listed as a Creole mulatto, aged 18, inventoried among the slaves of his deceased master Deslondes.

Source: From Gwendolyn, Midlo Hall. "The Franco-African Peoples of Haiti and Louisiana: Population, Language, Culture, Religion, and Revolution," in *Revolutionary Freedoms: A History of Survival, Strength and Imagination in Haiti* by Cécile Accilien, Jessica Adams, Elmide Méléance, and Ulrick Jean-Pierre. Coconut Creek, FL: Educa Vision Inc., 2006, p. 44.

Books

Ford, Lacy K. *Deliver Us from Evil: The Slavery Question in the Old South.* New York, NY: Oxford University Press, 2009. Book looks at how Southern whites tried to justify African slavery and how they often discredited legitimate revolts such as the one led by Charles Deslondes.

Loewen, James W. *Lies Across America: What Our Historic Sites Get Wrong.* New York, NY: Simon & Schuster, 2007. Loewen notes the 1811 rebellion and how it remains unacknowledged in local Louisianan history.

Websites

The Deslondes Revolt and the background information leading to it is commemorated at http://1811slaverevolt.com/.

The article "Drums in African American History," on the United Nations web link Breaking the Silence, Beating the Drum describes the importance of Deslondes' rebellion in pushing for an end to African slavery. http://www.un.org/en/slavery/drumsaa.shtml.

Also Noteworthy

1886

Timothy Drew is born in North Carolina. After a religious awakening, Drew changes his name to Noble Drew Ali and in 1913 founds The Moorish Science Temple of America in Newark, New Jersey. The Moorish Science Temple of America later moved its operations to Chicago, Illinois.

January 9

1866

The Nashville, Tennessee-based Fisk Free Colored School, which would become Fisk University, holds its first classes on January 9, 1866, in former Union army barracks in Nashville, Tennessee; the historically Black college (on the list of HBCUs) was incorporated on August 22, 1867. The school was named for General Clinton Bowen Fisk of the Kentucky-Tennessee Freedmen's Bureau; Fisk had provided the former army barracks that housed the original school. The school became internationally known when it organized the Fisk Jubilee Singers in 1867 and sponsored their tours of the United States and Europe in 1871 to raise money for the university. The Fisk Jubilee Singers helped popularize traditional African American gospel music.

. . . Just five years after opening its doors, the university was in such a financial bind many expected its closure; however, with the help of a professor and a band of students the university was saved. In 1871, Professor George L. White and nine students left Nashville to perform concerts throughout the United States in hopes of securing enough funds for the salvation of the newly formed university. Initial responses included ridicule and scorn, mostly due to the fact that the group of five women and four men were not performing in the "slap-happy" tradition of the minstrel show. In response to the atmosphere of despair, Professor White decided to name the group "Jubilee Singers," in reference to the biblical year of Jubilee.

Soon afterwards, the attitudes of whites began to change, and suddenly the reactions of the crowds were replaced with brick applause and standing ovations. The group's first official tour in the United States, which lasted three months and ended with a performance at the White House for President Ulysses S. Grant, not only brought national acclaim, it literally saved the university. Due to such recognition, subsequent tours both nationally and internationally would raise funds for the construction of the university's first permanent building, Jubilee Hall. Jubilee Hall was erected on the new location as the first permanent building in the nation solely dedicated to the higher education of African Americans.

Source: From Rodney T. Cohen. *Fisk University.* Mount Pleasant, SC: Arcadia Publishing, 2001, p. 8.

Books

Abbott, Lynn and Doug Seroff. *Out of Sight: The Rise of African American Popular Music, 1889–1895.* Jackson, MS: Univ. Press of Mississippi, 2003. Book looks at how Black musicians have historically faced racism and discrimination, yet found a way to have their music heard. The Fisk Jubilee Singers are featured prominently.

Richardson, Joe Martin. *A History of Fisk University, 1865–1946.* Tuscaloosa, AL: University of Alabama Press, 1980. Examines the founding of the school and how it survived.

Websites

The Fisk University Website provides the most up-to-date information on the school. http://www.fisk.edu.

The tradition of the Fisk University Jubilee Singers lives on today, as each year the school has a new troupe of singers. And the article on the Fisk University Jubilee Singers tells the story of how they began and the impact they made on their school and the world. http://www.fiskjubileesingers.org and http://frank.mtsu.edu/~baustin/jubilee.html.

Also Noteworthy

1914

Greek-letter fraternity Phi Beta Sigma (ΦΒΣ) is established by A. Langston Taylor, Leonard F. Morse, and Charles I. Brown at Howard University. Phi Beta Sigma Fraternity, Inc., was created with the motto: "Culture for Service and Service for Humanity."

January 10

1750

James Varick—the man who will become the first bishop of the African Methodist Episcopal Zion Church—is born in Orange County, New York. Varick was an original supporter for the United States' first Black newspaper, *Freedom's Journal*, and he presided over the Thanksgiving service for the final abolition of African enslavement in New York on July 4, 1827. Varick's remains are in a crypt in Harlem's African Methodist Episcopal Zion Church.

> In 1796 [Peter] Williams joined with James Varick and other Methodists of color to establish the Zion Chapel in a cabinetmaker's shop on Cross Street between Orange (Baxter) and Mulberry. The Zionites didn't intend to withdraw from the John Street congregation, merely to worship together in an atmosphere free of racial animosity, but by 1799 they had concluded that they would be better off on their own. Encouraged by the example of Richard Allen, who had just founded the African Methodist Episcopal Church in Philadelphia, they obtained permission from Bishop Francis Asbury to form a new congregation.
>
> In 1801 the dissidents incorporated as the African Methodist Episcopal Zion church and raised a house of worship on the corner of Leonard and Church Streets. In remembrance of the little Cross Street chapel, it would be known as "Mother Zion."
>
> *Source*: From Edwin G. Burrows and Mike Wallace. *Gotham: A History of New York City to 1898.* New York, NY: Oxford University Press, 2000, pp. 398–400.

Books

Lincoln, Charles Eric and Lawrence H. Mamiya. *The Black Church in the African-American Experience.* Durham, NC: Duke University Press, 1990. Book looks at how enslaved Africans adapted to Christianity and the ways Blacks used Christianity for worship, learning, and organizing in their community.

Sernett, Milton C. *African American Religious History: A Documentary Witness.* Durham, NC: Duke University Press, 1999. Book uses archival documents to look at African American religions and their effects on community in Africa and in the United States.

Websites

The Wesleyan University Website gives a description of the origin of the A.M.E. Zion

Church. http://www.wesleyan.edu/libr/schome/amezion/case1.htm.

The New York Public Library's Schomburg Center for Research in Black Culture has a description of James Varick's role in New York City's religious and African American history. http://abolition.nypl.org/images/celebrations/2/61.

1864

George Washington Carver is born near Diamond Grove, Missouri. Although born into slavery to Moses and Susan Carver, George Washington Carver became a leading agricultural chemist at Tuskegee Institute (later Tuskegee University). Carver developed a crop rotation method that helped restore nutrients in farmlands. He also developed more than 300 uses for peanuts and discovered several industrial uses for soybeans, pecans, and sweet potatoes.

> *From a child I had an inordinate desire for knowledge, and especially music, painting, flowers, and the sciences Algebra being one of my favorite studies.*
>
> *Day after day I spent in the woods alone in order to collect my floral beautis and put them in my little garden I had hidden in brush not far from the house, as it was considered foolishness in that neighborhood to waste time on flowers.*
>
> *And many are the tears I have shed because I would break the roots or flower of off some of my pets while removing them from the ground, and strange to say all sorts of vegetation succeed to thrive under my touch until I was styled the plant doctor, and plants from all over the country would be brought to me for treatment. At this time I had never heard of botany and could scerly read.*
>
> *Source*: From Gary R. Kremer, ed. *George Washington Carver In His Own Words*. Columbia, MO: University of Missouri Press, 1991, p. 20.

Books

Franchino, Vicky. *Compass Point Early Biographies: George Washington Carver*. Mankato, MN: Compass Point Books, 2001. Biography of George Washington Carver looks at his important agricultural inventions.

McMurray, Linda O. *George Washington Carver: Scientist and Symbol*. New York: Oxford University Press, 1981. McMurray looks at the life and times of George Washington Carver and how his inventions made him famous.

Websites

The National Park Service has a few Website pages regarding George Washington Carver. This site is devoted to the monument to Carver, in his hometown of Diamond, MO, and this site looks at his years of research. http://www.nps.gov/gwca/ and http://www.nps.gov/history/museum/exhibits/Tuskegee/gwcoverview.htm.

The U.S. Department of Agriculture has an online *George Washington Carver Coloring and Activity Book* that can be printed out and used to teach about the scientists' discoveries. http://www.da.usda.gov/oo/colorbook.htm.

1957

Martin Luther King, Jr., founds the Southern Christian Leadership Conference (SCLC) in New Orleans, Louisiana. The SCLC is established with the goal of redeeming "the soul of America" through nonviolent resistance.

> *To such stalwarts of the Old Left as Virginia Durr and Aubrey Williams, who witnessed King's rise firsthand, SCLC's emphasis on nonviolence and nonpartisanship seemed bafflingly naïve: blacks needed to work with the trade unions and with the Democrats, they argued, in order to fashion an interracial radical movement in the South. But this was precisely the strategy, Rustin and Levison believed, that had failed during the 1930s and 1940s. Black Southerners had to face the reality that white support would come from the North, not the South. They also had to adapt their tactics to the Cold War climate which had made radicalism a synonym for subversion.*
>
> *... SCLC was designed to be a "nonpolitical" organization that could win support from across the political spectrum. By emphasizing Christian*

principles and nonviolence it projected a non-controversial image of peace and moderation.

Source: From Adam Fairclough. *To Redeem the Soul of America: The Southern Christian Leadership Conference and Martin Luther King, Jr.* Athens, GA: University of Georgia Press, 1987, p. 41.

Books

Garrow, David J. *Bearing the Cross: Martin Luther King, Jr., and the Southern Christian Leadership Conference.* New York, NY: HarperCollins, 2004. This biography of Martin Luther King, Jr., examines his role in founding the SCLC and negotiating how it worked as a civil rights organization.

Marable, Manning and Leith Mullings, eds. *Let Nobody Turn Us Around: Voices of Resistance, Reform, and Renewal: An African American Anthology.* Lanham, MD: Rowman & Littlefield, 2000. This anthology looks at African American political perspectives from slavery through the twentieth century.

Websites

The Southern Christian Leadership Conference (SCLC) updates its events on its Website. http://sclcnational.org/net/content/default .aspx?s=0.0.12.2607&s=0.0.12.2607&db =system.

Stanford University's Martin Luther King, Jr., Research and Education Institute profiles the SCLC. http://mlk-kpp01.stanford.edu/index .php/encyclopedia/encyclopedia/enc_southern _christian_leadership_conference_sclc.

The SCLC Magazine is the official organ of the SCLC. http://www.sclcmagazine.com.

1924

Maxwell Lemuel Roach is born in the Township of Newland, North Carolina. Roach became famous as a member of the Charlie Parker quintet, which he played with from 1947 through 1949. He became known as a jazz percussion virtuoso, playing avant-garde, hard bop, post-bop, and bop styles of jazz. Roach also became a noted political activist, even using his music to advance the Civil Rights Movement, as with his album *We Insist! Freedom Now Suite.* When Roach was married to jazz singer Abbey Lincoln in the 1960s, the couple became hardcore activists. They famously helped organize the 1961 United Nations protests against Patrice Lumumba's assassination in the Congo.

Max Roach is arguably the greatest drummer of the century, and not just in jazz. He is a master musician of the first rank whose ability to lift a band with the propulsive surge of his drumming marked him out as the cream of the handful of truly great modern jazz percussionists. Even when simply playing fills behind a soloist in any of the many settings in which he has worked, his remarkably subtle and intricate drumming can set the music flowing and floating on a complex wave of polyrhythmic activity and rich tonal and timbral colouration. Equally, his solo performances have elevated the art of playing the jazz drum-set to a new level of musical achievement.

Source: From Kenny Mathieson. *Giant Steps: Bebop and the Creators of Modern Jazz 1945–65.* New York, NY: Canongate U.S., 1999, p. 125.

Books

Feather, Leonard G. *Inside Jazz, Roots of Jazz.* Cambridge, MA: Da Capo Press, 1977. Music critic Leonard Feather tells the story of the creation of bop and the musicians who made it famous.

Martin, Henry and Keith Waters. *Jazz: The First 100 Years.* Florence, KY: Cengage Learning, 2005. A look at the growth of jazz and its future as a musical style.

Websites

Drummerworld explains the importance of Max Roach in the field of percussion instruments. http://www.drummerworld.com/drummers/ Max_Roach.html.

HardBop presents a biographical sketch of Max Roach. http://hardbop.tripod.com/roach.html.

January 11

1961

A riot breaks out when two Black students—Charlayne Hunter and Hamilton Holmes—try to enter their classes at the University of Georgia. Hunter and Holmes were suspended, but a federal court ordered them reinstated. They returned to their classes on January 16.

> Charlayne Hunter and Hamilton Holmes broke the color line at the University of Georgia several months before Atlanta began its desegregation. Both Hunter and Holmes applied to the university after their 1959 graduation with honors from Atlanta's Turner High School. They were denied admission purportedly because they had applied too late, so Hunter entered Wayne State University and Holmes enrolled in Morehouse College, and they continued their attempts to enroll at Georgia. Holmes's mother, an Atlanta schoolteacher, received harassing phone calls when he applied for transfer and admission at Athens. Federal judge William Bootle ordered their admission on January 10, 1961, ruling in a case in which they were represented by Horace Ward and his partner Donal L. Hollowell, with assistance from veteran civil rights attorney Constance Baker Motley. Bootle then stayed his order; appeals judge Elbert Tuttle reversed the stay, and the Supreme Court backed Tuttle.
>
> Source: From Donald Lee Grant. *The Way it Was in the South: The Black Experience in Georgia*. Athens, GA: University of Georgia Press, 2001, p. 383.

Books

Boney, F. N. and Michael Adams. *A Pictorial History of the University of Georgia*. Athens, GA: University of Georgia Press, 2000. Book looks at the history of the University of Georgia from the 1800s to the present.

Bryant, Nicholas Andrew. *The Bystander: John F. Kennedy and the Struggle for Black Equality*. New York, NY: Basic Books, 2006. Examines how President John F. Kennedy confronted white resistance and those who wanted to stop the advancement of the Civil Rights Movement in the United States.

Websites

Our Georgia History has a timeline of important events in the state's history. http://ourgeorgia history.com/year/1961.

This newsfilm clip from Atlanta, Georgia, station WSB-TV shows the first time Charlayne Hunter and Hamilton Holmes were able to successfully register as students at the University of Georgia in Athens, Georgia, on January 9, 1961. http://crdl.usg.edu/cgi/crdl?action= retrieve;rset=001;recno=1;format=_video.

1966

A Ku Klux Klan bombing in Hattiesburg, Mississippi, kills Black community leader Vernon Dahmer.

> Vernon Dahmer was the thirty-second murdered civil rights worker in Mississippi since 1960. His murder was followed by four more, in the late 1960s. Indeed, what happened to him happened to numerous other civil rights workers.
>
> . . . .
>
> In the early 1940s, W. J. Cash concluded that "violence, intolerance, aversion and suspicion toward new ideas, an incapacity for analysis, an inclination to act from feeling rather than from thought, an exaggerated individualism and a too narrow concept of social responsibility, attachment to fictions and false values, above all too great attachment to racial values and a tendency to justify cruelty and injustice in the name of those values, sentimentality and a lack of realism—these have been its characteristic vices in the past."
>
> Source: From Laurence W. Moreland, Robert P. Steed, and Todd A. Baker. *Blacks in Southern Politics*. New York, NY: Praeger Publishers, 1987, p. 31.

Books and Papers

Estes, Carol Ann. *The Death of Vemon Dahmer: Klan Violence and Mississippi Justice in the 1960s*. University of Southern Mississippi, 1988. Examines the activist work Dahmer was engaged in and the Klan forces determined to stop him.

Newman, Mark. *Divine Agitators: The Delta Ministry and Civil Rights in Mississippi.* Athens, Georgia: University of Georgia Press, 2004. Recounts the story of the National Council of Churches' "Delta Ministry" and its work for civil rights in Mississippi, where Vernon Dahmer had a large influence.

The University of Southern Mississippi—McCain Library and Archives. *Dahmer (Vernon F.) Collection.* Hattiesburg, MS: University of Southern Mississippi Libraries Special Collections, 1999. Covers papers related to Vernon Dahmer's work for the years 1966 through 1998, up to his brutal death.

Websites

32 Years to Justice describes the 1950s Mississippi courtroom trial of KKK leader Sam Bowers, the man accused of the 1966 murder of civil rights activist Vernon Dahmer. http://gbgm-umc.org/response/articles/dahmer.html.

The Case of the 1966 KKK Firebombing provides a Headline Archive of the Federal Bureau of Investigation's inquest in the firebombing of Vernon Dahmer's home. http://www.fbi.gov/page2/jan06/dahmer010906.htm.

The article "Coverage of Dahmer proved the exception" argues that news reporting in Mississippi, at the time of Vernon Dahmer's murder, tended to be racist and to not prioritize the civil rights concerns of African Americans. http://www.hattiesburgamerican.com/apps/pbcs.dll/article?AID=/20071016/LIFESTYLE14/71016023.

1985

After becoming the first Black person to graduate from the University of Mississippi School of Law, on January 1, 1985, Reuben V. Anderson becomes the first African American to be appointed to the Mississippi Supreme Court.

> On January 11, 1985, Reuben Anderson became the first African American judge to be appointed to the Mississippi Supreme Court. Anderson, a native of Jackson, received his bachelor of arts

> degree from the University of Mississippi in 1967. He served as a municipal judge of the 7th Circuit Court, State of Mississippi from 1982 to 1985. Anderson served on the Mississippi Supreme Court from 1985 to 1990 and later served as president of the Mississippi Bar Association from 1997 to 1998.
>
> *Source:* From Turry Flucker and Phoenix Savage. *African Americans of Jackson.* Mount Pleasant, SC: Arcadia Publishing, 2008, p. 46.

Books

Anderson, Reuben and Charles C. Bolton. *An Oral History With Reuben V. Anderson; Volume 320, Part 2 of Mississippi Oral History Program of the University of Southern Mississippi.* Charlottesville, VA: AbeBooks, 2008. A look at Anderson's political career, told by Anderson himself.

Southern Women's Institute. *Golden Days: Reminiscences of Alumnae, Mississippi State College for Women.* Jackson, MS: Univ. Press of Mississippi, 2008. Interview with Lenore Loving, of the Mississippi State College Women's class of 1953, who recalls when Reuben Anderson was sworn in as a judge and talks about how this helped change Mississippi society.

Websites

Superlawyers profiles Reuben Anderson and gives his office contact information. http://www.superlawyers.com/mississippi/lawyer/Reuben-V-Anderson/f4b8fcb4-4825-40bb-a3f-92ef82055fd1.html.

Phelps Dunbar, the law firm Anderson currently works for, features a profile of the esteemed jurist. http://www.phelpsdunbar.com/attorney-profile/profile/anderson-40.html.

Also Noteworthy

1957

Darryl Dawkins is born in Orlando, Florida. A 6-foot 10-inch, 251 pounder—assets which made him a formidable National Basketball Association player—Dawkins played prominently with the New Jersey Nets and the Philadelphia 76ers. His powerful dunks broke basketball backboards on at least two occasions and led to fans nicknaming him "Chocolate Thunder" and "Double D."

January 12

1890

Mordecai Wyatt Johnson is born in Paris, Tennessee, on January 12, 1890, to Reverend Wyatt J. Johnson and Carolyn Freeman. As an educator, Mordecai served as the first president of African descent of the historically Black Howard University from June 20, 1926 to 1960.

> The university did not appoint its first African American president until June 1926, when Mordecai Wyatt Johnson began his thirty-four-year tenure. Headlines in the Washington Post read: "Negro at Last Heads Howard University. Acquisition of Dr. Mordecai W. Johnson as President Places Local University as Capstone of Negro Education in America."
>
> ....
>
> During his university presidency, Johnson concentrated on attracting African American scholars as administrators, deans, and heads of departments, but was also proud of the school's varied faculty and student body. A skilled orator and debater whose remarks sometime made enemies, Johnson often said, "The Lord told me to speak, but He did not tell me when to stop."
>
> Source: From Joan Potter. African American Firsts: Famous Little-Known and Unsung Triumphs of Blacks. New York, NY: Dafina Books/Kensington Publishing Corp., 2002, pp. 36–37.

Books

Mays, Benjamin Elijah. *The Relevance of Mordecai Wyatt Johnson for our Times: The Inaugural Address in the Mordecai Wyatt Johnson Lecture Series.* Washington, DC: Howard University, 1978. Looks at Mordecai Johnson's role at Howard University and how his influence continues among Black educators.

McKinney, Richard I. *Mordecai, the Man and His Message: The Story of Mordecai Wyatt Johnson.* Washington, DC: Howard University Press, 1997. This biography of Mordecai Wyatt Johnson also quotes extensively from his writings and speeches.

Websites

The Robinson Library has a biographical sketch of Mordecai Wyatt Johnson. http://www.robinsonlibrary.com/education/history/biography/johnson.htm.

The University of Mississippi's Center for Excellence in Teaching and Learning has a web page in homage to Mordecai Wyatt Johnson. http://www.olemiss.edu/depts/cetl/BlackHistory3.html.

1920

James Leonard Farmer, Jr., is born in Marshall, Texas. Farmer is one of the principal founders of the interracial, nonviolent resistance-oriented Congress of Racial Equality (CORE), a group of students in Chicago, Illinois. Farmer served as CORE's national chairman.

> But what was the organization to be called? There had to be a catchy name with an unforgettable acronym. Bob Chino, a university student who was half Chinese and half Caucasian, shouted, "I've got it! Let's call it CORE, because it will be the center of things, the heart of the action."
>
> The enthusiasm was unanimous. But now that we had an acronym, what did it stand for? The RE was easy: Racial Equality. The C had to be either Committee of Council, and we opted for Committee, because Council sounded more like a discussion group than one for action. But what was the O? On or of? On that question, the debate was lengthy and high-spirited. The discussion was philosophical, not frivolous. We believed, after all, that we were starting an organization that would soon become nationwide and would shake America and its roots; what it was called would be of utmost importance. On signified the subject of our efforts; but of—and this is what I argued—implied that

the organization, in its structure, its methods, and its very being, would reflect the objective it sought. Like a seed, a real core, it would germinate and radiate its equality in wider and wider circles until it encompassed the whole nation.

CORE became the Committee of Racial Equality.

Source: From James Farmer. *Lay Bare the Heart: An Autobiography of the Civil Rights Movement.* Fort Worth, TX: TCU Press, 1998, p. 105.

Books

Farmer, James. *Lay Bare the Heart: An Autobiography of the Civil Rights Movement.* Fort Worth, TX: TCU Press, 1998. Farmer's personal account of his involvement in the Civil Rights Movement.

Jakoubek, Robert E. *James Farmer and the Freedom Rides.* Minneapolis, MN: Millbrook Press, 1994. Biography of Farmer's activist work with CORE and with the organization of the Freedom Rides.

Websites

The Congress of Racial Equality's Website has a page devoted to James Farmer. http://www.core-online.org/History/james_farmer_bio.htm.

The James Farmer Project is a digital history project designed by students at the University of Mary Washington. http://www.umw.edu/cas/jfscholars/who/default.php or http://jamesfarmer.umwblogs.org/.

1948

The U.S. Supreme Court rules in *Sipuel v. University of Oklahoma* that African Americans have the right to study law at state institutions. The court ordered Oklahoma to provide Ada Lois Sipuel Fisher the same legal education it would provide a white student, after she was barred from entering the University of Oklahoma Law School. When she did finally attend the school, the administration did not make her feel welcome: she was appointed a

seat marked "colored" to sit in, and made to eat in a special chained-off section of the cafeteria.

I have tried to decide what racist action or situation over the years I have felt most acutely. There have been many, and all of them have hurt. Hate always hurts. I think perhaps walking past my classmates in the law school classroom and climbing the levels up to the "colored" chair was the most humiliating. I was finally there, enrolled as a student along with some one hundred other first-year law students. We all were young American citizens with at least a bachelor's degree. We all had met qualifications for admission, and we were there solely for the purpose of studying the law. I, however, was considered so different that I must sit apart from my peers. As I climbed the levels and rows of seats, I realized that all eyes were on me. What were they thinking? Was I walking erect and maintaining a calm demeanor? I must show no emotion. I had to be careful not to stumble. As I ascended the levels to my chair, I wondered why that particular experience was worse than others.

Source: From Ada Lois Sipuel Fisher and Danney Goble. *A Matter of Black and White: The Autobiography of Ada Lois Sipuel Fisher.* Fort Worth, TX: TCU Press, 1998, p. 148.

Books

Johnson, Hannibal B. *Acres Of Aspiration: The All-Black Towns In Oklahoma.* Waco, TX: Eakin Press, 2002. Looks at the all-Black towns of Oklahoma and their inspiration to the rest of the state's African American community.

Taylor, Quintard and Shirley Ann Wilson Moore, eds. *African American Women Confront the West, 1600–2000.* Norman, OK: University of Oklahoma Press, 2008. Authors look at the roles African American women have played in the formation of the western United States.

Websites

The Oklahoma Historical Society's Website has an entry on Ada Lois Sipuel Fisher. http://

digital.library.okstate.edu/encyclopedia/entries/F/FI009.html.

Stanford Law School's Robert Crown Library has a Women's Legal History Website, with a biographical sketch on Ada Lois Sipuel Fisher. http://womenslegalhistory.stanford.edu/profiles/FisherAda.html.

The University of Oklahoma's Graduate College Website dedicates a page to Ada Lois Sipuel Fisher's struggles to enter the law school. http://gradweb.ou.edu/History/Bios/Students/Fisher.asp.

January 13

1913

Twenty-two college women found the Delta Sigma Theta Sorority, Inc. (ΔΣΘ)—the second Black Greek-letter organization—at Howard University.

> ...When, in 1913, those twenty-two students organized Delta Sigma Theta, they added an important and vital dimension to the "Black sorority idea"—an idea that filled such a compelling need, that gained such wide currency among college-educated women, it became a full-fledged social movement.
>
> Source: From Paula J. Giddings. *In Search of Sisterhood: Delta Sigma Theta and the Challenge of the Black Sorority Movement*. New York, NY: HarperCollins Publishers, 2007, p. 17.

Books

Hill, Pauline Anderson Simmons. *Too Young to Be Old: The Story of Bertha Pitts Campbell, a Founder of Delta Sigma Theta Sorority, Inc.* Bloomington, IN: AuthorHouse/Peanut Butter Pub., 1981. Author looks at the life of Bertha Pitts Campbell, a founder of the public service organization, Delta Sigma Theta Sorority, Inc.

Marshall, Alice Jefferson, et al. *A Life of Quiet Dignity: Naomi Sewell Richardson.* New York, NY: Red Elephant Publishers, 1995. The story of the life of Naomi Sewell Richardson, a founder of the Delta Sigma Theta Sorority, Inc.

Websites

Delta Sigma Theta sorority's official Website and its Delta Research and Educational Foundation-DREF; give the most complete information about the organization. http://www.deltasigmatheta.org/ and http://www.deltafoundation.net/.

The LA South Bay Alumnae Chapter of Delta Sigma Theta has a history of the organization on its Website. http://lasouthbaydst.org/dst-history.php.

1777

"A Great Number of Blacks" in the state of Massachusetts submit a petition to the legislature calling for their freedom. The petition—believed to have been written by Prince Hall—notes that Blacks in Massachusetts understood that they "wher Unjustly Dragged by the hand of cruel Power from their Derest frinds and sum of them Even torn from the Embraces of their tender Parents—from A popolous Plasant And plentiful cuntry And in Violation of Laws of Nature and off Nations."

> ...On January 13, 1777, Prince Hall and seven other men publicly demanded that Massachusetts grant them "the Naturel Right of all men." Hall, born to a British father and a mixed-race mother in Barbados, had achieved freedom in 1770 before founding the first lodge of black Masons in the Americas. Well aware of proposals for gradual emancipation being discussed in other states, Hall pointedly called upon his white neighbors to practice "the mild Religion of Jesus" by liberating all "Slaves after they arrive at the age of Twenty one years." Hall's petition led a legislative committee to draft "an Act for preventing the practice of holding persons in Slavery," although the bill never came to a vote.
>
> Source: From Douglas R. Egerton. *Death Or Liberty: African Americans and Revolutionary America*. New York, NY: Oxford University Press, 2009, p. 103.

Books

Bruns, Roger, ed. *Am I Not a Man and a Brother: The Antislavery Crusade of Revolutionary America,*

1688–1788. New York, NY: Chelsea House, 1977. Collection of documents shows the virulence of the antislavery movement.

Patrick, John J. *Founding the Republic: A Documentary History.* Santa Anna, CA: Greenwood Publishing Group, 1995. Written documents showing the campaigns waged to push for freedom at the founding of the U.S. republic.

Websites

The Medford, Massachusetts Historical Society has an entry on Prince Hall (a former resident of the town) and his role in petitioning the state for African American freedom. http://www.medfordhistorical.org/princehall.php.

The official Prince Hall Memorial Project, which unveiled its memorial on September 12, 2009, gives a history of Prince Hall and his activism. http://www.princehall memorial.org/ph/index.php?option=com _content&view=article&id=50:ph-ceremony &catid=1:latest-news.

January 14

1916

The novelist John Oliver Killens is born in Macon, Georgia. His novels *Youngblood* (1954) and *And Then We Heard the Thunder* (1963) are considered to have given a stronger slant to the idea of social protest in African American literature.

If Richard Wright is the spiritual father of critical realism, John O. Killens was probably its contemporary moving force. Born on January 14, 1916, in Macon, Georgia, he was raised and educated primarily in the South. He also attended Howard, Columbia, and New York Universities. A major figure in the Harlem left-wing literary movement of the 1950s, Killens was one of the founders in 1951 of the Harlem Writer's Guild and a contributor to Paul Robeson's Freedom *newspaper. In the June 1952 issue of* Freedom *he revealed his belief in a rather dogmatic theory of socialist realism by denouncing the modernism of Ralph Ellison's* Invisible Man *as a "vicious distortion of Negro life." His commitment to the tradition of realism was expressed not only in his writings, but also in*

the creative writing workshops that he taught in the 1960s at the New School for Social Research and at Fisk, Howard, and Columbia Universities, where he encouraged the creative efforts of black women writers like Sarah Wright. Killens died of cancer on October 27, 1987, in Brooklyn, New York.

Source: From Bernard W. Bell. The Contemporary African American Novel: Its Folk Roots and Modern Literary Branches. *Amherst, MA: University of Massachusetts Press, 2004, pp. 142–143.*

Books

Gilyard, Keith. *Liberation Memories: The Rhetoric and Poetics of John Oliver Killens.* Detroit, MI: Wayne State University Press, 2003. Looks at Killens's roles as an inspirational writer and political activist as he worked for African American civil rights.

Lehman, Paul Robert. *The Development of the BlackPsyche in the Writings of John Oliver Killens, 1916–1987.* Lewiston, NY: Edwin Mellen Press, 2003. Author looks at Killens's understanding of his "Black psyche" and the ways it influenced his writings.

Websites

The Website for the African American Literature Book Club features a biographical entry on John Oliver Killens. http://aalbc.com/authors/killens.htm.

The official Harlem Writers Guild (HWG) Website acknowledges John Oliver Killens as one of its principal founders. http://theharlem writersguild.org/history.htm.

1990

Lawrence Douglas Wilder becomes governor of Virginia. Wilder takes office as Virginia's 66th governor and the nation's first African American elected U.S. governor since Reconstruction.

In January 1990, throngs of citizens crowded into Virginia's Capitol Square to witness Douglas Wilder's inauguration. African-Americans far outnumbered whites. The intense pride felt by

African-Americans was expressed again and again. Every day he served as governor of Virginia became an inspiration for all those who had historically been denied an equal opportunity to participate in the political process. The inauguration would set the tone for Wilder's symbolic impact.

Source: From Judson L. Jeffries. *Virginia's Native Son: The Election and Administration of Governor L. Douglas Wilder*. West Lafayette, IN: Purdue University Press, 2000, p. 96.

Books

Baker, Donald P. *Wilder: Hold Fast to Dreams: A Biography of L. Douglas Wilder*. Santa Ana, CA: Seven Locks Press, 1989. Author looks at Douglas Wilder's impact on Black politics in Virginia.

Edds, Margaret. *Claiming the Dream: The Victorious Campaign of Douglas Wilder of Virginia*. Chapel Hill, NC: Algonquin Books, 1990. This book closely examines the 1989 gubernatorial campaign in Virginia.

Websites

The Virginia Historical Society's Website has an entry on Douglas Wilder. http://www.vahistorical.org/sva2003/wilder.htm.

The National Governor's Association's Website contains a biographical sketch on Douglas Wilder. http://www.nga.org/portal/site/nga/menuitem.29fab9fb4add37305ddcbeeb501010a0/?vgnextoid=5c27ae3effb81010VgnVCM1000001a01010aRCRD.

The Virginia Foundation for the Humanities' online *Encyclopedia Virginia* dedicates a page to Wilder. http://www.encyclopediavirginia.org/Wilder_Lawrence_Douglas_1931-.

January 15

1908

Alpha Kappa Alpha (AKA), the first African American Greek-letter sorority, is founded at Howard University. College-trained women who wanted to be able to help strengthen and give service to their community

established the sorority. During the twentieth century, members participated in many programs, including the Alpha Kappa Alpha Mississippi Health Project—which brought treatment, supplies, and health education to Mississippi Delta residents from 1935 to 1942; the Cleveland Job Corps Center for women was created in 1965 as part of President Lyndon B. Johnson's "War On Poverty" and designed to help strengthen the educational and vocational skills of young women between the ages of 16 and 21; and the Ivy Reading AKAdemy focuses on early learning and mastery of basic reading skills by the end of third grade.

The second readily identifiable practice that influenced the establishment of BGLOs [Black Greek Letter Organizations] was a naming pattern that overtly affirmed the connection between black North American institutions, organizations, and people and their African ancestry. Like Hall and Allen in the eighteenth century, nineteenth-century citizens had continued to use the words Africa, Abyssinia, Canaan, Cush, Ethiopia, and other synonyms for Africa when naming institutions, denominations, sanctuaries, schools and other edifices. So even though these students were living in an era when the vagaries of racism and Jim Crowism had led to changes in racial designations (e.g., the National Association for the Advancement of Colored People), it is reasonable to conclude that many of the early-twentieth-century student-founders were the progeny of communities where institutions were named in honor of people and things "African." Moreover, they had likely been mentored by adults who valued political, social, and economic equity for "the race" and had probably observed many adult organizational models that promoted mutual aid, self-help, and support for the less fortunate. In fact, all the BGLOs defined a mission that included service, in sharp contrast to the social foci of the white fraternities and sororities. So strong was this commitment that, following Alpha Kappa Alpha's 1913 lead, other BGLOs also incorporated in order to establish chapters not only on other campuses but also in other cities. This allowed members to continue their affiliation beyond their undergraduate days, "for the good of the race."

Source: From Clarenda M. Phillips. *African American Fraternities and Sororities*. Lexington, KY: University Press of Kentucky, 2005, pp. 12–13.

Books

Parker, Marjorie H. *Alpha Kappa Alpha Through the Years, 1908–1988*. Chicago Mobium Press, 1990. Author gives historical information about the founding and growth of the AKA sorority throughout the twentieth century.

Smith, Susan Lynn. *Sick and Tired of Being Sick and Tired: Black Women's Health Activism in America, 1890–1950*. Philadelphia, PA: University of Pennsylvania Press, 1995. Author devotes a chapter to looking at the establishment and impact of the Alpha Kappa Alpha Mississippi Health Project.

Websites

Alpha Kappa Alpha Sorority, Incorporated's official Website is located at http://www.aka 1908.com.

Recognitions of the sorority's centennial are online at http://www.aka1908.com/centennial/index.html.

1929

The birthday of the African American Civil Rights Movement leader, Dr. Martin Luther King, Jr., has been observed as a federal holiday on every third Monday in January since 1986.

From beyond the borders of his own land, the Negro had been inspired by another powerful force. He had watched the decolonization and liberation of nations in Africa and Asia since World War II. He knew that yellow, black and brown people had felt for years that the American Negro was too passive, unwilling to take strong measures to gain his freedom. He might have remembered the visit to his country of an American head of state, who was called upon by a delegation of prominent American Negroes. When they began reciting to him their long list of grievances, the visiting statesman had waved a weary hand and said:

"I am aware of current events. I know everything you are telling me about what the white man is doing to the Negro. Now tell me: What is the Negro doing for himself?"

Source: From Martin Luther King, Jr. *Why We Can't Wait*. New York, NY: Penguin Group/Signet Classic, 2000, pp. 7–8.

Books

King, Jr. Martin Luther, edited by Clayborne Carson, Ralph E. Luker, and Penny A. Russell. *The Papers of Martin Luther King, Jr. Volume I: Called to Serve, January 1929– June 1951*. Berkeley, CA: University of California Press, 1992. Editors use the young Martin Luther King, Jr.'s correspondence, academic papers and other writings to demonstrate the growth of his thought process and early activism.

King, Jr. Martin Luther, edited by James Melvin Washington. *A Testament of Hope: The Essential Writings and Speeches of Martin Luther King, Jr*. New York, NY: HarperCollins, 1991. Editor uses King's writings, speeches, and interviews to examine King's thoughts about the African American Civil Rights Movement.

Websites

The Website for the Nobel Foundation has a biographical note on King, a 1964 recipient of the Nobel Prize. http://nobelprize.org/nobel _prizes/peace/laureates/1964/king-bio.html.

The King Center, established by King's widow, Coretta Scott King, maintains the legacy of the late Civil Rights leader. http://www.the kingcenter.org/KingCenter/Welcome.aspx.

Also Noteworthy

1890

Palmer C. Hayden is born in Wide Water, Virginia, under the name Peyton Hedgeman.

Hayden became a favored painter of the Harlem Renaissance; he used oils and watercolors to depict African American life.

1929

Earl Zebedee Hooker is born in Quitman County, Mississippi, and raised in Chicago, Illinois. As an adult, Hooker (who is a cousin of the another blues great, John Lee Hooker) was widely recognized as one of the best blues guitarists out of the Chicago music scene.

January 16

1865

The Union Army's General William Tecumseh Sherman issues orders to implement a restitution scheme that would help compensate the formerly enslaved. General Sherman and Secretary of War Edwin M. Stanton had met with 20 African American community leaders from Savannah, Georgia, on January 6, 1865, to discuss the plight of Blacks in the formerly Confederate southeastern states. Sherman's Special Field Order No. 15 designated the Sea Islands and some 30 miles of land from Charleston to the St. John's River in Florida for the exclusive settlement of newly freed Blacks. The order granted individual African American families 40 acres of land and a mule to help them start their new lives. President Andrew Johnson vetoed Sherman's scheme, but some Blacks did receive land under the Southern Homestead Act of 1866. The majority of that land, though, was former public land—land that had not been cultivated in the past, because it was poor in quality.

...Issued January 16, Sherman's Special Field Orders, No. 15 designated the sea islands and the rich plantation areas bordering rivers for thirty miles inland from Charleston down to Jacksonville for settlement by freedmen. Each head of family

could be granted forty acres of land, to which he would be given a "possessory title" until Congress "shall regulate their title." This land had of course belonged to slaveholders. Their dispossession of it by Sherman's order, like Lincoln's dispossession of their slaves by the Emancipation Proclamation, was a military measure carried out under "war powers." The thirteenth Amendment confirmed Lincoln's action; it remained to be seen how Court, Congress, and Executive would deal with the consequences of Sherman's Order No. 15. The army did not wait, however. During the next several months General Rufus Saxton, an abolitionist who commanded the Union occupation forces on the South Carolina sea islands, supervised the settlement of 40,000 freed men on land designated in Sherman's order.

Source: From James M. McPherson. Battle Cry of Freedom: The Civil War Era. Volume 6 of Oxford History of the United States. New York, NY: Oxford University Press, 2003, pp. 841–842.

Books

Ward, Andrew. *The Slaves' War: The Civil War in the Words of Former Slaves.* Orlando, FL: Houghton Mifflin Harcourt, 2008. Ward quotes the formerly enslaved and notes their reactions to the promised granting of 40 acres and a mule.

Zinn, Howard. *A People's History of the United States, 1492–Present.* New York, NY: HarperCollins, 2003. Zinn's coverage of the issuance of Sherman's Special Field Order No. 15 uses quotes from the African American leaders from Savannah, Georgia, and shows how they felt about the idea of freedom from enslavement.

Websites

The Ashland University Website (Teaching AmericanHistory.org) has the full text of General Sherman's Field Order No. 15. http://teachingamericanhistory.org/library/index.asp?document=545.

The Federation of Southern Cooperatives Land Assistance provides information on how land was gained and loss among African

Americans. http://www.federationsouthern coop.com/landloss.htm.

Also Noteworthy

1920

Zeta Phi Beta (ZΦB) sorority is founded at Howard University in Washington, DC. Zeta was created by Howard University coeds Arizona Cleaver, Myrtle Tyler, Viola Tyler, Fannie Pettie and Pearl Neal. Zeta Phi Beta was designed to emphasize the progressive social service aspects of being in a sorority, and in 1948 it became the first Greek-letter African American organization to establish a chapter on the continent of Africa.

1967

Lucius D. Anderson is sworn in as sheriff of Macon County (Tuskegee), Alabama, making him the first African American to serve as a sheriff in the southern United States in the twentieth century.

January 17

1759

The merchant, shipbuilder, and Black nationalist Paul Cuffee is born on Cutterhunkker Island, near New Bedford, Massachusetts. Cuffee was a successful ship-builder, and after an initial visit to Sierra Leone in 1811, he strongly advocated the emigration of Blacks in the Americas back to Africa. He founded the Friendly Society of Sierra Leone and in 1815 spent $4,000 transporting 38 African Americans from the United States to Sierra Leone and helping them get established there.

The consequence was, the formation of two societies, one in Philadelphia, and the other in New York, and the discovery of a number of proper persons, who were willing to go with him and settle in Africa. He however met with many difficulties in the accomplishment of his purpose, but having,

at length, by his perseverance, removed them all, he prepared for his departure, and in December 1815, took on board his brig 38 persons of the African Nation, and after a voyage of 55 days, landed them safely on the soil of their forefathers. Of these the African Society had engaged to defray the expenses only of eight, so that the outfit and support of the remaining 30 fell entirely on Paul Cuffee, and cost him no less a sum than 4000 dollars.

Source: From *The History of Prince Lee Boo: to which is Added the Life of Paul Cuffee, a Man of Colour, also Some Account of John Sackhouse, the Esquimaux.* Ann Arbor, MI: University of Michigan/ C. Crookes, 1820, pp. 166–167.

Books

Pinkney, Alphonso. *Red, Black, and Green: Black Nationalism in the United States.* New York, NY: Cambridge University Press, 1979. Author looks at the situations that made people of African descent think of themselves as a nation apart; he views Paul Cuffee as one of the United States' first Black nationalists.

Ward, Andrew. *The Slaves' War: The Civil War in the Words of Former Slaves.* Orlando, FL: Houghton Mifflin Harcourt, 2008. Ward quotes the formerly enslaved and notes their reactions to the promised granting of 40 acres and a mule.

Websites

The Website for the PBS production *Africans in America* describes and allows visitors to view the original version of "Memoir of Captain Paul Cuffee," an account of Cuffee's life and work published October 4-11, 1811, in the *Liverpool Mercury.* http://www.pbs.org/wgbh/aia/part3/3h485.html.

The UNESCO Website features a brief biography of Cuffee and talks about the importance of his life's work. http://portal.unesco.org/culture/en/ev.php-URL_ID=38524&URL_DO=DO_PRINTPAGE&URL_SECTION=201.html.

1942

Three-time World Heavyweight Champion boxer Muhammad Ali is born. At the time of his birth in Louisville, Kentucky, he was given the name Cassius Marcellus Clay, Jr., in honor of his father. (His father had been named after the nineteenth-century abolitionist and politician Cassius Clay.) The celebrated winner of an Olympic Light-heavyweight gold medal, Clay, Jr., went on to win his first heavyweight championship in a surprise defeat of Sonny Liston. Once he defeated Liston, Ali changed his name from Cassius after joining the Nation of Islam in 1964. He was a symbolic figure in the U.S. Civil Rights Movement after refusing to fight in Vietnam because of the way Black people were treated in America. He converted to Sunni Islam in 1975. In 1999, both *Sports Illustrated* and the BBC named Ali "Sportsman of the Century."

> *When you saw me in the boxing ring fighting, it wasn't just so I could beat my opponent. My fighting had a purpose. I had to be successful in order to get people to listen to the things I had to say.*
>
> *I was fighting to win the world heavyweight title so I could go out in the streets and speak my mind. I wanted to go to the people, where unemployment, drugs, and poverty were part of everyday life. I wanted to be a champion who was accessible to everyone. I hoped to inspire others to take control of their lives and to live with pride and self-determination I thought perhaps if they saw that I was living my life the way I chose to live it—without fear and with determination—they might dare to take the risks that could set them free.*
>
> Source: From Muhammad Ali and Hana Ali. *The Soul of a Butterfly: Reflections on Life's Journey*. New York, NY: Simon & Schuster, 2004, p. 69.

Books

Collings, Mark and Lennox Lewis, eds. *Muhammad Ali: Through the Eyes of the World*. New York, NY: Skyhorse Publishing Inc., 2007. Various celebrities and people who know Ali speak of his image and impact on the world.

Ezra, Michael. *Muhammad Ali: The Making of an Icon*. Chicago, IL: Temple University Press,

2009. Author looks at the cultural impact Muhammad Ali has had as a sports celebrity and as a social and political figure.

Websites

The Website for the Muhammad Ali Center is http://www.alicenter.org.

The Official Muhammad Ali Website features the latest news about and photos of Ali, plus a biography, interactive timeline, and newsletter for those who want information on the life of Ali. http://www.ali.com.

January 18

1938

Curtis Charles Flood is born in Houston, Texas. Signed to play professional baseball straight out of high school, Flood was a seven-time Major League Baseball Golden Glove winner for his work as a center fielder and played on three National League Champion teams and two World Series winning teams. Flood played for the Cincinnati Reds but spent most of his career with the St. Louis Cardinals. When he was told that he was being traded from the Cardinals—after 12 years of establishing a life and career in St. Louis—Flood refused the trade and became the first Major League Baseball (MLB) player to challenge the "reserve clause." Because the MLB's reserve clause tied a player to a single team and gave him no say in which team he wanted to play with, Flood termed it a "legal slavery." Flood's lawsuit—which went to the U.S. Supreme Court—brought about the end of the reserve clause and the beginning of free agency in baseball.

> *In November 1987, Flood and 60 black former players met for three days in Irving, Texas, to discuss their common experiences and to form their own organization, known as the Baseball Network. "Forty years after the debut of Jackie Robinson, bitterness is not what I am," Flood told the Baltimore Sun's Mark Hyman. "But I am a little embarrassed we have not gone further." When*

asked what kind of job he wanted in baseball, Flood replied that he wanted to be an owner.

Source: From Brad Snyder. *A Well-Paid Slave: Curt Flood's Fight for Free Agency in Professional Sports*. New York, NY: Penguin Group, 2007, p. 340.

Books

Moffi, Larry and Jonathan Kronstadt. *Crossing the Line: Black Major Leaguers, 1947–1959*. Lincoln NE: University of Nebraska Press, 2006. Provides a detailed overview of Flood's life, his baseball career and statistics, and his lawsuit against the MLB's reserve clause.

Weiss, Stuart L. *The Curt Flood story: The Man Behind the Myth*. Columbia, MO: University of Missouri Press, 2007. Author looks at Curt Flood's life and the circumstances that influenced his decision to sue Major League Baseball in 1970.

Websites

The Website for AOL Inc.'s MLB Fanhouse features the article "Curt Flood: An Extraordinary Man of Principle and Conviction," which focuses on the legacy of Curt Flood's suit against Major League Baseball. http://mlb.fanhouse.com/2009/10/06/curt-flood-an-extraordinary-man-of-principle-and-conviction/.

The Baseball Almanac provides baseball statistics and year-by-year salary for Flood during his playing years. http://www.baseball-almanac.com/players/player.php?p=floodcu01.

1966

Robert Clifton Weaver becomes the United States' first African American presidential cabinet member when sworn in as Secretary of Housing and Urban Affairs under the Lyndon Baines Johnson administration. Weaver wrote often about the lack of good housing or labor initiatives for people of African descent. He authored books with titles like *Negro Labor: A National Problem* (1946), *The Negro Ghetto* (1948), and

Dilemmas of Urban America (1965). In 2000, Weaver's work was honored when the HUD located at 451 Seventh Street headquarters building was renamed the Robert C. Weaver Federal Building.

Not only has there been a liberalization of attitude toward open occupancy but significant institutional developments have occurred. The first of these is the recent spontaneous rise of about a thousand fair housing committees, largely in the suburbs. These are groups of middle-class whites who have organized to recruit and welcome nonwhites as neighbors. President Kennedy's Executive Order on Equal Opportunity in Housing (1962), despite its limited coverage, has slowly opened new neighborhoods to nonwhites, supplementing the eighteen state laws, three territory laws, and thirty-four municipal ordinances for fair housing practices. Most recently, several thousand Americans have organized to provide financial resources in support of nonsegregated housing on a national scale.

Source: From Robert Clifton Weaver. *Dilemmas of Urban America*. Cambridge, MA: Harvard University Press, 1965, pp. 81–82.

Books

Kersten, Andrew Edmund. *Race, Jobs, and the War: The FEPC in the Midwest, 1941–46*. Champaign, IL: University of Illinois Press, 2000. Author shows Weaver's early role as an influential member of Franking Delano Roosevelt's New Deal and the struggle for fair employment.

Kryder, Daniel. *Divided Arsenal: Race and the American State During World War II*. New York, NY: Cambridge University Press, 2001. Author looks at Weaver's role in getting African Americans more involved in the Defense Industry.

Websites

The University of Virginia's Miller Center of Public Affairs features a short biography of Robert C. Weaver and his role in Lyndon Baines Johnson's administration. http://

millercenter.org/academic/americanpresident/lbjohnson/essays/cabinet/601.

Time magazine's March 4, 1966, cover featured Robert C. Weaver and celebrated his selection as Secretary of HUD and is archived on the Internet. http://www.time.com/time/covers/0,16641,19660304,00.html.

Also Noteworthy

1941

Davis Eli "David" Ruffin is born in Whynot, Mississippi. Later famed as the lead singer of the Motown band, The Temptations, Ruffin sang songs like "My Girl," "Beauty Is Only Skin Deep," and "I Wish It Would Rain."

1949

Rep. William L. Dawson (D., Ill.) is named chairman of the House Expenditures Committee. Dawson was the first African American to lead a standing committee of Congress.

January 19

1969

The University of California, Los Angeles, renames its social science buildings in honor of its famed alumnus Ralph Johnson Bunche. Bunche was a political science scholar who established the Howard University Political Science department and co-founded the National Negro Congress. After working as part of the delegation that wrote the charter for the establishment of the United Nations, Bunche served as a United Nations diplomat and became the first African American to be awarded the Nobel Peace Prize.

I abhor racism as a dangerous virus, whether it is spread by white or black peoples. I seek total integration, which to me means the Negro taking his place in the very mainstream of American life . . . .

My ancestors have contributed very much to the development of this country and therefore I have a vested interest in it that I intend to realize and protect.

Source: From Ralph Johnson Bunche, ed. *Ralph J. Bunche: Selected Speeches and Writings*. Ann Arbor, MI: University of Michigan Press, 1995, p. 290.

Books

Henry, Charles P. *Ralph Bunche: Model Negro or American Other?* New York, NY: NYU Press, 2005. Author, who serves as head of the Ralph J. Bunche Center for African American Studies, looks at Bunche's political odyssey from radicalism to moderation.

Urquhart, Brian. *Ralph Bunche: An American Odyssey*. New York, NY: W. W. Norton & Company, 1998. Biography utilizes Bunche's writings to portray his sense of his role in the world.

Websites

University of California, Los Angeles's Ralph Bunche Center for African American Studies and the school's Social Science building Bunche Hall were named in honor of Ralph J. Bunche. http://www.bunchecenter.ucla.edu/ http://www.english.ucla.edu/ucla1960s/6465/gilmour.htm.

The Famous People Website features a biography of Ralph J. Bunche. http://www.thefamouspeople.com/profiles/ralph-bunche-61.php.

January 20

1847

William Reuben Pettiford, the founder of the Alabama Penny Savings Bank, is born. This first African American-owned bank in Alabama expanded and soon had three branches. The Alabama Penny Savings Bank lasted some 25 years.

The [Alabama Penny Savings and Loan Company] was founded and presided over by the Reverend

W. R. Pettiford. He had been born a free Negro in North Carolina before the Civil War and was educated in Alabama at the State Normal School at Marion. A former schoolteacher and Baptist minister, Pettiford was also a close associate of Booker T. Washington and was active in the field of real estate. All of this eventually culminated in his founding of Alabama Penny and later in his presidency of the Negro Bankers Association. The key to the bank's and Pettiford's success lay in the fact that he tied the development of the black bank business with the advancement of the race and campaigned to educate the black masses to support black-owned businesses.

Source: From Antonio Fredrick Holland. *Nathan B. Young and the Struggle over Black Higher Education.* Columbia, MO: University of Missouri Press, 2006, p. 179.

Books

Culp, Daniel Wallace. *Twentieth Century Negro Literature: Or, A Cyclopedia of Thought on the Vital Topics Relating to the American Negro.* Ann Arbor, MI: J. L. Nichols & Co./University of Michigan, 1902. Book contains a biographical sketch of W.R. Pettiford.

McKiven, Henry M. *Iron and Steel: Class, Race, and Community in Birmingham, Alabama, 1875–1920.* New York, NY: UNC Press, 1995. Author looks at the role prominent African American business leaders like W. R. Pettiford played in influencing the Black community of Birmingham, Alabama.

Websites

The New York Public Library's Digital Gallery features a photograph of W. R. Pettiford. http://digitalgallery.nypl.org/nypldigital/dgkey searchdetail.cfm?trg=1&strucID=212276 &imageID=413983&total=104&num=0&word =African%20American%20educators&s=3 &notword=&d=&c=147&f=2&k=0&lWord =&lField=&sScope=Collection%20Guide &sLevel=&sLabel=Africana%20%26amp %3B%20Black%20History&imgs=20&pos=16 &e=w.

University of Illinois Press's online access to the Booker T. Washington papers features a biographical sketch of W. R. Pettiford by Washington. http://www.historycooperative .org/btw/Vol.5/html/388.html.

1977

Patricia Roberts Harris becomes U.S. Secretary of Housing and Urban Development; she is the first African American woman to hold a U.S. Cabinet position.

In only sixty years (by today's standard, a life cut short) Patricia Roberts Harris grew from being the daughter of a small-town railroad dining-car porter to a high-profile cabinet executive. In her amazing lifetime, Patricia Harris was a civil rights advocate, educator, and attorney. She was appointed ambassador to Luxembourg, cabinet secretary of U.S. Housing and Urban Development (HUD), and cabinet secretary of the then single-largest U.S. government agency, the Department of Health, Education, and Welfare (HEW). She was also a board member of Fortune 100 corporations and even a mayoral candidate in our nation's capital.

Source: From Claire L. Felbinger and Wendy A. Haynes. *Outstanding women in Public Administration: Leaders, Mentors, and Pioneers.* Armonk, NY: M.E. Sharpe, 2004, p. 103.

Books

Morin, Isobel V. *Women Chosen for Public Office.* Minneapolis, MN: The Oliver Press, Inc., 1995. Book features a biographical sketch of the life and work of Patricia Roberts Harris.

Smith, Jr. Clay J. *Rebels in Law: Voices in History of Black Women Lawyers.* Ann Arbor, MI: J. L. Nichols & Co./University of Michigan, 1902. Book contains a biographical sketch of Patricia Roberts Harris.

Websites

The Website for the National Women's Hall of Fame features a biographical sketch of Patricia Roberts Harris. http://www.greatwomen.org/ women.php?action=viewone&id=200.

When a U.S. postage stamp was named in honor of Patricia Roberts Harris on January 27,

2000, Howard University commemorated the event and archived it on its Website. http://www.huarchivesnet.howard.edu/0005huarnet/harris1.htm.

Source: From Jacqueline Bacon. *Freedom's Journal: The First African-American Newspaper*. Lanham, MD: Lexington Books, 2007, p. 42.

Also Noteworthy

2009

Barack Obama is sworn in as the 44th president of the United States; he is the nation's first-ever African American president.

January 21

1827

Freedom's Journal, the first African American-owned and operated newspaper to be published in the United States, begins publishing under editors Samuel Cornish and John B. Russwurm. In their first issue they wrote about why a Black-owned and operated newspaper was essential. "We wish to plead our own cause. Too long have others spoken for us," the editors wrote. *Freedom's Journal* was published weekly in New York City from 1827 to 1829.

...Cornish and Russwurm placed far greater emphasis on African American's self-determination and collective identity than on white racism. They noted on their "Prospectus" that African Americans were "daily slandered" and described themselves as "champions in defence of oppressed humanity" who would refute "the calumnies of [their] enemies"; and responses to white rhetoric, as we have seen, were included in the periodical. Yet the editors explicitly pointed to community concerns as their primary motivation in publishing Freedom's Journal. *"We deem it expedient to establish a paper," they remarked, "and bring into operation all the means with which our benevolent CREATOR has endowed us, for the moral, religious, civil and literary improvement of our race ... [T]he diffusion of knowledge, and raising our community into respectability, are the principal motives which influence us in our present undertaking."*

Books

Horton, James Oliver and Lois E. Horton. *Slavery and the Making of America*. New York, NY: Oxford University Press, 2005. Book notes that *Freedom's Journal* was founded in part to counter the efforts of the American Colonization Society, which urged people of African descent to leave the United States.

Hutton, Frankie. *The Early Black Press in America, 1827 to 1860*. Santa Barbara, CA: Greenwood Publishing Group, 1993. Origins of Black newspapers and magazines published between the 1830s and 1860s.

Websites

The Website for the Wisconsin Historical Society contains digitized copies of all 103 issues of *Freedom's Journal* in Adobe Acrobat format. http://www.wisconsinhistory.org/library archives/aanp/freedom/.

The PBS link for the documentary *The Black Press: Soldiers Without Swords* notes the founding of *Freedom's Journal* on its Website. http://www.pbs.org/blackpress/news_bios/newbios/nwsppr/freedom/freedom.html.

January 22

1931

Soul, rock-and-roll, and gospel singer Sam Cooke is born to Annie Mae and Charles Cook in Clarksdale, Mississippi. His family later moved to Chicago, Illinois, and his father served as the minister at the Church of Christ Holiness Church. Cooke first gained fame as the lead singer with the gospel group The Soul Stirrers. But when he began writing and singing rock and roll and soul music, Sam Cooke became famous around the world for songs like "You Send Me," "Stand By Me," "A Change Is Gonna Come," and "Shake, Rattle and Roll."

Cooke's shocking death came at the age of 33, when he was fatally shot under suspicious circumstances by the manager of a Los Angeles motel. Two funeral services—in Chicago, Illinois, and Los Angeles, California— brought more than 200,000 people out to pay their last respects to Cooke.

> Cooke reached [his] audience with a string of hits beginning with "You Send Me" and culminating in "A Change Is Gonna Come," which was released eleven days after his death. The song expresses the soul of the freedom movement as clearly and powerfully as King's "Letter from a Birmingham Jail." The opening measures verge on melodrama: a searching French horn rises over a lush swell of symphonic strings accompanied by tympani. But Cooke brings it back to earth, bearing witness to the restlessness that keeps him moving like the muddy river bordering the Delta where he was born. Maintaining his belief in something up there beyond the sky, Cooke draws sustenance from his gospel roots. He testifies that it's been a long, long time—the second "long" carries all the weight of a bone-deep gospel weariness. Then he sings the midnight back toward dawn. The hard-won hope that comes through in the way he uses his signature "whoa-whoa-whoa" to emphasize the word "know" in the climactic line—"I know that a change is gonna come"—feels as real as anything America has ever been able to imagine.
>
> Source: From Craig Hansen Werne. A Change Is Gonna Come: Music, Race & the Soul of America. Ann Arbor, MI: University of Michigan Press, 2006, p. 33.

Books

Cooke, Sam. *Portrait of a Legend 1951–1964: Piano/Vocal/Chords*. New York, NY: Warner Bros. in association with Abkco Music, 2004. Cooke's discography and musical compositions are compiled.

Greene, Erik. *Our Uncle Sam: The Sam Cooke Story from His Family's Perspective*. Bloomington, IN: Trafford Publishing, 2005. Sam Cooke's relatives share memories of the legendary artist.

Websites

The Abkco Music & Records, Inc., Website provides a biography of Sam Cooke, along with access to his samcooke.com/biography.php.

The history music and past reviews of his work. http://www.samcooke.com/biography.php of Rock 'n' Roll Website features a detailed biography of Sam Cooke. http://www.history-of-rock.com/cooke.htm.

January 23

1904

Benjamin Arthur Quarles, PhD, is born in Boston, Massachusetts. A scholar, teacher, administrator, mentor, and role model, Quarles centered on the contributions and achievements of African Americans to U.S. history. Quarles authored some 10 books and served as chair of the history department at Morgan State University; Quarles remains a major force in the legacy of Black Studies and of historically Black colleges and universities.

> Black studies, despite their tender years, can no longer be regarded as a controversial academic innovation, though coming-of-age ceremonies would certainly be premature at this "growing pains" stage. It is impossible for American society to be properly appraised if blacks are left out of the picture. "We cannot," writes Columbia historian Walter Metzger, "understand America without the help of those studies now called 'black.'" John W. Blassingame of Yale concurs, pointing out that "no American can truly understand his own society and culture without a knowledge of the roles Negroes have played in them." The black looms large in American letters, writes Jean Fagan Yellin: "His dark figure is ubiquitous in our fiction: the American imagination was as obsessed in the nineteenth century by the black as it is today." Since Jamestown, black-white relationships have been a central attribute of our national culture. The experiences of blacks and whites, though profoundly different, have always been intertwined and complementary, even symbiotic on occasion, however much whites may have monopolized the process and substance of power. Hence

American studies, properly perceived, must be viewed through a multiracial lens.

Source: From Benjamin Quarles. *Black Mosaic: Essays in Afro-American History and Historiography.* Amherst, MA: University of Massachusetts Press, 1988, p. 182.

Books

Quarles, Benjamin. *Allies for Freedom: Blacks and John Brown.* Cambridge, MA: Da Capo Press, 2001. Quarles looks at the impact and iconic stature of the famed abolitionist, John Brown.

Quarles, Benjamin. *The Negro in the Making of America.* New York, NY: Simon & Schuster, 1996. Quarles' definitive history of the African American contribution to American history.

Websites

The Library Thing Website lists all the books published by Benjamin Quarles. http://www.librarything.com/author/quarlesbenjamin.

The article "The Howard University Department of History, 1913–1973" depicts the creation and evolution of Howard University's History Department and the philosophical influence of the towering figure of Benjamin Quarles. http://www.howard.edu/explore/history-dept.htm.

1964

The Twenty-fourth Amendment to the U.S. Constitution, which abolished the poll tax, is ratified on January 23. The poll tax had been used by many states in the South to elude enforcement of the Fifteenth Amendment, which had given formerly enslaved African men the right to vote.

For all the wide-ranging provisions of the Civil Rights Act (1964), the measure failed to guarantee the black population in the South the right to vote. A move in this direction had been made with the ratification of the 24th Amendment in 1964 which abolished the poll tax. Prior to the ratification of the 24th Amendment several states had imposed a tax on voting to deny poor blacks the franchise.

Although the 24th Amendment removed one obstacle to the black population's exercise of the franchise, events at Selma, Alabama, where a march organized by the civil rights movement was violently broken up by police on 7 March 1965, provided an indication that voting rights needed to be further protected. The result was the passage of the Voting Rights Act (1965) which President Johnson signed into law on 6 August 1965.

Source: From Garson, Robert A. and Christopher J. Bailey. *The Uncertain Power: A Political History of the United States Since 1929.* Manchester, England: Manchester University Press, 1990, pp. 96–97.

Books

Griffith, Benjamin E. *America votes!: A Guide to Modern Election Law and Voting Rights.* Chicago, IL: American Bar Association, 2008. Book talks about passage of the Twenty-fourth Amendment and looks at the court cases that have upheld it.

Heath, David. *Elections in the United States.* Mankato, MN: Capstone Press, 1999. Notes the long history of various disqualifiers used to keep people of African descent from voting, and how the Twenty-fourth Amendment meant to enfranchise Black voters.

Websites

The U.S. Constitution Online's Notes on the Amendments Website summarizes the Twenty-fourth Amendment and talks about the legal fights for its passage. http://www.usconstitution.net/constamnotes.html#Am24.

Cornell University's Law School Website summarizes the importance of the Twenty-fourth Amendment and how it has been upheld. http://www.law.cornell.edu/anncon/html/amdt24_user.html#amdt24_hd1.

Also Noteworthy

1964

Twenty-fourth Amendment to the U.S. Constitution eliminates the use of any poll tax in all federal elections.

January 24

1962

Jack Roosevelt "Jackie" Robinson becomes the first African American to be inducted into Major League Baseball's Hall of Fame. Jackie Robinson was also the first African American to play in Major League Baseball, when he became a member of the Brooklyn Dodgers in 1947, and he was the first African American to win the National League Most Valuable Player Award in 1949. Outside of his playing career, Robinson became an advocate for African Americans being able to take on management roles in Major League Baseball. In his own life, he helped start the Black-controlled Freedom National Bank as well as the Jackie Robinson Construction Corporation.

> *I have to admit that this day, of all the unpleasant days in my life, brought me nearer to cracking up than I ever had been. Perhaps I should have become inured to this kind of garbage, but I was in New York City and unprepared to face the kind of barbarism from a northern team that I had come to associate with the Deep South. The abuse coming out of the Phillies dugout was being directed by the team's manager, Ben Chapman, a Southerner. I felt tortured and I tried just to play ball and ignore the insults. But it was really getting to me. What did the Phillies want from me? What, indeed, did Mr. Rickey expect of me? I was, after all, a human being. What was I doing here turning the other cheek as though I weren't a man? In college days I had had a reputation as a black man who never tolerated affronts to his dignity. I had defied prejudice in the Army. How could I have thought that barriers would fall, that, indeed, my talent could triumph over bigotry?*
>
> *Source*: From Jackie Robinson, edited by Alfred Duckett. *I Never Had It Made: An Autobiography of Jackie Robinson*. New York, NY: HarperCollins Publishers, 2003, pp. 58–59.

Books

Robinson, Jackie, edited by Michael G. Long. *First Class Citizenship: The Civil Rights Letters of Jackie Robinson*. New York, NY: Macmillan, 2007. Correspondence of Jackie Robinson shows his thoughts on the advancement of civil rights for African Americans.

Rutkoff, Peter M. and Alvin L. Hall, eds. *The Cooperstown Symposium on Baseball and American Culture, 1997 (Jackie Robinson)*. Jefferson, NC: McFarland, 2000. Book contains the papers presented at a Major League Baseball Hall of Fame symposium on the impact of Jackie Robinson on the national game as well as on U.S. life.

Websites

The Website sponsored by the estate of Jackie Robinson maintains the most up-to-date information of his life and legacy. http://www.jackierobinson.com/.

The Jackie Robinson Foundation (JRF) Website is a source for higher education scholarships for minority students. http://www.jackierobinson.org/.

January 25

1851

The abolitionist activist Sojourner Truth addresses the first Black Women's Rights Convention in Akron, Ohio. Sojourner Truth was given the name Isabella Baumfree when she was born into slavery in Swartekill, New York. In 1843, she gave herself the name Sojourner Truth and became renowned as an abolitionist and women's rights activist.

> *"What was thy name?"*
> *"Belle."*
> *"Belle what?"*
> *"Whatever my master's name was."*
> *"Well, thee says thy name is Sojourner?"*
> *"Yes."*
> *"Sojourner what?"*
> *Sojourner confessed that she hadn't thought of that, whereupon the Quaker woman "picked that name to pieces" so much that it looked different; and "didn't seem to be such a name after all." Crestfallen, and hastily excusing herself, Sojourner "plodded on over the sandy road and was very hot and miserable." In her frustration she cried, "Oh*

God, give me a name with a handle to it." After all, since God's voice had led her out of the city into an unknown region, she now needed God to give her a last name. At that moment of despair, it came to her "as true as God is true, Sojourner Truth." She "leapt for joy" and thanked God for the name. "Thou art my master, and Thy name is Truth, and Truth shall be my abiding name till I die." Finally, after five masters and five children, and over forty years on the earth, Sojourner recalled, "I was liberated."

Source: From Margaret Washington. *Sojourner Truth's America*. Champaign, IL: University of Illinois Press, 2009, pp. 8–9.

Books

Mabee, Carleton and Susan Mabee Newhouse. *Sojourner Truth: Slave, Prophet, Legend*. New York, NY: NYU Press, 1995. Biography of Sojourner Truth, which argues for her placement as an icon in U.S. history.

Truth, Sojourner with Olive Gilbert and Nell Irvin Painter. *Narrative of Sojourner Truth: A Bondswoman of Olden Time, with a History of Her Labors and Correspondence Drawn from Her Book of Life*. New York, NY: Penguin Classics, 1998. Sojourner Truth tells her own story of her life and her fight for Black emancipation from slavery.

Websites

The Sojourner Truth Institute of Battle Creek, Michigan's Website maintains the most up-to-date information and various artifacts on the life and legacy of Sojourner Truth. http://www.sojournertruth.org.

The Website for the Sojourner Truth Memorial Statue Project in Florence, Massachusetts, posts information about the life of Sojourner Truth and the campaign to honor her memory. http://www.sojournertruthmemorial.org/.

Also Noteworthy

1938

The singer Etta James is born Jamesetta Hawkins in Los Angeles, California. She was an American blues, soul, rhythm and blues (R&B), rock-and-roll, gospel, and jazz singer. James became an R&B singer at the young age of 14 with her 1954 hit, "Roll with Me Henry." She is widely considered the other "Queen of Soul" (other than Aretha Franklin). James is celebrated for her renditions of "At Last" and "I'd Rather Go Blind."

January 26

1863

The Massachusetts 54th Regiment, the first state regiment of Black troops, is formed. The African American men who formed the 54th regiment were, in the majority, free Blacks from Massachusetts. They formed to fight in the U.S. Civil War, but also carried the hopes and aspirations of Blacks throughout the States—they had to prove that people of African descent were brave fighters and loyal to the nation.

Black leaders across the North understood the magnitude of the opportunity facing them, and its burdens. Although Union regiments of former slaves already on the battlefield had proved their valor under fire, Northern resistance to the widespread use of black troops remained firm. The very idea of armed blacks left many white Union soldiers with "a chilling sensation" and provoked, as in one Pennsylvania unit, feelings "akin to disgust." As the volunteers of the Fifty-fourth Massachusetts Regiment assumed responsibility to refute the racist accusations that blacks could not or would not fight, black men and women from across the North felt the "eyes of the whole world" upon them. The New York Weekly Anglo-American, the era's most influential black newspaper, best summarized the challenge: "Civilized man everywhere waits to see if you will prove yourselves . . . . Will you vindicate your manhood?" African Americans understood that if the regiments should fail, "it will be a blow from which we Northern men would never recover." The regiment's success would constitute a fatal blow against slavery and racism; failure would mean disaster.

Source: From Donald Yacovone, "The Fifty-fourth Massachusetts Regiment the Pay Crisis," in Martin Henry Blatt, Thomas J. Brown and Donald Yacovone. *Hope & Glory: Essays on the Legacy of the Fifty-Fourth Massachusetts Regiment.* Amherst, MA: University of Massachusetts Press, 2001, p. 36.

Books

DeAngelis, Gina. *The Massachusetts 54th: African American Soldiers of the Union.* Mankato, MN: Capstone Press, 2002. Book explains how the 54th regiment was formed and how it performed in the U.S. Civil War.

Emilio, Luis Fenollosa. *A Brave Black Regiment: The History of the Fifty-fourth Regiment of Massachusetts Volunteer Infantry, 1863–1865.* Cambridge, MA: Da Capo Press, 1995. The author, Captain Luis F. Emilio, tells the story of the formation of the 54th regiment and how it survived even after many of its officers were killed during the famous charge on Fort Wagner.

Websites

The History of the Wild West's Website provides short biographies on the individuals who formed the Massachusetts' 54th regiment. http://www.black-hawk-design.net/wildwest/54Regement/page10.htm.

The Website for the New England-based Museum of African American History in Florence, Massachusetts, posts information about the life of Sojourner Truth and the campaign to honor her memory. http://www.afroammuseum.org/site1.htm.

1892

Elizabeth "Bessie" Coleman is born in the rural town of Atlanta, Texas. A civil aviator, popularly known as "Queen Bess," Coleman was the first African American to become an airplane pilot, and the first American of any race or gender to hold an international pilot's license. After returning to the United States, Coleman became a barnstormer—performing tricks and aerial feats for large audiences. She planned to use the income from her performances to open a flight school specifically geared toward African Americans. Regrettably, Coleman died when, on April 30, 1926, her engine got stuck and she fell out of her plane to her death near Jacksonville, Florida.

In November 1920, Coleman enrolled in the Aviation School of the Caudron Brothers in Le Cretoy, France. On June 15, 1921, she became the first African American to earn an international pilot's license. With this license Coleman was able to fly throughout the world.

Source: From Margo McLoone and Jacquelyn L. Beyer. *Women Explorers of the Air: Harriet Quimby, Bessie Coleman, Amelia Earhart, Beryl Markham, Jacqueline Cochran.* Mankato, MN: Capstone Press, 1999, p. 20.

Books

Duncan, Joyce. *Ahead of Their Time: A Biographical Dictionary of Risk-Taking Women.* Santa Barbara, CA: Greenwood Publishing Group, 2002. Author provides a biographical sketch of Bessie Coleman.

Handleman, Philip and Craig Kodera. *A Dream of Pilots.* Gretna, LA: Pelican Publishing Company, 2009. Book places Bessie Coleman among the pioneers of U.S. aviation.

Websites

The Website of the U.S. Centennial of Flight Commission provides a detailed and sourced biographical essay on Bessie Coleman. http://www.centennialofflight.gov/essay/Explorers_Record_Setters_and_Daredevils/Coleman/EX11.htm.

The BessieColeman.com Website provides information about Coleman's life and work. http://www.bessiecoleman.com/default.html.

1948

President Harry S. Truman signs Executive Order 9981, designed to end racial segregation in the U.S. Armed Forces.

When asked about the impact of Executive Order 9981, Dr. Height, the respected civil rights advocate who served for four decades as the president of the NCNW, explained, "Harry Truman's integration of the armed services represented the most significant institutional advance for the civil rights of black Americans since President Lincoln issued the Emancipation Proclamation." Height, who succeeded civil rights pioneer Mary McLeod Bethune at the council, recalled how Truman's decisive take-charge action in integrating the military provided a much-needed example for U.S. corporate leaders, who often were reluctant to force integration of their employees in the same bold manner that the commander in chief had used in integrating the U.S. military.

Source: From Michael R. Gardner, George M. Elsey, Kweisi Mfume. *Harry Truman and Civil Rights: Moral Courage and Political Risks.* Carbondale, IL: SIU Press, 2003, p. 36.

Books

Browne-Marshall, Gloria J. *Race, Law, and American Society: 1607 to Present.* Cambridge, MA: Da Capo Press, 1995. Author presents detailed information on the legislation and social actions that led up to Truman's signing of Executive Order 9981.

Pohlmann, Marcus D. and Linda Vallar Whisenhunt. *Student's Guide to Landmark Congressional Laws on Civil Rights.* Santa Barbara, CA: Greenwood Publishing Group, 2002. Book asserts that with passage of legislation like his Executive Order 9981, President Truman was the most assertive president to advocate for African American civil rights, even though he was of European descent.

Websites

Harry S. Truman Library and Museum's Website provides background on Executive Order 9981, as well as a link to a digitized copy of the original document. http://www.trumanlibrary.org/9981.htm.

Website of the U.S. Equal Employment Opportunity Commission (EEOC) provides the full text of Executive Order 9981. http://eeoc.gov/eeoc/history/35th/thelaw/eo-9981.html.

January 27

1961

Lyric soprano opera singer Leontyne Price makes her New York City Metropolitan Opera House (Met) debut singing in Verdi's opera, *Il Trovatore.* Leontyne was born Mary Violet Leontyne Price in Laurel, Mississippi, on February 10, 1927. Price was already a famed and internationally sought-after opera singer at the time of her Met debut and remained so throughout her career. Her last professional performance was broadcast live from New York City's Lincoln Center: Price sang the lead in Verdi's *Aida* on January 3, 1985.

Ms. Price made successful debuts in grand opera productions in Europe. She conquered audiences in Paris, Vienna, and London as well as in the United States. Following these triumphs, she was invited to star at the Metropolitan Opera in New York. When she finished singing the role of Leonora in Verdi's Il Trovatore, *the audience gave her the longest tribute of applause in the Metropolitan Opera's history. The ovation lasted forty-two minutes. Later she became the first African American artist to have the honor of opening a Metropolitan Opera season. She starred in the opera written by Samuel Barber,* Anthony and Cleopatra, *that opened at the new opera house, the $50 million Metropolitan Opera House at Lincoln Center.*

Source: From Martha Ward Plowden. *Famous Firsts of Black Women.* Gretna, LA: Pelican Publishing Company, 2001, pp. 102–103.

Books

McCants, Clyde T. *American Opera Singers and Their Recordings: Critical Commentaries and Discographies.* Jefferson, NC: McFarland, 2004. Author notes the critical importance of Leontyne Price in classical music history.

Woodstra, Chris, Gerald Brennan, and Allen Schrott. *All Music Guide to Classical Music: The Definitive Guide to Classical Music.* Milwaukee, WI: Hal Leonard Corporation,

2005. Book provides a biographical sketch of Leontyne Price's life and singing career.

Websites

Metropolitan Opera House Website provides a searchable database with playbills for Leontyne Price's performances at the Met. http://archives.metoperafamily.org.

National Endowment for the Arts Opera Honors Awards Website has a biography of Price, which was uploaded in time for her 2008 tribute as a Lifetime Honoree. http://www.arts.gov/honors/opera/price2.html.

January 28

1986

Dr. Ronald Ervin McNair is a National Aeronautics and Space Administration (NASA) astronaut who died onboard the Space Shuttle *Challenger* when it exploded.

Leading the Challenger crew was the commander, Francis "Dick" Scobee, who had already flown on a shuttle mission. Michael J. Smith was the pilot; Challenger was his first space flight. With them were Ronald E. McNair, Judith A. Resnik, and Ellison S. Onizuka. They were scientists who would make sure the shuttle worked properly and also carry out experiments in space. The payload specialists, who looked after the equipment the shuttle would put into space, were Gregory B. Jarvis and teacher Christa McAuliffe. All seven people had lots of training for the mission. After the disaster, their families formed the Challenger Organization in their memory. It gives money to Challenger Learning Centers to encourage students to find out about space. The Ronald McNair Foundation also encourages scientific study.

Source: From Kathleen Fahey. Challenger and Columbia. Strongsville, OH: Gareth Stevens, 2005, p. 7.

Books

Naden, Corinne J. *Ronald McNair*. New York, NY: Chelsea House, 1990. Author looks at McNair's life and legacy.

Sherrow, Victoria. *Uniquely South Carolina*. Chicago, IL: Heinemann-Raintree Library, 2004. Biographies of famous people from South Carolina include a feature on Ronald McNair.

Websites

National Aeronautics and Space Administration (NASA) Website has a biographical page dedicated to McNair. http://www.jsc.nasa.gov/Bios/htmlbios/mcnair.html.

The Ronald McNair Middle School's Website features biographical information on the fallen astronaut and information on why the school was named in his honor. http://novusites.admin.brevard.k12.fl.us/schools/mcnairmid/aboutmcnair.html.

January 29

1885

Huddie William "Leadbelly" Ledbetter is born to Wesley and Sallie Ledbetter on the Jeter Plantation in Mooringsport, Louisiana. He was a local harmonica and guitar player in and around Louisiana until he fell under the sway of "Blind" Lemon Jefferson and became a devotee of the blues. He inherited the name "Leadbelly" and began playing a 12-string guitar. After being convicted of murder and assault, Leadbelly ended up serving time in the Louisiana State Penitentiary at Angola. There he met white music anthropologist John A. Lomax, who was able to help win Leadbelly a pardon. Leadbelly then embarked on a musical career that would influence other folk, blues, and rock-and-roll musicians for generations to come. In 1988 Leadbelly was inducted into the Rock and Roll Hall of Fame.

Huddie had learned earlier that he could attract attention in prison by customizing songs—either by adapting an existing song or making up a song about local specific events or people, whether it was Governor Neff he wanted to get a pardon from or a girlfriend he wanted to seduce. His quick wit and musical versatility made this almost second nature. Indeed, Leadbelly probably improvised scores of topical songs, forgetting them in a couple of weeks after they served their purpose. He soon found that the people in New York were not all that different from the audiences in Angola or Sugarland: all got a kick out of instant songs about current topics. Huddie enjoyed reading the newspapers as much as anyone else and the headlines he saw gave him ideas for a whole genre of new songs. If people tired of hearing about Pat Neff, then he could give them Jean Harlow, Howard Hughes, the Hindenburg airship, or the Queen Mary luxury liner—not quite protest songs, but pieces offering a fresh take on current topics.

Source: From Charles K. Wolfe, Kip Lornell. *The Life and Legend of Leadbelly*. Cambridge, MA: Da Capo Press, 1999, p. 203.

Books

Handyside, Chris. *Folk*. Chicago, IL: Heinemann-Raintree, 2006. Book looks at the growth of folk music in the United States and points to Leadbelly's role in bringing a blues influence to folk.

Robinson, Tiny and John Reynolds. *Lead Belly: A Life in Pictures*. Santa Ana, CA: Seven Locks Press, 1989. Photographs, letters, and other memorabilia show Leadbelly's musical career.

Websites

The nonprofit Leadbelly Foundation provides information on Leadbelly's musical legacy and promotes music scholarship. http://www.leadbelly.org/.

The Houston Institute for Culture's Website contains a biographical sketch of Leadbelly and includes lyrics to his song "Midnight Special." http://www.houstonculture.org/cr/lead.html.

1954

Oprah Gail Winfrey is born in Kosciusko, Mississippi. Her mother was still a teenager at the time, so Oprah was initially raised on a farm by her grandmother. Later she was raised by her mother in an inner-city Milwaukee neighborhood, but then moved in with her father and his new wife in Nashville, Tennessee. After initially working at age 17 on WVOL radio in Nashville, Winfrey was hired to coanchor the local evening news on WTVF-TV when she was 19 years old. Her talent stood out, and she was hired in Baltimore, Maryland, to anchor the news and host WJZ-TV's daytime talk show *People Are Talking*. As she became more successful, Oprah founded her own production company, syndicated her talk show internationally, and at one point was the world's only billionaire of African descent.

At age 19, Oprah became the first woman and first African American to anchor the news at Nashville's WTVF-TV. After three years in that job, she advanced to a larger market, WJZ-TV in Baltimore to anchor the 6 o'clock news. After the show's producers decided her delivery of the news was too emotional, she was relegated to the morning show, People Are Talking.

"The minute the first show was over, I thought, 'Thank God, I've found what I was meant to do.' It's like breathing to me."

Source: From Janet Lowe. *Oprah Winfrey Speaks: Insights from the World's Most Influential Voice*. Hoboken, NJ: John Wiley & Sons, 2001, p. 32.

Books

Konchar Farr, Cecilia. *Reading Oprah: How Oprah's Book Club Changed the Way America Reads*. Albany, NY: SUNY Press, 2005. Author looks at how Oprah's Book Club has broadened the reach of the publishing world and changed the reading habits of the U.S. public.

Nagle, Jeanne M. *Oprah Winfrey: Profile of a Media Mogul*. New York, NY: The Rosen Publishing Group, 2007. Book examines the media career of Oprah Winfrey.

Websites

The Oprah.com Website has links to Oprah Winfrey's television show, magazine, book club, and more—all under her company,

Harpo, Inc. http://www.oprah.com/index
.html.

Oprah's Angel Network uses donations from the
public to promote philanthropy around the
world. http://www.oprahsangelnetwork.org.

1872

Francis Lewis Cardoza is elected to serve as
state treasurer of the state of South Carolina;
he served in this position until 1877. In
January 1868, Cardoza had been elected to
the position of Secretary of State of South
Carolina—he became the first person of
African descent to serve in a state-level position in South Carolina. The child of Lydia
Williams, a free African American, and Isaac
N. Cardozo, a wealthy white Sephardic
Jewish father, Cardoza was born on January 1, 1837, in Charleston, South Carolina.
After attending free Black private schools,
he worked as a journeyman carpenter and
was able to save his money so that he could
enroll at the University of Glasgow in Scot-
land in 1858 and study to become a minister.
When he returned to the United States, Cardoza took part in many efforts to further the
education and political inclusion of people of
African descent, including serving as principal
of the Avery Normal Institute (today's Avery
Research Center for African American History and Culture, www.avery.cofc.edu). In
March 1867, Cardoza helped found the
South Carolina state Republican Party.

*After he had served out the first term of the
treasurership, he was re-elected in 1876, but the
downfall of Republicanism at that time prevented
the exercises of the duties of the office. The trans-
fer of the Republican State of government of
South Carolina and Louisiana to the Democrats
by a coup d'etat is perfectly familiar to all. During
his treasureship he handled between six and seven
million dollars and eight million in bonds and
stocks. His books were carefully and thoroughly
examined by a committee of the Democratic
Legislature after his term of office expired, with
an expert accountant, and they reported his books
correct.*

Source: From William J. Simmons and Henry
McNeal Turner. *Men of Mark: Eminent, Prog-
ressive and Rising.* Cambridge, MA: Harvard
University, 2006, p. 430.

Books

Cox, Joseph. *Great Black Men of Masonry.* Bloomington, IN: Indiana University Press, 2002.
Book provides a brief profile of the life and
work of Francis Cardoza.

Zuczek, Richard. *Encyclopedia of the Reconstruction
Era: A-L.* Albany, NY: SUNY Press, 2005.
Biographical sketch of Cardoza includes a list
of books for further reading on the
Reconstruction era and Cardoza's prominent
role at that time.

Websites

The University of North Carolina at Chapel
Hill's Website, "A Portion of the People:
Three Hundred Years of Southern Jewish
Life" provides a profile of Francis Lewis Car-
doza. http://www.lib.unc.edu/apop/this
happyland.html?counter=90.

The edited selection of "Slave Narratives" by the
University of Houston professor Steven
Mintz quotes from the famous speech "Let
the Lands of the South Be . . . Divided,"
which Cardoza gave at the proceedings of
the Constitutional Convention of South
Carolina in 1868. http://www.vgskole.net/
prosjekt/slavrute/43.htm.

January 30

1911

David Roy Eldridge is born in Pittsburgh,
Pennsylvania. By the age of 16, Eldridge was
being paid to play music professionally as he
toured with a carnival band. As an adult, he
would become famous for his powerful
trumpet playing, which strongly influenced
the U.S.-based jazz swing movement. When
he played with Gene Krupa's orchestra
between 1941 and 1942, Eldridge would
become famous for his classic versions of
"Rockin' Chair" and "After You've Gone."

No one more ably personified . . . excitement than the indefatigably competitive Roy Eldridge, a paradigm of the music's volatility and joy, whose trumpet electrified the jazz skies of five decades, transforming its fevers with generosity, cunning, and unconstrained elation. He incarnated the love of playing and asserted the highest personal standards of excellence. No one was more esteemed by his peers: Elmer Snowden dubbed him "Little Jazz" in the early '30s. The Little referred to his size and was later dropped, but the moniker that equated him with jazz itself stuck.

Source: From Gary Giddins. *Visions of Jazz: The First Century.* New York, NY: Oxford University Press, 2000, p. 188.

Books

Dance, Stanley. *The World of Swing: An Oral History of Big Band Jazz.* Cambridge, MA: Da Capo Press, 2001. Book includes a biographical sketch of Roy Eldridge, presented in the musician's own words, as he recalls his playing days and the other musicians he learned from and played with.

Jordan, Steve and Tom Scanlan. *Rhythm Man: Fifty Years in Jazz.* Ann Arbor, MI: University of Michigan Press, 1993. Rhythm guitarist Steve Jordan recalls having worked with Roy Eldridge and notes Eldridge's impact on jazz.

Websites

Suite101.com provides a biography of Eldridge's life and work. http://www.suite101.com/article.cfm/jazz/54219.

The Verve Music Group site provides a short biography and samples of Eldridge's discography. http://vervemusicgroup.com/artist/music/detail.aspx?pid=9214&aid=2712.

January 31

1865

The Thirteenth Amendment to the Constitution abolishes African slavery in the United States. The Constitutional Amendment was the official follow-up to the Emancipation Proclamation and was meant to guarantee the abolition of slavery. The Thirteenth Amendment declared that "Neither slavery nor involuntary servitude, except as a punishment for crime whereof the party shall have been duly convicted, shall exist within the United States, or any place subject to their jurisdiction." The Amendment was ratified by the states on December 6, 1865.

Until the House voted on January 31, 1865, no one could predict which way it would go. As a few Democrats early in the roll call voted Aye, Republican faces brightened. Sixteen of the eighty Democrats finally voted for the Amendment; fourteen of them were lame ducks. Eight other Democrats had absented themselves. This enabled the Amendment to pass with two votes to spare, 119 to 56. When the result was announced, Republicans on the floor and spectators in the gallery broke into prolonged—and unprecedented—cheering, while in the streets of Washington cannons boomed a hundred-gun salute.

Source: From James M. McPherson. *Battle Cry of Freedom: The Civil War Era.* New York, NY: Oxford University Press, 2003, p. 839.

Books

Remini, Robert Vincent. *The House: The History of the House of Representatives.* New York, NY: Smithsonian Books/Library of Congress/HarperCollins, 2006. Book details how the vote on the Thirteenth Amendment progressed and the notable legislators who were on site to witness its passage.

Wolf, Naomi. *Give Me Liberty: A Handbook for American Revolutionaries.* New York, NY: Simon & Schuster, 2008. Author looks how political activism has helped create democracy in the United States.

Websites

The National Archives has a jpeg of the original Thirteenth Amendment online. http://

www.archives.gov/historical–docs/document
.html?doc=9&title.raw=13th%20Amendment
%20to%20the%20U.S.%20Constitution%3A
%20Abolition%20of%20Slavery.

The Website for *Harper's Monthly* has an article
titled "The End of Slavery: The Creation of
the Thirteenth Amendment," which details
the creation of the Thirteenth Amendment.
http://13thamendment.harpweek.com/.

Also Noteworthy

1925

Benjamin Lawson Hooks is born in Memphis, Tenessee. Hooks was an attorney and Baptist minister who for 16 years led the National Association for the Advancement of Colored People.

February

February 1

1902

James Mercer Langston Hughes is born in Joplin, Missouri. As a poet and author, Langston Hughes became one of the most influential writers on African American life during the first half of the twentieth century; his influence on jazz poetry and his role in the Harlem Renaissance made him a major force on Black literature throughout the Americas as well as in Africa. Hughes spent his last years at his home in Harlem, New York, at 20 East 127th Street; his former home has been landmarked by the New York City Preservation Commission and his street—East 127th Street—has been renamed "Langston Hughes Place."

Hughes . . . sought his material in the world around him. "Seventh Street in Washington," he wrote, was "the long, old, dirty street where ordinary Negroes hang out. On Seventh Street they played the blues, ate watermelon, shot pool, told tall tales, and looked at the Dome of the Capitol and laughed out loud. I listened to their blues. And I went to their churches and heard the tambourines play and the little tinkling bells of the triangle adorn the gay shouting that sent sisters dancing down the aisle for joy. I tried to write poems like the songs they sang on South Street, . . . songs that had the pulse beat of the people who keep going. Like the waves of a sea coming one after another, so is the undertow of black music with its rhythm that never betrays you, its strength like the beat of a human heart, its humor, and its living power."

Source: From Langston Hughes, Arnold Rampersad, and David Ernest Roessel. Langston Hughes: Poetry for Young People. New York, NY: Sterling Publishing Company, Inc., 2006, p. 5.

Books

Hughes, Langston. *Not Without Laughter.* New York, NY: Simon & Schuster, 1995.

Hughes's first novel looks at the joys and pressures of life for young men of African descent.

McLaren, Joseph. *Langston Hughes, Folk Dramatist in the Protest Tradition, 1921–1943.* Westport, CT: Greenwood Publishing Group, 1997. Author examines the 40-some-odd theatrical plays Langston Hughes wrote.

Websites

The Website for Yale University's Beinecke Library maintains digital copies of Hughes's literary work. http://beinecke.library.yale.edu/digitallibrary/hughes.html.

Books and Writers features a biography of Hughes along with a list of some of his published works. http://www.kirjasto.sci.fi/lhughes.htm.

1960

Four freshmen at the historically Black North Carolina A&T College—Ezell Blair, Jr. (a.k.a., Jibreel Khazan), Franklin McCain, Joseph McNeil, and David Richmond—begin a "sit-down protest" for Civil Rights at the Woolworth's in downtown Greensboro, North Carolina, on February 1. Their efforts inspired other sit-in demonstrations and helped spur the U.S. Civil Rights Movement.

None of the "Greensboro Four," as they would later be dubbed in history books and civil rights lore, expected to become celebrities or heroes of the civil rights movement. What they expected, in fact, was to be arrested or beaten up at best or lynched at worst. What happened instead when they arrived at the Woolworth's on South Elm Street at approximately 4 p.m. that Monday was that everyone else at the lunch counter ignored them. The pregnant black waitress behind the counter, Geneva Tisdale, refused to serve them, fearing for her job and her health. On order from the store manager, Curly Harris, the white employees likewise ignored them. One elderly white lady, however, walked past them on her way out, patted them on the back, and told them she was proud of them; somebody should have done this years ago, she said. That sentiment was echoed by a local white merchant, Ralph Johns, who had long been encouraging blacks to step up and challenge the Jim Crow system. It was he who tipped off the local newspaper that a major story was developing downtown. At 5 p.m. the store closed for the day as usual. The Greensboro Four hurried back to campus, hearts racing, pride swelling, feet not touching the ground from the surreal feeling of excitement over what they had just done. It would not be the end of their "sit-down protest," however, as the local newspaper called it, but just the beginning.

Source: From Thomas Adams Upchurch. *Race Relations in the United States, 1960–1980*. Westport, CT: Greenwood Publishing Group, p. 8.

Books

Chafe, William Henry. *Civilities and Civil Rights: Greensboro, North Carolina, and the Black Struggle for Freedom*. New York, NY: Oxford University Press, 1981. Author examines the Woolworth sit-ins as the start of the U.S. Civil Rights revolution, and then looks specifically at how the sit-ins influenced progressive change in Greensboro, North Carolina.

Gaillard, Frye. *The Greensboro Four: Civil Rights Pioneers: A Profile*. Charlotte, NC: Main Street Rag Pub. Co., 2001. The four activists who led the famous Greensboro protest are profiled.

Websites

The International Civil Rights Center and Museum is now located on the site of the former Woolworth's in Greensboro, North Carolina. http://www.sitinmovement.org/.

The documentary film *February One* gives the flavor of the atmosphere in Greensboro as the nonviolent sit-in protests began. http://www.februaryonedocumentary.com.

February 2

1995

Dr. Bernard Harris, Jr., is launched into space as a NASA astronaut/mission specialist on the US/Russian Shuttle-Mir Program's STS-63. Harris became the first African American to walk in space on February 9, 1995, when he spent some four hours testing the heat capacity of his spacesuit and helping to refine spacewalk techniques. In his six years of work as an astronaut from 1990 to 1996, Dr. Harris logged some 438 hours during two NASA space shuttle missions to space.

Bernard A. Harris Jr. was the first African American astronaut to walk in space. On February 9, 1995, Harris stepped outside the STS-63, the first flight of the joint Russian-American space program. He remained in space for four hours and 25 minutes. An astronaut since 1991, Harris had also flown in space in 1993.

Source: From Betty Kaplan Gubert, Miriam Sawyer, and Caroline M. Fannin. *Distinguished African Americans in Aviation and Space Science*. Westport, CT: Greenwood Publishing Group, 2002, p. 150.

Books

Allen, Carole H. *Dare to Dream: Biography of Dr. Bernard A. Harris, Jr.* Bloomington, IN: Xlibris Corporation, 2007. Biography shows how Harris started from humble roots yet pursued his education and was able to become an astronaut and medical doctor.

Tripp, L. O. *African-American Astronauts: Guion S. Bluford, Jr., Charles F. Bolden, Jr., Frederick D. Gregory, Bernard A. Harris, Jr., Mae C. Jemison*. Mankato, MN: Capstone Press, 2000. Book presents short biographies of African Americans who have served in the U.S. space program.

Websites

In 1998, Dr. Harris established the nonprofit Harris Foundation "to develop math/science education and crime prevention programs for America's youth." http://www.theharris foundation.org/.

The Website for NASA's Kennedy Space Center details the launch of the 67th Shuttle Mission

STS-63 and the experiments conducted during its orbit. http://science.ksc.nasa.gov/shuttle/missions/sts-63/mission-sts-63.html.

Also Noteworthy

1897

Alfred L. Cralle receives U.S. Patent No. 576,395 for his ice cream scooper.

February 3

1870

The Fifteenth Amendment to the U.S. constitution is ratified. The Amendment was meant to grant African American men the right to vote by basically reinforcing their citizenship. But because various efforts continued to be used to disenfranchise people of African descent, the Fifteenth Amendment had to be strengthened again—nearly 100 years later—by the 1965 Voting Rights Act.

> *The remaining three Southern states completed the reconstruction process in 1869 and 1870. Congress required them to ratify the 15th as well as the 14th Amendments. The 15th Amendment prohibited states from denying the right to vote on grounds of race, color, or previous condition of servitude. Its purpose was not only to prevent the reconstructed states from any future revocation of black suffrage, but also extend equal suffrage to the border states and to the North. With final ratification of the 15th Amendment in 1870, the Constitution became truly color blind for the first time in U.S. history.*
>
> *Source: From John M. Murrin, Paul E. Johnson, James M. McPherson, and Gary Gerstle. Liberty, Equality, Power: A History of the American People, Compact. Florence, KY: Cengage Learning, 2007, p. 640.*

Books

Carter, Patrick. *American History*. Toronto, Canada: Emond Montgomery Publication, 2007.

Author summarizes the campaign for and passage of the Fifteenth Amendment.

Stephenson, D. Grier. *The Right to Vote: Rights and Liberties under the Law*. Santa Barbara, CA: ABC-CLIO, 2004. Book looks at the laws and cases that lead to the creation and enforcement of the right to vote.

Websites

The Library of Congress has links to speeches, graphics, and documentation that supported efforts to pass the U.S. Fifteenth Amendment to the Constitution. http://www.loc.gov/rr/program/bib/ourdocs/15thamendment.html.

The Website for the Our Documents initiative details the campaign for and creation of the Fifteenth Amendment. http://www.ourdocuments.gov/doc.php?flash=old&doc=44.

1956

Autherine Juanita Lucy enrolls as the first African American student to attend the University of Alabama (UA). When the university found out she was of African descent, it rejected her admission. It took three and a half years of legal action by the NAACP for Lucy to be allowed to attend the school. But with a race riot ensuing, and the UA's board remaining intransigent, Lucy finally gave up. In 1980 the University of Alabama annulled her expulsion and in 1992, Lucy graduated with a master's degree from the school. The University of Alabama then created the "Autherine Lucy Foster Endowed Scholarship" in her honor.

> *In 1950, Autherine Lucy sued for admission after the University of Alabama rejected her application because of her race. After several years of procedural delay, federal judge Harlen Hobart Grooms ordered her admitted in 1955, and the university complied early in 1956. A race riot ensued. More than 1,000 students protested, and a cross was burned. The board of trustees promptly suspended Lucy from classes, insisting that it was for her own safety. She then began contempt proceedings against university officials,*

alleging that they had acted in bad faith in sus- pending her. The court dismissed the contempt motion but ordered Lucy reinstated. University officials then promptly expelled her, allegedly because she had filed "shocking and baseless" charges against them in the contempt proceed- ings. Judge Grooms upheld the university's posi- tion, and early in 1957 Lucy abandoned her quest to attend the University of Alabama.

Source: From Michael J. Klarman. *From Jim Crow to Civil Rights: The Supreme Court and the Strug- gle for Racial Equality.* New York, NY: Oxford University Press, 2004, pp. 258–259.

Books

Carter, Patrick. *But for Birmingham: The Local and National Movements in the Civil Rights Struggle.* Chapel Hill, NC: UNC Press, 1997. Book looks at Birmingham, Alabama's, central role in the Civil Rights Movement struggles. Autherine Lucy's case is summarized and shown to have affected other activists and leaders in the state.

Sargent, Frederic O. *The Civil Rights Revolution: Events and Leaders, 1955–1968.* Jefferson NC: McFarland, 2004. Book provides a quick analysis of Autherine Lucy's efforts to attend the University of Alabama, the work of her attorney Thurgood Marshall, and the end of the campaign.

Websites

The Library of Congress' America's Story Website features the article "Autherine Lucy and the University of Alabama." http:// www.americaslibrary.gov/aa/marshallthrgd/ aa_marshallthrgd_lucy_1.html.

The National Women's History Museum (NWHM) profiles Autherine Lucy and looks at her efforts to integrate the University of Alabama. http://www.nwhm.org/Education/ biography_alucy.html.

1977

February 3 is the eighth and final night for the televised miniseries based on Alex Haley's *Roots.* This final episode achieved the highest ratings ever for a single television program. Haley, the author of *Roots* (for which he was awarded the Pulitzer Prize on April 18, 1977) and *The Autobiography of Malcolm X,* was born on August 11, 1921.

On February 3, ABC airs the final episode of the miniseries Roots, *based on Alex Haley's genealogi- cal novel* Roots: The Saga of an American Family. *The final episode of* Roots *achieves the highest- ever ratings for a single program.* Roots, *which stars Maya Angelou, LeVar Burton, O.J. Simpson, and Louis Gossett Jr., would go on to win nine Emmys, a Golden Globe, and a Peabody Award.*

Source: From Molefi K. Asante. *It's Bigger Than hip-hop: The Rise of the Hip-Hop Generation.* New York, NY: Macmillan/St. Martin's Press, 2008, p. 87.

Books

Haley, Alex. *Roots: The Saga of an American Family.* Boulder, CO: Westview Press, 2007. The Pulit- zer Prize- and National Book Award-winning novel tells the story of Haley's family history.

Wolper, David L. with David Fisher. *Producer: A Memoir.* New York, NY: Simon & Schuster, 2003. In his memoirs, Wolper speaks about his work with Alex Haley and the impact of pro- ducing the successful television series, *Roots.*

Websites

The Website for "Roots—The Book That Changed America" commemorates the 30th anniversary edition of the book and offers a dis- cussion forum as well as further information on the book, on the miniseries, and on the author, Alex Haley. http://www.rootsthebook.com.

The Museum of Broadcast Communications pro- files Alex Haley and talks about his literary output and the miniseries based on his popular book, *Roots.* http://www.museum.tv/eotvsection .php?entrycode=haleyalex.

Also Noteworthy

1964

Over 400,000 African American and Puerto Rican students boycott New York City's public schools in an organized civil rights protest.

February 4

1913

Rosa Louise McCauley Parks is born Rosa Louise McCauley to James McCauley and Leona Edwards in Tuskegee, Alabama. On December 1, 1955, Rosa Parks refused to change seats in a Montgomery, Alabama, bus and was arrested. This event helped spark the Civil Rights Movement's famous Montgomery Bus Boycott.

Rosa Parks was born in Tuskegee, Alabama. She was a well-respected seamstress and an active member of the NAACP when she broke a local segregation ordinance, on December 1, 1955, by refusing to give up her seat on a Montgomery bus to a white man who had boarded after her. Her subsequent arrest helped spark the famous boycott and led her to earn the title "Mother of the Civil Rights Movement." Parks subsequently was employed by the Southern Christian Leadership Conference (SLC) in Detroit, Michigan, and later worked for Congressman John Conyers, Jr.

Source: From Manning Marable and Leith Mullings. *Let Nobody Turn Us Around: Voices of Resistance, Reform, and Renewal: An African American Anthology.* Lanham MD: Macmillan/Rowman & Littlefield, 2009, p. 352.

Books

Giovanni, Nikki and Bryan Collier. *Rosa.* New York, NY: Simon & Schuster, 2003. This biography by noted poet Nikki Giovanni lyrically portrays Parks's life and importance to the Civil Rights Movement. The text is reinforced by watercolor illustrations created by artist Bryan Collier.

Parks, Rosa with James Haskins. *Rosa Parks: My Story.* Newton, KS: Paw Prints, 2009. This biography of Rosa Parks details her early life and the injustices she saw then, all leading up to the Montgomery Bus Boycott.

Websites

The Website for the Rosa & Raymond Parks Institute for Self Development was co-founded by Rosa Parks. The Institute promotes civic activism among youth, and the Website has detailed information on Parks's life. http://www.rootsthebook.com.

The Rosa Parks Museum of Troy University in Montgomery, Alabama, provides information about the museum exhibitions, which feature artifacts from 1955, when the Montgomery Bus Boycott took place. http://montgomery.troy.edu/rosaparks/museum.

February 5

1934

Henry "Hammerin Hank" Louis Aaron is born in Mobile, Alabama. Following a career in the Negro Baseball League with the Indianapolis Clowns, he joined the Major League Baseball's Atlanta Braves in 1954 and won a World Series ring with the Braves in 1957. On April 8, 1974, Aaron set the record for most home runs in a career when he hit his 715th, surpassing the 714 mark previously set by Babe Ruth.

They called Henry Louis Aaron "Hammerin' Hank," and the name fit perfectly. In addition to the home run record, Aaron also hammered his way in to the record book for knocking in the most runs (2,297) and compiling the most total bases (6,856) and extra-base hits (1,477). He ranks second in at-bats (12,364), is tied for second with Ruth in runs (2,174), and is third in hits (3,771) and games played (3,298). He is the only player to hit at least 30 homers in 15 seasons and at least 20 homers in 20 seasons. He hit at least 40 homers eight times, with a career best of 47.

Source: From Fred McMane. *The 3,000 Hit Club.* Champaign, IL: Sports Publishing LLC, p. 22.

Books

Kappes, Serena. *Hank Aaron.* Breckenridge, CO: Twenty-First Century Books, 2005.

Biography of the life of baseball player, Henry Hank Aaron.

Nemec, David. *Players of Cooperstown: Baseball's Hall of Fame*. Lincolnwood, IL: Publications International, 1995. This book features Hank Aaron as one of the most important players in Major League Baseball's history.

Websites

Life magazine's Website has an online tribute entitled "Hank Aaron: One and Only." http://www.life.com/image/first/in-gallery/24671/hank-aaron-a-legend-looks-back.

ESPN.com features a profile of Hank Aaron and his legacy. http://espn.go.com/sports century/features/00006764.html.

February 6

1820

The American Society for Colonizing the Free People of Color of the United States organizes its first emigration back to Africa when the ship Elizabeth—which had been re-named the "Mayflower of Liberia"—set sail from New York harbor. The Mayflower of Liberia carried some 86 formerly enslaved African Americans on-board. It had been granted some $100,000 to establish a new colony by the U.S. Congress. The ship landed in West Africa, in the British colony of Freetown, Sierra Leone, on March 9.

> On February 6, the Mayflower of Liberia *(previously the brig* Elizabeth*) sailed from New York City to Sierra Leone on the western coast of Africa with eighty-six blacks who had agreed to return to Africa as part of a colonization scheme. The ship arrived in Sierra Leone on March 9. The British had established Sierra Leone as a colony where former slaves could be repatriated to Africa. The colony had been accepting freed blacks and fugitive slaves for the past three decades.*
>
> *Source: From Junius P. Rodriguez.* Slavery in the United States: a social, political, and historical encyclopedia, Volume 2. *Santa Barbara, CA: ABC-CLIO, 2007, p. 36.*

Books

Clegg, Claude Andrew. *The Price of Liberty: African Americans and the Making of Liberia*. New York, NY: University of North Carolina Press, 2003. Author examines the colonization movement and the people and politics behind the decisions of some 2,000 African Americans to take their chances establishing a new life in Liberia.

McPherson, J. H. T. *History of Liberia*. Whitefish, MT: Kessinger Publishing, 2004. Book looks at the history of Liberia, particularly the arrival of African American emigrants from the United States.

Websites

The Website for the United Nations Development Programme—Liberia has a page dedicated to the historical foundation of the nation. http://mirror.undp.org/liberia/liberia.htm.

Liberia: Past and Present of Africa's Oldest Republic provides information about the colonization and growth of Liberia. http://www.liberiapastandpresent.org/.

1898

The author and educator, Melvin Beaunorus Tolson, is born in Moberly, Missouri. Educated at Fisk, Lincoln, and Columbia universities, Tolson would later teach English at the historically Black Wiley College, where he mentored the school's award-winning debate team, the Wiley Forensic Society. In 1935 the Wiley Forensic Society defeated the debate team of the traditionally white University of Southern California, the first time a Black debate team won against the reigning debating school team. Tolson's first volume of poetry, *Rendezvous with America*, is published in 1944. But he will become famous for his *Libretto for the Republic of Liberia*, published in 1953.

> *Tolson's major poems, which have been widely pub. and anthologized, include "Dark Symphony," which won the National Poetry Contest, and*

Libretto for the republic of Liberia (a longer work, 1953), for which he was named Liberia's poet laureate. After retiring from Langston in the 1960s, he spent his remaining years in a specially created post in humanities at Tuskegee Inst. (AL).

He was recipient of numerous honors and awards in poetry and was also permanent Bread Loaf Fellow in Poetry and Drama (1954). He died in Dallas, TX, at age sixty-six.

Source: From Bernard L. Peterson. *Profiles of African American Stage Performers, 1816–1960.* Santa Barbara, CA: ABC-CLIO, 2000, p. 240.

Books

Glasrud, Bruce A. *Blacks in East Texas History: Selections from the East Texas Historical Journal.* College Station, TX: Texas A&M University Press, 2008. Book provides a short biography of Tolson's life and work.

Tolson, Melvin Beaunorus, edited by Raymond Nelson. *"Harlem Gallery" and Other Poems of Melvin B. Tolson.* Charlottesville, VA: University Press of Virginia, 1999. This complete collection of Tolson's poetry gives a broad portrayal of his themes and styles.

Websites

The Poetry Foundation's Website has a page dedicated to Melvin B. Tolson. http://www.poetryfoundation.org/archive/poet.html?id=6871.

The Modern American Poetry Website's article "Melvin B. Tolson: Biographical Note" provides information about Tolson's life and work. http://www.english.illinois.edu/maps/poets/s_z/tolson/bio.htm.

1961

The "jail-in" movement starts in Rock Hill, South Carolina. Four students—Charles Sherrod, J. Charles Jones, Diane Nash, Ruby Doris Smith—are arrested during a sit-in. Rather than pay the fines for their arrest, the students—who are members of the Student Nonviolent Coordinating Committee (SNCC)—demand to be jailed and are sentenced to 30 days.

Standing behind the belief in "jail versus bail," a total of ninety-nine students entered jail during the first week of February ... with the determination to remain there. Six of the students are in Virginia, in the Lynchburg City Jail, convicted of trespass after a drug-store sit-in. They went in on Feb. 6 to serve 30 days. Eighty-four of the students are in Georgia, in the Fulton Tower of Atlanta, convicted of trespass in a downtown cafeteria. They went in on Feb. 7 and 8 to serve 30 days. Thirteen of the students are in South Carolina, convicted of trespass in variety and drug stores. Nine of them, Friendship College students, went in on February 1. Four more went in February 7. These last four are members of SNCC who decided, during the February SNCC meeting, that "we have no alternative other than to join them." The South Carolina arrests occurred in Rock Hill. Convicted and sentenced, the students were divided—the boys sent to York County Prison Farm in York, S.C. They will serve 30 days for trespassing.

Source: From Clayborne Carson, ed. *The Student Voice, 1960–1965: Periodical of the Student Nonviolent Coordinating Committee.* Santa Barbara, CA: Greenwood Publishing Group, 1990, p. 33.

Books

Carson, Clayborne. *In Struggle: SNCC and the Black Awakening of the 1960s.* Cambridge, MA: Harvard University Press, 1995. Author examines the history of SNCC and looks at the internal and external politics that affected the organization.

Zinn, Howard. *SNCC: The New Abolitionists.* Cambridge, MA: South End Press, 2002. Author looks at the revolutionary importance of SNCC and its influence on other student activist organizations.

Websites

The Civil Rights Movement Veterans Website has an article by J. Charles Jones on the "Rock Hill & Charlotte Sit-ins." http://www.crmvet.org/info/rockhill.htm.

Liberia: Past and Present of Africa's Oldest Republic provides information about the colonization and growth of Liberia. http://www.liberiapastandpresent.org/.

February 7

1872

Alcorn Agricultural and Mechanical College (later Alcorn State University, http://www.alcorn.edu) opens in Claiborne County, Mississippi; it is the first state-supported institution for the higher education of African Americans in the United States. The state's senator, Hiram Revels—the first African American elected to the U.S. Senate—serves as the first president of this historically Black institution, which opens with eight faculty members and 179 students—all men. Alcorn began admitting women in 1895.

> Three competent professors were employed, and the institution was opened February 7, 1872. The experiment of the higher education of the colored youth could not have been tried under more favorable auspices.
>
> ...
>
> ...It was under the presidency of Hon. and Rev. Hiram R. Revels, D.D. and ex-Senator of the United States, and himself a negro. A high curriculum was devised. During the first session, 117 students were enrolled; during the second, 179; during the third, 172.
>
> Source: From Edward Mayes. *History of Education in Mississippi.* Charleston, SC: Nabu Press/BiblioBazaar, 2010, pp. 271 and 273.

Books

Guy Dunham, Melerson. *The Centennial History of Alcorn Agricultural and Mechanical College.* Hattiesburg, MS: University and College Press of Mississippi, 1971. Looks at the formation of the college and its successes over 100 years.

McCann Posey, Josephine. *Alcorn State University and the National Alumni Association.* Mount Pleasant, SC: Arcadia Publishing, 2000.

Review of the history and establishment of Alcorn State University.

Websites

The Alcorn State University official Website profiles the school. http://www.alcorn.edu.

Alcorn State University "Campus Chronicle Online" is written by students attending the University. http://alcorn.jeffeco.com/.

1883

James Hubert "Eubie" Blake is born in Baltimore, Maryland. As a composer and pianist, Blake produces Ragtime hits like "I'm Just Wild About Harry" and "Shuffle Along," together with his writing partner, Noble Sissle. In 1978, *Eubie!*, a musical based on his music, opened on Broadway.

> Among African Americans who recorded prior to 1920, two of the best remembered are the team of Noble Sisle and Eubie Blake. In their day they were major stars of vaudeville and the Broadway stage, but probably the chief reason their names live on is the extraordinary success (as a composer) and longevity of Eubie Blake. Blake became a major media celebrity in his eighties and nineties, playing and talking about the ragtime music he loved to a generation far removed from the era in which it was created. He lived to the age of one hundred, and his death in 1983 made national headlines. Sissle and Blake each first recorded in 1917, making them pioneers among black recording artists.
>
> Source: From Tim Brooks and Richard Keith Spottswood. *Lost Sounds: Blacks and the Birth of the Recording Industry, 1890–1919.* Champaign, IL: University of Illinois Press, 2004, p. 363.

Books

Carter, Lawrence T. *Eubie Blake: Keys of Memory.* Detroit: Balamp Publishing, 1979. A look at Blake's life and various events during the formation of jazz.

George, Luvenia A. "The Early Piano Rags (1899–1916) of James Hubert ("Eubie") Blake: A

Stylistic Study and Annotated Edition." PhD diss., Baltimore, MD: University of Maryland Baltimore County, 1995. Blake's music is examined in depth.

Websites

The Maryland Historical Society hosts an online collection related to Eubie Blake. http://www.mdhs.org/eubieblake/index.html.

The Eubie Blake National Jazz Institute and Cultural Center Website promotes Blake's legacy. http://www.eubieblake.org/.

February 8

1968

The "Orangeburg Massacre" takes place on the campus of South Carolina State University. When Black students protested the segregated bowling alley near their school in Orangeburg, South Carolina, police attempted to stop them. Students threw rocks at the police, but the police shot at the students. Three students—Samuel Hammond, Delano Middleton, and Henry Smith—were killed; 27 other students were injured.

On the night of eighth day of February 1968 an all-white throng of state police unleashed massive gunfire into a crowd of black students near the edge of the South Carolina State College campus in Orangeburg. Three students were killed, twenty-seven were injured. Most of the students were shot from the side or in the back with shotguns. Killed in the incident were Samuel Hammond, Jr., an eighteen-year-old freshman from Fort Lauderdale, Florida; Delano Middleton, a seventeen-year-old Orangeburg youth; and Henry Smith, an eighteen-year-old sophomore from Marion, South Carolina.

Source: From Cecil J. Williams. *Freedom and Justice*. Macon, GA: Mercer University Press, 1995, p. 221.

Books

Bass, James and Jack Nelson. *The Orangeburg Massacre*. Hattiesburg, MS: University and College Press of Mississippi, 1971. Looks at the laws and persistence of discrimination that led to the Orangeburg Massacre.

Durbin Christian, James. *Newspapers and the Orangeburg Massacre: Framing a Deadly Encounter*. Columbia, S.C.: University of South Carolina, 2004. Reviews how the media covered the Orangeburg Massacre and how the event now lives in history.

Websites

The Orangeburg Massacre 1968 is a Website containing a documentary about the tragedy. http://www.orangeburgmassacre1968.com/.

The Orangeburg Massacre is also commemorated at the Website, which is connected to the American Public Radio drama, "The Orangeburg Massacre." http://www.orangeburgmassacre.com.

February 9

1944

The author Alice Malsenior Walker is born in Eatonton, Georgia. On April 18, 1983, she won the Pulitzer Prize for her novel *The Color Purple*, which would also win the American Book Award for fiction 10 days later.

...Perhaps the best indicator of her feelings about the success of The Color Purple could be found in a short profile that accompanied the Prescott review. "It is my happiest book," Alice told Newsweek. "I had to do all the other writing to get to this point. I had to live a lot and...much of it was hurt. But I learned that you can get a lot out of whatever happens to you."

Source: From Evelyn C. White. *Alice Walker: A Life*. New York, NY: W. W. Norton & Company, 2004, p. 350.

Books

Lauret, Maria. *Alice Walker*. New York, NY: Palgrave Macmillan, 2000. A review of Walker's life's work as a writer and womanist activist.

Lazo, Caroline Evensen. *Alice Walker: Freedom Writer*. Breckenridge, CO: Twenty-First Century Books, 2000. A biography of Alice Walker, written for young adults.

Websites

The official Alice Walker Website has the author's current photos, videos, and lists of books and upcoming events. http://www.alicewalkersgarden.com.

Emory University maintains the "Alice Walker Archives." http://www.emory.edu/home/academics/libraries/alice-walker.html.

Also Noteworthy

1902

Juanita Craft is born Juanita Jewel Shanks. A towering figure in civil rights history in the Dallas, Texas, area, Craft is remembered for having helped to organize some 182 branches of the National Association of Colored People in just 11 years. Her one-story, wood-frame home in South Dallas's Wheatley Historic District is today a historic landmark, known as the Juanita J. Craft Civil Rights House.

February 10

1854

Joseph Charles Price is born in Elizabeth City, North Carolina. Price founded North Carolina's Livingstone University (http://www.livingstone.edu) and served as the historically Black college's president in 1882. He also used his oratorical skills to raise monies for African American schools throughout the nation.

It is doubtful if the nineteenth century produced a superior or more popular orator of the type that enlists the sympathies, entertains and compels conviction than Joseph C. Price. In little more than a brief decade he was known in Great Britain and the United States, both on the Pacific and the Atlantic, as a peerless orator. In 1881 he first rose to eminence as a platform speaker; in 1893 his star sank below the horizon. Yet he was more than orator: he was a recognized race leader; a most potential force in politics, though not a politician; a builder of a great school—a most conspicuous object lesson of "Negro Capabilities."

Source: From John W. Cromwell. *The Negro in American History; Men and Women Eminent in the Evolution of the American of African Descent*. Charleston, SC: BiblioBazaar, LLC, 2009, p. 171.

Books

Walls, William Jacob. *Joseph Charles Price: Educator and Race Leader, Founder of Livingstone College*. Hanover, MA: The Christopher Publishing House, 1943. This biography of Joseph Charles Price is written by an A.M.E. Zion Church Bishop.

Yandle, Paul David. *Joseph Charles Price and the Southern Problem*. New York, NY: Wake Forest University. Department of History, 1990. A look at how Joseph Charles Price was able to conduct his work in the U.S. South, when discrimination against African Americans still reigned.

Websites

StoppingPoints.com has a short biography and notes the location of Joseph C. Price's home and grave in Salisbury, North Carolina. http://www.stoppingpoints.com/north-carolina/sights.cgi?marker=Joseph+C.+Price+1854–1893&cnty=Rowan.

Livingstone University maintains a page dedicated to noting the biography of its founder and first president, Joseph Charles Price. http://www.livingstone.edu/cms/Founder+and+First+President/28.html.

Also Noteworthy

1835

John Keep, who serves as president of the Board of Trustees of Ohio State's Oberlin College, casts the deciding vote that leads to the passage of a resolution allowing African Americans to attend the school. Oberlin is the first predominately white school to include people of African descent in its student body.

February 11

1644

Eleven Black indentured servants petition the Council of New Netherlands (which later became New York City) for their freedom. Most indentured servants had been able to complete their service within 7 years, but these Blacks had served nearly 18 years and been constantly refused their freedom. The Council granted freedom to this "New York 11," whose names were recorded as Paul d'Angola, Big Manuel, Little Manuel, Manual de Gerrit de Rens, Simon Congo, Anthony Portuguese, Gracia, Peter Santome, John Francisco, Little Anthony, and John Fort Orange. All received land grants and established their homes in what is today Greenwich Village; yet they were still required to pay yearly for their continued freedom. Subsequently, African people were enslaved, rather than given a set period of indentured servitude.

In this case as well as most other cases of manumission, the company's conditions of freedom required the Blacks to render some type of service to the company after manumission. A portion of the first manumission act (1644) declared:

Therefore we, the Director and Council do release, for the term of their natural lives, the above named and their wives from Slavery, hereby setting them free and at liberty, on the same footing as other free people here in New Netherlands, where they shall be able to earn their livelihood by Agriculture, on the land shown and granted to them, on condition that they, the above named Negroes, shall be bound to pay for the freedom they receive each man for himself annually, as long as he lives, to the West India Company for its Deputy here, thiry skepels (barn baskets-22 ½ bushels) of Maize, or Wheat, Pease or Beans, and one Fat Hog, valued at twenty guilders (89) which thirty skepels and the hog they, the Negroes, each for himself, promises to pay annually, beginning from the date hereof, on pain, if anyone of them shall fail to pay the yearly tribute, he shall forfeit his freedom and return back into the said Company's slavery.

Source: From Oscar Renal Williams. *African Americans and Colonial Legislation in the Middle Colonies.* New York, NY: Taylor & Francis, 1998, p. 15.

Books

Foote, Thelma Wills. *Black and White Manhattan: The History of Racial Formation in Colonial New York City.* New York, NY: Oxford University Press, 2004. Book shows how race and class differences help determine how people fit into the early creation of New York City.

Harris, Leslie M. *In the Shadow of Slavery: African Americans in New York City, 1626-186.* Chicago, IL: University of Chicago Press, 2004. Examination of how people of African descent lived, worked, and died in New York City from the city's founding until the official end of slavery.

Websites

Digitized document on the BlackHistory Matters.com Website shows that a parcel of Manhattan land was given in 1644 to Groote (Big) Manuel. http://www.freemaninstitute .com/BCF%20Manhattanphoto.htm.

The Internet Archive has full texts of "Dutch records in the City clerk's office, New York." http://www.archive.org/stream/dutchrecords inci00bant/dutchrecordsinci00bant_djvu.txt.

1813

Abolitionist and author Harriet Ann Jacobs is born into slavery in Edenton, North

Carolina. She escaped from slavery, and the sexual torment from her enslaver, by hiding in her grandmother's attic for seven years. Ultimately, Jacobs escaped to freedom in Brooklyn, New York.

> A small shed had been added to my grandmother's house years ago. Some boards were laid across the joists at the top, and between these boards and the roof was a very small garret, never occupied by any thing but rats and mice. It was a pent roof, covered with nothing but shingles, according to the southern custom for such buildings. The garret was only nine feet long and seven wide. The highest part was three feet high, and sloped down abruptly to the loose board floor. There was no admission for either light or air. My uncle Philip, who was a carpenter, had very skillfully made a concealed trap-door, which communicated with the storeroom. He had been doing this while I was waiting in the swamp. The storeroom opened upon a piazza. To this hole I was conveyed as soon as I entered the house. The air was stifling: the darkness total. A bed had been spread on the floor. I could sleep quite comfortably on one side; but the slope was so sudden that I could not turn on the other without hitting the room. The rats and mice ran over my bed; but I was weary, and I slept such sleep as the wretched may, when a tempest has passed and night were all the same.
>
> Source: From Harriet A. Jacobs. *Incidents in the life of a Slave Girl, Written by Herself*. Whitefish, MO: Kessinger Publishing, 2004, p. 98.

Books

Garfield, Deborah M. and Rafia Zafar. *Harriet Jacobs and Incidents in the Life of a Slave Girl: New Critical Essays*. New York, NY: Cambridge University Press, 1996. Looks at the growing importance of Harriet Jacobs's *Incidents in the Life of a Slave Girl*.

Jean Fagan Yellin. *Harriet Jacobs: A Life*. New York, NY: Westview Press, 2005. Retraces the historical documents that detail how Harriet Jacobs survived slavery.

Websites

The Harriet Jacobs Website provides a biography of the abolitionist activist. http://www.harriet jacobs.org/.

A full digitized edition of *Incidents in the Life of a Slave Girl, Written by Herself* is available from the Documenting the American South Website (DocSouth). http://docsouth.unc.edu/fpn/jacobs/jacobs.html.

1977

Clifford Alexander, Jr., is confirmed as the first African American to serve as U.S. Secretary of the Army. He served from February 1977 through January 1981, during the Carter administration.

> Clifford Alexander, Jr., a distinguished lawyer and public servant, held positions in four presidential administrations during the 1960s and '70s.
>
> ...Alexander...practiced law until 1977, when President Jimmy Carter appointed him secretary of the Army. He was the first African American to hold that position. He served until Ronald Reagan took office, and later formed a consulting company, Alexander & Associates, Inc., that advised businesses on increasing minority hiring.
>
> Source: From Joan Potter. *African American Firsts: Famous Little-Known and Unsung Triumphs of Blacks in America*. New York, NY: Dafina Books, 2009, p. 160.

Books

Breuer, William B. *War and American Women: Heroism, Deeds, and Controversy*. Westport, CT: Greenwood Publishing Group, 1997. Book notes Alexander's role in advocating for women's service in the U.S. military.

U.S. Congress Senate Committee on Armed Services. *Nominations of Clifford L. Alexander, Jr., and W. Graham Clayton, Jr.* Washington, DC: U.S. Government Printing Office, 1977. A record of the Committee on Armed Services' hearings on Alexander's nomination to be Secretary of the Army.

Websites

The National Visionary Leadership Project Website features a biography of and a video interview with Clifford Alexander, Jr. http://www.visionaryproject.com/alexanderclifford/.

The American Presidency Project has a digitized version of the press release announcing President Jimmy Carter's decision to nominate Alexander as Secretary of the Army. http://www.presidency.ucsb.edu/ws/index.php?pid=7400.

February 12

1909

Formation of the National Association for the Advancement of Colored People (NAACP) by a group of multiracial activists. The group was originally called the National Negro Committee. The NAACP was formed in response to the Springfield, Illinois, race riot of 1908.

> We denounce the ever growing oppression of our 10,000,000 colored fellow citizens as the greatest menace that threatens the country. Often plundered of their just share of the public funds, robbed of nearly all part in the government, segregated by common carriers, some murdered with impunity, and all treated with open contempt by officials, they are held in some States in practical slavery to the white community. The systematic persecution of law-abiding citizens and their disfranchisement on account of their race alone is a crime that will ultimately drag down to an infamous end any nation that allows it to be practiced, and it bears most heavily on those poor white farmers and laborers whose economic position is most similar to that of the persecuted race.
>
> *Source*: From Marshall Cavendish Corporation. "Platform Adopted by the National Negro Committee, 1909" in *America in the 20th Century, Volume 12*. Tarrytown, NY: Marshall Cavendish, 2003, p. 1475.

Books

National Association for the Advancement of Colored People. *NAACP: Celebrating a Century—100 Years in Pictures*. Layton, Utah: Gibbs Smith, 2009. A photographic record of the NAACP's century of activism.

Zangrando, Robert L. *The NAACP Crusade Against Lynching, 1909–1950*. Philadelphia, PA: Temple University Press, 1980. Book details the NAACP's ultimately unsuccessful effort to get the U.S. government to enact a federal antilynching law.

Websites

The National Association for the Advancement of Colored People (NAACP) promotes local membership across the United States and organizes community activism. http://www.naacp.org.

Documents from the Niagara Movement—the organization which preceded the formation of the NAACP—are online with the University of Massachusetts Amherst Du Bois Papers Archives, http://www.library.umass.edu/spcoll/digital/niagara.htm.

1934

William Felton "Bill" Russell is born in Monroe, Louisiana, and when he was nine his family moved to Oakland, California. At 6 feet 9 inches, he was drafted in 1956 by the National Basketball Association's St. Louis Hawks but was traded and served some 13 years as the center for the Boston Celtics basketball team from. Russell's Celtics won 11 championships. Russell was voted the NBA's most valuable player five times and was the first African American player inducted into the Basketball Hall of Fame.

> He ended up signing with the Celtics for $19,500, a substantial bargain even at the modest salaries most top professional athletes were making in the 1950s. Russell just wanted to play ball and prove his worth as an NBA center. "When I signed my first pro contract," Russell later recounted, "Red [Auerbach] asked me whether I was concerned about my scoring. I had a reputation as not being much of a scorer in college, and I said I was a little worried. So he told me, 'From this day

on, every time we talk about contracts we will never discuss statistics. I want you to think about winning, not about scoring.' That took the pressure off me."

Source: From Thomas J. Whalen. *Dynasty's End: Bill Russell and the 1968–69 World Champion Boston Celtics.* Lebanon, NH: University Press of New England, 2005, p. 46.

Books

Nelson, Murry R. *Bill Russell: A Biography.* Santa Barbara, CA: Greenwood Publishing Group, 2005. Russell's life, basketball career, and ideas are profiled in this biography.

Russell, Bill with David Falkner. *Russell Rules: 11 Lessons on Leadership from the Twentieth Century's Greatest Winner.* New York, NY: Penguin, 2002. Russell uses his philosophy of winning at basketball to demonstrate how to win at life.

Websites

"Bill Russell Block Art" shows the player's talents as a defensive center. http://www.YouTube.com/watch?v=nWFsL4Y8RVA.

"Bill Russell Interview: Cornerstone of the Boston Celtics' Dynasty" includes a text and video interview with Russell. http://www.achievement.org/autodoc/page/rus0int-1.

February 13

1920

The first African American baseball league, known as the National Negro Baseball League (NNL), is established inside the Paseo YMCA in Kansas City, Missouri. The league's first game was played on May 2, 1920, between the Indianapolis ABCs and the Chicago American Giants at Washington Park in Indianapolis; the ABCs won the game by a score of 4 to 2. This was officially the third attempt to form a baseball league for people of African descent, who were not allowed to play in the country's major and minor baseball leagues. The NNL's motto was "We are the ship, all else the sea." The NNL was the first Black Baseball league to last for more than one year; it lasted from 1920 to 1931.

From 1920, when the first Negro National League was founded in Kansas City, until 1946, when Jackie Robinson formally stepped across the color line and into organized white baseball, the Negro leagues grew, matured, overcame hardship, and even flourished.

Black teams, representing black communities, formed a replica of major-league baseball, separate and unequal in everything but athletic ability. Though it was virtually ignored by the dominant white culture, in the black community the Negro league was a cultural institution of the first magnitude.

Source: From Donn Rogosin. *Invisible Men: Life in Baseball's Negro Leagues.* New York: Atheneum/Bison Books, 2007, p. 4.

Books

Lanctot, Neil. *Negro League Baseball: The Rise and Ruin of a Black Institution.* Philadelphia, Pennsylvania: University of Pennsylvania Press, 2004. This book looks at the long effort to establish successful Black baseball franchises, and how they later were destroyed by integration.

Nelson, Kadir. *We Are the Ship: The Story of Negro League Baseball.* Hyperion Book CH, January 8, 2008. In words and paintings, Kadir Nelson introduces readers to the thoughts and feelings of African American baseball players who battled through racism and discrimination.

Websites

The Negro League Baseball Players Association (NLBPA) celebrates the major players in the Negro Baseball League. http://www.nlbpa.com/history.html.

The Negro League Baseball Website promotes the history of Negro League Baseball. http://www.negroleaguebaseball.com/.

1923

Robert J. Douglas, a West Indian entrepreneur who lived in Harlem, creates the first all-Black professional basketball team. Douglas's team, the New York Renaissance, also known as the "Rens" or the "Renaissance Five," was the first African American basketball team with players who were paid to play the game. From 1932 through 1933, the Rens posted an 88-game winning streak. Douglas became known as the "Father of Black Basketball" and was eventually inducted into the NBA Hall of Fame.

> One of the first basketball dynasties, the New York Renaissance, was founded in 1923. The team's namesake came from their home court, the Harlem Renaissance Ballroom, in which they played 27 seasons. The Renaissance organized games each day of the week and twice on Sundays. Because the racial climate of the 1930s was often harsh and unforgiving, while away from their home court, the Rens were often refused food and board. Other barnstorming teams included the Harlem Globetrotters, the New York Enforcers and the Philadelphia Tribunes.
>
> Source: From United States of America Congressional Record: Proceedings and Debates of the 109th Congress. Volume 151, Part 16. Government Printing Office, p. 1153.

Books

Porter, David L. *Basketball: A Biographical Dictionary*. Santa Barbara, CA: Greenwood Publishing Group, 2005. Contains sketch of William "Wee Willie" Smith, the legendary center for the New York Renaissance team.

Thomas, Ron. *They Cleared the Lane: The NBA's Black Pioneers*. Lincoln, NE: University of Nebraska Press, 2004. Looks at the role racism played in keeping African Americans out of professional basketball.

Websites

Hoopedia, The Basketball Wiki Website http://hoopedia.nba.com/index.php?title =Renaissance_Five has an entry on the Renaissance Five.

Black Legends of Professional Basketball Foundation promotes the history of Black participation in organized basketball. http://jumpinjohnnykline.com/

February 14

1760

The activist/writer and minister Richard Allen is born in Germantown, Pennsylvania. Allen and Absalom Jones organized Philadelphia's Free Africa Society, a mutual self-help group in Philadelphia, Pennsylvania. Richard Allen also later founded the Bethel African Methodist Church in Philadelphia in 1794.

> Much depends upon us for the help of our color—more than many are aware. If we are lay and idle the enemies of freedom plead it as a cause why we ought not to be free, and say we are better in a state of servitude, and that giving us our liberty would be an injury to us; and by such conduct we strengthen the bands of oppression and keep many in bondage who are more worthy than ourselves. I entreat you to consider the obligations we lie under to help forward the cause of freedom. We who know how bitter the cup is of which the slave hath to drink, O, how ought we to feel for those who yet remain in bondage! Will even our friends excuse—will God pardon us—for the part we act in making strong the hands of the enemies of our color?
>
> Source: From Richard Allen and Absalom Jones. The Life, Experience, and Gospel Labors of the Rt. Rev. Richard Allen: To Which is Annexed, the Rise and Progress of the African Methodist Episcopal Church in the United States of America: Containing a Narrative of the Yellow Fever in the Year of Our Lord 1793: With an Address to the People of Color in the United States. Columbia University/ F. Ford and M.A. Riply, 1880, pp. 55–56.

Books

Newman, Richard S. *Freedom's Prophet: Bishop Richard Allen, the AME Church, and the Black*

Founding Fathers. New York: NYU Press, 2008. Thorough biography of Richard Allen examines the impact of his spiritual, abolitionist, and activist work.

Robert Wright, Richard and African Methodist Episcopal Church. *Richard Allen, 1760–1831: Greatest Negro Born in America*. Philadelphia, PA: St. George Methodist Church, 1960. Short biography recognizing the life and work of Richard Allen.

Websites

The full text of Richard Allen's *The Life, Experience, and Gospel Labours of the Rt. Rev. Richard Allen* is digitized and available online. http://docsouth.unc.edu/neh/allen/allen.html.

The Mother Bethel AME museum features artifacts from Allen's church as well as the Bishop's tomb. http://www.motherbethel.org/mus.php.

1817

The African American leader and abolitionist, Frederick Douglass, is born into slavery to Harriet Bailey. He was originally given the name Frederick Augustus Washington Bailey. Disguised as a sailor, Douglass liberated himself from slavery in Baltimore in 1838, and then spent the rest of his life speaking out against the institution of slavery. He was a major moral and social-reform force in the United States. After his freedom from slavery, Douglass played a major role in the nation's politics. On July 1, 1889, he was named U.S. Minister to Haiti. On February 24, 1922, Douglass's home was made a national shrine.

Very soon after I went to live with Mr. and Mrs. Auld, she very kindly commenced to teach me the A, B, C. After I had learned this, she assisted me in learning to spell words of three or four letters. Just at this point of my progress, Mr. Auld found out what was going on, and at once forbade Mrs. Auld to instruct me further, telling her, among other things, that it was unlawful, as well as unsafe, to teach a slave to read. To use his own words, further, he said, "If you give a nigger an inch, he will take an ell. A nigger should know nothing but to obey his master—to do as he is told to do. Learning would spoil the best nigger in the world. "Now" said he, "if you teach that nigger (speaking of myself) how to read, there would be no keeping him. It would forever unfit him to be a slave. He would at once become unmanageable, and of no value to his master. It would make him discontented and unhappy." These words sank deep into my heart, stirred up sentiments within that lay slumbering, and called into existence an entirely new train of thought. It was a new and special revelation, explaining dark and mysterious things, with which my youthful understanding had struggled, but struggled in vain. I now understood what had been to me a most perplexing difficulty—to wit, the white man's power to enslave the black man. It was a grand achievement, and I prized it highly. From that moment, I understood the pathway from slavery to freedom. It was just what I wanted, and I got it at a time when I the least expected it. Whilst I was saddened by the thought of losing the aid of my kind mistress, I was gladdened by the invaluable instruction which, by the merest accident, I had gained from my master. Though conscious of the difficulty of learning without a teacher, I set out with high hope, and a fixed purpose, at whatever cost of trouble, to learn how to read.

Source: From Frederick Douglass, edited by Henry Louis Gates. Des Moines. *Frederick Douglass: Autobiographies*. IA: Library of America, 1994, pp. 37–38.

Books

Lampe, Gregory P. *Frederick Douglass: Freedom's Voice, 1818–1845*. East Lansing, MI: Michigan State University Press, 1998. Examines the training and effort Douglass put into his career as a public speaker and advocate.

McFeely, William S. *Frederick Douglass*. New York, NY: W. W. Norton & Company, 1995. Biography of Douglass's life and work.

Websites

The nonprofit Fremarjo Enterprises, Inc., has an online biography on the life of Frederick Douglass. http://www.frederickdouglass.org/douglass_bio.html.

The Frederick Douglass Papers at the Library of Congress contains links to PDF documents of articles and speeches written by the activist. http://memory.loc.gov/ammem/doughtml/doughome.html.

1867

The Augusta Institute is established in the basement of the Springfield Baptist Church in Augusta, Georgia. Founded by Rev. William Jefferson White, the Institute was meant to prepare Black men to serve as educators and ministers. The Augusta Institute later moved to Atlanta, Georgia, and was renamed Morehouse College (http://www.morehouse.edu). Morehouse serves as a liberal arts college for African American men.

William Jefferson White, an Augusta Baptist minister and cabinetmaker, founded the Augusta Institute. With educating the recently emancipated Negroes as their mission, they started a campaign that was highly unpopular in the South. In addition to operating with inadequate facilities during its early years, the college also had to deal with protests from the recently formulated Ku-Klux-Klan.

However under the auspices of the American Baptist Home Mission Society and through the friendship of Rev. James Dixon, a white pastor of an Augusta church, the Institute faltered, but never failed. Dixon encouraged Rev. Dr. Joseph T. Robert, a white minister, to return to the South to run this Institute. Robert had left the South because he sought not to educate his children in a society that perpetuated slavery. With the approval of the Mission Society, Robert did return in 1871 to become the first president of the school.

Source: From Dereck Joseph Rovaris. *Mays and Morehouse.* Silver Spring, MD: Beckham Publications Group, Inc., 2004, p. 56.

Books

Jones, Edward Allen. *A Candle in the Dark; A History of Morehouse College.* Valley Forge, PA: Judson Press, 1967. A history of the founding and mission of Morehouse, from its earlier days to the 1960s.

Williams, David Salter. *From Mounds to Megachurches: Georgia's Religious Heritage.* Athens, Georgia: University of Georgia Press, 2008. Features a section on the founding of Morehouse and the college's impact on Georgia's religious tradition.

Websites

The Morehouse College Website features the article "Morehouse Legacy," which gives a history of the school, pointing to its beginnings as Augusta Institute. http://www.morehouse.edu/about/legacy.html.

The Atlanta, Georgia, information site features a page on Morehouse. http://acvbfoundation.com/detailPages/detail_page.aspx?accountnum=00086244.

February 15

1961

African Americans and African nationalists protest the assassination of Congo Premier Patrice Lumumba by disrupting and taking over sessions at the United Nations in New York City. Protestors assumed what has recently been confirmed—that Belgium and U.S. forces had played a major role in Lumumba's assassination.

On Wednesday evening, February 15, 1961, at the United Nations headquarters in Manhattan, a group of African Americans, the women wearing black veils and men black armbands, shocked Americans when they took their outrage right onto the floor of the Security Council meeting on the Congo Crisis. On several occasions, key officials in U.S. foreign policy circles had indicated that they were against Lumumba and favored the Belgian interests and the dismemberment of the Congo. Thus, while the U.S. Representative Adlai Stevenson was speaking, "about sixty men and women burst into the Security Council Chamber, interrupting the session, and fought with guards in a protest against the United Nations policies in the Congo and the slaying of Patrice Lumumba, former Congo Premier. After the violent clash between demonstrators and the special UN police force, twenty people were treated for injuries by United Nations medical personnel.

Source: From Komozi Woodard. *A Nation Within a Nation: Amiri Baraka (LeRoi Jones) and Black Power Politics.* Chapel Hill, NC: UNC Press Books, 1999, p. 139.

Books

Joseph, Peniel E. *The Black Power Movement: Rethinking the Civil Rights-Black Power Era.* New York, NY: CRC Press, 2006. Looks at the connections between U.S. Black nationalists and the African liberation movements.

Minter, William. *King Solomon's Mines Revisited: Western Interests and the Burdened History of Southern Africa.* New York, NY: Basic Books, 1986. While examining U.S. relations with governments in Africa, the author writes about the importance of the U.N. demonstration against Lumumba's assassination.

Websites

The article "Dedicated to the Struggle: Black Music, Transculturation, and the Aural Making and Unmaking of the third World" on the Black Music Research Journal Website describes the U.N protests by Black nationalists. http://bmrj.press.illinois.edu/28/2/njoroge.html.

The article "Longer, analytical article." D R Congo: New evidence on Lumumba death in AfricaFiles.org features excerpts from William Minter's *King Solomon's Mines Revisited,* which details the U.N. protests and their aftermath. http://www.africafiles.org/article.asp?ID=24137&ThisURL=./history.asp&URLName=History.

February 16

1923

Blues great Bessie Smith records the song "Down Hearted Blues" for Columbia Records. The song was written by Alberta Hunter and Lovie Austin and became so popular it sold more than 800,000 copies and introduced much of the nation to the blues.

Blues performers like Chattanooga native Bessie Smith, and Alberta Hunter, who was born in Memphis, honed their musical talents performing throughout the South but found prosperity performing in New York and Chicago. As black music moved northward with the Great Migration, blues attracted black and would-be hip white urban audiences. Smith's 1923 recording of Hunter's song, "Down Hearted Blues," sold over two million records, becoming one of the biggest hits of the decade.

Source: From Paul H. Bergeron, Stephen V. Ash, Jeanette Keith. *Tennesseans and Their History.* Knoxville, TN: University of Tennessee Press, 1999, p. 245.

Books

Davis, Angela Yvonne. *Blues Legacies and Black Feminism: Gertrude 'Ma' Rainey, Bessie Smith, and Billie Holiday.* New York: Pantheon, 1998. Campbell, CA: Paw Prints, 2008. Author looks at the theme of feminist freedom that can be found in the songs of Bessie Smith, Billie Holiday, and Ma Rainey.

Kay, Jackie. *Bessie Smith.* Portsmouth-Hampshire, UK: Playground, 2004. Biography of Bessie Smith's professional and personal life.

Websites

The Amoeblog Website celebrates Smith's April 15 birthday with a biography and some video of her recordings. http://www.amoeba.com/blog/2009/04/jamoeblog/happy-birthday-bessie-smith-empress-of-the-blues.html.

The Bessie Smith, Talking to the Day Website features biographical information along with links to Smith's music and lyrics. http://xroads.virginia.edu/~UG97/blues/bs.html.

Also Noteworthy

1812

The African Lodge of Boston, Massachusetts, issues a charter allowing for the establishment of the Boyer Grand Lodge in New York City. The name Boyer had been chosen to honor the Haitian President Jean

Pierre Boyer, who had helped liberate Haiti from France. The name of the Boyer Grand Lodge was changed to the United Grand Lodge of New York on October 13, 1848.

February 17

1942

Huey Percy Newton is born in Monroe, Louisiana. Newton's family moved to Oakland, California, when he was three years old. While attending college in October 1966, Newton and Bobby Seale formed the Black Panther Party for Self Defense.

From all of these things—the books, Malcolm's writings and spirit, our analysis of the local situation—the idea of an organization was forming. One day, quite suddenly, almost by chance, we found a name. I had read a pamphlet about voter registration in Mississippi, how the people in Lowndes County had armed themselves against Establishment violence. Their political group, called the Lowndes County Freedom Organization, had a black panther for its symbol. A few fays later, while Bobby and I were rapping, I suggested that we use the panther as our symbol and call our political vehicle the Black Panther Party. The panther is a fierce animal, but he will not attack until he is backed into a corner; then he will strike out. The image seemed appropriate, and Bobby agreed without discussion. At this point, we knew it was time to stop talking and begin organizing. Although we had always wanted to get away from the intellectualizing and rhetoric characteristic of other groups, at times we were as inactive as they were. The time had come for action.

Source: From Huey P. Newton, David Hilliard, Donald Weise. *The Huey P. Newton Reader*. New York, NY: Seven Stories Press, 2002, p. 52.

Books

Jeffries, Judson L. *Huey P. Newton: The Radical Theorist*. Jackson, MS: University Press of Mississippi, 2006. Outlines the life and political achievements of B. K. Bruce.

Morrison, Toni, ed. *To Die for the People: The Writings of Huey P. Newton*. New York, NY: Random House, 1972. Provides a collection of Newton's essays and speeches.

Websites

The Huey P. Newton Foundation is a nonprofit designed to continue Newton's legacy of advocacy for people of African descent. http://www.blackpanther.org.

PBS Website for the film *A Huey P. Newton Story* features a biography of Newton and information about the people and time period he lived in. http://www.pbs.org/hueypnewton/.

Also Noteworthy

1891

A. C. Richardson receives U.S. Patent No. 466,470 for his invention of the churn machine.

1909

Francisco "Pancho" Coimbre is born in Coamo, Puerto Rico, but raised in Ponce. After playing 13 seasons with the Leones de Ponce of the Puerto Rican Professional Baseball League (LBPPR)—where he won two LBPPR batting titles and the league's Most Valuable Player Award in 1943—Coimbre moved to New York City and joined the Negro Leagues' Puerto Rico Stars baseball team.

February 18

1948

Oliver Toussaint Jackson, the founder of the town of Dearfield, Colorado, dies. Jackson had created a colony for African Americans, after having been inspired by the philosophical teachings of Booker T. Washington. After a successful start, the Great Depression and the Dust Bowl ruined the agricultural opportunities in Dearfield and the community failed. Dearfield is now a National Historic District.

Jackson's new land, thirty miles east of Greeley, became the nucleus for the black colony of Dearfield. Jackson and his wife Minerva, organized the Negro Townsite and Land Company in 1909. With advertising and persuasion, Jackson inspired sixty settlers of color to join in his agriculture colony. He established the Dearfield Lodge, complete with the fashionable false front of the period.

Along with the farming, Jackson planned canning factories and a college. While these dreams never materialized, the community did prosper for a time, with a peak population of 700. Even Booker T. Washington visited the small community. Within five years Dearfield had forty-four wooden cabins and over 600 farm acres. The community had two churches, a school, a boardinghouse, a blacksmith shop, cement factory and a filling station.

Source: From Linda Wommack. *From the Grave: A Roadside Guide to Colorado's Pioneer Cemeteries.* Caldwell, ID: Caxton Press, 1998, p. 78.

Books

Picher, Margaret. *Dearfield, Colorado: A Story from the Black West.* Denver, CO: University of Denver, 1976. Looks at the founding and establishment of Dearfield, Colorado.

Tucker, Phillip Thomas. *Cathy Williams: From Slave to Buffalo Soldier.* Mechanicsburg, PA: Stackpole Books, 2002. While looking at Williams's life on the frontier, author notes the importance of Dearfield, Colorado.

Websites

The University of Northern Colorado Archival Services maintains a web page about Dearfield, Colorado. http://library.unco.edu/archives/dearfield.htm.

The article "Dearfield Colorado: Victim of the Dust Bowl" on the FencePost's Website describes what Dearfield looks like today. http://www.thefencepost.com/article/20060417/FEATURES/60417004.

1931

The author Toni Morrison is born as the second of four children to George Wofford and Ramah Willis Wofford in Lorain, Ohio. Born with the name Chloe Anthony Wofford, she took on the nickname "Toni," from her middle name, Anthony, while attending Howard University. Toni graduated with a B.A. in English from Howard in 1953, and earned a Master of Arts in English from Cornell University in 1955. She also became a member of the United States's oldest Black Greek-letter sorority, Alpha Kappa Alpha Sorority, Inc. In 1987 Morrison was named the Robert F. Goheen Professor in the Council of Humanities at Princeton University, becoming the first female writer of African descent to be named chair of an academic department at an Ivy League University. She has also worked as an editor for Random House, where she edited books by authors like Toni Cade Bambara, Angela Davis, and Gayl Jones. Her six-year marriage to Harold Morrison gave her two children, Harold and Slade. Among her best-known novels are *The Bluest Eye*, *Song of Solomon*, and *Beloved*. *Beloved* won the Pulitzer Prize for Fiction in 1988. In 1993, Toni Morrison received the Nobel Prize in Literature, becoming the eighth woman and the first woman of African descent to do so.

Race has always mattered a lot in Morrison's fiction. In six previous novels, including Beloved, Song of Solomon, *and* Jazz, *she has focused on the particular joys and sorrows of black American women's lives. As both a writer and editor—Morrison was at Random House for eighteen years—she has made it her mission to get African-American voices into American literature.*

Source: From Toni Morrison, Carolyn C. Denard. *Toni Morrison: Conversations.* Jackson, MS: University Press of Mississippi, 2008, p. 98.

Books

Morrison, Toni. *Lecture and Speech of Acceptance, Upon the Award of the Nobel Prize for Literature, Delivered in Stockholm on the Seventh of*

December, Nineteen Hundred and Ninety-Three. New York, NY: Random House, Inc., 1994. Full text of Morrison's Nobel Prize acceptance speech.

Morrison, Toni, ed. *To Die for the People: The Writings of Huey P. Newton.* New York, NY: Random House, 1972. Provides a collection of Newton's essays and speeches.

Websites

The Nobel Foundation's Website has a biography of Toni Morrison dated up to 1993, the year she won her Nobel Prize in Literature. http://www.Nobelprize.org.

ToniMorrison.org has a biography, photos, and video interviews featuring Toni Morrison. http://tonimorrison.org/videos.html.

1934

Audre Geraldine Lorde is born in Harlem, New York, to Grenadian-born parents, Linda Belmar and Frederick Byron Lorde. A self-described "Black lesbian, mother, warrior, poet," Lorde also used the occasion of an African naming ceremony to adopt the name "Gamba Adisa" (Warrior: She Who Makes Her Meaning Known). She was named New York State Poet Laureate for 1991–1993.

> . . . Lorde brought the perspective of a Black lesbian radicalized within the civil rights movement, the black power movement, the second wave of the U.S. women's movement, and the gay and lesbian movement. She was among the first black feminists to publicly self-identify as a lesbian and to position lesbianism as a legitimate and powerful standpoint from which to enunciate a radical and progressive politics of struggle. This accounted, in part, for the rock-star following and iconic status she enjoyed during her lifetime. While Lorde was not the first black lesbian feminist, she was among the first to live her life and to practice her politics in the public domain, that is to say, out of the closet.
>
> *Source*: From Audre Lorde, Rudolph P. Byrd, Johnnetta Betsch Cole, and Beverly Guy-Sheftall. *I Am Your Sister: Collected and Unpublished*

> *Writings of Audre Lorde.* New York, NY: Oxford University Press, 2009, p. 12.

Books

Lorde, Audre. *Zami, a New Spelling of my Name.* Berkeley, CA: Crossing Press, 1982. Lorde writes about her childhood and the women who have most influenced her in life.

Lorde, Audre and Cheryl Clarke. *Sister Outsider: Essays and Speeches.* New York, NY: Random House, Inc., 2007. A collection of essays and speeches by Audre Lorde.

Websites

Audre Lorde Project, a nonprofit activist group designed to organize queer people of color, is named in honor of Audre Lorde. http://alp.org/.

The Modern American Poetry Website has an entry on Audre Lorde. http://www.english.illinois.edu/maps/poets/g_l/lorde/lorde.htm.

February 19

1919

The Second Pan-African Congress meets in Paris, France, from February 19–21. After Henry Sylvester-Williams had organized the First Pan-African Congress in London, England, in 1900, there was a long gap before another Congress. The Second Pan-African Congress was organized by W. E. B. Du Bois of the United States and Blaise Diagne, a Senegalese man living in France. The Second Pan-African Congress helped to regroup African diaspora activists and led to several more Congresses in years to come.

> The second Pan-African Congress was held in Paris in 1919. It coincided with the Paris Peace Conference by the Allied Powers ending World War I and demanded the right to self-determination in the African colonies. It was also in the same year that there were widespread protests against the exclusion of racial equality from the Covenant of

> *the League of Nations, and delegates from the Pan-African Congress presented resolutions to the League of Nations demanding freedom and independence for Africans.*
>
> *Source*: From Godfrey Mwakikagile. *Relations Between Africans and African Americans: Misconceptions, Myths and Realities*. La Vergne, TN: Lightning Source Inc. 2007, p. 41.

Books

Singh, Nikhil Pal. *Black is a Country: Race and the Unfinished Struggle for Democracy*. Cambridge, MA: Harvard University Press, 2004. Looks at U.S.-based Pan-Africanist thought and how it influenced Black community ideology.

West, Michael Oliver, William G. Martin, and Fanon Che Wilkins. *From Toussaint to Tupac: The Black International Since the Age of Revolution*. Chapel Hill, NC: UNC Press Books, 2009. Essays and speeches demonstrate how Pan-Africanism has been interpreted throughout the African diaspora.

Websites

"The Pan-African Congresses, 1900–1945" details the reasons behind the Pan-African Congress and how each one was organized. http://www.blackpast.org/?q=perspectives/pan-african-congresses-1900–1945.

The United Nations Economic Commission for Africa explains the roots of Pan-Africanism and the desire for a united Africa that it eventually led to http://www.uneca.org/adfiii/riefforts/hist.htm.

1923

The U.S. Supreme Court's *Moore vs. Dempsey* decision is the first to guarantee due process of law to Black people in state courts. The case resulted from a series of death-penalty decisions against 12 African Americans who were nearly lynched after a race riot, but then given a 45-minute trial that led to death-penalty sentences.

> *. . . Although the Court had never treated them as race cases, there can be little doubt that the*

> *decisions in* Moore v. Dempsey, Powell v. Alabama, *and* Brown v. Mississippi *made new criminal procedure law in part because the notorious facts of each case exemplified the national scandal of racist southern justice. This conclusion is reinforced by Holmes' famous letter to Laski, in which he replied to Laski's lament on the execution of Sacco and Vanzetti:*
>> *Your last letter shows you stirred up like the rest of the world on the Sacco Vanzetti case. I cannot but ask myself why this so much greater interest in red than black. A thousand-fold worse cases of negroes [sic] come up from time to time, but the world does not worry over them.*
>
> *Source*: From Robert M. Cover. *Narrative, Violence, and the Law.* Ann Arbor, MI: University of Michigan Press, 1995, p. 36.

Books

Parrish, Michael E. *The Hughes Court: Justices, Rulings, and Legacy*. New York, NY: Vintage Books, 1982. Book looks at the important decisions made by the Charles Evans Hughes-led Supreme Court, particularly the *Moore vs. Dempsey* decision.

Stockley, Grif. *Blood in Their Eyes: The Elaine Race Massacres of 1919*. Fayetteville, AR: University of Arkansas Press, 2004. Examines the causes of the race-based riots that led to the decision in *Moore vs. Dempsey*.

Websites

Justia.com, a database of all U.S. Supreme Court decisions, has in-depth information on *Moore v. Dempsey*, 261 U.S. 86 (1923). http://supreme.justia.com/us/261/86/.

"Moore et al v. Dempsey Appeal: 1923—Studded Straps and Strangling Drugs, 'the Whole Proceeding Is a Mask.' " http://law.jrank.org/pages/2842/Moore-et-al-v-Dempsey-Appeal-1923.html summarizes the *Moore v. Dempsey* case.

Also Noteworthy

1948

On February 19, the Harlem Globetrotters defeat the National Basketball

Association's championship team—the all-white, George Mika-led Minneapolis Lakers—in front of an audience of 18,000 in Chicago Stadium.

February 20

1927

Sydney Poitier is born in Miami, Florida, in 1927 and then brought back to Cat Island, Bahamas, where he is raised. Poitier would become an actor when he moved to New York City and began performing with the American Negro Theater. In 1950, he became famous for his role in the film *No Way Out*. On April 15, 1964, Poitier became the first person of African descent to win an Academy Award for Best Actor—he received the award for his role in *Lilies of the Field*.

> *"I don't mean to be like some old guy from the olden days who says, 'I walked thirty miles to school every morning, so you kids should too.' That's a statement born of envy and resentment. What I'm saying is something quite different. What I'm saying is that by having very little, I had it good. Children need a sense of pulling their own weight, of contributing to the family in some way, and some sense of the family's interdependence. They take pride in knowing that they're contributing. They learn responsibility and discipline through meaningful work. The values developed within a family that operates on those principles then extend to the society at large. By not being quite so indulged and 'protected' from reality by overflowing abundance, children see the bonds that connect them to others."*
>
> *Source:* From Sidney Poitier. *The Measure of a Man: A Spiritual Autobiography.* New York, NY: HarperCollins, 2007, pp. 213–214.

Books

Goudsouzian, Aram. *Sidney Poitier: Man, Actor, Icon.* Chapel Hill, NC: UNC Press Books, 2004. Biography of Sidney Poitier.

Poitier, Sidney. *Life Beyond Measure: Letters to My Great-Granddaughter.* New York, NY:

HarperCollins, 2009. Poitier writes his life lessons in the form of letters to his great-granddaughter.

Websites

The IMDB profiles the life and cinematic career of Sidney Poitier. http://www.imdb.com/name/nm0001627/.

Filmbug has a biography of Poitier and notes his filmography. http://www.filmbug.com/db/21285.

1934

The first African American-performed opera on Broadway, *Four Saints in Three Acts*, by Virgil Thompson and Gertrude Stein, premieres.

> *The disjunction between the opera's setting and its cast attracted much critical attention. By 1934, New York theater audiences had seen many all-black shows, among them Marc Connelly's* Green Pastures *and Hall Johnson's* Run Little Chillun, *but blacks had not yet penetrated the upper reaches of the fine arts. Most white critics praised the black cast, acknowledging the power of the voices even as they were struck by the performers' appearance. Significantly, black critics almost completely ignored* Four Saints in Three Acts, *focusing instead on* They Shall Not Die, *a play about the Scottsboro trial. To these black critics, Stein and Thomson's opera seemed a terrible waste of talent and opportunity. History bore out their viewpoint: audiences viewed the black cast as a gimmick not to be repeated, and of the performers, only Edward Matthews (Saint Ignatius) enjoyed much acclaim afterward.*
>
> *Source:* From Cary D. Wintz, Paul Finkelman. *Encyclopedia of the Harlem Renaissance, Volume 1.* New York, NY: Taylor & Francis, 2004, p. 407.

Books

Dickstein, Morris. *Dancing in the Dark: A Cultural History of the Great Depression.* New York, NY: W. W. Norton & Company,

2010. Looks at the influence *Four Saints in Three Acts* had on other theatrical productions.

Watson, Steven. *Prepare for Saints: Gertrude Stein, Virgil Thomson, and the Mainstreaming of American Modernism*. New York, NY: Random House, 1998. Looks at how Virgil Thomson and Gertrude Stein came together to write *Four Saints in Three Acts* and the influence the opera had on the art world of the time.

Websites

Nonesuch links to excerpts from a 1981 recording of the opera. http://www.nonesuch.com/albums/four-saints-in-three-acts.

Discogs lists each song in the opera and provides background info. http://www.discogs.com/Virgil-Thomson-Gertrude-Stein-Orchestra-Of-Our-Time-Joel-Thome-Four-Saints-In-Three-Acts/release/1191825.

February 21

1936

Barbara Charline Jordan is born to Benjamin Jordan, a Baptist minister and Arlyne Jordan, who worked as a warehouse clerk. In 1966, Jordan became the first African American woman to serve as a Texas State Senator—she was the first person of African descent to serve in the Texas state legislature since Reconstruction. Jordan also later became the first African American woman to serve in the U.S. House of Representatives. She received three honorary doctorates and was awarded the Presidential Medal of Freedom in 1994. In 1999 *Texas Monthly Magazine* named Jordan the "Role Model of the Century."

Jordan's record in the state Senate shows a sensitivity to issues affecting the poor, the working-class, the disabled, racial minorities, and women. Though she had to accept many compromises in the political give and take, she knew in which direction she was headed and tried to bring the other politicians along with her, even if they had acted hidebound or racist in the past. Lieutenant Governor Ben Barnes appointed her chair of the Labor and Management Relations Committee, vice-chair of the Judicial, Congressional, and Legislative committees, and a member of ten other committees. Some of her successful bills created the Texas Fair Employment Practices Committee, gave the state its first minimum wage law, and increased workmen's compensation coverage for on-the-job injuries.

Source: From Ruthe Winegarten, Janet G. Humphrey, and Frieda Werden. Black Texas Women: 150 Years of Trial and Triumph. Austin, TX: University of Texas Press, 1995, p. 273.

Books

Jordan, Barbara, edited by Max R. Sherman. *Barbara Jordan: Speaking the Truth with Eloquent Thunder*. Austin, TX: University of Texas Press, 2007. Book contains examples of Barbara Jordan's political philosophy, viewed through some of her most famous speeches.

Jordan, Barbara with Shelby Hearon. *Barbara Jordan: A Self-Portrait*. New York, NY: Doubleday & Co., 1979. Jordan collaborated on the writing of her autobiography.

Websites

The Website for the Biographical Directory of the U.S. Congress, features a biographical sketch of Barbara Jordan. http://bioguide.congress.gov/scripts/biodisplay.pl?index=j000266.

Jordan is buried alongside past legislators and other famous Texans in the Texas State Cemetery in Austin, Texas. The Texas State Cemetery's Website features a biography of Jordan and notes the text on her headstone: "Barbara Jordan, 1936–1996; Eloquent Champion of Ethics and Justice; We The People Salute You." http://www.cemetery.state.tx.us/pub/user_form.asp?pers_id=6624.

Also Noteworthy

1965

El Hajj (Malcolm X) is assassinated while delivering a speech at the Audubon Ballroom in upper Manhattan, New York.

February 22

1839

Octavius Valentine Catto is born to William T. Catto (a formerly enslaved ordained Presbyterian minister) and Sarah Isabella Cain, in Charleston, South Carolina. A noted sportsman, educator, and civil rights activist, Catto worked alongside Frederick Douglass during the Civil War to create a Recruitment Committee, which urged young Black men to fight for their emancipation. Ultimately, Catto helped raise 11 regiments of "Colored Troops" in the Philadelphia, Pennsylvania, area and was even commissioned a major in the Union Army. Catto became the corresponding secretary of the Pennsylvania Equal Rights League in 1864 and was instrumental in the desegregation of Philadelphia's mass transit system. Though Pennsylvania passed the Fifteenth Amendment guaranteeing voting rights for African American men in October 1870, Catto was killed while trying to vote on October 10, 1871. White, predominately Democratic party voters had spent the day harassing Blacks, who tended to vote Republican. Catto was harassed by a white man, Frank Kelly, who approached him at the intersection of Ninth and South Streets and shot him three times.

Catto offered resolutions—"That we earnestly and unitedly protest against the proscription which excludes us from the city cars, as an outrage against the enlightened civilization of the age." He named the U.S. cities that had already opened their streetcars to Negroes.

Resolved, That while men and women of a Christian community can sit unmoved and in silence, and see women barbarously thrown from the cars—and while our courts of justice fail to grant us redress . . . we shall never rest at ease, but will agitate and work, by our means and by our influence, in court and out of court, asking aid of the press, calling upon Christians to vindicate their Christianity, and the members of the law . . . by granting us justice and right, until these invidious and unjust usages shall have ceased.

Source: From Daniel R. Biddle and Murray Dubin. *Tasting Freedom: Octavius Catto and the Battle for Equality in Civil War America.* Philadelphia, PA: Temple University Press, 2010, p. 350.

Books

Catto, Octavius V. and Institute for Colored Youth of Philadelphia, PA. Our Alma Mater: An Address Delivered at Concert Hall on the Occasion of the Twelfth Annual Commencement of the Institute for Colored Youth, May 10th, 1864. Philadelphia, PA: Rhistoric Publications, 1969. Catto's speech emphasized the importance of education for African Americans, and—by extension—for the United States.

National Equal Rights League. Proceedings of the First Annual Meeting of the National Equal Rights League Held in Cleveland, Ohio, October 19, 20, and 21, 1865. Charleston, SC: Nabu Press, 2010. Minutes of meeting where Catto served as recording secretary.

Websites

The Philadelphia-based U.S. History Website tells of Catto's life and work for African American civil rights, and highlights how Catto has been remembered in the city after his death. http://www.ushistory.org/people/catto.htm.

The Historical Society of Pennsylvania features a biography and portrait of Octavius Catto. http://www.hsp.org/default.aspx?id=994.

1989

Colonel Frederick Gregory becomes the first African American to command a space shuttle mission when he leads mission STS-33 on board the Orbiter Challenger. Gregory currently works as the deputy administrator of the National Aeronautics and Space Administration (NASA).

. . . Ronald E. McNair, Guion S. Bluford Jr., and Frederick D Gregory were the first African

Americans admitted to the NASA space program, in 1978.

Source: From Stephanie Maze. *I Want to Be an Astronaut.* New York, NY: Houghton Mifflin Harcourt, 1999, p. 41.

Books

Phelps, J. Alfred. *They Had a Dream: The Story of African American Astronauts.* Philadelphia, PA: Presidio/Random House, 1994. Frederick D. Gregory is among the pioneers of African Americans in space.

Reef, Catherine. *African Americans in the Military.* New York, NY: Infobase Publishing, 2009. Places Gregory's role in the context of NASA and U.S. military history for African Americans.

Websites

The HistoryMakers Website features a photo and biography of Frederick D. Gregory. http://www.thehistorymakers.com/biography/biography.asp?bioindex=1595&category=ScienceMakers&occupation=Astronaut%20%26%20NASA%20Administrator&name=Col.%20Frederick%20D.%20Gregory%2C%20Sr.

NASA's Website features biographical data on Gregory. http://www.jsc.nasa.gov/Bios/htmlbios/gregory-fd.html.

Also Noteworthy

1864

Dr. George Cleveland Hall is born to James W. and Emmaline Buck Hall in Ypsilanti, Michigan. Hall became a physician and served for 30 years as chief of staff at Chicago's Provident Hospital and Training School. He was a founder of the Cook County Physicians' Association and vice president of the National Urban League and the Chicago Urban League, and served as the first president of Carter G. Woodson's Association for the Study of Negro Life and History (ASNLH). Hall served on the board of directors for the Chicago Public Library and advocated the construction of a library branch to serve African Americans in the city's Bronzeville community. Dr. Hall died while the library was under construction, and the Library's board of directors named the branch in his honor.

1965

The day after the activist Malcolm X's assassination, Mosque No. 7—the Nation of Islam mosque that Malcolm used to preach at on 106 West 127th Street in Harlem, New York—is bombed and set on fire. Local activist Jesse Gray demanded that all of Harlem's stores be closed down as a tribute to Malcolm, and hundreds of people gathered in front of Lewis Michaux's National Memorial African Bookstore—the former site of Malcolm X's outdoor lectures—to commiserate together.

February 23

1868

The scholar/activist William Edward Burghardt (W.E.B.) Du Bois is born in Great Barrington, Massachusetts. He was the first African American to graduate from his high school. He studied at Fisk University in Tennessee on a full academic scholarship, graduated with honors in 1888, and then went on to Harvard to pursue a second undergraduate degree, which he received in 1890. DuBois received his master's degree at Harvard as well, in 1891. He became the first Black to receive a PhD from Harvard in 1895. Du Bois's Harvard University dissertation, *The Suppression of the African Slave Trade to the United States of America, 1638–1870*, was published as No. 1 in the Harvard Historical Series. After working as an assistant instructor in sociology at the University of Pennsylvania, Du Bois published *The Philadelphia Negro: A Social Study* (1899). Du Bois buttressed his scholarship with work as an activist: he was a founder and general secretary of the protest group known as the

Niagara Movement in 1905; in 1909 he helped found the National Association for the Advancement of Colored People (NAACP). Du Bois also edited the NAACP's monthly magazine, *The Crisis*, from 1910 to 1934. He became involved with the Pan-African movement, while continuing to write and, in 1961, joined the Communist Party. DuBois expatriated to Ghana in 1964, where he died on August 27, 1963, at age 95.

After almost twenty-five years editing The Crisis, *Du Bois left the NAACP in 1034 to return to Atlanta University; he published a slew of essays, editorials, and books, including* Black Reconstruction, The Gift of Black Folk, *and* Black Folk, Then and Now; *he took an active role in Pan-African Conventions that endeavored to wrench control of Africa away from European powers and put it in the hands of Africans themselves; he traveled to Africa, throughout Europe several times, and enjoyed a visit to Russia, where Communism demonstrated to him the possibilities of massive economic planning and racial harmony . . .*

Source: From Edward J. Blum. *W.E.B. Du Bois: American prophet.* Philadelphia PA: University of Pennsylvania Press, 2007, p. 40.

DuBois's work. http://www.webdubois.org/index.html.

1937

Claude Brown, author of the 1965 best seller *Manchild in the Promised Land*, is born to Henry Lee and Ossie Brock Brown in Harlem, New York.

Claude Brown the author of Manchild in the Promised Land *is also Claude Brown the central actor in the drama of his narrative. He belongs to the new breed of post-World War II black men, strong and confident but searching, individualistic shareholders in the ghetto experience, but not its prisoners. With the autobiographical* Manchild, *however, Brown creates a new and distinctive vehicle for expressing that experience. It is a clear product of the 1960s civil rights movement, during which the audience for the "experiences" of blacks grew exponentially.*

Source: From Jerry H. Bryant. *Born in a Mighty Bad Land: The Violent Man in African American Folklore and Fiction.* Bloomington, IN: Indiana University Press, 2003, p. 80.

Books

Du Bois, W.E.B. and David L. Lewis. *W.E.B. Du Bois: A Reader.* New York, NY: Macmillan, 1995. A collection of Du Bois's essays and editorials.

Lewis, David Levering. *W.E.B. DuBois—The Fight for Equality and the American Century, 1919–1963.* New York, NY: Macmillan, 2001. Biography looks at the last portion of Du Bois's life and career and his influence on a new generation of social activists.

Websites

The Website for the Kansas City, Missouri–based W.E.B. DuBois Learning Center features a biographical sketch of Du Bois. http://www.duboislc.org/html/DuBoisBio.html.

WEBDubois.org features biographical data on DuBois and links to other sites containing

Books

Brown, Claude. *Manchild in the Promised Land.* New York, NY: Simon & Schuster, 1999. Brown's autobiographical novel about life in Harlem.

Brown, Claude. *The Children of Ham.* New York, NY: Bantam/Random House, 1977. Brown's sequel to *Manchild in the Promised Land* depicts life for teens in Harlem.

Websites

The activist/author Haki R. Madhubuti penned an obituary about Claude Brown that can be found on the Website http://findarticles.com/p/articles/mi_m0DXK/is_1_19/ai_84429939/.

The *Telegraph*'s Website has an obituary of Claude Brown. http://www.telegraph.co.uk/news/obituaries/1386947/Claude-Brown.html.

Also Noteworthy

1874

The Kentucky General Assembly officially accepts the incorporation of the Franklin Colored Benevolent Society No.1 as an organization. Established with the purpose of furthering the "intellectual, moral, and social improvement of its members, and works of benevolence and charity," the Franklin, Kentucky-based Colored Benevolent Society No.1 was created with R. R. Burnley serving as president, William Butts as vice president, John H. Perdue as secretary, and King Boisseau as treasurer.

1892

Tuskegee University conducts its first Negro Farmers Conference, which was designed to allow Southern Black farmers to gather and talk about farming pros and cons, as well as their difficulties with racial restrictions. The conference has continued to be held for over 100 years.

February 24

1811

Bishop Daniel Alexander Payne is born in Charleston, South Carolina. Payne was ordained the sixth bishop of the African Methodist Episcopal Church (AME) on May 13, 1852, and in 1848 he was named the historiographer of AME. Payne also founded Wilberforce University and served as the school's first president. Wilberforce was the first Black-owned and Black-operated institution of higher learning in the country.

An orphan at ten, school instructor at nineteen, licensed preacher at twenty-six, and bishop at forty-one, Payne was born of free parents in Charleston, South Carolina. He left the South in 1834 and attended the Lutheran Theological Seminary at Gettysburg, Pennsylvania. Though ordained by the

Franckean Lutheran Synod, an abolitionist connection in New York State, Payne joined the church of Richard Allen in 1841. He became the official historian of the African Methodists, their greatest educator, and perhaps the most influential bishop of the nineteenth-century black denominations.

Source: From Milton C. Sernett. African American Religious History: A Documentary Witness. Durham, NC: Duke University Press, 1999, p. 232.

Books

Bishop, Dr. Rudine Sims. *Bishop Daniel A. Payne: Great Black Leader*. East Orange, NJ: Just Us Books, Inc., 2009. Biography of the life and work of Bishop Payne.

Rivers, Larry E. and Canter Brown. *Laborers in the Vineyard of the Lord: The Beginnings of the AME Church in Florida, 1865–1895*. Gainesville, FL: University Press of Florida, 2001. Authors note Bishop Payne's central role in the formation of the African Methodist Episcopal Church (AME).

Websites

Payne's *Recollections of Seventy Years* is available on the Internet. http://docsouth.unc.edu/church/payne70/payne.html.

The 7th District AME Church—South Carolina's Website features Payne as one of the principals in establishing the AME Church. http://www.ame7.org/history/4_horsemen.htm#DANIEL_A._PAYNE.

February 25

1870

Hiram Rhodes Revels, the first African American to serve as a U.S. Senator, takes his oath of office. Revels served as the Republican Party Senator from Mississippi from February 25, 1870, to March 3, 1871. After serving in the Senate, Revels became the first president of what is today Alcorn State University.

Hiram Revels (1822–1901) was the first black citizen to be elected to the US Senate. Born to free parents in Fayetteville, North Carolina, Revels had to go to Indiana and Illinois to obtain an education. He became an African Methodist Episcopal church pastor and the principal of a school for blacks in Baltimore, Maryland.

Source: From Shmoop. *Reconstruction: Shmoop US History Guide.* Sunnyvale, CA: Shmoop University Inc., p. 42.

Books

Sewell, George A. and Margaret L. Dwight. *Mississippi Black History Makers*. Jackson, MS: University Press of Mississippi, 1984. Looks at notable Blacks in Mississippi history, among them Hiram Revels.

Wynne, Ben. *Mississippi*. Northampton, MA: Interlink Books, 2007. This look at Mississippi's history has a segment highlighting Revels' significance as a senator both locally and nationally.

Websites

Revel's biography is available on the U.S. Congress's site. http://bioguide.congress.gov/scripts/biodisplay.pl?index=r000166.

The Digital History Home Website features a biography on Revels. http://www.digitalhistory.uh.edu/reconstruction/section4/section4_revels.html.

1853

Anthony Bowen establishes the first African American Young Men's Christian Association (YMCA) in Washington, D.C. Bowen had been born into slavery in Maryland, but after purchasing his own freedom he went on to become the first African American employee of the U.S. Patent Office. He used his resources to establish DC's first YMCA oriented toward Black males; in 1908 they began constructing the Twelfth Street YMCA Building, which was completed in 1912. In 1972, the Twelfth Street YMCA was renamed the Anthony Bowen YMCA,

and it was declared a National Historic Landmark in 1994.

. . . Bowen organized an association for African Americans and became its first president. The black YMCA owned no facilities and met in Bowen'ss home on Sunday afternoons. Limited by lack of funds and restricted by laws regulating the personal freedom of free blacks, the first African-American YMCA in the United States offered its members no more than Bible study meetings. The black association in Washington, DC, continued to exist throughout the Civil War but never evolved beyond club status.

Source: From Nina Mjagkij. *Light in the Darkness: African Americans and the YMCA, 1852–1946.* Lexington, KY: University Press of Kentucky, 2003, p. 18.

Books

Benedetto, Robert, Jane Donovan, and Kathleen Du Vall. *Historical Dictionary of Washington, Part 3*. Lanham, MD: Scarecrow Press, 2003. Has an excerpt on the Anthony Bowen YMCA, its founding, and history.

Savage, Beth L, ed. *African American Historic Places*. Hoboken, NJ: John Wiley & Sons, 1994. Excerpt on Bowen's establishing and fundraising for the YMCA that today bears his name.

Websites

The YMCA's history site features Bowen's founding of the first Black YMCA. http://www.ymca.net/history/1800–1860s.html.

The YMCA of Metropolitan Washington notes Bowen's efforts to found the first YMCA club. http://www.ymcadc.org/branches/DC/anthony_bowen/Pages/default.aspx.

Also Noteworthy

1907

Mechanics and Farmers (M&F) Bank http://www.mfbonline.com is chartered in North

Carolina and opens for business in August 1908 at 112 Parrish Street on Durham's "Black Wall Street." M&F Bank was created with a mission of helping to spur African American economic development.

1964

Muhammad Ali defeats Charles "Sonny" Liston for the World Heavyweight Championship.

February 26

1925

Robert Franklin Williams is born in Monroe, North Carolina. A Civil Rights leader, author, and the president of the Monroe, North Carolina, NAACP chapter in the 1950s and early 1960s, Williams was a key figure in promoting both integration and armed Black self-defense in the United States. Williams's 1962 book, *Negroes with Guns*, details Williams's experience with violent racism and the pacifist Civil Rights Movement philosophies he disagreed with. At one point in 1961, Williams was accused of kidnapping a Klansman and his wife, so he fled for Cuba. He spent the next eight years in exile; in Cuba from 1961 through 1966 and then in China from 1966 to 1969. Williams would strongly influence Black Power Movement organizations, like the Revolutionary Action Movement, Republic of New Africa, and the Black Panther Party.

A week after his death, Rosa Parks climbed slowly into a church pulpit in Monroe, North Carolina. Beneath her lay the body of Robert F. Williams, clad in a gray suit given to him by Mao tse-Tung and draped with a black, red, and green Pan-African flag. Rosa Parks told the congregation that she and those who marched with Martin Luther King Jr. in Alabama had always admired Robert Williams "for his courage and his commitment to freedom. The work that he did should go down in history and never be forgotten." Above the desk where Williams completed his memoirs

just before his death, there still hangs an ancient rifle—a gift, he said, from his grandmother.

Source: From Timothy B. Tyson. "Robert F. Williams: 'Black Power' and the Roots of the African American Freedom Struggle", in Susan M. Glisson, ed., *The Human Tradition in the Civil Rights Movement*. Lanham, MD: Rowman & Littlefield, pp. 227–248.

Books

Tyson, Timothy. *Radio Free Dixie: Robert F. Williams and the Roots of Black Power*. Minneapolis, MN: Demco Media/Sagebrush Corp, 1992. Tyson provides a thorough biography of Williams and looks at his effect of subsequent Black Power Movement groups.

Williams, Robert Franklin. *Negroes with Guns*. Detroit, MI: Wayne State University Press, 1962. Williams' first book tells about the struggles of Blacks in Monroe, North Carolina, to arm and protect themselves from race-based violence.

Websites

The University of Michigan's Bentley Historical Library maintains the papers from Robert F. Williams's estate. http://bentley.umich.edu/.

Williams's 1968 pamphlet "Listen, Brother!" is available as a download. http://www.archive.org/details/ListenBrother.

1928

Antoine "Fats" Domino, Jr., singer, is born in New Orleans, Louisiana. Famous as a rhythm and blues and rock-and-roll singer, Fats Domino songs like "I'm Walkin'," "Walkin' to New Orleans," and "Blueberry Hill" helped determine the rhythm and style of popular music for generations of listeners. Domino was inducted into the Rock and Roll Hall of Fame in 1986.

The lilt of his music is unmistakable. His piano-playing technique is pure New Orleans style. His voice—with that quality of munched rather than simply spoken words—is magnificently distinctive.

> The Fats Domino sound dominated American popular music for two decades. On the "rhythm and blues" side of the ledger, only Ray Charles and James Brown rivaled Fats Domino's hit-record production between 1950 and 1969.
>
> Source: From Brian Lee Cooper and Wayne S. Haney. *Rock Music in American Popular Culture, Volume 1*. New York, NY: Psychology Press/ Routledge, 1995, p. 217.

Books

Coleman, Rick. *Blue Monday: Fats Domino and the Lost Dawn of Rock 'n' Roll*. Cambridge, NY: Da Capo Press, 2006. Biography of Fats Domino details his life and his role in New Orleans and in rock-and-roll history.

Domino, Fats. *Fats Domino, a Man and His Music*. Hialeah, FL: Columbia Pictures Publications, 1985. A short autobiography of Fats Domino.

Websites

The History of Rock site shows Domino's influence and includes a biography of his life. http://www.history-of-rock.com/domino .htm.

The Songwriters Hall of Fame notes Domino's song catalog, photos from his career, and has some of his sheet music available. http:// www.songwritershalloffame.org/exhibits/ C109.

1965

Twenty-six-year-old Civil Rights activist Jimmie Lee Jackson dies after being shot by Alabama State Trooper James Bonard Fowler in Marion, Alabama. Because Jackson died after working to protest the arrest of a member of Martin Luther King's Southern Christian Leadership Council, King spoke at Jackson's funeral and called him "a martyred hero of a holy crusade for freedom and human dignity." Jackson's shooting death inspired the "Bloody Sunday" Selma-to-Montgomery voting rights protest of March 7, 1965. Fowler served a six-month plea-bargained prison term for the killing in 2010, some 45 years after the murder.

> One of those injured behind the church was eighty-year-old Cager Lee, past president of a branch of the Rising Star Association and one of the first black registrants in Marion. His grandson Jimmie Lee Jackson, twenty-six years old, had brought him to the mass meeting here that night. Jimmie Lee had returned to Marion from Indiana to be with his family. He liked to cook, hunt, and shoot pool. The previous winter he had also gone to the courthouse to register. That night Jimmie Lee was in Mack's Café, a sandwich place where his sister and mother worked down the hill from the church just in front of Lee's Funeral Home. When Jimmie Lee tried to get his grandfather to a doctor and resisted an attack on his mother, troopers cornered him in the café and shot him in the stomach as he was pinned against a cigarette machine.
>
> Source: From Townsend Davis. *Weary Feet, Rested Souls: A Guided History of the Civil Rights Movement*. New York, NY: W. W. Norton & Company, 1999, p. 122.

Books

Leonard, Richard D. *Call to Selma: Eighteen Days of Witness*. Boston, MA: Unitarian Universalist Association of Congregations, 2002. A look at the role the death of Jimmie Lee Jackson and the white Unitarian Universalist minister Rev. James Reeb played in passage of the Voting Rights Act.

Mendelsohn, Jack. *The Martyrs: Sixteen Who Gave Their Lives for Racial Justice*. New York, NY: Harper & Row, 1966. Book includes profiles of the major racial killings of the 1960s, including that of Jimmie Lee Jackson.

Websites

"The Death of Jimmy Lee Jackson" is recounted in this Alabama heritage site, http:// www.thatsalabama.com/civilwrongs/jimmy leejackson/.

National Public Radio covered jury selection for the trial of the trooper who killed Jackson. http://www.npr.org/2010/11/12/131270196/jury-selection-begins-for-civil-rights-cold-case.

Also Noteworthy

1931

George Alvin Wiley is born in Bayonne, New Jersey. While teaching chemistry at Syracuse University in 1960, Wiley founded a local chapter of the Congress of Racial Equality (CORE), and by 1964 he was named CORE's associate national director, just second to the national director, James Farmer. As an activist, Wiley later famously founded the National Welfare Rights Organization (NWRO), a group that challenged the popular perception of poor people and their civil rights. Wiley's organizing and militant civil rights tactics have been viewed as the models for later groups such as Association of Community Organizations for Reform Now (ACORN) and the U.S. Public Interest Research Group (U.S. PIRG) groups.

February 27

1988

Debra Janine "Debi" Thomas becomes the first African American to win an Olympic medal in figure skating. In 1986, Thomas won the U.S. National ladies' figure skating title and the World Figure Skating Championships while she was a freshman at Stanford University. Thomas won a bronze medal at the XV Olympic Winter Games in 1988 and was inducted into the U.S. Figure Skating Hall of Fame in Colorado, Springs, Colorado in 2000.

. . . It was a classic matchup between Witt and Stanford premed student Debi Thomas, who was seeking to become the first African-American athlete to win a medal in the Winter Olympic. Thomas, born in 1967 in New York, grew up in northern California and became fascinated with ice skating while watching ice clown Mr. Frick at a local show. She begged her parents for lessons, and they enrolled her at a nearby rink. She was a natural, and in 1986 she became the first African-American woman in history to win a gold medal at the world championships. The rivalry between Witt and Thomas grew fierce, and, ironically, at the 1988 Olympics both women chose to skate to the music from Carmen. *Witt went first and gave a brilliant artistic performance, but her lack of technical difficulty left the door open for Thomas, who had upset her at the 1986 world championships.*

Thomas unraveled under pressure, however, landing badly on her second jump and missing two more jumps later in the program. She seemed to give up after the second fall, and a worldwide television audience watched, stunned, as her dream shattered in four minutes. She was so upset when she left the ice that she brushed past her coaches. "The whole reason I came here was to be great," she said afterward.

Source: From Lissa Smith and Mariah Burton Nelson. *Nike Is a Goddess: The History of Women in Sports.* New York, NY: Atlantic Monthly Press, 1999, pp. 171–172.

Books

Bel Monte, Kathryn I. *African-American Heroes and Heroines: 150 True Stories of African-American Heroism.* New York, NY: W. W. Norton & Company, 1999. Author notes the historical importance of Thomas's role at the U.S. Women's Championship in 1986.

Ferguson, Carroy U. *Transitions in Consciousness from an African American Perspective: Original Essays in Psycho-Historical Context.* Lanham, MD: University Press of America/Rowman & Littlefield Publishing Group, 2004. Includes a short autobiography of Debi Thomas.

Websites

Thomas, who is now an orthopaedic surgeon, has her own Website: http://www.docdebithomas.com/.

Debi Thomas is a member of the U.S.Figure Skating Hall of Fame. http://www.worldskatingmuseum.org/ushof.htm.

1897

The singer, Marian Anderson, is born in Philadelphia, Pennsylvania, to John Rucker Anderson and the former Anna Delilah Rucker. In 1939 Anderson's attempt to give a concert at Constitution Hall in Washington, D.C., was cancelled by the Daughters of the American Revolution (DAR), who didn't want an African American to perform there. Eleanor Roosevelt, the wife of President Franklin D. Roosevelt, resigned her DAR membership and arranged for Anderson to give a concert at the Lincoln Memorial on April 9, 1939, which was Easter Sunday. Anderson sang to a crowd of some 75,000 people, and millions more listened to her concert on radio. On January 7, 1955, Anderson became the first Black singer to perform with the Metropolitan Opera when she took the stage as "Ulrica," the Gypsy fortune-teller, in Verdi's *Un ballo in maschera* (Masked Ball).

> *I report these things now because I have looked them up. All I knew then as I stepped forward was the overwhelming impact of that vast multitude. There seemed to be people as far as the eye could see. The crowd stretched in a great semicircle from the Lincoln Memorial around the reflecting pool on to the shaft of the Washington Monument. I had a feeling that a great wave of goodwill poured out from these people, almost engulfing me. And when I stood up to sing our National Anthem I felt for a moment as though I were choking. For a desperate second I thought that the words, well as I know them, would not come.*
>
> *Source*: From Marian Anderson. *My Lord, What a Morning: An Autobiography*. Champaign, IL: University of Illinois Press, 2002, p. 191.

Books

Arsenault, Raymond. *The Sound of Freedom: Marian Anderson, the Lincoln Memorial, and the Concert That Awakened America*. New York, NY: Bloomsbury Publishing USA, 2010. Examines Anderson's career and her historic Lincoln Memorial concert.

Ferris, Jeri. *What I had Was Singing: The Story of Marian Anderson*. Breckenridge, CO: Twenty-First Century Books, 1994. Author looks at the life of Marian Anderson and the historical impact of her career.

Websites

Marian Anderson Historical Society site is dedicated to maintaining Anderson's Philadelphia, Pennsylvania, home and promoting music education. http://www.mariananderson.org.

Photo essay about Anderson's Lincoln Memorial concert, with photos from the event. http://www.english.illinois.edu/maps/poets/s_z/.../anderson.htm.

1872

Charlotte Ray—the daughter of nationally known abolitionist and publisher of the *Colored American*, Rev. Charles B. Ray—becomes the first African American woman attorney when she graduates from Howard University School of Law at the age of 63. Although Ray was officially admitted to practice law in the District of Columbia on April 23, 1872, she never really got enough business as a lawyer and ended up having to end her law practice; she went back to teaching.

> *When Charlotte Ray decided she wanted to go to law school— unheard of for an African American woman in the 1800s— she applied as CE Ray. When the Howard University School of Law found out that she was a woman, they admitted her anyway. Ray, who was born in New York City in 1850, was such an outstanding student at Howard that she was inducted into Phi Beta Kappa, the national scholastic organization.*
>
> *Source*: From Joan Potter. *African American Firsts: Famous Little-Known and Unsung Triumphs of Blacks in America*. New York, NY: Dafina Books/Kensington Publishing Corp, 2009, p. 138.

Books

Flexner, Eleanor and Ellen Frances Fitzpatrick. *Century of Struggle: The Woman's Rights*

Movement in the United States. Cambridge, MA: Harvard University Press, 1996. Authors note the importance of Ray's efforts to become an attorney.

Jones, Martha S. *All Bound Up Together: The Woman Question in African American Public Culture, 1830–1900.* Sydney, Australia: ReadHowYouWant.com, 2009. The influence of Ray's minister father and devout mother is examined as part of her character building.

Websites

Ray's life is recalled by author/activist and former NBA star Kareem Abdul-Jabbar. http://latimesblogs.latimes.com/kareem/2008/02/charlotte-e-ray.html.

Duhaime.org has a short biography on Charlotte Ray. http://www.duhaime.org/LawMuseum/LawArticle-417/Ray-Charlotte-1850-1911.aspx.

Also Noteworthy

1883

The inventor W. B. Purvis receives U.S. Patent No. 273,149 for his hand stamp.

1942

Charlayne Alberta Hunter-Gault is born in West, South Carolina. Hunter-Gault and Hamilton E. Holmes became the first African Americans to attend Georgia University. Hunter-Gault would go on to become a journalist and international correspondent.

February 28

1942

Race riot erupts at the Sojourner Truth Homes in Detroit, Michigan. Local whites became enraged when they found out the federally subsidized Sojourner Truth Homes would encourage the housing of the families of Black defense workers in what had been a predominately white neighborhood.

The first serious race riot in Detroit during the war years took place at the Sojouner Truth Homes in

February 1942. The development was originally designated as a segregated public housing project to house black workers, located just north of the Polish-American suburb of Hamtramck in an area where black-white relations had been relatively friendly. It was briefly considered for white occupancy after local white residents expressed fear of property devaluation, and finally in January 1942 designated as a black project. The announcement in early February that the first residents were preparing to take occupancy provoked a violent reaction: the Ku Klux Klan burned a cross outside the project, vans carrying black tenants furniture were overturned, and when black youths form Detroit rallied to protect the trucks and tenants, local police arrested the blacks. In outrage, the N.A.A.C.P. and UAW, supported the black tenants, demanding police protection for their peaceful intent, and in April African-American defense workers began moving into the project in earnest.

Source: From Constance B. Schulz. *Michigan Remembered: Photographs from the Farm Security Administration and the Office of War Information, 1936–1943.* Detroit, MI: Wayne State University Press, 2001, p. 145.

Books

Shogan, Robert and Tom Craig. *The Detroit Race Riot: A Study in Violence.* Cambridge, MA: Da Capo Press, 1976. Details the issues and results of the race riot in 1942 and in 1943.

Sugrue, Thomas J. *Sweet Land of Liberty: The Forgotten Struggle for Civil Rights in the North.* New York, NY: Random House, Inc., 2009. Details how Black activists pushed for Black occupants at the Sojourner Truth Home, as a way for the United States to fulfill its New Deal promises.

Websites

The *Detroit News* recalls the 1942 riot on its history page. http://apps.detnews.com/apps/history/index.php?id=185.

Portfolio provides a photo essay on the 1942 Detroit Race Riots. http://ahp-portfolio.blogspot.com/2007/03/race-riots-in-1942-detroit-michigan.html.

February 29

1892

Augusta Savage is born Augusta Christine Fells in Green Cove Springs, Florida. The seventh of 14 children, Augusta's interest in sculpture started at a young age. As her talent increased, she was able to gain admittance as one of the first women to study at New York City's Cooper Union.

Savage's tenacious determination paid off: By 1921, she was studying sculpture under George Brewster at Cooper Union and was soon supported by scholarship funding. Even before she completed her four-year course of study at Cooper Union, savage had gained fame for a portrait of W.E.B. Du Bois, after which she received numerous other commissions for portraits of notable black Americans, including Marcus Garvey, who sat for her over a series of Sundays in his Harlem apartment. By 1923, her esteem among the black community of Harlem and especially among the figures of the Harlem Renaissance helped secure Savage a scholarship for summer study at the Palace of Fontainebleau art school in France. When it was learned that she was black, the scholarship money was withdrawn. Savage's fame turned to notoriety when the news of the French art school's withdrawal of its offer became front-page, cause célèbre material in the black and radical press of New York City. Although she did receive another offer for summer study in College Point, New York, and eventually did get to Paris by means of the Julius Rosenwald Fellowship, Savage also received an undeserved reputation as a troublesome agitator because of the press coverage, resulting in a generalized rebuff from the white art world that effectively shut Savage out of museum and gallery representation for the rest of her life.

Source: From Phoebe Farris. Women Artists of Color: A Bio-Critical Sourcebook to 20th Artists in the Americas. Santa Barbara, CA: Greenwood Publishing Group, 1999, p. 342.

Books

Hinnant, Denise Ellaine. *Sculptor Augusta Savage: Her Art, Progressive Influences, and African-American Representation.* Crestwood, KY: University of Louisville, 2003. Book looks at the influence of Savage's art on African American artists.

Schroeder, Alan. *In Her Hands: The Story of Sculptor Augusta Savage.* New York, NY: Lee & Low Books, 2009. Biography looks at Savage's youth, her training, and her artistic legacy.

Websites

Smithsonian American Art Museum has a photograph and information about Savage's "Gamin." http://americanart.si.edu/collections/search/artwork/?id=21658.

Bookrags provides a substantial biography of Savage. http://www.bookrags.com/biography/augusta-savage-aya/.

The Circle Association's African American History of Western New York state 1770 to 1830. http://www.math.buffalo.edu/~sww/0history/1770-1830.html.

Also Noteworthy

1940

The *Chicago Defender's* publisher, John H. Sengstacke, brings together a meeting of Negro newspaper publishers in Chicago from February 29 through March 2. The meeting is meant to unite the publishers into an organization. In the end, they form the National Negro Newspaper Publishers Association (NNPA; which is in 1956 renamed the National Newspaper Publishers Association).

1968

National Advisory Committee on Civil Disorders (formerly known as the Kerner Commission) issues its report on the effect of White racism on U.S. society and demonstrates that white racism is the major cause of African American riots in U.S. cities.

March

March 1

1841

Although born into slavery on this day, Blanche Kelso Bruce became the first African American to serve in the U.S. Senate—and became the first person of African descent to preside over Senate chambers on February 14, 1879. B. K. Bruce represented Mississippi from 1875 to 1881; he was a member of the Republican Party.

> ...I spent an evening with Congressman Cosgrove, of Missouri, at Willard's Hotel in Washington, who told me much of Mr. Bruce's boyhood. He said that many years before the war he (Cosgrove) was learning the printer's trade at Brunswick, Mo., and that Mr. Bruce was the 'devil' on the press, and whenever he was wanted, he was always found with his head buried in a book or a newspaper it was a difficult job to keep him at work. Having learned the trade of printer he (Cosgrove) left Brunswick and did not return until '82—nearly thirty years thereafter—when he thought he would visit the printer's office, where he found the same old man publishing the same little sheet, and said almost the first question he asked, was, 'Where is that colored boy—the "devil"? When the old man said, 'why, have you never seen or heard of him since?' and taking from his pocket a dollar bill, the old man pointed to the lower left-hand corner to the name 'B.K. Bruce, Register' and said: 'Not only is he the Register of the United States Treasury, and no bonds or paper money issued by this great government is valid without his name, but he has become a United States Senator and to-day stands as not only the recognized leader of his race, but one of the great men of this nation. Even you, Mr. Cosgrove, cannot get to Washington, to be sworn in, unless you have a "pass" from this "devil" of ante-bellum days.'
>
> *Source*: From John Wesley Cromwell. *The Negro in American History: Men and Women Eminent in the Evolution of the American of African Descent*. Ann Arbor, MI: University of Michigan/

The American Negro Academy, 1914, pp. 164–165.

Books

Hofstadter, Richard and Beatrice K. Hofstadter. *Great Issues in American History: From Reconstruction to the Present Day, 1864–1981*. New York, NY: Vintage Books, 1982. Features a section which looks at Kelso's March 31, 1876, Senate speech about election practices in Mississippi.

Sewell, George A. and Margaret L. Dwight. *Mississippi Black History Makers*. Jackson, MS: University Press of Mississippi, 1984. Outlines the life and political achievements of B. K. Bruce.

Websites

The U.S. Senate Website has an online biography on Blanche Kelso Bruce. http://www.senate.gov/artandhistory/art/artifact/Painting_32_00039.htm.

Black Americans in Congress features a biography and portrait of Blanche K. Bruce. http://baic.house.gov/member-profiles/profile.html?intID=127.

1875

The U.S. Congress passes the Civil Rights Act, which bans discrimination in places of public accommodation. The Civil Rights Act was signed into law by President Ulysses S. Grant and declared itself an effort "... to protect all citizens in their civil and legal rights," and professed that it was "essential to just government [that] we recognize the equality of all men before the law." A Republican Party-led Congress, which included African American representatives who had been elected after the Civil War, passed the Act. The Supreme Court overturned the Civil Rights Act of 1875 by declaring it unconstitutional in 1883.

. . . The Civil Rights Act of 1875 was enacted to provide African-Americans with equal access to public accommodations, including inns, public consequences, theaters, and "other places of public amusement." By its terms, the Act applied to private individuals, and made violations criminal misdemeanors. Several white owners of private hotels, theaters, and railroads had policies excluding African-Americans, and were indicted under the Act.

Source: From Kermit Hall. *Freedom and Equality: Discrimination and the Supreme Court.* New York, NY: Taylor & Francis/Routledge, 2000, p. 298.

March 2

1807

Abolition of the Atlantic Slave Trade in the United States. Thomas Jefferson signed a bill abolishing the slave trade, to take effect on January 1, 1808. The slave trade was not just a matter of national commercial policy, but a moral one as well.

Until the House voted on January 31, 1865, no one could predict which way it would go. As a few Democrats early in the roll call voted Aye, Republican faces brightened. Sixteen of the eighty Democrats finally voted for the Amendment; fourteen of them were lame ducks. Eight other Democrats had absented themselves. This enabled the Amendment to pass with two votes to spare, 119 to 56. When the result was announced, Republicans on the floor and spectators in the gallery broke into prolonged—and unprecedented—cheering, while in the streets of Washington cannons boomed a hundred-gun salute.

Source: From James M. McPherson. *Battle Cry of Freedom: The Civil War Era.* New York, NY: Oxford University Press, 2003, p. 839.

Books

Hoffer, Peter Charles. *The Law's Conscience: Equitable Constitutionalism in America.* Chapel Hill, NC: UNC Press Books, 1990. Looks at the reasons behind passage of 1875 Civil Rights Act and why it was overturned.

Lurie, Jonathan and Salmon Portland Chase. *The Chase Court: Justices, Rulings and Legacy.* Santa Barbara, CA: ABC-CLIO, 2004. Looks at the reasons behind passage of the Civil Rights Act of 1875.

Websites

The Center for History and New Media provides the text of The Civil Rights Act of March 1, 1875. http://chnm.gmu.edu/courses/122/recon/civilrightsact.html.

The history behind passage of the Civil Rights Act of 1875 is provided on the Website of the Clerk of the U.S. House of Representatives. http://clerk.house.gov/art_history/highlights.html?action=view&intID=294.

Also Noteworthy

1949

Joe Louis retires from professional boxing. Louis ended his career as an undefeated world heavyweight boxing champion.

Books

Remini, Robert Vincent. *The House: The History of the House of Representatives.* New York, NY: Smithsonian Books/Library of Congress/HarperCollins, 2006. Book details how the vote on the Thirteenth Amendment progressed and the notable legislatures who were on site to witness its passage.

Wolf, Naomi. *Give Me Liberty: A Handbook for American Revolutionaries.* New York, NY: Simon & Schuster, 2008. Author looks at how political activism has helped create democracy in the United States.

Websites

The National Archives has a jpeg of the original Thirteenth Amendment online. http://www.archives.gov/historical-docs/document

.html?doc=9&title.raw=13th%20Amendment
%20to%20the%20U.S.%20Constitution%3A
%20Abolition%20of%20Slavery.

The Website for *Harper's Monthly* has an article
on "The End of Slavery: The Creation of
the Thirteenth Amendment," which details
the creation of the Thirteenth Amendment.
http://13thamendment.harpweek.com/.

Also Noteworthy

1926

Carlos Manuel Santiago is born in Mayaguez, Puerto Rico. Santiago became a star
infielder while playing second base and
shortstop for the New York Cubans in the
Negro Leagues between 1945 and 1946.
Although he was invited to spring training
by the Cleveland Indians in 1951, Santiago
was drafted by the U.S. Army and sent to
fight in Korea. After two years, he was
honorably discharged as a sergeant. After
retirement he worked as a general manager
for three seasons at Puerto Rico's Mayaguez
Indians club and in 1993 became a Puerto
Rican Baseball Hall of Famer.

March 3

1865

The federal government's War Department
establishes a Bureau of Refugees, Freedmen,
and Abandoned Lands. From 1865 to 1872,
the Freedmen's Bureau, as it came to be
known, established field offices in Alabama,
Arkansas, the District of Columbia, Florida,
Georgia, Kentucky, Louisiana, Maryland,
Delaware, Mississippi, Missouri, North and
South Carolina, Tennessee, Texas, and Virginia. The bureau founded some 4,300
schools, among which were Clark Atlanta
University, Fisk University, Hampton Institute, and Howard University, which later
become historically Black institutions
(HBCUs). The Freedmen's Bureau was also
mandated to record the movements of

Blacks from community to community and
throughout the various states; its offices were
responsible for documenting, supervising,
and managing the transition of the formerly
enslaved from bondage to freedom; they
were to help establish educational programs
and provided medicine, food, and other
basic supplies to the nation's Blacks. For the
first time, the U.S. government funded an
agency that would formally recognize African Americans as individuals, with names
and families and life histories, rather than as
mere beasts of burden, listed only by sex,
age, and color.

Among the more controversial issues of
Reconstruction was the Freedmen's Bureau. In
March 1865, Congress established under the auspices of the War Department the Bureau for Refugees, Freedmen, and Abandoned Lands for the
purpose of bringing order to the emergent chaos
in parts of the South. Since the issuance of the
Emancipation Proclamation, hundreds of thousands of freedmen had left plantations and farms
in search of new opportunities. However, for these
masses of uneducated and largely sheltered people, and in the midst of war, there were few opportunities. Many flocked to cities; others settled in
makeshift refugee camps run by the U.S. military.
In Washington, those who had seen the situation
in the South claimed that direct action had to be
taken to address the growing crisis.

Source: From Jeffrey W. Coker. *Presidents from
Taylor Through Grant, 1849–1877: Debating the
Issues in Pro and Con Primary Documents*. Santa
Barbara, CA: Greenwood Publishing Group,
2002, p. 167.

Books

Cimbala, Paul Alan and Randall M. Miller. *The
Freedmen's Bureau and Reconstruction: Reconsider-
ations*. Bronx, NY: Fordham University Press,
1999. Examines the departments and looks at
some of the agents of the Freedmen's Bureau
and their work with the formerly enslaved.

Murrin, John M., Paul E. Johnson, James M.
McPherson, and Gary Gerstle. *Liberty,*

Equality, Power: A History of the American People, Compact. Independence, KY: Cengage Learning, 2007. Has detailed passage on the Freedmen's Bureau.

Websites

The University of South Florida and the Africana Heritage Project has an archive of names, stories, and lives of the Freedmen. http://www.africanaheritage.com/Freedmens_Bureau.asp.

The Freedmen's Bureau online contains records from the Bureau departments from various states. http://freedmensbureau.com/.

1865

President Abraham Lincoln signs the Freedman's Savings and Trust Company (Freedman's Bank) into law. Frederick Douglass is elected president of the bank on February 16, 1874. But by the time Douglass came to the presidency, the Freedman's Savings Bank was already in trouble—a victim of mismanagement and fraud by bank officials; it failed later that year. Nevertheless, the Freedman's Bank was the first savings vehicle established in the United States for people of African descent who had only recently left slavery.

Soon after Colored Troops were mustered into the service of the Government a question arose as to some safe method by which these troops might save their pay against the days of peace and personal effort. The noble and wise Gen. Saxton answered the question and met the need of the hour by establishing a Military Savings Bank at Beaufort, South Carolina. Soldiers under his command were thus enabled to husband their funds. Gen. Butler followed in this good work, and established a similar one at Norfolk, Virginia. These banks did an excellent work, and so favorably impressed many of the friends of the Negro that a plan for a Freedman's Savings Bank and Trust Company was at once projected. Before the spring campaign of 1865 opened up, the plan was presented to Congress; a bill introduced creating such a bank, was passed and signed by President Lincoln on the 3d of March.

Source: From George Washington Williams. *History of the Negro Race in America from 1619 to 1880: Negroes as Slaves, as Soldiers, and as Citizens; Together with a Preliminary Consideration of the Unity of the Human Family, an Historical Sketch of Africa, and an Account of the Negro Governments of Sierra Leone and Liberia, Volume 2.* New York, NY: G.P. Putnam's Sons, 1882, p. 403.

Books

Du Bois, William Edward Burghardt. *Some Notes on Negro Crime, Particularly in Georgia: Report of a Social Study Made under the Direction of Atlanta University; Together with the Proceedings of the Ninth Conference for the Study of the Negro Problems, Held at Atlanta University. May 24, 1904.* Atlanta, GA: Atlanta University Press, 1904. DuBois provides a breakdown of the 32 branches that were part of Freedman's Savings and their deposits.

Webster, Laura Josephine. *The Operation of the Freedmen's Bureau in South Carolina, Volume 1, Issue 2.* Northampton, MA: Department of History of Smith College, 1916. Author writes about the faith Blacks in South Carolina had in their branches of the Freedman's Savings bank, and who was responsible for its failures.

Websites

The Website for the National Center for White House History at Decatur House has an entry on the Freedman's Savings & Trust Co. that features digital images of the former bank building and of savings books once used by customers. http://www.preservationnation.org/travel-and-sites/sites/southern-region/decatur-house/freedmans-savings-trust.html.

The Family Search Website features an article on the African American Freedman's Savings and Trust Company records, with details about the information to be found in the records and how they can be searched. https://wiki.familysearch.org/en/African_American_Freedman%27s_Savings_and_Trust_Company_Records.

March 4

1912

Garrett Augustus Morgan is born in Paris, Kentucky, to Eliza Reed Morgan and the Rev. Garrett Reed. Garrett Morgan moved first to Cincinnati and then to Cleveland, Ohio, when he was 14, and his curiosity about machines led him to become an inventor. He created two very famous devices: on August 19, 1912, he filed a patent for the Morgan Safety Hood and Smoke Protector device, which is now more commonly called the Gas Mask, and on November 20, 1923, he was awarded a patent for a traffic light, which he called the Three-Position Traffic Signal. Morgan later became the publisher of the African American-oriented *Cleveland Call* newspaper.

> *Morgan's fortunes changed on July 25, 1916, when an explosion in a Cleveland water works tunnel 282 feet under Lake Erie left two dozen men trapped in a tunnel filled with smoke and pockets of asphyxiating natural gas. Two years earlier, Morgan had patented a safety hood, an early version of the gas mask. Now, together with his brother Frank, both wearing the airtight canvas hood with its breathing tube, they entered the tunnel. Thanks to the inhalator, they found three survivors among the dead bodies. When Morgan's heroic rescue was reported in the newspapers, fire and police departments across the country began ordering his hood.*
>
> *Source*: From Marshall Cavendish Corporation. *America in the 20th Century, Volume 12*. Tarrytown, NY: Marshall Cavendish, 2003, p. 211.

Books

Murphy, Patricia J. *Garrett Morgan: Inventor of the Traffic Light and Gas Mask*. Berkeley Heights, NJ: Enslow Publishers, 2004. This juvenile nonfiction biography of Morgan explains his inventions and how the inventor overcame difficulties to create them.

Oluonye, Mary N. *Garrett Augustus Morgan: Businessman, Inventor, Good Citizen*. Bloomington,

IN: AuthorHouse, 2008. Biography on the life of Garrett Morgan.

Websites

The Website for the Garrett A. Morgan Technology and Transportations Futures Program at the U.S. Department of Transportation's Federal Highway Administration contains a biography on Morgan and notes the importance of his inventions. http://www.fhwa.dot.gov/education/gamorgan.htm.

The Hopewell Museum of History & Fine Art in Paris, Kentucky (where Garrett Morgan was born), has a permanent exhibit of his life and work. http://hopewellmuseum.org/aboutus.html.

Also Noteworthy

1893

George Washington Murray is elected to serve in the U.S. House of Representatives from South Carolina's 7th district. Murray served from March 4, 1893, to March 3, 1895; he was the only African American member in the 53rd and 54th Congresses.

March 5

1770

The escaped-slave-turned-sailor, Crispus Attucks, becomes the first martyr of the American Revolution against the British when he is killed in the Boston Massacre.

> *Crispus Attucks, "the first to defy, . . . the first to die" in the American Revolution, had been a slave in Framingham, Massachusetts. He escaped in 1750, but little else is known about his life before March 5, 1770. That night he was in Boston, on King Street. He was one of a large group of Americans who crowded around a troop of British soldiers, calling them "lobsters" and "bloody backs" because of their red uniforms. The Patriots threw snow and chunks of ice at the soldiers. Crispus Attucks stepped forward, holding a think piece of wood. "Attack the main guard! Strike at*

the root!" Attucks called to the others. "Shoot if you dare!" he yelled at the soldiers.

The soldiers shot.

The Boston Globe reported that Attucks was hit with two bullets and "killed instantly . . . most horribly." That night, in what was later called the Boston Massacre, Attucks and four others were the first to die in the struggle for American independence.

Source: From David A. Adler. Heroes of the Revolution. New York, NY: Holiday House, 2003, p. 6.

Books

Hodgson, John. *The Trial of the British Soldiers, of the 29th Regiment of Foot, for the Murder of Crispus Attucks, Samuel Gray, Samuel Maverick, James Caldwell, and Patrick Carr, on Monday Evening, March 5, 1770.* University Park, PA: Pennsylvania State University. Details the murder of Crispus Attucks in legal terms and shows the charges brought against the soldiers who killed him.

Resnick, Abraham. *They Too Influenced a Nation's History: The Unique Contributions of 105 Lesser-Known Americans.* Lincoln, NE: iUniverse, 2003. Provides a small profile of Attucks and his importance to the U.S. Revolution.

Websites

The Framingham, Massachusetts, Website profiles Crispus Attucks. http://www.framingham.com/history/profiles/crispus/.

American Treasures of the Library of Congress provides details on Attucks life and how he came to be a martyr for the U.S. cause. http://www.loc.gov/exhibits/treasures/trr046.html.

March 6

1857

The Dred Scott decision is announced. The U.S. Supreme Court had decided to determine, once and for all, the question of Black citizenship in the *Dred Scott v. Sandford* case of 1856. Sanford's attorneys had previously argued that Scott had no right to bring a case

in federal court against Sanford, since Scott was not a citizen of Missouri, where the case first surfaced; or Illinois, the "slave-free" state he'd spent time enslaved in; or even of the United States. In his majority opinion deciding the case, Supreme Court Chief Justice Roger Taney found that, in the United States, Scott's—and any Black person's—legal rights were secondary to a white person's legal rights. For Taney, a supporter of continued African enslavement, "Neither that class of persons who had been imported as slaves nor their descendants, whether they became free or not, were a part of the People."

In Dred Scott, Chief Justice Taney tried to settle, with one sweeping decision, the volatile problem of slavery in the territories. He also tried to relegate American blacks to a permanent state of inferiority. Taney ultimately failed in both attempts. His decision led to a temporary diminution of the power of the Supreme Court. More permanently, the case was a catalyst for a fundamental alteration of the Constitution through the Thirteenth, Fourteenth, and Fifteenth Amendments, forever changing the nature of American law and race relations. The Thirteenth Amendment ended slavery. The Fourteenth Amendment made all people born in the United States—including former slaves—citizens of the United States and guaranteed them equal rights under the law. The Fifteenth Amendment prohibited discrimination in voting on the basis of race. In the aftermath of Dred Scott and the Civil War, the United States witnessed what Abraham Lincoln called "a new birth of freedom" for African Americans.

Source: From Paul Finkelman, ed. Dred Scott v. Sandford: A Brief History with Documents. New York, NY: Palgrave Macmillan, 1997, p. 2.

Books

Graber, Mark A. *Dred Scott and the Problem of Constitutional Evil.* New York, NY: Cambridge University Press, 2006. Looks at the problems with the U.S. Constitution that led to the Dred Scott decision.

Moses, Shelia P. and Bonnie Christensen. *I, Dred Scott: A Fictional Slave Narrative Based on the*

Life and Legal Precedent of Dred Scott. New York, NY: Simon & Schuster, 2005. Fictional account of the life and attempts by Dred Scott to declare his citizenship.

Websites

The Dred Scott Case Collection Website provides background and searchable texts on the case. http://library.wustl.edu/vlib/DredScott/.

The Missouri Digital Archive's "Missouri's Dred Scott Case, 1846–1857" provides background on the Dred Scott family and the court case. http://www.sos.mo.gov/archives/resources/africanamerican/scott/scott.asp.

March 7

1965

The civil rights "Selma-to-Montgomery March" begins on Sunday, March 7, 1965. Led by the SNCC (Student Nonviolent Coordinating Committee) and the SCLC (Southern Christian Leadership Conference), the march consisted of some 600 people who had come together to demonstrate for Black voting rights, who walked for 54 miles from Selma to Montgomery, Alabama.

> On Sunday, March 7, 1965, about 600 protesters began their march. They had barely started when they met a line of state troopers and policemen some on horseback, who ordered the crowd to turn back. When the marchers held their ground, the police attacked with tear gas, bullwhips, and billy clubs, driving the activists back into Selma.
>
> The nation was shocked by televised images of "Bloody Sunday," as the brutal assault came to be known. The Reverend Martin Luther King Jr. immediately called on civil rights activists to converge on Selma for another march.
>
> *Source*: From William J. Bennett and John T. E. Cribb. *The American Patriot's Almanac*. Nashville, TN: Thomas Nelson Inc., 2008, p. 78.

Books

Beschloss, Michael R. *Reaching for Glory: Lyndon Johnson's Secret White House Tapes, 1964–*

1965. New York, NY: Simon & Schuster, 2002. Shows the strategies devised by President Lyndon B. Johnson and U.S. Attorney General Nicholas Katzenbach during the Selma-to-Montgomery march.

Partridge, Elizabeth. *Marching for Freedom: Walk Together, Children, and Don't You Grow Weary.* New York, NY: Penguin, 2009. Photos and text tell the personal stories of the adults and children who participated in the Selma-to-Montgomery march.

Websites

The National Park Service commemorates the Selma-to-Montgomery National Historic Trail. http://www.nps.gov/semo/index.htm.

Bloody Sunday in Selma summarizes the importance of the day. http://www.america.gov/st/peopleplace-english/2008/December/20090106140544jmnamdeirf0.1943018.html.

March 8

1965

U.S. Supreme Court upholds provisions of the Voting Rights Act, which President Lyndon B. Johnson would sign into law on August 6, 1965. The Voting Rights Act put an end to literacy, lineage, and even pop quiz-type tests as a requirement of the right to vote, which frequently denied the franchise to people of African descent. On March 8, the U.S. Supreme Court upheld the Act as law.

> On 8 March 1965, only a few months before President Lyndon Johnson signed the Voting Rights Act, the Supreme Court unanimously concluded that Louisiana was guilty of unconstitutionally depriving its black residents of their right to vote. In Louisiana v. United States the state was enjoined from continuing to require potential voters to pass its constitutional "interpretation" test. The test required applicants for registration to "understand and give a reasonable interpretation" of a passage from either the three-volume state constitution or the federal Constitution. It was the latest in a series of unlawful devices that

the state had employed to disfranchise its black residents.

Source: From Chandler Davidson. *Quiet Revolution in the South: The Impact of the Voting Rights Acts, 1965–1990*. Princeton, NJ: Princeton University Press, 1994, p. 104.

Books

Garrow, David J. *Protest at Selma: Martin Luther King, Jr., and the Voting Rights Act of 1965*. New Haven, CT: Yale University Press, 1980. Looks at how the Martin Luther King, Jr.-led 1965 civil rights protests in Selma and Birmingham, Alabama, led to the creation of federal voting rights legislation.

Laney, Garrine P. *The Voting Rights Act of 1965: Historical Background and Current Issues*. Hauppauge, NY: Nova Publishers, 2003. Shows how and why the Voting Rights Act was created to protect the citizen's right to vote.

Websites

Audio and photos detail the August 6, 1965: Voting Rights Act Website. http://www.usm.edu/crdp/html/cd/vra65.htm.

The National Archives provides a readable, digital image of the Voting Rights Act. http://www.archives.gov/historical-docs/document.html?doc=18&title.raw=Voting%20Rights%20Act.

1977

Henry L. Marsh III becomes the first African American elected to serve as mayor of Richmond, Virginia, the city that had been the capital of the Southern Confederacy from May 1861 through April 1865. Marsh was born in Richmond on December 10, 1933, and went to law school to become a civil rights attorney who tried some 50 school desegregation cases in the state.

When African American citizens succeeded in electing a black majority to the city council in

1977 and council members subsequently selected the African American Henry L. Marsh III as mayor, a new era commenced in which blacks exercised direct political power.

Source: From Willie Avon Drake and Robert D. Holsworth. *Affirmative Action and the Stalled Quest for Black progress*. Champaign, IL: University of Illinois Press, 1996, p. 37.

Books

Persons, Georgia Anne. *Dilemmas of Black Politics: Issues of Leadership and Strategy*. New York, NY: HarperCollins, 1993. Marsh's influence on Black Richmonders is examined.

Silver, Christopher and John V. Moeser. *The Separate City: Black Communities in the Urban South, 1940–1968*. Lexington, KY: University Press of Kentucky, 1995. Looks at Marsh's emergence in Richmond city politics as a civil rights attorney and ultimately as a state senator.

Websites

State Senator Henry L. Marsh III is a member of the Democratic Party and represents the state's 16th District. http://sov.state.va.us/SenatorDB.nsf/d6b46280f207781785256b18005c429d/fa00661ac2e479ab85256aa000719976?OpenDocument.

The Library of Virginia records Marsh's impact on the state's history. http://www.lva.virginia.gov/public/trailblazers/2010/honoree.asp?bio=7.

Also Noteworthy

1911

The blues guitarist Robert Leroy Johnson is born in Hazlehurst, Mississippi.

March 9

1841

The U.S. Supreme Court upholds the freedom of the 35 Sierra Leone mutineers who had been enslaved aboard the *Amistad* ship.

The Court agreed with John Quincy Adams, the defense lawyer for the *Amistad* mutineers (the Congressman and former U.S. president), who argued that they were not slaves but free people who had been illegally kidnapped from their homes in Africa, and that they were not guilty of murder or piracy because they had simply fought in defense of their freedom. The *Amistad* revolt had been led by Sengbe Pieh (a.k.a., Joseph Cinque), the son of a Mende chief in Sierra Leone.

> *Most of the captives, including two of the girls and the young boy, were from the Mandingo region in and around Sierra Leone in western Africa. A few others, including one of the girls, were from the Congo. Cinque told Ferry that he had been kidnapped and taken to Spanish slave traders in western Africa. They put him aboard a ship, where he met the other Africans who were now in jail. A month and a half later, they landed in Havana. After a brief stay, they were taken aboard the* Amistad, *where the captain "beat them severely," according to Cinque.*
>
> *The Africans decided to take over the ship. He recounted how the Spaniards deceived them by steering the boat westward during the night. They had no idea where they were when they sighted land.*
>
> *Source*: From Susan Dudley Gold. *United States v. Amistad: Slave Ship Mutiny.* Tarrytown, NY: Marshall Cavendish, 2006, p. 50.

Books

Adams, John Quincy. *The* Amistad *Case: The Most Celebrated Mutiny of the Nineteenth Century.* Victoria, BC: AbeBooks/Johnson Reprint Corporation, 1968. Book cites primary sources to show how the argument was won for the *Amistad* mutineers.

Osagie, Iyunolu Folayan. *The* Amistad *Revolt: Memory, Slavery, and the Politics of Identity in the United States and Sierra Leone.* Athens, Georgia: University of Georgia Press, 2003. A look at how the legacy of the *Amistad* has been remembered by artists in the United States and Sierra Leone.

Websites

The text of the Supreme Court's decision in *United States v. The Libellants and Claimants of the Schooner* Amistad, *Her Tackle, Apparel, and Furniture, Together with Her Cargo, and the Africans Mentioned and Described in the Several Libels and Claims.* http://www.law.cornell.edu/background/amistad/opinion.html.

The nation of Sierra Leone features a likeness and remembrance of the Mende farmer Sengbe Pieh on its banknote for 5000 Leones. http://www.banknotes.com/sl28.htm.

Also Noteworthy

1987

Edward (Pork Chop) Davis dies after a long illness at age 65. Davis was a well-respected Harlem street-corner preacher up through the 1960s. He was famed for preaching Black Nationalism and Black Pride from his step-ladder on the corner of 125th Street and Seventh Avenue.

March 10

1913

Antislavery advocate and Underground Railroad "conductor," Harriet Tubman—who is also known as "Black Moses," "Grandma Moses," and "The Moses of Her People"—dies. At birth, Tubman had been given the name "Araminta Ross" by her parents, Harriet Green and Benjamin Ross. She was born on the Brodas Plantation in Dorchester County, Maryland, to parents who could trace their ancestry to the Ashanti (Asante) people of Ghana. At some point in 1844, Araminta Ross married a free Black named John Tubman. She adopted Tubman's last name and would later change her own first name to Harriet, in honor of her mother. Tubman liberated herself from slavery in July 1849, but she would return to the South at least 20 times over the following 10 years and lead more than 300 other

African Americans to freedom. She was so successful that at one point a reward of $40,000 was posted for her capture. Tubman worked as a Union soldier, spy, and nurse during the U.S. Civil War, but did not receive a pension for her services for some 30 years. Toward the end of her life she established a home for the aged in Auburn, New York. After Tubman died at age 93, the home was renamed the Harriet Tubman Home and its buildings still stand. The home is owned and operated by the African Methodist Episcopal Zion Church. On August 27, 2003, March 10 was legally established as "Harriet Tubman Day," a holiday in New York State.

Tubman was interviewed in St. Catharines by the Bostonian antislavery journalist Benjamin Drew when he visited in the summer of 1855. Remarkably, given the danger she faced in her Underground Railroad work, the brief testimonial she dictated about her experience in slavery was published over her own name. She did not reveal her clandestine role as a liberator of her family and friends, of course—as a matter of fact, she even claimed, somewhat disingenuously (given that she had already made several trips back to Dorchester Country to rescue family), that she had "no opportunity to see my friends in my native land." This testimony, though brief, is a strong expression of her antislavery views: "Now I've been free, I know what a dreadful condition slavery is. I have seen hundreds of escaped slaves, but I never saw one who was willing to go back and be a slave . . . . I think slavery is the next thing to hell. If a person would send another into bondage, he would, it appears to me, be bad enough to send him into hell, if he could." (Tubman, 1856)

Source: From Jean McMahon Humez. Harriet Tubman: The Life and the Life Stories. Madison, WI: University of Wisconsin Press, 2003, p. 25.

Books

Bradford, Sarah. *Harriet Tubman*. Carlisle, MA: Applewood Books, 1993. Biography of Tubman looks at her life and her antislavery work.

Lowry, Beverly. *Harriet Tubman: Imagining a Life.* New York, NY: Random House, Inc., 2008. As a novelist and biographer, Lowry re-imagines the life and events Tubman played a part in.

Websites

Harriet Tubman Biography has information and photos of scenes from Tubman's life and of the places she visited. http://www.harriet tubmanbiography.com.

The Harriet Tubman Website provides information about Tubman's life and work and has current information on news related to tributes related to Tubman and other abolitionists. http://www.harriettubman .com.

Also Noteworthy

1972

National Black Political Convention opens in Gary, Indiana.

March 11

1959

Lorraine Hansberry's *A Raisin in the Sun* opens at New York City's Ethel Barrymore Theatre. A story about how a Black family struggles to move out of a blighted Southside Chicago neighborhood and own their own home, *A Raisin in the Sun* was the first play written by a Black woman (Hansberry) and directed by a Black man (Lloyd Richards) to premier on Broadway.

RUTH:	*(Studying her mother-in-law furtively and concentrating on her ironing, anxious to encourage without seeming to)* Well, Lord knows, we're put enough rent into this here rat trap to pay for four houses by now . . .
MAMA:	*(Looking up at the words "rat trap" and then looking around and leaning back and sighing —in a suddenly reflective mood—)*

"Rat trap"—yes, that's all it is. (*Smiling*) I remember just was well the day me and Big Walter moved in here. Hadn't been married but two weeks and wasn't planning on living here no more than a year. (*She shakes her head at the dissolved dream*) We was going to set away, little by little, don't you know, and buy a little place out in Morgan Park. We had even picked out the house. (*Chuckling a little*) Looks right dumpy today. But Lord, child, you should know all the dreams I had 'bout buying that house and fixing it up and making me a little garden in the back—(*She waits and stops smiling*) And didn't none of it happen.

Source: From Lorraine Hansberry. *A Raisin in the Sun*. New York, NY: Random House, Inc., 1994, pp. 44–45.

Books

Carter, Steven R. *Hansberry's Drama: Commitment amid Complexity*. Champaign, IL: University of Illinois Press, 1991. Critical look at Hansberry's literary work and its importance on the U.S. political landscape.

Davis, Thadious M. and Trudier Harris. *Afro-American Writers after 1955: Dramatists and Prose Writers, Volume 2*. Victoria, BC: AbeBooks/Gale Research Co., 1985. As a novelist and biographer, Lowry re-imagines the life and events Tubman played a part in.

Websites

A news report on National Public Radio explains that *A Raisin in the Sun* was inspired by the attempts of Lorraine Hansberry's parents to purchase a home in a predominately white neighborhood. http://www.npr.org/programs/morning/features/patc/raisin/.

The *Chicago Tonight* program looks at the Hansberry House, which Lorraine's parents bought and through doing so tried to break the restrictions against African American home ownership in all white neighborhoods. http://www.wttw.com/main.taf?p=42,8,80&pid=MZBf72eyDEtTfrH_QGuCBiwu1YywkyXs&player=Chicago-Tonight.

March 12

1932

The activist, politician, and diplomat Andrew Young is born in New Orleans, Louisiana, to Andrew Young, a dentist, and Daisy Fuller Young, who had worked as a schoolteacher. After serving as an assistant to the civil rights leader Martin Luther King, Jr., in the 1960s, Young became a U.S. congressman, a U.N. ambassador in 1977, and a mayor of Atlanta, Georgia.

. . . In 1970, Young decided that the best way to continue his work for peace abroad and justice at home was to enter the national political fray himself. After losing that first election, he won a seat in the United States Congress in 1972. During his two terms in Congress, he applied the lessons he had learned in the 1950s and 1960s to influence U.S. foreign relations and to advocate peace and racial justice around the world. By 1976 he ranked as one of the leading congressional spokespersons for developing a new policy toward the Third World, particularly Africa. Young's accomplishments in Congress and his work in Jimmy Carter's campaign catapulted him to the post of U.S. ambassador to the United Nations in 1977, where he literally became America's "civil rights ambassador."

Source: From Andrew DeRoche. *Andrew Young: Civil Rights Ambassador*. Lanham, MD: Rowman & Littlefield, 2003, p. 41.

Books

Young, Andrew. *An Easy Burden: The Civil Rights Movement and the Transformation of*

America. Waco, TX: Baylor University Press, 2008. Young recounts his activist and political life in this autobiography.

Young, Andrew and Kabir Sehgal. *Walk in My Shoes: Conversations Between a Civil Rights Legend and His Godson on the Journey Ahead.* New York, NY: Macmillan, 2010. Young and his godson look at the lessons learned from the Civil Rights Movement and how they apply to life today.

Websites

The Andrew J. Young Papers are housed at the Auburn Avenue Research Library on African American Culture and History. http://www.afpls.org/aarl.

The Andrew Young Foundation furthers Young's philosophy of "equality, justice and peace for 'all of God's children.' " http://andrewyoungfoundation.org/.

Also Noteworthy

1859

Abolitionist activists Frederick Douglass and John Brown meet in the home of the Black Underground Railroad activist William Webb, on East Congress Street in Detroit, Michigan.

March 13

1802

Absalom Jones is ordained as the first African American priest in the Episcopal Church. Jones was born into slavery in Milford, Delaware, on November 6, 1746. He taught himself to read by reading the New Testament, and when his owner moved with him to Philadelphia, Pennsylvania, Jones hired himself out and earned enough to purchase his freedom and the freedom of his wife, Mary King, whom he married in 1770. They were also able to buy a home and later rent out homes for income. In 1787, Jones created the Free Africa Society, a mutual self-help group in Philadelphia, Pennsylvania, along with Richard Allen. Later, in 1792, they created the African Church, which on September 14, 1794, formally became the African Episcopal Church of St. Thomas.

Richard Allen recalled, Absalom Jones and he withdrew from Saint George's Methodist Episcopal Church in Philadelphia:

Meeting had begun, and they were nearly done singing, and just as we got to the seats, the elder said, "Let us pray." We had not been long upon our knees before I heard considerable scuffling and low talking. I raised my head up and saw one of the trustees ... having hold of the Rev. Absalom Jones, pulling him up off his knees, and saying, "You must not kneel here." Mr. Jones replied, ... "Wait until prayer is over, and I will get up and trouble you no more." With that he beckoned to one of the other trustees ... to come to his assistance ... By this time prayer was over, and we all went out of the church in a body, and they were no more plagued with us in the church.

Within six weeks of this 12 April incident, Jones and Allen had founded the Free African Society, a benevolent alliance that oversaw the spiritual welfare of its members. The society first met for devotional services in 1788 and for formal worship in 1791, and a few years later a church was built. But when in 1794 its members voted to associate their parish with the Episcopal church, Richard Allen departed and proceeded to build his own church, Bethel African Methodist Church (dedicated on 17 July 1794). Jones became the rector of the first black Episcopal congregation, named Saint Thomas African Episcopal Church, dedicated on 29 July 1794. The following year, Jones was ordained a deacon and nine years later a priest.

Source: From Jon Michael Spencer. *Black Hymnody: A Hymnological History of the African-American Church.* Knoxville, TN: University of Tennessee Press, 1992, p. 166.

Books

Hein, David and Gardiner H. Shattuck, Jr. *The Episcopalians.* Harrisburg, PA: Church Publishing, Inc., 2005. This overview of Episcopalian history contains information on how Jones founded St. Thomas African Episcopal Church.

Miller, Randall M. and William Pencak. *Pennsylvania: A History of the Commonwealth.* University Park, PA: Penn State Press, 2002. Citation looks at the impact of both Richard Allen and Absalom Jones on the formation of Black religious institutions in Pennsylvania.

Websites

The Philadelphia, Pennsylvania-based African Episcopal Church of St. Thomas (AECST) has a biography of Absalom Jones on its Website. http://www.aecst.org/ajones.htm.

The on-line Lectionary page for the Episcopal Church contains links to readings about Absalom Jones. http://satucket.com/lectionary/Absalom_Jones.htm.

Also Noteworthy

1938

Dorothy Brunson is born to Wadis and Naomi (Ross) Edwards in Glensville, Georgia, and raised in Harlem, New York. As an adult, Brunson worked with Inner City Broadcasting and is recognized for developing the "urban contemporary" format. Brunson was the first African American woman to own a radio station when she purchased WEBB-Radio in Baltimore, MD, in 1979. Under her company, Brunson Communications, she also bought WIGO-AM in Atlanta and WBMS-AM in Wilmington, North Carolina. In 1986, Brunson became the first African American woman to own and operate a television station, when she purchased WGTW-TV Channel 48 in Philadelphia, Pennsylvania.

March 14

1933

Quincy Delight Jones, Jr., is born in Chicago, Illinois. As a jazz trumpeter, record producer, and composer of music to some 33 different films, Jones is one of the most influential musical artists in the nation. In 1985, Jones famously gathered musical celebrities to sing parts of the song "We Are the World," which raised money for the victims of Ethiopia's famine. Jones helped establish the Institute for Black American Music, to create a national library of African American art and music. *The Autobiography of Quincy Jones* was published in 2001.

Always looking forward, Quincy has never been content to rest on past achievements, no matter how celebrated. He is most comfortable conquering uncharted territory. As vice president of Mercury Records in 1961, Quincy was the first high-level black executive at a major label. With the release of The Pawnbroker *in 1963, Quincy became the first African-American composer to score a major Hollywood movie. (He would ultimately score 33 before turning his attention to other pursuits.) Michael Jackson's* Thriller *album, produced by Quincy in 1982, sold in excess of 40 million copies —the best selling record in history. The list of gold and platinum records Quincy has worked on seems endless and includes titles from the 32 albums he has released as leader. A quick inventory of his awards reveals 27 Grammys, the Grammy Legend award, an Emmy, seven honorary doctorates, five NAACP Image awards, arts prizes from three foreign governments, and much more.*

Source: From Mark Small, Andrew Taylor, Jonathan Feist, and Berklee College of Music. *Masters of Music: Conversations with Berklee Greats.* Boston, MA: Berklee Press, 1999, p. 175.

Books

Jones, Quincy. *Q: The Autobiography of Quincy Jones.* New York, NY: Random House Digital, Inc., 2002. Jones tells of his life and work in this autobiography.

Jones, Quincy and Bill Gibson. *Q on Producing.* Milwaukee, WI: Hal Leonard Corp, 2010. One-on-one interviews with Jones on how to produce songs and albums.

Websites

The Quincy Jones Website has up-to-date information on Jones's life and work. http://www.quincyjones.com/.

Jones has an official MySpace page, which releases his latest music and updates news about his career. http://www.myspace.com/quincyjones.

March 15

1905

Blues singer Bertha "Chippie" Hill is born in Charleston, SC. As one of the 16 children of Ida and John Hill, Bertha was encouraged to pursuit her love of music, initially by way of the spiritual songs in church. By the age of 16, Hill was working as a dancer in Harlem, New York. "Chippie" Hill became one of the most respected blues singers of her generation.

Chippie Hill's career was minor compared to singers discussed previously, but her small record output was prestigious. She had a deep, heavy voice as big as Bessie Smith's but not as refined. The hard edge was developed from her experiences singing and dancing in dives and fending for herself in the city. A hard worker, Hill moved to Chicago in the mid-1920s and performed at the Plantation and Dreamland with the musicians Armstrong, Oliver and Austin.

Source: From Daphne Duval Harrison. *Black Pearls: Blues Queens of the 1920s*. Newark, NJ: Rutgers University Press, 1990, p. 232.

Books

Dahl, Linda. *Stormy Weather: The Music and Lives of a Century of Jazzwomen*. Milwaukee, WI: Hal Leonard Corporation, 1996. Book contains a short biography on the life of Bertha "Chippie" Hill.

Harris, Rex and Brian A. L. Rust. *Recorded Jazz: A Critical Guide*. New York, NY: Penguin Books, 1953. Looks at Bertha "Chippie" Hill's phenomenal career and then strange disappearance from the music scene.

Websites

Red Hot Jazz has a page dedicated to Bertha "Chippie" Hill and links to some of her recordings. http://www.redhotjazz.com/chippiehill.html.

Some of Bertha "Chippie" Hill recordings are available on the Internet, including "How Long Blues." http://www.YouTube.com/watch?v=8S3umP3LTCM.

March 16

1827

James Varick, Richard Allen, Alexander Crummel, Samuel Eli Cornish, and John Brown Russwurm begin publishing *Freedom's Journal* in New York City. The nation's first African American newspaper, *Freedom's Journal* began operating out of Varick's African Methodist Episcopal Zion Church. In the paper's first edition, Russwurm writes, "We wish to plead our own cause. Too long have others spoken for us."

In the inaugural issue of Freedom's Journal, *published March 16, 1827, editors Samuel Cornish and John Russwurm clearly outlined their intentions: "We wish to plead our own cause. Too long have others spoken for us." To claim their rights as Americans and determine their own destinies, they suggested, African Americans needed a voice in civic debates. It was a "real necessity" that they have "a public channel" shaped and controlled by African Americans themselves, "devoted exclusively to their improvement" and reflecting their "sentiments" on subjects affecting them. "Often has injustice been heaped upon us," they asserted, "but we believe that the time has now arrived, when the calumnies of our enemies should be refuted by forcible arguments."*

Source: From Jacqueline Bacon. *Freedom's Journal: The First African-American Newspaper*. Lanham, MD: Lexington Books, 2007, p. 13.

Books

Berry, Faith. *From Bondage to Liberation: Writings by and about Afro-Americans from 1700 to 1918*. London, England: Continuum International Publishing Group, 2006. Contains a chapter that gives background on Samuel

Cornish and John Russworm and discusses their rationale for the articles published in *Freedom's Journal*.

Reynolds, Amy and Brooke Barnett Ph.D. *Communication and Law: Multidisciplinary Approaches to Research*. New York, NY: Psychology Press, 2006. Shows the influence of David Walker, the author of "Walker's Appeal," on the editorial leanings of *Freedom's Journal*.

Websites

The Wisconsin Historical Society has digitized all 103 issues of *Freedom's Journal* and made them available here. http://www.wiscons inhistory.org/libraryarchives/aanp/freedom/.

Mapping the African American Past (MAAP) has a short article about *Freedom's Journal*, its founders, and the sites where it operated from. http://maap.columbia.edu/place/29.html.

1846

Rebecca Cole is born in Philadelphia, Pennsylvania. After studying science as a student of Philadelphia's Institute for Colored Youth (the city's first co-educational school for African Americans) and graduating in 1863, Cole attended and graduated from the Woman's Medical College of Pennsylvania in 1867 and became the second African American female to serve as a physician in the United States.

Rebecca Cole, the first known African American to receive her M.D. from WMC, practiced in Philadelphia; Columbia, South Carolina; and Washington, D.C. Early in her career, she worked for Elizabeth and Emily Blackwell's New York Infirmary for Women and Children as its "sanitary visitor," an assignment that entailed visiting poor women in their tenement homes. Later, Cole returned to Philadelphia, where with Dr. Charlotte Abbey, an English-born 1887 WMC graduate, she founded the "Woman's Directory," an entity offering social, medical, and legal services to pregnant women, aimed at avoiding "feticide and infanticide" and providing help to mothers who had been

abandoned by their partners. Cole was also active in the black women's club movement.

Source: From Jacqueline Bacon. A New and Untried Course: Woman's Medical College and Medical College of Pennsylvania, 1850–1998. Piscataway, NJ: Rutgers University Press, 2000, pp. 116–117.

Books

Macmillan Library Reference USA. *Black Women in America*. New York: Macmillan Library Reference USA, 1999. Contains a segment on Cole and examines her work as a physician and social reformer.

Tolley, Kimberley. *The Science Education of American Girls: A Historical Perspective*. New York, NY: Psychology Press, 2003. Shows how Cole's schooling in the sciences helped spark her career as a physician.

Websites

The National Library of Medicine has a biography of Rebecca J. Cole. http://www.nlm.nih .gov/changingthefaceofmedicine/physicians/biography_66.html.

The Faces of Science: African Americans in the Sciences has a biography of Rebecca Cole. https://webfiles.uci.edu/mcbrown/display/cole .html.

1916

Marcus Mosiah Garvey travels from Jamaica aboard the *S.S. Tallac* and arrives in New York City. With little money on hand, he takes up residence with a family in Harlem, New York. After traveling throughout the Caribbean and Latin America—and to England—Garvey had an understanding about the situation of people of African descent throughout the Americas and elsewhere. By 1919, Garvey had established the Universal Negro Improvement Association (UNIA) and African Communicates League (ACL) and became the United States' leading spokesman on Black Nationalism. On

October 14, 1919, Garvey was shot and wounded in New York in a racially driven assassination attempt by George Tyler. Tyler commited suicide while in jail on October 15. But by 1920, Garvey's UNIA was strong enough to hold a national convention in New York City from August 1 to 2. As the U.S. government tried to curb his power, it charged Garvey with mail fraud in 1923. He was convicted in 1925 and deported in 1927 after serving time in prison.

> By 1921 Garvey was unquestionably the leader of the largest organization of its type in the history of the race. He had succeeded as no one else had in gathering up the worldwide feelings of dismay at the loss of independence and defiance against colonialism and oppression, which characterized the "New Negro" spirit of the age. As of August 1, 1921, the UNIA contained 418 chartered divisions (up from 95 a year earlier) plus 422 not yet chartered. There were in addition 19 chapters (none the previous year), making a total of 859 branches.
>
> Source: From Tony Martin. *Race First: The Ideological and Organizational Struggles of Marcus Garvey and the Universal Negro Improvement Association*. Dover, MA: The Majority Press, 1986, p. 13.

Books

Garvey, Marcus and Amy Jacques Garvey. *The Philosophy and Opinions of Marcus Garvey, or, Africa for the Africans, Volume 1*. Dover, MA: The Majority Press, 1986. Garvey's philosophical groundings are explained via his writings.

Hill, Robert A., Marcus Garvey, and Barbara Bair. *Marcus Garvey Life and Lessons: A Centennial Companion to the Marcus Garvey and Universal Negro Improvement Association Papers*. Ewing, NJ: University of California Press, 1988. Book provides a thorough examination of Garvey's life and work.

Websites

The Marcus Garvey Foundation promotes education and knowledge of Black history. http://www.garveyfoundation.com/garvey.html.

Marcus Mosiah Garvey "A Defiant Symbol of Black Nationalism" by Jill Heather Winnick is posted on the University of Vermont's Website. http://www.uvm.edu/~debate/dreadlibrary/winnick.html.

Also Noteworthy

1864

Arkansas state voters ratify a new state constitution that abolishes African slavery. Arkansas is at the time a former Confederate state, now under the control of Union officers.

1960

San Antonio, Texas, becomes the first major southern city to integrate lunch counters when business owners voluntarily begin serving African American customers at previously segregated counters. The activists Harry Burns and the Reverend Claude Black had threatened to hold lunch counter demonstrations on March 17, 1960, if segregated counters were allowed to continue.

March 17

1806

Norbert Rillieux is born to Constant Vivant, an enslaved woman, and Vincent Rillieux, a white Frenchman, in New Orleans, Louisiana. Norbert's parents were in a French-style *plaçage*, or common-law marriage, and had a total of seven children together, with Norbert as the oldest. Rillieux was raised as a free Black—he was educated in Paris, France, and became the first to invent the multiple-effect evaporator, which he patented as an "Improvement in Sugar Works," a method of sugar refining.

> Evaporation in multiple effect is now universally used throughout the sugar industry as well as in other industries where the evaporation of liquids is an essential process. In the Rillieux evaporator,

a series of vacuum pans are so combined as to make use of the heat of the vapor of the evaporation of the juice in the first pan to heat the juice in the third, and so on; the degree of pressure in each successive pan being less. Since the pressure in succeeding pans is less, the liquid boils at a lower temperature, as previously explained. The number of syrup pans may be increased or decreased as needed so long as the last of the series is in conjunction with the condenser, and there is a sufficient temperature difference between the vapor and the liquid to be boiled. The fuel savings made by the use of this latent heat of vapors are enormous.

Source: From Louis Haber. *Black Pioneers of Science and Invention*. Boston, MA: Houghton Mifflin Harcourt, 1992, pp. 27–28.

Books

Pursell, Carroll W., ed. *A Hammer in Their Hands: A Documentary History of Technology and the African-American Experience*. Cambridge MA: MIT Press, 2005. Book has a section that explains Rillieux's invention and includes a copy of the original patent letter and description.

Reynolds, Amy and Brooke Barnett Ph.D. *Norbert Rillieux Collection*. New York, NY: Psychology Press, 2006. Provides documents, including copies of letters and newspaper articles, and a biography of Norbert Rillieux.

Websites

Rillieux's family history and his personal life's work are portrayed on this site about famous creoles. http://www.frenchcreoles.com/norbertrillieux/norbertrillieux.htm.

Rillieux is profiled on the online version of the *Engines of Our Ingenuity* radio program. http://www.uh.edu/engines/epi236.htm.

Also Noteworthy

2008

David Paterson is sworn in as New York State's 55th governor. Paterson is New York's first African American governor and the nation's first legally blind governor.

March 18

1821

The new $10,000 building of the African Methodist Episcopal Zion Church is established and dedicated in New York. Also known as the AME Zion Church, it was established by Black parishioners of the Episcopalian Church who wanted to worship without encountering racial discrimination. By June 21, 1821, the ministers representing the A.M.E. churches of New York, New Haven, Newark, and Philadelphia elected James Varick as their first bishop.

. . . In Oct. 1796, about 60 of the colored members withdrew from the first Methodist Episcopal Church established in America, in John Street, New York City, and, led by James Varick, formed the first Negro Methodist Society in America. Separate meetings from the regular services of the whites were held in their church in the intervals of the regular services. These meetings were subsequently transferred to a building fitted up on Orange Street.

. . . They erected their first church edifice in 1800 on the corner of Leonard and Church Streets. The A.M.E. Zion Church was incorporated Feb. 16, 1801, and articles of final separation from the M.E. Church were executed and confirmed, April 6, 1801.

Source: From Henry True Besse. *Church History*. Victoria, BC: H.T. Bess/AbeBooks, 1908, p. 216.

Books

African Methodist Episcopal Zion Church. *The A.M.E. Zion Hymnal: Official Hymnal of the African Methodist Episcopal Zion Church*. Charlotte, NC: A.M.E. Zion Publishing House, 1996. A catalogue of the hymns and spiritual songs regularly used in the African Methodist Episcopal church.

Walls, William J. *The African Methodist Episcopal Zion Church: Reality of the Black Church*. Charlotte, NC: A.M.E. Zion Publishing House, 1974. Walls provides the most extensive overview of the history of the African Methodist Episcopal Zion Church.

Websites

The Website for the African Methodist Episcopal Zion Church provides a short history of the church and a look at its mission. http://www.amez.org/news/amezion/aboutourchurch.html.

This Website for the African Methodist Episcopal Zion Church contains information about church history and current news. http://www.ame-church.com.

1833

The Phoenix Society, a literary and educational group, is founded by Blacks in New York City.

> The founders of New York's Phoenix Society, organized in 1833, called on "every person of color to unite himself, or herself, to [the Phoenix Society], and faithfully endeavor to promote its objects" ... The ultimate goal of the Phoenix Society was to transform New York City's entire black population into a "useful portion of the community". ... To do this they planned to "establish circulating libraries in each ward for the use of people of colour on very moderate pay—to establish mental feasts, and also lyceums for speaking and for lectures on sciences."
>
> Source: From Thomas Augst and Kenneth E. Carpenter. *Institutions of Reading: The Social Life of Libraries in the United States.* Amherst, MA: University of Massachusetts Press, 2007, p. 105.

Books

Swift, David E. *Black Prophets of Justice: Activist Clergy Before the Civil War.* Baton Rouge, LA: LSU Press, 1989. Looks at the success of the Phoenix Society and its efforts to establish branches across the nation.

West, Earle H. *The Black American and Education.* Columbus, OH: Charles E. Merrill Publishing Co., 1972. Provides a copy of the original constitution of the Phoenix Society.

Websites

The Website for *The Encyclopedia of New York City* gives information about how the Phoenix Society operated in New York. http://www.virtualny.cuny.edu/EncyNYC/Blacks_for_draft_riots.html.

The National Humanities Center has a link to a PDF document containing the Phoenix Society's goals. http://nationalhumanitiescenter.org/pds/maai/community/text5/text5read.htm.

1847

Susan Maria Smith is born on March 18, 1847, to Sylvanus and Anne Springsteel Smith in Brooklyn, New York's African American community of Weeksville. The seventh of 10 children, Smith saw two of her brothers die during the Civil War and had to nurse a sick niece back to health during the New York cholera epidemic of 1866. Many believe these events helped inspire her to become Dr. Susan Maria Smith McKinney Steward—the first African-American female doctor in the state of New York, and the third in the nation.

> Born Susan Maria Smith, in Brooklyn, Dr. Susan S. McKinney Steward was the first African American woman in New York to earn a medical degree and was a resident of Weeksville, Brooklyn's first African American community, which still exists today.
>
> Source: From Alexandra Kathryn Mosca. *Green-Wood Cemetery.* Mount Pleasant, SC: Arcadia Publishing, 2008, p. 116.

Books

Love, Dorothy M. *A Salute to Historic Black Women.* Chicago, IL: Empak Enterprises, 1984. This children's book provides a biography of Dr. McKinney-Steward.

Wilder, Craig Steven. *A Covenant with Color: Race and Social Power in Brooklyn.* New York, NY: Columbia University Press, 2000. Book demonstrates the social influence of Dr. Susan

Maria Smith McKinney Steward in African American society.

Websites

A photograph of Dr. Susan S. McKinney-Steward is featured on http://docsouth.unc.edu/neh/brownhal/ill33.html.

The Women in History page features a biography of Susan McKinney Steward. http://www.lkwdpl.org/wihohio/stew-sus.htm.

1991

The National Basketball Association's Philadelphia 76ers team retires the No. 13 jersey once worn by Wilton Norman "Wilt" Chamberlain. Chamberlain was born in Philadelphia in 1936, and his basketball talents won him a scholarship to the University of Kansas in Lawrence, where he played with the Jayharks. Chamberlain's court dominance—on both the offensive and defensive side—was so strong that both the National Collegiate Athletic Association (NCAA) and the National Basketball Association (NBA) changed their rules to try to control his supremacy. Known as "Wilt the Stilt," "Goliath," and "The Big Dipper," Chamberlain was the first player to earn $100,000 in the NBA, and he is the only player to ever score 100 points in a single game (on March 2, 1962, in a game against the New York Knicks). He was inducted into the NBA Hall of Fame in 1978, the first year he was eligible, and named one of the NBA's 50 Greatest Players in 1996.

> ... The National Collegiate Athletic Association (NCAA) had even changed some rules in anticipation of Wilt's skills. It outlawed offensive goaltending (when an offensive player touches a shot as it travels down toward the rim) and forced players to stay behind the free-throw line on foul shots. Wilt could jump from the free-throw line and dunk his foul shots, a skill that NCAA officials feared would allow him to make every free throw he ever took. An article in the Saturday Evening Post even asked the question: "Can basketball survive Wilt Chamberlain?"
>
> Source: From Matt Doeden. Wilt Chamberlain. Breckenridge, CO: Twenty-First Century Books, 2010, p. 19.

Books

Chamberlain, Wilt. *View from above: Sports, Sex, and Controversy.* New York, Dutton Books, 1992. Chamberlain's autobiography, in which he infamously claimed to have had sex with more than 10,000 women.

Cherry, Robert Allen. *Wilt: Larger Than Life.* Chicago, IL: Triumph Books, 2004. Biography of Chamberlain looks at his life and his strong personality.

Websites

NBA.com has a page dedicated to Wilt Chamberlain's prowess. http://www.nba.com/history/players/chamberlain_bio.htmlhttp://www.nba.com/history/players/chamberlain_bio.html.

Newsreel features Wilt Chamberlain at age 17. http://www.YouTube.com/watch?v=q9GPibuasw4.

March 19

1894

Loretta Mary Aiken—who won fame as Jackie "Moms" Mabley, a Chitlin' Circuit comedian who was later known nationwide —is born on March 19, 1894, in Brevard, North Carolina.

> Mabley began her career in the 1920s and performed through the 1970s. Mabley, who started performing in her early twenties, quickly adopted the stage character of "Moms," a salty granny who sang, danced, and told stories—often raunchy. In her early years, segregation forced her to confine her early performances to the Negro "chitlin circuit" (which white comics used to visit— often to steal her material).

Source: From Susan Horowitz. *Queens of Comedy: Lucille Ball, Phyllis Diller, Carol Burnett, Joan Rivers, and the New Generation of Funny Women.* New York, NY: Psychology Press/ Routledge, 1997, p. 139.

Books

Smith, Jessie Carney. *Powerful Black Women.* Canton, MI: Visible Ink Press, 1996. Profiles Moms Mabley and looks at the impact of her career as a stand-up comedian.

Williams, Elsie A. *The Humor of Jackie "Moms" Mabley: An African American Comedic Tradition.* New York, NY: Garland Publishing, 1995. Book testifies to "Moms" Mabley's talent as one of the nation's first African American women stand-up comedians.

Websites

The nonprofit Founders Academy has a page that explains why Moms Mabley was billed as "The Funniest Woman in the World." http://www.foundersacademy.org/Gallery_Go%20Writers/about_pages/MABLEY/about%20Mabley.html.

Video of Jackie Moms Mabley performing live in concert. http://www.YouTube.com/watch?v=KDbYI0tDGJ8.

1971

Rev. Leon Howard Sullivan is elected to the board of directors at General Motors Corp. This is but one of many methods through which Sullivan worked with corporate powers to enforce social change. Sullivan was born to Charles and Helen Sullivan on October 16, 1922, in Charleston, West Virginia. As an adult, he became a Baptist minister and worked hard to promote the rights of people of African descent. Sullivan famously established the Sullivan Principles— it was an essential element in his work as an anti-Apartheid activist. The six principles have broadened and become known as the Global Sullivan Principles, a guide for how multinational companies can operate fairly with foreign workforces. In 1991, Sullivan received a Presidential Medal of Freedom award.

The Rev. Mr. Sullivan wrote an international code of business conduct that helped fight apartheid. For more than 20 years, he crusaded against institutionalized racial oppression, backed by the white South African government. His "Sullivan Principles," written in 1977, called on U.S. firms conducting business in South Africa to establish fair-employment practices, train non-whites and promote them to management jobs, and to improve employees' lives outside of the work environment. He used his position as the first African-American to sit on the board of directors of General Motors Corp. to focus attention on racial segregation and deplorable living conditions of black workers in South Africa.

Source: From Congress. The Speech of Congresswoman Barbara Lee (D-CA) published in *Congressional Record.* New York, NY: Government Printing Office, 1966, p. 6618.

Books

Sethi, S. Prakash and Oliver F. Williams. *Economic Imperatives and Ethical Values in Global Business: The South African Experience and International Codes Today.* New York, NY: Springer, 2000. Book examines the Sullivan Principles, looks at its impact on U.S companies operating in South Africa, and how it affected the anti-apartheid movement.

Sullivan, Leon H. *Moving Mountains: The Principles and Purposes of Leon Sullivan.* Valley Forge, PA: Judson Press, 1998. Sullivan's autobiography examines his upbringing and his life of social justice activism.

Websites

The Leon H. Sullivan Foundation was established to further the social justice work of Rev. Leon Sullivan. http://www.thesullivanfoundation.org.

The full text of the Global Sullivan Principles. http://www.mallenbaker.net/csr/CSRfiles/gsprinciples.html.

March 20

1883

Jan Ernst Matzeliger patents a Lasting Machine that can mold and sew leather uppers to the soles of shoes. Matzeliger was born on September 15, 1852. in Paramaribo, Dutch Guiana (now Suriname), in South America. After moving to the United States, he worked as a cobbler's apprentice in Philadelphia, Pennsylvania, and later in Boston, Massachusetts. In 1876, Matzeliger moved to Lynn, Massachusetts, where he was the first to create a shoe-lasting machine that could produce 150 to 700 pairs of shoes a day. Matzeliger's patent reduced the high cost of shoes and made the purchase of shoes more available to average people.

> *Finally, he forwarded an application for a patent to Washington when he felt his invention was done. The reviewers sent an officer to Lynn to see the model when none could comprehend the mangled drawings and concoctions received. Jan E. Matzeliger was awarded patent number 274207 on March 20, 1883 when the reviewer convinced himself of the efficacy of the machine made with cigar boxes, wood and wire.*
>
> *Matzeliger's Lasting Machine turned out 200 to 600 shoes daily, competed with the best manual daily rate of 50. Unfortunately, having made Lynn the shoe capital of the world, and creating employment for thousands, the inspiration Matzeliger drew from the door of opportunity had caused him to overwork in the cold and dampness of the town. The resulting bout of tuberculosis killed him on August 24, 1887. But in between the day of his invention and the day of his death, he was nourished by the fact none ever called him by the derogatory terminology used for blacks.*
>
> *Source*: From Abraham K. Turkson. *Save American Jobs: New Business Ideas to Retain Jobs in America.* Bloomington, IN: iUniverse, 2005, p. 39.

Books

Cothran, John C. *A Search of African American Life, Achievement and Culture: First Search.* Carrollton, TX: Stardate Publishing, 2006. Book has an entry on Matzeliger's life and work.

Sullivan, Otha Richard and James Haskins. *African American Inventors.* Hoboken, NJ: John Wiley & Sons, 1998. Book provides a chapter that looks at Matzeliger's life and work.

Websites

Inventions.org profiles Matzeliger and talks about the importance of his invention. http://www.inventions.org/culture/african/matzeliger.html.

The city of Lynn, Massachusetts, has a remembrance of Matzeliger and his history-making shoe-machine invention. http://www.ci.lynn.ma.us/aboutlynn_shoemaking_history.shtml.

Also Noteworthy

1912

New Canton, Virginia-born Carter G. Woodson receives doctorate from Harvard University. Woodson was the second African American—and the first child of formerly enslaved parents—to receive a PhD in history from Harvard.

1916

Ota Benga commits suicide. Benga was from the Mbuti ethnic group in the Belgian Congo and was brought to the United States in 1904; he was to be placed on display at the Saint Louis World's Fair. After the Fair, Benga was exhibited in the Monkey House at New York City's Bronx Zoo. After being released from these displays, Benga ended up working in a tobacco factory, but because he was depressed he eventually killed himself at the age of 32.

March 21

1965

Civil Rights marchers complete the first leg of the Selma-to-Montgomery march, while being escorted by U.S. troops and federalized members of the National Guard. The march ends on March 25 with a rally of some 40,000 people in the Alabama

Capitol. Following the rally, white Civil Rights worker Mrs. Viola Liuzzo is shot to death.

Two weeks after Bloody Sunday, emboldened by their faith in God and the support of a white southerner in the Oval Office, Dr. King led 4,000 people across the Pettus Bridge on the 54-mile trek to Montgomery. And 6 months later, President Johnson signed the Voting Rights Act, proclaiming that the vote is the most powerful instrument ever devised for breaking down injustice and destroying the terrible walls which imprison men because they are different from other men. It has been said that the Voting Rights Act was signed in ink in Washington, but it first was signed in blood in Selma.

Source: From Editors of Black Issues In Higher Education. *The Unfinished Agenda of the Selma-Montgomery Voting Rights March.* New York, NY: Diverse Issues In Higher Education, 2005, p. 81.

Books

Lewis, P. H. *Selma: The Other Side of 1965.* Victoria, BC: AbeBooks/Factor Press, 2001. Looks at the importance of the Selma-to-Montgomery March in determining the right to vote for African Americans.

Partridge, Elizabeth. *Marching for Freedom: Walk Together, Children, and Don't You Grow Weary.* New York, NY: Penguin, 2009. Poignant black-and-white photographs and text detail the Selma-to-Montgomery march.

Websites

Selma-Montgomery March, 1965—Parts 1 and 2 are on YouTube. http://www.youtube.com/watch?v=T8reaKQgwKg.

"Selma-Montgomery March" is profiled on Civil Rights Digital Library. http://crdl.usg.edu/events/selma_montgomery_march/?Welcome.

Also Noteworthy

1856

Henry Ossian Flipper, the first African American to graduate from the U.S. Military Academy in West Point, New York, is born enslaved in Thomasville, Georgia.

1940

Soul music singer and songwriter Solomon Burke is born in Philadelphia, Pennsylvania. Burke is famed for his hit songs "Everybody Needs Somebody to Love" and "Cry to Me."

March 22

1943

Jazz guitarist and singer George Benson is born in Pittsburgh, Pennsylvania. Attracted to the guitar as early as age 8, Benson began playing with bands by age 10. His release of "Breezin' " in 1976 won him three Grammy Awards, and the album *This Masquerade* was granted the Grammy Award for Record of the Year. Other major selling songs include "On Broadway," "This Masquerade," and "Give Me the Night."

Given his background, George Benson remained inevitably fascinated by the ways in which the intricacies and ambiguities of jazz improvisation could be squared with the directness and physicality of rock music and funk. He hinted at some answers to those questions in his spare, brooding solo as a guest artist on Miles Davis's groundbreaking mid-1960s album Miles in the Sky. *But in the 1970s, Benson's career was to take a quite different turn. As with Wes Montgomery and Grant Green the record companies heard in Benson's deceptively lazy development of a solo and the voluptuousness of his tone the potential for a wider market.*

Source: From Charles Alexander. *Masters of Jazz Guitar: The Story of the Players and Their Music.* Milwaukee, WI: Hal Leonard Corporation, 2002, p. 80.

Books

Benson, George and Wolf Marshall. *Best of George Benson: A Step-By-Step Breakdown of His Guitar*

Styles and Techniques. Milwaukee, WI: H. Leonard Corporation, 2001. Book/CD combination breaks down Benson's guitar technique.

Chapman, Charles H. *Mel Bay Presents Interviews with the Jazz Greats—And More.* Pacific, MO: Mel Bay Publications, 2001. Book includes an interview with George Benson.

Websites

George Benson the Art of Jazz Guitar is on Youtube. http://www.YouTube.com/watch ?v=kThHgJNZmXg.

George Benson's official Website. http://www .georgebenson.com.

Also Noteworthy

1898

Joseph H. Smith receives U.S. Patent No. 601,065 for his updated lawn sprinkler design.

1930

Willie Lawrence Thrower is born in New Kensington, Pennsylvania. The 5 feet 11 inches Thrower became the first African American quarterback to complete a game in the NFL when he came into replace George Blanda for the Chicago Bears as they played against San Francisco on October 8, 1953.

1957

Stephanie Dorthea Mills is born in Brooklyn, New York. In 1974, Mills famously starred on Broadway as Dorothy in *The Wiz*. After *The Wiz*, Mills became a Grammy Award-winning singer, releasing songs like "What Cha Gonna Do with My Lovin," "Never Knew Love Like This Before," and "Sweet Sensation."

March 23

1955

Moses Eugene Malone is born and raised in the Delectable Heights neighborhood of Petersburg, Virginia. A Naismith Memorial Basketball Hall of Fame player, the 6 foot 10 inch Malone was the first ever basketball player to start playing professionally directly out of high school. He was drafted in 1974 by the American Basketball Association's (ABA) Utah Stars and would later also play for the league's Spirits of St. Louis team. Known for his offensive rebounding, Malone was donned "Chairman of the Boards." After the ABA and NBA merged, Malone played for several teams including six seasons with the Houston Rockets between 1976 and 1982. He ended his career with the Philadelphia 76ers where he won a 1983 NBA championship ring.

> In the early 1970s, 6'10" Moses Malone, a high school basketball star in Petersburg, Virginia, was pursued by more than 200 colleges and by pro sscouts as well. The recruiting frenzy began when Malone scored 32 points in his first game with the Petersburg High School varsity. With each succeeding year in high school, Malone gained more attention, especially after he earned the highest possible rating at Garkinkel's Five-Star basketball summer camp following his junior year. In the spring of 1974, shortly before his high school graduation, Malone signed a letter of intent to attend the University of Maryland. At the same time that Maryland was pursuing Malone, Bucky Buckwalter, general manager of the Utah Stars of the American Basketball Association, was trying to persuade the phenom to skip college and head straight to the pros. In August 1974, Buckwalter and Jim Collier, the owner of the Stars, met with Malone at his house, spread ten $100 bills across an orange crate, and showed Malone a photograph of a Lincoln Mark IV. A short time later, while meeting with the Stars in the Washington, D.C. offices of his agent, Malone agreed to a five-year contract worth $590,000.
>
> Source: From Frederick J. Day. *Sports and Courts.* Bloomington, IN: iUniverse, 2005, p. 118.

Books

Conner, Floyd. *Basketball's Most Wanted: The Top 10 Book of Hoops' Outrageous Dunkers, Incredible Buzzer-Beaters, and Other Oddities.*

Dulles, VA: Potomac Books, Inc., 2001. Book contines a short profile of Malone's basketball career information.

Lundgren, Hal. *Moses Malone: Philadelphia's Peerless Center.* San Francisco, CA: Children's Press, 1983. Biography of Malone examines his career and looks at his contributions to the 1983 Philadelphia 76ers championship team.

Websites

Remember the ABA has a tribute page for Moses Malone. http://www.remembertheaba.com/TributeMaterial/Malone.html.

Moses Malone—Chairman of the Boards. http://www.YouTube.com/watch?v=M1xlhGg-lCo.

Also Noteworthy

1928

Channing E. Phillips is born in Brooklyn, New York. Phillips served as minister of the Washington, D.C.-based Lincoln Temple, United Church of Christ. He was also a prominent social activist and on August 28, 1968, became the first African American placed in nomination for president of the United States by a major party, the Democratic Party.

1953

R&B and funk singer Chaka Khan is born Yvette Marie Stevens to Charles Stevens and Sandra Coleman in Chicago, Illinois. As a young woman, Chaka Khan and her sister Taka Boom (nee Yvonne Stevens) formed a group called Shades of Black; the two also became active in Chicago's Black Panther Party. Famed as the lead singer with the 1970's funk group Rufus, Khan later became a solo artist and is widely acclaimed as the "Queen of Funk."

March 24

1907

Nurse and aviator Janet Harmon Bragg is born in Griffin, GA. Bragg was the first African American female ever been issued a commercial pilot's license. Although she made many attempts to pursue her flying education and to work as a pilot, segregationist and racist institutions made constant efforts to put her off track. But Bragg always found ways to get past the racism. When she was not allowed to fly into white airports, she joined the Challenger Aero Club, a group of Black aviators, and purchased land in Robbins, Illinois—the group used the land to create its own airfield.

> *. . . When Janet Harmon Bragg (née Waterford, 1907–93), a registered nurse and licensed aviatrix, answered a recruitment telegram for women pilots in 1943 to transport military aircraft across the country and to England, she was rejected by Ethel Sheehy, vice president of the Ninety-Nines and the WFTD (Women's Flying Training Detachment) executive officer, because "she did not know what to do with colored girls." Through writing newspaper columns and lecturing nationally at churches, schools, museums, and civic organizations, Bragg continued for the remained of her life actively encouraging African Americans to undertake aviation careers.*
>
> *Source:* From Mankiller and Barbara Smith. *The Reader's Companion to U.S. Women's History.* New York, NY: Houghton Mifflin Harcourt, 1999, p. 53.

Books

Bragg, Janet Harmon and Marjorie M. Kriz. *Soaring above Setbacks: The Autobiography of Janet Harmon Bragg, African American Aviator Janet Harmon Bragg.* Washington, DC: Smithsonian Institution Press, 1996. Bragg's autobiography of her love of flying and her efforts to urge more African Americans into the field of aviation.

Smith, Sherri L. *Flygirl.* New York, NY: Penguin, 2008. In this book of historical fiction, the author notes Bragg's aviation prowess and the fact that she was not allowed to join the Women Airforce Service Pilots (WASP).

Websites

Hill Air Force Base dedicates a page to Janet Harmon Bragg. http://www.hill.af.mil/library/factsheets/factsheet.asp?id=5854.

Through Our Parents' Eyes: History & Culture of Southern Arizona provides an interview with Bragg and examination of her life. http://parentseyes.arizona.edu/esteban/bios_med-legal_bragg.html.

March 25

1843

Explorer Jacob Dodson sets out as a member of John C. Frémont's group of explorers in search of the Northwest Passage.

> *Jacob Dodson came from Washington, D.C., where he had been a free Negro. He was employed by the Senator Thomas Hart Benton family. When Benton's son-in-law, John C. Frémont, went on his second Western expedition in 1843, he took along young Dodson, then eighteen. Dodson accompanied Fremont again on his third expedition, which also went to California.*
>
> *Source:* From Rudolph M. Lapp. *Blacks in Gold Rush California.* New Haven, CT: Yale University Press, 1995, p. 7.

Books

Smithsonian Institution Press. *Blacks in the Westward Movement.* Victoria, BC: AbeBooks/Smithsonian Institution Press, 1975. Book looks at Dodson's work with the surveyor, John Charles Frémont.

United States, George Minot, and George P. Sanger. *The Statutes at Large and Treaties of the United States of America, Volume 34.* Victoria, BC: AbeBooks/Little, Brown, 1856. Document shows that the U.S. Government recognized and paid Dodson for his work with John Charles Frémont.

Websites

The Online Nevada Encyclopedia has an article on Jacob Dodson and the fact that he is the first known person of African descent to cross the Nevada territory. http://www.onlinenevada.org/jacob_dodson.

The Longcamp Website, about the expeditions of John Charles Frémont, has a page dedicated to Dodson and his service. http://www.longcamp.com/jacob_dodson.html.

1931

After an armed posse of white men stops a Southern Railroad train passing through Paint Rock, Alabama, nine young Black men are arrested and charged with assault and rape. The young men soon came to be known as the Scottsboro Boys, and attempts to have them declared innocent became an international cause célèbre. Most of the charges against the Scottsboro Boys were dropped by 1937.

> *Two young white women, 21-year-old Victoria Price and 17-year-old Ruby Bates, had sneaked into a boxcar on the same train. Both women were returning to their homes in Huntsville, Alabama, from Chattanooga, where they had unsuccessfully searched for work. By the time the train pulled out of Stevenson, Alabama, at least some of the black youths crossed paths with several young white men who were also on board. A fight broke out and all of the white youths except one were thrown or jumped from the train. The jettisoned youths made their way by foot to Stevenson and complained to the stationmaster. By this time, the train already had passed through Scottsboro and was approaching Paint Rock, some 40 miles west of Stevenson. The Stevenson stationmaster forwarded word that a gang of blacks had assaulted the young white men. A posse of white men were quickly deputized, armed themselves, flagged down the train at Paint Rock, and arrested all of the blacks they could find. The nine Scottsboro Boys were handcuffed, tied together with a rope, and transported in a flatbed truck to the Scottsboro jail.*
>
> *Source:* From Steven M. Chermak and Frankie Y. Bailey. *Crimes and Trials of the Century: From the Black Sox Scandal to the Attica Prison Riots.* Santa Barbara, CA: ABC-CLIO, 2007, p. 132.

Books

Carter, Dan T. *Scottsboro: A Tragedy of the American South*. Baton Rouge, LA: LSU Press, 2007. Author looks at the problems and resolutions posed by the Scottsboro trial, from the vantage point of the twenty-first century.

Miller, James A. *Remembering Scottsboro: The Legacy of an Infamous Trial*. Princeton, NJ: Princeton University Press, 2009. Author looks at how the Scottsboro trial became a defining moment in the U.S. cultural memory.

Websites

"The Scottsboro Boys Trials: A Chronology" is available on the University of Missouri-Kansas City's Law School Website. http://law2.umkc.edu/faculty/projects/ftrials/scottsboro/sb_chron.html.

The Trial of the "Scottsboro" Boys is summarized on the University of Pittsburgh's Law School Website. http://jurist.law.pitt.edu/famoustrials/Scottsboro.php.

Also Noteworthy

1942

Aretha Louise Franklin is born to Clarence LaVaughn (C.L.) and Barbara Franklin in Memphis, Tennessee. A singer/songwriter who famously grew up singing Gospel music in her father's Detroit, Michigan–based New Bethel Baptist Church, Franklin has been the acknowledged "Queen Of Soul" since the heyday of R&B in the 1960s. Franklin had numerous Top Ten hits, among them "Respect," "(You Make Me Feel Like) A Natural Woman," "Think," "Chain of Fools," "Rock Steady," "Spanish Harlem," and many more.

March 26

1911

President William H. Taft appoints William Henry Lewis as assistant U.S. Attorney General. Born in Berkley, Virginia, in 1868 to Ashley Henry Lewis and Josephine Baker—both formerly enslaved parents—Lewis grew up to be an American football star at both Amherst College and Harvard University and wrote the book *How to Play Football*, one of the first books on the techniques and strategies of American football. Lewis's football prowess led to his being the first African American to be named a "College Football All-American." As an attorney, Lewis was the first person of African descent admitted to the American Bar Association and started a law practice in 1913.

> Born in Norfolk in 1868, William H. Lewis served as captain of the Amherst College football squad. The young African American was accepted into Harvard Law School in 1892 and was named the first All-American of his race to excel on the gridiron. Despite his slight build and weight, William excelled as a defensive lineman when not studying for the bar. Following his Ivy League years, he continued to serve the school as a line coach and later authored a helpful guide to future gridiron stars titled *How to Play Football*. In 1911, with a Harvard degree in hand, William became the first African-American to be admitted to the American Bar Association and was appointed assistant attorney general under President Howard Taft.
>
> Source: From Clay Shampoe. *The Virginia Sports Hall of Fame: Honoring Champions of the Commonwealth*. Mount Pleasant, SC: Arcadia Publishing, 2005, p. 52.

Books

Cavendish, Marshall. *America in the 20th Century, Volume 12*. Tarrytown, NY: Marshall Cavendish, 2003. Book provides a section on the importance of Taft's appointment of William H. Lewis as assistant U.S. Attorney General.

Lewis, William H., edited by Alice Moore Dunbar-Nelson. "Abraham Lincoln" in *Masterpieces of Negro Eloquence, 1818–1913*. Mineola, NY: Courier Dover Publications, 2000. Lewis was invited to give a speech before the Massachusetts House of Representatives on February 12, 1913, to celebrate Abraham Lincoln.

Websites

Virginia Sports Hall of Fame profiles William H. Lewis. http://www.vshfm.com/hall/induct _lewisw.html.

Lewis's first alma mater, Amherst College, has a long article on his life and legacy. https:// www.amherst.edu/aboutamherst/magazine/ issues/2007_winter/blazing.

1937

William Hastie, first Black federal judge, is appointed in 1937. Born to Henry Hastie, Sr., and Roberta Childs on November 17, 1904, in Knoxville, Tennessee, Hastie was the first person of African descent to serve as governor of the United States' Virgin Islands. He was also the nation's first federal judge and federal appellate judge.

Truman's decision to nominate William Hastie was provocative and unprecedented and in time would prove to be inspired. Hastie, born on November 17, 1904, in Knoxville, Tennessee, had superb credentials and a distinguished record of service as dean of the Howard University Law School. With his impressive background as a lawyer who had argued before the Supreme Court with Thurgood Marshall, Hastie was an important symbol of professional success in the black community in the 1940s. President Truman had been personally impressed with Governor William Hastie during his presidential visit to the Virgin Islands, where Hastie had demonstrated strong leadership skills, as well as an affable personality. President Roosevelt had appointed Hastie to an obscure district court in the Virgin Islands for two years in the late 1930s, but President Truman took the unprecedented action of appointing Hastie to the federal appellate bench—an action that represented the first black American appointment to the federal bench in the continental United States.

Source: From Michael R. Gardner, George M Elsey, and Kweisi Mfume. *Harry Truman and Civil Rights: Moral Courage and Political Risks*. Carbondale, IL: SIU Press, 2003, p. 152.

Books

Anderson, Carol Elaine. *Eyes Off the Prize: The United Nations and the African American Struggle for Human Rights, 1944–1955*. New York, NY: Cambridge University Press, 2003. Book quotes from Hastie's talks with the NAACP about efforts to push for African American civil rights before the United Nations.

Cox, Graham. *What Irony! Herbert C. Pell, Crimes Against Humanity, and the Negro Problem*. Houston, TX: University of Houston/Pro-Quest, 2008. Book notes William Hastie's efforts for African American civil rights and the ways that white politicians responded to him.

Ware, Gilbert. *William Hastie: Grace under Pressure*. New York, NY: Oxford University Press, 1984. Biography of Hastie traces his legal career and its national impact.

Websites

The Harry S. Truman Library & Museum has an online oral history interview with Judge William H. Hastie. http://www.truman library.org/oralhist/hastie.htm.

Tennessee State University provides a biography of William Hastie. http://www.tnstate.edu/ library/digital/hastie.htm.

Also Noteworthy

1872

Thomas J. Martin of Dowagiac, Michigan, is awarded U.S. Patent No. 115,603 for his invention of the fire extinguisher. Martin was born on January 25, 1858.

March 27

1924

Sarah Lois "Sassy" Vaughan—later known as "The Divine Sarah"—is born to Ada and Asbury "Jake" Vaughan in Newark, New Jersey. Her father was a carpenter and amateur guitarist while her mother worked as a laundress. Sarah grew up playing piano and singing in the choir at her local New Mount Zion Baptist Church. After winning the famed Harlem's Apollo Theatre Amateur Night talent contest at age 18, Vaughan was lauded by the singer Billy Eckstine. Eckstine recommended Vaughan to Earl "Fatha" Hines, and Hines took Vaughan on as a singer for his big band and as his second pianist. Vaughan went on to have a 50-year career as one of the most distinctive and sultriest jazz singers of all time.

> *Throughout her career, she was affectionately known as "Sassy" or "Sass" or "the Divine Sarah." The first two nicknames reflected her kittenish sense of humor and a mischievous sensuality that was frequently apparent on the stage. The third acknowledged her virtuoso performances and the unique beauty and range of her voice with all her inventions and dramatic colorings that brought to mind the legendary actress Sarah Bernhardt, who had been as phenomenal in the theater as this Sarah was in the arena of music. Her friend Paula Kelly has pointed out that Sarah could go "from Divine to Sassy in the same song; listen to her majestic, impressive, royal sounds and then the sudden switch into coyness and sassiness and sexiness. No, she could do no wrong—not when it came to music!"*
>
> *Source*: From Marianne Ruuth. *Sarah Vaughan.* Los Angeles, CA: Holloway House Publishing, 1994, p. 20.

Books

Brown, Denis. *Sarah Vaughan: A Discography.* Santa Barbara, CA: Greenwood Publishing Group, 1991. Author provides a detailed discography of Vaughan's music throughout her career.

Gourse, Leslie. *Sassy: The Life of Sarah Vaughan.* Cambridge, MA: Da Capo Press, 1994. Author profiles Sarah Vaughan based on interviews with friends, family, and bandmates.

Websites

Sarah Vaughan sings "Speak Low". http://www.YouTube.com/watch?v=yTKXEtOWFlk&feature=autoplay&list=MLGxdCwVVU LXdNHsTZVNq3EY2xAEiWyGKC&index =7&playnext=1.

Verve Music Group has a page dedicated to Sarah Vaughan. http://www.vervemusic group.com/artist/default.aspx?aid=2864.

1934

Arthur Mitchell is born on March 27, 1934. Mitchell was the first dancer of African descent to join the New York City Ballet. His skill in dance and choreography led him to create the Dance Theatre of Harlem, the first African American classical ballet company. In 1969, Mitchell founded the Dance Theatre of Harlem (DTH), and he serves at the DTH's artistic director. In 1993, Mitchell became one of the youngest-ever recipients of the Kennedy Center Honors.

> *The black theatrical male dancer had to. . . . navigate a labyrinth of racism that emanated from dance audiences, historians, and critics. Basically, the black male's dance body was seen as a location of "primitivism" that, it was thought, could not embody Western ideals of classical perfection. This racist notion prevailed in ballet establishment until the Civil Rights movement . . . Denied access to traditional white ballet companies, in the 1930s, 1940s, and 1950s, black male dancers performed in companies created for and by black dance artists such as Aubrey Hitchens (1906–1969). These companies were short-lived, but provided an opportunity for black dancers to perform and for audiences to see them expressing their physicality outside of racial stereotypes. Arthur Mitchell (b. 1934) danced for the New York City Ballet in the 1950s and 1960s, and was the first black man to reach the level of principal dancer in an American ballet company. When New York City Ballet's cofounder and artistic director, George Ballanchine (1904–1983), partnered Mitchell with a white woman in the 1950s, it was an artistic triumph and a strong political statement. In 1968 Mitchell founded the Dance Theatre of Harlem as a reaction to the assassination of Martin Luther King Jr. and his desire to fight for the place of the black dancer in ballet.*

Source: From Michael S. Kimmel and Amy Aronson. *Men and Masculinities: A Social, Cultural, and Historical Encyclopedia, Volume 1.* Santa Barbara, CA: ABC-CLIO, 2004, p. 200.

Books

Gruen, John. *People Who Dance: 22 Dancers Tell Their Own Stories.* Hightstown, NJ: Princeton Book Co., 1988. Book profiles Mitchell as one of modern dance's celebrities.

Tobias, Tobi and Carole M. Byard. *Arthur Mitchell.* Porter, ME: Crowell, 1975. Biography of Mitchell's life and his impact on dance in the United States.

Websites

Mitchell founded the Dance Theatre of Harlem in response to the assassination of Martin Luther King, Jr. htp://www.dancetheatreofharlem.org.

Arthur Mitchell & Dance Theatre of Harlem Ballet are profiled in this short documentary. http://www.YouTube.com/watch?v=rhk-MxSE3TQ.

March 28

1870

Jonathan Jasper Wright becomes South Carolina's first Black state Supreme Court justice. Wright was born to Jane and Samuel Wright in Lancaster, Pennsylvania, and attended college in New York. Wright became the first African American attorney in the state of Pennsylvania. Wright was part of the American Missionary Society as it went South during the Reconstruction era after the Civil War. In Beaufort, South Carolina, he helped teach formerly enslaved Blacks and members of the colored troops to read and later served as a delegate to create a new constitution for South Carolina. After being elected as the state senator from Beaufort, Wright resigned from the South Carolina Senate on February 1, 1870, after he was elected to serve as a South Carolina state Supreme Court justice, fulfilling the term of a justice who had left to run for Congress. After serving for one year, Wright was re-elected and served a total of seven years (from 1870 to 1877) as South Carolina's first Black state Supreme Court justice.

. . . *Wright joined the American Missionary Society and was sent to Beaufort County, South Carolina, to establish schools for illiterate black military personnel stationed there. Wright was apparently successful in his efforts as within a year he wrote that all of the men could read the New Testament. In addition, he participated in civic activities and gave public lectures including one to a crowd of 5,000 on the anniversary of emancipation. . . .*

Source: From John R. Vile. *Great American Judges: An Encyclopedia, Volume 1.* Santa Barbara, CA: ABC-CLIO, 2003, p. 829.

Books

Bryant, Lawrence Chesterfield. *South Carolina Negro Legislators: A Glorious Success: State and Local Officeholders; Biographies of Negro Representatives, 1868–1902.* Orangeburg, SC: South Carolina State College, 1974. Book includes a biographical profile of Jonathan Jasper Wright.

Toal, Jean Hoefer, et al. *Jonathan Jasper Wright and the Early African American Bar in South Carolina: A Retrospective.* Columbia, SC: South Carolina Supreme Court Historical Society, 1998. Historical society reviews the impact of Wright on law in the state.

Websites

Claflin University established the Jonathan Jasper Wright Institute for the Study of Southern African American History, Culture, and Policy. http://www.claflin.edu/academic/J.J.Wright Institute.html.

South Carolina African American History Calendar provides a biography of Wright. http://scafricanamerican.com/honorees/view/2002/12/.

March 29

1799

The state of New York passes the Act for the Gradual Abolition of Slavery, the first law to end the enslavement of people of African descent in the state.

> *By 1799, however, changing economic and political conditions, as well as the continuing agitation of slaves, made New Yorkers more open to emancipation. The growing European immigrant population gave employers a new labor force, one less foreign than African slaves. The foreignness of Africans, as well as the general difficulty of holding slaves, may have been exacerbated for white New Yorkers by the influx of refugee slave masters and their slaves from the Saint Domingue rebellions. New Yorkers, like other slave owners throughout the Americas, listened in fear to the reports from Saint Domingue and wondered if the "French" slaves in their midst would incite native slaves to rebellion. These factors, as much as Manumission Society attempts to encourage New Yorkers to free their slaves, left to the passage of New York's first gradual emancipation law.*
>
> *Source: From Leslie M. Harris. In the Shadow of Slavery: African Americans in New York City, 1626–1863. Chicago, IL: University Of Chicago Press, 2004, p. 70.*

Books

Berlin, Ira and Leslie Maria Harris. *Slavery in New York*. New York, NY: New Press, 2005. Thorough examination of the move to end African slavery in the state of New York.

Gellman, David Nathaniel. *Emancipating New York: The Politics of Slavery and Freedom, 1777–1827*. Baton Rouge, LA: LSU Press, 2006. Author covers the debates and looks at the activism that led to the abolition of African slavery in the state of New York.

Websites

"Somewhere in Between: Alexander Hamilton and Slavery" examines Hamilton's stance on New York state's abolition of slavery. http://www.earlyamerica.com/review/2011_winter_spring/hamilton-and-slavery.html.

New York's archives Website has a copy of the Act for the Gradual Abolition of Slavery. http://iarchives.nysed.gov/dmsBlue/viewImageData.jsp?id=177879.

Also Noteworthy

1898

William J. Ballow receives U.S. Patent No. 601,422 for his combined hatrack and table.

March 30

1870

The Fifteenth Amendment to the U.S. Constitution is ratified: its passage granted African American men the right to vote. The amendment ostensibly outlawed the denial of any man's right to vote, yet through the use of threats, violence, and murder African Americans would remain disenfranchised throughout the nation for nearly 100 more years.

> *With the adoption of the Fifteenth Amendment, many radical Republicans considered their work to be completed and the Northern Republican party began to abandon its preoccupation with the Southern reconstruction issue soon after the election of 1866. With the adoption of the Fifteenth Amendment there was widespread acceptance of the belief that radicalism was superfluous; the Negro could not take care of himself, and there was no further need for vigilance. . . . Although the Fifteenth Amendment was narrow in its scope and a negatively worded measure that was largely nullified in the 1870s and 1880s, the radicals should be credited for their "vision of the equality of all citizens" and for the foundations they erected for the "achievement of their goals" in the twentieth century.*
>
> *Source: From Kenneth Milton Stampp, Robert H. Abzug, and Stephen E. Maizlish. New Perspectives on Race and Slavery in America: Essays in Honor*

of Kenneth M. Stampp. Lexington, KY: University Press of Kentucky, 1986, pp. 210–211.

Books

Banfield, Susan. *The Fifteenth Amendment: African-American Men's Right to Vote.* Berkeley Heights, NJ: Enslow Publishers, 1998. Book looks at the struggle for the voting rights of African American men.

Foner, Eric. *A Short History of Reconstruction, 1863–1877.* New York, NY: HarperCollins, 1990. Book looks at the Democratic Party's belief that the Fifteenth Amendment was the culmination of a Radical Republican attempt to promote Black rights.

Websites

Annenberg Classroom features text of the Fifteenth Amendment. http://www.annenberg classroom.org/page/fifteenth-amendment.

The background to the Fifteenth Amendment is summarized on the Awesome Stories Website. http://www.awesomestories.com/assets/ us-constitution-15th-amendment.

1914

Sonny Boy Williamson is born John Lee Curtis Williamson just outside of Jackson, Tennessee. Williamson won fame as a blues harmonica player, particularly with his first recording, "Good Morning, School Girl," which was a hit in 1937. Williamson was inducted into the Blues Hall of Fame in 1980.

March 31

1855

The lawyer/journalist/poet/activist Robert Charles O'Hara Benjamin is born in the island of St. Kitts. After working as a ship-hand, Benjamin arrived in New York City in 1869. This initiated his itinerant life of agitation for Black rights: he worked for, edited, and helped distribute newspapers in New York, California, and throughout the South. Bemjamin was the first person of African descent to pass the California bar; he published several books and authored poetry and worked as an advocate for Black rights.

> *... The killing of a black by a white mob served as a warning to Afro-American everywhere of what would happen to them for certain transgressions. As explained by a militant lawyer/journalist, Robert Charles O'Hara (RCO) Benjamin, the lynching of blacks resulted from a determination by whites to keep blacks at the bottom of society: "It is only since the Negro has become a citizen and a voter that this charge has been made. It has come along with the pretended and baseless fear of Negro supremacy." Tragically, Benjamin, who moved to Lexington in 1897 to assume control of a weekly newspaper, was killed in a manner that suggested a lynching; and that nothing was done to his assailant was a clear indication of white disregard for black life.*
>
> *Source:* From James C. Klotter. *Our Kentucky: A Study of the Bluegrass State.* Lexington, KY: University Press of Kentucky, 2000, p. 125.

Books

Rummel, Jack. *African-American Social Leaders and Activists.* New York, NY: Infobase Publishing, 2003. Book contains a detailed biographical entry on R.C.O. Benjamin.

Smith, Jr., J. Clay and Thurgood Marshall. *Emancipation: The Making of the Black Lawyer, 1844–1944.* Baton Rouge, LA: LSU Press, 2007. Includes reference to R.C.O. Benjamin and the fact that he was the first person of African descent admitted to the California bar.

Websites

The University of Kentucky Libraries Website features a profile of Benjamin. http:// www.uky.edu/Libraries/NKAA/record.php ?note_id=1748.

Benjamin's "The Farmer's Soliloquy" is available on the Poetry Foundation site. http://www.poetryfoundation.org/archive/poem.html?id=185827.

1870

Thomas Mundy Peterson of Perth Amboy, New Jersey, becomes the first African American to vote in an election under the just-enacted provisions of the Fifteenth Amendment to the U.S. Constitution.

> *Thomas Mundy Peterson is known as the first black man to vote in the United States because he voted on March 31, 1870, in a Perth Amboy election to revise the city charter, one day after the Fifteenth Amendment to the Constitution barring race as a qualification for voting went into effect. In later years, Peterson served on the charter commission, and was a delegate to the Republican convention.*
>
> *Source*: From Russell Roberts. *Discover the Hidden New Jersey*. Piscataway, NJ: Rutgers University Press, 1995, p. 340.

Books

Capo, Fran. *It Happened in New Jersey*. Guilford, CT: Globe Pequot, 2003. Book notes Peterson's role as first African American to cast a vote.

Harris, Middleton A., Morris Levitt, Ernest Smith, and Toni Morrison. *The Black Book: 35th Anniversary Edition*. New York, NY: Random House Digital, Inc., 2009. Excerpt on Thomas Mundy Peterson looks at his claim as the first African American voter in the United States and at the other Black voters who also voted at that time.

Websites

Peterson's gravesite in Perth Amboy's Saint Peters Churchyard is noted, along with a short bio. http://www.findagrave.com/cgi-bin/fg.cgi?page=gr&GRid=6935257.

The Colonial Williamsburg site details the medal Peterson was awarded as the first African American to cast a vote in the United States.

http://www.history.org/history/teaching/enewsletter/volume4/september05/primsource.cfm.

1878

John Arthur "Jack" Johnson—later also known as the "Galveston Giant"—is born in Galveston, Texas. Johnson became the first African American world heavyweight champion when he defeated a white Canadian named Tommy Burns in the 14th round on December 26, 1908, at the World Boxing Championship in Sydney, Australia. Johnson's victory was so devastating to the predominantly white media that a worldwide search for a "Great White Hope" was soon started. On July 4, 1910, Jack Johnson defeated that supposedly invincible "Great White Hope"—Jim Jeffries—in Reno, Nevada.

> *John Arthur "Jack" Johnson of Galveston, Texas, had a national reputation by 1902, but three consecutive heavyweight champions, Jim Jeffries, Robert Fitzsimmons, and Tommy Burns, refused to fight him on racial grounds. Finally, in Australia in 1908, Burns gave in to the size of the prize that was offered; he was badly defeated.*
>
> *Source*: From Joseph R. Conlin. *The American Past: A Survey of American History*. Independence, KY: Cengage Learning, 2008, p. 571.

Books

Johnson, Jack and Christopher Rivers. *My Life and Battles*. Santa Barbara, CA: Greenwood Publishing Group, 2007. Book is a translation of a series of articles Jack Johnson wrote and which were originally published in French.

Ward, Geoffrey C. *Unforgivable Blackness: The Rise and Fall of Jack Johnson*. New York, NY: Random House Digital, Inc., 2006. Book looks at the life and career of Jack Johnson.

Websites

Famous Texans recalls Jack Johnson as the first Black person and the first Texan to hold the

U.S. Heavyweight Boxing Championship title. http://www.famoustexans.com/jackjohnson.htm.

The Cyber Boxing Zone has an article on Jack Johnson, which lists his fights and provides photos of Johnson during his heyday. http://www.cyberboxingzone.com/boxing/jjohn.htm.

The video "Jack Johnson vs. James J. Jeffries (1909)" is available to view on YouTube. http://www.YouTube.com/watch?v=BnMJL36_oCs.

Also Noteworthy

1948

The civil rights leader A. Philip Randolph initiates a nonviolent, civil disobedience campaign to protest racial segregation in the U.S. Armed Forces.

April

April 1

1899

North Carolina Mutual Life (NCML), which was initially known as the North Carolina Mutual and Provident Association, opens its doors for business in Durham, North Carolina. NCML was established as an African American life insurance company, because Blacks were rarely able to own life insurance through the existing companies.

The occasion for the organization of the North Carolina Mutual and Provident Association came on an October evening in 1898 when seven black men, at the call of John Merrick, gathered in the office of Dr. Aaron McDuffie Moore, Durham's Negro physician. Assembled with Merrick and Dr. Moore were William Gaston Pearson, teacher, principal, and business colleague of Merrick; Edward Austin Johnson, historian, attorney, and dean of the Law School at Shaw University in nearby Raleigh; James Edward Shepard, preacher-politician-pharmacist, and future founder of North Carolina College; Pinckney William Dawkins, Durham schoolteacher; and Dock Watson, a local tinsmith. Merrick presided over the meeting and declared its purpose was to devise a means "to aid Negro families in distress"; thus "an insurance association similar to the two organized by Negroes in Richmond in 1893 and 1894 should be organized in Durham."

Source: From Walter B. Weare. *Black Business in the New South: A Social History of the North Carolina Mutual Life Insurance Company*. Durham, NC: Duke University Press, 1993, p. 29.

Books

Brown, Leslie. *Upbuilding Black Durham: Gender, Class, and Black Community Development in the Jim Crow South*. Chapel Hill, NC: UNC Press Books, 2008. Looks at the progress of Durham's Black community, particularly with its establishment of organizations like the NCML.

Butler, John Sibley. *Entrepreneurship and Self-Help among Black Americans: A Reconsideration of Race and Economics*. Albany, NY: SUNY Press, 1991. The importance of NCML as one of the nation's first Black businesses is noted.

Websites

North Carolina Mutual Life (NCML) is still in operation today. http://www.ncmutuallife.com/.
The North Carolina History Project has an article on the NCML. http://www.northcarolinahistory.org/commentary/220/entry.

Also Noteworthy

1966

The first Festival Mondial des Arts Negres/ World Festival of Black Arts is held in Dakar, Senegal, and presided over by Leopold Senghor, the nation's president.

April 2

1939

Marvin Pentz Gay, Jr.—later famed as the Motown legend and R&B singer, Marvin Gaye—is born. Gaye's career spanned the beginning of rhythm and blues as a musical form in the early 1960s and extended to the heights of soul music in the 1980s. Gaye left an indelible imprint on popular music in the United States.

"The biggest result of *What's Going On*, though, had to do with my own freedom. I'd earned it, and no one could take it away from me. Now I could do whatever I wanted. For most people that would be a blessing. But for me—with all my hot little games—the thought was heavy. They said I'd reach the top, and that scared me 'cause Mother used to say, 'first ripe, first rotten.'

No, I needed to keep going up—raising my consciousness—or I'd fall back on my behind."

Source: From David Ritz. *Divided Soul: The Life of Marvin Gaye.* New York, NY: Da Capo Press, 2003, p. 153.

Books

Dyson, Michael Eric. *Mercy, Mercy Me: The Art, Loves and Demons of Marvin Gaye.* New York, NY: Basic Civitas Books, 2005. This biography of Marvin Gaye also puts his life and music in political context.

Gaye, Frankie and Fred E. Basten. *Marvin Gaye, My Brother.* Milwaukee, WI: Hal Leonard Corporation, 2003. Marvin Gaye's brother recalls intimate moments in the life and career of the famous singer.

Websites

Classic Motown's Marvin Gaye page provides information on Gaye's musical career. http://classic.motown.com/artist.aspx?ob=ros&src=lb&aid=1

The History of Rock 'n' Roll Website sums up Gaye's musical career. http://www.history-of-rock.com/marvin_gaye.htm.

1984

Georgetown University basketball coach John Thompson, Jr., becomes first African American coach to win the National Collegiate Athletic Association (NCAA) basketball tournament. Thompson's Georgetown Hoyas defeated the University of Houston for the Men's Division I Basketball Championship by featuring future National Basketball Association Hall of Famer, Patrick Ewing as the team's center.

When considering that there has always been this lingering suspicion about urban Black men and their perceived propensity for violence, Thompson instructed his team to play in a way that reinforced this perception. He did not shy away from the stereotype; he embraced it. This style was such that while it intimidated a lot of people, it also

endeared the Hoyas to a large number of Black fans who otherwise would probably not have paid much attention to the game. This is evidenced by the way that Georgetown's athletic gear became the hottest apparel on inner-city streets. The game that the Hoyas played was very much like the game played on playground blacktops all over urban America. Thompson simply put it front and center, and made it a mainstream attraction.

Source: From Todd Boyd. *Young, Black, Rich, and Famous: The Rise of the NBA, the Hip Hop Invasion, and the Transformation of American Culture.* Lincoln, NE: University of Nebraska Press, 2008, p. 84.

Books

Reiser, Howard. *The Georgetown Hoyas Men's Basketball Team.* Berkeley Heights, NJ: Enslow Publishers, 1999. Author looks at Thompson's Georgetown coaching career and the team he put together, which featured Patrick Ewing as the center.

Shapiro, Leonard. *Big Man on Campus: John Thompson and the Georgetown Hoyas.* New York, NY: Henry Holt, 1991. Book profiles John Thompson and looks at his impact on Georgetown's men's basketball program.

Websites

"Coaching legacy: The John Thompsons" looks at the legacy of John Thompson, Jr., and his son, John Thompson III, who have both served as Georgetown basketball coaches. http://sports.espn.go.com/espn/commentary/news/story?page=johnson/100223.

Hoopedia features an entry on the 1984 championship team, along with a photograph of the teammates. http://hoopedia.nba.com/index.php?title=Georgetown_University

April 3

1826

The poet-orator James Madison Bell is born. On first appearance, Bell seemed a humble plasterer from Ohio, but he was also an accomplished poet and lecturer who spoke out forcefully against African slavery and advocated for Black educational and legal rights.

James Madison Bell (1826–1902), the "Bard of the Maumee," was a native of Gallipolis, Ohio, where he spent his first sixteen years. He worked as a plasterer in Cincinnati (1842–53) and there married Louisiana Sanderlin with whom he had several children. From 1854 to 1860, Bell plied the plasterer's trade in Canada West, Ontario (where he became a friend, ally, and fundraiser for John Brown), then in San Francisco from 1860 to 1865 and in several other cities, North and South. He returned to Toledo about 1890. During all these years, Bell wrote, published, and gave public readings of his poetry; he lectured nationwide for abolitionism and black educational and legal rights; he served as a prominent lay worker for the A.M.E. church; and in the 1870s he was briefly active in Republican politics. All in all, Bell was one of the century's most articulate witnesses to racial oppression and to the African-American struggle for equality.

Source: From Joan R. Sherman. African-American Poetry of the Nineteenth Century: An Anthology. Champaign, IL: University of Illinois Press, 1992, p. 192.

Books

Bell, James Madison and Benjamin William Arnett. *The Poetical Works of James Madison Bell.* Charleston, SC: Nabu Press, 2010. Reprint of James Madison Bell's 1923 publication of poetical works.

Taylor, Quintard. *In Search of the Racial Frontier: African Americans in the American West, 1528–1990.* New York, NY: W. W. Norton & Company, 1999. Author shows the role of James Madison Bell's poetry, following the official end of African slavery.

Websites

"Publication List for Bell, James Madison" is available on the Electronic Poetry Portal Website. http://poetry.emory.edu/epoet-Author.xml ?search=Bell%2C+James+Madison.

GenealogyForum.com provides a biography of James Madison Bell. http://www.genealogy forum.rootsweb.com/gfaol/resource/African Am/BellJ.htm.

Also Noteworthy

1858

Matthew Oliver Ricketts is born in Henry County, Kentucky. A noted politician and physician, Dr. Ricketts became the first African American man to graduate from the University of Nebraska College of Medicine and was later elected the first African American to serve as a state senator in the Nebraska State Legislature. Ricketts became the most influential Black politician in Omaha at the start of the twentieth century.

1888

A. B. Blackburn receives U.S. Patent No. 380,420 for a spring seat for chairs.

1892

Arturo Schomburg, Rosendo Rodriguez (both Afro-Puerto Ricans), and Rafael Serra (who was Afro-Cuban) organize the Club Politico Puertoriqueño Las Dos Antillas. The Las Dos Antillas political club was created to promote the liberation of both Puerto Rico and Cuba and was led by Blacks.

1928

Earl Francis "The Big Cat" Lloyd is born in Alexandria, Virginia. A star on the West Virginia State College championship basketball teams of 1948 and 1949, Lloyd was named "Player of the Decade" for the 1940s by the school's conference, the Central Intercollegiate Athletic Association (CIAA). On October 31, 1950, Lloyd became the first African American to play in a National Basketball Association game when he played forward for the Washington Capitols in a game against the Rochester Royals, during the 1950–1951 NBA season. Lloyd played for the Washington Capitols from 1950 to

1951, for the Syracuse Nationals from 1952 to 1958, and then for the Detroit Pistons from 1958 to 1960.

April 4

1915

McKinley Morganfield is born to Ollie Morganfield and Berta Grant in Rolling Fork, Mississippi. Because he enjoyed playing in mud as a child, his grandmother, Della Grant, nicknamed him "Muddy." Under the name Muddy Waters he became one of the legendary blues guitarists of the twentieth century and was recognized as the "Father of the Electric Guitar."

> British players got their first remarkable glimpse of a real live Telecaster in October 1958 when Muddy Waters visited, bringing from Chicago his piano player Otis Spann . . . and his Fender Telecaster. The sonic bombardment of real, loud, aggressive R&B came as a shock to many in the London audiences. "There were some who could not hear [Muddy's] voice properly over the powerfully amplified guitar, and others who simply do not care for the electric instruments at all," wrote a baffled reviewer. "I liked some of the violent, explosive guitar accompaniment—although there were times when my thoughts turned with affection to the tones of the acoustic guitar heard on his first record. . . . Muddy seemed able to forget where he was standing as, eyes closed, he built up patterns, sometimes walls, of electrified sound."
>
> Source: From Tony Bacon. *Six Decades of the Fender Telecaster: The Story of the World's First Solid Body Electric Guitar.* Winona, MN: Hal Leonard Corporation, 2005, p. 40.

Books

Oliver, Paul. *The Story of the Blues.* Lebanon, NH: UPNE/Northeastern University Press, 1998. History of the blues focuses on Muddy Waters's central role in the style and feel of the genre.

Tooze, Sandra B. *Muddy Waters: The Mojo Man.* Toronto, Canada: ECW Press, 1997. Detailed look at Muddy Waters's life and his influence on blues music.

Websites

The official Muddy Waters Website is dedicated to perpetuating his memory. http://www.muddywaters.com/home.html.

The Delta Blues Museum in Clarksdale, Mississippi, features a life-size sculpture depicting Muddy Waters, and a wing of the museum is named after the musician. http://www.deltabluesmuseum.org.

1928

Maya Angelou is born Marguerite Ann Johnson to Bailey Johnson and Vivian (Baxter) Johnson in St. Louis, Missouri. She grew up in St. Louis and later Stamps, Arkansas. As an adult, Angelou became a world-renowned author, poet, historian, songwriter, playwright, dancer, stage and screen producer, director, performer, singer, and civil rights activist.

> On January 20, 1993, Bill Clinton became the forty-second president of the United States. At least 250,000 people watched the ceremony, waving flags and cheering. Maya Angelou became the first African American woman to recite her poetry at a U.S. presidential inauguration. She called her poem "On the Pulse of Morning."
>
> Source: From L. Patricia Kite. *Maya Angelou.* Minneapolis, MN: Lerner Publications, 2006, pp. 5–6.

Books

Angelou, Maya. *I Know Why the Caged Bird Sings.* New York: Random House Digital, Inc., 2009. The first in Angelou's series of autobiographical-fiction books.

Angelou, Maya. *The Heart of a Woman.* New York: Random House Digital, Inc., 2009. The fourth book in Angelou's series of autobiographical-fiction books.

Websites

Maya Angelou's official Website provides updates about her latest publications and interviews. http://www.mayaangelou.com.

The Academy of Achievement provides a biography of Angelou's life and work. http://www.achievement.org/autodoc/page/ang0bio-1.

Also Noteworthy

1863

Alexander T. Augusta, the first African American surgeon in the Union Army, is commissioned regimental surgeon of the 7th Regiment of U.S. Colored Troops, with the rank of Major. Dr. Augusta became the first African American to head a hospital in the United States when he directed Freedmen's Hospital between 1863 and 1864 and was the only African American among Howard University College of Medicine's first five faculty members, where he served from 1869 to 1877.

1948

Richard Parsons is born in Brooklyn, New York's Bedford-Stuyvesant neighborhood. Parsons became the first African American CEO of a U.S. savings institution that was not owned by people of African descent, when he was named CEO of the Dime Savings Bank of New York. He also later served as the chairman of both Citigroup and Time Warner, two major Fortune 500 companies.

1968

Martin Luther King, Jr., is assassinated on the terrace of the Lorraine Motel in Memphis, Tennessee. The shock and anger caused by his murder led to a week of riots in some 125 cities throughout the United States.

1972

The former Harlem congressman and civil rights activist Adam Clayton Powell, Jr., dies in Miami, Florida.

April 5

1856

Booker Taliaferro Washington is born enslaved in Hale's Ford in Franklin County, Virginia. As an educator, Washington was a founder of Tuskegee Institute, and as a nationally recognized leader of African Americans just after emancipation from slavery, Washington's council that Blacks should work for economic freedom was extremely popular.

It was a Sunday school rather than a day school that Booker first saw the inside of. One Sunday morning as he played marbles in the main street of Malden an old black man passed by and spoke harshly to the boys about playing on the Sabbath when they should be in Sunday school. His explanation of the benefit they would derive so impressed Booker that he gave up his game and followed the old man. He began to attend regularly the African Zion Baptist Church in Tinkersville, as did his whole family. Elder Lewis Rice, the pastor, baptized him, and he became a "pillar of the church."

Source: From Raymond Smock. *Booker T. Washington in Perspective: Essays of Louis R. Harlan*. Jackson, MS: University Press of Mississippi, 2006, p. 30.

Books

Norrell, Robert Jefferson. *Up from History*. Cambridge, MA: Harvard University Press, 2009. Biography of Washington looks at his popular push for Black economic independence.

Washington, Booker T. *Up from Slavery: An Autobiography, an African American Heritage Book*. Radford, VA: A&D Publishing/Wilder Publications, 2008. Washington's autobiography was written as a blueprint for how people of African descent could work hard to make their lives better.

Websites

Cengage Learning provides a biographical sketch of Booker T. Washington. http://www.gale.cengage.com/free_resources/bhm/bio/washington_b.htm.

The Booker T. Washington Virtual Museum and Storybook is oriented toward teaching young children about the life and influence of Booker T. Washington. http://score.rims .k12.ca.us/activity/bookertwashington/book ertwashington.html.

April 6

1712

After meeting in a tavern sometime near midnight, 23 Blacks set out with guns, hatchets, and swords. In the early morning hours of April 7, they set fire to buildings in Manhattan, and, when white colonists came to put the fires out, the enslaved Blacks attacked them. Nine whites were shot, stabbed, or beaten to death; six more were injured. It was the start of what would be called the New York Slave Revolt. Soldiers were sent to put down the rebellion; some 27 Blacks were captured, and six of them committed suicide. The others were soon executed; some were even burned alive. Following the revolt, new legislation restricted Black life in New York. Only three Blacks could meet together at any one time, and slave-owners were given permission to punish enslaved Blacks any way they saw fit. Yet for years, the arsonist plot to start a slave revolt kept tensions high in New York. Some 30 years later, on March 8, 1741, Fort George was destroyed by fire— and then a house went up in flames a week later. By early April, a total of five houses had caught fire, and local whites began to fear this was the start of another revolt. By 1741, New York City had become more diverse, including free and enslaved Blacks (from other U.S. states and from Spanish and Caribbean countries) as well as poor and working-class whites. A reward was posted for anyone with information about the fires and Mary Burton, a 16-year-old white indentured servant, was promised the money and her freedom if she revealed the "conspiracy." Burton's accusations led to the

hanging of 18 Blacks, the deportation of 70, and 13 Blacks being burned alive.

> *In 1712, during Governor Hunter's administration, there was an attempt at a slave insurrection. A party of negroes, armed with guns, knives, and hatchets, assembled one evening, in an orchard near Maiden Lane, and set fire to an outhouse. At sight of the flames people came running to the spot, and as fast as they came were shot or slashed. Nine had been killed and six wounded when a squad of soldiers came upon the scene and captured the murderers. Many negroes were arrested, and twenty-one were executed in ways intended to strike terror. One was broken on the wheel, and several were burned alive at the stake, while the rest were hanged.*
>
> *Source:* From John Fiske. *Historical Works . . . : The Dutch and Quaker Colonies in America, Volume 2.* New York, NY: Houghton Mifflin Co., 1899, p. 288.

Books

Davis, Thomas Joseph. *A Rumor of Revolt: The "Great Negro Plot" in Colonial New York.* Amherst, MA: University of Massachusetts Press, 1990. Book sets the scene for the background of the slave uprisings in New York City.

Johnson, Mat. *The Great Negro Plot: A Tale of Conspiracy and Murder in Eighteenth-Century New York.* New York, NY: Bloomsbury Publishing USA, 2007. Book about the 1741 Slave Revolt in New York focuses on the 1712 revolt as an antecedent.

Websites

Columbia University's "Mapping the African American Past" explains the 1712 revolt and provides maps of the location of the revolt. http://maap.columbia.edu/place/34.html.

NBC news' "The Slave Revolt of 1712 in New York" provides a short description of the revolt. http://www.nbcnewyork.com/news/ local/The-Slave-Revolt-of-1712-in-New -York—An-Anniversary-90028817.html.

1798

Explorer James Pierson Beckwourth is born in Fredericksburg, Virginia, to a mother who is of African descent and is enslaved on the plantation of his Anglo-Irish father, Sir Jennings Beckwith. Beckwourth's family moved to Missouri when he was a teen, and because he wanted to become an explorer, he began traveling farther west by the age of 18. After working as a trapper, fur trader, and hunter, Beckwourth was adopted by the Crow Indian nation and given the names "Bloody Arm" and "Bull's Robe." He later married a Crow Indian woman and lived and fought in wars alongside the Crow for some six years. Beckwourth went on to California in search of gold, and while working as a scout for General John Fremont, he discovered a route through the Sierra Nevada Mountains, which is still known as the Beckwourth Pass. The small town of Beckwourth, California, is also named in his honor. Beckwourth dictated his autobiography to Thomas D. Bonner, who published the narrative in the 1856 book, *The Life and Adventures of James P. Beckwourth, Mountaineer, Scout, and Pioneer, and Chief of the Crow Nation of Indians.*

> *Beckwourth tells of his discovery of the pass through the Sierra Nevada, which bears his name:*
> *It was the latter end of April when we entered upon an extensive valley at the northwest extremity of the Sierra range. The valley was already robed in freshwater verdure, contrasting most delightfully with the huge snow-clad masses of rock we had just left. Flowers of every variety and hue spread their variegated charms before us; magpies were chattering, and gorgeously-plumaged birds were caroling in the delights of unmolested solitude. Swarms of wild geese and ducks were swimming on the surface of the cool crystal stream, which was the central fork of the Rio de las Plumas, or sailed the air in clouds over our heads. Deer and antelope filled the plains, and their boldness was conclusive that the hunter's rifle was to them unknown. Nowhere visible were any traces of the white man's approach, and it is probable that our steps were the first that ever marked the spot.*
>
> *Source: From T. D. Bonner. The Life and Adventures of James P. Beckwourth, Mountaineer, Scout,*

> *and Pioneer, and Chief of the Crow Nation of Indians.* Chestnut Hill, MA: Adamant Media Corporation, 2005. p. 1856.

Books

Gregson, Susan. *James Beckwourth: Mountaineer, Scout, and Pioneer.* Mankato, MN: Compass Point Books/ Red Brick Learning, 2006. This juvenile nonfiction book provides a biography of one of the first African American explorers.

Sabin, Louis and Troll Books Staff. *Jim Beckwourth: Adventures of a Mountain Man.* Minneapolis, MN: Demco Media/ Sagebrush Corporation, 1992. A young-adult biography of the mountain man.

Websites

The Plumas National Forest Service has a page devoted to the Beckwourth Trail. http://www.fs.fed.us/r5/plumas/recreation/hiking/bkrd_trails.php.

The article "James P. Beckwourth and the Mythology of the West" is on the Utah History to Go Website summarizes Beckwourth's life and adventures. http://historytogo.utah.gov/utah_chapters/trappers,_traders,_and_explorers/jamespbeckwourthandthemythologyofthewest.html.

1964

Final day of recording for the album *Nina Simone in Concert*, a live concert performed at Carnegie Hall on March 21 and April 1 and 6, 1964. Simone released her major protest song "Mississippi Goddam" on this album and would continue to play a large part in the Civil Rights Movement as she recorded other famous songs like "Four Women" and "To Be Young, Gifted and Black." The singer-activist was born Eunice Kathleen Waymon on February 21, 1933.

> *I went down to the garage and got a load of tools and junk together and took them up to my apartment. Andy came in an hour later, saw the mess and asked me what I was doing. My explanation*

didn't make sense because the words tumbled out in a rush—I couldn't speak quickly enough to release the torrents inside my head. He understood, though, and was still enough of a cop to see I was trying to make a zip gun, a home-made pistol. I had it in my mind to go out and kill someone, I didn't know who, but someone I could identify as being in the way of my people getting some justice for the first time in three hundred years. Andy didn't try to stop me, but just stood there for a while and said, 'Nina, you don't know anything about killing. The only thing you've got is music.' He left me alone while I calmed down enough to think straight. The idea of fighting for the rights of my people, killing for them if it came to that, didn't disturb me too much—even back then I wasn't convinced that non-violence could get us what we wanted. But Andy was right: I knew nothing about killing and I did know about music. I sat down at my piano. An hour later I came out of my apartment with the sheet music for 'Mississippi Goddam' in my hand. It was my first civil rights song, and it erupted out of me quicker than I could write it down. I knew then that I would dedicate myself to the struggle for black justice, freedom and equality under the law for as long as it took, until all our battles were won.

Source: From Nina Simone and Stephen Cleary. *I Put a Spell on You: The Autobiography of Nina Simone.* Cambridge, MA: Da Capo Press, 2003, pp. 89–90.

Books

Cohodas, Nadine. *Princess Noire: The Tumultuous Reign of Nina Simone.* New York, NY: Random House Digital, Inc., 2010. Biography of Simone and her life in jazz.
Simone, Nina. *The Nina Simone Piano Songbook.* London, England: Faber Music, 2008. Book provides sheet music for the songs of Nina Simone.

Websites

L'hommage: Nina Simone is dedicated to the life and music of Nina Simone. http://www.high-priestess.com.
Nina Simone performing "Ain't Got No . . . I've Got Life." http://www.YouTube.com/watch?v=GUcXI2BIUOQ.

Also Noteworthy

1864

The state of Louisiana abolishes African slavery.

April 7

1917

Billie Holiday, the blues/jazz singer known as "Lady Day," is born to Sadie Harris and either Frank DeViese or Clarence Holiday in East Baltimore, Maryland. Holiday appeared in the films *The Emperor Jones* and *New Orleans*. Her voice and phrasings of songs like "Strange Fruit" and "God Bless the Child"—alongside the memorable events of her life—left an indelible mark on the history of jazz.

If Holiday's sparklingly clear enunciation made her an irresistible interpreter of lyrics, it also gave her a powerful set of rhythmic sounds with which to interlace her tunes. Rolling r and l sounds, flashed of d, s, and t sounds, and well-measured, full-toned vowels infused her music with a subtly nuanced play of rhythmical beats. Lest there be any question of the truth of Carmen McRae's unequivocal assertion that Holiday could "swing you into bad health," listen to her "Swing, Brother, Swing" on the live air check from Harlem's Savoy Ballroom of 1937. On that number, Holiday's propulsive delivery of the lyrics swings the band and, one feels, the dancers as well. But also listen to the studio version of the more gingerly swinging "Miss Brown to You," with its quick, light rhythmical drive. Holiday's first records were cut for the burgeoning jukebox market, as the Depression had made the private retail record-buying market almost nonexistent. Put a nickel in the machine, that was the idea: dance to Billie's mysteriously subtle and many-tempoed songs.

Source: From Robert G. O'Meally. *Lady Day: The Many Faces of Billie Holiday.* Cambridge, MA: Da Capo Press, 1991, pp. 38–40.

Books

Blackburn, Julia. *With Billie: A New Look at the Unforgettable Lady Day.* New York, NY: Vintage Books, 2006. Author looks at the career and remaining impact of Billie Holiday's persona and music.

Holiday, Billie with William Dufty. *Lady Sings the Blues.* New York, NY: Random House Digital, Inc., 2006. Holiday's autobiography describes her youth in East Baltimore and her rise as a jazz artist.

Websites

"Billie Holiday: The Official Site of Lady Day" provides a biography, photos, and purchasable memorabilia about Lady Day. http://www.billieholiday.com.

Billie Holiday singing "Fine and Mellow" on YouTube. http://www.YouTube.com/watch?v=nCDbl_Wg1g0&feature=related.

April 8

1920

Carmen McRae is born on April 8. After winning an amateur contest at Harlem's legendary Apollo Theatre in her hometown of New York City, McRae went on to become a noted jazz singer with Earl Hines, Mercer "Duke" Ellington, and Benny Carter bands, among others, and recording more than 20 albums. She died on November 10, 1994.

> One of the top jazz singers of all time, Carmen McRae may not have had quite the range and depth of an Ella Fitzgerald or a Sarah Vaughan but she had something of her own to offer, including her influential behind-the-beat phrasing. McRae studied piano as a youth, wrote the song "Dream of Life" (recorded by Billie Holiday in 1939), and sang with the Benny Carter big band in 1944. But it would not be until 1954 that she began to get much notice. ... McRae's voice was higher during that era than it would be later on, and she was influenced by Billie Holiday and (to a lesser extent) Sarah Vaughan, but she was already quite distinctive, often adding irony to the lyrics that she interpreted.

> *Source*: From Scott Yanow. *Bebop*. Milwaukee, WI: Hal Leonard Corporation, 2000, p. 310.

Books

Gourse, Leslie. *Carmen McRae: Miss Jazz.* New York, NY: Billboard Books, 2001. A look at McRae's career and life.

McClellan, Lawrence. *The Later Swing Era, 1942 to 1955.* Santa Barbara, CA: Greenwood Publishing Group, 2004. Book contains a biographical sketch of Carmen McRae.

Websites

"Carmen McRae, the definitive Website" provides a biography and essays about McRae. http://www.carmenmcrae.com.

The Complete Carmen McRae Discography lists every song McRae recorded in each decade of her career. http://www.carmenmcraediscography.com/.

Also Noteworthy

1965

Sixteen-year-old Lawrence Bradford of New York City is appointed to serve as the first Page to the U.S. Senate who is of African descent.

1974

Atlanta Braves slugger Henry "Hank" Aaron hits his 715th home run in Atlanta stadium, which puts him in the record books as surpassing Babe Ruth as the game's all-time home-run leader.

April 9

1898

The singer, actor, athlete, writer, and civil rights activist Paul LeRoy Bustill Robeson is born on April 9, 1898, in Princeton, New Jersey, to the Rev. William Robeson and Maria Louisa Bustill. Robeson's father had liberated himself from slavery after escaping from a North Carolina plantation; his mother had been raised in an abolitionist Quaker family. Reared in an educated family, Paul Robeson won a four-year academic scholarship to Rutgers University in 1915 (becoming the third Black student to attend Rutgers) and later went on to get a law degree at Columbia University. Robeson spoke out against the racism and lynchings suffered by African Americans (for which he won the Spingarn Medal and was named a Lenin Peace Prize laureate), but he was vilified in the larger U.S. society as a Communist sympathizer for doing so.

Robeson quotes in his autobiography from the testimony he gave on June 12, 1956, before the House Committee on Un-American Activities:

I stand here struggling for the rights of my people to be full citizens in this country. They are not —in Mississippi. They are not—in Montgomery. That is why I am here today. . . . You want to shut up every colored person who wants to fight for the rights of his people!

Source: From Paul Robeson. *Here I Stand*. Boston, MA: Beacon Press, January 1, 1998; originally published in 1958, p. 42.

Books

Robeson, Paul. *Here I Stand*. Boston, MA: Beacon Press, January 1, 1998; originally published in 1958. Robeson gives an account of his life and his beliefs in this autobiography, which was initially ignored in the mainstream white press but heralded in the Black press, particularly in newspapers like the *New York Amsterdam News* and the *Pittsburgh Courier*.

Robeson Jr., Paul. *The Undiscovered Paul Robeson, An Artist's Journey, 1898–1939*. Hoboken, NJ: John Wiley & Sons; 1 edition. March 2, 2001. The son of the famous actor/activist writes about his father's life and its affect on the people around him.

Robeson, Paul. *Paul Robeson Speaks: Writings, Speeches, and Interviews, a Centennial Celebration*. By presenting Robeson's own writings and interviews, this book gives readers a chance to understand the activist on an intimate level.

Websites

The not-for-profit Paul Robeson Foundation, Inc., has sponsored exhibitions that feature the life and work of Robeson. The foundation is currently creating a digital archive of Robeson memorabilia. http://www.paul robesonfoundation.org.

The Paul Robeson Cultural Center (PRCC) at Rutgers University promotes academic studies and features online archives of the work of famous African American writers. http://prcc.rutgers.edu/index.html.

Penn State also has a Paul Robeson Cultural Center, which sponsors programs that promote multicultural learning. http://www.sa.psu.edu/prcc/.

Also Noteworthy

1866

The Civil Rights Act grants citizenship and equal rights to all male persons in the United States. The Act was created "to protect all Persons in the United States in their Civil Rights, and furnish the Means of their Vindication." President Andrew Johnson attempted to veto the Act but that veto was overturned.

1895

The Page Fence Giants—a traveling Black baseball team based out of Adrian, Michigan, and sponsored by the Page Woven Wire Fence Company—play their first organized game. The Page Fence Giants were one of the best Black teams prior to the creation of the National Negro League.

1911

Arthur Schomburg and John Edward Bruce found the Negro Society for Historical Research, an institute designed to collect and maintain archives on the history and culture of people of African descent.

1947

The Congress of Racial Equality (CORE) sends an interracial test group of "Freedom Riders" to the South to test the country's segregation laws.

April 10

1926

Johnnie Tillmon Blackston is born in Scott, Arkansas. After spending some time in Little Rock she moved to Los Angeles, California, in 1963. After having been a welfare recipient, Blackston became a central organizer in promoting dignity for African American women who were welfare recipients, and in 1972 she became the director of the National Welfare Rights Organization (NWRO).

> Johnnie Tillmon articulated a variant of Black Power politics that placed female independence and power at the center. Although Tillmon did not endorse black nationalism, she modeled a positive black identity that integrated class, gender, and sexuality. She rejected calls to restore the two-parent heterosexual black family and for black men to reassert their masculinity. Her radical black feminism proposed autonomy for poor women to make decisions about childbearing, child rearing, and their intimate lives. She waged campaigns to enable poor women to live their lives with dignity, respect, and economic security. And she worked tirelessly to debunk the stereotypes that had become associated with receipt of welfare. If Black Power, at its core, is about empowering black people, striving for self-determination, and giving them a sense of self-worth, then Johnnie Tillmon was one of its most important advocates.
>
> Source: From Dayo F. Gore, Jeanne Theoharis, Komozi Woodard. Want to Start a Revolution?: Radical Women in the Black freedom Struggle. New York, NY: NYU Press, 2009, p. 334.

Books

Lanker, Brian and Barbara Summers. *I Dream a World: Portraits of Black Women Who Changed America*. New York, NY: Stewart, Tabori & Chang, 1989. Contains a biographical sketch of Johnnie Tillmon Blackston and her work.

Ware, Susan. *Modern American Women: A Documentary History*. New York, NY: McGraw-Hill, 2001. Author features a look at the work of Johnnie Tillmon Blackston to organize poor women into a political movement.

Websites

Tillmon is profiled on the site Social Work/Social Action. http://socialworkaction.blogspot.com/2008/04/johnnie-tillmon.html.

The *Los Angeles Times* article "The Sunday Profile: A Dreamer and Her Dream Lose Ground" provides background on Tillmon and her work. http://articles.latimes.com/1995-07-09/news/ls-21958_1_welfare-rights/6.

April 11

1881

The private, four-year liberal arts institution for women, Spelman College—now on the list of historically black colleges and universities (HBCU)—is founded in Atlanta, Georgia. Initially named the Atlanta Baptist Female Seminary, the school opened with $100 in funding and 11 students enrolled to train as teachers in the basement of Friendship Baptist Church. After receiving donations from John D. Rockefeller, the school was renamed Spelman Seminary to honor Rockefeller's mother-in-law, Lucy Henry Spelman, who had been an Antislavery Movement activist. The school's name was changed to Spelman College in 1924.

> When the Atlanta Baptist Seminary for Girls (as Spelman was originally named) opened on April 11, 1881, it was the only private single-sex institution of higher education for black women. Its founders, Sophia B. Packard and Harriet E. Giles, were white schoolteachers and missionaries for the Women's American Baptist Home Missionary Society (WABHMS) in Boston, Massachusetts. After seeing the struggles for black women during a mission trip to New Orleans, Packard and Giles

> decided to open a school for black women and girls so that they could take care of themselves and their families.
>
> Source: From Leslie Miller-Bernal. *Challenged by Coeducation: Women's Colleges Since the 1960s.* Nashville, TN: Vanderbilt University Press, 2006, p. 234.

Books

Guy-Sheftall, Beverly and Jo Moore Stewart. *Spelman: A Centennial Celebration 1881–1981.* Atlanta, HA: Spelman College, 1981. Book looks at the history and traditions of life at Spelman College.

Read, Florence Matilda. *The Story of Spelman College.* Victoria, BC: AbeBooks /Georgia, 1961. A look at the reasons behind the founding of Spelman College.

Websites

The Spelman College Website provides historical information about the school. http://www.spelman.edu/about_us/facts/.

Inside Spelman is the college's online newsmagazine. http://insidespelman.com/.

Also Noteworthy

1899

Percy Lavon Julian is born to James Sumner Julian and Elizabeth Adams Julian in Montgomery, Alabama. Dr. Julian's work as a scientist, medical researcher, and chemist led to the understanding of ways to extract ingredients from soybeans that aid in the treatment of arthritis. With the establishment of his international company, Julian Laboratory, Inc., he developed synthetic cortisone, which is used to treat rheumatoid arthritis; sex hormones, which paved the way to birth control pills; and synthesized physostigmine, which is used to treat glaucoma.

1933

Talk show host Tony Brown is born in Charleston, West Virginia. In 1971, Brown was the founding dean of Howard University's School of Communication. Brown also served as the host and producer of the Public Broadcasting Service longest-running series, *Tony Brown's Journal.*

1966

Emmett Ashford becomes the first African American umpire in the major leagues.

1968

Civil Rights Act of 1968 is signed into law. Title VIII of this Act is the Fair Housing Act, which bans discrimination in the sale, rental, and financing of housing.

April 12

1787

Blacks in Philadelphia, Pennsylvania publish the "Preamble" and "Articles" of the Free African Society (FAS). Two of the central organizers were the religious leaders Absalom Jones and Richard Allen, who would later help to form the African Methodist Episcopal (AME) Church.

> The Free African Society, the first mutual aid organization for African Americans, was founded in Philadelphia in 1878 by Richard Allen and Absalom Jones, who later became prominent religious leaders. Members of the Free African Society promised to lead orderly, sober lives, characterized by decorum and marital fidelity, and to contribute to the assistance of those who became widowed, orphaned, or ill.
>
> Source: From Joan Potter. *African American Firsts: Famous Little-Known and Unsung Triumphs of Blacks in America.* New York, NY: Dafina Books/Kensington Publishing Corp, 2009, p. 92.

Books

Lincoln, Charles Eric and Lawrence H. Mamiya. *The Black Church in the African-American Experience.* Durham, NC: Duke University Press,

1990. Book looks at the history and traditions of the African American church.

Willson, Joseph, edited by Julie Winch. *The Elite of Our People: Joseph Willson's Sketches of Black Upper-Class Life in Antebellum Philadelphia.* University Park, PA: Penn State Press, 2000. Author examines the class structure in eighteenth-century Philadelphia and writes about noted leaders like those who founded the Free African Society.

Websites

The Website for PBS's *Africans in America* series provides a copy of the text from the *Preamble of the Free African Society.* http://www.pbs.org/wgbh/aia/part3/3h465.html.

The Pennsylvania History and Tourism Website provides background on the founding of the Free African Society and notes the location of sites where society members met. http://explorepahistory.com/hmarker.php?markerId=853.

1882

James "Jimmy" Winkfield is born in Chilesburg, Kentucky. Winkfield is the last-known African American thoroughbred jockey to win the Kentucky Derby, and he was the second jockey ever to win two Kentucky Derbies in a row. Winkfield was faced with virulent racism during his career, but he famously took his talents elsewhere—first living and racing in Czarist Russia, and then after Russia's Bolshevik Revolution he lived in other parts of Europe, before finally ending up in France.

By the time Winkfield had reached the end of his riding career, he had won an astounding 2,600 races, mostly on two-year-old horses all across the European continent. Had he stayed in America, he almost certainly would have been in more Kentucky Derbies than the four that he actually ran in. As it turns out, he left the United States in 1903, but continued racing horses until 1930. One can only guess what his Derby record would have been had he remained in America for just half of the years that he continued riding in Europe. He might easily have been the greatest jockey of his or any other era.

Source: From James Robert Saunders and Monica Renae Saunders. *Black Winning Jockeys in the Kentucky Derby.* Jefferson, NC: McFarland, 2003, p. 95.

Books

Drape, Joe. *Black Maestro: The Epic Life of an American Legend.* New York: Morrow, 2006. Biography of the life and career of Winkfield.

Hotaling, Edward. *Wink: The Incredible Life and Epic Journey of Jimmy Winkfield.* New York, NY: McGraw-Hill Education, 2004. Winkfield biography looks at his love of horse racing.

Websites

The Jimmy Winkfield Stakes at New York's Aqueduct Racetrack is named in honor of Wakefield. http://www.allhorseracing.com/stakes?name=Jimmy_Winkfield_Stakes.

CBS News's "A Racing Legend, Remembered" profiles Winkfield's life. http://www.cbsnews.com/video/watch/?id=667413n.

Also Noteworthy

1983

Harold Washington wins election as the first African American mayor of Chicago, Illinois, on April 12, 1983. He served as the 42nd mayor in the history of Chicago and won re-election in 1987, but Washington died of a heart attack on November 25, 1987.

April 13

1891

Nellallitea Larsen is born in Chicago, Illinois, to Marie Hanson, a Danish immigrant and Peter Walker, who was from Saint Croix. As Nella Larsen, she played an important role in the Harlem Renaissance, particularly with her publication of the novels *Quicksand* and *Passing*, both of which dealt with the conflicts of not acknowledging African ancestry.

> As Passing *went through production, Larsen began to enjoy a small measure of celebrity. At the 135th Street Library,* Quicksand *was in "continuous demand," and she was lined up to give a lecture there at the end of January, publicized throughout the library system, on "what present-day negro writers are saying, and how." On the first or second of January, she learned that she had won the Harmon Foundation's bronze medal (for second place), with a $100 honorarium. On the fifth, the announcements came out in the* New York Age, *and these were soon followed by scores of notices and articles in newspapers across the country. The January issue of* Opportunity *featured James Allen's most flattering portrait of her (identified as "Nella Larsen" rather than "Nella Imes") on the first page of its lead essay, Alain Locke's "1928: A Retrospective Review."*
>
> *Source:* From George Hutchinson. *In Search of Nella Larsen: A Biography of the Color Line.* Cambridge, MA: Harvard University Press, 2006, p. 311.

1946

Albert Leornes Green is born to Robert and Cora Green in Forest City, Arkansas. Famed as the rhythm and blues (and later Gospel) singer Al Green, he made classic songs like "Love and Happiness," "Take Me to the River," "Call Me," and "Let's Stay Together." Green was a major sex symbol in the 1970s, and in 1995 he was inducted into the Rock and Roll Hall of Fame.

> *Green rose to international fame with timeless hits such as "Let's Stay Together," "Call Me," "Take Me To The River," "I'm Still In Love With You," "Tired of Being Alone," and "Love and Happiness." His eclectic collection of covers included the Doors' "Light My Fire," the Beatles' "I Wanna Hold Your Hand," and the Bee Gees' "How Can You Mend a Broken Heart." In the early 1970s, he was the Prince of Love, the man with the trademark smile that made women swoon in near-riotous concerts as he tossed long stem red roses to adoring fans.*
>
> *Source:* From Various. *Spiritual Journeys: How Faith Has Influenced Twelve Music Icons.* Winter Park, FL: Relevant Media Group, 2003, p. 84.

Books

Larsen, Nella. *Passing.* New York: Random House Digital, Inc., 2002. Larsen's 1929 novel about an African American woman who chooses to pass for white, rather than acknowledge her family and culture.

Larsen, Nella. *Quicksand.* New York, NY: Penguin, 2002. Larsen's first novel, published in 1928, is a semi-autobiographical look at racial identity among African Americans in the early twentieth century.

Websites

Nella Larsen is profiled on the Swarthmore College Website. http://www.sccs.swarthmore .edu/users/08/ajb/tmve/wiki100k/docs/ Nella_Larsen.html.

New York City Women's Biography Hub has a biography on Larsen. http://www.library.csi .cuny.edu/dept/history/lavender/386/nlarsen .html.

Books

Green, Al and Davin Seay. *Take Me to the River: An Autobiography.* Chicago, IL: Chicago Review Press, 2009. Autobiography of the soul singer, Al Green.

Otfinoski, Steven. *African Americans in the Performing Arts.* New York, NY: Infobase Publishing, 2003. Contains a small biography of Al Green's life and career.

Websites

The Al Green's official Website. http://www .algreenmusic.com/.

Al Green's performance of "Love and Happiness" on Soul Train in 1972. http://www .YouTube.com/watch?v=mFHjF0TZkhA &feature=related.

Also Noteworthy

1669

The first African American man to be baptized in the Lutheran Church is baptized on Palm Sunday, April 13, of 1669. Named Emmanuel, the man was baptized before a Lutheran congregation in New York City.

1854

Lucy Craft Laney is one of 10 children born to Louisa and David Laney. Her father had purchased his own and his wife's freedom 20 years before her birth, so Lucy did not grow up enslaved. She learned to read and write and became a staunch advocate for Black education. Laney was the founder and principal of the Haines Normal and Industrial Institute in Augusta, Georgia for 50 years (1883–1933).

1873

Colfax Massacre takes place on Easter Sunday morning in Grant Parish, Louisiana. Some 300 white Louisianans stormed the local courthouse, where African American officials were in charge. After shots rang out, the Blacks in the courthouse tried to get away, but some 80 people were shot dead.

1964

Sidney Poitier is awarded an Oscar for Best Actor for his work in the film *Lilies of the Field*.

April 14

1969

Members of the Student Afro-American Society (SAS) seize the Columbia College admissions office and demand a special admissions board and staff. SAS styled itself as a Black militant protest group, which took part in the occupation of Hamilton Hall during the 1968.

In 1968, Columbia's few African American students formed a Students Afro-American Society (SAS) to demand more black faculty and students as well as more courses in African American studies. They also joined the Harlem community in opposing Columbia's plans to build a gymnasium on public land in Morningside Heights Park. As originally arranged with Robert Moses, Columbia would clean up the park and allow the Harlem community some access to the facility using a separate community entrance. In April 1968 student and community pickets managed to stop construction amid accusations of "Gym Crow."

Source: From Joanne R. Reitano. *The Restless City: A Shorty History of New York from Colonial Times to the Present*. Boca Raton, FL: CRC Press/ Taylor & Francis, 2006, p. 174.

Books

Bradley, Stefan. *Harlem vs. Columbia University: Black Student Power in the Late 1960s*. Champaign, IL: University of Illinois Press, 2009. Book looks at how concepts of Black Power influenced Columbia University's African American students and their relationship with Black residents in Harlem.

McCaughey, Robert A. *Stand, Columbia: A History of Columbia University in the City of New York, 1754–2004*. New York, NY: Columbia University Press, 2003. A look at the 1968–1979 campus protests from the point of view of the university's administration.

Websites

The documentary film 1968 *Columbia University Protest*, which shows how members of the SAS conducted their protest, is available online. http://www.YouTube.com/watch?v=tEKK2iByi5w.

1968: Columbia in Crisis is Columbia University's look at the crisis on its campus. https://ldpd.lamp.columbia.edu/omeka/exhibits/show/1968.

Also Noteworthy

1775

The Society for the Relief of Free Negroes Unlawfully Held in Bondage, the very first abolitionist society established in the United States, is founded in Philadelphia, Pennsylvania. The group, which was founded by Quakers, also had Benjamin Franklin serve as its president and would eventually be renamed the Pennsylvania Society for Promoting the Abolition of Slavery and the Relief of Free Negroes Unlawfully Held in Bondage.

April 15

1915

Elizabeth Catlett Mora is born in Washington, DC. Famed as a sculptor and printmaker, Catlett's work was highlighted because it showed the lives of African Americans in a sociopolitical context. After working and teaching in the United States (at schools like Howard University), Catlett moved to Mexico, where she became a citizen in 1962, continued her work by joining the Taller de Grafica Popular (Popular Graphic Arts Workshop) and teaching at the Universidad Nacional Autonoma de Mexico, and married the artist Francisco Mora and raised a family.

Like many African American artists of the 1930s and 1940s, Catlett's interest in the work of Mexican artists had begun many years before her decision to establish permanent residence in Mexico in 1947. Catlett was first introduced to the work of Mexican artists while a student at Howard University in the 1930s, when her teacher, James Porter, arranged for her and another student to paint a mural as part of the PWAP in Washington, D.C. In doing research for that project, Catlett familiarized herself with the work of Mexican muralists. As Melanie Herzog writes, Catlett was attracted to the work of the muralists because of "their social commitment, direct engagement with the experiences of ordinary people, deliberately accessible style, and choice of medium."

Source: From Rebecca Mina Schreiber. *Cold War Exiles in Mexico: U.S. Dissidents and the Culture of Critical Resistance*. Minneapolis, MN: University of Minnesota Press, 2008, p. 35.

Books

Gedeon, Lucinda H., Michael Brenson, Lowery Stokes Sims, and Neuberger Museum of Art. *Elizabeth Catlett Sculpture: A Fifty-Year Retrospective*. New York, NJ: Neuberger Museum of Art, Purchase College, State University of New York, 1998. An examination of the work produced by Catlett between the years of 1946 and 1996.

Herzog, Melanie. *Elizabeth Catlett: An American Artist in Mexico*. Seattle, WA: University of Washington Press, 2000. Herzog looks at the work and life Catlett has led in both the United States and Mexico.

Websites

The Sculpture of Elizabeth Catlett is featured—with a catalog and career highlight information—on the Ann Norton Sculpture Gardens Website. http://elizabethcatlett.net/.

Elizabeth Catlett is profiled on the Website of the National Museum of Women in the Arts, Washington, DC. http://www.nmwa.org/collection/profile.asp?LinkID=129.

Also Noteworthy

1889

Asa Phillip Randolph is born in Crescent City, Florida. Randolph was the founder of the Brotherhood of Sleeping Car Porters in 1925. Prior to that he had founded and co-edited the monthly magazine *The Messenger*, an antilynching publication that was also against U.S. participation in World War I. Randolph was the impetus behind a proposed march on Washington to protest racial discrimination in 1945, but after President Franklin Roosevelt issued the Fair

Employment Act the march was cancelled. Randolph later participated in the organization of the 1963 March on Washington for Jobs and Freedom.

1947

Jackie Robinson becomes the first African American to play Major League Baseball when he debuts as the Brooklyn Dodgers' first baseman on Ebbets Field. Wearing No. 42, Robinson would become a hero for the African American community, and the fact that he played with the Brooklyn Dodgers made that team the most favored in the Black community. Even after enduring threats and taunts as a baseball player, Robinson also became an important voice in the world of African American politics.

1960

During a conference in Raleigh, North Carolina, from April 15 to 17, the Student Non-Violent Coordinating Committee (SNCC) is founded. Black college students who wanted to use nonviolent protests and "sit-ins" to help end segregation and advance the Civil Rights Movement created SNCC under the guidance of the activist Ella Baker.

April 16

1861

Isaac (Ike) Burns Murphy is born to the freedman and Union Army soldier James Burns and an enslaved mother on a farm in Bourbon County, Kentucky. Murphy—who is still considered one of the best horseracing jockeys who ever lived—was highly successful and scrupulously honest; he became the first jockey to win the Kentucky Derby both back-to-back and then three times in a row, when he did so on May 13, 1891.

The superabundance of talented black jockeys made it difficult for Murphy to acquire his first

mount, but in 1875 at the age of fourteen he won his first race as a replacement rider. Murphy soon dominated the sport. He won the St. Leger Stakes at Louisville's Churchill Downs in 1877 and a record thirty-five races entered in 1879, including the Travers Stakes in Saratoga, New York. In 1882 he won forty-nine of fifty-one starts at Saratoga, and on several cards he rode winners in every race, feats that acquired him the best mounts of the era. Murphy won the Latonia Derby in northern Kentucky five times, the Clark Stakes in Louisville four times, and four of the first five runnings of the American Derby at Washington Park in Chicago. In 1884, at a time when black patrons were segregated and often harassed in the grandstands at Kentucky racetracks, Murphy won his first Kentucky Derby aboard Buchanan, a horse prepared by black trainer William Bird. Murphy became the first back-to-back and three-time Derby winner by riding Riley to victory in 1890 and Kingman in 1891, and he finished in the money on three other occasions.

Source: From John E. Kleber. The Kentucky Encyclopedia. Lexington, KY: University Press of Kentucky, 1992, p. 663.

Books

Brodowsky, Pamela K., Tom Philbin, and Churchill Downs Inc. *Two Minutes to Glory: The Official History of the Kentucky Derby.* New York, NY: HarperCollins, 2009. An examination of the history of the Kentucky Derby includes an extensive look at Murphy's legacy.

Dunnigan, Alice Allison. *The Fascinating Story of Black Kentuckians: Their Heritage and Traditions.* Victoria, BC: Associated Publishers/Abe-Books, 1982. History of African Americans in Kentucky contains a biography of Isaac Burns Murphy.

Websites

The 150th birthday of Isaac Burns Murphy is celebrated with remembrances of his impact on the horseracing world. http://www.isaacmurphy.org/IMMAG/Legacy.html.

Isaac Burns Murphy is profiled by the Kentucky Horse Park. http://kyhorsepark.com/legends-of-the-park/isaac-burns-murphy.

1947

A 12-pound, 11-ounce Ferdinand Lewis Alcindor, Jr., is born in New York City. When he attends Power Memorial High School in New York City, Lewis Alcindor shines as a basketball star; he won three All-American selections and led the Power Memorial team to a 95-6 record. After growing to 7 feet, 2 inches, Alcindor went to California and played college basketball with the UCLA Bruins. A three-time college All-American, he led the Bruins to three consecutive NCAA titles (1967, 1968, and 1969) and became the first and only player named the NCAA Tournament's Most Outstanding Player three different times. Alcindor used the dunk shot so well that the NCAA eventually banned its use. After his conversion to Islam in 1971, Lewis Alcindor changed his name to Kareem Abdul-Jabbar, which means "noble, powerful servant." Jabbar played in the National Basketball Association with the Milwaukee Bucks and the Los Angeles Lakers; he won five NBA championships with the Lakers. In 1990, Jabbar retired from professional basketball but turned to other pursuits, including becoming a bestselling author.

Aside from my family, I have four major passions that define who I am. First, I was born in Harlem, which has been the capital city of the African-American community since the start of the Harlem Renaissance back in the 1920s. More important to me than anything else I do, or have ever done (yes, including basketball), is my active participation in improving the lives of and opportunities for all members of the black community.

Source: From Kareem Abdul-Jabbar and Raymond Obstfeld. On the Shoulders of Giants: My Journey Through the Harlem Renaissance. New York, NY: Simon & Schuster, 2007, p. 4.

Books

Abdul-Jabbar, Kareem and Alan Steinberg. *Black Profiles in Courage: A Legacy of African American Achievement*. New York, NY: HarperCollins, 2000. Jabbar profiles African Americans who have played major roles in U.S. history.

Abdul-Jabbar, Kareem and Stephen Singular. *A Season on the Reservation: My Soujourn with the White Mountain Apache*. New York, NY: W. Morrow and Co., 2000. Book follows Abdul-Jabbar as he lives among members of an Apache tribe.

Websites

The official Website of Kareem Abdul Jabbar contains information on his basketball career plus updates about his media appearances. http://www.kareemabduljabbar.com/.

Kareem Abdul-Jabbar highlights video is available on YouTube. http://www.youtube.com/watch?v=h1yVfJs6OcI.

Also Noteworthy

1845

Mary Eliza Mahoney is born in Boston, Massachusetts. Mahoney wanted to be a nurse, but because schools were not open to people of African descent, she worked as a de facto nurse for white families for many years before finally being permitted to enter the nurse training program at the New England Hospital for Women and Children.

1862

President Abraham Lincoln signs the District of Columbia's Compensated Emancipation Act, which outlawed slavery in Washington, DC: the bill was signed nine months before the Emancipation Proclamation. Abolitionists had frequently said it was a "national shame" to have African slavery in the nation's capital. The law freed some 3,100 enslaved Africans, and the federal government paid their former owners $300 per person in compensation. A total of $993,407 in compensation was paid to slave owners for their lost "property." Celebrations of Emancipation Day were held yearly from 1866 to 1901 and then resumed in 2002 when organized by District Council-member Vincent Orange. On January 4, 2005, Mayor Anthony Williams signed legislation that named April 16 as "Emancipation Day," an official public holiday in the District of Columbia.

1868

Voters in Louisiana elect Oscar J. Dunn as the state's first African American lieutenant governor (he served in office from 1868 to 1871) and Antoine Dubuclet as its first African American state treasurer.

1869

Ebenezer Don Carlos Bassett is named Consul General to Haiti and the Dominican Republic—a post he held for 12 years. He is the first African American to serve as a U.S. diplomat.

1973

Lelia Smith Foley becomes the first African American female elected mayor of a U.S. city. Foley took office as mayor in the small town of Taft, Oklahoma, and held the position for 13 years.

April 17

1872

Activist William Monroe Trotter is born to James Monroe Trotter and Virginia Isaacs Trotter in Chillicothe, Ohio. The Trotters moved back to Boston, Massachusetts, after having their son. Although born into relative economic ease, as an adult Trotter became a long-term crusader for African American equality. He was co-founder—with George Forbes—of *The Boston Guardian*, a national weekly newspaper that covered Black life, spoke out against discrimination, and was

specifically in opposition to what Monroe considered the accomodationist teachings of Booker T. Washington. Trotter was also a co-founder of the Niagra Movement and a close friend of the scholar/activist W. E. B. Dubois. Monroe's former home, located in the Dorchester section of Boston, is today the William Monroe Trotter House, a National Historic Landmark.

The year 1901 brought Boston a militant new newspaper, whose founder and managing editor, twenty-nine-year-old Monroe Trotter, had as his role model William Lloyd Garrison and the Liberator. Trotter's new weekly was the Guardian, *and its motto was "For Every Right with All Thy Might." For three decades he tried to abide by it, as one of the first Afro-American editors to make a life-long career with a weekly newspaper in the twentieth century.*

Source: From Faith Berry. *From Bondage to Liberation: Writings By and about Afro-Americans from 1700 to 1918.* London, England: Continuum International Publishing Group, 2006, p. 418.

Books

Fox, Stephen R. *The Guardian of Boston: William Monroe Trotter.* Victoria, BC: Atheneum/Abe Books, 1970. Biography of the life and work of William Monroe Trotter.

Schneider, Mark. *Boston Confronts Jim Crow, 1890–1920.* Lebanon, NH: University Press of New England (UPNE), 1997. This look at how racism progressed in Boston includes a significant section on the life and work of William Monroe Trotter.

Websites

The National Park Service has a site for the William Monroe Trotter House. http://tps.cr.nps.gov/nhl/detail.cfm?ResourceId=1681&ResourceType=Building.

The Trotter Institute is a grouping of African American editorialists formed in recognition of the media efforts of Trotter. http://www.trottergroup.org/trotter.htm.

Also Noteworthy

1983

Alice Walker wins the Pulitzer Prize for fiction for *The Color Purple*.

1990

Playwright August Wilson wins his second Pulitzer Prize for drama with the play *The Piano Lesson*. Wilson previously won the Pulitzer Prize for drama in 1987 for his play *Fences*.

April 18

1924

Clarence "Gatemouth" Brown is born in Vinton, Louisiana. A Grammy-winning blues musician, best known for his hits "Okie Dokie Stomp," "Boogie Rambler," "Just Before Dawn," "Dirty Work at the Crossroads," and "Gatemouth Boogie," Gatemouth was known for his prowess in playing blues, country, jazz, and Cajun music.

Gatemouth was born into a musical family in 1924 near the Louisiana border at Vinton, Louisiana, and raised in Orange, Texas, a hop, skip and jump across the Sabine River. After life in Texas and even Nashville, he settled in Slidell, Louisiana, where he resided until Hurricane Katrina forced him to evacuate to Orange. He passed away shortly after that on September 10, 2005.

Brown played guitar, fiddle, viola, drums, mandolin, and harmonica, to name a few instruments; he learned to love music from his father, a railroad worker who sang and played fiddle in a Cajun band. Brown always named his father as his greatest musical influence.

Source: From Ron Yule, Bill Burge, and Mary Evans. *Louisiana Fiddlers*. Jackson, MS: University Press of Mississippi, 2009, p. 39.

Books

Aswell, Tom. *Louisiana Rocks!: The True Genesis of Rock & Roll*. Gretna, LA: Pelican Publishing, 2009. Contains an excerpt on the musical impact of Clarence "Gatemouth" Brown.

Obrecht, Jas. *Rolling and Tumbling*. Milwaukee, WI: Hal Leonard Corporation, 2000. Author provides a detailed profile of Clarence "Gatemouth" Brown.

Websites

Alligator Records has a biography of Clarence "Gatemouth" Brown. http://www.alligator .com/index.cfm?section=artists&artistid=12.

Clarence "Gatemouth" Brown in concert. http://www.YouTube.com/watch?v=PVK _nSrxhiQ.

Also Noteworthy

1813

James McCune Smith is born in New York City to a mother who was self-emancipated and a white father. Smith attended New York's African Free School and, after earning a medical degree at the University of Glasgow, became the first licensed African American doctor in the United States. Smith was the first person of African descent to operate a pharmacy in the United States. He also worked as an abolitionist and author.

1864

More than 200 Black Union troops are massacred by Confederate forces at Fort Pillow, Tennessee. On April 18, 1864, the First Kansas Colored Volunteers had broken through Confederate lines at Poison Spring, Arkansas, but the unit later suffered heavy losses after being captured: Confederate troops murdered the African American soldiers, rather than take them in as POWs, which was the standard treatment for captured white Union soldiers.

1877

Six African American settlers in north-western Kansas establish the Nicodemus

Town Company in Graham County, Kansas, along the Solomon River. Rev. W. H. Smith, a Kentucky minister, had organized the town and named it after the ballad "Wake Nicodemus!" by abolitionist Henry Clay Work. The first settlers were recruited at Kentucky church meetings, and among them was Z.T. Fletcher, who became Nicodemus's first postmaster and who in 1880 established the town's St. Francis Hotel. Fletcher's wife, Jenny Smith—the town's first postmistress and schoolteacher—was the daughter of Rev. W. H. Smith.

1941

After a four-week boycott led by Rev. Adam Clayton Powell, Jr., of Harlem's Abysinnian Baptist Church, New York City, bus companies agree to hire some 200 African Americans to serve as drivers and mechanics.

1956

The Bandung Conference of leaders of colored nations begins in Indonesia.

1966

Bill Russell is named coach of the Boston Celtics; he became the first-ever African American coach in professional athletics.

April 19

1969

Student members of Cornell University's Afro-American Society (AAS) occupy Willard Straight Hall during Parents' Weekend in their quest to have the school administration open a Black Studies department. White students tried to attack the Black students, so the Black students received guns to protect them during their occupation. AAS students held Straight Hall

for 36 hours before winning a concession that the school would establish what is today the Cornell University Africana Studies & Research Center.

> *Saturday, April 19: The AAS takes over Willard Straight Hall at 6:00 a.m. A day of tense negotiations, rumors, and ominous events ensues. Brothers from the Delta Upsilon fraternity invade the Straight in an attempt to liberate it from the AAS. After repelling the invaders, AAS allies begin bringing weapons into the building. Administrators find out later that evening that guns have been brought into the Straight, making it "a whole new ballgame."*
>
> *Sunday, April 20: A deal is struck between administrators Keith Kennedy and Steven Muller and the AAS to end the takeover. The key provisions entail amnesty for the takeover and nullification of the judicial board's reprimands by the faculty as whole. At 4:00 p.m. the AAS walks out of Straight in a military procession, guns held high.*
>
> *Source*: From Donald Alexander Downs. *Cornell '69: Liberalism and the Crisis of the American University*. Ithaca, NY: Cornell University Press, 1999, p. 313.

Books

Brisbane, Robert H. *Black Activism: Racial Revolution in the United States, 1954–1970*. Victoria, BC: AbeBooks/Judson Press, 1974. Provides a detailed look at the Straight Hall takeover and its results.

Margulis, Dan. *A Century at Cornell: Published to Commemorate the Hundredth Anniversary of the Cornell Daily Sun*. Victoria, BC: AbeBooks/ Cornell Daily Sun, 1980. Book contains original reporting regarding the Straight Hall takeover.

Websites

The Cornell University Africana Studies & Research Center. http://asrc.cornell.edu/.

The Cornell University Library Guide has a history about the Straight Hall takeover. http:// guides.library.cornell.edu/wshtakeover.

Also Noteworthy

1837

Cheyney University is founded as the first historically Black (HBCU) institution of higher learning in the United States. It is also the first college in the United States to receive official state certification as an institution of higher academic education for African Americans. Cheyney began its existence in Philadelphia as the Institute for Colored Youth. In 1902, the school was moved to George Cheyney's farm, 24 miles west of Philadelphia. In 1913, its name was changed to Cheyney Training School for Teachers; in 1921, the Normal School at Cheyney; in 1951, Cheyney State Teachers College; and in 1959, Cheyney State College. In 1983, Cheyney joined the State System of Higher Education (SSHE) as Cheyney University of Pennsylvania.

1866

Nearly 5,000 Washington, DC-based African Americans celebrate the abolition of slavery and call for the enforcement of civil rights for their people. After a crowd assembled at the White House, President Andrew Johnson addressed them. Then, led by two African American regiments, they marched up Pennsylvania Avenue to Franklin Square, held religious services, and listened to political speeches. The services and speeches were delivered from a platform that read: "We have received our civil rights. Give us the right of suffrage and the work is done."

1942

Atlanta University held its first exhibition of African American art, which would soon come to be known as the "Atlanta Annual."

1972

Stationed in Germany, Major Gen. Frederic E. Davidson becomes the first Black to lead an army division.

April 20

1908

Lionel Leo Hampton is born in Louisville, Kentucky. Though trained as a drummer, Hampton fell in love with the sound of the vibraphone in 1930, while in a recording session with Louis Armstrong. Hampton became famous for his work as a jazz vibraphonist.

> "When we went to the studio to record with Louis [Armstrong], we saw the vibes standing in the corner. He asked me if I knew anything about that instrument. 'Well, you know, I've been playing the bells behind you,' I answered, 'and it's got the same keyboard, only bigger.' So Louis said, 'Play some behind me!' And that's how I first started playing vibes . . ."
>
> Source: From Stanley Dance. *The World of Swing.* Cambridge, MA: Da Capo Press, 2001, p. 268.

Books

Hampton, Lionel, James Haskins, and Vincent Pelote. *Hamp: An Autobiography.* New York, NY: Amistad/HarperCollins, 1999. Hampton writes about his life in music and the famous jazz musicians he worked with.

Pener, Degen. *The Swing Book.* New York, NY: Hachette Digital, Inc., 1999. Contains an excerpt explaining Hampton's musical career.

Websites

The University of Idaho holds an annual Lionel Hampton Jazz Festival. http://www.uidaho.edu/jazzfest.

Lionel Hampton's "Bongo Interlude" is available on YouTube. http://www.YouTube.com/watch?v=ox48uLLo_-A&NR=1.

Also Noteworthy

1853

Antislavery activist Harriet Tubman begins working with the Underground Railroad, the network of activists who helped Black people escape from slavery.

1871

Third Enforcement Act defines Klan conspiracy as a rebellion against the United States and empowers the president to suspend the writ of habeas corpus and declare martial law in rebellious areas.

April 21

1878

Some 260 Black emigrants, who had purchased stock in the Liberian Exodus Association's joint stock company, leave for Monrovia, Liberia, in Africa on the *Barque Azor*. The *Azor* debarked from Charleston, South Carolina.

> *On the twenty-first of April the Azor left Charleston for Liberia, having on board 260 colored emigrants, of whom one hundred and fifty-two (77 males and 75 females) were over twelve years of age. The officers and crew, fifteen in number, made 275 persons on the vessel. Nearly as many, eager to go, were left behind, for want of room. On board the vessel were two organized churches, one known as the "Azore African Methodist Episcopal Church," with Rev. Mr. Flegler as their pastor, and the other known as the "Shiloh Baptist Church," with seven deacons and a clerk, but no pastor. With one hundred Bibles and Testaments from the American and Foreign Bible Society, Sunday-school books from the American Baptist Publication Society, and hymn books from kind friends, the emigrants left for their fatherland, singing the songs of Zion.*
>
> *Source*: From American Colonization Society. *The African Repository and Colonial Journal, Volumes 54–56*. Victoria, BC: Way & Gideon/AbeBooks, 1878, p. 19.

Books

Dray, Philip. *Capitol Men: The Epic Story of Reconstruction Through the Lives of the First Black Congressmen*. New York, NY: Houghton Mifflin Harcourt, 2008. This look at the United States' first African American congressmen also contains information about the Liberia Exodus Association and the excitement many people felt for it.

Tindall, George Brown. *South Carolina Negroes, 1877–1900*. New York, NY: University of South Carolina Press, 2003. Book contains information from the local historian George Tindall about the impact of the ideas and work of the Liberian Exodus Association on African Americans in South Carolina.

Websites

The University of North Carolina at Chapel Hill has digitized a copy of the 1878 document "The Liberian Exodus. First Voyage of the Azor. Liberia a Delightful Country. Climate, Soil and Productions. Character of the People in Liberia; and How They Live. Full Information of the Exodus Movement." http://docsouth .unc.edu/church/liberian/liberian.html.

The *New York Times* article "Sailing of Negroes for Liberia" is available as an abstract and/or as a full article. http://query.nytimes.com/ gst/abstract.html?res=F30615FA3A5E137B9 3C0AB178FD85F4C8784F9.

Also Noteworthy

1892

More than 2,000 African American longshoremen begin a strike for higher wages in St. Louis, Missouri.

1966

Pct. Milton L. Olive III is posthumously awarded the Congressional Medal of Honor for valor in Vietnam. Olive, the first African American ever awarded the Medal of Honor, had dived onto a live grenade and saved the lives of his fellow soldiers.

1974

Lee Elder wins the Monsanto Open and becomes the first African American professional golfer to qualify to play in the Masters Golf Championship Tournament.

2003

The great singer-activist Nina Simone dies.

April 22

1922

Jazz bassist and composer Charles Mingus is born on a military base in Nogales, Arizona. Though raised in Watts, California, Mingus is known for having played with the jazz legends of the 1950s in the New York City area.

> Sadly, the story of Mingus's music lessons was repeated in his schooling, and one of his constant themes in later life was the way in which he (and so many others) had been disadvantaged. As an articulate and sensitive adult, he felt strongly that he had missed out, and that he was misjudged by others as a direct result. 'People may not underestimate my intelligence, but they overestimate my education,' was one of his more concise expositions of this grievance.
>
> Source: From by Brian Priestley. Mingus, A Critical Biography. Cambridge, MA: Da Capo Press, 1984, p. 5.

Books

Jenkins, Todd S. *I Know What I Know: The Music of Charles Mingus*. New York, NY: Greenwood Publishing Group, 2006. This book is a chronological look at the more than 100 recordings by Mingus.

Santoro, Gene. *Myself When I Am Real: The Life and Music of Charles Mingus*. New York, NY: Oxford University Press, 2001. Biography of Charlie Mingus and his tumultuous life.

Websites

Charles Mingus: The Official Site has complete information on the artist. http://www.mingusmingusmingus.com.

Charles Mingus's "Moanin" is available on YouTube. http://www.YouTube.com/watch?v=__OSyznVDOY.

Also Noteworthy

1526

The first slave revolt in the United States takes place in South Carolina.

2004

Professional golfer Charlie Sifford—the first African American to win the PGA (Professional Golfers' Association) Tour—becomes the first person of African descent elected to the World Golf Hall of Fame.

April 23

1856

Granville T. Woods is born in either Columbus, Ohio, or, some say, in Australia. As an adult, Woods became a skilled inventor and was awarded more than 60 patents. A few of his inventions include Steam Boiler Furnace, Electric Railway, Tunnel Construction for Electric Railway, and Railway Telegraphy.

> . . . Granville T. Woods. Six years ago Mr. Woods sent me a list of his inventions patented up to that time, and there were then about thirty of them, since which time he has added nearly as many more, including those which he perfected jointly with his brother Lyates. His inventions relate principally to electrical subjects, such as telegraphic and telephonic instruments, electric railways and general systems of electrical control, and include several patents on means for transmitting telegraphic messages between moving trains.
>
> The records of the Patent Office show that for valuable consideration several of Mr. Woods' patents have been assigned to the foremost electrical corporations of the world, such as the General Electric Company of New York, and the American Bell Telephone Company of Boston. These records also show that he followed other lines of thought in the exercise of his inventive faculty, one of his other inventions being an incubator, another a complicated and ingenious amusement device,

another a steam-boiler furnace, and also a mechanical brake.

Source: From Henry E. Baker. *The Colored Inventor: A Record of Fifty Years*. St. Peter Port, Guernsey: Dodo Press/The Book Depository, 2009, p. 7.

Books

Sluby, Patricia Carter. *The Inventive Spirit of African Americans: Patented Ingenuity*. Santa Monica, CA: Greenwood Publishing Group, 2004. Book includes references to Granville T. Woods and his wide recognition as the "Black Edison."

Sullivan, Otha Richard and James Haskins. *African American Inventors*. New York, NY: Wiley, 1998. Contains a long profile on the life of Granville T. Woods.

Websites

The Faces of Science: African Americans in the Sciences. https://webfiles.uci.edu/mcbrown/display/woods.html has a biography of Granville T. Woods.

Inventions.org looks at the importance of Granville T. Woods' life and work. http://www.inventions.org/culture/african/gtwoods.html.

Also Noteworthy

1895

The inventor, Clatonia Joaquin Dorticus—who was born on April 16, 1823, in Cuba—patents the photographic print wash. Dorticus is awarded U.S. Patent No. 537,968.

1899

Brutal lynching of Sam Hose takes place in Coweta County, Georgia. Hose was chopping wood for a white man named Alfred Cranford when he asked for time off so that he could visit his sick mother. Cranford refused and threatened him with a gun, and Hose took the ax he was using and threw it at Cranford, killing him with that throw.

Hose tried to run away from the area, but a mob of whites tracked him down, and he was eventually tortured and executed; parts of Hose's body were later sold as souvenirs.

1913

The historic civil rights organization, the National Urban League http://www.nul.org/, is founded in New York City via the merger of three organizations: the National League for the Protection of Colored Women, the National League on Urban Conditions Among Negroes, and the Niagra Movement.

April 24

1898

Andrew "Lefty" Lewis Cooper is born in Waco, Texas. As a 6-foot 2-inch, 220-pound man, Cooper became a seminal left-handed pitcher for the Detroit Stars and later for the Kansas City Monarchs in the National Negro Baseball Leagues.

From 1920 through 1927 and again in 1930, the Stars' staff included one of the game's greatest pitchers, Andy "Lefty" Cooper. . . . With 123 official league victories, Cooper ranks second on the all-time wins list behind only Hall of Famer Willie Foster. The six-foot two-inch, 220 pound Cooper had exceptional control and a vast array of pitches that secured him the role of pitching staff ace during his tenure in the Motor City. Cooper compiled a record of 92 wins and 47 losses with the Stars.

Source: From Larry Lester, Sammy J. Miller, and Dick Clark. *Black Baseball in Detroit*. Mount Pleasant, SC: Arcadia Publishing, 2000, p. 31.

Books

Bak, Richard. *A Place for Summer: A Narrative History of Tiger Stadium*. Detroit, MI: Wayne State University Press, 1998. Contains a profile of Andrew "Lefty" Cooper.

Bak, Richard. *Turkey Stearnes and the Detroit Stars: The Negro Leagues in Detroit, 1919–1933*. Detroit, MI: Wayne State University Press, 1995. Book looks at the impact the Negro League's Detroit

Stars had on the local Black community; Andy Cooper and his exploits are highlighted.

Websites

Negro Leagues Baseball Museum and Kansas State University College of Education has a profile of Andrew "Lefty" Cooper. http://www.coe.ksu.edu/nlbemuseum/history/players/cooper.html.

Baseball-reference.com provides Andrew "Lefty" Cooper's player statistics. http://www.baseball-reference.com/bullpen/Andy_Cooper.

Also Noteworthy

1884

The National Medical Association (The Association for African American Physicians; www.nmanet.org) is founded in Atlanta, Georgia. The organization was originally named the National Medical Association of Black Physicians.

1944

The United Negro College Fund (UNCF; www.uncf.org) is founded to raise college tuition money and grant scholarships to financially challenged Black students. The UNCF has a general scholarship that funds 39 historically Black colleges and universities (HBCUs).

1986

University of Southern California (USC) guard Cheryl Miller is picked in the 15th round to play with the Staten Island Stallions of the United States Basketball League (USBL). Miller became the first women drafted to play in a predominately men's professional basketball league.

April 25

1918

Ella Jane Fitzgerald is born to William and Temperance Fitzgerald in Newport News,

Virginia. After winning the Apollo Theater amateur contest in Harlem, New York, on November 21, 1934, Ella Fitzgerald became a member of the Chick Webb orchestra. Fitzgerald famously recorded the song "A-tisket, A-tasket" and became known as the "First Lady of Song" because she would tour non-stop and was considered a skilled interpreter of the *American Songbook*.

> With "A-Tisket, A-Tasket" Ella was now the most popular female vocalist in America. In three short years she had risen from obscurity to stardom, and although she was only twenty-one, she had the world at her feet. Her needs were simple: All she wanted was to sing and have a good time, and these were being fulfilled beyond her wildest dreams.
>
> Source: From Stuart Nicholson. *Ella Fitzgerald: A Biography of the First Lady of Jazz*. Cambridge, MA: Da Capo Press, 1994, p. 55.

Books

Fritts, Ron and Ken Vail. *Ella Fitzgerald: the Chick Webb Years and Beyond*. Lanham, MD: Scarecrow Press, 2003. Chronicles Ella Fitzgerald's rise to stardom during the period of her work with Chick Webb.

Stone, Tanya Lee. *Ella Fitzgerald*. New York, NY: Penguin, 2008. Biography of Ella Fitzgerald.

Websites

The official Website of Ella Fitzgerald provides her biography and career highlights. http://www.ellafitzgerald.com.

The GAS Audio Edition virtual museum contains a biography, essays, and MP3s of Ella Fitzgerald's music. http://museum.media.org/ella/index.html

Also Noteworthy

1959

Mack Parker is lynched in Poplarville, Mississippi.

April 26

1886

Gertrude Pridgett "Ma" Rainey is born to Thomas and Ella Pridgett in Columbus, Georgia. By the age of 14 Gertrude had joined a traveling show called the "Bunch of Blackberries." She later married William "Pa" Rainey and took on her iconic "Ma" Rainey name. As a vaudeville blues singer, "Ma" Rainey became one of the first African American female recording stars.

For her audience, Ma Rainey was a folk figure. . . . The span of her career witnesses the uprooting of thousands of black people from their homes in the South and their movement to alien environments in major cities of the North and Midwest, and her lyrics frequently reflect this dislocation: the sentimentalized yearning for the South; the attraction to, yet fear of, the North; the man who takes his country woman to the city, only to abandon her there; the working woman whose sweet man cheats her of her savings; the young girl who heads South to her parents when her Northern love affair goes sour.

Source: From Sandra R. Lieb. *Mother of the Blues: A Study of Ma Rainey.* Amherst, MA: University of Massachusetts Press, 1983, p. 169.

Books

Dorsey, Brian. *Spirituality, Sensuality, Literality: Blues, Jazz, and Rap as Music and Poetry.* Vienna: Braumüller, 2000. Contains a profile "Ma" Rainey.

Stewart-Baxter, Derrick. *Ma Rainey and the Classic Blues Singers.* New York, NY: Stein and Day, 1970. Biography of "Ma" Rainey.

Websites

Ma Rainey singing " 'Ma' Rainey's Black Bottom" is available on YouTube. http://www.YouTube.com/watch?v=-fizLgmUHmw.

Wild Women Don't Have the Blues provides background on "Ma" Rainey and how she became a major celebrity. http://www.YouTube.com/watch?v=ieEN44N0PZ0&feature=related.

Also Noteworthy

1886

William Levi Dawson is born in Albany, Georgia. Trained as a lawyer, Dawson became a Congressman in the U.S. House of Representatives. He represented Chicago, Illinois's, First Congressional District for over 27 years.

April 27

1945

The playwright August Wilson is born to Daisy Wilson, an African American, and Frederick August Kittel, Sr., a German immigrant, and given the name Frederick August Kittel. On January 31, 1986, Wilson's *Fences*, starring James Earl Jones, opened at Chicago's Goodman Theatre.

When August Wilson got off the train in New Haven, Connecticut, en route to the first Yale Repertory Theater rehearsal of Ma Rainey's Black Bottom, his demeanor in no way foreshadowed that this was a man who would later win two Pulitzer Prizes in drama and make a serious impact upon the course of American theater. Frankly, his biggest concern at this point in his career was steadying himself to meet the cast and the director of this fledgling work-in-progress. He had just undergone an extensive and rigorous ten-week crash course in playwrighting at the prestigious Eugene O'Neill Center. He had already attracted the attention of prominent producers, and now his play about black jazz musicians of the 1920s was to be staged at one of the nation's top drama schools by noted director Lloyd Richards—then Dean of the Yale School of Drama and Artistic Director of the Yale Repertory Theater. Even though Wilson had received the equivalent of a Ph.D. degree in playwrighting, he apparently still felt vulnerable and, to some extent, overwhelmed by all that success in the theater business entails.

Source: From Marilyn Roberson Elkins. *August Wilson: A Casebook.* New York, NY: Psychology Press/Garland Publishing Inc., 2000, p. 183.

Books

Nadel, Alan. *May All Your Fences Have Gates: Essays on the Drama of August Wilson.* Iowa City, IA: University of Iowa Press, 1994. Critical essays looking at the work of August Wilson.

Wilson, August with an introduction by Toni Morrison. *The Piano Lesson.* New York, NY: Theatre Communications Group, 2007. August Wilson's Pulitzer Prize-winning play tells the story of the intergenerational bonds that unite an African American family.

Websites

The August Wilson Center for African American Culture is a museum and inter-disciplinary art institution. http://www.augustwilsoncenter.org.

AugustWilson.net is a searchable database related to the works of August Wilson. http://www.augustwilson.net.

Also Noteworthy

1916

Three white nuns—Sisters Mary Thomasine Hehir, Mary Scholastica Sullivan, and Mary Beningus Cameron of the Sisters of St. Joseph—teachers at the St. Benedict the Moor Catholic School, are arrested for defying a 1913 law that prohibited white teachers from teaching children of African descent. The nuns were later acquitted when a judge determined the law did not apply to private schools. St. Benedict the Moor Catholic was an all-African American private Catholic school that welcomed students of any religion, from kindergarten up through the eighth grade. Open from 1898 through 1968, the school was closed in 1964 when Catholic schools were desegregated. In 1991, St. Benedict the Moor Catholic School was placed on the National Register of Historic Places.

April 28

1847

George Boyer Vashon becomes the first person of African descent to enter New York State Bar and be allowed to practice law. Vashon had also been the first Black person to graduate with a bachelor of arts degree from Oberlin College and the first Black professor to teach at Howard University.

> *About the middle of the last century George Boyer Vashon was prominent, first as teacher, then as lawyer and man of letters. He was enrolled in Oberlin College from 1840 to 1844, and then spent a year in the theological seminary. He received the A.B. degree in 1844, and the A.M. was conferred on him in 1849. For some time he was one of the three Negro professors (the other two being Charles L. Reason and William G. Allen) employed at New York Central College, McGrawville, N.Y., an institution established by the abolitionists. Becoming interested in the law, he had as preceptor Judge Walter Forward, later Secretary of the Treasury of the United States, and in 1847 was admitted to the bar in New York City. Soon after that event Vashon sailed to the West Indiess, and for the next three years he taught at College Faustin, Port-au-Prince, Hayti. Returning to the United States in the fall of 1850, he contributed to a number of periodicals and engaged in the practice of his profession at Syracuse, N.Y.; but before long he became principal of the one school for Negro children in Pittsburgh, Penn.*
>
> *Source: From Benjamin Griffith Brawley. Early Negro American Writers: Selections with Biographical and Critical Introductions. Manchester, NH: Ayer Publishing, 1968, p. 261.*

Books

Glasco, Laurence Admiral and Federal Writers' Project (Pa.). *The WPA History of the Negro in Pittsburgh.* Pittsburgh, PA: University of Pittsburgh Pre, 2004. Notes Vashon's influence and work in Pittsburgh.

Wells Brown, William. *The Black Man: His Antecedants, His Genius, and His Achievements.* Boston, MA: J. Redpath, 1863. Contains a long section recalling Vashon's life and career.

Websites

A biography of George Boyer Vashon is available on the University of Pittsburgh Library's

Website. http://www.library.pitt.edu/freeat-last/abolition.html.

"After 163 Years, African-American Legal Scholar and Abolitionist George B. Vashon to Be Admitted to Pennsylvania Bar" notes that Vashon was only recently, posthumously, admitted to the Pennsylvania Bar. http://www.pittsburghurbanmedia.com/After-163-Years-African-American-Legal-Scholar-and-Abolitionist-George-B-Vashon-to-Be-Admitted-to-Pennsylvania-Bar/.

Also Noteworthy

1839

Sengbe Pieh (a.k.a., Joseph Cinque) leads a mutiny aboard the slave ship *Amistad* just off the coast of Long Island, New York.

1911

Prudencio Mario Bauzá is born in Havana, Cuba. When he turned 19 in 1930, Bauzá moved to New York City and reportedly learned to play the trumpet in a matter of weeks. As a trumpeter, Bauzá is credited with melding classical Cuban music with Afro-Cuban styles and African American jazz. Bauzá recorded his last CD in 1993; entitled *944 Columbus*, it was named after the last building he called home in Manhattan, New York.

1971

Samuel Lee Gravely is appointed the U.S. Navy's first African American admiral.

April 29

1899

Edward Kennedy "Duke" Ellington is born to James Edward Ellington and Daisy Kennedy Ellington in Washington, DC. Ellington's celebrity as a jazz musician and composer lasted some 50 years.

Not content to rest on his laurels, Ellington continued to expand his musical horizons, composing

for films, ballet, musical comedy, stage productions, and symphony orchestras. Three major sacred works were the culmination of the last decade of his life. On his deathbed, Ellington was still attempting to finish an opera, as well as edit the recording of his last sacred composition. No composer of note in any field was able to write as much music while simultaneously putting a great dance orchestra through a nonstop schedule of working in nightclubs, theaters, concert halls, and dance palaces in virtually every country in the Western world. This orchestra, a collection of temperamental virtuosi, had within its ranks men who preeminence on their instruments was a direct result of their relationship with Ellington. When Ellington died in 1974, there were men whose entire musical lives were spent in collaboration with him, from twenty years, in the case of Russell Procope, to forty-seven for Harry Carney.

Source: From A. H. Lawrence. Duke Ellington and His World. New York, NY: Roudedge/Psychology Press, 2003, p. xiii.

Books

Hasse, John Edward. *Beyond Category: The Life and Genius of Duke Ellington.* New York, NY: Simon & Schuster, 1993. Biography of Duke Ellington.

Tucker, Mark. *Ellington: The Early Years.* Champaign, IL: University of Illinois Press, 1995. Biography looks at Duke Ellington's youth and his early years as a musician.

Websites

The Duke Ellington Society, NY (TDES, Inc.), a non-profit devoted to studying Ellington's life and musical legacy, was established in 1955. http://www.thedukeellingtonsociety.org.

A recording of the Duke Ellington Orchestra playing "Take The A Train" is on YouTube. http://www.YouTube.com/watch?v=wnurVNkg62Q.

1992

First day of the five days of riots in South Central Los Angeles, California, that would come to be known as the Rodney King Rebellion. The rebellion was sparked by the acquittal of four white LAPD officers in the beating of Rodney Glen King, who had been beaten with batons after not pulling his car over when officers signaled him to. The King beating was videotaped and shown around the world. Once the officers were acquitted, the ensuing rebellion led to some 50 deaths, the injury of thousands, and estimates of up to $1 billion in property damage.

These different images underlying people's first impressions of the King videotape help make sense of the various reactions to the verdict. Of course, the sharpest contrast was between those who responded to the verdict by taking to the streets in Pico and South Central and, at the opposite pole, the police-department personnel who cheered the news. But most across the spectrum of mainstream culture who deplored the "rioting" didn't do so because they agreed with the verdict or with the cheering police. To the contrary, for the most part, they sought to preserve the very value that they thought the Simi Valley jury had impugned—the value of the rule of law. The dominant public discourse of the "L.A. riots" quickly became articulated as an opposition between those urging restraining and advocating respect for the "rule of law" and those articulating an alternative first principle of "no justice, no peace." The contrast between the rhetoric of "rule of law" and "no justice, no peace" was soon translated by the dominant culture into a contest between an objective, reasoned, responsible reaction and an emotional, passionate, irresponsible one. These strands of narrative culminated in the symbolic conflict between whether the people out in the streets should be seen as "mob" "rioting" or as part of an "insurrection."

Source: From Robert Gooding-Williams. *Reading Rodney King/Reading Urban Uprising.* New York, NY: Psychology Press, 1993, p. 67.

Books

Cannon, Lou. *Official Negligence: How Rodney King and the Riots Changed Los Angeles and the LAPD.* Boulder, CO: Westview Press, 1999. Journalist interviews participants and looks at

the results of the Rodney King Rebellion in South Central Los Angeles.

Wall, Brenda. *The Rodney King Rebellion: A Psychopolitical Analysis of Despair and Hope.* Victoria, BC: African American Images/AbeBooks, 1992. Examines the various viewpoints on the reaction to the verdict in the Rodney King case.

Websites

Time magazine looked at the King Rebellion on its 15-year anniversary. http://www.time.com/time/specials/2007/la_riot/0,28757,1614117,00.html#ixzz1SwLNc9VF.

Rodney King Riots on YouTube. http://www.YouTube.com/watch?v=FCfmkAGlj0o.

Also Noteworthy

1985

Colonel Frederick Drew Gregory becomes the National Aeronautics and Space Administration's (NASA) first Black astronaut to pilot a space craft when he pilots the STS-51B/Spacelab-3 Challenger mission out of the Kennedy Space Center in Florida.

1845

The attorneys Macon B. Allen Jr. and Robert Morris Jr. become the first people of African descent to open a law practice.

April 30

1961

Isiah Lord Thomas III is born in Chicago, Illinois. Known for his prowess as a professional basketball player, Isiah "Zeke" Thomas was an All-American point guard, named the NCAA Men's Basketball's Most Outstanding Player in 1981 when he led the Indiana University Hoosiers to the NCAA national championship. In what would have been his sophomore year in college, Thomas became the first round, second pick of the National Basketball Association's

(NBA) Detroit Pistons, and from 1981 to 1994 he played point guard for the team. He led the Pistons to two consecutive championships in 1989 and 1990; and when leading the Pistons in the 1988 NBA Finals, Thomas famously greeted his professional rival/good friend Magic Johnson with a kiss on the cheek. Thomas retired from the Detroit Pistons on May 2, 1994. He was named one of the 50 Greatest Players in NBA History in 1996 and was inducted into the Naismith Memorial Basketball Hall of Fame in 2000.

> *For his part, Isiah seemed pretty confident that he would be up to the task of running a big-time basketball team. After all, he'd done it numerous times on the court on the West Side, at St. Joe's, and at IU. For countless years with the Pistons, his leadership was rarely questioned. But knowing how to beat a full-court press only goes so far when the shorts and tank-top are traded in for a suit and tie. . . . .*
>
> *Everyone knew that as a player, Isiah Thomas moved quickly off the dribble and toward the hoop. But that was nothing compared to the speed with which he moved out of the Piston's backcourt and into the Raptor's front office. In an unbelievably quick turnaround, Isiah was announced as the Raptor's GM on May 24, 1994 —just three weeks after his last game as a Piston and only two weeks after announcing his retirement as a player.*
>
> Source: From Paul Challen. *From the Back Court to the Front Office: The Isiah Thomas Story.* Toronto, Ontario: ECW Press, 2004, pp. 157–158.

Books

Farrell, Perry A. *Tales from the Detroit Pistons.* Champaign, IL: Sports Publishing LLC, 2004. Book includes excerpts about Thomas's leadership of the championship Pistons teams.

Thomas, Isiah and Matt Dobek. *Bad Boys.* Dallas, TX: Masters Press, 1989. Thomas gives his first-hand account of his championship years with the Detroit Pistons.

Websites

Isiah Thomas page at the Naismith Memorial Basketball Hall of Fame. http://www.hoophall.com/hall-of-famers/tag/isiah-l-thomas.

"NBA Best Guards Isiah Thomas" on YouTube. http://www.YouTube.com/watch?v=LtNi0rj7Zg4&feature=related.

Also Noteworthy

1932

Opening Day takes place in Pittsburgh, Pennsylvania, for businessman William "Gus" Greenlee's Greenlee Field, the first African American-owned baseball stadium in the nation. Located at 2500 Bedford Avenue, the brick, steel, and wood Greenlee Field ballpark featured seats for some 7,500 patrons. Opening Day features the Negro National League's Pittsburgh Crawfords with their pitcher, Leroy Robert "Satchel" Paige; catcher, Josh Gibson; and famed centerfielder, James Thomas "Cool Papa" Bell.

1952

The surgeon Dr. Louis Tompkins Wright— the first person of African descent to become a fellow of the American College of Surgeons—is honored by the American Cancer Society for his work in cancer research.

1983

Robert Clyve Maynard gains controlling interest in a major metropolitan newspaper when he buys the *Oakland Tribune*, a newspaper he had initially come to as an editor four years earlier. Under Maynard, the once-failing newspaper won a Pulitzer Prize in 1990.

1992

After eight seasons and 197 episodes, *The Cosby Show* television situation comedy comes to an end.

May

May 1

1867

Howard University, one of the nation's most prominent historically Black universities (HBCU), opens in Washington, DC. It is named after Oliver Otis Howard, a former general in the Union Army during the U.S. Civil War who later served as head of the Freedmen's Bureau. General Howard's efforts to build schools and to help the formerly enslaved restore their lives was widely recognized, and he was asked to help establish the university. Howard served as the school's third president from 1869 to 1874. Granted a charter by an act of the Thirty-ninth Congress on March 2, 1867, the school was originally called Howard Normal and Theological Institute for the Education of Preachers and Teachers. Noted Black Greek-letter organizations such as Alpha Kappa Alpha and Delta Sigma Theta were each initially established at Howard and the university houses at the Moorland-Spingarn Research Center, one of the largest Black history research libraries in the world. Although established as a theological seminary for African American ministers, the university's first four students were young white females.

> One of the most cherished traditions asserts that the first students were four white girls, the daughters of members of the Faculty. . . .
> . . . . Dr. Mordecai Johnson, President of the University from 1926 to 1960, frequently and eloquently underscored the significance of the fact. It was a personal commitment that Howard University was to be truly a "University for the education of youth," where white girls would go to school with the sons and daughters of freemen and freedmen.
>
> Source: From Rayford W. Logan. Howard University: The First Hundred Years 1867–1967. New York: NYU Press, 2004, p. 34.

Books

Logan, Rayford W. Howard University: The First Hundred Years 1867–1967. New York: NYU Press, August 2004. A Howard University history professor from 1938 to 1965, Rayford Logan compiled one of the first histories of Howard University.

Robinson, Harry G. and Hazel Ruth Edwards. The Long Walk: The Placemaking Legacy of Howard University. Washington, DC: Moorland-Spingarn Research Center, Howard University, 1996. The Long Walk examines Howard's history and looks at some of the alumnae who have made impacts beyond the school's border.

Websites

Howard University is today one of the preeminent predominately Black schools of higher education. This site is the schools' official Website. http://www.howard.edu.

U-S-History.com provides background on the school's founding and the degree programs Howard University offers today. http://www.u-s-history.com/pages/h3244.html.

Howard University Press, which was established in 1972, is—according to its Website—"Dedicated to publishing noteworthy new scholarship that addresses the contributions, conditions, and concerns of African Americans, other people of African descent, and people of color around the globe." The press is known as the first Black University Press in the United States. http://www.hupress.howard.edu.

Howard University's Moorland-Spingarn Research Center is one of the largest collections of photographs and documents about people of African descent in Africa and the Americas. http://www.howard.edu/msrc/.

Also Noteworthy

1866

Former Confederate soldiers go on a two-day race riot in Memphis, Tennessee. The riot left 46 Blacks and 2 whites dead, 5 Black women were raped, and more than 90 buildings were burned to the ground.

1950

The poet Gwendolyn Brooks is awarded a Pulitzer Prize for her second book of poetry, *Annie Allen*.

1967

The "Long Hot Summer" takes place between May 1 and October 1, as Black community members riot in 40 different U.S. cities. Each riot was sparked by a unique cause, but in general many believe the overall reason was the growing frustration about a lack of peaceful change in U.S. policies toward African American lives.

May 2

1883

Nannie Helen Burroughs is born to John and Jennie Burroughs in Orange, Virginia. An outspoken educator, orator, and activist, Nannie came to national renown at the age of 21 when she delivered the speech "How the Sisters are Hindered from Helping" at the National Baptist Convention in Richmond, Virginia in 1900. In 1909, Nannie Helen Burroughs founded the National Training School for Women and Girls in Washington, DC. The school was later renamed in her honor as the Nannie Helen Burroughs School (http://www.nhburr oughs.org/). Since 1975, Washington's District of Columbia has celebrated every May 10 as "Nannie Helen Burroughs Day."

As a church and organization leader, school founder and educator, women's advocate and race champion, Nannie Helen Burroughs was a pragmatic warrior and outspoken public intellectual who defied conventional female confinements of her era. Through her newspaper commentary, speeches, and writings she inserted herself into the male-centered discourse on race advancement. Her work paralleled that of better-known black women predecessors and contemporaries including Annie Julia Cooper, Mary Church Terrell, and Mary McLeod Bethune, and her accomplishments and zeal for racial uplift were just as impressive. Burroughs brought into the public sphere a deep concern for the black working class who lacked "social or economic pull" and a belief in self-help that caused people to compare her with Booker T. Washington. Burroughs, however, was more like W.E.B. DuBois in agitating for justice. "Hound dogs are kicked, not bull dogs," she wrote.

Source: From Clarence L. Mohr and Charles Reagan Wilson. The New Encyclopedia of Southern Culture: Volume 17: Education. Chapel Hill, NC: UNC Press Books, 2011, p. 34.

Books

Ventura, Varla. *Sheroes: Bold, Brash, and Absolutely Unabashed Superwomen from Susan B. Anthony to Xena*. San Francisco, CA: Conari Press, 1998. Book contains a biography of Nannie Helen Burroughs and points to the impact of her work on the lives of young women.

Wimbush, Vincent L. and Rosamond C. Rodman. *African Americans and the Bible: Sacred Texts and Social Textures*. Harrisburg, PA: Continuum International Publishing Group, 2001. Contains a chapter on the influence of the Bible on the work of Nannie Helen Burroughs.

Websites

Nannie Helen Burroughs School has a biographical sketch of the school's namesake. http://www.nhburroughs.org/id1.html.

The Library of Congress page "Nannie Helen Burroughs—Discovering Hidden Washington: A Journey Through the Alley Communities of the Nation's Capital." The Website shares the activists story. http://www.loc.gov/loc/kidslc/sp-burroughs.html.

1844

Elijah J. McCoy is born to George and Emillia McCoy in Colchester, Ontario, in Canada; McCoy's parents had fled to Canada from Kentucky via the Underground Railroad. As an inventor and engineer, McCoy became so well known for the great quality of his many inventions that the expression "the real McCoy" became a way for stores to advertise the validity of McCoy's products. Initially an African Canadian, McCoy became a U.S. citizen and held more than 57 U.S. patents.

Elijah saw how much time was wasted in stopping his train, so he designed an automatic lubricating device that would oil the moving parts while they were moving. He got a patent for the invention in 1872. With his "lubricating cup" in place, machines did not have to be stopped to be oiled. This invention was used for years in factories, on steam locomotives and steam ships around the world. Trains and ships could get to their destinations faster and factories could make more things in the same amount of time.

Source: From Jan Hansen. Moments in Canadian Black History. Napanee, Ontario: S&S Learning Materials, 2004, p. 42.

Books

Moodie, Andrew. *The Real McCoy*. Toronto, ON: Playwrights Canada Press, 2006. Playwright retells the story and importance of Elijah McCoy.

Towle, Wendy. *The Real McCoy: The Life of an African-American Inventor*. Logan, IA: Perfection Learning Corporation, 1995. Illustrated children's book serves as an introduction to McCoy's life and work.

Websites

Northern California Council of Black Professional Engineers has a short biography on the life and work of Elijah McCoy. http://www .ncalifblackengineers.org/Elijah%20McCoy .htm.

Elijah McCoy's first patent, for a Self-Regulating Lubricator, U.S. Patent No. 129,843. http:// www.usi.edu/science/engineering/emccoy/ index.htm.

Also Noteworthy

1920

First game of National Negro Baseball League is played between the Indianapolis ABCs and the Chicago Giants at Washington Park in Indianapolis, Indiana. The ABCs defeat the Giants 4 to 2.

May 3

1898

Septima Poinsette Clark is born to Victoria Anderson and Peter Poinsette in Charleston. Clark's mother was of Haitian descent and gave her the name Septima because it means "sufficient" in Haitian Creole. As an educator and civil rights activist, Septima promoted Black education among her pupils and was fired from the Charleston public school system because she would not give up her NAACP membership. Clark is also famous for serving as the director of nonviolent civil disobedience workshops at the Highlander Folk School in Monteagle, Tennessee, where Rosa Parks once sat in her class. Clark worked with the Southern Christian Leadership Conference and became a close associate of Dr. Martin Luther King, Jr.,—she even went with him to Oslo, Norway, when King won the Noble Peace Prize.

Septima Clark did not limit her usefulness to the school board. After five children died in five separate Charleston house fires, she joined the city's clubwomen to raise money to build a day care center and to hire a qualified teacher for it. When a car accidentally killed a young girl as she crossed the street, Clark persuaded friends in her civic organizing circle to donate a dollar a month to employ fifteen women as crossing guards at busy intersections. By 1975, Clark served on the Charleston Committee for Day Care; two years later, Alleen Brewer Wood, Bernice Robinson, and Ethel Grimball, the first three Citizenship School teachers on the Sea Islands, sat on the same board. As a member of the Advisory Council for the Aging, Clark voiced her concern with the lack of care for the elderly who lived alone. One woman had drowned when she left her house and walked into a marsh, another had spent two nights sleeping naked by the Ashley River, and another had fallen in her bathtub. Clark made a series of phone calls and composed a list of volunteers willing to call older people to check on them. She also stayed active in her sorority, Alpha Kappa Alpha. By 1978, members had launched a program called Parental Involvement Now, designed to increase participation in school and community activities, for which they had secured federal funding. They anticipated using home visits to educate parents on how they might "strengthen their children's skills in reading, language, and arithmetic." Finally, Clark remained involved in the nonpartisan League of Women Voters and signaled her partisan affiliation by becoming a member of the Democratic Women of Charleston County.

Source: From Katherine Mellen Charron. Freedom's Teacher: The Life of Septima Clark. Chapel Hill, NC: The University of North Carolina Press, 2009, pp. 347–349.

Books

Brown, Cynthia Stokes, ed. *Ready from Within: A First Person Narrative: Septima Clark and the Civil Rights Movement.* Lawrenceville, NJ: Africa World Press, 1990. Septima Clark's remembrances of her work in the Civil Rights Movement.

Clark, Septima Poinsette with Legette Blythe. *Echo in My Soul*, 1st edition. New York: Dutton, 1962. Septima Clark's autobiography looks at the many aspects of her work as a teacher in the segregated South.

Websites

Septima P. Clark Papers are available at Avery Research Center for African American History and Culture at the College of Charleston. http://avery.cofc.edu/clarkpapers.htm.

The University of South Carolina–Aiken dedicates a page to Septima Poinsette Clark. http://www.usca.edu/aasc/clark.htm.

1933

James Joseph Brown, Jr., is born in Barnwell, South Carolina, and then raised in Augusta, Georgia. By blending gospel, rhythm and blues, and soul rhythms, James Brown—the "Godfather of Soul" (a.k.a "The Hardest-Working Man in Show Business" and "Soul Brother #1")—was a seminal influence on various musical styles, including afrobeat, jazz, reggae, disco, dance, and hip hop. A few of his most famous songs include "Get Up (I Feel Like Being a) Sex Machine," "Papa's Got a Brand New Bag," "It's a Man's Man's Man's World," and "Papa Don't Take No Mess." Brown was inducted into the Rock and Roll Hall of Fame Museum in 1986.

The heightened sociopolitical atmosphere of the times emboldened Brown to release "Say It Loud—I'm Black and I'm Proud," an anthem for a generation, which placed Brown squarely in the vanguard of black leadership. With Dr. Martin Luther King Jr.'s assassination, blazing urban riots, and the conflicting philosophies that marked the black nationalist era, Brown's vision of economic self-reliance and his naive politics were respected and even envied.

Source: From Nelson George and Alan Leeds. The James Brown Reader: 50 Years of Writing about the Godfather of Soul. New York, NY: Penguin, 2008, p. 163.

Books

Brown, James with Marc Eliot. *I Feel Good: A Memoir of a Life of Soul.* New York: New American Library, 2005. James Brown recounts his own story of his life and career.

Brown, Geoff and Chris Charlesworth. *James Brown: Doin' It to Death: A Biography.* London: Omnibus Press, 1996. Biography of James

Brown shows his impact on the world of entertainment.

Websites

James Brown's "Papa Don't Take No Mess & My Thang" is on YouTube. http://www.youtube.com/watch?v=FKeY88YLBUU.

James Brown's "Say It Loud I'm Black and I'm Proud" is on YouTube. http://www.youtube.com/watch?v=2VRSAVDlpDI.

Augusta, Georgia, where James Brown grew up, had the "James Brown Statue and Plaza" created in his remembrance. http://www.augustaga.com/augusta_recreation/jamesbrownstatue.php.

1948

The U.S. Supreme Court delivers a landmark decision in *Shelley v. Kraemer*, the first case to challenge the legality of restrictive real estate covenants.

For many years in St. Louis, blacks were denied housing by the extensive use of restrictive covenants—written agreements among property owners with the expressed purpose of restricting property ownership to whites. The 1940s case of J.D. and Ethel Shelley in St. Louis offered a significant challenge to this practice. The Shelleys had moved to St. Louis from Starksville, Mississippi, in 1930 in search of a better place to raise their children. They first lived with relatives and then rented substandard housing in an overcrowded, segregated area. In August 1945, the Shelleys bought a home at 4600 Labadie and thought they had finally found a decent home for their family. In October the Shelleys moved into the modest, two-story brick dwelling. A day later, two of their neighbors, Louis and Fern Kraemer sued to evict the Shelleys from their new home, citing a restrictive covenant attached to the house's deed. The restriction, dating back to 1911, barred any owners of the property, their heirs, legal representatives, or subsequent owners from selling or renting the property to people who were not of the "Caucasian Race." This restrictive agreement was binding for fifty years and specifically prohibited the transferring in anyway of the property to "persons of the Negro and Mongolian Race."

Source: From Lorenzo Johnston Greene, Gary R. Kremer, and Antonio Frederick Holland. *Missouri's Black Heritage*. Columbia, MO: University of Missouri Press, 1993, p. 163.

Books

Hyatt, Wayne S. *Condominium and Homeowner Association Practice: Community Association Law*. Philadelphia, PA: ALI-ABA, 1988. Contains information on the importance of the ruling in *Shelley v. Kraemer*.

Vose, Clement. *Caucasians Only: The Supreme Court, the NAACP, and the Restrictive Covenant Cases*. New York: University of California Press, 1992. The book includes extensive coverage of the *Shelley v. Kraemer* case.

Websites

The Shelley House, at 4600 Labadie Avenue in St. Louis, Missouri, is today a National Historic Landmark. http://www.cr.nps.gov/nr/travel/civilrights/mo1.htm.

Case Briefs summarizes the issues in *Shelley v. Kraemer*. http://www.casebriefs.com/blog/law/property/property-law-keyed-to-cribbet/role-of-property-in-society/shelley-v-kraemer/.

Also Noteworthy

1845

Macon B. Allen passes the Massachusetts bar, thus becoming the first African American lawyer to pass a state bar and the first Black person permitted to practice law in the United States. Allen was born in Indiana, but after the Civil War he moved to South Carolina, where he was elected a judge in 1873.

1964

Frederick O'Neal becomes first Black president of the Actor's Equity Association.

May 4

1891

Dr. Daniel Hale Williams founds the Provident Hospital and Training Center in

Chicago, Illinois. It becomes a major training center for Black doctors and nurses. Williams is best known, however, for performing the nation's first open-heart surgery on July 9, 1893. Williams operated on a man injured in a knife fight; his patient would live for another 20 years after the surgery. Williams also help establish the National Medical Association (NMA), which was established to serve people of African descent in the medical professions, who were denied membership in the American Medical Association.

> *Surgery interested him most. Daniel Hale Williams employed the latest methods of using carbolic acid to prevent infections in wounds and washing his hands and soaking the instruments before surgery. In 1883, he received his medical degree, set up a practice, worked on the surgical staff of South Side Dispensary, and taught at Chicago Medical College. He also began operating on some patients at home. At the time, many hospitals refused to treat African Americans. In addition, some people were afraid to enter hospital because in the [1]800s that was where people went to die. Williams had a plan and on May 4, 1891. Provident Hospital and Training School opened its doors to become the country's first interracial hospital and first training school for African-American nurses.*
>
> *Source*: From Mary Ellen Sterling. *Focus on Scientists*. Westminster, CA: Teacher Created Resources, 1994, p. 73.

Books

Buckler, Helen. *Daniel Hale Williams: Negro Surgeon*. New York: Pitman, 1968. Biography of Williams and his pioneering work in cardiology.

Fenderson, Lewis H. *Daniel Hale Williams: Open-heart Doctor*. New York: McGraw-Hill, 1971. Book examines the life of the first medical professional to perform open-heart surgery, Daniel Hale Williams.

Websites

Gibbs Magazine provides a profile of Daniel Hale Williams. http://www.gibbsmagazine.com/DrWilliams.htm.

The Provident Foundation, which perpetuates the work of the Provident Hospital, has a biography of Daniel Hale Williams. http://providentfoundation.org/history/williams.html.

Also Noteworthy

1897

Joseph H. Smith receives U.S. Patent No. 581,785 for his first lawn sprinkler design.

1943

Nickolas Ashford is born in Fairfax, South Carolina. After meeting Valerie Simpson, Ashford became a songwriter and singer, responsible for famous soul music songs like "Ain't No Mountain High Enough," "Love Don't Make It Right," "You're All I Need to Get by," and "Ain't Nothing Like the Real Thing."

1961

Thirteen "Freedom Riders" begin bus trips through the South to test Southern compliance with a 1960 U.S. Supreme Court ruling outlawing segregation in interstate transportation facilities. They were soon joined by hundreds of other Freedom Riders of all ages and races. Despite the Court decision, dozens of Freedom Riders were arrested as the South attempted to hang onto its segregationist ways. CORE began freedom rides from Washington, DC, to force desegregation of southern bus terminals, 1961. Freedom Riders were protesting segregation of interstate bus travel in the South.

May 5

1905

Robert Sengstacke Abbott publishes first issues of the *Chicago Defender* newspaper with an initial press run of only 300 copies. The *Chicago Defender* quickly became the largest circulation nationally syndicated newspaper for the Black community, and Abbott deemed it "the world's greatest weekly." The *Defender* is credited with helping to promote the "Great Migration" of African Americans from the South to the North, with its many editorials touting the opportunities available in the northern United States.

> The Chicago Defender, *a Negro weekly edited by Robert S. Abbott, a native of Georgia who had come north in the Nineties and made good, played a leading role in stimulating the migration. It coaxed and challenged, denounced and applauded. It organized a "Great Northern Drive" and succeeded in getting itself banned from many a southern community. It scoffed at the Southerner's reforms under duress:*
>
> *Turn a deaf ear to everybody . . . . You see they are not lifting their laws to help you. Are they? Have they stopped their Jim Crow cars? Can you buy a Pullman sleeper where you wish? Will they give you a square deal in court yet? Once upon a time we permitted other people to think for us— today we are thinking and acting for ourselves with the result that our "friends" are getting alarmed at our progress. We'd like to oblige these unselfish (?) souls and remain slaves in the South, but to their section of the country we have said, as the song goes, "I hear you calling me," and have boarded the train singing, "Good-bye, Dixie Land."*
>
> Source: *From St. Clair Drake and Horace R. Cayton.* Black Metropolis: A Study of Negro Life in a Northern City. *New York: Harcourt, Brace & World, Inc., 1970, p. 59.*

Books

Ellis, Charlesetta Maria. *Robert S. Abbott's Response to Education for African-Americans via the Chicago Defender, 1909–1940.* Book looks at the political impact of the *Chicago Defender* in the area of education for African Americans.

Ottley, Roi. *The Lonely Warrior: The Life and Times of Robert S. Abbott.* Chicago, IL: H. Regnery Co., 1955. Biography of the founder of the *Chicago Defender.*

Websites

The *Chicago Defender* has a profile of its founder, Robert Sengstacke Abbott. http://www .chicagodefender.com/article-1369-about-us .html.

The "Abbott-Sengstacke Family Papers, 1847– 1997" are available from the Chicago Public library. http://www.chipublib.org/cplbooks movies/cplarchive/archivalcoll/abbott_seng1 .php.

Also Noteworthy

1988

Eugene Marino becomes the first African American to be installed as a Roman Catholic archbishop in the United States.

May 6

1812

The Black nationalist/abolitionist Dr. Martin Robison Delany is born in Charles Town, Virginia. Delany's mother was free, but his father had had to purchase himself out of slavery in 1823. Delany was an ardent abolitionist and published the newspaper *The Mystery* between 1843 and 1846 before also working with Frederick Douglass on the *North Star* in Rochester, New York. In 1850, Delany went to Harvard Medical School and became a medical doctor. In 1859, he went to Africa to search for areas he could promote emigration. When the U.S. Civil War broke out, Delany became the nation's first Black military officer when, on February 8, 1865, he received the commission of Major in the Federal Army. Most importantly, Delany is remembered as "the father of Black Nationalism," the man who coined the phrase "Africa for the Africans," and the man who Frederick Douglass once recalled by stating "I thank God for making me a man, simply, but Delany always thanks Him for making him a Black man."

At the 1854 National Emigration Convention of Colored Men in Cleveland, Delany, who served as chairman of the business committee, delivered the keynote address, "Political Destiny" (reputedly over a seven-hour period). The address, which is presented here in its entirety, counseled African Americans to emigrate to Central or South America, or the Caribbean, on the grounds that white racists would never allow blacks to become U.S. citizens. But much more is going on in the speech than a call for emigration. "Political Destiny" provides acute political commentary on race relations in the United States and an eloquent Pan-African vision of blacks' potentially regenerative role in the Americas.

Source: From Martin Robison Delany and Robert Steven Levine. *Martin R. Delany: A Documentary Reader*. Chapel Hill: University of North Carolina Press, 2003, p. 245.

Books

Delany, Martin Robison. *The Origin of Races and Color*. Mobile, AL: Black Classic Press, 1879. One of Delany's most famous books, it points to the African influences on biblical history, archaeology, and anthropology.

Ullman, Victor. *Martin R. Delany: The Beginnings of Black Nationalism*. Boston, MA: Beacon Press, 1971. Book looks at the legacy of Delany's political ideology.

Websites

A close-up portrait of Martin R. Delany and his Underground Railroad activities. http://explorepahistory.com/displayimage.php?imgId=1-2-3D2.

"A Brief Biography of Martin R. Delany." http://hierographics.org/mrdelanyabbeokuta.htm.

Also Noteworthy

1787

Prince Hall organizes the nation's first Black Masonic lodge in Boston, Massachusetts—African Lodge #459. Hall would go on to become the father of Black Masons in America and a major Black leader in the Northeast.

1991

The Smithsonian Institution approves the creation of the National African American Museum.

May 7

1895

Black jockey James "Soup" Perkins guides Halma to victory in the Kentucky Derby. The 15 year old joined fellow Black jockey Alonzo Clayton as the youngest jockey to ride a Derby winner.

Perhaps more telling than the fall from his horse was the regimen of "flipping" that he, like Murphy, was regularly engaged in, requiring him to eat and then purge so as to get his weight down as low as possible for particular races. Though he only needed to get to 122 pounds for the 1895 Derby, on other occasions he was able, through what were actually bouts of bulimia, to reduce his weight all the way down to 88 pounds, the optimum weight for riding two-year-old horses. Murphy drank champagne to keep his energy level up while depriving his body of the calories and nutrition he would have needed to keep himself healthy. Soup must have served the same purpose for Perkins. In fact, that light meal became such a staple in his diet that it eventually became part of his name as he soon became known as "Little Soup" or, somewhat more formally, James "Soup" Perkins.

Source: From James Robert Saunders and Monica Renae Saunders. *Black Winning Jockeys in the Kentucky Derby*. Jefferson, NC: McFarland, 2003, p. 73.

Books

Bolus, Jim. *Kentucky Derby Stories*. New York: Harper, 2010. Contains a profile of James "Soup" Perkins.

Hotaling, Edward. *The Great Black Jockeys: The Lives and Times of the Men Who Dominated America's First National Sport.* New York: Forum, 1999. Book includes excerpts about African American athletes, like James "Soup" Perkins, who dominated the sport of horse racing.

Websites

Black Horsemen profiles James "Soup" Perkins. http://www.blackhorsemen.com/otherfamilies/Perkins.html.

University of Kentucky Libraries has a short biography of Perkins. http://www.uky.edu/Libraries/nkaa/record.php?note_id=669.

Also Noteworthy

1700

William Penn begins urging his fellow Quakers in Philadelphia to start having monthly meetings advocating for the emancipation of enslaved Africans.

1800

Jean Baptiste Point DuSable sells his estate for $1,200 and returns to Peoria, Illinois. DuSable's prosperous settlement will one day become the city of Chicago.

1878

Joseph F. Winters of Chambersburg, Pennsylvania, receives U.S. Patent No. 203,517 for his improvements in firemen's ladder and fire-escape, which "provide[d] an apparatus that may be readily transported from place to place, and by means of which a series of ladders may be expeditiously raised to the upper stories of a burning building without dismounting said ladders from the truck."

1943

The Liberty Ship *George Washington Carver,* named after the scientist, is launched.

May 8

1951

Thirty-five-year-old Willie McGee is electrocuted in Laurel, Mississippi. McGee was accused of raping a white woman named Willette Hawkins. After an initial trial in 1945 that saw his conviction within the space of two-and-a-half minutes, there was an international pressure for government authorities to declare McGee innocent. After three trials in six years and time spent in various Mississippi jails, McGee was ultimately electrocuted to death in 1951.

> The Daily Worker of 3/27/51 described WILLIE McGEE as a Mississippi Negro victim of a rape frame-up who was seeking an appeal of a death sentence before the US Supreme Court.
>
> According to the Worker of 4/22/51 ... EINSTEIN stated in part: "In the face of the evidence, any unprejudiced human being must find it difficult to believe that this man really committed the rape of which he has been accused. Moreover, the punishment must appear unnaturally harsh to anyone with any sense of justice. [Informant blacked out] advised the WILLIE McGEE was a Negro convicted of rape and executed in the State of Mississippi for this crime.
>
> *Source:* From Fred Jerome. *The Einstein File: J. Edgar Hoover's Secret War Against the World's Most Famous Scientist.* New York, NY: Macmillan, 2003, p. 129.

Books

Heard, Alex. *The Eyes of Willie McGee: A Tragedy of Race, Sex, and Secrets in the Jim Crow South.* New York: Harper, 2010. The book provides a thorough examination of the famed legal case that led to the death of Willie McGee.

Levine, Suzanne and Mary Thom. *Bella Abzug: How One Tough Broad from the Bronx Fought Jim Crow and Joe McCarthy, Pissed off Jimmy Carter, Battled for the Rights of Women and Workers, Rallied Against War and for the Planet, and Shook Up Politics along the Way: An Oral History.* New York: Macmillan, 2007. Oral biography of the activist attorney Bella Abzug includes her account of her work as an attorney for Willie McGee.

Websites

"My Grandfather's Execution" is an audio remembrance of the Willie McGee execution by his granddaughter, Bridgette McGee-Robinson. http://www.npr.org/templates/story/story.php?storyId=126539134.

"A Legal Lynching" is a review of the book *The Eyes of Willie McGee* and provides an overview of the facts in the Willie McGee case. http://www.chapter16.org/content/legal-lynching.

Also Noteworthy

1901

Norman Thomas "Turkey" Stearnes is born in Nashville, Tennessee. Stearnes, who reportedly ran the bases in a waddle similar to a turkey's, was a favored player with the National Negro League's Detroit Stars.

1925

A. Philip Randolph organizes the Brotherhood of Sleeping Car Porters.

1983

Lena Horne is awarded the Springarm Medal for a distinguished career in the field of entertainment.

May 9

1899

John Albert Burr of Agawam, Massuchusetts, receives U.S. Patent No. 624,749 for an improved rotary-blade lawn mower. With this rotary blade, his device was one of the first to replace the reel-type mower, which had always allowed grass to get stuck in the blades.

Then, on May 9, 1899, an African American inventor named John Albert Burr was granted US Patent No. 624749 on yet another improvement in lawn mowers. Unlike the reel mowers, Burr's mower had a rotary blade, which spun parallel to the ground. His design also included traction wheels, making it possible to mow closer to the edge of buildings and walls.

Source: From Marshall Cavendish Corporation. Inventors and Inventions, Volume 1. Tarrytown, NY: Marshall Cavendish, 2007, p. 188.

Books

Ford, Roderick O. *The Evasion of African American Workers*. Bloomington, IN: Xlibris Corporation, 2008. Contains references to Burr's lawn mower invention.

Ikenson, Ben. *Patents: Ingenious Inventions: How They Work and How They Came to Be*. New York, NY: Black Dog & Leventhal Publishers, 2004. The book provides a breakdown of Burr's invention and looks at his patent.

Websites

The design for John Albert Burr's patent is available on the following Website: http://inventors.about.com/library/inventors/bl_John_Albert_Burr.htm.

The BKFK (By Kids For Kids) Website has a short bio of John Albert Burr. http://www.bkfk.com/inventor/burr-johnalbert.asp.

Also Noteworthy

1800

The white abolitionist John Brown, who was so violently opposed to African slavery that he led a raid on the U.S. military arsenal at Harper's Ferry, is born in Torrington, Connecticut.

May 10

1837

Pinckney Benton Stewart (P.B.S.) Pinchback is born in Macon, Georgia. His father, William Pinchback, was a white plantation owner who had fallen in love with Eliza Stewart, who was a manumitted Black woman. The two lived together as husband and wife. Elected as a U.S. congressman from Louisiana, Pinchback became the first African American to become governor of a state and was the first biracial governor of Louisiana. He served for 35 days, from December 9, 1872, to January 13, 1873. P.B.S. Pinchback was Louisiana's 24th governor; his famous grandson was the writer, Jean Toomer.

In 1871, P.B.S. Pinchback, the charismatic black lieutenant-governor of Louisiana, characterized blacks as sandwiched "between the hawk of Republican demogogism and the buzzard of Democratic prejudices." Pinchback was the son of an aristocratic white plantation owner and mulatto slave whose freewheeling gambling and love life involved him in several gun fights and six formal duels. Pinckney was a newspaper publisher, civil rights leader, university founder and lawyer. He served as a delegate to the Louisiana Constitutional Convention of 1867–1868 and the Republican National Conventions of 1868 and 1892. He was the only politician to contend simultaneously for seats in the House of Representatives and the U.S. Senate. He previously was elected to the Louisiana State Senate and served as president of that body. He served as the first black governor ever in the United States and accomplished more in his eight-four years than most men.

Source: From Stanley Turkel. *Heroes of the American Reconstruction: Profiles of Sixteen Educators, Politicians and Activists*. Jefferson, NC: McFarland, 2009, p. 124.

Books

Dawson, Joseph G. *The Louisiana Governors: From Iberville to Edwards*. Baton Rouge, LA: LSU Press, 1990. Contains a chapter on the life and career of P.B.S. Pinchback.

Haskins, James. *Pinckney Benton Stewart Pinchback*. New York, NY: Macmillan, 1973. Biography of the first Black governor of Louisiana.

Websites

Louisiana's Secretary of State has a biography of P.B.S. Pinchback. http://www.sos.louisiana .gov/tabid/383/Default.aspx.

P. B. S. Pinchback, Governor of Louisiana 1872, La-Cemeteries.

. . .www.la-cemeteries.com/. . ./Pinchback, %20Pickney%20Benton%20S.

Also Noteworthy

1944

The *Smith v. Allwright* case, which dealt with attempts by the local Democratic Party to exclude Blacks from primary voting in the state of Texas, is decided. The U.S. Supreme Court found that the whites-only primaries held in Texas were illegal because they violated the Fifteenth Amendment. The NAACP's attorney, Thurgood Marshall, argued the case.

1950

Boston Celtics selects Chuck Cooper as the first African American player drafted to play in the National Basketball Association.

May 11

1895

European classical composer William Grant Still is born to Carrie Lena Fambro Still and William Grant Still in Woodville, Mississippi. Although his father died when he was young, Still's mother moved to Arkansas and was remarried to a man who instilled in him a love for European opera. Still became the first African American to conduct a major U.S. symphony orchestra and is referred to as "The Dean of Afro-American Composers."

In addition to the variety of Still's titles, additional verbal cues appear in his program notes and sometimes in his scores, suggesting more about *the music. The best-known example of this is the Afro-American Symphony, composed in late 1930. One of the descriptions Still provided as a program note for this work has this symphony portraying the "sons of the soil, . . . who have not responded completely to the transforming effect of progress." The symphony may be taken as a record of that transformation as he saw it, progressing from "Longing" and "Sorrow" through "Humor" to "Aspiration," the four subtitles he suggested for its four movements. A blues-type theme is his basic building block for all four movements. Blues were still considered to be disreputable in 1930 because of their "lowly origin"; thus, he felt the need to defend this choice for its true reflection of "the anguish of human hearts" . . . .*

Source: From Catherine Parsons Smith. *William Grant Still*. Champaign, IL: University of Illinois Press, 2008, p. 48.

Books

Reef, Catherine. *William Grant Still: African-American Composer*. Greensboro, NC: Morgan Reynolds, 2003. Biography of Still and his career in music.

Still, Judith Anne, Michael J. Dabrishus, and Carolyn L. Quin. *William Grant Still: A Bio-bibliography*. Santa Barbara, CA: Greenwood Publishing Group, 1996. Contains excerpts from reviews and written material that covered William Still.

Websites

A detailed biography of William Still is available on AfriClassical.com. http://chevalierdesaint georges.homestead.com/still.html.

The Mississippi Writers & Musicians page has a biography of William Still. http://www .mswritersandmusicians.com/musicians/ william–still.html.

May 12

1939

Mamie Katherine Phipps Clark completes her Howard University master's thesis, "The Development of Consciousness of Self

in Negro Preschool Children." Mamie and her husband Kenneth Bancroft Clark, who were both psychologists, published the results of this and their famous doll experiments, both of which revealed a lack of self-esteem in children of African descent. Fifteen years later, their work would be cited in the May 17, 1954, *Brown v. Board of Education* decision as one of many reasons for school desegregation. The Clarks founded the Northside Center for Child Development in Harlem to further their work.

In exploring the language of consciousness of skin color in children three to seven years of age the Clarks, who had joined forces in their research, gave children a coloring test and a dolls test. Children were given a sheet of paper with the drawings of a leaf, an apple, an orange, a mouse, a boy, and a girl plus a box of twenty-four crayons including brown, black, white, yellow, pink, and tan. Each child was asked to color the leaf, orange, apple, and mouse. If the child responded correctly, the child was tested further: "See this little boy? Let us make believe he is you. Color this little boy the color you are." After the child responded, he was told, "Now this is a little girl. Color her the color you like little girls to be." These questions were also, appropriately, asked of girls. In the coloring test, all black children with medium-to-dark-brown skin colored their own figure with either white or a yellow crayon or with some bizarre color like red or green. These children's choice of an inappropriate color for themselves is "an indication of emotional anxiety and conflict in terms of their own skin . . . because they wanted to be white, they pretended to be."

Source: From Agnes N. O'Connell and Nancy Felipe Russo *Women. Psychology: A Bio-bibliographic Sourcebook*. Westport, CT: Greenwood Publishing Group, 1990, p. 68.

Books

Clark, Kenneth B. and Cook, Stuart W. *Prejudice and Your Child*. Middletown, CT: Wesleyan University Press, 1988. The book looks at how racism and race relations in U.S. society affect the mental health of children of all ethnicities.

Markowitz, Gerald E. and David Rosner. *Children, Race, and Power: Kenneth and Mamie Clark's Northside Center*. Charlottesville, VA: University Press of Virginia, 1996. Authors write about the establishment of the Northside Center for Child Development and the struggles its founders waged to keep its doors open as they confronted other major social agencies who belittled the impact of racism and poverty on mental health.

Websites

The Northside Center for Child Development, Inc., which was established by Kenneth and Mamie Clark in 1946, continues to promote "the healthy development of children and families and seeks to empower them to respond constructively to negative societal factors including racism and its related consequences." http://www.northsidecenter.org/v4/aboutus.php.

Columbia University celebrates the Clarks as the first African Americans to receive doctorates in psychology at the school. http://www.c250.columbia.edu/c250_celebrates/remarkable_columbians/kenneth_mamie_clark.html.

1914

Joseph Louis Barrow is born in Lafayette, Alabama; he is the seventh of eight children born to Lillie Reese Barrow and Munroe "Mun" Barrow, a local sharecropper. After the family moved to Detroit in 1924, Joseph started taking part in amateur boxing contests and became known to the world as Joe Louis, the "Brown Bomber." The 6-foot one-and-a-half inch, 197-pound Louis would earn some $5 million during his 12-year reign as the world heavyweight-boxing champion from 1937 through 1949. Louis retired undefeated in 1949, but he came out of retirement twice—in 1950 and 1951—attempting to regain the heavyweight championship, but was unable to win the title.

> *It exploded in other places as well. "Like a gigantic spring unloosed," the black population of "St. Louis' Harlem" began celebrating "after Joe Louis'*

> *hand was raised as heavyweight boxing champion of the world. "They blocked traffic, forming long dancing parades, weaving through the streets shouting "Who won the fight?" and "Who's the champeen?" Thousands of celebrants did much the same thing along South Street in Philadelphia, shouting themselves hoarse cheering for the new champion. The scene was repeated in cities and towns across the country. In Lansing, Michigan, twelve-year-old Malcolm Little swelled with pride during the celebration. Years later, after he had changed his name to Malcolm X and converted to the Nation of Islam, he remembered, "All the Negroes in Lansing, like Negroes everywhere, went wildly happy with the greatest celebration of race pride our generation had ever known. Every Negro boy old enough to walk wanted to be the next Brown Bomber."*

> *Source: From Randy Roberts. Joe Louis: Hard Times Man. New Haven, CT: Yale University Press, 2010, p. 68.*

Books

Bak, Richard. *Joe Louis: The Great Black Hope*. Cambridge, MA: Da Capo Press, 1998. Book looks at Louis's biography and at how his success as a boxer helped to bring down the walls of racism in the United States.

Mead, Chris. *Joe Louis: Black Champion in White America*. Mineola, NY: Dover Publications, 2010. Biography of the heavyweight champion Joe Louis, a.k.a "The Brown Bomber."

Websites

The Estate of Joe Louis established a Website in his honor. http://www.cmgww.com/sports/louis/index.php.

The CyberBoxingZone profiles Joe Louis and provides video clips from his fights. http://cyberboxingzone.com/boxing/jlouis.htm.

Also Noteworthy

1940

Norman Jesse Whitfield, the famed writer and producer of numerous Motown recording hits, is born in Harlem, New York.

Whitfield and lyricist Barrett Strong wrote the song "Cloud Nine" for the Temptations and became one of Motown's lead songwriting duos. Once he left Motown, Whitfield started his own company—Whitfield Records—and produced the successful group, Rose Royce.

1968

Participants in the Poor People's Campaign march on Washington, DC.

May 13

1989

George Augustus Stallings becomes the first archbishop and founder of the Imani Temple African-American Catholic Congregation, a group that broke away from the Roman Catholic Church and was designed to cater to the needs of Black parishioners. The Imani Temple permits its priests to choose between being celibate or not and allows for women priests. Stallings was born to George Augustus, Sr., and Dorothy Stallings (née Smith) in New Bern, North Carolina.

After 1970, African Americans in most mainstream denominations were faced with an identity crisis, in that they felt distant and outside of the religious culture of what was defined by some as "authentic" black American Christianity. As they struggled to find themselves in an everchanging society, modifications were made in the preaching, music, polity, liturgy, and patterns of congregational life. In 1989, Father George Augustus Stallings, pastor of a Catholic church in Washington, D.C., introduced the "African-American Catholic Congregation" at a service held at the Howard University School of Law. At least four thousand people attended the ceremony, which included an African-based liturgy and chants to African saints and ancestors. Father Stallings was suspended and later excommunicated for violating the laws of the Catholic Church. Stallings created quite an uproar with his charges of racism in the Catholic Church and the subsequent creation of the Imani

Temple. During the 1990s, his black Catholic congregation spread to a number of cities, including Baltimore, Philadelphia, Richmond, New Orleans, and Columbia, South Carolina.

Source: From Bettye Collier-Thomas. *Jesus, Jobs and Justic: African American Women and Religion*. New York, NY: Random House Digital, Inc., 2010, p. 484.

Books

Alexander, Estrelda Y. *Black Fire: One Hundred Years of African American Pentecostalism*. Downers Grove, IL: InterVarsity Press, 2011. Book includes a long look at the reasons behind the creation of the Imani Temple.

Lawrence, Beverly Hall. *Reviving the Spirit: A Generation of African Americans Goes Home to Church*. Jackson, TN: Grove Press, 1997. Author looks at the rise of African American Pentecostals and includes information about the founding of the Imani Temple.

Websites

The Defining Moment features an interview with Rev. Stallings. http://www.defining moment.tv/defining-moment-shows/index -218.html.

The *Chicago Tribune* article "Renegade Spirit" profiles Rev. Stallings. http://articles.chicago tribune.com/1989-07-16/features/89021706 85_1_american-catholic-stallings-jr-father -stallings.

Also Noteworthy

1950

Stevland Hardaway Morris is born Stevland Hardaway Judkins to Calvin Judkins and Lula Mae Hardaway in Saginaw, Michigan. As the singer/songwriter Stevie Wonder, he was a child prodigy who, although blind from birth, was initially signed to record under the Motown label at a mere 11 years of age. More than just an entertainer, Stevie Wonder's work as a political activist led to his work with Coretta Scott King in advocating the creation of Martin Luther King, Jr., Day as a U.S. federal holiday; Wonder notably released the 1980 song "Happy Birthday" to promote the cause.

May 14

1923

Southern California–based architect Paul Revere Williams became the first African American member of the Southern California chapter of the American Institute of Architects and in 1957 became the first African American elected to the AIA College of Fellows. Williams famously designed important African American institutions like the 28th Street YMCA, the Second Baptist Church, and Los Angeles' First A.M.E. Church. But he also designed the homes of famous white celebrities like Desi Arnaz and Lucille Ball and Frank Sinatra's "Trousdale" estate.

> . . . Paul Revere Williams, a Los Angeles native, was one of the foremost commercial and domestic architects of southern California and the first African-American architect to be admitted as a fellow in the American Institute of Architects. Williams graduated from the University of Southern California in 1919, became a licensed architect in 1921, and opened his own firm just a year later. His numerous commissions to design homes for Hollywood celebrities led to his nickname, "the Architect to the Stars." His clients included such motion picture and television stars as Lon Chaney, Bill "Bojangles" Robinson, Tyrone Power, and, in later decades, Frank Sinatra, Lucille Ball and Desi Arnaz, and Zsa Zsa Gabor. Over the course of his long and productive career, Williams designed close to 3,000 homes, commercial buildings, and government structures and became one of the most successful African-American architects of the twentieth century.
>
> Source: From Kathleen Morgan Drowne and Patrick Huber. The 1920s. Westport, CT: Greenwood Publishing Group, 2004, p. 92.

Books

Hudson, Karen E. *Paul R. Williams, Architect: A Legacy of Style*. New York, NY: Rizzoli, 2000. The niece of Williams, the author writes about his life and the challenges he faced as the first prominent African American architect.

Williams, Paul R. *The Small Home of Tomorrow*. Santa Monica, CA: Hennessey & Ingalls, 2006. Williams's first book, originally published in 1945, provides his philosophy on the small-house format.

Websites

The Paul Revere Williams Project promotes knowledge and scholarship about Williams's life and work. http://www.paulrwilliams project.org/.

The American Institute of Architects has an archival page dedicated to Williams's correspondence with the organization. http://communities.aia.org/sites/hdoaa/wiki/Wiki%20Pages/ahd1048713.aspx.

Also Noteworthy

1897

Jazz saxophonist and clarinetist Sidney Bechet is born in New Orleans, Louisiana, and grows up in the city's 7th Ward. Bechet was a notably forceful saxophonist and was one of the first to record New Orleans-style Dixieland jazz music.

1970

The Jackson State Tragedy takes place when some 100 students on the campus of Mississippi's Jackson State College gather for a protest just 10 days after the killings at Kent State. After holding antiwar and antiracism protests into the early morning, Jackson city police and Mississippi state police decided to disperse the crowd. As they shot into the area, bullets ended up killing a 21-year-old pre-law student named Phillip Layfayette

Gibbs and a 17-year-old high school student named James Earl Green.

May 15

1916

Seventeen-year-old Texas farmhand Jesse Washington is dragged from a Waco, Texas, courtroom, lynched, mutilated, and burned to death. The murder of Washington was so horrific, that it was known as the "Waco Horror"; it became one of the central cases the National Association for the Advancement of Colored People used to organize against the use of lynch laws.

> *Now that they had their chance, it seemed that nearly every man in Waco wanted to take his turn at Jesse Washington. Along the way, people in the crowd beat him with shovels, bricks, clubs, and anything else that came to hand. One paper reports that "a yellow negro boy who was raised here in Waco" hit Jesse on the head and cried, "You're getting just what's coming to you, you d——— rascal." Despite their delicacy in not printing words like damned in full, the Waco newspapers spared their readers none of the details of the lynching. Such details became as much a part of the "folk pornography" of the time as details of rapes.*
>
> *Part of the crowd surged toward the bridge, thinking Jesse would be hanged where Sank Majors had been hanged eleven years earlier, but the ring-leaders already had another plan in mind. Hanging would be too easy a death. They turned on Second Street, to take Jesse to the town square by City Hall and burn him alive. Piles of kindling and wood had been left along the way; dry goods boxes and inflammable material like excelsior seemed to appear of out of nowhere.*
>
> *Source:* From Patricia Bernstein. *The First Waco Horror: The Lynching of Jesse Washington and the Rise of the NAACP.* College Station, TX: Texas A&M University Press, 2006, p. 108.

Books

Durocher, Kristina. *Raising Racists: The Socialization of White Children in the Jim Crow South.*

Lexington, KY: University Press of Kentucky, 2011. Book looks at how the socialization of white children during Jim Crow led to lynchings like that of Jesse Washington.

Waldrep, Christopher. *Racial Violence on Trial: A Handbook with Cases, Laws, and Documents.* Santa Barbara, CA: ABC-CLIO, 2001. Contains an overview of the Washington case and trial and looks at the resulting lynching.

Websites

National Public Radio has an online interview regarding the lynching, "Waco Recalls a 90-Year-Old 'Horror'." http://www.npr.org/templates/story/story.php?storyId=5401868.

Washington is remembered by the Texas State Historical Association in an article, "Jesse Washington Lynching." http://www.tsha online.org/handbook/online/articles/jcj01.

Also Noteworthy

1820

U.S. Congress declares foreign slave trade an act of piracy, punishable by death.

1946

Camilla Williams appears as Madame Butterfly with the New York City Opera.

2007

Yolanda King, eldest daughter of the Rev. Martin Luther King, Jr., and Coretta Scott King, dies of heart failure. During her life, Yolanda King was a motivational speaker and occasionally worked as an actress: she famously took on the role of Rosa Parks in the 1978 television miniseries *King.*

May 16

1929

John Conyers, Jr., is born in Highland Park, Michigan. Conyers was elected to the U.S. House of Representatives in 1964 and re-elected 22 times. As a congressman, Conyers served as Chairman of the House Government Operations Committee from 1989 to 1995 and Chairman of the House Judiciary Committee from 2007 to 2011. In 1969, Conyers was one of the 13 founding members of the Congressional Black Caucus (CBC), and he introduced the Martin Luther King Holiday Act of 1983, the bill that made Martin Luther King's birthday a national holiday.

For a number of years Michigan was represented in the Congress by a single black member, Charles Diggs, Jr. By 1956 Diggs was one of three blacks "sitting in the House of Representatives" who "were wielding their seniority effectively," the other two being the venerable William Dawson of Chicago and the flamboyant Adam Clayton Powell of New York. In the latter part of 1963, the state legislature was compelled by the U.S. Supreme Court's apportionment decisions to redraw the boundaries of congressional district lines. Before the new district boundaries were drawn, however, the firm of George Crockett and Maurice Sugar encouraged a young black lawyer to enter a primary contest against an incumbent congressman, Lucien Nedzi. The district had not yet been drawn, but it was expected to contain if not a majority of blacks, at least a sufficient number to make the candidacy worth the effort. Thus, a year before the election, John Conyers, Jr., began a campaign to unseat an incumbent white congressman in a congressional district not yet created.

Source: From Dudley W. Buffa. Union Power and American Democracy: The UAW and the Democratic Party, 1935–72. Ann Arbor, MI: University of Michigan Press, 1984, p. 148.

Books

Schraff, Anne. *Rosa Parks*. Costa Mesa, CA: Saddleback Educational Publishing, 2008. This biography of Rosa Parks includes a look at how, because she respected John Conyers, she convinced Martin Luther King, Jr., to make a speech for Conyers's campaign.
Evans, Janet Lynn. *"We'll Take Care of the Counting*★*": A Cultural, Rhetorical and Critical*

Analysis of Electronic Voting Technology. Boulder, CO: University of Colorado at Boulder, 2007. Book notes Rep. Conyers's work regarding investigating the problems in the state of Ohio during the 2004 Presidential elections.

Websites

Rep. John Conyers maintains an office Website http://conyers.house.gov/index.cfm?FuseAction=About.Biography.
The *Chicago Tribune* maintains a page dedicated to news and information about Rep. John Conyers, Jr. http://www.chicagotribune.com/topic/politics/john-jr-conyers-PEPLT001287.topic.

Also Noteworthy

1840

James Milton Turner is born enslaved in St. Louis, Missouri. He became a politician after the Civil War and worked for the Missouri Department of Education, where he helped establish over 30 schools for African Americans. In 1871, President Ulysses S. Grant appointed Turner to serve as U.S. Minister to Liberia, making him the first-ever African American consul. After returning from Liberia in 1878, Turner helped create the Colored Emigration Aid Association, which supported African Americans as they migrated from the South.

1883

Very first issue of the weekly Detroit *Plaindealer*—Detroit, Michigan's first African American newspaper—is published. The newspaper becomes known for emphasizing use of the term "Afro-American," instead of "Negro," to point to the ethnic origin of people of African descent.

1887

Laura Wheeler Waring is born in Hartford, Connecticut. As a teacher and painter,

Waring founded the State Normal School's art and music departments at Cheyney University and served as the lead teacher for 30 years.

1927

William Harry Barnes becomes the first African American certified by any American surgical board when the American Board of Otolaryngology certifies him. Otolaryngologists are doctors who treat diseases and disorders of the ear, nose, and throat (ENT).

1929

The jazz singer Betty Carter is born under the name Lillie Mae Jones in Flint, Michigan. Carter was raised in Detroit and studied piano at the Detroit. Her cool, sexy voice led Carter to be featured with jazz greats like Charlie Parker and Ray Charles. In 1980, the documentary film *But Then, She's Betty Carter* looked at her career, and, in 1997, President Bill Clinton awarded her the National Medal of Arts.

1966

Stokely Carmichael is named chairman of the Student Nonviolent Coordinating Committee (SNCC).

1966

Janet Damita Jo Jackson is born in Gary, Indiana. As an actress and recording artist, Janet Jackson initially performed with her famous family band the Jackson Five and later became a solo artist.

1966

Thurman Lee Thomas is born in Houston, Texas. Thomas played with the National Football League's Buffalo Bills and was inducted into the Pro Football Hall of Fame in 2007.

1979

Asa Phillip Randolph, civil rights leader and founder of the Brotherhood of Sleeping Car Porters, dies.

1990

The singer and dancer Sammy Davis, Jr., dies of lung cancer after years as a smoker. Davis was 64 years old.

May 17

1925

Ira Tucker, Sr., is born in Spartanburg, South Carolina. Tucker joined the a cappella-style gospel group the Dixie Hummingbirds at age 13 and served as their lead singer for the next 70 years, throughout the rest of his life. The Dixie Hummingbirds gained fame with songs like "Thank You for One More Day," "Trouble in My Way," "I Just Can't Help It," and "Bedside of a Neighbor." The Dixie Hummingbirds were inducted into the Gospel Music Hall of Fame in 2000.

What group anywhere has the track record of the Dixie Hummingbirds? Since 1939, the Birds have been the favorites of gospel quartet fans. For versatility, imagination, and harmony few groups play in their league. Their bass, William Bobo, is the lowest, their guitarist, Howard Carroll, gospel's answer to B.B. King. But the Bird's most powerful member is their lead singer, Ira Tucker. Tucker is the virtuoso of quartet. He looks to seduce his audience vocally. So, within a few bars of his opening note, he will scoop down between beats in a dizzying combine of wit and breath. It takes a split second before the audience responds, and then orgiastic "Oohs" and "Help yourself, son" inform Tucker he's home safe.

Source: From Anthony Heilbut. *The Gospel Sound: Good News and Bad Times*. Milwaukee, WI: Hal Leonard Corporation, 2002, p. 37.

Books

Darden, Robert and Bob Darden. *People Get Ready!: A New History of Black Gospel Music*. New York, NY: Rizzoli, 2000. Book contains a profile of the Dixie Hummingbirds.

Zolten, Jerry. *Great God A'Mighty! The Dixie Hummingbirds: Celebrating the Rise of Soul Gospel Music*. Santa Monica, CA: Oxford University Press, 2003. Williams's first book, originally published in 1945, provides his philosophy on the small house format. Book looks at the history of the Dixie Hummingbirds, from their start in Greenville, South Carolina, to their international fame as Grammy-award winning gospel singers.

Websites

The Dixie Hummingbirds' "Our Prayer For Peace" is on Vimeo. http://vimeo.com/481575.

The Vocal Group Hall of Fame features information about the Dixie Hummingbirds. http://www.vocalgroup.org/inductees/dixie_hummingbirds.html.

Also Noteworthy

1875

Oliver Lewis wins the first Kentucky Derby riding the thoroughbred horse *Aristides*.

1903

Birthdate of James "Cool Papa" Bell. Bell was born in Starksville, Mississippi, and was a famed baseball outfield player with the Negro National Leagues' St. Louis Stars.

1954

U.S. Supreme Court declares segregation in public schools unconstitutional in the *Brown v. Board of Education* decision.

1957

The Prayer Pilgrimage for Freedom brings some 250,000 demonstrators to Washington, DC, to demonstrate for the protection of civil rights for African Americans.

May 18

1896

U.S. Supreme Court upholds the doctrine of "separate but equal" education and public accommodations in the *Plessy v. Ferguson* case. The *Plessy v. Ferguson* case was initiated by Homer Plessy, a 30-year-old man who worked as a shoemaker in Louisiana.

> *Plessy v. Ferguson tested the constitutionality of this recent trend in Southern legislation. Plessy was a mulatto who, on June 7, 1892, bought a first-class ticket on the East Louisiana Railway for a trip from New Orleans to Covington, Louisiana, and sought to be seated in the "white" coach. Upon conviction of a violation of the 1890 statute, he appealed to the Supreme Court of Louisiana, which upheld his conviction, and finally to the U.S. Supreme Court, which pronounced the Louisiana law constitutional, on May 18, 1896.*
>
> *Source*: From Paula S. Rothenberg. *Race, Class, and Gender in the United States: An Integrated Study*. New York, NY: Macmillan, 2006, p. 570.

Books

Anderson, Wayne. *Plessy v. Ferguson: Legalizing Segregation*. Santa Monica, CA: The Rosen Publishing Group, 2003. Williams first book, originally published in 1945, provides his philosophy on the small house format.

Thomas, Brook. *Plessy v. Ferguson: A Brief History with Documents*. New York, NY: Bedford Books, 1997. Book retells the story of *Plessy v. Ferguson* with supporting documentation.

Websites

Plessy v. Ferguson is summarized at http://www.watson.org/~lisa/blackhistory/post-civilwar/plessy.html.

Looks at how the U.S. Supreme Court's upholding of Louisiana state law upholding "separate but equal." http://www.ourdocuments.gov/doc.php?flash=true&doc=52.

May 19

1925

Malcolm X is born under the name Malcolm Little in Omaha, Nebraska. As a Pan-African and religious activist, Malcolm X became the charismatic spokesman for the Nation of Islam. After breaking with the Nation of Islam, Malcolm made the journey to Mecca, Saudi Arabia, and took the name El-Hajj Malik El Shabazz. Back in the United States, El-Hajj Malik El Shabazz formed the Muslim Mosque, Inc., on March 12, 1964 (just four days after leaving the Nation of Islam), and he formed the Organization of Afro-American Unity (OAAU) on June 28, 1964. Malcolm X was assassinated on February 21, 1965, at Harlem's Audobon Ballroom.

> The civil-rights struggle involves the black man taking his case to the white man's court. But when he fights it at the human-rights level, it is a different situation. It opens the door to take Uncle Sam to the world court. The black man doesn't have to go to court to be free. Uncle Sam should be taken to court and made to tell why the black man is not free in a so-called free society. Uncle Sam should be taken into the United Nations and charged with violating the UN charter of human rights.
>
> Source: From Malcolm X and George Breitman. *Malcolm X Speaks: Selected Speeches and Statements.* New York, NY: Grove Press, 1965, pp. 53–54.

Books

Malcolm X with Alex Haley. *Autobiography of Malcolm X.* New York, NY: Penguin Popular Classics, 2007. Classic autobiography tells how Malcolm went to jail and was born again through the teachings of the Nation of Islam.

Terrill, Robert. *Malcolm X: Inventing Radical Judgment.* East Lansing, MI: MSU Press, 2004. Author looks at the ideological formation of Malcolm X's thought.

Websites

Comprehensive Website on the life and legacy of Malcolm X. http://www.brothermalcolm.net/.

The Malcolm X & Dr. Betty Shabazz Memorial & Educational Center is established on the site of the Audobon Ballroom. www.theshabazzcenter.net/.

Also Noteworthy

1918

The lynching of Mary Turner—who was eight months pregnant and 20 years old—takes place in Brooks County, Georgia. Mary was lynched after protesting and threatening to go to police authorities and report who had lynched her husband, Hayes Turner.

1965

Patricia R. Harris is named ambassador to Luxembourg—she is the first African American woman named to serve as an ambassador.

2006

The Uptown Lounge at Minton's Playhouse opened in the same building as the original Minton's Playhouse, the jazz club at 210 West 118th Street in Harlem, New York, where BeBop was born.

May 20

1952

The boxer Marvin Hagler is born in Newark, New Jersey. He famously had his name legally changed to Marvelous Marvin Hagler.

> "Marvelous" [Marvin Hagler]. One of the greatest of his era, Marvin Hagler originally had a name as frill-free as his style. That is, until he decided he wanted to be known as "Marvelous" as in

"awe-inspiring." So, starting in the middle of his career, he insisted on being introduced as "Marvelous" Marvin Hagler. But before his 1982 title defense against William "Caveman" Lee, one of the ABC-TV directors snapped, "If he want to be announced as 'Marvelous' Marvin, let him change his name." And so, after dispatching of Lee in 67 seconds, Marvin headed down to the registrar's office to change his name officially to Marvelous Marvin Hagler, his nickname becoming part of his legal name.

Source: From Bert Randolph Sugar and Teddy Atlas. *The Ultimate Book of Boxing Lists.* New York, NY: Running Press, 2011, p. 15.

Books

Arnold, Peter. *All-Time Greats of Boxing.* New York, NY: Gallery Books/Simon & Schuster, 1987. Contains a profile of the "Master of Disaster," Marvelous Marvin Hagler.

Pacheco, Ferdie, Mills Lane, and Jim Moskovitz. *The 12 Greatest Rounds of Boxing: The Untold Stories.* Kingston, NY: Total/Sports Illustrated, 2000. Book looks at the famous April 15, 1985, fight between Marvelous Marvin Hagler and Thomas "Hitman" Hearns.

Websites

Marvelous Marvin Hagler has his own Website www.marvelousmarvin.com.

The International Boxing Hall of Fame profiles Marvin Hagler. http://www.ibhof.com/pages/about/inductees/modern/hagler.html.

Also Noteworthy

1704

The French colonist Elias Neau, who was a religious Huguenot, establishes the Society for the Propagation of the Gospel. The Society was designed to educate enslaved Africans and indigenous people and teach them Christian values. Neau felt that Indians and Africans were being worked to death without anyone having concern for their souls.

1910

Benjamin Sherman Crothers—the actor and singer later widely known as "Scatman" Crothers—is born in Terre Haute, Indiana.

1958

Robert Nelson Cornelius Nix, Sr., is elected to Congress as the Democratic Party representative for the 2nd district of Pennsylvania, which covers Philadelphia, Pennsylvania. Nix, Sr., was Pennsylvania's first African American congressman and the 28th African American to serve in the U.S. Congress; he served from 1958 to 1980. His son, Robert Nix, Jr., served as a Pennsylvania Supreme Court Chief Justice for 24 years.

1961

U.S. Attorney General Robert Kennedy sends U.S. Marshals into Montgomery, Alabama, to restore order after Student Non-Violent Coordinating Committee "Freedom Riders" is beaten. The Freedom Riders had planned to ride from Washington, DC, to New Orleans, Louisiana, but were stopped by two instances of mob violence.

May 21

1904

Thomas Wright Waller, the jazz musician later famously known as "Fats" Waller, is born to Adaline Locket Waller and the Reverend Edward Martin Waller, who was a Baptist minister. Fats Waller was born and raised in Harlem, New York, and began playing piano and organ at a young age. Waller became famous playing swing music and writing songs like "Honeysuckle Rose" and "Ain't Misbehavin'."

Johnson, Razaf, Edgar Dowell, and Spencer Williams were the principal lyricists with whom Fats wrote during these formative years. There were others, of course, and on nearly five hundred *known compositions credited to Fats Waller, publishers' and producers' names appear as co-composers. These latter were, as often as not, courtesy credits, or given in order to obtain publication fees. In addition, much material written by Waller has never been published under his name. Rumour persists, and indeed Fats confirmed it during his lifetime, that at least three of the main hits of the Twenties are in reality Fats' own compositions, picked off publishers' shelves by hack writers and turned into great hits. This cannot be passed off as mere hearsay; it is due to the fact that Waller sold many tunes for trivial amounts, often surrendering all subsequent rights for ready cash. Andy Razaf can well remember the days when his partner would walk into a music office and say, 'I'll write you a song for $2.50.' Whatever he needed at that moment was to him sufficient payment, and buyers were not normally anxious to jack up prices for his benefit. When, later in his career, he did begin to realize the tremendous returns that were being made from these cheaply sold compositions of his, he began to re-appraise his value to himself and others. Harry Link and Irving Berlin were always eminently fair with Fats, the former claiming to have given him his first royalty contract for a song. 'Fats,' he said, 'didn't even know what it was to sell a song and continue to reap benefits from it, before I put him wise.' Further evidence in support of his claim to authorship of many 'anonymous' hits lies in the fact that many of them were written in the years when he and Razaf were partners. They did the scores for whole shows both in Harlem and on Broadway, for this was the time when he and Andy were selling melodies right and left. It is impossible, of course, to list these lost songs by name but it is fortunate that he left behind him compositions which match and, it is hoped, even surpass the stolen ones. Such tunes as Honeysuckle Rose, Ain't Misbehavin', and Black And Blue—all from the same period—will surely perpetuate the memory of their composer when the men who performed petty thievery on his works will be long gone and forgotten.*

Source: From Ed Kirkeby. *Ain't Misbehavin': The Story of Fats Waller.* Cambridge, MA: Da Capo Press, 1975, pp. 92–93.

Books

Shipton, Alyn. *Fats Waller: The Cheerful Little Earful.* Harrisburg, PA: Continuum, 2002. Biography of Waller argues for greater recognition of his musical talents.

Taylor, Stephen. *Fats Waller on the Air: The Radio Broadcasts and Discography.* Lanham, MD: Scarecrow Press, 2006. Book looks at Fats Waller's radio and television broadcasts, which began when he was as young as 19.

Websites

Thomas "Fats" Waller commemorative site www.fatswaller.org.

Fats Waller's "Your Feet's Too Big" is on YouTube. http://www.youtube.com/watch?v=in1eK3x1PBI.

Also Noteworthy

1917

Leo Pinckney becomes the first African American drafted to serve in the U.S. Army for World War I.

1975

Lowell W. Perry is confirmed as chairman of the Equal Opportunity Commission (EEOC). Perry was nominated to serve by President Gerald Ford; he became the EEOC's sixth chairman and served from May 27, 1975, through May 15, 1976.

May 22

1921

Shuffle Along, the first successful African American musical starring an all-Black cast, opens on Broadway in New York City. *Shuffle Along* had some 504 performances at the 63rd Street Music Hall and ran from May 23, 1921, through July 15, 1922. The team of Eubie Blake and Noble Sissle wrote the music and lyrics.

Blake and Co.'s musical comedy made history in several ways. Most obviously, since black musicals were usually large-cast shows, Shuffle Along and its successors provided steady, well-paying work for large numbers of African American performers on the mainstream New York stage. This employment afforded a real opportunity for numerous blacks to achieve true recognition, even stardom, in a theatre world dominated by whites both on stage and in the audience. Further, the success of Shuffle Along "legitimized the black musical. It proved to [white] producers and theatre managers that audiences would pay to see black talent on Broadway. As a result, Shuffle Along spawned a series of imitators, and black musicals became a Broadway staple" ... And audiences were paying the same top dollar ($3.00) for the best seats to black shows as they were for other musicals.

Source: From John Bush Jones. Our Musicals, Ourselves: A Social History of the American Musical Theatre. Lebanon, NH: UPNE, 2003, p. 70.

Books

Bloom, Ken. *Broadway: Its History, People, and Places: An Encyclopedia.* New York, NY: Taylor & Francis, 2004. Book includes information on the performances of *Shuffle Along.*

Stearns, Marshall Winslow and Jean Stearns. *Jazz Dance. The Story of American Vernacular Dance.* Cambridge, MA: Da Capo Press, 1968. Book contains information on the dance styles featured in musicals like *Shuffle Along.*

Websites

The controversies around *Shuffle Along* and its featured songs are presented at http://www.musicals101.com/1920bway3.htm.

The Internet Broadway Database profiles *Shuffle Along.* http://www.ibdb.com/production.php?id=9073.

Also Noteworthy

1948

The novelist and poet, Claude McKay, dies of heart failure in Chicago, Illinois. McKay was a poet, novelist, and journalist and became a major figure in the Harlem Renaissance.

May 23

1900

Sgt. William H. Carney is awarded the Congressional Medal of Honor for Valor for his bravery at Fort Wagner, SC, in 1863. Carney served with the 54th Massachusetts Regiment during the Civil War battle. Carney is the first African American ever awarded this medal.

Two of the most desperate battles of the war in which coloured troops were engaged were the assault of Fort Wagner, July 18, 1863, in which the Fifty-fourth Massachusetts, the first regiment of coloured soldiers to be recruited in the North, was engaged, and the battle of Honey Hill, South Carolina, November 30, 1864, in which the Fifty-fifth Massachusetts, the second coloured regiment raised in the North, was engaged. It was in the assault of Fort Wagner that the gallant Colonel Robert G. Shaw fell dead at the head of his Negro regiment and mingled some of the best blood of New England with that of these black men whom he had volunteered to lead in the fight for the freedom of their race. It was in this same battle that Sergeant William H. Carney of the Fifty-fourth Massachusetts, though wounded in the head and in the shoulder and in both legs, carried the National flag of his regiment across the open field which separated him from safety, where he handed it over with the words which made him famous: "Dey got me boys, but de old flag neber touched de groun!"

Source: From Booker T. Washington. The Story of the Negro: The Rise of the Race from Slavery, Volume 1. New York, NY: Doubleday, Page & Co., 1909, p. 328.

Books

Cashin, Herschel V. *Under Fire with the Tenth U.S. Cavalry.* Manchester, NH: Ayer Publishing, 1969. Book looks at the famous Fort

Wagner battle and Sergeant William H. Carney's actions to hold the flag high.

Coffin, Charles Carleton. *Stories of Our Soldiers: War Reminiscences, Volume 1.* New York, NY: Taylor & Francis, 2004. Book includes an excerpt profiling Sergeant William H. Carney.

Websites

William H. Carney: 54th Massachusetts Soldier and First Black U.S. Medal of Honor Recipient. http://www.historynet.com/william-h -carney-54th-massachusetts-soldier-and-first -black-us-medal-of-honor-recipient.htm.

Survivor of Famous Union Regiment Became First Black Recipient of Medal of Honor. http://www.military.com/Content/More Content?file=ML_carney_bkp.

Also Noteworthy

1952

Wendell Oliver Scott of Danville, Virginia, breaks the color line in Southern stock car racing when he wins the National Association for Stock Car Auto Racing's (NASCAR's) "Grand National" event.

May 24

1963

African American celebrities meet with U.S. Attorney General Robert Kennedy to talk about the government's civil rights policies. Kennedy asked the writer James Baldwin to invite prominent Black celebrities to the meeting.

In an effort to gauge the pulse of the black community, Robert Kennedy asked Baldwin to organize a meeting with leading cultural and literary figures. Baldwin dutifully rounded up a guest list that included Harry Belafonte, Lena Horne, Lorraine Hansberry, Professor Kenneth Clark, and Clarence Jones, King's personal attorney.

Designed as a discreet way for Kennedy to assess the collective black psyche through

Baldwin's celebrity proxies, the May 24, 1963 encounter devolved into a raucous shouting match over the progress of the Kennedy administration's civil rights policies and the limits of black patience....

Source: From Peniel E. Joseph. Waiting 'til the Midnight Hour: A Narrative History of Black Power in America. New York: Henry Holt/Owl Books, 2006, p. 72.

Books

Kennedy, Robert F., Edwin O. Guthman, and Jeffrey Shulman. *Robert Kennedy, in His Own Words: The Unpublished Recollections of the Kennedy Years.* New York: Bantam, 1988. Contains Robert Kennedy's reflections on his Civil Rights meeting with Baldwin, Lorraine Hansberry, Harry Belafonte, and Lena Horne.

Russell, Dick and Alvin F. Poussaint. *Black Genius: Inspirational Portraits of America's Black Leaders.* New York: Skyhorse Publishing Inc., 2009. Book contains a look at the meeting between Baldwin, Kennedy, and members of the African American community.

Websites

James Baldwin's "A Soul on Fire" looks at the meeting with Robert Kennedy. http://www.seanohalloran.com/jbasof/Story.html.

Water Man Spouts recalls the historic Baldwin-Kennedy meeting. http://h2oman.blogspot .com/2008/06/listening.html.

Also Noteworthy

1854

Lincoln University, Pennsylvania, the first African American college in the United States, is founded by Presbyterians.

1916

The Lincoln Motion Picture Company is founded; it is the first film company controlled by Black filmmakers. Created by the actor Noble Johnson and his brother George Johnson, the Lincoln Motion Picture Company was incorporated in January 1917 and remained in operation until 1921.

1944

The rhythm and blues/soul singer Patti LaBelle is born Patricia Louise Holt Edwards in Philadelphia, Pennsylvania.

1951

Washington, DC, Municipal Court of Appeals outlaws segregation in restaurants.

1991

Harold Abraham McRae, a former left-field outfielder who played with Major League Baseball's Cincinatti Reds and Kansas City Royals for a total of 19 years, is named manager of the Kansas City Royals.

May 25

1926

Miles Dewey Davis III is born in Alton, Illinois, to Cleota Mae (Henry) Davis and Dr. Miles Henry Davis, a dentist. As a jazz trumpeter, Miles Davis was one of the seminal figures in the BeBop and Cool Jazz movements.

His music displayed many contradictions, too. Miles was never either hot or cool: he could be both, or neither. When bebop trumpeters were loud, fast and high, he was quiet, steady, hovering in the middle register. He softened his trumpet with a device—the Harmon mute—which gave his sound a sneaky, inward-facing timbre which could seem tremendously vulnerable one moment, mockingly acerbic the next. He played ballads better than most other musicians, but he never gave his listeners the easy option of a simple, romantic identification with a poignant lyric: whether it was 'My Funny Valentine' or 'Time After Time', he simply adapted the setting to his own

inscrutable thing he did, unwilling to accept even the word 'jazz', yet he refused to admit the anarchy of free jazz and its supposed liberations from imposed rule. He is often thought of as a restrained musician, but he could be bitingly expressive, frequently sounding sour and aggressive, and at many points in his career he played the trumpet with something approaching venom: he made sure that his sound was always the one that cut through to the audience.

Source: From Richard Cook. *It's about That Time: Miles Davis On and Off Record*. New York, NY: Oxford University Press, 2005, p. 132.

Books

Davis, Miles with Quincy Troupe. *Miles, the Autobiography*. New York, NY: Simon & Schuster, 1990. Davis retells the highlights of his musical career.

Szwed, John. *So What: The Life of Miles Davis*. New York, NY: Simon & Schuster, 2004. Biography of Miles Davis looks at the impact and legacy of his musical ideas.

Websites

The Official Miles Davis Site www.milesdavis.com.

Miles Davis at the Isle of Wight '70 "Call It Anything." http://www.dailymotion.com/video/x2njlh_miles-davis-at-the-isle-of-wight-70_music.

Also Noteworthy

1878

Famed tape dancer and actor, Bill "Bojangles" Robinson, is born in Richmond, Virginia.

May 26

1899

Aaron Douglas is born to Aaron and Elizabeth Douglas in Topeka, Kansas. After moving to New York City in 1925, Douglas became the leading proponent of the new, strong, and dignified Harlem Renaissance-style portrayals of African Americans in the visual arts.

> One of the first American painters who can be considered an Africanist, Douglas, during the late 1920s, devoted much of his time to studying the African art then available at a few nearby institutions. The Barnes Foundation in Philadelphia was prominent among these. However, despite his great interest in African art and its cubistic forms, Douglas felt that his knowledge of Africa was too superficial to become the sole focus of his work. He preferred to dedicate himself to painting African Americans, with a new measure of dignity and pride.
>
> Source: From Samella S. Lewis. *African American Art and Artists*. Berkeley, CA: University of California Press, 2003, p. 61.

Books

Kirschke, Amy Helene and Aaron Douglas. *Aaron Douglas: Art, Race, and the Harlem Renaissance*. Jackson, MS: University Press of Mississippi, 1995. Book looks at the strong influence Douglas had on ideas of visual art during the Harlem Renaissance.

Nadell, Martha Jane. *Enter the New Negroes: Images of Race in American Culture*. Cambridge, MA: Harvard University Press, 2004. Book looks at how the imagining of people of African descent changed, particular during the Harlem Renaissance.

Websites

Douglas's work is featured on this site about the Harlem Renaissance. http://robinurton.com /history/Harlem.htm.

The Art Institute of Chicago profiles Douglas and looks at his "Study for Aspects of Negro Life: The Negro in an African Setting." http://www.artic.edu/artaccess/AA_AfAm/ pages/AfAm_3.shtml.

Also Noteworthy

1961

Marvin Cook is named ambassador to the Niger Republic; he is the first Black envoy named by the Kennedy Administration to an African nation.

May 27

1849

Thomas Greene Wiggins is born to Charity and Mingo Wiggins on a plantation in Harris County, Georgia. Thomas and his parents were enslaved, and together they were sold to General James Neil Bethune of Columbus, Georgia. Thomas was blind from birth and an autistic savant, who was intuitively attracted to making music on the piano. By age eight, Gen. Bethune had rented Thomas out as "Blind Tom" and was making estimates of $100,000 a year from Blind Tom's concerts and compositions. Thomas Wiggins made money for the Bethune family for some 40 years before becoming incapacited by a heart attack.

> A career in chains? Perhaps. Once Tom's master discovered that the worthless runt he had purchased out of pity was a musical prodigy, he lost no time in licensing the eight-year-old to a Barnum-style showman, under whom Tom raised thousands of dollars for the Confederate War effort. Emancipation failed to deliver Tom from the shackles of slavery, his master's son merely morphing into the role of guardian and manager. Legally adjudged insane, Tom spent much of his life in perpetual motion, performing to packed houses across the continent—the profits of which financed his guardian's extravagant lifestyle.
>
> Source: From Deirdre O'Connell. *The Ballad of Blind Tom, Slave Pianist*. New York, NY: Overlook Hardcover, 2009, p. 10.

Books

Blair, Montgomery. *The Marvelous Musical Prodigy, Blind Tom, the Negro Boy Pianist*. Ithaca, NY: Cornell University Library, 1867. Manuscript of articles about Blind Tom Wiggins and his concerts.

Southall, Geneva Handy. *Blind Tom, the Black Pianist-Composer: Continually Enslaved*. Lanham, MD: Scarecrow Press, 2002. Author looks as the enslavement of Wiggins and his life as a concert pianist.

Websites

Africlassical profiles Thomas Wiggins and has a link to one of his song compositions. http://chevalierdesaintgeorges.homestead.com/wiggins.html.

The Columbus State University Archives Website has archival information concerning Blind Tom. http://archives.columbusstate.edu/findingaids/mc169.php.

Also Noteworthy

1837

Cheyney University, the oldest institution of higher education for African American students, is founded.

1861

The educator, Victoria E. Matthews, is born in New York. Matthews, who lived at 9 Murray Street in Manhattan, was a vocal proponent of African American civil rights and served as the editor of *The Woman's Era of Boston*.

1919

Cosmetics manufacturer Madame C.J. Walker dies.

May 28

1831

Eliza Ann Gardner is born in New York City but raised in Boston, Massachusetts. Gardner worked as a dressmaker and allowed her home (at 20 North Anderson Street in Boston) to serve as a "station" on the Underground Railroad prior to the Civil War. A relative of W. E. B. DuBois, Gardner often spoke as an abolitionist alongside Frederick Douglass, Sojourner Truth, and William Lloyd Garrison. Gardner was a member of Boston's African Methodist Episcopal Zion Church, and she served as the founder of the A. M. E. Zion Missionary Movement. She later wrote the "Historical Sketch of the A. M. E. Zion Church of Boston."

> *Eliza Ann Gardner's long life spanned nine turbulent decades, during which she was involved in many of the most pressing causes of her time. She was born in New York City thirty years before the start of the Civil War and became active in the abolition movement in Boston when she was quite young; the Gardner family home, in fact, was a station on the Underground Railroad. Throughout most of her life she was a member of the African Methodist Episcopal (AME) Zion Church in Boston. As a religious leader, she was influential locally, nationally, and internationally. She was known in the denomination as the "Mother" of the AME Zion Missionary Society, which raised money for the first church missionaries to visit Africa, and she also served as vice-president of the society's New England Conference.*
>
> **Source:** From Jessie Carney Smith. *Notable Black American Women*. Bonn, Germany: VNR AG, 1996, p. 239.

Books

Brown, Hallie Quinn. *Homespun Heroines and Other Women of Distinction*. New York, NY: Oxford University Press, 1926. Book profiles Eliza Ann Gardner and her work for African American civil rights.

Walls, William Jacob (Bp.). *The African Methodist Episcopal Zion Church: Reality of the Black Church*. Charlotte, NC: A. M. E. Zion Pub. House, 1974. Contains a profile of Eliza Ann Gardner and looks at her contributions to the A. M. E.'s work.

Websites

Columbus Avenue A. M. E. Zion Church profiles Eliza Ann Gardner. http://columbusaveamez.org/Columbus_Avenue_Website/History__The_Boston_Riots.html.

The Pittsburgh Courier provides a profile of Eliza Gardner. http://courier-pittsburgh.

vlex.com/vid/this-week-in-black-history-21
0031871.

May 29

1973

Thomas J. Bradley is elected to serve as the 37th mayor of Los Angeles, California. Bradley was Los Angeles' first African American mayor; he won election in a landslide victory over incumbent white mayor Sam Yorty with over 56 percent of the vote. The son of Crenner Hawkins and Lee Bradley, Thomas was born in Calvert, Texas, where his father worked as a sharecropper. The family moved to California while Thomas was a youth. Thomas Bradley—who was also the first African American to serve in the Los Angeles City Council—served as Los Angeles' mayor for five terms, for a total of some 20 years. Bradley was the first African American mayor of a majority white city; in his memory, Los Angeles International Airport dedicated the Tom Bradley International Terminal.

> *In 1973 Los Angeles elected Tom Bradley as its first African-American mayor. His ascension to the mayoralty was remarkable in light of the heterogeneous nature of the city's population. Unlike other large cities that had elected black mayors—among them, Cleveland, Newark, and Atlanta—African Americans comprised only a small portion of Los Angeles's population—less than 18 percent. To win the election Bradley needed support from a large percentage of non-black voters. His campaign strategy was to appeal to the majority electorate without alienating his black support base. His mild manner, moderate political views, and states as a member of the city council and former police officer attracted white voters, but his five consecutive terms as mayor witnessed a gradual deterioration in his relationship with the black community.*
>
> *Source: From Jeffrey S. Adler. African-American Mayors: Race, Politics, and the American City. Champaign, IL: University of Illinois Press, 2001, p. 153.*

Books

Payne, James Gregory and Scott C. Ratzan. *Tom Bradley, the Impossible Dream: A Biography.* Santa Monica, CA: Roundtable Pub., 1986. Biography of Thomas Bradley's life and political career.

Starr, Kevin. *The Dream Endures: California Enters the 1940s.* New York, NY: Oxford University Press, 1926. Book includes a profile of Tom Bradley from his youth after his family initially moved to California through his adulthood and five terms as Los Angeles' mayor.

Websites

UCLA's Spotlight has a profile, "Tom Bradley, Mayor of Los Angeles." http://spotlight.ucla.edu/alumni/tom-bradley_mayor/.

"Bridging the Divide: Tom Bradley and the Politics of Race" is a biography of Thomas Bradley. http://mayortombradley.com/biography.

Also Noteworthy

1888

Granville T. Woods receives U.S. Patent No. 383,844 for an overhead conducting system for the electric railway.

1973

Maynard Jackson is elected to serve as mayor of Atlanta, Georgia.

May 30

1822

The West African-born Telemanque, who is known to history as Denmark Vesey, is betrayed when his planned insurrection against African slavery is discovered. Denmark had been enslaved in Haiti and then in Charleston, South Carolina, by a man named Joseph Vesey but purchased his freedom for $600 after winning a $1,500 Charleston city lottery. Although free and able to live on his own by working as a carpenter, Denmark Vesey's abhorrence of slavery led to an elaborate plot that was to include thousands of Charleston's Blacks. After the insurrection was discovered, some 131 Blacks and 4 whites were arrested. Denmark Vesey and five of his aides were put to death by hanging at Blake's Landing, Charleston, South Carolina.

On such slender evidence and testimony was Vesey's fate determined. Particularly troublesome to historians has been the lack of weapons produced as evidence during Vesey's trial or those of his conspirators. Of the "hundreds" of pikes, guns, and daggers about which numerous slaves testified later that Vesey had arranged to have them cached throughout the city for use on the night of the revolt, the prosecution was able eventually to present only six pike poles (not yet fitted with blades), less than a dozen hammered daggers or swords, and a keg of musket balls discovered accidentally underneath a wharf. The judges apparently concluded, as have many historians since, that Vesey simply had exaggerated the number of weapons available to his recruits, hoping that, once committed, they would continue fighting even if inadequately armed. Like all revolutionaries, Vesey believed that a well-armed cadre, not a fully equipped people army, precipitated revolt. "Let us assemble a sufficient number to commence work with spirit," Vesey often told his earliest recruiters, "and we'll not want men. They'll fall in behind us fast enough."

Source: From David Robertson. *Denmark Vesey*. New York, NY: Random House Digital, Inc., 2000, p. 132.

Books

Pearson, Edward A. *Designs Against Charleston: The Trial Record of the Denmark Vesey Slave Conspiracy of 1822*. Chapel Hill, NC: University of North Carolina Press, 1999. Documentation from the trial of Denmark Vesey.

Starobin, Robert S. *Denmark Vesey: The Slave Conspiracy of 1822*. Englewood Cliffs, NJ: Prentice Hall, 1970. Looks at Vesey's plot to free enslaved Africans in South Carolina.

Websites

LCV Cities Tour—Charleston: Denmark Vesey Slave Rebellion YouTube video about Vesey's rebellion. http://www.youtube.com/watch?v=ok4_Wdqym24.

Documents on the slave rebellions of Denmark Vesey and Nat Turner. http://teachergenius.teachtci.com/documents-on-the-slave-rebellions-of-denmark-vesey-and-nat-turner/.

Also Noteworthy

1903

The poet Countee Cullen is born in Baltimore, Maryland.

1943

African-American Civil Rights Movement activist James Chaney is born. His work to help register Mississippi's Blacks to vote led to his murder—alongside Michael Schwerner and Andrew Goodman—in Philadelphia, Mississippi, on June 21, 1964.

1965

Vivian Malone becomes the first African American to graduate from the University of Alabama.

May 31

1921

From May 31 through June 1, Tulsa, Oklahoma's Greenwood section—which was so prosperous it had been deemed the "Black Wall Street"—suffers the effects of a race riot as whites rampage through the 35-square block area. Today, many believe the Tulsa Race Riot was one of the worst domestic terrorist acts in modern U.S. history: the race riot led to the deaths of at least 300 African Americans. Greenwood's "Black Wall Street" never recovered from the destruction of over 1,200 homes, 35 grocery stores, eight doctor's offices, and five hotels. The riot cost the district an estimated 1.8 million in 1921 dollars.

> *Tulsa's saga promotes the best in self-reliance and talent that black Americans have to offer. These were universal and successful themes that would apply later in all businesses, including the securities industry. Ironically, what drew the best out of these individuals was the harsh reality of segregation. Restricted from hair salons, supermarkets, restaurants, and other white-owned business establishments, the black residents of Tulsa built their own. Other black communities spent their dollars at white businesses, despite being viewed as inferior. In contrast, the people of Tulsa realized the power of ownership. Because black shop-owners provided all the needed services to cater to the black community, all monies and investment stayed within the community and it blossomed. In that 35-block span, there were 1,500 black-owned businesses and houses, including 10 millionaires and many families with substantial savings.*
>
> *Source*: From Gregory S. Bell. *The Black: A History of African Americans on Wall Street.* Hoboken, NJ: John Wiley & Sons, 2002, p. 21.

Books

Hirsch, James S. *Riot and Remembrance: America's Worst Race Riot and Its Legacy.* New York, NY: Mariner Books, 2003. Author looks at the history of Tulsa's Greenwood District and why it was destroyed.

Wilson, Jay Jay and Ron Wallace. *Black Wallstreet: A Lost Dream.* Boca Raton, FL: Black Wallstreet Publishers, 1992. Book covers the rise and violent destruction of Black Wall Street.

Websites

The Black Holocaust Society Website looks at "A Black Holocaust in America." http://www.blackwallstreet.freeservers.com/.

Black Wall Street in Tulsa, Oklahoma - Pt. 1. http://www.youtube.com/watch?v=Nssa5B 79784.

Also Noteworthy

1870

Congress passes the first Enforcement Act, providing stiff penalties for those who deprive others of their civil rights.

1909

The National Negro Committee (today known as the NAACP) holds its first conference in New York.

1955

U.S. Supreme Court orders desegregation of the nation's public schools "with all deliberate speed."

2002

President George W. Bush proclaims June as Black History Music Month.

June

June 1

1966

President Lyndon Johnson convenes a two-day White House Conference on Civil Rights, titled "To Fulfill These Rights," which is designed to look at discrimination against African Americans in areas of housing, economic security, education, and justice. The conference included more than 2,400 participants from major civil rights organizations.

> Promised during Lyndon Johnson's historic Howard University commencement address of June 1965, the White House Conference on Civil Rights, "To Fulfill These Rights," was originally scheduled for November 1965. Envisaged as a forum in which black leaders, academics, and government officials discuss eliminating the remaining obstacles to black equality, the conference was postponed in the aftermath of the Watts riot. The November gathering became a planning conference, with the main event moved to June 1966.
>
> Source: From Simon Hall. *Peace and Freedom: The Civil Rights and Antiwar Movements in the 1960s.* Philadelphia, PA: University of Pennsylvania Press, 2006, p. 67.

Books

Anderson, Alan B. and George W. Pickering. *Confronting the Color Line: The Broken Promise of the Civil Rights Movement in Chicago.* Athens, GA: University of Georgia Press, 2008. Authors note the tensions evident even as President Johnson held his White House Conference on Civil Rights.

Behnken, Brian D. *Fighting Their Own Battles: Mexican Americans, African Americans, and the Struggle for Civil Rights in Texas.* Chapel Hill, NC: UNC Press Books, 2011. Author looks at the African American and Chicano Civil Rights movements and shows how each was accepted at the White House Conference on Civil Rights.

Websites

President Lyndon B. Johnson's Commencement Address at Howard University: "To Fulfill These Rights," June 4, 1965. http://www.lbjlib.utexas.edu/johnson/archives.hom/speeches.hom/650604.asp.

Civil Rights During the Johnson Administration, 1963–1969, contains documentation from the White House Conference. http://library.truman.edu/microforms/civil_rights_johnson.asp.

Also Noteworthy

1843

After having been "overwhelmed with the greatness of the Divine presence," the formerly enslaved Isabella Baumfree (or Bomefree) changes her name to Sojourner Truth and becomes a traveling preacher, focused on preaching against African slavery.

1881

A dispensation is issued allowing for the establishment of the El Sol De Cuba Masonic Lodge No. 38. The New York-based El Sol De Cuba (the Sun of Cuba) was a Spanish-speaking freemason lodge founded by Manuel R. Coronado, Sixto Pozo, Andrew N. Portos, John Johnson, Abraham Seino, and Lafayette Marcus, all of Mt. Olive Lodge No. 2, and Abony Brown of Celestial Lodge No. 3. On November 27, 1914, the El Sol De Cuba Masonic Lodge No. 38 officially changed its name to the Prince Hall Masonic Lodge No. 38.

1937

Morgan Porterfield Freeman, Jr., is born in Memphis, Tennessee. He won an Academy Award as Best Supporting Actor for his role in *Million Dollar Baby* (2004).

1939

Cleavon Jake Little is born in Chickasha, Oklahoma. As a film and stage actor, Cleavon Little won the Tony Award for Best Actor in a Musical for his performance in *Purlie* in 1971.

1968

Henry Lewis becomes first Black musical director of a U.S. symphony orchestra, when he is named to head the New Jersey Symphony.

1973

The first Black-owned television station, WGPR-TV 62, is granted a permit to begin operating. WGPR-TV is based in Detroit, Michigan.

June 2

1967

Race riot in Roxbury, Massachusetts. Three days of rioting and violence followed a sit-in demonstration by the Mothers for Adequate Welfare (MAW) at the Grove Hall Office welfare center on Blue Hills Avenue in Roxbury, Massachusetts.

> On Friday, June 2, 1967, in late afternoon, MAW arrived at the center with a delegation of twenty-five black and white welfare mothers and a small contingent of college students. They brought with them a list of demands printed on mimeograph sheets, and expressed their refusal to remain powerless. "We're here," they said, "because we're sick and tired of the way the Welfare Dept.—and especially Grove Hall—treats us. We're tired of being treated like criminals, of having to depend on suspicious and insulting social workers and of being completely at the mercy of a department we have no control over." They presented a long list of demands and then, at 4.20 p.m., they chained the doors shut from the inside, preventing fifty-eight welfare workers from leaving the building.

> Source: From Jack Tager. *Boston Riots: Three Centuries of Social Violence*. Lebanon, NH: UPNE, 2001, p. 179.

Books

Cort, John C. *Dreadful Conversions: The Making of a Catholic Socialist*. Bronx, NY: Fordham University Press, 2003. A look at Cort's work as a journalist on the staff of the *Catholic Worker* and as an organizer, including his part working with the Roxbury riots.

Weinberger, Paul E. *Perspectives on Social Welfare: An Introductory Anthology*. New York, NY: Macmillan, 1974. Book includes a look at the Roxbury riots.

Websites

Roxbury, Quiet in Past, Finally Breaks into Riot; Why Did Violence Occur? http://www.thecrimson.com/article/1967/6/15/roxbury-quiet-in-past-finally-breaks/.

Boston police arrest the rioters who create violence on the streets during race riots in Boston, Massachusetts. http://www.criticalpast.com/video/65675072478_race-riots_smash-stores-glass_buildings-on-fire_police-arrests-victims.

Also Noteworthy

1863

Anti-slavery activist Harriet Tubman leads Union Army guerillas into Maryland and is able to free some 700 enslaved Africans.

1875

James Augustine Healey becomes the first Black Catholic Bishop in the United States.

1971

Samuel L. Gravely, Jr., becomes the first African American admiral in the U.S. Navy.

June 3

1944

Welterweight Boxing Champion Sugar Ray Robinson is honorably discharged from the U.S. Army. Robinson had been born Walker Smith Jr. on May 3, 1921 in Ailey, Georgia, and then raised in the North. As he trained to become a boxer—all the while idolizing Joe Louis—Robinson's fluid technique caused watchers to refer to him as "sweet as sugar," which led to his nickname. Robinson turned professional at age 19 and within six years was the World Welterweight Champion. When drafted to serve in the Army, he was able to tour and perform in boxing matches with Joe Louis. But Robinson was discouraged by the degree of racism he encountered in the armed forces and often disobeyed his superiors. Robinson won 91 fights in a row and held the Welterweight Championship for five years. Robinson also became World Middleweight Champion in 1951.

> *"Joe Barrow was the big hero in the neighborhood,"* Sugar recalled. He had demolished nearly all the amateur fighters he met, knocking them out without breaking a sweat. Barrow lived only a few blocks from Sugar, so it was easy for Sugar to keep tabs on him, to wait outside his idol's house and to grab his boxing equipment and carry it for him. According to Joe, "Little kids on my block followed me around all the time. There was one kid in particular who seemed to know my schedule. He'd be there, Johnny-on-the-spot, asking to carry my bag. I felt embarrassed and silly and proud, but anyway I let him carry it to Brewster Center for me. When he moved to New York, I missed him. He was a real nice kid. His name was Walker Smith. Later they changed his name to 'Sugar' Ray Robinson."
>
> *Source*: From Herb Boyd. *Pound for Pound: A Biography of Sugar Ray Robinson*. New York, NY: HarperCollins, 2005, p. 14.

Books

Haygood, Wil. *Sweet Thunder: The Life and Times of Sugar Ray Robinson*. Chicago, IL: Chicago Review Press, 2011. Biography of Sugar Ray Robinson.

Robinson, Sugar Ray and Dave Anderson. *Sugar Ray*. Cambridge, MA: Da Capo Press, 1994. Book looks at Sugar Ray's life and his battles with discrimination as well as his profile as a hero in the African American community.

Websites

The Official Site of Sugar Ray Robinson. http://www.cmgww.com/sports/robinson/.

Sugar Ray Robinson fight with Jake LaMotta is on YouTube. www.youtube.com/watch?v=KUYhjX64pDo.

Also Noteworthy

1904

Dr. Charles Richard Drew is born in Washington, DC, to Richard Thomas Drew and Nora Rosella Burrell. As a physician and medical researcher, Drew researched blood transfusions and developed a way of transfusing blood plasma that is today used internationally to make blood donations.

1949

Wesley Brown became the first African American to graduate from the U.S. Naval Academy; it had taken more than a century for the first Black to graduate from Annapolis. Brown originally wanted to go to the U.S. Military Academy at West Point.

1968

Martin Luther King, Jr.'s "Poor People's March" takes place in Washington, DC.

June 4

1972

University of California professor and Black prison-rights activist Angela Yvonne Davis is acquitted of all murder and conspiracy charges. Davis had been charged with assisting and conspiring with the young men involved in a deadly 1970 shootout at the Marin County courthouse in California. The assault on the courthouse was an attempt to free imprisoned African American activist George Jackson. At least three people were killed during the escape attempt. Davis, a Birmingham, Alabama, native who became a member of the Communist Party, spent 18 months in prison but was found not guilty of all charges by an all-white San Jose jury.

> *In February 1972, after intense and lengthy lobbying by activists to end dehumanizing prison conditions and judicial racism in sentencing, the state Supreme Court abolished the death penalty in California, a decision that would facilitate Davis's release on bail. Organizers had effectively mobilized a massive, (inter)national campaign, inundating the trial judge with demands for immediate bail, including a telegram signed by all thirteen of the African-American US Congressmen, at that time, the entire membership of the Congressional Black Caucus. On February 23, 1972, noting the magnitude of the public demands, the presiding judge granted bail. Given that her release undermined the presumption of guilt, which had been promoted in most media, prosecutors sought, and were denied, a delay in the trial proceedings. The trial, which progressed throughout 1971 and into the following year, ended just as the Soledad Brother's trial had: Angela Yvonne Davis was acquitted of all charges when the jury rendered its "not guilty" verdict on June 4, 1972.*
>
> *Source*: From Angela Yvonne Davis and Joy James. *The Angela Y. Davis Reader.* Hoboken, NJ: Wiley-Blackwell, 1998, p. 12.

Books

Davis, Angela Y. *Angela Davis—An Autobiography.* New York, NY: Random House, 1974. Angela Davis's autobiography.

Davis, Angela Y. *Women, Race, & Class.* New York, NY: Random House Digital, Inc., 2011. Davis looks at the history of the Feminist Movement in the United States.

Websites

"The Example of Angela Davis" (June 3–4, 1972) looks at the international appeal of Davis's civil rights work. http://germanhistorydocs.ghi-dc.org/sub_image.cfm?image_id=622.

Angela Davis's biography is on this Website. http://socialjustice.ccnmtl.columbia.edu/index.php/Angela_Davis_Biography.

Also Noteworthy

1922

Samuel L. Gravely is born. Gravely became the first African American admiral in the U.S. Navy and the first African American to command a U.S. warship.

1951

Mississippi Valley State University is founded.

June 5

1966

James Meredith, the first African American to enroll at the University of Mississippi, begins his "March Against Fear." To combat the ongoing sense of intimidation African Americans felt in the South, Meredith began walking alone from Memphis, Tennessee, toward Jackson, Mississippi. Meredith was shot and wounded on the second day of his march as he walked along Mississippi's Highway 51, but his courage inspired other Civil Rights Movement activists to descend upon the South and continue his efforts.

> *James Meredith wore a pith helmet against the Mississippi sun and carried an ivory-headed African cane as he walked down U.S. 51 on June 6, 1966. Just the day before, the thirty-two-year-old civil rights veteran had set out on a 220-mile "March Against Fear" from Memphis, Tennessee, to Jackson, Mississippi. His announced purpose is to encourage blacks in his home state to register and vote. Four years earlier, when Meredith had integrated the Oxford campus of Ole Miss, he*

had strong support from the major civil rights organizations and the federal government. Then, this was a cause the movement was ready to embrace. Now, at the beginning of his 1966 march, Meredith, a man few could get close to or understand, was ignored by almost all of his former allies "A black Don Quixote," Newsweek called him.

Source: From Henry Hampton, Steve Fayer, Sarah Flynn. *Voices of Freedom: An Oral History of the Civil Rights Movement from the 1950s Through the 1980s.* New York, NY: Random House Digital, Inc., 1991, p. 12.

Books

Axelrod, Alan. *Minority Rights in America.* Washington, DC: CQ Press, 2002. Includes a look at Meredith's march.

Stanton, Mary. *Freedom Walk: Mississippi or Bust.* Jackson, MS: University Press of Mississippi, 2003. Looks at the marches and protests that led to the transformative Civil Rights Movement.

Websites

The Meredith Mississippi March–June 1966. http://www.jofreeman.com/photos/meredith.html.

James Meredith Talks about His 1966 March Against Fear on YouTube. http://www.youtube.com/watch?v=YB_kezlxv2w.

Also Noteworthy

1894

G.W. Murray receives U.S. Patent No. 520,888 for a cotton chopper.

1987

Dr. Mae C. Jemison becomes the first African American female astronaut.

June 6

1966

Kwame Ture (a.k.a. Stokely Carmichael) launches the "Black Power" movement.

Born Stokely Carmichael on June 29, 1941, in Port of Spain, Trinidad, Ture did not come to the United States until age 11. After attending schools in Bronx, New York, Ture majored in philosophy at Howard University. He became an activist when he joined Howard University's Nonviolent Action Group (NAG), which was an affiliate of the Student Nonviolent Coordinating Committee (SNCC). Kwame Ture was named "Honorary Prime Minister" of the Black Panther Party and famously popularized the term "Black Power" as he participated in Martin Luther King, Jr.'s "March Against Fear." Ture officially changed his name in 1978; he chose names that honored Ghana's president, Kwame Nkrumah, and Guinea's president, Ahmed Sékou Touré.

The point is obvious: black people must lead and run their own organizations. Only black people can convey the revolutionary idea—and it is a revolutionary idea—that black people are able to do things themselves. Only they can help create in the community an aroused and continuing black consciousness that will provide the basis for political strength. In the past, white allies have often furthered white supremacy without the whites involved realizing it, or even wanting to do so. Black people must come together and do things for themselves. They must achieve self-identity and self determination in order to have their daily needs met.

Source: From Stokely Carmichael and Charles V. Hamilton. *Black Power: The Politics of Liberation in America.* New York, NY: Random House Digital, Inc., 1992, p. 16.

Books

Carmichael, Stokely. *Stokely Speaks: From Black Power to Pan-Africanism.* Chicago IL: Lawrence Hill Books, 2007. A collection of some of the best speeches made by Kwame Ture.

Carmichael, Stokely with Michael Thelwell. *Ready for Revolution: The Life and Struggles of Stokely Carmichael (Kwame Ture).* New York, NY: Simon & Schuster, 2003. Autobiography of Kwame Ture.

Websites

Stokely-Carmichael.com recalls the ideology of Black Power, as established by Kwame Ture. http://stokely-carmichael.com/.

University of Washington has a full-text speech with photos of Kwame Ture. http://courses .washington.edu/spcmu/carmichael/.

Also Noteworthy

1831

First annual "People of Color" convention is held in Philadelphia.

1935

Grant Thomas Green is born in St. Louis, Missouri. Green was a guitarist, known for his distinctive technique: he played jazz, hard bop, soul jazz, and funk styles.

June 7

1917

Gwendolyn Elizabeth Brooks is born to David and Keziah Brooks in Topeka, Kansas. Her family moved to Chicago, Illinois, shortly after her birth, and Brooks is known for her association with Chicago's South Side neighborhood. A poet, Brooks became the first African American to win the Pulitzer Prize for Poetry, in 1950.

> *At a young age, Brooks was a disciplined and prolific writer, once listing as her New Year's resolution to "write some poetry everyday" (Kent 27). She already considered herself a poet, but now that she had outside endorsement, she felt others were also taking her seriously. When she was sixteen, she began publishing her poems in the Chicago Defender, a black newspaper, and in two years, the newspaper had published seventy-five of her poems.*
>
> *Source: From Gwendolyn Brooks by Harold Bloom. New York, NY: Infobase Publishing, 2005, p. 16.*

Books

Brooks, Gwendolyn and Gloria Jean Wade Gayles. *Conversations with Gwendolyn Brooks.* Jackson, MS: University Press of Mississippi, 2003. Writings and thoughts of Gwendolyn Brooks over the decades.

Wright, Stephen Caldwell. *On Gwendolyn Brooks: Reliant Contemplation.* Ann Arbor, MI: University of Michigan Press, 2001. Author looks at the life and works of Gwendolyn Brooks.

Websites

Chicago State University has established the Gwendolyn Brooks Center for Black Literature and Creative Writing. http://www.csu .edu/gwendolynbrooks/index.htm.

Gwendolyn Brooks's biography is available on Modern American Poetry. http://www.english .illinois.edu/maps/poets/a_f/brooks/life.htm.

Gwendolyn Brooks "We Real Cool" is available on YouTube. http://www.youtube.com/ watch?v=BqlTXdvNPzY&NR=1.

Also Noteworthy

1880

Chester Arthur Franklin is born to George F. and Clara Belle Williams Franklin in Texas. In April of 1919, Franklin founded Kansas City's African American newspaper *The Call* (http://www.kccall.com/), and to help with financing it, his mother went out and sold subscriptions.

1892

George T. Sampson receives U.S. Patent No. 476,416 for a clothes dryer. Sampson would also receive U.S. Patent No. 312,388 for a sled propeller on February 17, 1885.

1953

At age 90, long-time civil rights leader Mary Church Terrell helps win a lawsuit that ends segregation in public restaurants in Washington, DC.

June 8

1892

Homer Adolph Plessy refuses to move to a segregated railroad coach in New Orleans, initiating the infamous *Plessy v. Ferguson* case. The Supreme Court decision in this case established the segregationist doctrine of "Separate But Equal."

At 4:35 p.m., twenty minutes after the train's scheduled departure, Detective Cain and others forcibly dragged the neatly dressed Plessy from the whites-only coach and executed his arrest at Royal and Press Streets. The East Lousiana number eight train resumed its otherwise uneventful trip to Covington sans Homer Plessy. Detective Cain was conducting him to the Fifth Precinct station on Elysian Fields—a block away from where his father lived on Burgundy Street and two blocks from where Joseph Guillaume protested segregated star cars in 1867. At the station house, Plessy submitted to the same booking procedure applied to the array of drunks, petty larcenists, and foul-mouthed New Orleanians arrested that day on the city's streets. But his charge of "Violating Section 111 of the Separate Car Act" was anything but a typical Tuesday-evening New Orleans petty crime. Members of the Comité des Citoyens—Eugene Luscy, treasurer Paul Bonseigneur, Rodolphe Desdunes, L.J. Joubert, and Louis Martinet—all converged at the Fifth Precincy station, perhaps somewhat giddy over the success of Plessy's ticket purchase, train boarding, arrest, and being booked with a charge they could scrutinize with the Fourteenth Amendment. Now they had a case to take before the courts. Furthermore, they convinced Judge Moulin to release a disheveled Plessy on temporary bail, sparing him a night in parish prison. Homer still held his first-class ticket as he and his compatriots walked from the Fifth Precinct station and made their way across Elysian Fields and back toward Tremé. They had just purposefully, intentionally, and openly defied Gov. Murphy Foster; Francis Nicholls, chief justice of the state supreme court; and the 1890 Louisiana legislature.

Source: From Keith Weldon Medley. *We as Freemen: Plessy v. Ferguson*. New York, NY: Infobase Publishing, 2005, pp. 142–143.

Books

Fireside, Harvey and Marc H. Morial. *Separate and Unequal: Homer Plessy and the Supreme Court Decision That Legalized Racism*. New York, NY: Basic Books, 2005. Book looks at *Plessy v. Ferguson* decision and includes a profile of Homer Plessy.

Thomas, Brook. *Plessy v. Ferguson: A Brief History with Documents*. New York, NY: Bedford Books/St. Martin's Press, 1999. Full text of *Plessy v. Ferguson* decision with other documentation.

Websites

"Separate but equal" *Plessy v. Ferguson* 1896. http://www.lawbuzz.com/can_you/plessy/plessy.htm.

Homer Adolph Plessy: Civil rights activist is profiled on his church's Website. http://www.staugustinecatholicchurch-neworleans.org/plessy.htm.

Also Noteworthy

1886

First Civil Rights Act is passed.

1953

Supreme Court ruling bans discrimination in Washington, DC, restaurants.

June 9

1845

James Carroll Napier is born enslaved in Nashville, Tennessee. Napier became Nashville's first African American attorney and served on Nashville City Council. Napier was the founder of Nashville's One-Cent Savings Bank and Trust Company.

The Morris Memorial Building at Fourth and Charlotte was designed by the African American firm of McKissack & McKissack from 1923 to 1925. It housed one of the first African American-owned banks in the country, the One Cent Savings Bank, founded in 1904. . . . James Carroll Napier was one of the founders of the One Cent Savings Bank, which is now the Citizens Savings Bank and Trust Company. He was appointed by President Theodore Roosevelt to serve as registrar of the U.S. Treasury, and served from 1911 to 1915. He was a delegate to four Republican National Conventions, and was a trustee of Fisk, Howard and Meharry Universities.

Source: From James A. Hoobler. *A Guide to Historic Nashville, Tennessee.* Stroud, Gloucestershire: The History Press, 2008, p. 93.

Books

Lamon, Lester C. *Black Tennesseans, 1900–1930.* Knoxville, TN: University of Tennessee Press, 1976. Includes a profile of Napier and his founding of the One Cent Savings Bank.

Lamon, Lester C. *Blacks in Tennessee, 1791–1970.* Knoxville, TN: University of Tennessee Press, 1981. Covers the importance of the founding of the One Cent Savings Bank.

Websites

Citizens Savings Bank and Trust Company (1865–1874). http://ww2.tnstate.edu/library/digital/CITIZEN.HTM.

Citizens Savings Bank and Trust Company. http://www.hmdb.org/marker.asp?marker=4222.

Also Noteworthy

1995

Lincoln J. Ragsdale, pioneer fighter pilot of World War II, dies.

June 10

1904

Clarence "Pine Top" Smith is born in Troy, Alabama, on June 11, 1904. "Pine Top" was a major blues and boogie-woogie musician, best known for his 1928 tune "Pine Top's Boogie Woogie."

. . . Clarence "Pine Top" Smith (b Troy, Alabama, 11 Jan 1904; d Chicago, 15 March 1929) was the first to popularize the style and the original issue of Pine Top's Boogie Woogie (Vocalion 1245, 1928) was probably the most influential and widely imitated of all blues records. It is a piano solo with spoken comments, suggesting that it was the accompaniment to a dance. Smith was an entertainer and tap-dancer as well as a musician, and this is evident in the monologue style of Now I ain't got nothin' at all (Vocalion 1298, 1929). Only his Pine Top's Blues (Vocalion 1245, 1928) is in traditional blues vein and he sings it in a high, even petulant and childlike voice.

Source: From Paul Oliver, Max Harrison, and William Bolcom. *The New Grove Gospel, Blues and Jazz: With Spirituals and Ragtime.* New York, NY: W. W. Norton & Company, 1997, p. 76.

Books

Oliver, Paul, Max Harrison, and William Bolcom. *The New Grove Gospel, Blues and Jazz: With Spirituals and Ragtime.* New York, NY: Dafina Books/Kensington Publishing Corp, 2002. An extensive history of African American music in the United States.

Spencer, Frederick J. *Jazz and Death: Medical Profiles of Jazz Greats.* Washington, DC: University Press of Mississippi, 2002. Author examines the myths about the deaths of several famous jazz musicians and debunks them with medical evidence.

Woods, Tricia. *Complete Blues Keyboard Method: Beginning Blues Keyboard, Book & CD.* Van Nuys, CA: Alfred Publishing, 1999. Book and CD demonstrate how blues and boogie woogie music can be played.

Websites

The Alabama Jazz Hall of Fame promotes a musical journey through the history of jazz that begins with "the beginnings of boogie woogie with Clarence 'Pinetop' Smith." Pinetop was inducted into the Alabama Jazz

Hall of Fame in 1991. http://wwwjazzhall
.com/jazzhalloffame/jazzhalloffame.htm.

There are several recorded versions of "Pine Top's Boogie Woogie" on YouTube. http://www.youtube.com/watch?v=BZgS03Md3mQ and http://www.youtube.com/watch?v=JQix tqDdyLs.

Also Noteworthy

1854

The first African American Roman Catholic bishop, James Augustine Healy, is ordained.

1895

Hattie McDaniel is born in Wichita, Kansas. Both a singer and actress, McDaniel was frequently criticized for accepting stereotypical roles that demeaned Blacks, but McDaniel once said, "I'd rather play a maid than be one." In 1940, McDaniel's work as an actress led to her becoming the first performer of African descent to win an Academy Award, which she won for Best Supporting Actress for her role as Mammy in *Gone with the Wind* (1939).

1910

Chester Arthur Burnett is born in White Station, Mississippi. As an adult, Burnett won fame as the legendary blues singer and harmonica player Howlin' Wolf.

June 11

2000

Former interim senior administrator of the National Association for the Advancement of Colored People (NAACP), Earl Theodore Shinhoster dies in a car accident outside Montgomery, Alabama. Shinhoster was born on July 5, 1950, in Savannah, Georgia, and began his activist career by working with the NAACP's youth council in Savannah. He served as the NAACP's interim director from 1994 to 1995 and was praised for raising funds and increasing membership.

> *Instead of fighting for racial justice and equality, Shinhoster spent his time and energy trying to resolve the NAACP's internal problems, "so we can live to fight another day," he was quoted as saying in the Atlantic Journal-Constitution in 1995. All the while, Shinhoster knew he was only in the top spot temporarily. "If they don't solve some of these real serious organizational problems we have," one chapter president told the Journal-Constitution, "it won't matter who runs the organization." During Shinhoster's tenure, the NAACP erased over $1 million in debt from its books, and membership grew from 600,000 to nearly one million. According to writer Jamie Stockwell in the Washington Post, "Shinhoster has been credited with steadying the organization and easing the financial crisis and political infighting that threatened to . . . it."*
>
> *Source: From Saudah Aziz. Highway Robbery: Life before and after an SUV Rollover Accident—The Ford and Firestone Tire Cover-up Story. Pittsburgh, PA: Dorrance Publishing, 2011, p. 81.*

Books

Gunderson, Gary. *Boundary Leaders: Leadership Skills for People of Faith.* Minneapolis, MN: Fortress Press, 2004. Book includes a look at the leadership abilities shown by Earl Shinhoster.

Long, Kristi S. and Matthew Nadelhaft. *America under Construction: Boundaries and Identities in Popular Culture.* Abingdon, Oxfordshire, England: Taylor & Francis, 1997. Includes a look at Shinhoster's campaigns to end use of the South's Rebel flag.

Websites

Georgia Legislature passes resolution establishing the Earl T. Shinhoster Interchange and Bridge. http://www1.legis.ga.gov/legis/2003_04/fulltext/sr6.htm.

Southern Changes article "Peace and Power: Earl Theodore Shinhoster (1950–2000)." http://beck.library.emory.edu/southern changes/article.php?id=sc22-2_024.

Also Noteworthy

1912

Joseph Hunter Dickinson patents improvements to the player piano. His pianola, or self-playing piano, is awarded U.S. Patent No. 1,028,996.

June 12

1823

Louis Charles Roudanez is born in Saint James Parish, Louisiana, to Aimee Potens, who was of Haitian descent, and Louis Roudanez, a French-born merchant. Roudanez became the publisher of the United States' first daily African American newspaper with his creation of the *Tribune de la Nouvelle Orleans* (the *New Orleans Tribune*).

. . . The creation of a new organ was imperative if the movement for black rights were to continue. Therefore, the bilingual New Orleans *Tribune was inaugurated by Dr. Roudanez twelve days later, on July 21, 1864. A bilingual publication, it first appeared triweekly, but after October 4, 1864, it became a daily except Mondays—the first black daily in America. It employed essentially the same staff as L'Union, including editor Paul Trévigne. Its first crusade was against both the ratification of the constitution and Lincoln's 10 percent plan. The* Tribune's *first editorial was, however, an all out attack on the discriminatory laws in Louisiana. Under the heading, "Is the Black Code Still in Force" the editor remarked: "The black code of Louisiana is as bloody and barbarous as the laws against witchcraft . . . and far behind the spirit of our times." The editor pointed out that the Emancipation Proclamation was the law and observed that the judge who considered the Black Code still in force "must be so tangled up in legal cobwebs as to be quite disabled for all practical purposes; so involved in mental obscurity as to be positively 'inepacitated [sic]to act."*

Source: From Charles Vincent. *Black Legislators in Louisiana During Reconstruction*. Carbondale, IL: Southern Illinois University Press, 2011, p. 24.

Books

Houzeau, Jean-Charles, edited by David C. Rankin and translated by Gerard F. Denault. *My Passage at the New Orleans "Tribune": A Memoir of the Civil War Era*. Baton Rouge: LSU Press, 2001. Jean-Charles Houzeau's look at his years of work as editor of the *New Orleans Tribune*.

Scott, Rebecca Jarvis. *Degrees of Freedom: Louisiana and Cuba after Slavery*. Cambridge, MA: Harvard University Press, 2005. Book profiles political influence of the *New Orleans Tribune*.

Websites

Dr. Louis Charles Roudanez: Publisher of America's First Black Daily Newspaper. http://theneworleanstribune.com/roudaneztext.htm.

The French Creoles of America Website. http://www.frenchcreoles.com/CreoleCulture/famouscreoles/dr.%20roudanez/dr%20roudanez.htm has a profile of Roudanez *New Orleans Tribune* Website. http://theneworleanstribune.com/aboutus.htm.

Also Noteworthy

1963

Medgar W. Evers, civil rights leader, is assassinated in Jackson, Mississippi.

1963

Civil rights groups protest discrimination in trades unions by holding demonstrations at a Harlem construction site.

June 13

1911

Albert Buford Cleage, Jr., is one of seven children born to Albert Buford and Pearl (Reed) Cleage in Indianapolis, Indiana. Ordained as a Christian minister, Cleague presented a new interpretation of his beliefs when on March 26, 1967, he installed an 18-foot religious painting depicting the

Madonna and baby Jesus as people of African descent. With this effort, Cleage, who also changed his name to Jaramogi Abebe Agyeman, initiated the Black Christian Nationalist Movement. He is said to have created the term "Black Liberation Theology," and his work led to the founding of the Shrine of the Black Madonna Church and Cultural Centers, which today has locations in Detroit, Houston, and Atlanta.

> As black people, we don't have a lot of separate dignities. We have one dignity. If you mess it up, you mess it up for all of us. Or you see our black kids acting a fool out on the streets. They are messing up our dignity. You know why they are doing it? Because they don't understand. Because they are living in a world in which they have been shattered—leaning walls, tottering fences. So they are out there fighting back in their own little way, making a fool of themselves for the man.
>
> Source: From David Turley, ed. *American Religion: Literary Sources & Documents*. New York, NY: Taylor & Francis US, 1998, p. 439.

Books

Cleage, Albert B. Jr. *The Black Messiah*. New York, NY: Sheed and Ward, 1968. Cleage's book of sermons about the African descent of Jesus and how Christianity can aid the Black community.

Cleage, Albert B. Jr. and George Bell. *Black Christian Nationalism: New Directions for the Black Church*. New York: W. Morrow, 1972. Cleage's leadership on the Black Liberation Theology is spelled out.

Websites

The Shrines of the Black Madonna of the Pan-African Orthodox Christian Church. http://www.theshrineonline.org/.

Biography of Albert Cleage, Jr., is available at the Detroit African American History Project. http://www.daahp.wayne.edu/biographiesDisplay.php?id=50.

Also Noteworthy

1868

Oscar James Dunn is elected lieutenant governor of Louisiana, the first person of African descent to be elected a lieutenant governor of any U.S. state.

1894

Provident Hospital and Free Dispensary is established at 419 Orchard Street in Baltimore, Maryland, with 10 beds. Provident's 1897 annual report stated that "The hospital is intended to fulfill three purposes: to be an institution where people of color may be attended by physicians of their own race; secondly—the colored physicians may have an opportunity to develop themselves along the lines of specialty, thereby become proficient in them and thirdly—that there may be a well-organized training school for nurses where young ladies may obtain instruction pertaining to their calling."

1967

Thurgood Marshall is nominated by President Lyndon Johnson to serve as the first person of African descent to sit on the U.S. Supreme Court.

June 14

1833

The Blackburn Riots—the first race riots in the recorded history of Detroit, Michigan—take place from June 14 through 15. The rioting took place following the arrest of Thornton and Ruthie (Lucie) Blackburn, who had escaped enslavement in Louisville, Kentucky, but been tracked down by slave hunters. The Blackburns had escaped slavery by boarding the steamboat *Versailles* on July 3, 1831; they settled in the free territory of Detroit on July 6, 1831. Antislavery activists had been able to free Lucie and get her into Canada, but it took a protest of 400 African Americans—armed with stones, bricks, and guns—to free Thornton. By July 1834, Thornton and Lucie were able to establish themselves in Toronto, and Thornton eventually created the city's first horse-and-buggy taxi service. Other than returning to Kentucky to liberate his mother, Sibby, Thornton spent the rest of his days in Canada growing his businesses and working toward Black liberation.

> *Some four hundred people, more than the entire black population of the Michigan territory, moved toward the jail.* The Detroit Courier *claimed that a large contingent of blacks had come over from Canada to take part in the uprising, including members of the "negro settlement near Malden, composed almost exclusively of fugitive slaves." And elderly woman carrying a stake wrapped with a white rage led the charge.*
>
> *Source:* From Betty DeRamus. *Forbidden Fruit: Love Stories from the Underground Railroad.* New York, NY: Simon & Schuster, 2005, p. 69.

Books

Farmer, Silas. *History of Detroit and Wayne County and Early Michigan: A Chronological Cyclopedia of the Past and Present.* New York: Muncell & Co., 1890. History of Detroit contains a recounting of the incidents that created the Blackburn Riots.

Frost, Karolyn Smardz. *I've Got a Home in Glory Land: A Lost Tale of the Underground Railroad.* New York, NY: Macmillan, 2008. Author tells the story of Thornton and Ruthie Blackburn.

Websites

Provides a timeline showing the Thornton's route from enslavement to freedom in Canada. http://www.homeingloryland.com/timeline .swf.

Slavery in Canada details the Blackburn story. http://www.canadachannel.ca/slavery/index .php/Thornton_Blackburn

1877

Henry Ossian Flipper became the first African American to graduate from the U.S. Military Academy in West Point, New York, and thus became the first Black commissioned officer in the U.S. Army. Flipper had been born into slavery in Thomasville, Georgia, and suffered harassment and discrimination during his training at West Point. Even though he graduated and was assigned to a post at Fort Davis in western Texas, he ended up being accused of embezzlement and dishonorably discharged. It took until 1976 to have that discharge reversed, and in 1999 his descendants had President William Clinton issue him a posthumous pardon.

> *The life of Henry Flipper spanned 84 years; he was born a slave before the Civil War and died after World War II began in Europe. He lived through 14 presidencies—from Franklin Pierce to Franklin Roosevelt. He was born before the telephone, radio or phonograph were invented and died when all had become a part of American life. He was born a slave, graduated from an elite institution of higher education, had a promising career in the army, was court-martialed, achieved success in the Southwest, then in Washington, as an assistant to a cabinet secretary, worked in the oil industry when that was becoming an essential part of the national economy, died in poverty during the Great Depression, and was honored years after his death.*
>
> *Source:* From Don Cusic. *The Trials of Henry Flipper, First Black Graduate of West Point.* Jefferson, NC: McFarland, 2009, p. 189.

Books

Black, Lowell Dwight and Sara Harrington Black. *An Officer and a Gentleman: The Military Career of Lieutenant Henry O. Flipper.* Victoria, BC: AbeBooks/Lora Co., 1985. Biography of Erroll Garner.

Flipper, Henry Ossian. *The Colored Cadet at West Point. Autobiography of Lieut. Henry Ossian*

Flipper, U.S.A., First Graduate of Color from the U.S. Military Academy. New York, NY: Cherry Lane Music, 2003. Book provides a look at the life of Henry Ossawa Turner and his work.

Websites

The U.S. Army Center of Military History profiles Lieutenant Henry Ossian Flipper's military service. http://www.history.army.mil/html/topics/afam/flipper.html.

BuffaloSoldier.net profiles Henry Ossian Flipper. http://www.buffalosoldier.net/HenryO.Flipper2.htm.

Also Noteworthy

1864

U.S. Congress passes legislation authorizing equal pay for African American troops and makes this rule retroactive to January 1, 1864.

1891

John Standard receives U.S. Patent No. 455,891 for improvements to the refrigerator.

1919

Evelio Grillo, Sr., is born in Ybor City (now Tampa), Florida. Grillo would grow up to work as an activist and organizer with the Community Service Organization (CSO), the Mexican American Political Association (MAPA), and the Spanish-speaking Unity Council in Oakland, California. Grillo also authored the book *Black Cuban, Black American—A Memoir.*

1986

Some 60,000 people marched in New York City's Central Park demanding that the United States impose economic sanctions against South Africa, which was governed by a race-based Apartheid regime.

June 15

1921

Erroll Louis Garner is born in Pittsburgh, Pennsylvania, to Ernest and Estella Garner. Garner came from a family of musicians, and was so gifted himself that he had learned to play the piano by age 3. At age 7, Garner played for the first time on the radio. As a famed jazz pianist, Garner was the first person of African descent to perform a jazz concert in New York City's Carnegie Hall.

> Born on June 15, 1921, Errol Garner was one of the most popular jazz musicians and composers of the 1950s. The self-taught pianist moved to Los Angeles from Pennsylvania. Garner's gift for music and melody led to his recordings of several popular songs, including the pop hit "Misty," which became a hit for five different artists between 1959 and 1975. In 1971, Garner rerecorded "Misty" for Clint Eastwood's feature directorial debut, Play Misty for Me. Garner formed his own band and performed throughout Europe.
>
> *Source:* From Karin L. Stanford. *African Americans in Los Angeles.* Mount Pleasant, SC: Arcadia Publishing, 2010, p. 44.

Books

Doran, James M. *Erroll Garner: The Most Happy Piano (Studies in Jazz).* Lanham, MD: Scarecrow Press, 1985. Biography of Erroll Garner.

Garner, Erroll and Sy Johnson. *The Erroll Garner Anthology: The First Anthology of Erroll Garner's Compositions.* New York, NY: Cherry Lane Music, 2003. Book provides a look at the life of Henry Ossawa Turner and his work.

Websites

Last.fm features a biography, discography, and photos of Erroll Garner. http://www.last.fm/music/Erroll+Garner/+wiki.

Erroll Garner plays "Misty" on this YouTube video. http://www.youtube.com/watch?v=P_tAU3GM9XI&feature=related.

Also Noteworthy

1789

The abolitionist Josiah Henson is born enslaved in Charles County, Maryland. Henson wrote an autobiography about his life entitled *The Life of Josiah Henson, Formerly a Slave, Now an Inhabitant of Canada, as Narrated by Himself.*

1864

Freedmen's Hospital first appears on official government records on this date, but it was probably established sometime in 1863. Freedmen's began as a U.S. Army medical unit during the Civil War as an auxiliary of the Freedmen's Bureau; it is the nation's oldest medical institution designed to care for and provide professional medical training to people of African descent. In 1967, the U.S. Congress transferred Freedmen's Hospital and the Freedmen's Hospital School of Nursing over to Howard University's College of Medicine.

1913

Dr. Effie O'Neal is born. O'Neal is the first African American woman to hold an executive position in the American Medical Association.

1943

The Congress of Racial Equality (CORE) is founded in Chicago by a group of students attending the University of Chicago. Among the founders were James Farmer and Bayard Rustin. Originally called the Chicago Committee of Racial Equality, the group was composed of interracial members who believed in direct, nonviolent action—in the vein of the Indian activist Mahatma Gandhi—to gain civil rights for African Americans.

June 16

1970

Kenneth Allen Gibson is elected to serve as the mayor of Newark, New Jersey. Gibson, who became Newark's 34th mayor and the first African American mayor of a major eastern U.S. city, served as Newark's mayor for some 16 years.

> After a protracted struggle for power, the Modern Black Convention Movement defeated the Addonizio political machine in June 1970. It had been a long and difficult dogfight. Although the black convention candidates received the majority of votes in the predominately African American wards as early as the November 1968 elections, the white extremist candidates Anthony Imperiale and Anthony Giuliano outpolled them in the heavily Italian American wards. However, in the May and June elections of 1970, with Puerto Rican allies and progressive white coalitions, Mayor Kenneth Gibson became the city's first African American mayor. Specifically, on June 16, 1970, Mayor Hugh J. Addonizio lost the election with 43,086 votes, and Kenneth Gibson won with 55,097. The voter turnout reached an unprecedented 73 percent of the electorate. Some 7,000 white voters felt uncomfortable with Addonizio on election day, casting their ballots for Gibson alongside some 48,000 African American and Puerto Rican voters. Thus, with the solid support of 19 out of every 20 black votes, Kenneth A. Gibson broke a key executive color bar in the power structure by becoming the first black mayor of a major eastern seaboard city.
>
> Source: From Jeanne Theoharis and Komozi Woodard. *Freedom North: Black Freedom Struggles Outside the South, 1940–1980.* New York, NY: Palgrave Macmillan, 2003, pp. 305–306.

Books

Gibson, Kenneth A. *The First Twelve Months: A Look at the Past, a Strategy for the Future: The Remarks of the Honorable Kenneth A. Gibson,*

Mayor, Newark, New Jersey, Upon Completion of His First Year in Office, July 1, 1971. Victoria, BC: AbeBooks, 1971. Book provides Gibson's comments about his first year in office.

Tuttle, Brad R. *How Newark Became Newark: The Rise, Fall, and Rebirth of an American City.* Piscataway, NJ: Rutgers University Press, 2009. Book includes a look at Gibson's rise to power and his administration of the city.

Websites

Gibson recalls the incidents that led up to the Newark riots. http://blog.nj.com/ledgernewark/2007/07/ken_gibson_sharing_a_mayors_vi.html.

Ken Gibson Political Ad (1986). http://www.youtube.com/watch?v=MhK9TLhxJzM.

Also Noteworthy

1822

West African born Telemanque, who is known to history as Denmark Vesey, leads a rebellion of enslaved Africans in Charleston, South Carolina.

June 17

1871

James Weldon Johnson is born under the name James William Johnson in Jacksonville, Florida. A writer/poet/activist, Weldon Johnson was the first African American attorney in the state of Florida and was one of the initial founders of the National Association for the Advancement of Colored People (NAACP). Weldon Johnson famously co-authored the song "Lift Every Voice and Sing," which is known as the African American National Anthem.

The platform of the Association startled a great many Negroes. Many there were who, while longing for the objectives set forth, felt timid about the methods proposed for attaining them. They feared that a full statement of the Negro's case, and an open avowal of the determination to

prosecute it, would retard rather than hasten the results aimed at; that a frontal attack would do the Negro's cause more harm than good. And many there were who definitely opposed the association, who fought it covertly and openly. This particular opposition to the organization was, in a large degree, an inheritance from the Niagara Movement. It was the Niagara Movement, inaugurated by Dr. Du Bois in 1905, that marked, with respect to the question of the Negro's civil rights, a split of the race into two well-defined parties— one, made up from the prepondering number of conservatives, under the leadership of Booker T. Washington and the other, made up from the militant elements, under the leadership of W.E.B. Du Bois. Between these two groups there were incessant attacks and counter-attacks; the former declaring that the latter were visionaries, doctrinaires, and incendiaries; the latter charging the former with minifying political and civil rights, with encouraging opposition to higher training and higher opportunities of Negro youth, with giving sanction to certain prejudiced practices and attitudes toward the Negro, thus yielding up in fundamental principles more than could be balanced by any immediate gains.

Source: From James Weldon Johnson. *Along This Way: The Autobiography of James Weldon Johnson.* Cambridge, MA: Da Capo Press, 2000, p. 313.

Books

Johnson, James Weldon. *Black Manhattan.* Cambridge, MA: Da Capo Press, 1991. Weldon Johnson's famous look at the history of African Americans in New York City.

Johnson, James Weldon. *The Autobiography of an Ex-Colored Man.* Minneapolis, Minnesota: Filiquarian Publishing, LLC., 2007. Weldon Johnson's fictional yet autobiographical account of the issues facing people of African descent.

Websites

University of South Carolina profiles James Weldon Johnson, 1871–1938. http://library.sc.edu/spcoll/amlit/johnson/johnson1.html.

James Weldon Johnson—National Portrait Gallery. www.npg.si.edu/exh/harmon/johnharm.htm.

Also Noteworthy

1775

Massachusetts Militia Minuteman Peter Salem fights in the Battle of Bunker Hill.

Salem was born enslaved in Framingham, Massachusetts, but was granted his freedom because he joined the army.

June 18

1877

Simon P. Roundtree arrives in Nicodemus, Kansas. He became the town's first settler. Nicodemus, Kansas, is today a National Historic Site because it is the only remaining western community established by African Americans who were attempting to establish their lives as free people at the end of the Civil War. Nicodemus holds an annual Emancipation Day celebration that has been taking place since August 1, 1881. The town is named in honor of an enslaved African named Nicodemus who foretold the advent of the Civil War.

One of the most successful Exoduster settlement arose at Nicodemus in Graham County, Kansas. Colonists from Kentucky established the town in July 1877. Although lacking needed tools, seed, and money, they survived their first winter on the plains. Some sold buffalo bones; some traveled 35 miles to work for the Kansas Pacific Railroad at Ellis. By 1880, however, Nicodemus held a population of 400 determined settlers. Their descendants and buildings from the early pioneers remain there today.

Source: From Richard W. Slatta. *The Mythical West: An Encyclopedia of Legend, Lore, and Popular Culture.* Cambridge, MA: Da Capo Press, 2000, p. 138.

Books

Athearn, Robert G. *In Search of Canaan: Black Migration to Kansas, 1879–80.* Lawrence, KS: Regents Press of Kansas, 1978. Book looks at African American History in the West and the founding of Nicodemus, Kansas.

Painter, Nell Irvin. *Exodusters: Black Migration to Kansas after Reconstruction.* New York: Knopf, 1976. Painter looks at the African Americans who fled the South after emancipation and looked to create homesteads in Kansas.

Websites

Nicodemus Historical Society. www.nicodemus historicalsociety.com.
Nicodemus Kansas. www.nicodemuskansas.org/.

Also Noteworthy

1822

West African-born Telemanque, who is known to history as Denmark Vesey, and his co-conspirator Peter Poyas are arrested in Charleston, South Carolina, and charged with planning an insurrection against African slavery.

1863

The 54th Massachusetts Colored Infantry attacks Fort Wagner, S.C.

1889

William H. Richardson receives U.S. Patent No. 405,600 for his improvements to the baby carriage.

1909

Nannie Burroughs founded national training School for Women.

1937

Barbara Ann Teer is born in East St. Louis, Illinois. After enrolling at the historically Black Bennett College for Women at the age of 16, she transferred to the University of Illinois. With a bachelor's degree in dance education, Teer went on to appear in several Broadway productions—but she did not like the roles written for people of African descent. In 1968, Teer founded the National Black Theatre in Harlem.

June 19

1865

Enslaved Africans in Texas are finally told that the Emancipation Proclamation had been issued on January 1, 1863. Union Army Major General Gordon Granger and some 2,000 federal troops arrived in Galveston, Texas, to read General Order No. 3, announcing that "all slaves are free" and to enforce President Abraham Lincoln's Emancipation Proclamation. Juneteenth is a commemoration of this day and is the oldest known African American celebration of the end of slavery in the United States—Texas was the first state to declare Juneteenth an official state holiday.

Four regional celebrations began with the issuance of varied proclamations of Emancipation. On May 9, 1862, General David Hunter, Commander of the Department of the South, issued an order freeing all the slaves in South Carolina, Georgia, and Florida; on September 22, 1862, President Abraham Lincoln issued his "preliminary proclamation" which gave the seceding states one hundred days to abandon their pro-slavery position; on January 1, 1863, President Lincoln issued his historic Emancipation Proclamation and set in motion the hallowed "Day of Days" celebrations; and on June 19, 1865, General Gordon Granger landed at Galveston, Texas, and read the following General Order Number 3 from the balcony of the Ashton Villa:

The people of Texas are informed in accordance with a Proclamation from the Executive of the United States, all slaves are free. This involves an absolute equality of rights of property between masters and slaves, and the connection heretofore existing between them becomes that between employer and free laborer. The freedmen are advised to remain at their present homes and work for wages. They are informed that they will

not be allowed to collect at military posts, and that they will not besupported in idlenss, either there or elsewhere. . . .

Source: From Francis Edward Abernethy and Texas Folklore Society. Juneteenth Texas: Essays in African-American Folklore. Denton, TX: University of North Texas Press, 1996, pp. 238–239.

Books

Preszler, June. *Juneteenth: Jubilee for Freedom.* Mankato, MN: Capstone Press, 2006. Young people's book explaining the importance and reasons for the Juneteenth celebration.

Taylor, Charles A. *Juneteenth: A Celebration of Freedom.* Greensboro, NC: Open Hand Publishing, LLC, 2002. In depth look at the Juneteenth celebrations.

Websites

19th of June. www.19thofjune.com/.

Juneteenth.com reprints General Order No. 3. http://www.juneteenth.com/general_order _no_3.htm.

June 19, 1865 "all slaves are free." http://www .thevindicator.com/history/article_ca6f5fdc -9797-11e0-80dc-001cc4c002e0.html.

Also Noteworthy

1912

Tennessee State University (TSU) opens in Nashville as the Tennessee Agricultural and Industrial State Normal School. TSU is the state's only historically Black school (HBCU).

June 20

1894

The industrial food chemist Dr. Lloyd Augustus Hall, who held some 80 U.S. and international patents for his inventions on the preservation of food products, is born to Augustus and Isabel Hall in Elgin, Illinois. Hall had a grandmother who had used the

Underground Railroad to come to Illinois and a grandfather who was a founder of Chicago's Quinn Chapel A.M.E. Church. Born to parents who were both high school graduates, Lloyd himself graduated from high school and then studied pharmaceutical chemistry at Northwestern University and at the University of Chicago. As a chemist, Lloyd worked for the Chicago Board of Health, the U.S. Ordinance Department, and was the chief chemist and research director for Griffith Laboratories Inc. for 34 years. Lloyd also served as a consultant to the United Nations' Food and Agriculture Organization and was the first African American to become a fellow of the American Institute of Chemists.

The preservation of food, especially meat, without altering its taste has been one of the biggest problems that industrial chemists have been called upon to solve. One solution that was used for years, the treatment of meat with crystals containing sodium chloride and various nitrates, was developed by Lloyd Hall. Hall also contributed to food science by developing a method for sterilizing spices and other products, discovering why fatty and oily foods become rancid, and developing some of the first artificial flavors.

Source: From Charles W. Carey. *African Americans in Science: An Encyclopedia of People and Progress, Volume 1*. Santa Barbara, CA: ABC-CLIO, 2008, p. 97.

Books

Carey, Charles W. *American Scientists*. New York, NY: Infobase Publishing, 2006. Book contains a biographical sketch on Dr. Hall's work.

Kessler, James H. *Distinguished African American Scientists of the 20th Century*. Santa Barbara, CA: Greenwood Publishing Group, 1996. Book contains a substantive biographical look at Dr. Hall's career as an industrial food chemist.

Websites

Hall's career is remembered on the Massachusetts Institute of Technology Website. http://web.mit.edu/invent/iow/hall2.html.

Griffith Laboratories has a biographical remembrance of Dr. Hall. http://www.griffith laboratories.com/United_States/en-US/people/Profiles+In+Excellence/Dr+Lloyd+A+Hall .htm.

Also Noteworthy

1953

Albert Walter Dent, who served as the third president of the historically black Dillard University, is elected president of the National Health Council.

June 21

1859

Henry Ossawa Tanner is born in Pittsburgh, Pennsylvania, to Sarah Miller Tanner and Reverend Benjamin Tucker Tanner, who served as a bishop in the African Methodist Episcopal Church. Although Tanner was not exposed to the world of art and artists until age 12, he quickly became a disciple, studying at the Pennsylvania Academy of Fine Arts and later moving to Paris, France, and becoming a member of the Paris Society of American Painters and the Société Internationale Peinture et Sculpture. Tanner became the first internationally known painter of African descent.

Henry Ossawa Tanner managed to break the rigid racial barriers of his time and achieved international renown.

Born on the eve of the Civil War and raised in a segregated society, Tanner was immersed in the issues of race in America. In fact, his parents gave him the name "Ossawa" in honor of the abolitionist John Brown, who, along with 40 followers, was attacked in Osawatomie, Kansas, by more than 400 pro-slavery vigilantes in 1856.

For much of his life Tanner associated with famous African-American intellectuals such as W.E.B. Du Bois and Booker T. Washington, and he supported groups such as the National Association for the Advancement of Colored People. Nevertheless, Tanner never returned to genre scenes of African-American life after the 1890s.

For most of his career he was more concerned with religious issues than social and racial issues.

Source: From Thomas Brothers. *Artists, Writers, and Musicians: An Encyclopedia of People Who Changed the World*. Santa Barbara, CA: Greenwood Publishing Group, 2001, p. 176.

Books

Mathews, Marcia M. *Henry Ossawa Tanner: American Artist*. Chicago, IL: University of Chicago Press, 1995. This extensively researched book looks at Henry Ossawa Turner's international fame and the disappointment he became for many in the Black community as he committed himself to artwork based on religion, rather than race.

Museum of African Art. *Art of Henry Ossawa Tanner, 1858–1937*. Victoria, BC: Museum of African Art/AbeBooks, 1970. Book provides a look at the life of Henry Ossawa Turner and his work.

Websites

ExplorePAhistory.com has posted information about the life of Henry Ossawa Tanner and about a marker in Philadelphia that notes where he studied art: http://explorepahistory.com/hmarker.php?markerId=622.

The Smithsonian's Archives of American Art has digitized the papers of Henry Ossawa Tanner. http://www.aaa.si.edu/collectionsonline/tannhenr/.

Also Noteworthy

1915

Supreme Court case of *Guinn v. United States* rules against grandfather clauses that had been used in the Maryland and Oklahoma constitutions to deny African Americans the right to vote.

1945

Col. Benjamin O. Davis, Jr., becomes the first African American to command a U.S. Army Air Corps base.

June 22

1909

The "Matriarch of Black Dance," Katherine Mary Dunham, is born in Chicago and then raised in Joliet, Illinois. Dunham is famed for enhancing the understanding and highlighting the importance of African diaspora dance within U.S. choreography.

At a given moment Téoline set the rhythm for the 'zepaules. La place catapulted into the air, landed on his knees, circles the altar kissing the emblems painted on it, then whirled, bent at right angles, the circumference of the room, miraculously avoiding vévés and drummers. At each vévé he lifted arms and legs high in a whiplash movement so convulsive that we wondered how his head remained attached to his body. He cross-stepped and turned around himself, flailing the air with arms and legs. These "breaks" or feints are common at the high point of all ceremonial dances in Haiti, serving both to release the tension of the dancer and to clear the air of unwanted spirits. The drummers take complete control of these feints once the dance has indicated, consciously or not, that he is ready for them, breaking the rhythm, sucking air in and hissing it out, ejaculating glottal sounds which are supposed to beat the "broken" or out-of-rhythm dancer or group of dancers back in line and to show that it is they, the drummers, who dominate the rhythms. I regard the feints as release periods for both drummers and dancers, and have seen signals calling for the broken beat pass between the two when one or the other is overtaxed.

Source: From Katherine Dunham. *Island Possessed*. Chicago, IL: University of Chicago Press, 1969, p. 130.

Books

Aschenbrenner, Joyce. *Katherine Dunham: Dancing a Life*. Champaign, IL: University of Illinois Press, 2002. A look at the career and influence of Katherine Dunham.

Beckford, Ruth. *Katherine Dunham, a Biography*. Chicago, IL: M. Dekker, 1979. Biography of the life of Katherine Dunham.

Websites

The Katherine Dunham Collection at the Library of Congress. http://lcweb2.loc.gov/diglib/ihas/html/dunham/dunham-timeline.html.

Katherine Dunham—YouTube. www.youtube.com/watch?v=W23MYjH92co.

The Katherine Dunham Centers for Arts & Humanities. http://kdcah.org/.

Also Noteworthy

1897

William Barry receives U.S. Patent No. 585,075 for his postmarking and canceling machine.

1938

The "Brown Bomber" Joe Louis defeats the German boxer Max Schmeling in a little over two minutes in a match that was pitted as a battle of African Americans versus whites. This was a rematch fight, allowing Louis to return and fight the only boxer who had defeated him up until that point.

1943

W. E. B. Du Bois becomes the first African American member of National Institute of Letters.

1951

Pfc. William Thompson is posthumously awarded the Congressional Medal of Honor for his heroism in the Korean conflict. Thompson was the first African American awarded the Congressional Medal since the Spanish-American War.

June 23

1940

Wilma Glodean Rudolph is born the 20th of 22 children in Clarksville, Tennessee. As a young child, she suffered from polio but her mother famously nursed her by massaging her legs and encouraged Wilma's siblings to help her regain leg muscle strength. Encouraged to play sports and to run, Wilma grew to be 5 feet 11 inches and 130 pounds. After becoming a star basketball player at her high school, she was encouraged to take up track and field. Wilma Rudolph became the first woman in the United States to win three gold medals, when she did so on September 7 at the 1960 Summer Olympics.

Wilma Rudolph received many honors in her lifetime. Some of the most meaningful came from her hometown and home state. For instance, the city of Clarksville recognized Wilma Rudolph as one of its most famous natives. The city named an important street Wilma Rudolph Boulevard and raised a bronze statue of Wilma at the corner of College Street and Riverside Drive. On December 2, 1980, Tennessee State University named its indoor track after her.

Source: From Tom Streissguth. *Wilma Rudolph (Sports Heroes and Legends).* Minneapolis, MN: Lerner Classroom, 2007, p. 92.

Books

Rudolph, Wilma. *Wilma.* New York: New American Library, 1977. Wilma Rudolph's autobiography.

Ruth, Amy. *Wilma Rudolph.* Minneapolis, MN: Lerner Publications, 1999. Biography of the life of Wilma Rudolph.

Websites

Wilma Rudolph is profiled on Women in History. http://www.lkwdpl.org/wihohio/rudo-wil.htm.

"ESPN.com: Rudolph Ran and World Went Wild." http://espn.go.com/sportscentury/features/00016444.htm.

Also Noteworthy

1872

Matilda Arabelle Evans is born to Harriet and Andy Evans as the oldest of three children. Evans earned her medical degree at the Women's Medical College of Pennsylvania and returned to South Carolina. Evans famously took in patients at her home until she was able to establish a hospital for them. In 1901, she established the Taylor Lane Hospital and Training School for Nurses in Columbia, South Carolina.

June 24

1964

Carl Thomas Rowan is appointed the director of the U.S. Information Agency. Rowan was born in 1925 in Ravenscroft, Tennessee. After serving as deputy assistant secretary of state for public affairs in the Kennedy administration, Rowan became director of the USIA under President Lyndon B. Johnson. He was next appointed U.S. ambassador to Finland and ultimately spent many years as an influential nationally syndicated columnist.

The interest of the African-American community in the appointment of blacks to, and promotion of blacks within, the foreign policy making bureaucracy of the United States was evident by the amount of newspaper and magazine coverage dedicated to the subject. Nearly each appointment or promotion was cited by the black media as another example of a barrier breached or a new precedent set. The attention given to the career of journalist Carl Rowan provides a good example of this. When Rowan was selected to be deputy assistant secretary of state for public affairs by the incoming Kennedy administration, Jet magazine proudly noted that that would make him "the highest-ranking Negro in the U.S. State Dept." Two years later, when he was named as ambassador to Finland, the Afro-American reported that Rowan saw his appointment "as a challenge to help blaze a trail in the foreign service for other colored citizens." He was quoted as saying that "doors might be opened to more colored students' in the foreign service if he and others of his race demonstrate that colored citizens can serve America's interest abroad with as much distinction and skill as any other citizen."

Source: From Michael L. Krenn. *Black Diplomacy: African Americans and the State Department, 1945–1969*. Armonk, NY: M.E. Sharpe, 1999, pp. 123–124.

Books

Rowan, Carl T. *Just Between Us Blacks*. New York, NY: Random House Inc, 1974. Rowan offers advice about social and economic survival for African Americans, following the Civil Rights Revolution.

Rowan, Carl T. *The Coming Race War in America: A Wake-up Call*. New York, NY: Little, Brown, 1996. Rowan examines the antagonisms between African Americans and whites in the United States.

Websites

Reporting Civil Rights: Reporters and Writers: Carl T. Rowan. http://reportingcivilrights .loa.org/authors/bio.jsp?authorId=67.

The Oberlin College Archives holds the personal papers of Carl T. Rowan. http://www.oberlin .edu/archive/WWW_files/rowan_i.html.

June 25

1908

Beatrice Murphy is born Beatrice Madeline Murphy Campbell in Monessen, Pennsylvania. As an editor and author, Murphy was instrumental in creating the Negro Bibliographic and Research Center (NBRC), which later became known as the Minority Research Center. Today, the Beatrice Murphy Campbell Community Service Award is presented to the individual, organization, or business in the District of Columbia with a demonstrated service toward advancements for people with disabilities.

Like many artists and writers during the 1950s, Murphy was persecuted during the McCarthy era, a time when the U.S. government, following the lead of Senator Jospeh McCarthy, actively sought out members of the Communist Party. Murphy was accused of membership in a subversive community organization, but she successfully disproved the charges and, unlike many of her peers, was able to clear her name. During the 1960s, Murphy gained prominence in the black literary community through her work with the Negro Bibliographic and Research Center (NBRC), which eventually became known as the Minority Research Center. The Negro Bibliographic and Research Center aimed to chronicle the works of African American writers and published a journal titled the Negro in Print, a bibliographic survey. Murphy served as editor of this journal between 1965 and 1972. After Murphy moved on to other endeavors, the NBRC continued to chronicle the black community through a variety of bibliographic tomes covering subjects including black English and the black church.

Source: From Elizabeth Ann Beaulieu. *Writing African American Women: An Encyclopedia of Literature by and about Women of Color, Volume 1.* Santa Barbara, CA: Greenwood Publishing Group, 2006, p. 656.

Books

Honey, Maureen. *Shadowed Dreams: Women's Poetry of the Harlem Renaissance.* Piscataway, NJ: Rutgers University Press, 2006. Contains a short biography of Beatrice M. Murphy alongside selections of her poetry.

Murphy, Beatrice M. *Love is a Terrible Thing.* Victoria, BC: AbeBooks/Hobson Book Press, 1945. Murphy's book of poetical writings.

Websites

The Arc of DC provides a definition of the Beatrice Murphy Campbell Community Service Award. http://www.arcdc.net/newsannoc.html.

Murphy's Valentine's Day poem, "The Letter." http://webspace.webring.com/people/cs/starchaser-m/val/letter.html.

Also Noteworthy

1864

President Abraham Lincoln signs bill providing schools for Black children.

1876

Isaiah Dorman, who had been born free in Philadelphia, Pennsylvania, in 1832, dies on June 25 as a cavalry scout. Dorman died on Reno Ridge fighting for the troops of George Armstrong Custer.

1885

Samuel David Ferguson is ordained the first African American bishop of the Episcopal Church. Ferguson was born in Charleston, South Carolina, but raised and educated in Liberia. Rev. Ferguson also founded Cuttington College in Liberia in 1889.

1941

President Franklin D. Roosevelt issues Executive Order 8802 establishing the Fair Employment Practices Commission (FEPC), which required that companies with government contracts not discriminate on the basis of race or religion. It was intended to help African Americans and other minorities obtain jobs in the U.S. war industry.

1948

The "Brown Bomber" Joe Louis is crowned World Heavyweight Boxing Champion in Chicago, Illinois.

June 26

1939

The novelist, poet, and visual artist Barbara Chase-Riboud is born in Philadelphia, Pennsylvania, to Vivian May Chase and Charles Edward Chase. Chase-Riboud became an expatriate as an adult, but most of her writings and artwork deal with the lives and struggles of African Americans in the United States.

Of course, all of the studies of the Jefferson-Hemings scandal were based on white supremacy.

As previously mentioned, Brodie's Thomas Jefferson: An Intimate History was published five years before Sally Hemings, and was the revolutionary investigation of the alleged affair. Upon reading Brodie's biography, Chase-Riboud decided to breath life into Sally Hemings with the power of the literary arts. Chase-Riboud stated: "I started thinking about the story after I read the Fawn Brodie biography of Jefferson and I just knew somebody was going to write it . . . I'm going to write an epic poem about Thomas Jefferson and Sally Hemings" (J. Wilson 12). Chase-Riboud wanted to retrieve the identity and dignity of Sally Hemings. She tried to put Sally Hemings on an equal footing with Thomas Jefferson by depicting a relationship of equality between lovers, rather than that of coercion under slavery in the antebellum South. Her attitude to this is similar to Brodie's. In the Author's Note to the 1994 edition of Sally Hemings, Chase-Riboud shows her respect for Brodie, writing, "dedicated to the memory of Fawn Brodie." It is no exaggeration to say that it was these two volumes, Thomas Jefferson: An Intimate History by Fawn Brodie and Sally Hemings by Barbara Chase-Riboud, that drew public attention to Sally Hemings. Their works were rebuttals to traditional historians who refused to discuss the Jefferson-Hemings affair or who denied that the liaison had actually occurred. Chase-Riboud constructed Sally Hemings by drawing on her own extensive research, and on Brodie's findings.

Source: From Yoriko Ishida. Modern and Postmodern Narratives of Race, Gender, and Identity: The Descendants of Thomas Jefferson and Sally Hemings. New York, NY: Peter Lang, 2010, p. 47.

Books

Chase-Riboud, Barbara. *Hottentot Venus: A Novel*. New York, NY: Random House Digital, Inc., 2004. Chase-Riboud tackles the story of Sarah Baartman, a South African woman who was brought to Europe and presented as a freak of nature, labeled the "Hottentot Venus."

Chase-Riboud, Barbara. *Sally Hemings: A Novel*. Chicago, IL: Chicago Review Press, 2009. Chase-Riboud's look at the 38-year relationship between Thomas Jefferson, the principal author of the Declaration of Independence,

and Sally Hemmings, a woman he owned as a slave.

Websites

Cornell University has a page about Barbara Chase-Riboud. http://www.law.cornell.edu /background/amistad/bcr.html.

Barbara Chase-Riboud reading from her works on YouTube. www.youtube.com/watch ?v=T9t05m7Hvco.

Also Noteworthy

1964

African Americans and whites riot over continuing racial segregation in St. Augustine, Florida.

1975

Samuel Blanton Rosser becomes the first African American certified in pediatric surgery.

June 27

1872

The poet and novelist Paul Laurence Dunbar is born in Dayton, Ohio, to Matilda and Josiah Dunbar, who had each escaped enslavement in the state of Kentucky. Dunbar's father had served in the 55th Massachusetts Infantry Regiment and the 5th Massachusetts Colored Cavalry Regiment during the Civil War. His parents instilled in him a love of learning and history, and Paul Laurence Dunbar would grow up attending predominately white schools and excelling as a literary stand-out. Dunbar first won national recognition for his 1896 book of poetry, *Lyrics of a Lowly Life*. He was recognized for his skilled use of African American dialect in his poetry.

As for the temper which fostered Dunbar's hopes, it is derived from Frances Ellen Watkins and consists in the awakening artistic consciousness, which in its perfect state permits of no racial limitations of matter and method. Through Dunbar and James Weldon Johnson this consciousness flows strong but less pure to the group of young writers who have been called "New Negroes." That the New Negroes have not attempted to to do what Dunbar did in prose is perhaps a mark of their wisdom. But their spirit is much the same. Many years must elapse before white America (the audience for whom books are published and to whom books are sold) will accept white American novels by Negroes. Poetry has moved less slowly, and certain Negro poets stand today as proof that Dunbar's spirit was right. As regards his white audience in general, Dunbar's words in, "The Poet," will probably remain true:

He sang of love when earth was young,
And Love, itself was in his lays.
But ah, the world, it turned to praise
A jungle in a broken tongue.

Source: From Jay Saunders Redding. *To Make a Poet Black*. Ithaca, NY: Cornell University Press, 1939, p. 67.

Books

Dunbar, Paul Laurence and Lida Keck Wiggins. *The Life and Works of Paul Laurence Dunbar: Containing His Complete Poetical Works, His Best Short Stories, Numerous Anecdotes and a Complete Biography of the Famous Poet*. Kila, MT: Kessinger Publishing, 2006. Dunbar's collected works of poetry.

Dunbar, Paul Laurence and William Andrew. *The Sport of the Gods*. New York, NY: Penguin, 2011. Dunbar's novel about southern African American efforts to survive in Harlem, New York.

Websites

The University of Dayton hosts a Paul Laurence Dunbar site. http://www.dunbarsite.org/.

Wright State University has a detailed biography of Paul Laurence Dunbar. http://www.libraries.wright.edu/special/dunbar/further_study/detailed_bio.html.

1936

The poet/children's book author Lucille Clifton is born Thelma Lucille Sayles in Depew,

New York, on June 27, 1936. Clifton served as Poet Laureate of Maryland from 1979 to 1985, became the first African American woman to win the Ruth Lilly Poetry Prize in 2007, and received the Frost Medal of the Poetry Society of America in 2010.

When I first started writing, when Good Times was first accepted by Random House, someone knew I had children and wanted to know if I had ever tried writing for children. I had not. But I did tell my kids stories. And so I started thinking about what could I do in the field, and I came up with the first book of Everett Anderson, Some of the Days of Everett Anderson. I found that I was able to write for children. It seems very easy, but it's not necessarily so. And so I thought, "Well, here's two different things." And, to me, they are absolutely two different things, two different careers entirely. They impact on each other, of course. But they are two different careers. People who know me as a children's author tend to not know me as a poet.

Source: From Hilary Holladay. *Wild Blessings: The Poetry of Lucille Clifton*. Baton Rouge, LA: LSU Press, 2004, pp. 184–185.

Books

Johnson, Hannibal B. *Acres of Aspiration: The All-black Towns in Oklahoma*. Waco, TX: Eakin Press, 2002. Looks at the all-Black towns of Oklahoma and their inspiration to the rest of the state's African American community.

Taylor, Quintard and Shirley Ann Wilson Moore, eds. *African American Women Confront the West, 1600–2000*. Norman, OK: University of Oklahoma Press, 2008. Authors look at the roles African American women have played in the formation of the western United States.

Websites

The Maryland Women's Hall of Fame Website has an entry on Lucille Clifton. http://www.msa.md.gov/msa/educ/exhibits/womenshall/html/clifton.html.

Stanford Law School's Robert Crown Library has a Women's Legal History Website, with a biographical sketch on Ada Lois Sipuel

Fisher. http://womenslegalhistory.stanford
.edu/profiles/FisherAda.html.

The University of Oklahoma's Graduate College
dedicates a page to Ada Lois Sipuel Fisher's
struggles to enter the law school. http://gradweb
.ou.edu/History/Bios/Students/Fisher.asp.

Also Noteworthy

1939

Frederick McKinley Jones receives U.S. Patent No. 2,163,754 for a ticket dispensing
machine.

June 28

1960

Peace and civil rights activist Bayard Taylor
Rustin resigns from the board of the Southern
Christian Leadership Conference (SCLC).
Rustin was a civil rights leader and one of
the principle organizers of the 1963 march
on Washington for Jobs and Freedom. Born
March 17, 1912, in West Chester, Pennsylvania, Rustin was a noted pacifist who worked
with the Congress of Racial Equality
(CORE) and the Fellowship of Reconciliation to push for an end to segregationist policies. In 1957, Rustin had helped Martin
Luther King, Jr., organize the SCLC but
resigned after Rep. Adam Clayton Powell,
Jr., threatened to expose Rustin's arrests for
homosexuality and Communist Party affiliation work.

On February 20, 1956, the executive committee of
the War Resisters League learned that "a request
had been received for Bayard Rustin to go to
Montgomery, Alabama." The league did not indi-
cate who made the request or to whom it was
directed. Did King or Abernathy want him back?
The executive committee voted "unanimously to
send Bayard, since he has had considerable experience with non-violent resistance in both the
North and South." The War Resisters League saw
the potential for the Montgomery Improvement
Association and Martin Luther King to create a

mass movement, a nonviolent mass movement.
King, they said, "is developing a decidedly
Gandhi-like view," but he was not all the way
there yet. The WRL could do many things to help
King, and one of them was to send Bayard. The
WRL may have been unanimous, but the Fellowship of Reconciliation had serious qualms. Rustin
was vulnerable to being framed. They were
worried that perhaps some sort of issue might
erupt—were they imagining a homosexual incident?—that would make Rustin a focal point of
the opposition. The FOR leadership agreed not to
interfere with him but forbade Glenn Smiley from
having anything to do with his old friend.

Source: From Daniel Levine. *Bayard Rustin and
the Civil Rights Movement*. Piscataway, NJ:
Rutgers University Press, 2000, p. 80.

Books

Anderson, Jervis. *Bayard Rustin: Troubles I've Seen:
A Biography*. New York, NY: HarperCollins-
Publishers, 1997. Biography of Bayard Rustin.

Rustin, Bayard, Devon W. Carbado, and Donald
Weise. *Time on Two Crosses: The Collected Writings of Bayard Rustin*. Berkeley, CA: Cleis Press,
2003. Writings and editorial writings describe
the life and activism of Bayard Rustin.

Websites

Website for the documentary "Brother Outsider." http://rustin.org/.

Bayard Rustin Civil Rights Leader. http://
www.quakerinfo.com/quak_br.shtml.

Also Noteworthy

1864

Fugitive slave laws are repealed by the U.S.
Congress.

June 29

1886

James Augustus Joseph Van Der Zee is born
to John VanDerZee and Susan Elizabeth

Egberts in Lenox, Massachusetts. As a photographer, James Van Der Zee became a famed recorder of African Americans in Harlem of the early twentieth century.

> The business continued to prosper after the end of World War I, when an even greater number of southern blacks migrated north to Harlem, stimulating the creative explosion of the Harlem Renaissance. Van Der Zee made portraits of heavyweight champion Jack Johnson, the Reverenend Adam Clayton Powell Sr., dancer and "Mayor of Harlem" Bill "Bojangles" Robinson, singers Florence Mills and Mamie Smith, and countless numbers of ordinary Harlemites. Every photograph presented a positive image of its sitter. There was no ugliness in James Van Der Zee's world. He once said, "I tried to see that every picture was better-looking than the person." He also told stories in his pictures, explaining, "I wanted to make the camera take what I thought should be there."
>
> Source: From James Haskins, Eleanora E. Tate, Clinton Cox, Brenda Wilkinson. *Black Stars of the Harlem Renaissance*. New York, NY: John Wiley & Sons, 2002, p. 46.

Books

Van Der Zee, James, Owen Dodson and Camille Billops. *The Harlem Book of the Dead*. Dobbs Ferry, NY: Morgan & Morgan, 1978. Van Der Zee's look at the burial practices of African Americans in Harlem, NY.

Willis-Braithwaite, Deborah and Rodger C. Birt. *VanDerZee: Photographer: 1886–1983*. New York, NY: Harry N. Abrams, 1998. Biography of VenDerZee includes a look at his photographs.

Websites

James Van Der Zee photos are on YouTube. http://www.youtube.com/watch?v=QSLMZ 3igO-c.

Wedge Gallery has a biography of Van Der Zee. http://wedgegallery.netfirms.com/JHarticle .php.

June 30

1921

Charles Sidney Gilpin is awarded the National Association for the Advancement of Colored People's Springarm Medal for his performance as "Brutus Jones" in Eugene O'Neill's play *Emperor Jones*. Gilpin's performance was so widely applauded that he was also received at the White House.

> He is generally acknowledged to be America's first "serious" Negro actor, and many say he was the greatest. For his performance as Emperor Jones, the Drama League named him one of the ten persons who, in 1920, had contributed the most to the theater.
>
> As the first Negro to be so honored, he was at first reluctant to attend the Drama League dinner. He thought he might not be welcome. But he went, and his speech was the hit of the evening.
>
> I like to keep the footlights between me and the public. I don't go in much for hobnobbing . . . I have my own little circle of friends and I love them. I live quietly in Harlem where I belong. I am really a race man, a Negro, and proud of being one . . . .
>
> Source: From William M. Dwyer. *So Long for Now: A World War II Memoir*. Bloomington, IN: Xlibris Corporation, 2009, p. 149.

Books

Brawley, Benjamin Griffith. *The Negro in Literature and Art: In the United States*. Whitefish, MT: Kessinger Publishing, 2006. Book presents a look at the theatrical career and biography of Charles S. Gilpin.

Cullen, Frank, Florence Hackman, and Donald McNeilly. *Vaudeville Old & New: An Encyclopedia of Variety Performances in America, Volume 1*. Boca Raton, FL: Routledge, Taylor & Francis Group/Psychology Press, 2004. Book contains an analysis of Gilpin and his role in the U.S. theater.

Websites

Schomburg Center profiles "Charles S. Gilpin (1878-1930) actor, as 'The Emperor Jones'." http://www2.si.umich.edu/chico/Harlem/text/gilpin.html.

The New York Public Library's Digital Collections has "Charles S. Gilpin as Emperor Jones. (1920)" http://digitalgallery.nypl.org/nypldigital/dgkeysearchdetail.cfm?trg=1&strucID=337952&imageID=490047&word=19724&s=1&notword=&d=&c=&f=13&k=0&lWord=&lField=&sScope=Name&sLevel=&sLabel=Vandamm%20Studio&total=2576&num=80&imgs=20&pNum=&pos=84.

July

July 1

1893

Walter Francis White is born to George W. White, who was a postal carrier, and Madeline Harrison, who was a teacher, in Atlanta, Georgia. White was a journalist and civil rights activist who served as a leader of the National Association for the Advancement of Colored People.

Walter White reveled in the disorientation caused by his apparent whiteness. He loved to tell of the time he was on a train and an ostensibly cultured southern man assured him that he could tell if a Negro was trying to pass simply by looking at his fingernails; examining White's, the man told him that unlike his, blacks' fingernails had pink crescents at the cuticles. He recounted with glee the bafflement on prominent whites' faces when he unexpectedly revealed to them his racial identity. He derived great satisfaction from this masquerade, this putting one over on whites. At the same time he could make himself the punch line of the joke. His autobiography is titled A Man Called White. *He enjoyed his work with Algernon Black, the leader of the Ethical Culture Society, with whom he served in the wake of the 1943 Harlem riot. White appreciated Black's comment that "the Black-White Committee is an ideal combination, especially since the man named 'Black' is white and the man named 'White' is black—or calls himself black."*

Source: From Kenneth Robert Janken. *Walter White: Mr. NAACP.* Chapel Hill, NC: UNC Press Books, 2006, p. 2.

Books

Dyja, Thomas. *Walter White: The Dilemma of Black Identity in America.* Lanham, MD: Ivan R. Dee Publisher, 2010. Biography of Walter Francis White.

Walter, White. *A Man Called White.* Athens, GA: University of Georgia Press, 1995. White's autobiography of his civil rights work.

White, Walter Francis. *Rope and Faggot: A Biography of Judge Lynch.* Notre Dame, IN: University of Notre Dame Press. Walter White's account of how lynching was used to intimidate and control African Americans in the U.S. South. Book presents excerpts from Ashe's diary, written between 1973 and 1974.

Websites

Yale University's Beinecke Library profiles Walter White. http://beineckejwj.library.yale.edu/2009/06/02/walter-white-papers/.

Walter White, Mr. NAACP. http://www.loc.gov/loc/lcib/0304/white.html.

Also Noteworthy

1899

Thomas Andrew Dorsey is born in Villa Rica, Georgia. Dorsey is known as the "father of gospel music," because he was the first to meld secular blues music with religious text.

1942

Andraé Crouch is born in San Francisco, California. Crouch became a seven-time Grammy Award-winning gospel singer, songwriter, arranger, and recording artist.

1970

Kenneth Gibson becomes the first black mayor of an Eastern city when he assumes the post in Newark, New Jersey.

July 2

1908

Thurgood Marshall is born to William Marshall and Norma Williams Marshall in Baltimore, Maryland. After attending Howard University Law School, Marshall became chief counsel for the National Association for the Advancement of Colored People (NAACP); he argued and won the landmark 1954 *Brown v. Board of Education of Topeka, Kansas,* decision before the U.S. Supreme Court and in 1961 was appointed to the U.S. Court of Appeals for the Second Circuit by President John F. Kennedy. In 1967, Thurgood Marshall was named the first African American to sit as a U.S. Supreme Court Judge; he served from 1967 to 1991.

America, Marshall reasoned, had to be sued to enforce its own Constitution, and he believed that if the NAACP put enough legal pressure on Jim Crow, racist institutions would collapse. Court-ordered integration would be extremely unpopular in the South, but Marshall felt it would work because "even in the most prejudiced communities, I think the majority of people have some respect for truth and some sense of justice, no matter how deeply hidden it is at times."

Source: From Chris Crowe. *Thurgood Marshall.* New York, NY: Penguin, 2008, pp. 152–153.

Books

Haugen, Brenda. *Thurgood Marshall: Civil Rights Lawyer and Supreme Court Justice.* Mankato, MN: Compass Point Books, 2007. Biography of Justice Thurgood Marshall's life and career.

Williams, Juan. *Thurgood Marshall: American Revolutionary.* New York, NY: Random House Digital, Inc., 2000. Author looks at Justice Marshall as one of the most influential African Americans of the twentieth century.

Websites

The Oyez Project has a biography of Justice Thurgood Marshall. http://www.oyez.org/justices/thurgood_marshall.

Thurgood Marshall, Supreme Court Justice is available on the Roy Rosenzweig Center for History and New Media site. http://chnm.gmu.edu/courses/122/hill/marshall.htm.

Also Noteworthy

1777

Vermont becomes the first U.S. territory to abolish African slavery.

1839

The Sierra Leone-born Sengbe Pieh (who would become known in the Americas as "Joseph Cinque") leads 53 other captured Africans in a revolt on the Spanish slave-trading ship *Amistad.* Sengbe was the son of a local chief in Sierra Leone; he was married, the father of three children, and busy working as a rice farmer when slave-traders captured him in 1839. After being taken to Cuba, Sengbe was purchased by Jose Ruiz. Ruiz wanted Sengbe and the other enslaved Africans he had purchased taken to Cuba's Puerto Principe. But while being transported there, Sengbe orchestrated a mutiny. The *Amistad* mutiny led to a trial in the U.S. state of Connecticut, which found that the Africans were justified in fighting against their kidnappers. The antislavery movement raised funds to help the 35 Africans who survived to mutiny return to Sierra Leone. The group arrived back in Africa in January 1842, along with a group of Christian missionaries. Sengbe's wife and three children had been killed while he was held in the Americas. and he was last known to have traveled down the coast in search of other relatives.

1917

Racist violence against African Americans erupts in East St. Louis. Tensions had been growing in the months leading up to the one of the bloodiest race riots in U.S. history.

On July 2nd, racist violence reached its cruelest crescendo as wanton rioting broke out after two white detectives were shot and killed the day before. White mobs assembled and marched into East St. Louis, burning black homes while beating and killing any African Americans they could encounter. Interviews with eyewitnesses conducted by Ida B. Wells reveal horrific details of the racial massacre as she noted the violence effectively made black skin a death warrant. Wells reported that between 40 and 150 African Americans had been killed, with thousands more fleeing their homes. The National Guard of Illinois and the police of East St. Louis stood by complacently as the carnage raged on, proving that deadly race riots were not the sole providence of the South.

1935

The playwright Ed Bullins is born in Philadelphia, Pennsylvania. Bullins wrote more than 100 plays and—because he served as the Black Panthers' Minister of Culture—most of his themes were focused on Black Nationalism.

1964

The U.S. Congress passes Public Law 82-352 (78 Stat. 241), also known as the Civil Rights Act of 1964. The Civil Rights Act is designed to help enforce the Fourteenth Amendment to the U.S. Constitution.

July 3

1904

Charles Richard Drew is born to Richard and Nora Drew in Washington, DC. After writing a dissertation on the idea of a "Blood Bank," Dr. Charles Drew was named director of the British Blood Plasma Project, and created a way to collect a central depository for blood during World War II. Drew became the world's pioneer in blood preservation when he developed the Blood Bank program, which is still in use today.

> *Dr. Drew was one of the first in his profession to research body fluid balance and to administer early plasma transfusions to trauma patients in emergency situations. Charles Drew and his research colleagues developed standard methods for banking blood and techniques for transporting plasma overseas. The process proved to be extremely valuable during World War II when servicemen wounded in battle were in urgent need of blood transfusions. In the aftermath of the war and to the present, plasma collected by blood banks saved millions of lives.*
>
> *Source*: From Abraham Resnick. *They Too Influenced a Nation's History: The Unique Contributions of 105 Lesser-Known Americans*. Bloomington, IN: iUniverse, 2003, p. 32.

Books

Love, Spencie. *One Blood: The Death and Resurrection of Charles R. Drew*. Chapel Hill, NC: UNC Press Books, 1997. Biography of Dr. Drew looks at his medical contributions and the legend surrounding his death.

Trice, Linda. *Charles Drew: Pioneer of Blood Plasma*. New York, NY: McGraw-Hill, 2000. Biography on the contributions of Dr. Charles Drew.

Websites

Charles Drew University of Medicine and Science. www.cdrewu.edu/about-cdu/dr-charles-drew.

American Red Cross Museum—Dr. Charles Drew. www.redcross.org/museum/history/charlesdrew.asp.

Also Noteworthy

1688

The Quakers in Germantown, Pennsylvania, make the first formal protest against the enslavement of Africans.

1775

Prince Hall founds Africa Lodge No. 1. Hall was the father of Black Masons in the United States and a major African American leader in the Northeast.

1962

Jackie Robinson becomes the first African American named to enter the Major League Baseball Hall of Fame.

1966

Race riots erupt in Omaha, Nebraska.

July 4

1845

The sculptor Mary Edmonia Lewis is born in Newark, New Jersey, to a father of African American descent and a mother who was of mixed African American and Ojibwe descent. Because both her parents died when she was young, Lewis was raised by her mother's sisters. After attending Oberlin College and then living and creating art in Rome, Italy, Lewis gained international fame with her piece "The Death of Cleopatra," which was featured at the 1876 Centennial Exposition in Philadelphia.

During her first decade in Rome, she continued to portray themes of emancipation and slavery and also executed a number of pieces drawing directly or indirectly upon Longfellow's Hiawatha. Among her portraits were busts in terra-cotta of Longfellow, John Brown, Abraham Lincoln, Charles Sumner, Garrison, and Hosmer. Her largest known piece, and perhaps her best, was The Death of Cleopatra, which, along with six smaller figures, was shown at the 1876 Philadelphia Centennial Exposition. "Cleopatra" was "lost" for well over a hundred years, during which time it was vandalized, exposed to the elements and, finally, painted. After its rediscovery, it was restored in 1995 and is now in the Smithsonian's National Museum of American Art.

Source: From Mary Sayre Haverstock, Jeannette Mahoney Vance, Brian L. Meggitt, Jeffrey Weidman, and Oberlin College Library. *Artists in Ohio, 1787–1900: A Biographical Dictionary*. Kent, OH: Kent State University Press, 2000, p. 526.

Books

Buick, Kirsten Pai. *Child of the Fire: Mary Edmonia Lewis and the Problem of Art History's Black and Indian Subject*. Durham, NC: Duke University Press, 2010. Biography of the life of Mary Edmonia Lewis.

Wolfe, Rinna. *Edmonia Lewis: Wildfire in Marble*. Scottsdale, AZ: Dillon Press, 1998. Focuses on Lewis's achievements at a time when her African/Chippewa heritage might have held her back.

Websites

Women in History profiles Mary Edmonia Lewis. http://www.lkwdpl.org/wihohio/lewi-edm.htm.

Art HERstory: Mary Edmonia Lewis. http://www.missomnimedia.com/2010/01/art-herstory-mary-edmonia-lewis/.

Also Noteworthy

1881

Booker T. Washington opens the Tuskegee Normal Institute (originally known as the Normal School for Colored Teachers) in Alabama's Zion Negro Church. Over the years, Washington's fundraising efforts would lead to Tuskegee owning land and building its own school buildings.

July 5

1892

Andrew Jackson Beard, who was born enslaved on a farm in Eastlake, Alabama—just outside Birmingham—patents the rotary engine with U.S. Patent No. 478,271. On November 23, 1897, Beard would also create a device he called the Janney, or Jenny Coupler (U.S. Patent No. 594,059; officially known as the "Automatic Railroad Car Coupler"), which could automatically join railroad cars. Beard sold the rights to his Jenny Coupler for $50,000.

Andrew Jackson Beard, a slave born in Jefferson County, Alabama, owned a farm near Birmingham. Once he tried to sell apples in Montgomery using a team of oxen to pull his wagon, but after the trip took three weeks, he quit farming and constructed a flour mill in Hardwick, Alabama. Experimenting with plow designs, Beard patented a plow in 1881, and then sold it in 1884 for $4,000—a fantastic sum at the time. He continued to refine plow designs, then, with his total savings— approximately $30,000—Beard entered the real estate market. Still, he continued to invent, creating a remarkable rotary steam engine patented in 1892. Early work in railroad yards provided Beard with a firsthand exposure to the hazards of hooking railroad cars together. The process was done entirely by hand, requiring a worker to stand between cars and place a metal pin in the coupling devices at the very instant that the cars came together. Fingers, hands, and arms all fell prey to accidents with the metal couplers, and Beard suffered the loss of a leg in a coupler accidents, focusing him on a solution. In 1897, he received a patent for the famous "Jenny" coupler, in which the coupling devices secured themselves when bumped together, like in a handshake. An improved version of the Jenny remains the foundation for the modern automatic coupler, and Beard saved untold hundreds of railroad employees from severe personal injury.

Source: From Larry Schweikart and Lynne Pierson Doti. American Entrepreneur: The Fascinating Stories of the People Who Defined Business in the United States. New York, NY: AMACOM Division of American Management Association, 2010, p. 163.

Books

Bailey, Richard. *They Too Call Alabama Home: African American Profiles, 1800–1999*. Victoria, BC: AbeBooks/Pyramid Pub., 1999. Book includes information about Andrew Jackson Beard.

Shaw, Charles E. *The Untold Stories of Excellence*. Bloomington, IN: Xlibris Corporation. Book includes a look at Andrew Jackson Beard and his inventions.

Websites

HALL OF FAME/inventor profile of Andrew Jackson Beard. http://www.invent.org/hall _of_fame/245.html.

National Railroad Hall of Fame profiles Andrew Jackson Beard. http://www.nrrhof.org/pages/ beard.php.

Also Noteworthy

1975

Tennis player Arthur Ashe wins the men's singles championship at Wimbledon's All England Lawn Tennis Club.

July 6

1868

The South Carolina House becomes the first and only legislature to have an African American majority. Whites continued to control the Senate though and regained the majority in the House in 1874.

The Constitutional Convention of 1868 met in Charleston, South Carolina, in January. Its delegates were made up of 76 Negroes and 48 Whites. This proportion was natural, for African American voters outnumbered the Whites. Among the African Americans were exceptionally capable men. Some of the most notable men were Francis L. Cardozo, Robert B. Elliott, Richard H. Cain and Jonathan J. Wright. It was also noted that:

The Constitution of 1868 was more democratic than any previous one in South Carolina history. It included universal male-suffrage and omitted all property qualifications for office holding. It likewise provided for popular election of many officials formerly appointed by the governor or legislature . . . The new legislature met in July, 1868. In the Senate ten of the 31 members were

Negroes; in the House, 78 of 124 were colored. The Negro legislators remained in the majority until 1874.

Source: From Emmanuel Ike Udogu. *African American Politics in Rural America: Theory, Practice, and Case Studies from Florence County, South Carolina*. Lanham. MD: Rowman & Littlefield Publishing Group/University Press of America, 2006, p. 59.

Books

Cothran, John C. *A Search of African American Life, Achievement and Culture: Over 1,800 Facts, Questions and Answers over 400 Photographs and Illustrations*. Carrollton, TX: Stardate Publishing, 2006. Book includes information about the African American politicians who served as part of the South Carolina House of Representatives.

Megginson, W. J. *African American Life in South Carolina's Upper Piedmont, 1780–1900*. Columbia, SC: University of South Carolina Press, 2006. Book looks at the development of African American political strength in South Carolina.

Websites

Robert Brown Elliott—Representative, 1871–1874, Republican from South Carolina. http://baic.house.gov/member-profiles/profile.html?intID=4.

Joseph Hayne Rainey—Representative, 1870–1879, Republican from South Carolina. http://baic.house.gov/member-profiles/profile.html?intID=11.

Also Noteworthy

1971

Henry Thomas Sampson receives U.S. Patent No. 3,591,860 for his co-invention (along with George H. Miley) of the gamma-electric cell. Dr. Sampson's invention consists of a nuclear fusion process that converts nuclear radiation into electric energy.

July 7

1906

Leroy Robert "Satchel" Paige is born to John and Lula Page in Mobile, Alabama. After his father died, Lula Page changed the family's last name to "Paige." Satchel Paige is known as the greatest pitcher in the history of the Negro Leagues—and possibly even in the history of professional baseball. Major League Baseball's Cleveland Indians signed Paige on July 7, 1948, when he was 42 years old. Paige pitched for the St. Louis Browns up to the age of 47 and even threw three scoreless innings for the Kansas City Athletics in 1965, when he was 59.

Talking to base runners became part of Satchel's routine. Normally he shouted from the mound but when he really wanted to make a point or stir up fans, he walked his message to the base. He did that once in Dayton, Ohio, when Dizzy tripled off him with a blooper over first and nobody out. "The fans were yellin' their head off for me," Dean told a radio audience, "when ol' Satch walks over and says to me, 'I hope all your friends brought plenty to eat, Diz, because if they wait for you to score, they're gonna be here past dark. You ain't goin' no further.' Then he fanned the next three." Satchel came back with a story of his own set out west, where he had heard Dizzy on the radio before the game arguing that Satch had no clue how to throw a curve. The truth was that Satchel had been quietly perfecting that pitch and others to go along with his trademark fastball. When Dean came up to bat that afternoon, Satchel yelled, "Hear say you're goin' around tellin'-people I ain't got a curve . . . Well, then, you tell me what this is." He threw three curves, with Dizzy swinging at air each time. "How's that," Satchel screeched, "for a guy who ain't got a curve ball?"

Source: From Larry Tye. *SATCHEL: The Life and Times of an American Legend*. New York: Random House, 2009, pp. 92–93.

Books

Paige, Leroy "Satchel." *Maybe I'll Pitch Forever*. Lincoln, NE: University of Nebraska Press/

Bison Books, 1993. Autobiography of Satchel Paige, by Satchel Paige.

Ribowsky, Mark. *Don't Look Back: Satchel Paige in the Shadows of Baseball.* New York: Da Capo Press, 1994. Biography looks at Paige's life outside of baseball, and how it affected his professional career and persona.

Websites

The Official Satchel Paige Home Page. http://www.satchelpaige.com/.

"Satchel Paige Pitching Footage" YouTube video shows Paige's pitching form. http://www.youtube.com/watch?v=I3q2TeFuTq8&feature=related.

1920

William Thaddeus Coleman, Jr. is born July 7, 1920, in Philadelphia, Pennsylvania. Coleman became the first African American on the Harvard Law Review and the first Black clerk to the U.S. Supreme Court. He was the co-author of the 1954 legal brief for the appellants in the U.S. Supreme Court case *Brown v. Board of Education* and served as president of the NAACP Legal Defense and Education Fund, and on January 14, 1975, President Gerald Ford appointed Coleman the U.S. Secretary of Transportation (Coleman was the second African American to hold a U.S. cabinet post.)

In 1948, William Thaddeus Coleman Jr., who graduated first in his class at Harvard Law School, was appointed a clerk to United States Supreme Court Justice Felix Frankfurter. He was the first African American ever to serve as a law clerk to a Supreme Court justice.

Source: From Joan Potter. *African American Firsts: Famous Little-Known and Unsung Triumphs of Blacks in America.* New York: Kensington Publishing/Dafina Books, 2002, p. 141.

Books

Harley, Sharon. *The Timetables of African-American History: A Chronology of the Most*

Important People and Events in African-American History. New York: Simon & Schuster, 1996. In this illustrated chronology of famous events, the author notes Coleman's ascendancy as a U.S. Supreme Court clerk.

Kane, Joseph Nathan. *Famous First Facts: A Record of First Happenings, Discoveries and Inventions in the United States.* Victoria, BC: AbeBooks/H. W. Wilson, 1964. In this reference book, the author notes that Justice Felix Frankfurter appointed William Thaddeus Coleman, Jr., of Philadelphia, Pennsylvania, the first African American clerk to the U.S. Supreme Court.

Websites

The National Leadership Project's Oral History Archive features a biographical entry on William T. Coleman, Jr. http://www.visionaryproject.com/colemanwilliam/.

Coleman was the featured lecturer at Harvard University's Charles Hamilton Houston Institute for Race and Justice, where he spoke about his legal career. http://www.law.harvard.edu/news/2008/04/16_coleman.php.

Also Noteworthy

1957

Althea Gibson wins the Women's Singles tennis championship at Wimbledon's All England Lawn Tennis Club.

1949

New Orleans's style jazz trumpeter William Gary "Bunk" Johnson dies. Johnson's birth date has never been factually determined, but many believe it was December 27, 1889.

July 8

1908

Jazz bandleader and songwriter Louis Thomas Jordan is born to James Aaron and Adell Jordan in Brinkley, Arkansas. Often referred to as the "father of rhythm and blues" and "king of the jukebox," Jordan

From a distance, it may appear that Louis Jordan instigated the most important transition of American pop music, that from a swing-and-show music foundation to a rhythm and blues foundation. But Jordan, who was himself also displaced when blues-driven pop took over the marketplace in the mid-fifties,was too idiosyncratic, too individual, and too flat-out swinging—too Petootie Pie—to represent various kinds of cultural forces impacting upon one another. More than that of any other figure, Louis Jordan's music belongs equally to the worlds of swing and the blues, but in the end it's wrong to try and make it part of a larger equation that explains the ebbs and flows of pop music. It's just too singular.

Source: From Will Friedwald. *A Biographical Guide to the Great Jazz and Pop Singers.* New York: Random House Digital, Inc., 2010, p. 141.

Books

Chilton, John. *Let the Good Times Roll: The Story of Louis Jordan and His Music.* Ann Arbor, MI: University of Michigan Press, 1997. Biography of Louis Jordan.

Pener, Degen. *The Swing Book.* New York, NY: Hachette Digital, Inc., 1999. Contains a short biography of Louis Jordan.

Websites

LouisJordan.com is the official Website commemorating the jazz great. www.louisjordan .com/.

Louis Jordan and his Tympani Five perform "Let The Good Times Roll." http://www.youtube .com/watch?v=YdQJ3Q0uhYE.

Also Noteworthy

1914

William Clarence "Billy" Eckstine is born in Pittsburgh, Pennsylvania. As Billy Eckstine he became famous as a jazz- and swing-era ballad singer.

1923

William Harrison Dillard is born in Cleveland, Ohio. Dillard, who claimed that Jesse Owens inspired him, was only the second male athlete to ever win Olympic titles in both sprinting and hurdling events. Dillard won a gold medal in the 100 meter dash at the 1948 Olympics in London and later won gold in the 4 × 100-meter relay at the 1952 Olympics in Helsinki.

1938

Julia Carson is born Julia May Porter in Louisville, Kentucky. After starting out in poverty, Carson was working as a secretary for the United Auto Workers union when Indiana Democratic Party Rep. Andy Jacobs hired her to work with him. After serving as Jacobs's office manager, Carson ran for office herself: she was elected to the Indiana House of Representatives in 1972 and the State Senate in 1976. In 1997, Carson was elected to represent Indiana's Seventh Congressional District in the U.S. House of Representatives.

1943

Faye Wattleton, the first African American director of Planned Parenthood, is born Alyce Faye Wattleton in St. Louis, Missouri.

July 9

1893

Dr. Daniel Hale Williams performs the first successful open heart surgery at Provident Hospital. Daniel Hale Williams was born in Hollidaysburg, Pennsylvania, in 1856. After receiving an MD from Chicago Medical College (which became Northwestern Medical School) in 1883, Williams became a respected surgeon in Chicago's Black community. After Emma Reynolds was repeatedly denied admission to local nursing schools because she was Black, she and her brother, the Reverend Louis Reynolds of St. Stephen's African Methodist Episcopal Church, enlisted Dr. Williams for help.

Eventually, Williams won the support of local Black organizations and some whites to contribute toward the founding of the Provident Hospital and Training School for Nurses on May 4, 1891. Today, Provident is the oldest Black-owned hospital in the United States: it was Chicago's first racially integrated hospital (employing both Black and white doctors) and the first nursing school for Black women in the United States. In 1893, Williams pioneered open-heart surgery when he successfully removed a knife from the heart of a stabbing victim; his patient was able to live another 50 years after the surgery. In 1913, Dr. Williams was the sole African American in a group of 100 charter members to the American College of Surgeons, and he founded and became the first vice-president of the National Medical Association. In 1970, the U.S. Congress issued a commemorative stamp in Dr. Williams's honor.

> On January 23, 1891, medical history was made. The first interracial hospital in the United States was founded. Articles of incorporation were drawn up in the name of the Provident Hospital and Training School Association. The trustees, executive committee, and finance committee were all colored. The hospital itself opened its doors in May 1891—a three-story building at Twenty-ninth Street and Dearborn, with room for twelve beds. The first year, out of 175 applicants for nurse training, Dr. Dan accepted seven, the sister of the Reverend Reynolds among them. All were high school graduates. The training period was for eighteen months.
>
> Source: From Louis Haber. *Black Pioneers of Science and Invention*. New York, NY: Houghton Mifflin Harcourt, 2007, p. 785.

Books

Byrd, W. Michael and Linda A. Clayton. *An American Health Dilemma: A Medical History of African Americans and the Problem of Race, Beginnings to 1900*. New York, NY: Routledge, 2000. Authors look at how health care has been denied and then fought for and created by African Americans.

Northington Gamble, Vanessa. *Making a Place for Ourselves: The Black Hospital Movement, 1920–1945*. New York, NY: Oxford University Press, 1995. Vanessa Northington Gamble tells the story of how Black physicians started a movement to create hospitals and medical programs to ensure good health in their community.

Websites

The Website for the Provident Foundation, which furthers the legacy of the historical Provident Hospital and Training School, provides a biography of Dr. Daniel Hale Williams. http://www.providentfoundation.org/history/williams.html.

The Chicago Tribute Markers of Distinction features a short biography of Dr. Daniel Hale Williams. http://chicagotribute.org/Markers/Williams.htm.

July 10

1943

Arthur Robert Ashe, Jr., is born in Richmond, Virginia. In 1963, Ashe became the first African American ever selected to play on the U.S. Davis Cup team and would go on to win the inaugural U.S. Open Tennis Championship on September 9, 1968. Ashe became famous as an athlete—he won three Grand Slam titles (the Australian Open, the French Open, Wimbledon, and the US Open)—but also because of his social activist work, particularly his work around the South Africa anti-apartheid movement.

> By 1985, I was at last satisfied that the anti-apartheid movement, once exotic, was blossoming in America. Arrested along with me that January 11 were sixteen other demonstrators, including teachers, municipal workers, and trade union officials. And we were only one small part of an ongoing national effort since November of the previous year, when three prominent blacks had staged a sit-in at the South African embassy

in Washington. Behind the national effort was the Free South Africa Movement, coordinated by Randall Robinson, who had been one of the three people in that sit-in. Since November, a host of well-known figures, including Belafonte, Coretta Scott King, and myself, had walked the picket lines outside the embassy complex. The picketing continued long after my arrest, with demonstrations and arrests taking place in other cities.

Source: From Arthur Ashe with Arnold Rampersad. *Days of Grace: A Memoir.* New York, NY: Random House, Inc., 1994, p. 122.

Books

Ashe, Arthur with Frank Deford. *Arthur Ashe: Portrait in Motion.* New York, NY: Carroll & Graf Publishers/R. Gallen, 1993. Book presents excerpts from Ashe's diary, written between 1973 and 1974.

Ashe, Arthur with Neil Amdur. *Off the Court.* New York, NY: New American Library, 1981. Focuses on the highlights of Ashe's tennis career and his social activist work upon retirement.

Websites

The Arthur Ashe Learning Center (AALC) Website promotes Ashe's sports and human rights activism legacy. www.ArthurAshe.org.

Arthur Ashe Institute for Urban Health was created to forward the healthcare-oriented concerns Ashe promoted, particularly as they relate to the United States' ethnic minorities. www.arthurasheinstitute.org.

Also Noteworthy

1875

Mary McLeod Bethune, Black educator and founder of the National Council for Negro Women, is born in Mayesville, South Carolina. Bethune was an educator and school founder who served as an unofficial advisor on African American issues to Presidents

Franklin D. Roosevelt and Harry S. Truman. She worked in Georgia and South Carolina and then founded Florida's Daytona Normal and Industrial Institute for Girls in 1904. The school merged with the Cookman Institute for Men in 1923 and became Bethune-Cookman College, one of the few black colleges in the country at that time.

1905

From July 11 to 13, W. E. B. Du Bois and William Monroe Trotter were among the leaders of the meeting from which sprung the Niagara Movement, the forerunner of the National Association for the Advancement of Colored People.

July 12

1920

The actress/playwright/activist Beah Richards is born Beulah Richardson in Vicksburg, Mississippi. Richards received an Academy Award nomination for her role as Sidney Poitier's mother in *Guess Who's Coming to Dinner* (1967). She also received two Emmy awards. But Richards is also known for her poetry, her writing, and her political activism.

In 1951, Thompson Patterson with actor Beulah Richardson and journalist Charlotte Bass founded the Sojourners for Truth and Justice, an all-black women's progressive civil rights organization. The group issued a call for African American women to join in a demonstration "to call upon our government to prove its loyalty to its fifteen million Negro citizens" . . . The stifling anti-Communist political atmosphere of the era partially contributed to the Sojourner's demise.

Source: From Mark Christopher Carnes. *American National Biography: With a Cumulative Index by Occupations and Realms of Renown, Volume 26.* New York, NY: Oxford University Press, 2005, p. 431.

Books

Jerome, Fred and Rodger Taylor. *Einstein on Race and Racism*. Piscataway, NJ: Rutgers University Press, 2006. Book demonstrates the importance of the Sojourners for Truth and Justice on efforts to promote human rights for African Americans.

Smith, Judith E. *Visions of Belonging: Family Stories, Popular Culture, and Postwar Democracy, 1940–1960*. New York, NY: Columbia University Press, 2004. Focuses on the idea of inclusion and how African Americans formulated it for themselves in the twentieth century, particularly strategies used by groups like Sojourners for Truth and Justice.

Websites

A portion of *Beah: A Black Woman Speaks* is available on YouTube. http://www.youtube.com/watch?v=V_lxaQsAda0.

Media: The documentary *Beah: A Black Woman Speaks* (2003) features Beah talking about the major events in her life. http://www.wmm.com/filmcatalog/pages/c626.shtml.

1967

A rebellion takes place in the city of Newark, New Jersey, between July 12 and July 17. The six days of rioting, looting, and destruction left 26 dead and hundreds injured. Newark's rebellion was followed by a rebellion in Detroit on July 28. As both ended, President Lyndon Johnson ordered an investigation into the disturbances. The report they created, called the Kerner Commission, spoke of the United States as "moving toward two societies, one black, one white—separate and unequal."

> The latest confrontation grew out of the mayor's plan to condemn and turn over 150 acres in the almost all-Black Central Ward to keep the expanding College of Medicine and Dentistry from leaving Newark, forcing the relocation of thousands of residents. With that crisis and others simmering in the background, the police beating of a black cabdriver who resisted arrest for a minor traffic violation on the night of Wednesday, July 12,

> 1967, exploded into five days of revolt in the streets. By the end, $15 million in property had been lost, including at least seven hundred stores, hundreds of people had been injured, and twenty-six were killed, all but three by the hands of the Newark Police, the New Jersey State Police, and the National Guard, who battled fiercely to reassert their control over the main shopping district of the ward.
>
> *Source*: From Lizabeth Cohen. *A Consumer's Republic: The Politics of Mass Consumption in Postwar America*. New York: Random House/ Vintage Books, 2003, p. 375.

Books

Hayden, Tom. *Rebellion in Newark: Official Violence and Ghetto Response*. New York, NY: Vintage Books, 1967. Hayden looks at causes and results of Newark Rebellion.

Tuttle, Brad R. *How Newark Became Newark: The Rise, Fall, and Rebirth of an American City*. Newark, NJ: Rutgers University Press, 2009. History of the founding and development of Newark includes details about the 1967 rebellion.

Websites

The 1967NewarkRiots.com Website provides links to photographs, documents, and videos related to the rebellion. http://www.1967newarkriots.com/.

Newark 1967 riots anniversary from the Star-Ledger. http://www.nj.com/newark1967/.

Also Noteworthy

1905

From July 11 through 13, W. E. B. Du Bois and William Monroe Trotter were among the leaders of the meeting that created the Niagara Movement. The Niagara Movement would later become the National Association for the Advancement of Colored People.

1943

Famed National Basketball Association player Paul Theron Silas is born in Prescott,

Arizona. Silas played power forward and won three separate NBA championship rings with the Boston Celtics and with the Seattle SuperSonics.

1949

Frederick McKinley Jones receives U.S. Patent No. 2,475,841 for an automatic air-conditioning unit in trucks, which allows for the transportation of food for long distances.

July 13

1863

The New York City Draft Riots start; they would last from July 13 to July 16. Initially intended to express anger at the first federal military draft in U.S. history, which was created to get soldiers for the Civil War, the protests turned ugly and degraded into "a virtual racial pogrom, with uncounted numbers of blacks murdered in the streets." Numerous buildings were destroyed, including an orphanage for black children. Many of the protesters were immigrants and viewed freed African Americans as competition for scarce jobs. Order was restored after four days, but it is estimated that 120 people were killed and 2,000 injured.

The riot began in New York on July 11. After two days of rioting, at 4:00 pm the 13th, a mob numbering in the hundreds, if not thousands, reached the Colored Orphan Asylum at Fifth Avenue between 43d and 44th streets where 233 children were housed. After breaking down the front door with an ax, the mob looted the building and set several fires. Chief Engineer John Decker of the NYC Fire Department arrived with ten or fifteen men and proceeded to extinguish the fires. He was told if he attempted to do so again, he would be killed. Decker and his men persisted in their efforts for more than one hour but were unable to save the building from the mob. The asylum, a four-story brick building, was totally destroyed.

While the firemen confronted the mob, the 233 children and their 8 caretakers, after a silent prayer, quietly left the building and went out into the streets, which were filled with rioters. The group did not know where to seek refuge but finally reached a police station on 35th Street where they remained for three days. Friends of the asylum sent in food to supply the orphans and other Black New Yorkers who had sought refuge in the police station. The refugees, both orphans and adults, were placed under the care of the superintendant of the asylum. When peace was restored in New York, the orphanage was moved to Carmansville, in upper Manhattan.

Source: From Hugh Barbour. *Quaker Crosscurrents: Three Hundred Years of Friends in the New York Yearly Meetings.* Syracuse, NY: Syracuse University Press, 1995, pp. 194–195.

Books

Schecter, Barnet. *The Devil's Own Work: The Civil War Draft Riots and the Fight to Reconstruct America.* London, England: Bloomsbury Publishing USA, 2007. Author looks at the social and political situation in New York City at the time of the Draft riots.

Spann, Edward K. *Gotham at War: New York City, 1860–1865.* Lanham, MD: Rowman & Littlefield, 2002. A looks at New York City during the Civil War, which contains a look at the Draft Riots.

Websites

New York City Draft Riots (July 11–13, 1863). http://www.civilwarhome.com/draftriots.htm.

Virtual New York covers the New York Draft Riots. http://www.vny.cuny.edu/draftriots/Intro/draft_riot_intro_set.html.

Also Noteworthy

1787

Congress outlaws slavery in Northwest Territory.

1956

Michael Spinks is born in St. Louis, Missouri. At 6 feet 3 inches, Spinks won a Gold medal in the Middleweight division at the 1976 Montreal Summer Olympic Games. Spinks turned professional in 1977 and won the Heavyweight Championship in 1985.

1965

Thurgood Marshall becomes the first African American appointed to serve as the U.S. solicitor general.

1966

The singer/songwriter Gerald Edward Levert is born in Philadelphia, Pennsylvania, and then raised in Cleveland, Ohio. With his group, LeVert, Gerald released seven albums and had his first solo album in 1991.

July 14

1914

Kenneth Bancroft Clark Social is born in the Panama Canal Zone to Arthur Bancroft Clark and Miriam Hanson Clark. As a scientist and educator, Clark and his wife, Mamie Phipps Clark, created the Harlem, New York-based Northside Center for Child Development and Harlem Youth Opportunities Unlimited (HARYOU). The Clarks also developed a doll test that demonstrated the power of attitudes about race at a very young age.

Human beings who are forced to live under ghetto conditions and whose daily experience tells them that almost nowhere in society are they respected and granted the ordinary dignity and courtesy accorded to others will, as a matter of course, begin to doubt their own worth. Since every human being depends upon his cumulative experiences with others for clues as to how he should view and value himself, children who are consistently rejected understandably begin to question

and doubt whether they, their family, and their group really deserve no more respect from the larger society than they receive. These doubts become the seeds of a pernicious self- and group-hatred, the Negro's complex and debilitating prejudice against himself.

Source: From Kenneth Bancroft Clark and William Julius Wilson. *Dark Ghetto: Dilemmas of Social Power*. Middletown, CT: Wesleyan University Press, 1989, pp. 63–64.

Books

Clark, Kenneth. *A Possible Reality: A Design for the Attainment of High Academic Achievement for Inner-City Students*. New York, NY: Emerson Hall/D. White, 1972. Clark looks at how children in deprived community can succeed academically.

Clark, Kenneth. *Prejudice and Your Child*. Middletown, CT: Wesleyan University Press, 1988. Clark looks at how prejudices in the larger society affect the psychological development of all children and ways to fix this problem.

Websites

"Teachers' Domain: Kenneth Clark" transcript of interview with Clark. http://www.teachersdomain.org/resource/iml04.soc.ush.civil.clark/.

Columbia University Oral History Project provides interviews with Kenneth Clark. http://www.columbia.edu/cu/lweb/digital/collections/nny/clarkk/.

Also Noteworthy

1885

Sarah E. Goode receives U.S. Patent No. 322,177 for her creation of the "hide away" bed. Goode, who was born into slavery and freed after the Civil War, moved to Chicago, Illinois, where she owned a furniture store. After listening to her customers complain about the small apartments they lived in, Goode created a bed that folded up into a cabinet. Goode's invention was a precursor to the Murphy bed.

1955

George Washington Carver Monument, first national park honoring an African American, is dedicated in Joplin, Missouri.

July 15

1867

The businesswoman Maggie Lena Walker is born. The first African American to become president of a bank in the United States, in 1903 Walker chartered the St. Luke Penny Savings Bank, which was created to help African Americans save money.

> It cost fifty thousand dollars to get a banking charter (a legal contract). Walker directed the sale of fifty thousand dollars worth of stock in the bank to people willing to invest in a black-owned bank. This was no small achievement for a woman. The charter for the St. Luke Penny Savings Bank was granted on July 28, 1903. The executive committee of the Right Worthy Grand Council was named to be the bank's board of directors.
>
> Source: From Candice F. Ransom. *Maggie L. Walker: Pioneering Banker and Community Leader.* Breckenridge, CO: Twenty-First Century Books, 2008, p. 63.

Books

Dabney, Wendell P. *Maggie L. Walker and the IO of Saint Luke: The Woman and Her Work.* Cincinnati, OH: Dabney, 1927. Biography of Maggie Walker and a look at her organizing work.

Drachman, Virginia G. and National Heritage Museum (Lexington, MA). *Enterprising Women: 250 Years of American Business.* Chapel Hill, NC: UNC Press Books, 2002. Contains a biography of Walker and a look at her establishment of the St. Luke Penny Savings Bank.

Websites

Maggie L. Walker National Historic Site commemorates Walker's life and maintains her former home. The site was named a National Historic Site on November 10, 1978. http://www.nps.gov/malw/.

Maggie Lena Walker | The Story of Virginia, An American Experience. www.vahistorical.org/sva2003/walker.htm.

Also Noteworthy

1822

Public schools for African Americans open in Philadelphia, Pennsylvania.

July 16

1862

Anti-lynching activist Ida Bell Wells Barnett is born in Holly Springs, Mississippi. The future civil rights activist will become the leading opponent of lynching, an organizer of the Niagara Movement, a founder of Chicago's Alpha Suffrage Club, and a co-founder of the National Association for the Advancement of Colored People (NAACP). Wells–Barnett's militancy made her too radical for the NAACP, however, and she was eased out of the new organization.

> In addition to a vindication of black manhood, *Southern Horrors* made African American women visible in the dynamics of southern lynching and sexualized racism. Wells documented not sideline suffering but attacks—lynching and rape—on black women and girls. In so doing, Wells staked a claim of outraged womanhood for African American women, a claim first articulated by opponents of slavery but becoming unthinkable under white supremacist ideology at century's end. She stressed the general public's ignorance of black women's experiences of sexual attack and declared that even if the facts were known, "when the victim is a colored woman it is different." Americans knew "nothing of assaults by white men on black women, for which nobody is

lynched and no notice is taken." Welss identified the white South as a hypocritical "apologist for lynchers of the rapists of white women only."

Source: From Patricia Ann Schechter. Ida B. Wells-Barnett and American Reform, 1880–1930. Chapel Hill, NC: UNC Press Books, 2001, p. 87.

Books

Welch, Catherine A. *Ida B. Wells-Barnett: Powerhouse with a Pen*. Breckenridge, CO: Twenty-First Century Books, 2000. Biography of Wells and her struggle for African American Civil Rights.

Wells-Barnett, Ida B., edited by Miriam DeCosta-Willis. *The Memphis Diary of Ida B. Wells*. Boston, MA: Beacon Press, 1995. DeCosta-Willis places the contents of Ida B. Wells's biography in the context of the political times she was living in.

Websites

Ida B. Wells-Barnett's pamphlet "Lynch Law in Georgia" has been digitized. http://lincoln.lib.niu.edu/cgi-bin/philologic/navigate.pl?lincoln.4804.

Ida B. Wells-Barnett Museum and Ida B. Wells Memorial Foundation. www.idabwells.org/.

Also Noteworthy

1951

The George Washington Carver National Monument is dedicated in Joplin, MO. It is the first national monument honoring an African American. George Washington Carver, noted scientist, was born on July 12, 1864. Carver was a teacher and agricultural botanist at Booker T. Washington's Tuskegee Institute in Alabama.

1964

James Powell, a 15-year-old African American resident of Harlem, New York, is shot and killed by an off-duty white police officer, NYDP Lieutenant Thomas Gilligan. The incident led to the 1964 Harlem riots.

July 17

1935

Diahann Carroll is born Carol Diahann Johnson in the Bronx, New York. As an actress and singer, Carroll appeared in many films and television shows. She most famously starred in the 1968 television program *Julia*, a breakthrough role that showed Carroll playing the role of a dignified, non-stereotypical African American woman.

In September 1968 Ms. Carroll starred in the television series Julia on NBC, the first African-American to star in a television program. The success of the program was remarkable. Many African-Americans criticized the program because it did not include an African-American father. In this series Ms. Carroll was cast as a nurse and war widow.

Source: From Martha Ward Plowden. Famous Firsts of Black Women. Gretna, LA: Pelican Publishing, 2002, p. 41.

Books

Carroll, Diahann with Bob Morris. *The Legs Are the Last to Go: Aging, Acting, Marrying, and Other Things I Learned the Hard Way*. New York, NY: HarperCollins, 2009. Carroll looks at her Hollywood career.

Carroll, Diahann with Ross Firestone. *Diahann!* Breckenridge, CO: Ballantine Books, 1987. Biography of Diahann Carroll looks at the racial barriers she was able to break in the world of entertainment.

Websites

Diahann Carroll Official Website. www.diahanncarroll.net/.

The Many Images of Diahann Carroll. http://www.tcf.ua.edu/Classes/Jbutler/T577/Students/dcweb.html.

Also Noteworthy

1953

Jesse D. Locker, a lawyer who became a city councilman in Cincinnati, Ohio, is appointed U.S. Ambassador to Liberia.

1959

Billie Holiday dies at age 44 in New York City's Metropolitan Hospital. Holiday's last recorded address was 26 West Eighty-Seventh Street, and she was married at the time to Louis McKay.

1967

John Coltrane dies at Huntington Hospital in Huntington, Suffolk County, Long Island, New York. The legendary saxophone player and composer was 40 years old.

July 18

1939

Saxophonist Coleman Hawkins records "Body and Soul," one of the classics of jazz. Coleman Randolph Hawkins, known as the "father of the tenor saxophone," was born in Saint Joseph, Missouri, on November 21, 1904.

Some artists are acclaimed during their lifetimes, then soon forgotten. Others live in the shadows and are discovered posthumously. A lucky few are admired and honored in life as well as in death. Coleman Hawkins (1904–1969) began his professional career in his teens, was the leading practitioner of his chosen instrument by his mid-twenties, an international star (when jazz had just a few) at thirty one of the very few established greats accepted by the young jazz modernists in his (and the century's) forties, and a universally admired "grand old man" of jazz in his sunset years. Today, he is an unassailable icon of jazz—a landmark in no need of a protective commission.

Source: From Dan Morgenstern and Sheldon Meyer. *Living with Jazz*. New York, NY: Random House Digital, Inc., 2004, p. 38.

Books

Chilton, John. *The Song of the Hawk: The Life and Recordings of Coleman Hawkins*. Ann Arbor, MI: University of Michigan Press, 1990. Biography of Coleman Hawkins.

James, Burnett. *Coleman Hawkins*. Staplehurst, UK: Spellmount, 1984. Biography of the life of Coleman Hawkins.

Websites

Coleman Hawkins' "Body and Soul" 1967. http://www.youtube.com/watch?v=SfJ5Ut-PoMcg&feature=related.

Coleman Hawkins profiled on All About Jazz. http://www.allaboutjazz.com/php/article.php?id=305.

Also Noteworthy

1753

Lemuel Haynes is born; he will become the first African American to serve as minister to a white congregation when he takes helm of a church in Middle Granville, New York.

1822

Violette A. Johnson is born. She will be the first African American woman to argue a case before the U.S. Supreme Court.

1863

Kelly Miller, the first African American mathematics graduate student, is born in Winnsboro, South Carolina.

1892

Frank R. Crosswaith is born in St. Croix, Danish West Indies. He will be a prominent labor organizer and political activist.

1923

Mari Evans is born in Toledo, OH. Deeply race conscious, she will publish several volumes of poetry as well as books for children.

1934

Donald Payne is born in Newark, New Jersey. Payne will be the first African American Congressperson from New Jersey.

1939

William Bell is born in Memphis, Tennessee. He will cut the hit R&B record "You Don't Miss Your Water till the Well Runs Dry."

July 19

1925

The Paris debut of Josephine Baker, entertainer, activist, and humanitarian. Baker was born Freda Josephine McDonald to Carrie McDonald and Eddie Carson in St. Louis, Missouri, on June 3, 1906. After years spent working in chorus lines in the United States, Baker became a sensation with her *La Revue Nègre* and later with her *La Folie du Jour* at the Follies-Bergère Theater in Paris, France.

> Her opening-night appearance in that show is still remembered as one of the great moments in music hall history. The curtain rose to reveal a steamy jungle setting: kapok trees, a winding river, birdcalls, heavy swinging vines. Native drumbeats could be heard in the distance. Then, high above the stage, Baker made her entrance, crawling backward, catlike, down one of the painted trees. She was not wearing a feathered headdress, like most Folie stars. Springing to the stage, landing on all fours like a panther, Baker was wearing nothing but a skirt of brilliant yellow bananas.
>
> *Source*: From Alan Schroeder and Heather Lehr Wagner. *Josephine Baker*. New York, NY: Infobase Publishing, 2006, pp. 37–38.

Books

Baker, Jean-Claude and Chris Chase. *Josephine: The Hungry Heart*. New York, NY: Cooper Square Press, 2001. One of Baker's sons tells the story of her life and career.

Jules-Rosette, Bennetta. *Josephine Baker in Art and Life: The Icon and the Image*. Champaign, IL: University of Illinois Press, 2007. A look at Baker's career in Paris, France, and the image she created.

Websites

The Official Josephine Baker Website—CMG Worldwide, www.cmgww.com/stars/baker/.

Josephine Baker's banana dance, http://www.youtube.com/watch?v=wmw5eGh888Y.

Also Noteworthy

1866

U.S. Government signs the Treaty with the Cherokee. Under Article 9 of the Cherokee treaty, people of African descent who were formerly enslaved are accepted into the tribe: "The Cherokee Nation having, voluntarily, in February, eighteen hundred and sixty-three, by an act of the national council, forever abolished slavery, hereby covenant and agree that never hereafter shall either slavery or involuntary servitude exist in their nation otherwise than in the punishment of crime, whereof the party shall have been duly convicted, in accordance with laws applicable to all the members of said tribe alike. They further agree that all freedmen who have been liberated by voluntary act of their former owners or by law, as well as all free colored persons who were in the country at the commencement of the rebellion, and are now residents therein, or who may return within six months, and their descendants, shall have all the rights of native Cherokees: Provided, That owners of slaves so emancipated in the Cherokee Nation shall never receive any compensation or pay for the slaves so emancipated."

July 20

1967

The National Conference on Black Power opens in Newark, New Jersey, bringing together more than 1,000 delegates representing 286 organizations and institutions. The conference was held from July 20th to the 23rd and included workshops, papers, and programs to promote the political, economic, and cultural advancement of the African American community. The conference ended with a "Black Power Manifesto."

Malcolm's idea of a Black nationalist conference was not put into effect until 1967 with the convening of the National Black Power conference in Newark, New Jersey. Coming close on the heels of the Newark rebellion, it had the characteristic crisis atmosphere that prompted the periodic gathering of Black activists in national conferences from as far back as the antebellum Black conventions. As with the second Black Power conference in Philadelphia in 1968, all manner of nationalists and even integrationists were present at these gatherings. The dominant theme was networking in pursuit of Black power. The slogan, "Black power," revolutionary in timbre, was more often than not reformist in content. Its militancy was rhetorical, its content reformist, and not always in the progressive sense of reform that Malcolm would have endorsed. It was not necessarily anti-capitalist since it often oriented itself to struggling to give Black people a bigger piece of the pie. The driving force of the Newark conference was an Episcopal priest who secured underwriting for the conference from the Revlon Corporation. SNCC had initiated Black Power to test the limits of reform. By the Black Power conferences, Black Power sounded more and more like conservative Black economic nationalism.

Source: From William W. Sales. From Civil Rights to Black Liberation: Malcolm X and the Organization of Afro-American Unity. Cambridge, MA: South End Press, 1994, p. 192.

Books

Joseph, Peniel E. *The Black Power Movement: Rethinking the Civil Rights-Black Power Era.* Boca Raton, FL: Taylor & Francis Group, LLC/CRC Press, 2006. Looks at the people who played part in the Newark Black Power Conference in 1967.

Marshall, Herbert and Mildred Stock. *Black Power Conference Reports.* Victoria, BC: Abe-Books/Action Library, Afram Associates, 1970. Documents from the Black Power Conference.

Websites

Rethinking the Black Power Movement. http://exhibitions.nypl.org/africanaage/essay-black-power.html.

Experiencing History: "Black Power." http://experiencinghistory.blogspot.com/2011/07/black-power.html.

Also Noteworthy

1874

William Henry Ferris is born to David H. and Sarah Ann Ferris in New Haven, Connecticut. William Henry Ferris received master's degrees from both Yale and Harvard and in 1913 would publish *The African Abroad, or, His Evolution in Western Civilization, Tracing His Development under Caucasian Milieu.* Ferris served as assistant president general of Marcus Garvey's Universal Negro Improvement Association and African Communities League and in 1919 became literary editor of Garvey's *Negro World.*

1950

The first U.S. victory in Korea is won by the African American troops of the 24th Infantry Regiment.

1988

U.S. presidential candidate Jesse L. Jackson receives 1,218 delegate votes at the Democratic National Convention. The number needed for the nomination, which went to Michael Dukakis, was 2,082.

July 21

1896

Mary Church Terrell is elected first president of the National Association of Colored Women. Terrell was born in 1863 to Robert Church and Louisa Ayers just outside of Memphis, Tennessee. Though both of her parents had been enslaved, Mary Church Terrell became one of the first African American women to earn a college degree when she graduated from Ohio's Oberlin College in 1884. As an activist, Terrell was an active member of the National American Woman Suffrage Association, she was the first president of the National Association of Colored Women, and she was also a founding member of the National Association for the Advancement of Colored People (NAACP). In 1895, Church Terrell was the first woman of African descent appointed to sit on the District of Columbia's Board of Education, and she was the first Black member of the American Association of University Women.

Mary Church Terrell was a pioneer in America's civil rights struggle whose activism spanned the late nineteenth and early twentieth centuries. As the daughter of the South's first black millionaire and the first president of the National Association of colored Women, Terrell recognized early in life that African Americans faced limitations in mainstream society solely because of their race. Her childhood in Memphis demonstrated clearly how African Americans were increasingly restricted to lives little better than what many had known as slaves. Furthermore, Terrell's personal and family experiences with racism and racial violence in the city left an indelible mark that necessitated and informed her lifelong activism.

Source: From Sarah Wilkerson Freeman and Beverly Bond. *Tennessee Women: Their Lives and Times.* Athens, GA: University of Georgia Press, 2009, p. 122.

Books

Church Terrell, Mary. *Colored Woman in a White World.* Waco, TX: Eakin Press, 2002. Church Terrell's autobiography of her life as an activist.

Fradin, Dennis B. and Judith Bloom Fradin. *Fight On!: Mary Church Terrell's Battle for Integration.* New York, NY: Houghton Mifflin Harcourt, 2003. Biographical profile of Church Terrell and her social impact.

Websites

The American Experience has a biography of Mary Church Terrell. http://www.pbs.org/wgbh/amex/1900/peopleevents/pandeA-MEX46.html.

The Mary Church Terrell House located at 326 T Street NW, in Washington, DC, is a landmark structure, though currently under threat of demolition. http://www.marychurchterrellhouse.org/

July 22

1946

Danny Lebern Glover is born in San Francisco, California. An actor and director, Glover is a celebrity for his appearances in well-known films like *The Color Purple* (1985) and in the role of Detective Roger Murtaugh in the *Lethal Weapon* series of films of the late '80s. But he is also known for his political activism. Glover has been active on the boards of organizations like The Algebra Project, The Black AIDS Institute, and TransAfrica Forum. Glover notably won the backing of the Venezuelan government for the production of a biopic on Haitian Revolutionary, *Toussaint Louverture.*

My fight against HIV/AIDs is a personal one. I have a brother who is affected by the disease. As an artist, I also have had numerous friends and colleagues who have suffered from it and died. As a result, I have learned about its path of destruction through individuals into families and extending into communities, societies, and nations. I know about its obvious and not so obvious impact on those it leaves behind. It was for these reasons that I decided two years ago to focus a good portion of my work as UNDP's Goodwill Ambassador on building a global movement to fight HIV/AIDS wherever it surfaces and—particularly—in Africa, which has been hardest hit.

Source: From Danny Glover. "HIV/AIDS and African's Poverty" in W Publishing Group, ed. *The Awake Project: Uniting Against the African AIDS Crisis.* Nashville, TN: Thomas Nelson Inc., 2005, p. 115.

Books

Blakely, Gloria. *Danny Glover.* New York, NY: Infobase Publishing, 2001. Biographical profile of Danny Glover.

Harrison, Paul Carter, Bill Duke, and Danny Glover. *Black Light: The African American Hero.* New York, NY: Thunder's Mouth Press, 1993. Glover co-authored this look at famous African Americans.

Websites

The *Washington Post* has Danny Glover Filmography. http://www.washingtonpost.com/wp-srv/style/longterm/filmgrph/danny_glover.htm.

InnerVIEWS with Ernie Manouse: Danny Glover. http://video.google.com/videoplay?docid=-4206391669338575300&q=innerviews.

Also Noteworthy

1861

President Lincoln reads the first draft of his Emancipation Proclamation to his Cabinet.

1939

Thirty-one-year-old Jane Matilda Bolin of New York City is appointed the first African American female judge. Bolin is sworn in by New York City Mayor Fiorello LaGuardia to serve as a judge of the Domestic Relations Court.

1941

The singer/songwriter George Clinton is born in Kannapolis, North Carolina. Clinton formed Parliament-Funkadelic in the 1970s, a supergroup that would advance Funk music with songs like "Give Me the Funk (Tear the Roof off the Sucker)" (1976), "Flashlight" (1977), and "One Nation under a Groove" (1978).

1943

The poet/journalist/educator Quincy Thomas Troupe is born in St. Louis, Missouri. Troupe authored *Miles: The Autobiography of Miles Davis* (1989), and his poetry led to his being named California's first Poet Laureate in 2002.

July 23

1909

Norman W. Lewis is born in Harlem, New York. As a painter and scholar, Lewis was a founding member of the SPIRAL Group, which included artists like Romare Bearden and Hale Woodruff. With the SPIRAL Group, Lewis promoted African American art that contributed to the Civil Rights Movement.

As black Americans, the artists of Spiral were greatly influenced by both the civil rights and the Black Power movements as well as by the charismatic leaders and highly charges issues involved in those struggles. As stated in the group's 1965 exhibition catalogue, they "could not fail to be touched by the outrage of segregation, or fail to relate to the self-reliance, hope, and courage of those persons who were marching in the interest of man's dignity." Yet the Spiral artists did not wish to create art whose raison d'être was protest. While individually committed to black progress and freedom, they wanted to be a part of the cultural and social reawakening of the era as artists, not as civil rights foot soldiers.

Source: From William Edward Taylor, Harriet Garcia Warkel, and Margaret Taylor Burroughs. *A Shared Heritage: Art by Four African Americans*. Bloomington, IN: Indiana University Press, 1996, p. 151.

Books

Conyers, James L. *Engines of the Black Power Movement: Essays on the Influence of Civil Rights Actions, Arts, and Islam*. Jefferson, NC: McFarland & Co., 2007. Contains a look at the Spiral Group and its role in the Civil Rights Movement.

O'Meally. Robert G. *The Jazz Cadence of American Culture*. New York, NY: Columbia University Press, 1998. Book contains a profile of the members of the Spiral Group.

Websites

NGA|Bearden: A Leader in the Arts Community—The Spiral Group. http://www.nga .gov/education/classroom/bearden/lead1 .shtm.

The Spiral Group: Paul R. Jones Collection of American Art. http://www.flickr.com/photos/uaart/sets/72157624874320555/.

Also Noteworthy

1778

More than 700 Blacks participate in the Battle of Monmouth in Monmouth, New Jersey.

1872

Elijah McCoy receives U.S. Patent No. 129,843 for his automatic oil cup.

1891

The physician Louis Tompkins Wright is born in La Grange, Georgia. Wright became the first African American surgeon admitted to the American College of Surgeons and the first African American physician named to join the staff of a New York City municipal hospital.

1913

Carlos Alexander Cooks is born in San Pedro de Macorís, Dominican Republic. After his family brought Cooks and his brother, Lorenzo, to the United States in 1929, Cooks and his father became prominent followers of Marcus Garvey's Pan-Africanist United Negro Improvement Association (UNIA). After the demise of Garvey, Cooks created the African Nationalist Pioneer Movement (ANPM). In 1959, the ANPM famously held a conference calling for the end of the use of the word "Negro" and demanded that "African" or "Black" be used to describe people of African descent.

1915

Hallie Almena Lomax, journalist and civil rights activist, is born in Galveston, Texas, but raised in Chicago, Illinois. Lomax studied journalism at Los Angeles City College but was unable to get a job at a newspaper. In 1941, she started the *Los Angeles Tribune*, a weekly newspaper targeted at the African American community. The *Tribune* had a reputation for fearless reporting publishing articles about racism in the Los Angeles Police Department and at its peak had a circulation of 25,000. In 1946, Lomax won the Wendell L. Willkie Award for Negro Journalism for a column that challenged the stereotype of black men's sexual prowess. Lomax closed the *Tribune* in 1960 and died March 25, 2011.

1984

Vanessa Williams returns her Miss America crown. Williams had won the Miss America pageant in 1983, making her the first woman of African American descent to wear the crown—but she was stripped of her Miss America label when nude photos of her surfaced. Williams went on to become a popular singer, dancer, and actress.

July 24

1807

Ira Frederick Aldridge is born in New York. Aldridge became famous as a nineteenth-century actor, particularly known for his interpretation of the role of Othello. Though faced with racism throughout most of his career, Aldridge's theatrical abilities were so widely esteemed that a bronze plaque of him was placed at the entrance to the Shakespeare Memorial Theatre at Stratford-upon-Avon in south Warwickshire, England.

Of the visitors who pause to glance at the statue, a few recognize the bronze plaque's legend: Ira Aldridge, the Tragedian, The names, if not the accomplishments, of great nineteenth-century actors (Booth, Kean, Bernhardt) are familiar to many Americans. Ira Aldridge, whom Herbert Marshall calls "a dark star whose brilliance has been dimmer by sins of omission and commission of the white world," was remembered through a hundred years of silence by a few writers who would remind America during Negro History Week that Aldridge was the first Black American honored by the Republic of Haiti for service to his race. They remembered also that he had received the Prussian Gold Medal for Arts and Science from King Frederick, and that he had been awarded the Medal of Ferdinand from Franz Joseph of Austria for his performance of Othello.

Source: From Ted Shine. Black Theatre USA: Plays by African Americans. New York, NY: Simon & Schuster, 1996, p. 3.

Books

Lindfors, Bernth. *Ira Aldridge: The African Roscius.* Rochester, NY: Boydell & Brewer Inc., 2010. Essays on the work and importance of Ira Aldridge.

Marshall, Herbert and Mildred Stock. *Ira Aldridge: The Negro Tragedian.* Washington, DC: Howard University Press, 1993. Biography of Ira Aldridge looks at his struggles to be an actor.

Websites

Aldridge, who became a British citizen, is recalled as a Great Black Briton. http://www.100greatblackbritons.com/bios/ira_aldridge.html.
Ira Aldridge is profiled on this personal Website. http://www.wayneturney.20m.com/aldridgeira.htm.

Also Noteworthy

1816

Fort Apalachicola is defeated by U.S. federal forces following a four-day siege by troops from the 4th U.S. Infantry and Navy gunboats that were stationed along the Apalachicola River. The Fort was also known as the "Negro Fort" and stood outside of Holy Trinity, Alabama; it had been built and maintained by some 300 self-liberated Africans and some 20 Native American Choctaw. Today, the Negro Fort Gadsden is officially the Fort Gadsden Historic Site, a National Historic Landmark.

1847

Hark Lay, Green Flake, and Oscar Crosby were the three African Americans in the advance company of Mormon pioneers accompanying Brigham Young as he entered the Great Salt Lake Valley in Utah.

1914

Frank Silvera is born in Kingston, Jamaica. Because of his light skin tone, Silvera was able to get work in theater and on stage at a time when most people of African descent were segregated in acting. Later, as a theatrical director, Silvera became famous for his work establishing the Frank Silvera Writers' Workshop Foundation.

July 25

1972

Front page *New York Times* article exposes the Tuskegee Syphilis Experiment. Peter Buxton, a venereal disease investigator with the U.S. Public Health Service (PHS), had written letters to the Centers for Disease Control (CDC) about the Tuskegee experiment as far back as 1966. But when the CDC failed to respond by 1972, Buxton exposed the experiment to Jean Heller of the *Associated Press* and the story made the front page of the *New York Times*. Public outrage led to an investigation by the Department of Health, Education, and Welfare, and the TSUS was declared ethically unjustified.

> In July 1972, while flying from Washington, D.C., home to Montgomery, I was reading the newspaper when my eye was caught by an article about a medical experiment in my adopted hometown of Tuskegee, Alabama. The article, by Associated Press reporter Jean Heller, described how the study was initiated by the United States Public Health Service in 1932 with the intent of collecting data about the effects of untreated syphilis. According to the article, the study used as subjects some six hundred African American males from the rural areas in and around Macon County, of which Tuskegee is the county seat. More than half of the 623 men had syphilis; the others, a control group, did not.
>
> Source: From Fred D. Gray, Tuskegee Institute. *The Tuskegee Syphilis Study: The Real Story and Beyond*. Montgomery, AL: NewSouth Books, 1998, p. 23.

Books

Jones, James Howard and Tuskegee Institute. *Bad Blood: The Tuskegee Syphilis Experiment.* New York, NY: Simon & Schuster, 1993. Book looks at how and why the U.S. government Public Health Service infected Black sharecroppers with syphilis.

Reverby, Susan M. *Examining Tuskegee: The Infamous Syphilis Study and Its Legacy*. Chapel Hill, NC: UNC Press Books, 2009. An examination of the 40-year Tuskegee Syphilis Study and the legacy it left of medical racism.

Websites

U.S. Public Health Service Syphilis Study at Tuskegee. www.cdc.gov/tuskegee/timeline.htm.

Tuskegee Syphilis Study. . . .www.brown.edu/Courses/Bio. . ./TUSKEGEESYPHILISSTUDY.htm.

Also Noteworthy

1943

The first U.S. warship named for a person of African descent, the *SS Leonard Roy Harmon*, is launched in Quincy, Massachusetts.

1946

Roger and Dorothy Malcolm and George and Mae Dorsey, two couples who worked as sharecroppers, are shot to death by a mob of 12 to 15 white men with shotguns in Walton County, Georgia. No one was ever convicted of the crime.

1948

President Harry S. Truman issues Executive Order 9981, ending segregation in the U.S. armed forces.

1970

Charles Cordone wins a Pulitzer Prize for his play *No Place to Be Somebody*.

July 26

1838

Maria Fearing is born into slavery on a cotton plantation near Gainesville, Alabama. She served as a house slave until age 27, but during that time she was fascinated by stories about the continent of Africa and became determined to go there. At age 38, she graduated from Talladega College, a Freedmen's Bureau School, and became a teacher. Fearing traveled to teach in present-day Zaire while in her 50s—the children she taught referred to her as Mama Wa Mputu, or "mother from far away"; she remained in the Congo for the next 20 years. Even after returning to the United States in her 70s, Fearing continued to teach until she died at age 99.

> Maria Fearing taught and preached not only at the Luebo mission stations, but in scores of nearby villages, where she sang and played with children lovingly. She also literally became the mother of some one hundred kidnapped or orphaned girls whom she raised in her newly created Pantops House for Girls. She was so loved that she became widely known to as "the foreign mother."
>
> Source: From Robert B. Edgerton. *The Troubled Heart of Africa: A History of the Congo*. New York: Macmillan, 2002, pp. 147–148.

Books

Brown Edmiston, Althea. *Maria Fearing, a Mother to African Girls* in *Four Presbyterian Pioneers in Congo*. Anniston, AL: First Presbyterian Church, 1965. This book is from a 1938 portrait of Fearing's missionary work and its legacy.

Sammon, Patricia. *Maria Fearing: a Woman Whose Dreams Crossed an Ocean*. Huntsville, AL: Writers Consortium Books, 1989. Biography of Maria Fearing and her missionary work in a missionary in the Belgian Congo.

Websites

The Alabama Women's Hall of Fame's Website has a page devoted to Maria Fearing. http://www.awhf.org/fearing.html.

The Westminster Presbyterian Church's site features a sermon that was preached about the life of Maria Fearing. http://westminster sermons.blogspot.com/2006/02/life-and-witness-of-maria-fearing.html.

Also Noteworthy

1948

President Harry S. Truman issues Executive Order 9981, ending segregation in the U.S. armed forces.

July 27

1816

One of the first battles of the Seminole Wars began when a U.S. Army detachment attacked Fort Blount, a Seminole fort on Apalachicola Bay, on Florida's northwest coast. Three hundred fugitive African slaves and some 20 of their Native American allies held Fort Blount for several days before it was attacked by U.S. troops. To punish the Seminoles for having helped self-liberated Africans, Fort Blount was completely destroyed. Indians and African Americans fought together against the United States during the three Seminole Wars. Notably, on December 25, 1831, a force of Black Seminole Indians defeated U.S. troops at Okeechobee, Florida, during the Second Seminole War.

> By the last quarter of the eighteenth century, people of African and Native American descent had established a number of settlements along the Suwannee and Apalachiola Rivers, in addition to those of longer standing in eastern and central Florida. Tensions between Georgia and the Seminoles over the status of absconded slaves led to even greater affinities between the latter and their African refugees. In 1812, Seminoles and Africans were successful in defeating an army raised in Georgia, and by 1814 the former alliance had gone on to create, with British assistance, a fortified position thirty miles above the mouth of the Apalachiola River, "generally called the Negro Fort" but officially named Fort Blount. The fort provided security for a number of Afircan Seminole farming settlements. Such was the threat of the African Seminoles that Andrew Jackson personally led an assault on Fort Blount in July 1816.

When Florida was claimed by the United States in 1821, Africans and Native Americans responded by retreating more deeply into the "fastnesses of the Florida swamps and forest." The so-called Seminole Wars ensued, lasting until 1842.

Source: From Michael Angelo Gomez. Exchanging Our Country Marks: The Transformation of African Identities in the Colonial and Antebellum South. Chapel Hill, NC: UNC Press Books, 1998, pp. 182.

Books

Foreman, Grant. *Indian Removal: The Emigration of the Five Civilized Tribes of Indians.* Norman, OK: University of Oklahoma Press, 1972. Book includes a look at the Seminole attempts to live with freed Africans and fend of U.S. government attacks.

McDonogh, Gary W. and Federal Writers' Project. *The Florida Negro: A Federal Writers' Project Legacy.* Jackson, MS: University Press of Mississippi, 1993. Looks at African American life in Florida, with a profile of the Black Seminole insurgency.

Websites

Tour of the Florida Territory during the Florida Seminole Wars, 1792–1859. http://www.southernhistory.us/index.html.

Negro Fort—Ghost Town. www.ghosttowns.com/states/fl/negrofort.html.

Also Noteworthy

1880

Alexander P. Ashbourne patents process for refining coconut oil.

1898

Queen Mother Audley E. Moore is born in New Liberia, Louisiana. In the 1950s, Queen Mother Moore presented petitions to the United Nations charging genocide and demanding reparations to descendants of former slaves.

July 28

1917

The first large-scale African American protest in U.S. history takes place along New York City's Fifth Avenue when the NAACP organizes some 10,000 men, women, and children to take part in a "Silent Protest Parade" to show their anger about the East St. Louis, Illinois, massacre of July 2, 1917. The protest was also designed to speak out against lynchings in Waco, Texas, and Memphis, Tennessee.

From the ashes of East St. Louis arose a cry of righteousness indignation. One expression of protest was a large "silent parade" organized by the National Association for the Advancement of Colored People in New York on July 28, 1917. The parade formation imitated countless military parades of the time—a drum corps out front, precise ranks and files, and American flags held aloft. In place of regimental banners, signs read, "Mr. President, why not make America safe for democracy?"

Source: From Alan Dawley. Changing the World: American Progressives in War and Revolution. Princeton, NJ: Princeton University Press, 2003, p. 164.

Books

Ellis, Mark. *Race, War, and Surveillance: African Americans and the United States Government During World War I.* Bloomington, IN: Indiana University Press, 2001. Looks at the importance and impact of the Silent Parade on progressive politics.

Tuck, Stephen G. N. *We Ain't What We Ought to Be: The Black Freedom Struggle from Emancipation to Obama.* Cambridge, MA: Harvard University Press, 2010. This book looks at the Silent Parade as one of a series of efforts to advance Black progress in the United States.

Websites

This "Harlem 1900–1940" photo exhibit contains a short description and photos from the

Silent Parade. http://www2.si.umich.edu/chico/Harlem/text/silentprotest.html.

Voices of Education page provides background on the "Silent Parade of Protest." http://www.voiceseducation.org/category/tag/silent-parade-protest.

Also Noteworthy

1868

The Fourteenth Amendment granting Blacks full citizenship rights is adopted as part of the U.S. Constitution.

July 29

1909

Chester Bomar Himes is born in Jefferson City, Missouri. While spending time in prison for armed robbery, Himes wrote short stories that he was able to publish in national magazines. Once out of prison, Himes became famous for novels like *If He Hollers Let Him Go* (1945) and *Cotton Comes to Harlem* (1965).

> *Himes probably began writing fiction in late 1931. His first pieces were published in 1932 and 1933 in Negro publications: Abbott's Monthly and Illustrated News, Bronzeman, The Pittsburgh Courier, and Atlanta Daily World. A couple of them, such as "A Modern Marriage" and "Hero: A Football Story," told rather acidly of youthful chivalric delusions. Most were vignettes and sketches about convicts and prison life, although a few dealt with the criminal world outside. One, "Prison Mass" required three successive issues of Abbott's Monthly because of its near novella length.*
>
> *More prestigious and lucrative was the publication in Esquire Magazine (April 1934) of "Crazy in the Stir," for which Himes was paid seventy-five dollars. Later that yeaer Esquire published "To What Red Hell." For Esquire, Himes's principal figures are white and their author's race is not identified. Possibly Himes of Arbold Gingrich, the editor of Esquire, thought the magazine's readership would not be especially drawn to Negro characters different from the then popular Amos 'n'*

> *Andy stereotypes. Meyer Levin, Gingrich's assistant, told Himes that "To What Red Hell" received greater response than any other fiction published in Esquire that year. This success did wonders for Himes's ego. He was now more than a prison number; he had a name, an identity. He was a writer. Wardens and guards had better be wary. Even his fellow convicts grudgingly respected him—although they seldom read his work.*
>
> *Source: From Edward Margolies and Michel Fabre. The Several Lives of Chester Himes. Jackson, MS: University Press of Mississippi, 1997, pp. 36–37.*

Books

Himes, Chester B., Michael Fabre, and Robert E. Skinner. *Conversations with Chester Himes.* Jackson, MS: University Press of Mississippi, 1995. Interviews with Chester Himes demonstrate his understanding of the African American political movements of the late twentieth century.

Himes, Chester B. *The Autobiography of Chester Himes: The Quality of Hurt.* New York, NY: Doubleday, 1972. Himes's autobiography goes over his youth and his life as a writer.

Websites

Article profiles Chester Himes and his impact on African American literature. http://aalbc.com/authors/chesterhimes.htm.

GIVEADAMN CHESTER HIMES PAGE. http://www.nsm.buffalo.edu/~sww/HIMES/CHESTER.html.

Also Noteworthy

1895

First National Convention of Black Women is held in Boston, Massachusetts.

1919

The first convention of the National Association of Negro Musicians (NANM; www.nanm.org/purposes.htm) is held.

1916

Charles Henry Christian is born in Bonham, Texas, and then raised in Oklahoma City, Oklahoma. Hired to play with Benny Goodman in the Goodman sextet, Christian became a favored jazz and swing guitarist among fans and his peers.

July 30

1936

George "Buddy" Guy is born to Isabell Toliver and Sam Guy in Lettsworth, Lousiana; Guy moved to Chicago, Illinois, in 1957, when he was 21. A blues guitarist and singer, Buddy's "Chicago blues" style is seen as a bridge between blues music and rock and roll. In 2003, Buddy Guy was awarded the National Medal of Arts, and in 2005 he was inducted into the Rock and Roll Hall of Fame.

> George "Buddy" Guy was born on July 30, 1936, in Lettsworth, Lousiana. He picked cotton during most of his youth and would listen to records like John Lee Hooker's "Boogie Chillen" when he could afford them. As a teenager Guy taught himself guitar and eventually found work playing in small clubs around Baton Rouge. As his instrumental prowess grew, he decided his musical future was not to be found in the South. Barely 20 years old, he took a train to Chicago and played in any club that would have him.
>
> As a way to win bar bets and guitar duels with established players such as Magic Sam and Otis Rush, Guy learned to wow the crowds with fingerboard flash and showmanship. He bought a 150-foot-long cord (an accessory first popularized by Magic Sam and also used by Albert Collins), which allowed him to walk through the audience—and right out of the bar—while playing his solos. Other blues guitarists, many of whom remained seated while performing, scratched their heads at what young Buddy was doing. But Guy never failed to drive the crowds wild.
>
> Source: From H. P. Newquist and Rich Maloof. *The Blues-Rock Masters*. Milwaukee, WI: Hal Leonard Corporation, 2002, p. 15.

Books

Cramer, Alfred W. *Musicians and Composers of the 20th Century—Volume 2.* Ipswich, MA: Salem Press, 2009. Contains a biography of Buddy Guy and his rise to prominence as a blues musician.

Wilcock, Donald E., Buddy Guy, and Rick Siciliano. *Damn Right I've Got the Blues: Buddy Guy and the Blues Roots of Rock-and-Roll.* New York, NY: Woodford Press, 1993. Biography of Buddy Guy looks at his influence on rock and roll.

Websites

Buddy Guy Home. www.buddyguy.net/.

Buddy Guy—Stormy Monday (Live 2004). http://www.dailymotion.com/video/xfhk9q_buddy-guy-stormy-monday-live-2004_music.

Also Noteworthy

1822

James Varick becomes the first bishop of African Methodist Episcopal Zion Church.

1885

Eugene Kinckle Jones is born in Richmond, VA. Jones later became the first executive secretary of the National Urban League.

1866

Edwin G. Walker and Charles L. Mitchell are elected to the Massachusetts Assembly from Boston. They were the first African Americans to sit in the Legislature of a U.S. state.

1961

Laurence John Fishburne III is born in Augusta, Georgia. An actor, playwright, director, and producer, Fishburne started acting at the age of 12 and has appeared on television, stage, and film.

July 31

1921

Whitney Moore Young Jr. is born to Whitney Sr. and Laura Young in Lincoln Ridge, Kentucky. In 1960, Whitney Young was appointed as executive director of the National Urban League, making him prominent in the Civil Rights Movement of the 1960s.

> ... *By involving the National Urban League in the March on Washington, Whitney Young not only linked the NUL with other Negro organizations but metamorphosed the NUL into a civil rights and economic and social organization, gaining—as never before—"the respect of the masses of Negro citizens."*
>
> *Whitney Young's role in this metamorphosis of the NUL into a civil rights partnership with other black civil rights groups during the sixties and seventies justifies his ranking here. Nancy J. Weiss assessed the impact of Young in redirecting the NUL to the needs of the black masses during his ten-year tenure as its leader. "Through jobs and training programs, Young enlarged the economic opportunities available to black Americans. He gave powerful whites in the private sector a means of comprehending the problems of the ghetto and, in the most successful instances, making some contribution toward their amelioration. He threw his weight behind public policies to combat discrimination and poverty. He encouraged communication and understanding across racial lines at a time when turmoil and misunderstanding were driving whites and blacks apart."*
>
> *Source*: From Columbus Salley. *The Black 100: A Ranking of the Most Influential African-Americans, Past and Present.* New York, NY: Citadel Press, 1999, p. 164.

Books

Dickerson, Dennis C. *Militant Mediator: Whitney M. Young Jr.* Lexington, KY: University Press of Kentucky, 2004. Book looks at Young's effort to use both interracial mediation and direct protest to advance the cause of African American Civil Rights.

Weiss, Nancy Joan. *Whitney M. Young, Jr., and the Struggle for Civil Rights.* Princeton, NJ: Princeton University Press, 1989. Biography of Whitney Young and his civil rights work.

Websites

Whitney M. Young Jr.: Little Known Civil Rights Pioneer. http://www.defense.gov/news/newsarticle.aspx?id=43988.

"One Handshake at a Time" documentary about Whitney M. Young. http://www.whitneyyoungfilm.com/.

Also Noteworthy

1874

Patrick Francis Healy, who was the first Black man to receive a PhD, is inaugurated as president of Georgetown University in Washington, DC.

1918

Henry "Hank" Jones is born on July 31, in Vicksburg, Mississippi, and then raised in Pontiac, Michigan. As a jazz pianist, he worked with Ella Fitzgerald and then spent 16 years as a pianist with CBS studio.

1960

Nation of Islam leader Elijah Muhammad calls for the establishment of an all-Black state within the United States during a meeting in New York City.

August

August 1

1894

Dr. Benjamin Elijah Mays is born in Epworth, South Carolina, the youngest of eight children; his parents had been enslaved. Mays received a PhD and became a minister, scholar, and social activist. He served as president of Morehouse College for 27 years (where he was so influential that one of his students, Martin Luther King, Jr., called him "my spiritual mentor and my intellectual father"), was dean of Howard University's School of Religion from 1934 to 1940, and was elected the first African American president of the Atlanta, Georgia, Board of Education on January 20, 1970.

> Dr. Clinton Warner, a freshman during Mays's first year as president, recalls one of Mays's sermons vividly:
>
> He stated a freshmen from Mars would likely be appalled and horrified at the attitude of students that I see everyday—bad study habits, no interest in learning, time spent having a good time, cutting classes and just laziness.
>
> Subsequently, he gave inspiring reasons why we all should be proud of ourselves and strive to do the best job that we could—at Morehouse and in the world. Mays advised, "Whatever you do, strive to do it so well that no man living and no man dead and no man yet to be born could do it any better." If this advice did not create the "Morehouse Mystique," it certainly enhanced it.
>
> Source: From Carrie M. Dumas and Julie Hunter. Benjamin Elijah Mays: A Pictorial Life and Times. Macon, GA: Mercer University Press, 2006, pp. 33–34.

Books

Mays, Benjamin Elijah, edited by Freddie C. Colston. *Dr. Benjamin E. Mays Speaks: Representative Speeches of a Great American Orator.* Lanham, MD: University Press of America, 2002. Speeches presented by Dr. Benjamin Mays.

Mays, Benjamin Elijah, edited by Orville Vernon Burton. *Born to Rebel: An Autobiography.* Victoria, BC: University of Georgia Press, 2003. Mays autobiography looks at his youth as the son of a sharecropper and his rise to become one of the most prominent African American scholars of the late twentieth century.

Websites

Dr. Mays Alma Mater, Bates College, has a profile of him. http://www.bates.edu/benjamin-mays.xml.

Dr. Benjamin E. Mays Historic Preservation Site contains a museum and Mays' birth home. www.mayshousemuseum.org/Page3.htm.

Also Noteworthy

1879

Mary Eliza Mahoney graduates from the New England Hospital for Women and Children, becoming the first professional nurse of African descent in the United States.

1960

Carlton Douglas Ridenhour is born in Roosevelt, Long Island, New York. As the lead rapper with the hip-hop group Public Enemy, Carlton became known as Chuck D. Under Public Enemy, Chuck D worked with Flavor Flav, Professor Griff, the S1W group, and Terminator X to create hip hop music that spoke about the social and political life of African Americans.

August 2

1924

James Arthur Baldwin is born to Emma Jones in Harlem, New York. His mother married the Baptist minister David Baldwin, when James was three years old. As a writer, Baldwin's novel *Go Tell It on the Mountain* and his essays about the 1960s African America protest movement, *The Fire Next Time*, explored the racial situation African Americans faced during the mid-twentieth century. Baldwin became a celebrity and spokesperson about the Black Protest era.

> *What Baldwin, in fact, offers is inside knowledge of how religious people think and act. He understood, perhaps only as a religious outsider who once believed could, the architecture of religious thought and how it shaped black people's collective aspirations and their connections to the larger society and world. In much of his early work, Baldwin describes a Christianity that equates the black with the ugly and damned, even as it paradoxically provides the rhetorical and institutional space for black resistance and black humanity. And even in the often-incendiary* The Fire Next Time *(1963), where his condemnation of his experience within Christianity is at its most strident, Baldwin demonstrates the continued vitality of black Christianity's moral voice by translating its religious language into a secular one. Martin Luther King's call for his fellow ministers and non-violent activists "to redeem the soul of America" . . . became, in Baldwin's hands, a broader plea to "relatively conscious whites and the relatively conscious blacks" to come together "like lovers" to "create" a new "consciousness" (*Fire Next Time 141*). Despite rejecting traditional Christian beliefs and institutions, Baldwin found that his religious heritage provided him a vocabulary to engage areas as varied as sex and politics. It provided a perch from which to condemn both a wayward nation and Christianity itself for betraying the sons and daughters of African slaves. In reckoning with his lost faith, Baldwin managed in his literary work to illuminate both the possibilities and restrictive limitations of evangelical culture in black American life, even as he defined much of what was best in his own art and social criticism.*
>
> *Source*: From Douglas Field. *A Historical Guide to James Baldwin*. New York, NY: Oxford University Press, 2009, pp. 65–66.

Books

Baldwin, James. *The Fire Next Time*. New York, NY: Random House Digital, Inc., 1963. Baldwin's look at the politics of late-twentieth-century United States and its effects on the lives of African Americans.

Leeming, David Adams. *James Baldwin: A Biography*. New York, NY: Knopf, 1994. Biography of Baldwin, his literary career, his personal life, and his impact on mid to late twentieth centrury politics.

Websites

University of Illinois profiles James Baldwin. http://www.uic.edu/depts/quic/history/james_baldwin.html.

Excerpt from the documentary "James Baldwin: the Price of the Ticket" is on YouTube. http://www.youtube.com/watch?v=4_hYraYI2J8.

Also Noteworthy

1850

William Still begins using his home in Philadelphia, Pennsylvania, as a major station on the Underground Railroad. Still was a child of Levin and Sidney Steel; Levin had purchased his freedom, and Sidney escaped enslavement in Maryland. The family changed their name to "Still," and Sidney changed her name to "Charity." After William left his parent's home in New Jersey he moved to Philadelphia, taught himself to read, and married Letitia George. William became the secretary and janitor of the all-white Pennsylvania Society for the Abolition of Slavery and worked his way up to being elected the Society's chairman—a position he maintained for 10 years. As Still ran his Underground Railroad he was careful to take information about the people he helped, so that he could re-unite them with family members later. In 1872, his notes were published as *The Underground Railroad* (1872). According to his notes, Still had helped 649 Blacks escape from slavery. Still also founded an orphanage for the children of African American soldiers and sailors and was later so successful in business that he was elected to the Philadelphia Board of Trade.

August 3

1492

Alonzo Pietro—an African Italian who was known as "Alonzo Il Negro"—captains Christopher Columbus's ship *Niña* as it sailed toward what was supposed to be a new trade route to China. Columbus's *Santa Maria*, *Pinta*, and *Niña* ships left from the Castilian Palos de la Frontera in southern Spain. Columbus was aboard the *Niña* when he came across the first island in the Americas.

> *Alonzo Pietro, a Negro is credited by some authorities as having been the pilot of the ship,* Nina, *of the fleet of Columbus in the discovery of America. It is further reported that he accompanied Columbus on his second voyage to America. His name is said to appear in the list of the names of those who sailed with Columbus. Pietro's name appeared in the "Libretto," 1504, as Pietro Alonzo, il nigro. This is repeated in "Paesi Nouamente Retrouati," Venice, 1507, also in Simon Grynaeus' "Novus Orbis Regionum," Basle, 1532, also Peter Martyrs' "Decades" Seville, 1511.*
>
> *Source*: From Tuskegee Institute. *Negro Year Book, Volume 6*. Department of Records and Research. Tuskegee Institute, AL: Negro Year Book Pub. Co., 1922, p. 123.

Books

Bussard, Paul C. and College of St. Thomas (Saint Paul, MN). *The Catholic Digest: Volume 8*. Victoria, BC: AbeBooks/College of St. Thomas, 1944. Book provides a summary of Pietro's role as the pilot of the *Niña* and notes that he played no part in the attempted mutiny against Columbus.

Eleazer, Robert Burns and Southern Regional Council. *America's Tenth Man: A Brief Survey of the Negro's Part in American History*. Victoria, BC: AbeBooks/Southern Regional Council, Inc., 1944. Book has an entry on Alonzon Pietro and his importance to the voyage of Columbus.

Websites

Columbus and "The Negro" takes on the claim that Alonzon Pietro was of African descent. http://www.jstor.org/pss/273057.

1492 In History puts Alonzon Pietro's steerage of the *Niña* in context. http://1492columbus .blogspot.com/2006/04/1492-in-history .html

August 4

1961

Barack Hussein Obama is born in Honolulu, Hawaii, to Barack Hussein Obama, Sr., and Stanley Ann Dunham. After spending the early years of his life in Jakarta, Indonesia, Obama's family returned to Hawaii, and he later attended schools in Los Angeles and New York City. As a law student at Harvard University, he became the first person of African descent to serve as president of the *Harvard Law Review*. In 2004 he was elected to the U.S. Senate as the representative for Illinois, and on November 4, 2008, he became the 44th president of the United States and the first U.S. president of African descent. On December 10, 2009, Obama won the Nobel Peace Prize.

> *That my father looked nothing like the people around me—that he was black as pitch, my mother white as milk—barely registered in my mind.*
>
> *In fact, I can recall only one story that dealt explicitly with the subject of race; as I got older, it would be repeated more often, as if it captured the essence of the morality tale that my father's life had become. According to the story, after long hours of study, my father had joined my grandfather and several other friends at a local Waikiki bar. Everyone was in a festive mood, eating and drinking to the sounds of a slack-key guitar, when*

a white man abruptly announced to the bartender, loudly enough for everyone to hear, that he shouldn't have to drink good liquor "next to a nigger." The room fell quiet and people turned to my father, expecting a fight. Instead, my father stood up, walked over to the man, smiled, and proceeded to lecture him about the folly of bigotry, the promise of the American dream, and the universal rights of man. "This fella felt so bad when Barack was finished," Gramps would say, "that he reached into his pocket and gave Barack a hundred dollars on the spot. Paid for all our drinks and puu-puus for the rest of the night—and your dad's rent for the rest of the month."

Source: From Barack Obama. *Dreams from My Father: A Story of Race and Inheritance.* New York, NY: Random House Digital, Inc., 2007, pp. 10–11.

Books

Obama, Barack. *Barack Obama: What He Believes in from His Own Works.* Rockville, MD: Arc Manor LLC, 2008. Book reviews the Senate bills and resolutions Senator Barack Obama sponsored or co-sponsored during 2007, in the first term of the 110th Congress.

Obama, Barack edited by Tim Davidson. *The Essential Obama: The Speeches of Barack Obama.* Chicago, IL: Aquitaine Media Corp, 2009. Excerpts from Obama's many speeches examine his understanding of politics.

Websites

The text and video of President Barack Obama's Inaugural Address as delivered on January 20, 2009. http://www.whitehouse.gov/blog/inaugural-address/.

Barack Obama Biography. http://www.obama-biography.info/.

Also Noteworthy

1810

Robert Purvis is born in Charleston, South Carolina, to Harriet Judah, a free woman of color, and William Purvis, an immigrant from England who became wealthy as a cotton broker. Purvis identified as a person of African descent and worked as an abolitionist—he helped found Philadelphia's American Anti-Slavery Society and helped those fleeing from slavery along their way as part of the Underground Railroad.

1897

Henry A. Rucker is appointed by President William McKinley to serve as the Collector of Internal Revenue; he is the first African American to serve in this position. Rucker was born on November 14, 1852, to enslaved parents in Wilkins County, Georgia.

1901

Louis Daniel "Satchmo" Armstrong is born in New Orleans, Louisiana. As a cornet and trumpet player, Louis Armstrong would come to define not just New Orleans' jazz but the idea of jazz itself.

1964

The bodies of James Earl Chaney, Andrew Goodman, and Michael Schwerner are found on a farm outside of Philadelphia, Mississippi. The three young men were civil rights workers, and they had been investigating the firebombing of an African American church when they disappeared on June 21, 1964. It took the FBI 44 days to break what it had code-named the "MIBURN" case when they found the body of James Earl Chaney buried 15 feet deep in an earthen dam alongside the bodies of Andrew Goodman and Michael Schwerner. Three years later, 21 members of the local White Knights of the Ku Klux Klan were charged in federal court with conspiracy and with violating the civil rights of the three young men. Only 7 of those 21 men were convicted.

August 5

1830

James Augustine Healy is born in Jones County, Georgia, to Michael Morris Healy (a Georgia cotton planter and slaver) and Mary Eliza Clark Healy, who was enslaved. Healy's parents lived together as husband and wife, although there are no records of an official church marriage. And, because the mother was a slave, the 10 children the Healys had were legally supposed to be enslaved. Healy's father had his children educated in the North to avoid these problems. As an adult, the Most Rev. James A. Healy, D.D., was consecrated as Bishop of Portland on June 2, 1875. Bishop James Augustine Healy was the first person of African descent to serve as a Catholic Bishop in the United States.

James Augustine Healy was born in 1830 near Macon, Georgia, but was educated in the North, having passed several years in Quaker schools on Long Island and New Jersey. He then entered the college of the Holy Cross at Worcester, Massachusetts, where he was graduated in 1849. Feeling that he was called by God to the ecclesiastical state, he then entered the theological seminary in Montreal directed by the Sulpitians, and completed his course in the institution at Paris directed by the same association of learned priests.

On returning to the diocese of Boston, to which he had become attached, he was stationed at the cathedral, where he acted for many years as chancellor and secretary. He then became pastor of St. James' Church, Boston, holding the position for nine years, winning the respect of his fellow-priests and the attachment of the flock confided to him. From this position he was summoned by the voice of the Holy Father to assume the burden of the episcopate. He was consecrated Bishop of Portland on the 2d of June, 1875.

Source: From John Gilmary Shea. *The Hierarchy of the Catholic Church in the United States: Embracing Sketches of All the Archbishops and Bishops from the Establishment of the See of Baltimore to the Present Time. Also, an Account of the Plenary Councils of Baltimore, and a Brief History of the Church in the United States.* Victoria, BC: AbeBooks/Office of Catholic Publications, 1886, pp. 345–346.

Books

Foley, Albert Sidney. *God's Men of Color.* Victoria, BC: AbeBooks/Arno Press, 1969. Book includes a profile of the life and work of Bishop James A. Healey; it also points to the progress of Healy's siblings in the Catholic Church, Father Alexander Sherwood Healy of New York and Boston, and Father Patrick F. Healy, who served as president of Georgetown University.

Paradis, Wilfrid H. *Upon This Granite: Catholicism in New Hampshire, 1647–1997.* Manchester, NH: Kevin Donovan, 1998. Contains a profile of Bishop James A. Healy and his career.

Websites

James Healy, Black Priest and Bishop. http://burlington1677.blogspot.com/2011/09/james-healy.html.

Bishop James Augustine Healy—Roman Catholic Diocese of Portland. www.portlanddiocese.net/info.php?info_id=132.

Also Noteworthy

1946

Sherry Ann Jackson is born in Washington, DC. Jackson is the first African American woman to receive a PhD from the Massachusetts Institute of Technology (MIT).

August 6

1930

Abbey Lincoln (née Anna Marie Wooldridge) is born in Chicago, Illinois. As a jazz vocalist, songwriter, and actress, Lincoln was famous for both writing and performing her own work. When Lincoln was married to jazz musician Max Roach in the 1960s, the couple became hardcore civil rights/Black Nationalist activists. Lincoln sang on Roach's famous album, *We Insist!—Freedom Now Suite* (1960). Zaire's minister of culture gave Lincoln the name Aminata Moseka; she became the best-known member of the group Cultural Association for Women of African Heritage; and, as a couple, Roach and Lincoln famously helped organize the United Nations protests against Patrice Lumumba's assassination in 1961. Lincoln co-starred in *Nothing but a Man* (1964) with Ivan Dixon and with Sidney Poitier in *For Love of Ivy* (1968).

In 1956, Liberty Records introduced recording artist Abbey Lincoln as a high-glamour black counterpart to their star sexpot, Julie London. Then, like a sixties honor student who drops out to join the radical underground, Lincoln reemerged at the end of the decade as a socially significant songstress advocating musical and political reform in the company of Sonny Rollins, Kenny Dorham, and her then husband, Max Roach.

That was in the fifties and sixties. Throughout the nineties and into the new millennium, Abbey Lincoln reigned as one of the most imposing presences on the jazz scene, both for how she sang and what she sang: The magnificence of her musical style was enhanced by the consistently high quality of the songs she wrote. Her sound is something way beyond special: Like Billie Holiday, Lincoln has a dark, hypnotic timbre, and while her range may be limited, her intonation is more than sufficiently accurate within it. More important, she has a dramatic ability to command a listener's attention that's far in excess of raw vocal technique (the ability to hit and sustain notes).

Source: From Will Friedwald. A Biographical Guide to the Great Jazz and Pop Singers. New York, NY: Random House Digital, Inc., 2010, p. 60.

Books

Lincoln, Abbey. *Abbey Lincoln Songbook.* Milwaukee, WI: Hal Leonard Corporation, 1994. Songbook of Abbey Lincoln's greatest songs.

Monson, Ingrid Tolia. *Freedom Sounds: Civil Rights Call Out to Jazz and Africa.* New York, NY: Oxford University Press, 2007. Contains a look at Abbey Lincoln's contributions to Max Roach's famous *We Insist!—Freedom Now Suite.*

Websites

Abbey Lincoln Discography. www.jazzdisco graphy.com/Artists/Lincoln/index.html.
Abbey Lincoln and Max Roach performing "Freedom Day." http://www.youtube.com/watch?v=4AGQQhFSy5g.

Also Noteworthy

1872

Elijah McCoy receives U.S. Patent No. 130,305 for his first self-lubricating locomotive engine. The quality of his inventions helped coin the phrase "the real McCoy."

1965

President Baines Lyndon Johnson signs the Voting Rights Act of 1965 (S 1564-PL 89-110). The Voting Rights Bill ended the use of literacy tests as a prerequisite for voting in an election and provided for the use of federal examiners to ensure that African Americans, specifically, and others could participate in elections in the South.

August 7

1970

Jonathan Jackson is gunned down during a shootout outside the Marin County California courthouse. Jackson had been attempting to free the Black Liberation Fighters, James McClain, William Christmas, and Ruchell Magee. The UCLA professor/political activist Angela Davis was accused of taking part in the incident and went into hiding to avoid arrest. On June 4, 1972, Davis was acquitted of all charges, but this incident—and other problems that took place in California prisons (particularly the assassination of George Jackson on

August 21, 1971, by San Quentin prison guards), led to the creation of "Black August," a coordinated community sunrise-to-sunset fasting and series of educational events designed to honor and commemorate the lives and deaths of Black Liberation Freedom Fighters and to promote the revolutionary teachings of the New African struggle.

> ...In the black community we observe Black August, originally in memory of Jonathan and George Jackson and the August 7th and August 21st incidents, and then it just kept expanding because the MOVE Nine were busted in August, on August 8th, 1978. I think Nat Turner did his thing in August, and we discovered there were a whole host of August dates in our history that we needed to commemorate. So Black August kind of became a tradition. . . .
>
> Source: From Ron Sakolsky. *Seizing the Airwaves: A Free Radio Handbook.* Oakland, CA: AK Press, 1998, p. 123.

Books

Chang, Jeff. *Can't Stop, Won't Stop: A History of the Hip-Hop Generation.* New York, NY: Macmillan, 2006. Book includes a profile of the Black August Malcolm X Grassroots Movement and looks at how it helped hip-hop artists connect with Black political prisoners.

Paradis, Wilfrid H. *Black August: Origins, History, and Significance.* Victoria, BC: AbeBooks/Books 4 Prisoners Crew, 2004. Looks at the reasons for the origins of Black August.

Websites

Black August Organizing Committee. http://www.dragonspeaks.org/.

The History of Black August. http://mxgm.org/blackaugust/blackaugust-history/.

Also Noteworthy

1894

Joseph Lee receives U.S. Patent No. 524,042 for his improvements to the dough-kneading machine.

1904

Ralph Johnson Bunche is born in Detroit, Michigan. He became the first African American to serve on the U.S. delegation to the first General Assembly of the United Nations. In 1949, Bunche negotiated a truce to the Arab-Israeli conflict. For his efforts, Bunche was awarded the Nobel Peace Prize. He is the first person of African descent to win the Nobel Peace Prize.

1935

Rahsaan Roland Kirk is born Ronald Theodore Kirk in Columbus, Ohio. Kirk became a famed jazz artist, able to play numerous instruments, and his interest in various musical styles made him a celebrated and enigmatic musical artist.

August 8

1866

Matthew Alexander Henson, the first person of African descent to reach the North Pole, is born in Charles County, Maryland. In 1909 Henson was part of a six-person expedition; he reached the North Pole 45 minutes before Commandeer Robert E. Peary.

> The memory of those last five marches, from the Farthest North of Captain Bartlett to the arrival of our party at the Pole, is a memory of toil, fatigue, and exhaustion, but we were urged on and encouraged by our relentless commander, who was himself being scourged by the final lashings of the dominating influence that had controlled his life. From the land to 87° 48' north, Commander Peary had had the best of the going, for he HAD brought up the rear and had utilized the trail made by the preceding parties, and thus he had kept himself in the best of condition for the time when he made the spurt that brought him to the end of the race. From 87° 48' north, he kept in the lead and did his work in such a way as to convince me that he was still as good a man as he had ever been. We marched and marched, falling down in our tracks repeatedly,

until it was impossible to go on. We were forced to camp, in spite of the impatience of the Commander, who found himself unable to rest, and who only waited long enough for us to relax into sound sleep, when he would wake us up and start us off again. I do not believe that he slept for one hour from April 2 until after he had loaded us up and ordered us to go back over our old trail, and I often think that from the instant when the order to return was given until the land was again sighted, he was in a continual daze.

Source: From Matthew A. Henson, Robert E. Peary, Deirdre C. Stam, and Booker T. Washington. *Matthew A. Henson's Historic Arctic Journey: The Classic Account of One of the World's Greatest Black Explorers*. Guilford, CT: Globe Pequot, 2009, pp. 156–157.

Books

Bryce, Robert M. *A Negro Explorer at the North Pole*. New York, NY: Cooper Square Press, 2001. Biography of Henson includes a foreword by Robert E. Peary and introduction by Booker T. Washington.

Miller, Floyd. *Ahdoolo; the Biography of Matthew A. Henson*. New York, NY: Dutton, 1963. Biography of Henson, one of the greatest Black explorers.

Websites

Matthew Henson's family established a memorial Website to his work. http://www.matthewhenson.com/.

San Jose State University provides a biography of Matthew Henson. http://www.sjsu.edu/depts/Museum/henson.html.

Also Noteworthy

1907

The jazz saxophonist Bennett Lester "Benny" Carter is born in New York City, New York. Known as "the king," Carter is remembered for his tunes "When Lights Are Low" (1936) and "Blues in My Heart" (1931).

1988

The N.W.A. (Niggaz With Attitude) debut album, *Straight Outta Compton*, is released. The album introduced group members Ice Cube, Dr. Dre, Eazy-E, DJ Yella, and MC Ren and officially broadcast the sound of West Coast hip hop's Gangsta Rap.

August 9

1869

Annie Minerva Turnbo Malone is born the tenth of 11 children in Metropolis, Illinois. Malone developed cosmetics and hair-straightening techniques—including the first patented hot comb—for African Americans. Her hair care products, which she named "Poro" (meaning "strength" in Western Africa), were so successful that Malone became a millionaire and was able to open Poro College, the first school dedicated to teaching the care of Black hair. Malone is also remembered as an ardent philanthropist toward African American causes.

. . . Annie Malone, the first celebrated black pioneer in beauty culture, was the nation's first black millionaires and was the nation's first major black philanthropist. Madame C.J. Walker, a former washerwoman, was one of the first students to enroll in Annie Malone's beauty culture courses at Poro College, founded in 1900 as the first black institution in the United States to train black women, future Poro agents, in the Poro method of beauty culture, and to manufacture toiletries for persons of African descent.

Source: From Vincent P. Franklin. *Cultural Capital and Black Education: African American Communities and the Funding of Black Schooling, 1865 to the Present*. Charlotte, NC: IAP, 2004, p. 104.

Books

Malone, Ross. *Tales from Missouri and the Heartland*. Bloomington, IN: AuthorHouse, 2010. This book includes a short biography about Annie Malone.

Wright, John. *The Ville, St. Louis*. Mount Pleasant, SC: Arcadia Publishing, 2001. Book notes Malone's contributions toward the creation and functioning of the Annie Malone Children's Home.

Websites

Annie Malone Children and Family Service Center, which Malone helped to found and once sat on the board of, is still in operation and sponsors an annual parade in May to recall Malone's contributions. http://www.anniem alone.com/about-us.html.

The St. Louis-based Western Historical Manuscript Collection Photo Database has several images related to Annie Malone and her work. http://tjrhino1.umsl.edu/whmc/view .php?description_get=Annie+Malone.

Also Noteworthy

1936

Jesse Owens wins four gold medals—in the 100-meter and 200-meter races, the long jump, and the 400-meter relay—at the Summer Olympics in Berlin, Germany.

1961

James B. Parsons is named to serve as the first African American federal district judge in the continental United States.

August 10

1858

Anna Julia Cooper is born Anna Julia Haywood in Raleigh, North Carolina, to an enslaved African woman, Hannah Stanley, and her white master. Cooper was interested in learning from a young age and, as early as kindergarten, decided to become a teacher. Cooper's persistence kept her in the field of education until 1925, when she earned a PhD from the Sorbonne University in Paris, France, at the age of 67.

Only the BLACK WOMAN can say "when and where I enter, in the quiet, undisputed dignity of my womanhood, without violence and without suing or special patronage, then and there the whole Negro race enters with me." Is it not evident then that as individual workers for this race we must address ourselves with no half-hearted zeal to this feature of our mission. The need is felt and must be recognized by all. There is a call for workers, for missionaries, for men and women with the double consecration of a fundamental love of humanity and a desire for its melioration through the Gospel; but superadded to this we demand an intelligent and sympathetic comprehension of the interests and special needs of the Negro.

Source: From Anna Julia Cooper. *A Voice from the South*. Xenia, Ohio: The Aldine Printing House, 1892, p. 31.

Books

Cooper, Anna Julia edited by Frances Richardson Keller. *Slavery and the French and Haitian Revolutionists: L'attitude De La France a L'egard De L'esclavage Pendant La Revolutio.*Lanham, MD: Rowman & Littlefield, 2006. Republication of Cooper's dissertation, which interpreted the importance of the French Revolution.

May, Vivian M. *Anna Julia Cooper, Visionary Black Feminist: A Critical Introduction.* Boca Raton, FL: CRC Press/Taylor & Francis Group, LLC, 2007. Critical analysis of Cooper's contribution to feminist and African American civil rights work.

Websites

Anna Julia Cooper is profiled on Women's Intellectual Contributions to the Study of Mind and Society. http://www.webster.edu/ ~woolflm/cooper.html.

University of New Mexico profiles Anna Julia Cooper. http://www.unm.edu/~erbaugh/ Wmst200fall03/bios/Cooper.html.

Also Noteworthy

1829

Some 2,000 African Americans leave the city of Cincinnati, Ohio, for Canada following a vicious race riot and years of racial persecution that had required Blacks to register with the county or leave the state. The mass exodus led to the establishment of the African American colony of Wilberforce, outside Ontario, Canada, and to the creation of the National Negro Convention movement. The first National Negro Convention was a 10-day event that took place at Richard Allen's Bethel AME Church in Philadelphia, Pennsylvania, in 1830.

1867

Shakespearean actor Ira Frederick Aldridge dies in Łódź, Poland.

1880

Clarence Cameron White is born in Clarksville, Tennessee. White became one of the founding members of the National Association of Negro Musicians.

1989

General Colin Powell is nominated chairman of the Joint Chiefs of Staff, becoming the first person of African descent to hold the post.

August 11

1965

The Watts Rebellion begins in Los Angeles, California's, South Central neighborhood when police officers pull over an African American named Marquette Frye on suspicion of drunk driving. As a crowd gathered to watch, Marquette, his brother Ronald, and later even their mother Rena Frye who came to support her sons were beaten and arrested. When the police left, the crowd that had witnessed the abuse began rampaging through the businesses in the area. Their anger lasted six days. By the time the rebellion was over, some 34 people had died, 1,032 were injured, and there was an estimated $50–$100 million in property damage.

The fury and rage of the rebellion grew out of long-standing unaddressed tensions between law enforcement officials and Black citizens, but also from the collective, continuing, and cumulative consequences of systemic racial discrimination in housing, employment, and education. Yet while the community lashed out, it did not do so blindly. A Black-owned bank was left untouched on a block where every other building was destroyed. A furniture store owned by whites was looted and burned to the ground, but the storefront next door housing an Urban League employment project remain untouched by the rioters. Inside stores known for charging deceptively high interest rates for installment purchases, looters first demolished the establishments' credit records sections before helping themselves to the clothing, furniture, and appliances on display. The riot demolished many commercial buildings, but almost no private homes, libraries, or churches.

Contemporary observers noted that despite its destructive fury and tragic consequences, the insurrection also produced a collective sense of pride and power. A psychologist conducting interviews with riot participants found that they did not think of themselves as criminals, but as "freedom fighters liberating themselves with blood and fire."

Source: From George Lipsitz. *How Racism Takes Place*. Philadelphia, PA: Temple University Press, 2011, pp. 144–145.

Books

Horne, Gerald. *Fire This Time: The Watts Uprising and the 1960s*. Cambridge, MA: Da Capo Press, 1997. Traces the causes that led to and the results following the Watts Rebellion.

Marable, Manning. *Race, Reform, and Rebellion: The Second Reconstruction and Beyond in Black America, 1945–2006*. Jackson, MS: University Press of Mississippi, 2007. Marable provides a look at the Watts rebellion and its meaning to the African American Civil Rights Movement.

Websites

Politics of the Watts Rebellion. http://dornsife
.usc.edu/cdd/civic/bmus/Politics%20of%20
the%20Watts%20Rebellion%20%281965%29
.html.

Six Days of Watts Race Riot 1965/08. http://
www.youtube.com/watch?v=BbElAfALWbM.

Also Noteworthy

1866

U.S. Government's Treaty with Creek Nation is officially declared. The treaty notes in Article 2 that: "The Creeks hereby covenant and agree that henceforth neither slavery nor involuntary servitude, otherwise than in the punishment of crimes, whereof the parties shall have been duly convicted in accordance with laws applicable to all members of said tribe, shall ever exist in said nation; and inasmuch as there are among the Creeks many persons of African descent, who have no interest in the soil, it is stipulated that hereafter these persons lawfully residing in said Creek country under their laws and usages, or who have been thus residing in said country, and may return within one year from the ratification of this treaty, and their descendants and such others of the same race as may be permitted by the laws of the said nation to settle within the limits of the jurisdiction of the Creek Nation as citizens [thereof,] shall have and enjoy all the rights and privileges of native citizens, including an equal interest in the soil and national funds, and the laws of the said nation shall be equally binding upon and give equal protection to all such persons, and all others, of whatsoever race or color, who may be adopted as citizens or members of said tribe."

1873

John Rosamond Johnson is born in Jacksonville, Florida. An author, actor, and co-composer, Johnson famously co-wrote the African American national anthem, "Lift Every Voice and Sing," along with his brother James Weldon Johnson.

1921

Alexander Murphy Palmer Haley is born to Simon Alexander and Bertha Palmer Haley in Ithaca, New York. Under the name Alex Haley, he became a writer and authored *Roots* (for which he was awarded the Pulitzer Prize on April 18, 1977) and *The Autobiography of Malcolm X*. When *Roots* was televised as a miniseries, the final episode achieved the highest ratings ever for a single television program.

August 12

1891

Annie Wilson Lillian Evans-Tibbs (Evanti) is born the daughter of Wilson B. Evans in Washington, DC. A lyric soprano, Evanti graduated with a music degree from Howard University in 1913, and because she could sing and speak in five different languages, Evanti went on to become an international opera singer. She moved to France in 1925, where she became the first African American woman to sing with a European opera company. Although racism kept her from performing with U.S. companies, she gave a special command performance at the White House for President Franklin D. and Eleanor Roosevelt in 1934. To combat the persistent racism against African American opera performers, Evanti created The National Negro Opera Company along with Mary Caldwell Dawson in 1941.

When Evans performed in France, Italy, and Germany with the Paris Opera Company, she became the first African American opera singer to gain international recognition. In spite of her success and growing stature in Europe, when she returned to the United States, she was not invited to join any American opera company. Some national leaders, however, recognized her talent and provided opportunities for her to perform. Evanti performed in the White House for Eleanor Roosevelt and later performed for Presidents Harry S. Truman and Dwight D. Eisenhower. Evanti traveled throughout South America with Arturo Toscanini's orchestra as part of the Roosevelt Administration's Goodwill Ambassador Program. During World War II she gave morale-building vocal performances for Black troops.

Most of Evanti's appearances, however, were in local theaters. Recognizing that other Black singers needed opportunities to perform classical music, she helped to establish the National Opera Company in 1942. She also participated in the Pan-African movement by promoting knowledge of African American culture in Latin America.

Source: From Nancy C. Curtis. *Black Heritage Sites: The South*. New York, NY: The New Press, 1998, p. 65.

Books

Nettles, Darryl Glenn. *African American Concert Singers before 1950*. Jefferson, NC: McFarland, 2003. Book contains a look at Evanti's singing career.

Savage, Beth L. and National Register of Historic Places. *African American Historic Places*. Hoboken, NJ: John Wiley & Sons, 1994. Contains a profile of Madame Evanti's career and looks at the home she grew up at 1910 Vermont Ave., N.W., in Washington, DC.

Websites

Madame Lillian Evanti (Lillian Evans Tibbs) Residence, African American Heritage Trail. http://www.culturaltourismdc.org/things-do -see/madame-lillian-evanti-lillian-evans-tibbs -residence-african-american-heritage-trail.

Lillian Evanti. http://beinecke.library.yale.edu/ cvvpw/gallery/evanti.html.

Also Noteworthy

1855

Clinton Greaves is born in Madison County, Virginia. Greaves received a Medal of Honor for his work as corporal fighting Apache Indians along with the 9th Cavalry Regiment on January 24, 1877.

1922

Emma Ophelia DeVore is born to John Walter DeVore and Mary Emma Strother in Edgefield, South Carolina. DeVore became the first prominent African American model in the United States, and in 1946, she established the Grace Del Marco Agency to promote models of color. DeVore said she wanted the Grace Del Marco Agency to help people of color be "recognized as attractive human beings who can do a job in any field."

1959

Lynette Woodard is born in Wichita, Kansas. A four-time All-American college basketball player at the University of Kansas, Woodard won a Gold medal as a member of the U.S. women's basketball team at the Los Angeles Olympic Games of 1984. In 1985, she famously became the first female member of the Harlem Globetrotters.

August 13

1883

Ernest Everett Just is born in Charleston, South Carolina. A biologist, Just was famous for his non-conformist ideas about cell development, division, and fertilization. Just set up and served as the first head of Howard University's Department of Zoology and was part of the creation at Howard University of the Alpha chapter of the Black Greek-letter organization, Omega Psi Phi, on December 15, 1911.

Ernest Everett Just came into the world at a time of jubilation, but it would not be long before he would be brought face to face with the reality that political and social conditions for his race in the state were difficult and growing worse. A better time had been right after the Civil War, when blacks took a share in the political power of the state, joined the ranks of the Republican Party, began to vote and enjoy public education, became legislators and officials in the South Carolina government. It was the time of Black Reconstruction. In 1876, however, things changed. The election that year brought in the period of the so called White Redemption. At noon on 10 April 1877, United States soldiers filed out of the State House in Columbia by order of President Rutherford B. Hayes, symbolically ending the period of Black Reconstruction. Whites began to usurp power and enlarge the Democratic Party through political chicanery. Throughout the state, and especially in Charleston, blacks were disenfranchised, legislators lost office, and the practices of jim crow emerged.

Source: From Kenneth R. Manning. *Black Apollo of Science: The Life of Ernest Everett Just*. Oxford University Press, New York, p. 5.

Books

Haber, L., *Black Pioneers of Science and Invention: Odyssey Book*. Boston, MA: Houghton Mifflin Harcourt, 1991. Traces the lives of 14 black scientists and inventors who have made significant contributions in the various fields of science and industry.

Just, Ernest Everett. *Studies of Fertilization in Platynereis Megalops*. Chicago, IL: University of Chicago, 1915. Ernest Everett Just's doctoral thesis at the University of Chicago.

Websites

The Medical University of South Carolina has a brief biography on the life of Ernest Everett Just. http://www.musc.edu/eeo/justbio.html.

Howard University reference library information on Ernest Everett Just and his scientific research. http://www.howard.edu/library/reference/cybercamps/camp99/Marcus/defaultw3.htm.

Also Noteworthy

1892

The *Baltimore Afro-American* newspaper is founded. The formerly enslaved John Henry Murphy, Sr., merged his church's publication, *The Sunday School Helper*, with two other church publications, *The Ledger* (owned by George F. Bragg of Baltimore's St. James Episcopal Church) and *The Afro-American* (published by Reverend William M. Alexander, pastor of Baltimore's Sharon Baptist Church) to create the *Baltimore Afro-American* newspaper.

1920

Marcus Mosiah Garvey's Universal Negro Improvement and Conservation Association and African Communities League (UNIA-ACL) officially proclaims its "Declaration of Rights of the Negro Peoples of the World," during its international convention held at Liberty Hall in New York City. On top of its Declaration, the UNIA established the Universal Negro Catechism of the African Orthodox Church. The red, black, and green flag—also known as the "liberation flag"—was adopted as the "national colors" of African people. The African Orthodox Church's Rev. George Alexander McGuire—who was also the chaplain-general of the UNIA—noted the symbolic meaning of the colors: "Red is the color of the blood which men must shed for their redemption and liberty; black is the color of the noble and distinguished race to which we belong; green is the color of the luxuriant vegetation of our motherland."

1933

Joycelyn Elders is born in Wichita, Kansas. In 1993, Elders became the first African American U.S. Surgeon General when President Bill Clinton appointed her to that office.

1948

Kathleen Battle is born in Portsmouth, Ohio. As a lyric soprano opera singer, Battle's talent was never denied, but in 1994,

New York City's Metropolitan Opera famously fired her for "unprofessional" conduct, because she had a diva-like personality and was difficult to work with during a production of Donizetti's *The Daughter of the Regiment*.

August 14

1959

Earvin "Magic" Johnson is born in Lansing, Michigan. At 6 feet 9 inches tall, Magic Johnson became a celebrated basketball player. Johnson led his college basketball team, the Michigan State University Spartans, to the 1979 national championship and then became the No. 1 pick in the 1979 National Basketball Association draft. Johnson won five NBA championships and three MVP titles with the Los Angeles Lakers. Magic Johnson retired from professional basketball in November 1881 when he discovered he was infected with HIV; he was named one of the 50 greatest players of all-time in 1996. Following basketball, Johnson became an international entrepreneur.

> *Partnerships should always add value to your brand. I look for partners who buy in to my brand and my vision for economic development in urban America. Ken Smikle, the president of Target Market News, the Chicago-based marketing research firm that monitors black consumer trends, told Black Enterprise that my success with Starbucks would help other African-American entrepreneurs break into the urban market.*
>
> *"He's opened the door for creating partnerships with major retailers interested in black consumers," Smikle told B.E. "Many are interested, but they don't understand [the market] and frankly are a little frightened by it. So there's a possibility that because of his success, corporations will look for a Magic to help them do their deals in the urban community."*
>
> *Source*: From Earvin Magic Johnson. *32 Ways to Be a Champion in Business*. New York, NY: Random House Digital, Inc., 2008, p. 139.

Books

Bird, Larry, Earvin Johnson, with Jackie MacMullan. *When the Game Was Ours*. New York, NY: Houghton Mifflin Harcourt, 2009. Earvin "Magic" Johnson and Larry Bird write about their epic basketball battles of the 1980s and the legacy it left the NBA.

Johnson, Earvin with William Novak. *My Life*. New York, NY: Random House Digital, Inc., 1993. Johnson's autobiography looks at his 12 years in the NBA and his private family life.

Websites

The non-profit Magic Johnson Foundation promotes health and social, educational, and physical well-being among urban youth. www.magicjohnson.com.

Earvin Magic Johnson Story & Highlights on YouTube. http://www.youtube.com/watch?v=TS2zZZKRvCI.

Also Noteworthy

1966

Maria Halle Berry is born in Cleveland, Ohio. An award-winning actress and model, Halle Berry won an Academy Award for Best Actress for her performance as Leticia Musgrove in the 2001 film *Monster's Ball*. She was the first woman of African descent to win the Academy Award's top prize.

1989

The North Carolina Black Repertory Company hosts the first National Black Theater Festival in Winston-Salem, NC.

August 15

1925

Oscar Emmanuel Peterson is born in Montreal, Canada. As a jazz pianist and composer, Peterson performed for some 65 years, taking the stage with jazz legends like Count

Basie, Ella Fitzgerald, Louis Armstrong, Dizzy Gillespie, Nat King Cole, and Duke Ellington. Ellington once declared Peterson the "maharaja of the keyboard." With his famed Oscar Peterson Trio, the "maharaja" released songs like "Hymn to Freedom" (1962) and "Canadian Suite" (1964).

> Only when it was absolutely necessary, Oscar Peterson wrote, would he go on stage before a concert to check out the piano, because doing so "might lead to preconditioned ideas, and they can in turn interfere with the creative process so essential to a creative jazz concert."
>
> For Peterson, who died on December 23, 2007, at age eighty-two, his full mastery of the instrument enabled him to keep striving for what to him was his ultimate reason for being. In his equally masterful autobiography, A Jazz Odyssey: The Life of Oscar Peterson (Continuum, 2002), he said of the "dare-devil enterprise [the jazz experience]" in which he engaged for so many years that it "required you to collect all your senses, emotions, physical strength and mental power, and focus them totally on the performance . . . every time you play . . . Uniquely exciting, once it's bitten you, you never get rid of it. Nor do you want to; for you come to believe that if you get it all right, you will be capable of virtually anything. That is what drives me, and I know it always will do so."
>
> Source: From Nat Hentoff. At the Jazz Band Ball: Sixty Years on the Jazz Scene. Berkeley, CA: University of California Press, 2010, p. 42.

Books

Peterson, Oscar. *Oscar Peterson—Jazz Exercises, Minuets, Etudes and Pieces for Piano.* Milwaukee, WI: Hal Leonard, 2005. Peterson's selection of jazz songs that work for the piano.

Peterson, Oscar with Richard Palmer. *Jazz Odyssey: My Life in Jazz.* New York, NY: Continuum Intl Pub Group, 2006. Peterson's autobiography covers his understanding of the growth in jazz over the twentieth century.

Websites

The Official Website of Oscar Peterson. www .oscarpeterson.com.

Oscar Peterson's "Hymn to Freedom" is on YouTube. http://www.youtube.com/watch ?v=5-mIHk2rM0Q.

Also Noteworthy

1824

Formerly enslaved African Americans—who are part of the Cape Mesurado colony—push forward into what will become the colony of Liberia. The Cape Mesurado colony had been originally created by members of the American Society for Colonizing the Free People of Color of the United States (or American Colonization Society [ACS]).

1817

George Washington is born in Virginia to enslaved parents. After his father was sold, his mother had a white couple, the Cochrans, adopt him. Raised by the Cochrans, Washington was well schooled but faced discrimination in the East. He traveled northwest and became the founder of the town of Centerville, a town later renamed Centralia, in Lewis County in Southwest Washington state. Washington sold lots for those wanting to live in his town for $10 each.

1818

Bridget "Biddy" Mason is born enslaved in Hancock County, Georgia. When her enslaver moved to California, which was a free state, Biddy took him to court; she sued for and won her freedom as well as that of her three daughters. Mason remained in Los Angeles and went on to become a nurse/ midwife. As a real estate entrepreneur, she became one of the first African Americans to purchase land in the city. Mason helped found an African American elementary school, and in 1872, she donated the land for the founding of the First African Methodist Episcopal Church.

1919

Melba Alvarado is born in Oriente, Cuba. On September 17, 1945, Alvarado was a founding member of the Bronx, New York-based El Club Cubano Inter-Americano, http://www.ecciny.org/, a predominantly Afro-Cuban-led cultural and social club. El Club Cubano Inter-Americano was established as a club for people of color.

1935

Vernon Eulion Jordan, Jr., is born in Atlanta, Georgia. Jordan served as the executive director of the United Negro College Fund from 1971 to 1981 and next as president of the National Urban League. Following a stint advising President William Clinton from 1992 to 1993, Jordan turned to business and worked with the investment-banking firm Lazard Freres & Co. LLC.

1938

Maxine Waters (née Maxine Moore Carr) is born in St. Louis, Missouri. Waters has served as a Democratic member of the U.S. House of Representatives from California since 1991. She represents California's 35th Congressional District.

1945

Eugene Thurman Upshaw, Jr., is born in Robstown, Texas. Upshaw grew to 6 feet 5 inches, 255 pounds, and after graduating from Texas A&I University he became the No. 1 draft pick to the Oakland Raiders in the 1967 AFL Draft. Upshaw played from 1967 to1981 and was a two-time Super Bowl champion. He was inducted into the Pro Football Hall of Fame in 1987. In 1983, he became the executive director of the NFL Players' Association and kept that position until his death on August 20, 2008.

August 16

1922

Louis E. Lomax is born in Valdosta, Georgia. A famed television journalist and author, Lomax began his journalism career writing for the *Afro-American* and the *Chicago Defender* newspapers. He became the first African American television journalist in 1958, when he began reporting for WNTA-TV in New York. Lomax also famously worked with *60 Minutes'* journalist Mike Wallace on the documentary about the Nation of Islam, entitled "The Hate That Hate Produced."

Lomax's speeches were built on a central, compelling argument: African Americans of the 1960s were damn mad because of their mistreatment by whites. They simply were not going to take it any more. Although the law of the land in the 1950s said "separate but equal," African-Americans were treated then, and continued to be treated in the 1960s, as "separate and unequal." They were still forced to endure an almost endless list of indignities as the 1960s began: they were forced to sit at the back of the bus, they could not eat at the same lunch counters with whites, segregation in housing prevailed, they frequently could not find overnight accommodations when they traveled, and a number of the South's largest public universities were still segregated. . . .

The Negro revolt represented more than a strong rejection of the segregationist attitudes and racist practices of many whites, however. It also represented a strong rejection by Lomax and many other African-Americans of the old-line, conservative Negro leadership that refused to use direct, mass-action programs to get full civil rights immediately. . . . . .

Source: From Richard W. Leeman. *African-American Orators: A Bio-Critical Sourcebook.* Westport, CT: Greenwood Publishing Group, 1996, p. 243.

Books

Lomax, Louis E. *Mississippi Eyewitness; The Three Civil Rights Workers, How They Were Murdered.*

Oxnard, CA: Layman's Press, 1964. Book examines the murders of the civil rights workers James Earl Chaney, Andrew Goodman, and Michael Henry Schwerner.

Lomax, Louis E. *The Negro Revolt*. New York, NY: Harper & Brothers, 1962. Lomax's look at the causes behind the Civil Rights Revolution.

Websites

Reporters and Writers profiles Lomax and his role in the Civil Rights Movement. http://reportingcivilrights.loa.org/authors/bio.jsp?authorId=45.

Harper's Magazine has the articles Louis Lomax wrote for the publication available via pdf. http://harpers.org/subjects/LouisELomax.

Also Noteworthy

1887

Granville T. Woods receives U.S. Patent No. 368,265 for his electro mechanical brake.

1970

The activist Angela Davis is named in a federal warrant issued on August 16, in connection with George Jackson's attempted escape from San Quentin prison. In 1967, Davis had joined the Student Nonviolent Coordinating Committee (SNCC) and the Black Panther Party. The following year she became involved with the American Communist Party. Davis began working as a lecturer of philosophy at the University of California in Los Angeles in 1970. When the FBI informed her employers, the California Board of Regents, that Davis was a member of the American Communist party, they terminated her contract. Davis went on the run and the FBI named her as one of its "most wanted criminals." She was eventually arrested in New York, but at trial was acquitted of all charges.

August 17

1849

Lawyer-activist Archibald Henry Grimké is born in Charleston, South Carolina, to Henry Grimké, a white slaver, and Nancy Weston, who was his slave. Henry Grimké had two sons—Archibald and Francis—with Nancy Weston and had them freed upon his death. Grimké graduated from Harvard Law School and famously challenged the segregationist policies of President Woodrow Wilson.

> . . . But Archibald Henry Grimké, who became the outstanding Negro leader in the years between the death of Frederick Douglass and the ascendancy of Booker T. Washington, always credited his aunts with having made him "a liberal in religion, a radical in the woman suffrage movement, in politics and on the race question."
>
> Source: From Gerda Lerner. *The Grimké Sisters from South Carolina: Pioneers for Women's Rights and Abolition*. Chapel Hill, NC: UNC Press Books, 2004, p. 261.

Books

Bruce, Dickson D. *Archibald Grimké: Portrait of a Black Independent*. Baton Rouge, LA: Louisiana State University Press, 1993. Biography of Grimké and his impact on the African American community.

Grimké, Angelina Weld and Carolivia Herron. *Selected Works of Angelina Weld Grimké*. New York, NY: Oxford University Press, 1991. Angelina Ward Grimké includes a portrait of her father and his life.

Grimké, Archibald. "A Madonna of the South" in *The Southern Workman*. Victoria, BC: AbeBooks/Hampton Institute Press, 1900. Grimké's portrait of African American life in the South.

Websites

Archibald Grimke biography. http://www.usca.edu/aasc/grimke.htm.

Archibald Grimke: Portrait of a Black Independent. http://findarticles.com/p/articles/mi_m2838/is_n1_v29/ai_17276640/.

Also Noteworthy

1887

Marcus Mosiah Garvey, Jr., is born in St. Ann's Bay, Jamaica. After traveling to various nations to understand the plight of people of African descent, Garvey became a world-renowned Black Nationalist.

1939

Luther Allison is born in Widener, Arkansas. Raised in Chicago, Illinois, Allison taught himself to play the blues guitar and would record the blues on the Motown record label.

1970

The dance-music show *Soul Train* premieres on Chicago, Illinois-based WCIU-TV. This first program was hosted by Don Cornelius and featured Jerry Butler, the Chi-Lites, and the Emotions. Although the first program was filmed in Chicago and sponsored by Sears Roebuck and Company the show was picked up for national syndication by the Johnson Products Company, the makers of African American hair care products, and transferred to Los Angeles, California.

August 18

1934

Roberto Clemente Walker is born to Luisa Walker Clemente and Melchor Clemente in the San Anton neighborhood of Carolina, Puerto Rico—Roberto is the last of the couple's four children. At age 18, Clemente signed up with the Cangrejeros de Santurce (Santurce Crabbers) in the Puerto Rican Professional Baseball League (LBBPR), but he was eventually offered a Major League Baseball contract via the Brooklyn Dodgers. Clemente was later drafted by the Pittsburgh Pirates on November 22, 1954, and ended up playing 18 seasons with them, making 12 All-Star game appearances, winning 12 Gold Glove Awards, winning the National League's Most Valuable Player Award in 1966, and leading the league in batting averages some four different seasons. On December 31, 1972, after his 3,000th hit in the last game of the 1972 season, Clemente died in an airplane crash while on a mission to bring supplies to earthquake victims in Managua, Nicaragua. The plane crashed off the coast of Puerto Rico. Clemente was selected for the Hall of Fame in 1973. Clemente was the first Latino ever to be elected to the Baseball Hall of Fame.

> The founder of the Santurce Cangrejos (which means Crabbers) in 1939, Zorrilla continued to operate the franchise in 1952. He had also managed to establish good working relationships with a number of major league teams, including the Brooklyn Dodgers of the National League. One day, 72 players gathered at Santurce's Sixto Escobar Stadium for a tryout camp that was sponsored by both the Dodgers and Zorrilla's Santurce Crabbers. Alex "Al" Campanis, the Dodger's chief scout in the Caribbean, didn't expect much; most tryout camps produced a collection of hungry, but untalented athletes who had no business playing professional baseball at any level.
>
> The group of hopefuls included the 17-year-old Clemente, who showed up wearing a plain T-shirt, wrinkled baseball pants and an awkward-looking duck-billed cap. Campanis watched all 72 players as they participated in the first phase of the workout. "The first thing we do at the tryout is ask the kids to throw from the outfield," Campanis told Dick Young of the New York Daily News in 1971. "This one [kid] throws a bullet from center on the fly. I couldn't believe my eyes."
>
> Source: From Bruce Markusen. *Roberto Clemente: The Great One.* New York, NY: Sports Publishing LLC, 2002, p. 9.

Books

Darraj, Susan Muaddi and Rob Maaddi. *Roberto Clemente*. New York, NY: Infobase Publishing, 2008. Traces the life of Roberto Clemente from Puerto Rico to Pittsburgh, Pennsylvania, and emphasizes his humanitarian work.

Maraniss, David. *Clemente: The Passion and Grace of Baseball's Last Hero*. New York, NY: Simon & Schuster, 2007. Looks at Clemente as one of Major League Baseball's last true heroes.

Websites

Roberto Clemente Walker page at National Baseball Hall of Fame. http://baseballhall.org /hof/Clemente-Roberto.

Roberto Clemente Walker-Puerto Rican/ American Baseball Hall of Fame. http:// www.metacafe.com/watch/403275/roberto _clemente_walker_puerto_rican_american _baseball_hall_o/.

Also Noteworthy

1859

Harriet Wilson's *Our Nig* becomes the first novel published by an African American writer.

1911

Educator and civil rights pioneer Amelia Boynton Robinson is born to George and Anna Eliza Hicks Platts in Savannah, Georgia. In 1933, Robinson was a co-founder, with Rev. Frederick Reece, of the Dallas County Voters League (DCVL), which aimed to help register African Americans to vote. She later helped Martin Luther King, Jr., and members of the Southern Christian Leadership Conference (SCLC) organize the Selma-to-Montgomery march, which would later help lead to passage of the 1965 Voting Rights Act.

August 19

1946

Charles Frank Bolden, Jr., is born in Columbia, South Carolina. Bolden served in the military during the Vietnam War and became an astronaut in 1981. Bolden would command the *Discovery*, the first joint U.S./Russian space shuttle mission, in 1994. In 2009, President Barack Obama made Bolden the first person of African descent to serve as administrator of the National Aeronautics and Space Administration.

> A decorated military pilot, Charles Bolden completed four scientific missions as an astronaut in NASA's STS program before returning to active duty in the Marine Corps. In 2002, Bolden rejoined NASA as deputy administrator, and seven years later he became the first African-American permanent head of the space agency.
>
> *Source*: From Catherine Reef. *African Americans in the Military*. New York, NY: Infobase Publishing, 2009, p. 36.

Books

Mattocks, Carolyn Regennia Mpa. *I Can Do Anything*. Bloomington, IN: Xlibris Corporation, 2009. Includes a short profile of Charles Bolden, Jr.

Webster, Raymond B. *African American Firsts in Science and Technology*. Farmington Hills, MI: Gale Group, 1999. Includes a look at Bolden's contributions to the U.S. space program.

Websites

NASA biography of Charles F. Bolden, Jr., NASA Administrator. http://www.nasa.gov/ about/highlights/bolden_bio.html.

Encyclopedia Astronautica profiles Charles F. Bolden. http://www.astronautix.com/astros/ bolden.htm.

Also Noteworthy

1791

Benjamin Banneker posts a letter to U.S. Secretary of State Thomas Jefferson pointing out the hypocrisy of African slavery. Banneker wrote, "I apprehend you will embrace every opportunity, to eradicate that train of absurd and false ideas and opinions, which so generally prevails with respect to us; and that your sentiments are concurrent with mine, which are, that one universal Father hath given being to us all; and that he hath not only made us all of one flesh, but that he has also, without partiality, afforded us all the same sensations and endowed us all with the same faculties; and that however variable we may be in society or religion, however diversified in situation or color; we are all of the same family, and stand in the same relation to him."

1814

Mary Ellen Pleasant is born in Philadelphia, Pennsylvania. Pleasant challenged racial segregation in California's public streetcars in her *Pleasant v. North Beach & Mission Railroad Company* lawsuit of 1866. Pleasant is recognized as the "mother of the Civil Rights Movement in California."

1882

The 42-year-old political activist Jack Turner is lynched by a white mob in Choctaw County, Alabama. Turner had been enslaved and was only freed because of the Civil War. He had married a woman named Chloe and taught himself to read and write, even while remaining a farmer. But Turner was also a powerful orator and was able to organize local Blacks to vote. His leadership was so well noted that local white nationalists started calling him "Captain Jack" and "Gen. Jack Turner"—military names to denote his apparent aggressiveness. Turner's enemies soon developed the story that he was the leader of a conspiracy to kill all whites in the area. Authorities arrested Turner, and he was dragged from jail and hanged in front of the county courthouse.

1950

President Harry Truman appoints Edith Spurlock Sampson an alternate U.S. delegate to the United Nations. Sampson is the first African American to officially represent the United States at the United Nations.

1955

Bo Diddley makes his first appearance at Harlem's Apollo Theater.

1963

NAACP Youth Council begins sit-ins at lunch counters in Oklahoma City, Oklahoma.

August 20

1619

Some 20 Africans arrive in Old Point Comfort, Fort Monroe, in what is today Hampton, Virginia, aboard a Dutch ship named *White Lion* led by Captain Jope. They were sold as involuntary laborers to plantation owners along the James River and in Jamestown itself. They became the first Blacks to be forcibly settled as involuntary laborers in the North American British Colonies. In his journal, the Jamestown farmer John Rolfe noted, ". . . there came a Dutch man of war that sold us (20) Negars." At the time, servants were required to provide services for seven years before being given provisions and land to work for themselves. Although most of the servants were treated very poorly, they were at least treated as fellow human beings instead of mere property. The full concept of slavery had not yet become the rule of the land. Capt. William Tucker, the commander of Point Comfort purchased Antonio and Isabella, and in 1623 they became the parents of the first African American child, William Tucker.

Unlike the Spanish, who had developed a slave system in the Caribbean, English settlers establishing colonies along the East Coast brought no Africans—slave or free—with them. Not until a little more than a decade after the first English settlement in American at Jamestown did the first Africans arrive among the English. Slaves joined the colony on August 20, 1619, when a Dutch ship anchored at the Virginia colony and offered twenty individuals, recently captured in Africa, in exchange for provision.

Source: From Michael Lee Lanning. *The African-American Soldier: from Crispus Attucks to Colin Powell.* New York, NY: Citadel Press, 2004, p. 5.

Books

Lanning, Michael Lee. *The American Revolution 100: The People, Battles, and Events of the American War for Independence, Ranked by Their Significance.* Naperville, IL: Sourcebooks, Inc., 2009. Contains information on the arrival of the first people of African descent in the North American colonies.

Rodriguez, Junius P. *Slavery in the United States: A Social, Political, and Historical Encyclopedia, Volume 2.* Santa Barbara, CA: ABC-CLIO, 2007. Includes details about the August 1619 landing of indentured Africans.

Websites

The Project 1619 Committee commemorates the 1619 landing of Africans in North America. http://project1619.org/default.aspx.

Jamestown myth event in Hampton looks to claim Hampton as the landing ground for the nation's first Africans. http://www.wavy.com/dpp/news/local_news/jamestown-myth-event-in-hampton.

Also Noteworthy

1856

Wilberforce University is established with funds from the African Methodist Episcopal Church (AME) and the Methodist Episcopal Church; it is the first higher education school in the United States owned and operated by people of African descent. Originally based in Xenia, Ohio, Wilberforce was the first private university created for the education of African Americans.

1993

Dr. David Satcher is named director of the Centers for Disease Control and Prevention. Satcher also served as the 16th Surgeon General of the United States and as director of the Satcher Health Leadership Institute.

August 21

1831

Nat Turner begins his revolt in Southampton, Virginia. Because Turner had been viewed as religious, his May 12, 1828, vision that he "should arise and prepare myself and slay my enemies with their own weapons," helped him gain followers for his mission. Turner's failed rebellion took place in Southampton, Virginia, from August 21 to 22; it included some 75 Blacks and led to the death of 55 whites. More than 3,000 state militia members were sent to quell the rebellion. In retaliation, more than 100 innocent slaves were killed. Turner went into hiding but was captured six weeks later on October 30—he and some 18 of his followers were later hanged in Jerusalem, Virginia, on November 11, 1831. Turner's efforts were a strong example of resistance to enslavement.

Nat Turner's Rebellion, also known as the Southampton County rebellion, began on August 21, 1831, in Virginia, about 70 miles southeast of Richmond. It is remembered as one of a handful of antebellum slave revolts that profoundly changed the attitudes of white Americans toward slavery, and may, in fact, have had the most significant lasting impact on the politics of slavery and on the way slavery is remembered as an institution in American cultural memory. The insurrection's apparent mastermind, Nat Turner, is a man with multiple identities in the historical record, his personality and motives endlessly shaped by the legions of historians who have attempted to place the rebellion in the wider context of American history and, for that matter, in the context of human social relationships in the 19th and 20th centuries. Turner is remembered as a hero, a villain, a remorseless monster, a brave and bold visionary, a crazed madman, and a liberator—all depending on the perspective of the person remembering Turner and his exploits. He had been lionized as a hero of the abolitionist movement and condemned as a mass murderer of innocent women and children. His personality, and the insurrection he led, suffuses American popular culture, at once representing both the tragic consequences of humans holding other humans in bondage while at the same time symbolizing principled resistance to inhuman suffering through cunning, ingenuity, and guile. While certain incontrovertible facts of the rebellion remain, little is actually known of Nat Turner and the motives that caused him to undertake his mission, leaving historians to piece together incomplete accounts of what Turner did and why he did it.

Source: From Steven Laurence Danver. *Revolts, Protests, Demonstrations, and Rebellions in American History: An Encyclopedia*. Santa Barbara, CA: ABC-CLIO, 2010, p. 269.

Books

French, Scot. *The Rebellious Slave: Nat Turner in American Memory*. New York, NY: Houghton Mifflin Harcourt, 2004. Book looks at Turner's Rebellion and how it affected African American movements for Civil Rights and Black Power.

Greenberg, Kenneth S. *Nat Turner: A Slave Rebellion in History and Memory*. New York, NY: Oxford University Press, 2004. Essays on Turner look at his life and the legacy of his rebellion.

Websites

The Nat Turner rebellion imprinted on a woodcut. http://historymatters.gmu.edu/d/6811.

The Library of Virginia has the online documentation "Nat Turner's Rebellion 'To Rebel and Make Insurrection'. " http://www.lva .virginia.gov/exhibits/DeathLiberty/natturner/.

Also Noteworthy

1904

William Count Basie is born in Red Bank, New Jersey. As a pianist and big band orchestra leader, Basie became famous as the leader of a Kansas City style swing band.

1927

Andrew W. Cooper is born in Brooklyn, New York. Cooper famously sued under the Voting Rights Act against the racial gerrymandering that had locked African Americans and Latinos out of congressional representation. The *Cooper v. Power* lawsuit helped establish New York's 12th Congressional District, which took up most of Brooklyn's Bedford-Stuyvesant neighborhood. In 1968, the new 12th Congressional District elected Shirley Chisholm as the first African American woman to serve in the U.S. Congress. Andrew Cooper also created the Trans-Urban News Service (TUNS), which trained journalists of color, and in 1984 he founded *The City Sun*, a weekly newspaper that published until 1996.

1971

Black Panther Party Field Marshal George Lester Jackson is killed in San Quentin prison as he is, reportedly, trying to escape.

August 22

1917

John Lee Hooker is born to William Hooker and Minnie Ramsey in Coahoma County, Mississippi, just outside the town of Clarksdale. He was the last of 11 children born to a family of sharecroppers. After running away from home at age 15, Hooker spent time in Memphis, Tennessee, and Detroit, Michigan. He developed and became famous for a distinctive boogie-woogie style of blues guitar playing.

> ... *"Boom Boom"* is, if nothing else, the greatest pop tune he ever wrote, not to mention the first to break him into the pop charts: its comparatively modest placing at Number 60 fails to convey the magnitude of his achievement in getting there at all. It was also the most memorable, the most instantly appealing, and the one which has proved the most adaptable to the needs of other performers.
>
> So what's so great about *"Boom Boom?"* For a start, it has just about the tightest musical structure of any Hooker composition: its verses sedulously adhere to the twelve-bar format over which Hooker generally rides so roughshod, albeit with a neat bar-for-bar call-and-response.
>
> *Source*: From Charles Shaar Murray. *Boogie Man: The Adventures of John Lee Hooker in the American Twentieth Century.* New York, NY: MacMillan, p. 239.

Books

Hooker, John Lee. *John Lee Hooker: Vintage Blues Guitar.* Pacific, MO: Mel Bay Publications, 1996. Collection of Hooker's 20 greatest hit songs.

Shea, Therese. *John Lee Hooker: Master of Boogie and Blues.* New York, NY: Gareth Stevens, 2010. Traces the life and career of John Lee Hooker.

Websites

Hooker is remembered through this memorial Website http://www.johnleehooker.com/home.htm.

John Lee Hooker's "Boom boom" is on YouTube. http://www.youtube.com/watch?v=rOyj4ciJk34.

Also Noteworthy

1843

Henry Highland Garnett told delegates to the National Negro Convention in Buffalo, New York, that fighting for Black liberation would be more worthy than asking for it. In his "Call to Rebellion" speech, Garnet urged enslaved Africans to take up arms and fight for their freedom: "Brethren, arise, arise! Strike for your lives and liberties. Now is the day and the hour. Let every slave throughout the land do this, and the days of slavery are numbered. You cannot be more oppressed than you have been—you cannot suffer greater cruelties than you have already. Rather die freemen than live to be slaves. Remember that you are *four millions!*"

August 23

1917

African American soldiers are stationed at Camp Logan's army training camp in Houston, Texas, and take up arms to go after white police officers who have attacked them. The soldiers, who were part of the third battalion of the all-Black 24th Infantry Regiment, had gotten tired of the Jim Crow laws they faced in Houston—particularly when they were training to go and defend democracy abroad, in France. Sixty-four of the soldiers were tried for murder and mutiny; 13 received death sentences, and the rest got life imprisonment.

> News of discord between black newcomers in Houston and local white police officers first reached a national audience in the summer of 1917. On August 23 of that year, following weeks of conflict between white civilians and the black soldiers, a white police officer pistol-whipped two unarmed African American men from the Third Battalion of the Twenty-fourth Infantry stationed at Houston's Camp Logan in two separate incidents. News of the assaults, along with rumors that a white mob would attack Camp Logan, reached the soldiers. "Forget France," one infantryman declared. "Let's go clean up the God damned city. Let's get to work!" That night, approximately one hundred armed black soldiers left camp and marched through the streets of Houston in military formation, killing or wounding over a dozen

> *white people as they searched for the officers who had wounded their comrades.*
>
> Source: From Tyina Leaneice Steptoe. *Dixie West: Race, Migration, and the Color Lines in Jim Crow Houston.* Madison, WI: The University of Wisconsin/ProQuest, 2008, pp. 19–20.

Books

Christian, Garna L. *Black Soldiers in Jim Crow Texas, 1899–1917.* College Station, TX: Texas A&M University Press, 1995. Book's examination of how African American troops were treated in Jim Crow Texas includes a look at how the 1917 race riot in Houston took place.

Haynes, Robert V. *A Night of Violence: The Houston Riot of 1917.* Baton Rouge: Louisiana State University Press, 1976. Reviews the events that led up to the 1917 race riot in Houston, Texas.

Websites

HOUSTON RIOT OF 1917. http://www.tshaonline.org/handbook/online/articles/jch04.

The Tragic Violence along Buffalo Bayou in 1917. http://users.hal-pc.org/~lfa/BB55.html.

Also Noteworthy

1861

James Stone becomes the first person of African descent to fight for the Union Army during the Civil War.

1900

The educator and economic development promoter, Booker T. Washington, establishes the National Negro Business League (NNBL) in Boston, Massachusetts.

1998

UNESCO (the United Nations Educational, Scientific and Cultural Organisation) recognizes this day as the "International Day for the Remembrance of the Slave Trade and Its Abolition." The date commemorates the uprising by enslaved Africans that began on the night of August 22, 1791, and ended on August 23,1791, on the island of Santa Domingo (modern Haiti and the Dominican Republic). Slavery Remembrance Day was first celebrated in countries like Haiti (on August 23, 1998) and Goree in Senegal (August 23, 1999). UNESCO encourages all United Nations' member states to help commemorate the day enslaved Africans officially began fighting for their liberation.

August 24

1965

Reginald Wayne Miller is born to Saul and Carrie Miller in Riverside, California. Miller played for 18 years with the National Basketball Association (NBA)'s Indiana Pacers. Miller played the shooting guard position, and by the time he retired he set the NBA record for career three-pointers made (2,560). Miller's No. 31 jersey was retired by the Indiana Pacers.

> *Reggie Miller had a long and rare career, spending it with just one NBA team. This feat, in today's sports culture is very uncommon. Miller lead the league in shooting categories in many different seasons, with his accuracy at both the free-throw line and 3-point arc carrying him through his career. Miller was the 4th (and most likely final) player to wear the Pacer's No. 31. Phil Chenier (1979), Granville Waiters (1983–1985), and Walker Russell (1986–1987) were the other three.*
>
> Source: From Indy-Tech Staff. *Reggie Miller: Shooting Star.* Indianapolis, IN: Indy Tech Publishing, 2005, p. 8.

Books

Frisaro, Joe. *Reggie Miller: From Downtown.* New York, NY: Sports Publishing LLC, 2000. Profiles Reggie Miller and the impact of his play and his character on the NBA.

Miller, Reggie, Gene Wojciechowski, and Spike Lee. *I Love Being the Enemy: A Season on the*

Court with the NBA's Best Shooter and Sharpest Tongue. New York, NY: Simon & Schuster, 1999. Miller's journal about a year as a guard with the Indiana Pacers.

Websites

Reggie Miller, Indiana Pacers legend. http://www2.indystar.com/library/factfiles/people/m/miller_reggie/reggie.html.

Reggie Miller—It is Miller Time. http://www.youtube.com/watch?v=yKSeoARswig.

Also Noteworthy

1969

Last day of the Harlem Arts Festival is held in Marcus Garvey/Mount Morris Park. The event—which is also referred to as the Harlem Cultural Festival or the Black Woodstock—was a celebration of African American music and culture. The concert series took place from June 29 through August 24 and featured a mixture of gospel, soul, and comedy routines. Some of the artists featured were Nina Simone, Gladys Knight and the Pips, Stevie Wonder, Sly & the Family Stone, Abbey Lincoln & Max Roach, Mahalia Jackson, and Moms Mabley.

August 25

1927

Althea Gibson is born in Silver, South Carolina. In 1956, she became the first African American to win the Wimbledon tennis tournament. At the age of 20, she won her first of 10 consecutive Black national championships. During her illustrious career, she would win the Italian Open, two U.S. Open championships, and multiple doubles championships at Wimbledon. She was named the Associated Press Female Athlete of the Year twice and inducted into the International Tennis Hall of Fame in 1971.

Set against the heights that Althea eventually scaled in her career, including five major singles

titles, it is difficult to put that first Wimbledon doubles title in its proper context. It was as difficult then as it is now. "Doubles gets you on the board, but it isn't like winning the singles," Angela Mortimer says; she eventually managed to do both at Wimbledon. In Althea's autobiography, there isn't a word about the 1956 Wimbledon doubles final. When you've just won the singles at both Wimbledon and Forest Hills two years in succession, as Althea had when that book was published, some two-year-old doubles title hardly seems crucial anymore.

Source: From Bruce Schoenfeld. *The Match: Althea Gibson and Angela Buxton: How Two Outsiders—One Black, the Other Jewish—Forged a Friendship and Made Sports History.* New York, NY: HarperCollins, 2004, p. 230.

Books

Gibson, Althea. *I Always Wanted to Be Somebody.* New York, NY: Harper, 1958. Gibson's autobiography of her life as a groundbreaking sportswoman.

Roskill, Andrew. *Althea Gibson: Breaking the Color Barrier in Tennis.* New York, NY: Webster's Digital Services, 2010. Book covers Gibson's progress as a Black tennis player, during a time of extreme discrimination.

Websites

The Althea Gibson Foundation has a Website in her remembrance. http://www.altheagibson.com/.

Althea Gibson: Tennis. http://www.womentalksports.com/athlete/690/Althea-Gibson.

Also Noteworthy

1868

Archibald James Carey, Sr., is born to Jefferson Alexander Carey and Anna Bell Carey in Atlanta, Georgia. Educated and eventually ordained a religious leader while in Georgia, Carey Sr. eventually moved to Chicago, Illinios, where he became the pastor of the Quinn Chapel African Methodist Episcopal Church. Carey's leadership also led to his strong ties with the Republican Party, it led to his appointment as head of Illinois' 50th anniversary celebration of emancipation from slavery in 1915, and he was named the chief examiner of claims for the City of Chicago.

1908

National Association of Colored Graduate Nurses (NACGN) is established. Founded by Martha Minerva Franklin the NACGN was created to support African Americans in the nursing profession, since they were not allowed to join the predominately white American Nurses Association (ANA).

2008

U.S. Senator Barack H. Obama is nominated at the Democratic National Convention in Denver, Colorado, as the Democratic candidate for the president of the United States.

August 26

1900

Hale Aspacio Woodruffis is born to Augusta and George Woodruff in Cairo, Illinois. Woodruff's beginning work as a painter was inspired by African traditions and by his admiration for Henry O. Tanner. After traveling to Paris, France, just to meet Tanner, Woodruff also became a fan of the work of Pablo Picasso. In 1931, he became the first art instructor of the Atlanta University Center. Woodruff is also known for the murals on Black history he created for Atlanta University and Alabama's Talladega College. Woodruff's *The Amistad Murals* tell the story of the mutiny of enslaved Africans aboard the slave ship *Amistad*. While in Atlanta, he began a national exhibition of work by Black artists, which was held annually for over 25 years. In his later years he was heavily influenced by abstract expressionism.

In 1925 Woodruff submitted five paintings to the Amy Springarn Competition at the Crisis under the fictitious name Icabod [sic] Crane. One of his landscapes won the ten-dollar third prize for illustration. These paintings so impressed Du Bois that he not only requested that Woodruff submit cover designs for the Crisis from time to time, but he also hung them in his office and was, as he said, "loathe to depart with them" when the 135th Street branch library in New York requested them for a solo exhibition in 1925.

Source: From Theresa A. Leininger-Miller. New Negro Artists in Paris: African American Painters and Sculptors in the City of Light, 1922–1934. Piscataway, NJ: Rutgers University Press, 2001, p. 108.

Books

Bey, Sharif. *Aaron Douglas and Hale Woodruff.* Saarbrücken, Germany: VDM Verlag, 2008. Looks at both Aaron Douglas and Woodruff's work and influences.

Studio Museum in Harlem. *The Hale Woodruff Memorial Exhibition: Curators' Choice: The Studio Museum in Harlem July 20–December 31, 1994.* New York, NY: Studio Museum in Harlem, 1994. Publication features Woodruff's work selected by curators.

Websites

The New Georgia Encyclopedia profiles Hale Woodruff. http://www.georgiaencyclopedia.org/nge/Article.jsp?id=h-1039.

The Van Gogh Gallery profile Woodruff and his work. http://www.vangoghgallery.com/artistbios/Hale_Woodruff.html.

Also Noteworthy

1920

The 19th Amendment to the Constitution is ratified, giving women the right to vote.

1946

Valerie Simpson is born in the Bronx, New York. With her songwriting partner and later husband, Nickolas Ashford, Simpson is known for composing some of the most famous soul music songs like "Ain't No Mountain High Enough," "Love Don't Make It Right," "You're All I Need to Get by," and "Ain't Nothing Like the Real Thing."

August 27

1909

Lester Willis Young is born in Woodville, Mississippi. After making his name playing with different bands, Young rose to national fame playing the saxophone with Count Basie & His Orchestra and would famously be nicknamed "Prez" or "President of the Saxophone" by the Jazz singing legend Billie Holiday.

The tenor stylist acquired a growing reputation not only as the band's special feature and hot soloist, but as a crowd-pleasing showman. No numbers were written specifically for him, but he could solo as much as he wanted. On "Tiger Rag," his specialty with the orchestra, his solo might last as long as ten choruses. To get over with his presentation, Young "used to take his mouthpiece off the horn and turn it around, and play it like he was smoking a pipe," according to Phillips. In other words, he "turned his mouthpiece upside down so the bottom of the reed would still be on his lip" and the bell of his horn was "pointing straight down to the floor." At the climax of his solo, he would throw in an acrobatic stunt: holding "his left arm behind his back . . . he would finger the bottom of the tenor saxophone, and his right hand would be in the front, fingering . . . the top."

Source: From Douglas Henry Daniels. Lester Leaps in: The Life and Times of Lester "Pres" Young. Boston, MA: Beacon Press, 2003, p. 524.

Books

Delannoy, Luc. *Pres: The Story of Lester Young.* Fayetteville, AR: University of Arkansas Press, 1993. Biography of Young looks at his impact on Jazz.

Porter, Lewis. *Lester Young.* Ann Arbor, MI: University of Michigan Press, 2005. Biography of the life of Lester Young.

Websites

Lester Young performing "Polka Dots and Moonbeams." http://www.youtube.com/watch?v=A6ogRiaWXaU.

Lester Young's Last Interview 1959 ~ On Reading Music. http://www.youtube.com/watch?v=oVLMR3ffNSQ&feature=related.

Also Noteworthy

1935

Mary McLeod Bethune establishes the National Council of Negro Women.

1963

W. E. B. DuBois dies in Accra, Ghana.

August 28

1818

Jean Baptiste Pointe du Sable—"the father of Chicago"—dies in St. Charles, Missouri. Born sometime in 1745 in St. Marc, Saint-Domingue—in what is today Haiti, du Sable was the first person of African descent and the first nonindigenous person, to settle in the area of what is now Chicago, Illinois. Du Sable is recorded as founding Chicago on March 13, 1773. In 1961, the DuSable Museum of African American History was founded in Du Sable's honor, and on October 26, 1968, Du Sable was declared the Founder of Chicago by the State of Illinois and the City of Chicago. The Du Sable homesite was declared a National Historic Landmark on May 11, 1976.

Pointe de Sable married a Pottawatomie woman named Catherine and had two children; they lived on the north bank of the Chicago River, near what would later be Michigan Avenue and Pioneer Court. The family had considerable material possessions: several buildings, including a milk house, a chicken house, and a barn that housed thirty head of livestock. Most importantly, de Sable maintained a gathering place for Indian and fur trader alike. He kept up good relations with the Pottawatomie and provided supplies to anyone who could pay on the frontier.

Source: From Dominic A. Pacyga. Chicago: A Biography. Boston, MA: University of Chicago Press, 2009, p. 12.

Books

Owens, L. L. *The Great Chicago Fire.* Edina, MN: ABDO, 2007. Contains a section on Du Sable's founding of Chicago and his role as the city's first true settler.

Marsh, Carole. *Jean Baptiste Pointe Du Sable: Father of Chicago.* Peachtree City, GA: Gallopade International, 1998. Examines the life and adventures of DuSable.

Websites

DuSable Heritage Association provides a short biography of DuSable. http://www.dusable heritage.com/history.htm.

Chicago Tribute Markers of Distinction notes a marker for Jean Baptiste Pointe Du Sable in the city of Chicago. http://www.chicago tribute.org/Markers/Sable.htm.

Also Noteworthy

1895

The Frederick Douglass Memorial Hospital and Training School is founded in Philadelphia, Pennsylvania, by Dr. Nathan F. Mossell.

1888

Granville T. Woods receives U.S. Patent No. 88,803 for his railway telegraphy invention.

1900

Granville T. Woods receives U.S. Patent No. 656,760 for his incubator.

1955

The 14-year-old Emmett Till is lynched in Money, Mississippi.

1963

The March on Washington was the largest civil rights demonstration ever. Over 250,000 people gathered in the nation's capital. Dr. Martin Luther King, Jr., would deliver his famous "I Have a Dream" speech at the event on the steps of the Lincoln memorial, a historical milestone in the constant struggle for equality.

August 29

1958

Michael Joseph Jackson is born in Gary, Indiana. As a recording artist and entertainer, Michael came to be known as the "king of op" and garnered multiple Guinness World Records—including one for "Most Successful Entertainer of All Time." He won 13 Grammy Awards, had 13 number one singles in his solo career—more than any other male artist in the Hot 100 era—and had sales of over 750 million albums worldwide. In his earlier career he was the youngest of the Jackson 5 and the seventh child of nine siblings. A renowned singer, songwriter, and producer, Jackson's 1982 album, *Thriller,* is currently the best-selling album in history, with 60 million copies sold worldwide. His number one hits included "Remember the Time," "Don't Stop Til' You Get Enough," and "Black and White."

The success of Thriller really hit me in 1984, when the album received a gratifying number of nominations for the American Music Awards and the Grammy Awards. I remember feeling an overwhelming rush of jubilation. I was whooping with joy and dancing around the house, screaming. When the album was certified as the best-selling album of all time, I couldn't believe it. Quincy Jones was yelling, "Bust open the champagne!"

We were all in a state. Man! What a feeling! To work so hard on something, to give so much and to succeed! Everyone involved with Thriller *was floating on air. It was wonderful.*

Source: From Michael Jackson. *Moonwalk*. New York, NY: Random House, Inc., 2009, p. 230.

Books

Campbell, Lisa D. *Michael Jackson: The King of Pop*. Wellesley, MA: Branden Books, 1993. Author looks at the Jackson family structure and how it influenced the trajectory and longevity of Michael Jackson's career.

Jackson, Michael. *My World: The Official Photobook, Volume 1*. New York, NY: MJ Licensing LLC, 2006. Traces the career of Michael Jackson in an authorized photobook.

Websites

The Official Michael Jackson Website features his music, news, and videos. www.michael jackson.com/

YouTube has an official channel for Jackson's music videos, www.youtube.com/user/michaeljackson.

1963

On August 29, 1963, Freedom Now Party activists and journalist James Worthy meet with Federal Bureau of Investigations director J. Edgar Hoover one day after the famed March on Washington to promote the enforcement of basic civil rights for people of African descent.

The day after the march, Worthy and seven Freedom Now Party representatives held an unscheduled meeting with J. Edgar Hoover. The impromptu summit took place following an early-morning news conference in which the FNP attorney Conrad Lynn announced plans for a "symbolic sit-in" at the FBI director's office to protest waves of antiblack violence in the South. In response, the FBI suggested a meeting to defuse what bureau files described as a "sudden and fast-developing" situation.

Source: From Peniel E. Joseph. *Waiting 'Til the Midnight Hour: A Narrative History of Black Power in America*. New York, NY: Macmillan, 2007, p. 85.

Books

Joseph, Peniel E. *Waiting 'Til the Midnight Hour: A Narrative History of Black Power in America*. New York, NY: Macmillan, 2007. Traces the rise, fall, and legacy of the Black Power movement.

Lynn, Conrad J. *There Is a Fountain: The Autobiography of a Civil Rights Lawyer*. Westport, CT: L. Hill, 1979. Lynn writes about his work as a civil rights attorney and political activist with organizations like the Freedom Now Party.

Websites

The virtual library on African-American involvement in the Vietnam War shows how the Freedom Now Party was classified upon its formation by the House Un-American Activities Committee, as "[f]ormed by former Communist Party member Conrad Lynn and Red China travel-ban violator William Worthy for the purpose of running an all-Negro slate of electors in the 1964 elections." http://www.aavw.org/protest/subversive_huac_abstract03_excerpt.html

The Institute for Democratic Renewal/Project Change features a speech delivered by Grace Lee Boggs, the coordinator of the Michigan all-black Freedom Now Party. http://www.race-democracy.org/CATCH_MARTIN.htm

1979

The Sheridan Broadcasting Corp purchases Mutual Black Network, making it the first completely Black-owned radio network in the world.

Founded at Pittsburgh in 1972, the Sheridan Broadcasting Corporation, parent of the Sheridan Broadcasting Network (SBN), grew out of four radio stations owned by businessman-attorney-academician Ronald R. Davenport, Sr., and his

wife, Judith. Programming and advertising was specifically designed to appeal to African American listeners. By 1976, the firm owned half the Mutual Black Network, buying the remainder in 1979. On March 1, 1992, a business journal announced the merger of dual black-oriented radio webs, NBN Broadcasting, Inc., and SBN, to form American Urban Radio Networks. Davenport was named co-chairman in a venture that included a trio of added chains (STRZ Entertainment Network, SBN Sports Network, SPM Radio Network). Black Enterprise reported that "the new company could be the nation's largest media vehicle targeted to black consumers." Davenport stated that the joint venture "could reach approximately 90% of all African-Americans . . . Clearly, we are stronger together than we are separately." The joint venture continued to prosper in the modern age, boasting several hundred affiliated stations with a diversity of formats.

Source: From Jim Cox. American Radio Networks: A History. New York, NY: McFarland, 2009, p. 200.

Books

Barlow, William. *Voice over: The Making of Black Radio*. Philadelphia, PA: Temple University Press, 1999. This history of Black radio includes a profile of the founding and importance of SBN.

Sterling, C. *Encyclopedia of Radio*. New York: Taylor & Francis, 2003. Book includes a look at the formation of the SBN network.

Websites

"Ron Davenport Jr. and Susan Austin: At Sheridan Broadcasting, It's a Family Affair." http://www.radioink.com/listingsEntry.asp?ID=311216&PT=industryqa.

Also Noteworthy

1920

Be-bop saxophonist Charlie "Yardbird" or "Bird" Parker, Jr., is born to Charles and Addie Parker on August 29, 1920, in Kansas City, Kansas.

1957

U.S. Congress passes the Civil Rights Act, the first federal civil rights legislation since 1875.

August 30

1800

Gabriel Prosser initiates his planned revolt against slavery in Richmond, Virginia. Prosser was a literate but enslaved blacksmith who was deeply religious. By meditating on his Bible, he envisioned a day when Virginia would be ruled by what were then enslaved Blacks. During the spring and summer of 1800 he worked with Jack Bowler to put plans for an uprising into place. The two were ready to assemble more than 1,000 enslaved Blacks and have them march with clubs and swords in hand on Richmond, Virginia—it was to be one of the largest rebellions up to that time. Two slaves betrayed the conspiracy and Prosser's rebellion was suppressed. As the marchers gathered six miles outside of Richmond several were arrested, 35 were executed, and 1 committed suicide. Prosser and 15 of his followers were hanged on October 7, but the episode scared local authorities so much that they passed new laws to ban the education of people of African descent. In the twenty-first century, Virginian authorities officially recognized and honored Prosser's efforts.

Probably the most fateful year in the history of American Negro slave revolts is that of 1800, for it was then that Nat Turner and John Brown were born, that Denmark Vesey bought his freedom, and it was then that the great conspiracy named after Gabriel, slave of Thomas H. Prosser of Henrico County, Virginia, occurred.

This Gabriel, the chosen leader of the rebellious slaves, was a twenty-four year old giant of six feet two inches, "a fellow of courage and intellect above his rank in life," who had intended "to purchase a piece of silk for a flag, on which they would have written 'death or liberty'." Another leader was Jack Bowler, four years older and three inches taller than Gabriel, who felt that "we had as much right to fight for our liberty as any men." Gabriel's wife, Nanny, was active, too, as were his brothers, Solomon and Martin. The former conducted the sword making, and the latter bitterly opposed all suggestion of delaying the outbreak, declaring, "Before he would any longer bear what he had borne, he would turn out and fight with his stick."

Source: From Herbert Aptheker. American Negro Slave Revolts. New York, NY: International Publishers Co, 1993, pp. 219–220.

Books

Egerton, Douglas R. *Gabriel's Rebellion: The Virginia Slave Conspiracies of 1800 and 1802.* Chapel Hill, NC: University of North Carolina Press, 1993. Author shows Gabriel Prosser to have been a literate blacksmith who was determined to end the oppression of slavery.

Miller, Frederic P., Agnes F. Vandome, and John McBrewster. *Gabriel Prosser.* Mauritius: VDM Publishing House Ltd., 2010. Book looks at the Prosser-led planned revolt and the effect that even it's planning had on Virginia.

Websites

Gabriel's Conspiracy, 1799–1800. http://shs.westport.k12.ct.us/jwb/HonorsUS/Slavery/Prosser.htm.

The Library of Virginia has the online article Gabriel's Conspiracy "Death or Liberty." http://www.lva.virginia.gov/exhibits/DeathLiberty/gabriel/.

Also Noteworthy

1901

Roy Wilkins is born in St. Louis, Missouri. Wilkins was the second executive director of the National Association for the Advancement of Colored People (NAACP) and was a major civil rights leader during the middle of the twentieth century.

1967

Thurgood Marshall is confirmed by the U.S. Senate to serve as an associate justice of the U.S. Supreme Court.

1983

Guion Stewart Bluford, Jr., becomes the first African American in space. His first mission was aboard the STS-8 Challenger, the first mission to be launched and land at night. Bluford served as mission specialist aboard two other flights during his career.

August 31

1935

Leroy Eldridge Cleaver is born to Leroy and Thelma Hattie Robinson Cleaver in Wabbaseka, Arkansas, and later raised in California. As Eldridge Cleaver, he became famous for his book of prison essays, *Soul on Ice*, and for having served as the Minister of Information for the Oakland-based Black Panther Party. Cleaver called for Black liberation via a militant revolution, and at one point, after being reportedly in a shootout with the Oakland police in 1969, he fled the United States and was given political exile for six years in Algiers.

Cleaver made it clear that black America owns or controls very little of anything of importance to the nation at large. Black America is still the stepchild that has to stand aside and watch media tycoons from foreign lands, British industrialists, and bankers from every corner of the world in every ethnic variety come to this land of opportunity and prosper, with nothing to hinder them save chance and their own failings. In all seasons, there are still two Americas, one black and one everything else. That was Cleaver's point, and it is his legacy. He didn't tell us anything we don't know. He just said it so well that whenever we read his words, we know that when we stop saying it, we're become the lap dog.

Source: From Clifford Mason. *The African-American Bookshelf: 50 Must-Reads from Before the Civil War Through Today*. New York, NY: Citadel Press, 2004, p. 249.

Books

Cleaver, Eldridge. *Soul on Ice*. Miami, FL: San Val, Incorporated, 2003. Cleaver's classic autobiographical look at life for African Americans in the United States.

Cleaver, Eldridge, Kathleen Cleaver, and Cecil Brown. *Target Zero: A Life in Writing*. New York, NY: Macmillan, 2007. Book looks at Cleaver's life as both a writer and a politically active citizen.

Websites

Leroy Eldridge Cleaver (1935–1998). http://encyclopediaofarkansas.net/encyclopedia/entry-detail.aspx?entryID=2743.

Eldridge Cleaver—YouTube. www.youtube.com/watch?v=XnCaO2ErCFQ.

Also Noteworthy

1836

Henry Blair of Glen Ross, Maryland, receives U.S. Patent No. 15 for his "new and useful Machine, called the 'Cotton-Planter'."

September

September 1

1977

Ethel Waters dies in Chatsworth, California. Waters was a celebrated singer and dancer who was born October 31, 1896, in Chester, Pennsylvania. Waters's mother was mere 13 years old when she was raped and became pregnant, giving birth to Ethel. Waters became famous for her blues and jazz singing, and her work as an actress led to her becoming the second African American nominated for an Academy Award when she was recognized for her role in the 1949 film *Pinky*.

> ... [H]er strongly Anglicized enunciation enabled Waters to break racial barriers as a pop singer. She was the first black singer to perform on major radio programs in the South, and she was the first black singer to receive top billing at a "white" theater. In the process, and despite her critics' claims of musical Uncle Tomism, Waters cracked open the door for future black performers such as Louis Armstrong and Billie Holiday, who would begin to stretch white listeners' ears with music in the African-American tradition. In a sense, then, Ethel Waters is contrapuntal to Bing Crosby in the evolution of classic-pop singing. While Crosby drew upon African-American musical techniques as a white artist, Waters adopted white musical techniques to help advance African-American artists.
>
> Source: From Roy Hemming and David Hajdu. *Discovering Great Singers of Classic Pop: A New Listener's Guide to the Sounds and Lives of the Top Performers and Their Recordings, Movies, and Video*. New York, NY: Newmarket Press, 1999, p. 19.

Books

Bourne, Stephen. *Ethel Waters: Stormy Weather.* Lanham, MD: Scarecrow Press, 2007. Biography of Waters looks at her blues and jazz career and her talent as an actress.

Waters, Ethel with Charles Samuels. *His Eye Is on the Sparrow: An Autobiography.* Cambridge, MA: Da Capo Press, 1989. Waters writes about her life, from bad times to good.

Websites

Ethel Waters singing "Am I Blue" in the 1929 motion picture *On with the Show.* http://www.youtube.com/watch?v=FN8-Yy8Rl3s.
Ethel Waters. http://www.jazzateria.com/roots/ewaters.html.

Also Noteworthy

1867

Robert T. Freeman becomes the first person of African descent to graduate from Harvard Dental School.

1891

Halle T. D. Johnson becomes the first woman of any race to practice medicine in Alabama.

1904

George Coleman Poage wins bronze medals in the 200-meter and 400-meter hurdles at the Olympic Games in St. Louis, Missouri. Poage was the first African American athlete to ever win an Olympic medal.

September 2

1911

Romare Bearden is born in Charlotte, North Carolina, but raised in Harlem, New York. His father worked for the City of New York and his mother, Bessye Bearden, was the New York City correspondent for the *Chicago Defender*. After attending classes at the Art Students League and initially attempting to make political cartoons, Bearden began producing paintings that dealt with African American roots in the southern United States.

> At the time of his passing, Romare Howard Bearden was described by the New York Times as one of America's preeminent artists and the nation's foremost collagist. Bearden had, as Lowery Sims of New York's Metropolitan Musuem put it, "raised the medium of collage to a mode of expression so intensely personal that it is difficult to think of another artist so closely associated with it." Bearden was awarded the National Medal of Arts in 1987. Today, his works remain on display at every major New York art museum and over a dozen more across the United States.
>
> Source: From Dick Russell and Alvin F. Poussaint. Black Genius: Inspirational Portraits of America's Black Leaders. New York, NY: Skyhorse Publishing Inc., 2009, p. 75.

Books

Bearden, Romare and Harry Brinton Henderson. *A History of African-American Artists: From 1792 to the Present.* New York, NY: Pantheon Books, 1993. Bearden's look at the history of African American art in the United States.

Bearden, Romare, Ruth Fine, Mary Lee Corlett, and National Gallery of Art (U.S.). *The Art of Romare Bearden.* Washington, DC: National Gallery of Art in association with Harry H. Abrams, New York, 2003. Book looks at the life and times of Romare Bearden.

Stewart, Frank. *Romare Bearden.* Wilmington, NC: Pomegranate, 2004. Visual biography of Bearden shows him creating work and relaxing with family and friends.

Websites

The Romare Bearden Foundation. http://www.beardenfoundation.org/index2.shtml.

National Gallery of Art—The Art of Romare Bearden. http://www.nga.gov/exhibitions/beardeninfo.htm.

Smithsonian Institution Archives of American Art contains the Romaire Bearden papers. http://www.aaa.si.edu/collections/romare-bearden-papers-5881/more.

Also Noteworthy

1958

Frederick McKinley Jones receives U.S. Patent No. 2,850,001 for his "Control Device for Internal Combustion Engine."

1975

Amadou Bailo Diallo is born in Guinea. Though unarmed at the time, the 23-year-old immigrant to the United States was shot to death in the Soundview section of the Bronx by four New York City plain-clothed police on February 4, 1999. Diallo's murder leads to marches, protests, and cries of outrage about police brutality and racial profiling in New York City. Even though Diallo was unarmed at the time of his killing, the officers—who fired a total of 41 shots at Diallo—were exonerated by jury trial and did not serve one day in jail for his murder.

1975

Joseph W. Hatchett becomes the first African American Supreme Court Justice in the South since Reconstruction. He serves in Florida.

September 3

1846

The American Missionary Association is founded in Albany, New York. After working towards the abolition of slavery, the group founded the Freedmen's Aid Society to promote education among formerly enslaved Blacks and their children.

> The honor of founding the first school for the Freedmen belongs to the American Missionary Association. That school was opened at Hampton, VA. . . . That spot on the Hampton Roads, where that school was located, had witnessed

(two hundred and forty-one years before) the entrance of the first slave-ship into the line of the American continent. That ship brought to our land slavery and all its woes—the curse that cast its baleful blight over the South, that stirred up enmity between the two sections of the country, which it aggravated into direful civil war. . . . That school on the Hampton Roads, the harbinger of all the freedmen's schools that followed, was the morning-star that heralded the dawn of knowledge and of a pure Gospel for the colored race in America, and that is destined to shed its effulgence over benighted Africa.

Source: From Rev. M. E. Strieby. "History of the Educational Work of the American Missionary Association," in Joseph Crane Hartzell, ed. *Christian Educators in Council: Sixty Addresses by American Educators.* Cambridge, MA: Harvard University, 2007, pp. 174–175.

Books

Gause Boone, Richard. *Education in the United States: Its History from the Earliest Settlements.* Manchester, NH: Ayer Publishing, 1971. This look at the education movement shows the importance of the Freedmen's Aid Society.

Stowell, Jay S. *Methodist Adventures in Negro Education.* Ann Arbor, MI: The Methodist book concern/University of Michigan, 2007. Shows how the Methodist Episcopal Church. played a strong role in setting up the second largest Freedmen's Aid Society.

Websites

The Internet Archive Website has a copy of the "Eighth annual report of the Freedmen's Aid Society of the Methodist Episcopal Church." http://www.archive.org/details/eighthannualrepo00meth.

A digitized version of The Freedmen's Record, April, 1865, 49–56 and 61–65. http://mac110.assumption.edu/aas/reports/fr4-65.html.

Also Noteworthy

1979

Robert Maynard becomes the editor-publisher of the *Oakland Tribune* (in California), becoming the first African American to head a daily newspaper.

September 4

1848

Lewis Howard Latimer is born in Chelsea, Massachusetts, to Rebecca and George Latimer. Lewis's parents had escaped from slavery by fleeing from Virginia in 1842, and they migrated to Massachusetts. In 1873, he invented the Water Closet for Railroad Cars, a toilet system to be used on trains. In 1876, Latimer drafted the designs for Alexander Graham Bell to receive a patent for the telephone. In January 1882 he patented the "Process of Manufacturing Carbons," which improved the carbon filaments used in light bulbs, and on January 12, 1886, Howard Latimer received U.S. Patent No. 334,078 for an "Apparatus for cooling and disinfecting."

Lewis Howard Latimer was one of the great pioneers in the development of electricity. To him goes the honor of having solved the problem of transforming the electric current into light through the invention of the incandescent light. Latimer became an associate of the pioneer inventor Thomas A. Edison in 1878. He invented a carbon filament for the Maxim electric bulb and was assigned to supervise the installation of electric lighting of streets for New York, Philadelphia, London, England, and several other cities in the eighteen eighties.

Source: From Ivan Van Sertima. *Blacks in Science: Ancient and Modern.* Piscataway, NJ: Transaction Publishers, 1983, p. 230.

Books

Deitch, JoAnne Weisman. *A Nation of Inventors.* Carlisle, MA: Applewood Books, 2001. Contains a profile of Latimer and his work as a member of the Edison Pioneers.

Haber, Louis. *Black Pioneers of Science and Invention.* New York, NY: Houghton Mifflin

Harcourt, 1992. Contains a look at Lewis
Latimer, including the lives of his parents.

Websites

Super Scientists—Lewis Howard Latimer. http://
www.energyquest.ca.gov/scientists/latimer
.html.

Lemelson Center Invention features Lewis
Latimer. www.invention.smithsonian.org/
centerpieces/ilives/latimer/latimer.html.

Also Noteworthy

1905

African American jazz pianist Meade Lux
Lewis is born in Chicago, Illinois.

1908

Richard Nathaniel Wright is born to
Nathaniel Wright and Ella Wilson on the
Rucker's Plantation, near Natchez, Missis-
sippi. Wright authored the famed African
American novels *Native Son* and *Black Boy*.

1962

New Orleans Catholic schools are integrated.

September 5

1917

On September 5 and September 19 the
radical Nevis-born immigrant Cyril Valentine
Briggs—who would later found the African
Blood Brotherhood for African Liberation
and Redemption (ABB)—publishes a two-
part editorial in the *New York Amsterdam News*
calling for the creation of a Black nation
within the United States.

*Born in St. Kitts, West Indies, in 1887, Briggs,
migrated to New York City. In 1919, he founded
the African Blood Brotherhood, a paramilitary,
revolutionary nationalist fraternity. Through his*

*involvement with the ABB, Briggs asserted a range
of strategies for Black empowerment, including
cooperative economics, trade unionism, armed
self-defense and the creation of a sovereign Black
state within the boundaries of the United States.
When the ABB dissolved in approximately 1924–
25, Briggs assumed the post of national secretary
for the National Negro Labor Congress.*

Source: From Ronald W. Walters and Cedric
Johnson. *Bibliography of African American Lead-
ership: An Annotated Guide.* Santa Barbara, CA:
Greenwood Publishing Group, 2000, p. 113.

Books

Gottesman, Isaac Herschel. *Cyril V. Briggs and the
American Left: 1917–1925.* Madison, WI:
University of Wisconsin–Madison, 2000.
Looks at Briggs's role as a radical race activist
willing to work with communists, socialists,
and anyone else to further the progress of people of African descent.

Soloon, Mark I. *The Cry Was Unity: Communists
and African Americans, 1917–36.* Jackson, MS:
University Press of Mississippi, 1998. Book
looks at Cyril Briggs's role working with the
Communist Party to liberate people of African descent.

Websites

"Black and Red—A Journey Through
Communism in the Black Community" contains a profile of Cyril Briggs. http://www
.tcnj.edu/~fisherc/black_and_red.html.

Programme of the African Blood Brotherhood.
http://www.marxists.org/history/international/
comintern/sections/britain/periodicals/commun
ist_review/1922/06/african.htm.

Also Noteworthy

1846

John Wesley Cromwell is born to Willis
Hodges Cromwell and Elizabeth Carney
Cromwell in Portsmouth, Virginia. Cromwell was born enslaved, but his father was
able to get the entire family out of slavery.

Cromwell went on to attend Howard University Law School and helped create the Virginia Educational and Historical Association, the National Colored Press Association, and the American Negro Academy. Cromwell's 1914 book, *The Negro in American History: Men and Women Eminent in the Evolution of the American of African Descent*, influenced Carter G. Woodson to create the Association for the Study of Negro Life and History in 1915.

1962

The former home of abolitionist leader and African American civil rights advocate Frederick Douglass is added to the U.S. National Park Service system. The property, which is located at 1411 W Street, SE 14th in Washington, D.C.'s Anacostia Historic District, was designated as the Frederick Douglass National Historic Site on February 12, 1988. In 1900, Douglass's last wife, Helen Pitts, had petitioned the U.S. Congress to charter the Frederick Douglass Memorial and Historical Association, and Pitts gave the house to the association.

September 6

1880

The Jamaican American author, journalist, and historian Joel Augustus Rogers is born in Negril, Jamaica. Rogers had no formal higher education but became a self-taught scholar. Rogers's books—including *From "Superman" to Man, 100 Amazing facts about the Negro with Complete Proof. A Short Cut to the World History of the Negro*, and *World's Greatest Men and Women of African Descent*—challenged prevailing ideas about people of African descent and focused on their many achievements.

The spirit of a blossoming racial consciousness could also be seen in scholarly writings of the period. Despite (perhaps even because of) the Eurocentric education forced on Caribbean children, there was a long tradition of Afrocentric journalism and scholarly writing. In the inter-war years J.A. Rogers of Jamaica and the United States traveled the world in search of obscure information on African history. . . . Roger's books, beginning with From "Superman" to Man *in 1917, are still immensely popular.*

Source: From Bridget Brereton. *General History of the Caribbean: The Caribbean in the Twentieth Century*. Paris, France: UNESCO, 2004, p. 248.

Books

Rogers, Joel Augustus. *From "Superman" to Man*. Ann Arbor, MI: AbeBooks/Helga M. Rogers, 1957. Rogers's famous book debunking myths about Black inferiority.

Rogers, Joel Augustus. *World's Great Men of Color, Volume 2*. New York, NY: Simon & Schuster, 1996. Looks at people of African descent who are historical figures and have changed world history.

Websites

Joel Augustus Rogers, 1883 to 1966. http://aalbc.com/authors/jarogers.htm.

Joel Augustus Rogers, Renaissance Man. http://www.aaregistry.org/historic_events/view/joel-augustus-rogers-renaissance-man.

September 7

1919

Jacob Lawrence is born in Atlantic City, New Jersey. As a painter and educator, Lawrence used his art to depict the history and struggles of people of African descent. He created paintings in series that would celebrate the lives of heroes like Harriet Tubman, Haitian general Toussaint L'Ouverture, Frederick Douglass, and John Brown or look at events like the migration of African Americans from the south to the North, such as in "The Migration of the Negro" series.

When he was only twenty-three years old Jacob Lawrence completed the best-known work of his life—*The Migration of the Negro*. *Consisting of 60 individual panels this series told "... the story of an exodus of African-Americans who left their homes and farms in the South around the time of World War I and traveled to northern industrial cities in search of better lives." Today, the series is divided between two different museums. All of the even-numbered paintings can be found in The Museum of Modern Art in New York City while the odd-numbered paintings can be seen at The Phillips Collection in Washington, D.C. In 1993, a special tour to several U.S. cities reunited all 50 pieces of the Migration series.*

Jacob's own life is reflective of the series' title. His parents met while they were on their separate ways north from Virginia and South Carolina. Lawrence was born in Atlantic City, New Jersey, on September 17, 1917. When he was two years old the family moved to Easton, Pennsylvania, where his father abandoned them. Later, his mother moved them to Philadelphia; they came to New York City when Jacob was 13. There, he attended an after-school arts and crafts program at the Utopia Children's House—Jacob's mother wanted him to keep busy while she was at work. Later, a full scholarship enabled him to attend the American Artists School in New York. Most of his spare time was spent in the Schomburg Collection at the New York Public Library on 135th Street where he gathered information and material to produce material for a pictorial biography of Frederick Douglass. With his subsequent Rosenwald Fellowship, Jacob was able to research southern migrants in the North after World War I. In just one year he finished his now-famous Migration series which is based on this research.

Source: From Mary Ellen Sterling and Karen Goldfluss. Focus on Artists. Westminster, CA: Teacher Created Resources, 1994, p. 75.

Books

Lawrence, Jacob. *The Great Migration: An American Story*. New York, NY: HarperCollins, 1995. Lawrence's *Migration* series in a pictorial book.

Nesbett, Peter T., Michelle DuBois, and Patricia Hills. *Over the Line: The Art and Life of Jacob Lawrence*. Seattle, WA: University of Washington Press in association with Jacob Lawrence Catalogue Raisonné Project, 2000. Contains essays by art historians who examine Lawrence's life and art work.

Websites

Whitney Museum of American Art: Jacob Lawrence. http://www.whitney.org/jacob lawrence/.

The Jacob Lawrence Virtual Archive & Education Center. http://www.jacoblawrence.org.

Jacob Lawrence Migration Series. http://www .phillipscollection.org/migration_series/.

Also Noteworthy

1930

The jazz tenor saxophonist and composer, Theodore Walter "Sonny" Rollins, is born in New York City. Rollins would become a seminal jazz master who composed songs like "Oleo" and "Airegin," which are jazz standards today.

1944

Street basketball legend Earl "The Goat" Manigault is born in Charleston, South Carolina, and later raised in Harlem, New York. Manigault played basketball for Benjamin Franklin High School, which was in the Public School Athletic League; Manigault averaged 24 points and 11 rebounds per game. As a player on New York City's basketball playgrounds, Manigault was credited with making ferocious two-handed dunks on his opponents. Although he played with some of the National Basketball Association's most famous members, Earl "The Goat" never played professionally, but he is remembered as one of the best players ever.

1954

Integration of public schools begins in Washington, DC, and Baltimore, Maryland.

September 8

1925

Thirty-year old dentist Dr. Ossian Sweet, with his wife, Gladys, and infant daughter, Ivy, take possession of their new home at 2905 Garland, Detroit, Michigan's East Side. Sweet had purchased the brick house for $18,500—it was in a predominately white, working-class neighborhood. On the very first night they moved in, neighborhood whites tried to drive the family out of the neighborhood by forming crowds who yelled and threw rocks. On their second night in the house, as the mob began to attack the building, Dr. Sweet shot his gun into the crowd, killing a white man. Sweet was tried by the state of Michigan, but his acquittal proved that—even for African Americans—there was a right to protect one's self and property.

> Gladys Sweet was tougher than Ossian and the other men, a lot tougher. She wasn't intimidated the way Kennedy must have expected her to be, the way her husband had been. She didn't have excuses to offer or an unlikely story to tell. On the contrary, she seemed proud of what she and her husband had done, that they'd taken a stand. And she resented being questioned, as if there were no reason to investigate the night's events, as if it were painfully obvious what had occurred, as if the Negroes had a right to shoot into a crowd of white people.
>
> Source: From Kevin Boyle. *Arc of Justice: A Saga of Race, Civil Rights, and Murder in the Jazz Age.* New York, NY: Macmillan, 2005, p. 176.

Books

Detroit, Michigan Recorder's Court. *Ossian Sweet Collection.* Victoria, BC: AbeBooks, 1925. Proceedings of the *People v. Ossian Sweet, et al.* in the Recorder's Court of Detroit, Michigan.

Vine, Phyllis. *One Man's Castle: Clarence Darrow in Defense of the American Dream.* New York, NY: HarperCollins, 2005. Looks at how the attorney Clarence Darrow defended Ossian Sweet, who protected his family and home from racist mob violence.

Websites

"I have to die a man or live a coward"—the saga of Dr. Ossian Sweet. http://apps.detnews.com/apps/history/index.php?id=201.

The Sweet trials of 1925 and 1926. http://law2.umkc.edu/faculty/projects/ftrials/sweet/sweet.html.

Also Noteworthy

1907

Negro Leagues baseball star Walter Fenner "Buck" is born in Rocky Mount, North Carolina Leonard played with the Brooklyn Elite Giants in 1933 and with the Homestead Grays from 1934 through 1950.

1954

Ruby Nell Bridges is born in Tylertown, Mississippi. She played an important part in the Civil Rights Movement. When she was four years old, she and her parent moved to New Orleans, Louisiana. When she was six, in 1960, her parents allowed her to participate in an NAACP call for volunteers to integrate the New Orleans School system. Ruby Bridges—who, as an adult, married and became Ruby Bridges Hall—was the first African American child to attend New Orleans' William Frantz Elementary School and the first African American child to attend an all-white school in the South.

September 9

1739

Some 20 enslaved Africans gather near the Stono River in St. Paul's Parish, less than 20 miles from Charlestown, South Carolina. They marched down the road in Stono, South Carolina, carrying banners that read

"Liberty!" Led by an enslaved Angolan named Jemmy, the men and women continued marching south, recruiting more enslaved Blacks along the way. Fed up with their enslavement, Stono's Blacks went to a shop that sold firearms and ammunition, armed themselves, and then killed the two men working in the shop. After one slave told the ruling whites about the rebelllion, some 100 whites gathered to come after the Stono rebels. They caught up with some and killed 30. Other Stono rebels were captured over the next six months and executed; one rebel was able to remain in hiding for almost three years. Following the Stono Rebellion, whites in the area passed a Negro Act that limited the liberties granted to enslaved Africans: they could no longer grow their own food, assemble in groups, earn their own money, or learn to read.

> Early on the morning of September 9, a column of armed men marched west along Pon Pon Road. In the troop, slaves from Ann Drayton's William Gattell's and John William's plantations bordering the Horse Savannah walked alongside those from the plantations of Henry Williamson, Frederick Grimke, John Smith, Thomas Sacheverrall, and Benjamin Wilkinson along the Stono. They were less than a disciplined troop and more than a ragged band of enslaved men, some exhausted but exhilarated from their night's labors, two drummers announcing their progression and a flag bearer at their head. They called out to to others like them to join their enterprise, and some—but not many—had come. Surely by now, if not before, the band had a leader, or more likely, a group of leaders. Jemmy, or Cato, later accounts recalled, were the boldest and the most well spoken of the rebels.
>
> Source: From Peter Charles Hoffer. *Cry Liberty: The Great Stono River Slave Rebellion of 1739 (New Narratives in American History)*. New York, NY: Oxford University Press, USA, 2010, pp. 103–104.

Books

Smith, Mark Michael. *Stono: Documenting and Interpreting a Southern Slave Revolt*. Columbia, SC: University of South Carolina Press, 2005. Book includes documentation from the period that looks into the causes and results of the Stono Rebellion.

Thornton, John K. "African Dimensions of the Stono Rebellion." In *A Question of Manhood: A Reader in U.S. Black Men's History and Masculinity, Volume 1*. edited by Darlene Clark Hine and Earnestine Jenkins. Bloomington, IN: Indiana University Press, 1999. Looks at the African dimensions of the Stono Rebellion of 1739.

Websites

Stono Rebellion—Teaching American History in South Carolina http://www.teachingus history.org/lessons/documents/StonoRebellion .html.

Library of Congress review of the Stono Rebellion http://memory.loc.gov/ammem/today/ sep09.html.

Also Noteworthy

1915

Carter G. Woodson founded the Association for the Study of Negro Life and History in Chicago.

1926

Radical Hubert Harrison delivers his last lecture on "World Problems of Race" for the Institute for Social Studies (ISS). The St. Croix, Virgin Islands-born Harrison was famed as the founder of the International Colored Unity League, an organization that urged a celebration of people of African descent as a way to combat racism.

1971

Thirty-two inmates and 11 prison employees are killed during riots at Attica prison from September 9 through 10. The four-day riot was put to a violent end when law enforcement officials stormed the prison.

September 10

2010

Ronald G. Walters dies of lung cancer. As a scholar, author, and political consultant, Walters was known as a frequent commentator on political and economic issues that affected African Americans. Walters was born July 20, 1938, in Wichita, Kansas. After receiving a PhD in international studies at American University, Walters taught at Howard University and Johns Hopkins University. He served as director of the African American Leadership Institute at the University of Maryland and worked as the campaign manager for Jesse Jackson during Jackson's presidential bids of 1984 and 1988.

. . . Some of the main points about post-1830 abolitionism were especially well made by Ronald G. Walters. In keeping with the line of scholarship that began with Barnes, Walters acknowledged the importance of revivalism in the lives of some abolitionists, but he stressed difficulties in defining the connections. To start with, a good many abolitionists came from Quaker, Unitarian, Calvinist, or other non-evangelical backgrounds. Furthermore, most people converted in revivals never became abolitionists, and those who did seldom did so immediately and often agonized over choosing between commitments to revivalism and the cause of the slave. They found themselves in conflict with Finney, who sought to keep abolitionism subsidiary to revivalism, and with other evangelists, who took little interest in social problems. Some moved toward abolitionsims out of disillusionment with the individual self-absorption that revivals fostered. Further disappointment followed the high hopes of the early 1830s that the churches would take a leading role in condemning the immorality of slaveholding (Walters 1976: chap. 3). Before long, some abolitionists were ready to denounce the clergy and the churches, as well as the mainstream benevolent and missionary organizations, as bulwarks of slavery. Despite schisms in the abolitionist movement and in major national denominations, efforts to persuade northern churches to take at least a moderate anti-slavery stance did not cease. Even after southern churches split from their northern counterparts, and even in the midst of the Civil War, few northern denominations could be moved to condemn slavery or endorse emancipation, let along racial equality (McKivigan 1984).

Source: From Karen Halttunen. *A Companion to American Cultural History* by Hoboken, NJ: John Wiley & Sons, 2008, p. 89.

Books

Smith, Mark Michael. *Stono: Documenting and Interpreting a Southern Slave Revolt.* Columbia, SC: University of South Carolina Press, 2005. Book includes documentation from the period that looks into the causes and results of the Stono Rebellion.

Thornton, John K., Darlene Clark Hine and Earnestine Jenkins. "African Dimensions of the Stono Rebellion." In *A Question of Manhood: A Reader in U.S. Black Men's History and Masculinity, Volume 1.* Bloomington, IN: Indiana University Press, 1999. Looks at the African dimensions of the Stono Rebellion of 1739.

Websites

Stono Rebellion—Teaching American History in South Carolina. http://www.teachingushistory.org/lessons/documents/StonoRebellion.html.

Library of Congress review of the Stono Rebellion. http://memory.loc.gov/ammem/today/sep09.html.

Also Noteworthy

1855

John Mercer Langston is elected township clerk of Brownhelm, Ohio, making him the first African American to hold an elective office in the United States.

1884

Congressman John R. Lynch presides over the Republican National Convention.

1945

Marlin Oliver Briscoe is born in Oakland, California. Briscoe became the first quarterback of African descent to start a game for an American Football League team when he played the position as a rookie with the Denver Broncos in 1968.

September 11

1851

The Christiana Resistance occurs. This was the first recorded open resistance to the 1850 Fugitive Slave Law; it was a resistance that many later considered a harbinger of the U.S. Civil War. A group of African Americans fought off a Maryland slaveowner named Edward Gorsuch who had traveled to Christiana, Pennsylvania, alongside U.S. marshals and deputies in an attempt to re-enslave four men he had formerly held in slavery. Gorsuch and his slave-catchers showed up at the house of William Parker, a man who had fled from slavery himself and who was devoted to keeping all the people in his home away from slavery's lash. Gorsuch was killed during the incident, and one other white person was wounded.

> *According to plan, four members of the posse staked out the corners of the house, so that none of the inhabitants could sneak through a back window or door. That left Marshal Kline and Edward Gorsuch to confront the blacks directly, to present the four warrants, explain the law, and take custody of the two fugitives whom they believed to be cowering upstairs. The front door was still open; the stairs were immediately inside. The situation called for some courage, creativity, and good judgment. Gorsuch had the courage. Kline was creative, if nothing else.*
>
> *The marshal called for the owner of the house. The imposing figure of William Parker appeared on the landing: "Who are you?"*
>
> *"I am the United States Marshal," Kline replied.*
>
> *"If you take another step," Parker warned, "I'll break your neck."*

> *Source*: From Thomas P. Slaughter. *Bloody Dawn: The Christiana Riot and Racial Violence in the Antebellum North*. New York, NY: Oxford University Press, USA, 1994, p. 60.

Books

Katz, Jonathan, edited by Darlene Clark Hine and Earnestine Jenkins. *Resistance at Christiana: The Fugitive Slave Rebellion, Christiana, Pennsylvania, September 11, 1851: A Documentary Account*. New York, NY: Crowell, 1974. Looks at the documents related to the Christiana Rebellion.

Rosenburg, John. *William Parker: Rebel Without Rights*. Minneapolis, MN: Millbrook Press, 1996. Detailed look at the Christiana Rebellion from the point of view of William Parker.

Websites

The Lancaster County Historical Society maintains documents and photographs in the Christiana Resistance Collection. http://www.lancasterhistory.org/index.php?option=com_wrapper&view=wrapper&Itemid=208.

Christiana Underground Railroad Center self-guided museum. http://www.padutchcountry.com/members/christiana_underground_railroad_center.asp.

September 12

1913

James Cleveland "Jesse" Owens is born to Henry and Emma Owens in Oakville, Alabama. Owens's family moved to the state of Ohio when he was nine years old. He became a track-and-field athlete at Ohio State University, and with his speed and agility, the 5-foot 10-inch, 165-pound Owens was nicknamed "The Buckeye Bullet." He famously won four Olympic Gold medals in the 100- and 200-meter races, the 4-by-100 meter relay race, and in the long jump at the 1936 Summer Olympic Games in Berlin, Germany.

. . . Suddenly Owens realized that he was in a real race, even as he knew that the top two finishers would advance. Running slightly scared, he somehow reached within himself to find a gear he had never before located. The sight of him running at breakneck speed sucked the air out of the stadium, and as he broke the tape, 4 yards in front of Hänni, yet another roar rose in appreciation. His time was posted a moment later: 10.2 seconds, a new world record.

"No European crowd had ever seen such a combination of blazing speed and effortless smoothness, like something blown in a gale," Grantland Rice wrote. "You could hear the chorus of gasps as he left all rivals far behind."

As the crowd showered Owens with adulation, as he and Snyder embraced, Leni Riefenstahl shook her head in frustration. She wasn't disappointed that Owens had run so brilliantly; she was disappointed that that she had not allotted enough cameras to his quarterfinal and would have to make the race more prominent in her film. "I've got to chuck my manuscript," she said. "I'll need all the 100-meter heats for this cutting. This is totally crazy!" It was becoming apparent to her that any documentary about the games would have to celebrate the remarkable black athletes from the United States. This meant another battle with Goebbels, which she dreaded.

Source: From Jeremy Schaap. *Triumph: The Untold Story of Jesse Owens and Hitler's Olympics.* New York, NY: Houghton Mifflin Harcourt, 2007, p. 177.

Books

Baker, William J. *Jesse Owens: An American Life.* Champaign, IL: University of Illinois Press, 2006. Biography of Jesse Owens looks at how he became an international superstar by exploding Hitler's myth of Aryan supremacy and winning gold medals at the Berlin Olympics of 1936.

Katz, Jonathan. *Jesse Owens: A Biography.* Ed. Darlene Clark Hine and Earnestine Jenkins. Santa Barbara, CA: Greenwood Publishing Group, 2007. Biography of Jesse Owens and how his athletic abilities inspired the world.

Websites

JesseOwens.com. http://www.jesseowens.com/.
Jesse Owens, Berlin 193636 in the 100-meter race. http://www.youtube.com/watch?v=K1 XclGwJY8s&NR=1.

Also Noteworthy

1944

Barrence Eugene Carter is born in Galveston, Texas. As the R&B singer/songwriter Barry White, he won five Grammy Awards and had major hit songs like "Never Gonna Give You Up" (1974) and "You're the First, the Last, My Everything" (1975).

1958

Wilfred Benitez is born in New York, New York. Benitez became a Hall of Fame boxer by winning the WBA Light Welterweight championship at the age of 17 and later winning the WBC Welterweight championship and the WBC Super Welterweight championship. Benitez was the youngest three-time world champion in boxing history.

1992

Dr. Mae C. Jemison becomes the first African American woman to travel in outer space.

September 13

1886

Alain LeRoy Locke is born to Pliny Ishmael Locke and Mary Hawkins Locke in Philadelphia, Pennsylvania. After studying at Harvard University, in 1907 Locke was the first-ever African American to be named a Rhodes scholar. Locke became a literary critic and philosopher and the lead voice of the New Negro Movement and the Harlem Renaissance.

One of the most difficult features of Locke's complex explication of race and culture is his insistence that they were not always identical. "The fallacy of the 'new' as of the 'older' thinking is that there is a type Negro who, either qualitatively or quantitavely, is the type symbol of the entire group. To break arbitrary stereotypes it is necessary perhaps to bring forward counter-stereotypes, but none are adequate substitutes for the whole truth." The counterstereotypes Locke refers to are the simplistic pictures of blacks as emotive and spiritual that are the dominant images of blacks in his The New Negro (1925). Locke was promoting black proletarian folk art at the writing of this article, but not because it represented the "real Negro." What makes a work of art or literature Negro, that is, socially African or Afro-American, are primarily its main theme, idiom, style, and form, which are not biological products, unchanging social phenomena, or the necessary property of a race.

Locke explores how artistic works are characterized as peculiarly Negro African because of their theme, author, or idiom. Negro art, as a social medium for Locke, is continually engaged in a search for what is truly Negro. The search is itself one of the defining characteristics of Afro-centric art.

Source: From Alain LeRoy Locke, edited by Leonard Harris. *The Philosophy of Alain Locke: Harlem Renaissance and Beyond*. Philadelphia, PA: Temple University Press, 1991, p. 207.

Books

Buck, Christopher. *Alain Locke: Faith and Philosophy 1*. Los Angeles, CA: Kalimat Press, 2005. Looks at the interplay of Locke's philosophies and his Bahá'í faith.

Harris, Leonard and Charles Molesworth. *Alain L. Locke: Biography of a Philosopher*. Chicago, IL: University of Chicago Press, 2008. Biography of Alain Locke looks at his influence among Harlem Renaissance figures like Jacob Lawrence, Langston Hughes, Zora Neal Hurston, et al.

Websites

Alain Locke Society. http://www.alainlocke.com/.

Alain Leroy Locke Biobibliography. http://www.howard.edu/library/Assist/Guides/Alain-Locke.htm.

Also Noteworthy

1663

The first serious attempt by enslaved Blacks to liberate themselves in colonial North America takes place in Gloucester County, Virginia. Known as the Servant's Plot, it included enslaved Africans, white indentured servants, and indigenous Virginians.

1881

Lewis Latimer receives U.S. Patent No. 247,097 for an electric lamp with a carbon filament he created along with Joseph V. Nichols.

1926

Andrew Felton Brimmer is born on September 13, 1926. Brimmer became the first Black person to serve as a member of the Board of Governors of the Federal Reserve System.

September 14

1921

Constance Baker Motley is born in New Haven, Connecticut, on September 14, 1921. Constance was the ninth of 12 children; her mother, Rachel Baker, was one of the founders of the New Haven branch of the National Association for the Advancement of Colored People (NAACP). While attending Columbia University law school, Motley began working with the NAACP Legal and Defense Educational Fund, Inc. Motley became an important contact and legal advocate for civil rights activists during the 1960s—one of her most famous clients was Martin Luther King, Jr. In 1964, she was elected to the New York State Senate—making her the first African American woman elected to serve in the senate in the history of New York state. In 1965 she was unanimously voted to serve as Manhattan Borough president by the city council, and on January 25, 1966, she became the first African American appointed to a federal judgeship. In 1993, Motley was inducted into the National Women's Hall of Fame.

> *One of the first cases I worked on at LDF after graduation was a suit against the University of Texas Law School. Our plaintiff, Herman Marion Sweatt, had applied for admission to the law school, and, under the "separate but equal" standard of* Plessy v. Ferguson, *the university hurriedly established a separate law school for blacks—in effect, just for him. Thurgood planned to use expert testimony to demonstrate that this school, in the basement of a building in Austin, was not equal, in any respect, to the long-established, high-quality law school for whites on the University of Texas campus.*
>
> Source: From Constance Baker Motley. *Equal Justice under Law: An Autobiography.* Lanham, MD: Farrar, Straus and Giroux, 1998, p. 61.

Books

Brenner, Marie. *Great Dames: What I Learned from Older Women.* New York, NY: Random House, Inc., 2001. Author includes a biographical interview with Constance Baker Motley.

Salokar, Rebecca Mae and Mary L. Volcansek. *Women in Law: A Bio-Bibliographical Sourcebook.* Santa Barbara, CA: Greenwood Publishing Group, 1996. Book includes a biographical sketch of Motley's life and work.

Websites

Columbia University's "Columbia 250" Website honors Constance Baker Motley as an alumna who helped change the face of law and its effects on the lives of people of African descent. http://www.c250.columbia.edu/ c250_celebrates/remarkable_columbians/ constance_motley.html.

The National Women's History Project notes on its Website Motley's work as a judge and civil rights attorney. http://www.nwhp.org/whm/ motley_bio.php.

1964

President Lyndon B. Johnson presents the activist and labor organizer Asa Philip Randolph with the Presidential Medal of Freedom. A. Philip Randolph was the founder of the Brotherhood of Sleeping Car Porters (BSCP) labor union in 1925. The BSCP organized African American Pullman car porters and became the first Black labor union to sign a collective bargaining agreement with a major U.S. corporation. Randolph's organizing abilities extended to the civil rights arena. He famously threatened a March on Washington in 1941 to protest racial segregation in the U.S. Armed Forces and in businesses who were employed to produce war products for the federal government. President Franklin D. Roosevelt's issuing of Executive Order 8802, the federal government's Fair Employment Act, was the only reason Randolph's march was canceled.

> *In March, 1941, Randolph issued the official call for the march, to take place on July 1:*
>
> *... be not dismayed in these terrible times. You possesss power, great power. Our problem is to hitch it up for action on the broadest, daring and most gigantic scale. In this period of power politics, nothing counts but pressure, more pressure and still more pressure. ... To this end we propose that 10,000 Negroes MARCH ON WASHINGTON FOR JOBS IN NATIONAL DEFENSE AND EQUAL INTEGRATION IN THE FIGHTING FORCES ... Mass power can cause President Roosevelt to issue an Executive Order abolishing discrimination.*
>
> Source: From Jervis Anderson. *A. Philip Randolph: A Biographical Portrait.* Berkeley, CA: University of California Press, 1986, p. 250.

Books

Kersten, Andrew Edmund. *A. Philip Randolph: A Life in the Vanguard*. Lanham, MD: Rowman & Littlefield, 2007. Author includes a biographical interview with Constance Baker Motley.

Pfeffer, Paula F. *A. Philip Randolph, Pioneer of the Civil Rights Movement*. Baton Rouge, LA: Louisiana State University Press, 1996. Book includes a biographical sketch of Motley's life and work.

Websites

The A. Philip Randolph Institute maintains the activist's legacy. http://www.apri.org/ht/d/sp/i/225/pid/225.

The A. Philip Randolph Pullman Porter Museum. http://www.aphiliprandolphmuseum.com.

Also Noteworthy

1940

President Franklin Delano signs the Selective Service Act, which allows African Americans to enter all branches of the U.S. Military Service.

September 15

1963

Four African American schoolgirls are killed in a bombing at the Sixteenth Street Baptist Church in Birmingham, Alabama. The girls—Denise McNair, aged 11, and Addie Mae Collins, Christiana Resistance Carol Robertson, and Cynthia Wesley, who were all aged 14—were preparing to serve as ushers for "Youth Day" at the Sunday morning church services when they lost their lives.

> *The bomb destroyed the stairs leading to a side entrance to the building and collapsed part of the basement wall. It crushed cars on the street nearby. It blew out all but one of the stained-glass windows upstairs. The only remaining window showed Jesus leading little children. His face was blown out.*
>
> . . . .
>
> *People all over Birmingham heard the explosion. Some later said they had thought it had been thunder or noises from a nearby factory. The explosion hurt at least 20 other people. Some were in the church, and others just happened to be walking by at the wrong moment.*
>
> Source: From Lisa Klobuchar. *1963 Birmingham Church Bombing: The Ku Klux Klan's History of Terror*. Mankato, MN: Compass Point Books, 2009, pp. 12–13.

Books

Sikora, Frank. *Until Justice Rolls Down: The Birmingham Church Bombing Case*. Tuscaloosa, AL: University of Alabama Press, 1991. Book examines the Birmingham 16th Street Baptist Churchbombing case.

McKinstry, Carolyn Maull and Denise George. *While the World Watched: A Birmingham Bombing Survivor Comes of Age During the Civil Rights Movement*. Bloomington, IN: Xlibris Corporation, 2010. Remembrances of Carolyn Maull who was 14 years old and in attendance at the 16th Street Baptist church when it was bombed.

Websites

Information about the 16th Street Baptist Church and its bombing in 1963 is available from the National Park Service. http://www.nps.gov/nr/travel/civilrights/al11.htm.

The Birmingham Public Library has documentation regarding the bombing. http://www.bplonline.org/resources/Digital_Project/SixteenthStBaptistBomb.asp.

Also Noteworthy

1830

The first National Negro Convention begins in Philadelphia, Pennsylvania.

1889

Festus Claudius McKay is born to Thomas Francis McKay and Hannah Ann Elizabeth Edwards in Clarendon, Jamaica. As a writer and poet, Claude McKay became a major influence on the Harlem Renaissance. He is remembered for his book, *Home to Harlem*, as well as for his poem, "If We Must Die," which was written about the lynching of African Americans but became famous after England's Winston Churchill recited it in reference to England's struggle to win World War II.

1928

Julian Edwin "Cannonball" Adderley was a jazz alto saxophonist of the hard-bop era of the 1950s and 1960s.

1965

The actor/comedian Bill Cosby co-stars in the television show *I Spy*. Cosby is the first person of African descent to star in a U.S. television program.

September 16

1889

Claude Albert Barnett is born in Sanford, Florida. In 1919, Barnett founded the Associated Negro Press (ANP), a service that helped circulate the information provided in African American newspapers.

After college Barnett held various jobs, and upon hearing about growing opportunities for blacks in Chicago he moved to the North. Chicago was a place where Barnett could put down roots and build his business. In 1916 he formed the Associated Negro Press (ANP), the first major wire service for nationwide coverage of news in the black community. To Barnett, the ANP was not just a news service, it was a resource for the development of other business ventures. Using the ANP as a negotiating tool, Barnett made several arrangements

with black newspapers and magazines around the country, stipulating that the ANP would provide them with stories in exchange for advertising space. Through this mechanism Barnett became a key advertising figure in the black community. His clients included many of the larger black businesses of his time, such as Annie Minerva Turnbo-Malone's Poro Colleges.

Source: From Robert Mark Silverman. Doing Business in Minority Markets: Black and Korean Entrepreneurs in Chicago's Ethnic Beauty Aids Industry. New York, NY: Psychology Press/Routledge, 2000, p. 47.

Books

Barnett, Claude. *The Claude A. Barnett Papers: Part 3: Subject Files on Black Americans, 1918–1967; Series B: Colleges and Universities, 1918–1966.* Bethesda, MD: University Publications of America, 1986. Documents from Claude Barnett files.

Collier-Thomas, Bettye. *Jesus, Jobs, and Justice: African American Women and Religion.* New York, NY: Random House Digital, Inc., 2010. Includes a look at Barnett's view of the power and abilities of African American organizations, like the NAACP, Urban League, and the ANP.

Websites

The Claude A. Barnett Papers—University of Maryland Libraries. http://lib.umd.edu/MICROFORMS/claude_barnett.html.

Claude A. Barnett Papers—Fondren Library—Rice University. http://www.library.rice.edu/collections/folder.2008-11.../claude-a-barnett-papers.

Also Noteworthy

1923

The St. Augustine Seminary, the first Catholic seminary created for the training of African American priests, is dedicated in Bay St. Louis, Mississippi. The seminary was operated by the Divine Word Missionaries, also known as the Societas Verbi Divini.

September 17

1879

Andrew "Rube" Foster is born in Calvert, Texas. After leaving school in the eighth grade, Foster became a pitcher for the Fort Worth Yellow Jackets. Foster later became the owner and manager of the Chicago American Giants, and, by 1920, Foster had created the Negro National League. Foster was inducted into the National Baseball Hall of Fame in Cooperstown, New York, in 1981.

> In 1917 the Freeman, a black paper in Indianapolis, made a public appeal for a "Moses to lead the baseball children out of the wilderness." Three years later, Foster answered its call. The increasing vibrancy of black communities in the North created new possibilities, and Foster understood the benefits of a league with fixed schedules, high-profile rivalries, and championships. Unhappy with allowing white promoters to dictate the terms by which he played in the East, Foster gathered black club owners and sportswriters at the Kansas City YMCA in February 1920. They formed the eight-team Negro National League and elected Foster as the NNL's first president.
>
> Source: From Rob Ruck. Raceball: How the Major Leagues Colonized the Black and Latin Game. Boston, MA: Beacon Press, 2011, p. 122.

Books

Cottrell, Robert Charles. *The Best Pitcher in Baseball: The Life of Rube Foster, Negro League Giant.* New York, NY: NYU Press, 2004. Biographical profile of Andrew Rube Foster.

Dixon, Phil S. *Andrew "Rube" Foster, a Harvest on Freedom's Fields.* Bloomington, IN: Xlibris Corporation, 2010. Biography about the life of Rube Foster.

Websites

The Negro League BaseBall Players Association has a biography of Andrew Rube Foster. http://www.nlbpa.com/foster__andrew_-_rube .html.

The Negro Leagues Baseball Museum provides a profile of Foster. http://coe.ksu.edu/nlbemuseum/history/players/fostera.html.

Also Noteworthy

1868

Hampton Normal and Agricultural Institute (now Hampton Institute) is founded by General Samuel Armstrong on the site where Blacks who had run away from slavery had gathered during the Civil War. The Congregationalists' American Missionary Association (AMA) founded Hampton as one of eight teacher-in-training schools created for freed people in the South.

1937

Orlando Manuel Cepeda Pennes is born in Ponce, Puerto Rico. As a Major League Baseball first baseman, Cepeda played with the San Francisco Giants (1958–66), St. Louis Cardinals (1966–68), Atlanta Braves (1969–72), Oakland Athletics (1972), Boston Red Sox (1973), and Kansas City Royals (1974). Cepeda was selected to play in seven Major League Baseball All-Star Games and became the first player from Puerto Rico to start one. The Veterans Committee inducted Cepeda into the National Baseball Hall of Fame in 1999.

1968

Diahann Carroll stars in the title role in the television series *Julia.* This makes Carroll the first African American actress to star in a television program role where she was not a domestic servant.

1983

Vanessa Lynn Williams becomes the first African American woman to win the "Miss America" pageant.

September 18

1882

George Wells Parker is born to Abraham W. Parker and Augusta Bing. Parker was one of the first African Americans to graduate from Harvard University and is known for his scholarship on African history and his support for the Marcus Garvey movement. Parker helped relocate Blacks to Omaha, Nebraska, in 1916 and 1917 and helped found the Hamitic League of the World in 1917. Under the auspices of the Hamitic League, Parker published the pamphlet *The Children of the Sun* in 1918.

> *...Robert A. Hill described Parker as "a medical student in Omaha and scion of one of that city's oldest black families."*
>
> *On 1 April 1917 Parker delivered a speech before the Omaha Philosophical Soceity entitled "The African Origin of the Grecian Civilization." Still referenced today, "The African Origin of the Grecian Civilization" was published in the* Journal of Negro History *in July 1917.*
>
> *George Wells Parker was an exceptional scholar, perhaps even ahead of his time, who wrote with a pronounced degree of confidence, clarity and sharpness. In 1918, the Hamitic League of the World published a twenty-nine page pamphlet by Parker entitled* The Children of the Sun, *which contained an enlightening section highlighting the ethnic composition of classical Asian civilizations.*
>
> *Source*: From Ivan Van Sertima and Runoko Rashidi. *African Presence in Early Asia, Volume 7, Issue 1.* Piscataway, NJ: Transaction Publishers, 1988, p. 264.

Books

Martin, Tony. *Literary Garveyism: Garvey, Black Arts, and the Harlem Renaissance.* Bloomington, IN: Majority Press, 1983. Book includes profile of Parker and his literary contributions to the Garvey movement.
Parker, George Wells. *The Children of the Sun.* Victoria, BC: AbeBooks/Black Classic Press, 1981. Book looks at the African scientific influences on ancient civilizations.

Websites

George Wells Parker—The African Origin of the Grecian Civilization. http://retakeyour fame.blogspot.com/2008/06/george-wells -parker-african-origin-of.html.
George Wells Parker, Race Man and Pioneer to the Past. http://www.cwo.com/~lucumi/ parker.html.

Also Noteworthy

1850

The U.S. Congress passes the Fugitive Slave Law as part of the Compromise of 1850.

1895

Booker T. Washington presents his "Atlanta Exposition" speech, which promoted the importance of vocational education in providing economic security for Blacks. Washington gave the speech at the Cotton States Exposition, which was nationally covered by the media, and he was famously quoted as saying, "In all things that are purely social we can be as separate as the fingers, yet one as the hand in all things essential to mutual progress." Washington's self-help model was widely accepted by white nationalists and some African Americans, while other Black activists criticized him for leading the Black community toward second-class citizenship.

1951

Benjamin Solomon "Ben" Carson, Sr., MD, is born in Detroit, Michigan. Known as a gifted surgeon, Dr. Carson was named director of pediatric neurosurgery at Johns Hopkins Hospital in Baltimore, Maryland, at the age of 33. In 1987, Carson famously led a 70-member surgical team during a

22-hour successful operation to separate conjoined twins who were connected at the cranium.

September 19

1865

Atlanta University is founded. Today, it is one part of the private, historically African American Clark Atlanta University (CAU) that was officially consolidated on July 1, 1988. The original Clark College was founded in 1869.

> Other money came from the North through the channels of philanthropic and church missionary societies. Of the $89,000 spent by Atlanta University in its first two years, $19,000 had come from the American Missionary Association. In the case of Clark University, entire support, such as it was, came from the Freedmen's Aid Society of the Northern Methodist Church. There was no endowment and growth was slow, but the limited income of the little school was secure and free from the constant demands of begging. The help of the American Baptist Home Mission Society which sponsored the Atlanta Baptist Seminary was hardly enough, however, for even a decent beginning. President Robert struggled continuously for a bare existence. Some classrooms were entirely unfurnished. Many pledges for the Atlanta building were never collected. Its usual expenditures in the seventies shifted between $2,000 and $4,000 a year. When the first college student was graduated in 1883, its expenditures reached the sum of only $7,000 while Atlanta University had $32,000 to spend.
>
> Source: From Willard Range. The Rise and Progress of Negro Colleges in Georgia, 1865–1949. Athens, GA: University of Georgia Press, 2009, p. 36.

Books

Bacote, Charles A. *The Story of Atlanta University: A Century of Service, 1865–1965*. Atlanta, GA: Atlanta University Press, 1969. Book includes information about the first 100 years of Atlanta University.

Brooks, Erik F. and Glenn L. Starks. *Historically Black Colleges and Universities*. Santa Barbara, CA: ABC-CLIO, 2011. Book includes information about the founding of both Atlanta and Clark Universities.

Websites

Clark Atlanta University. http://www.georgia encyclopedia.org/nge/Article.jsp?id=h-1447.

Clark Atlanta University. http://www.cau.edu/.

Also Noteworthy

1893

Elbert R. Robinson receives U.S. Patent No. 505,370 for his electric railway trolley.

1963

Iota Phi Theta (IΦΘ) is created by 12 older students on the campus of Morgan State College, now Morgan State University. The students—Alfred Hicks, Lonnie Spuill, Jr., Charles Briscoe, Frank Coakley, John Slade, Barron Willis, Webster Lewis, Charles Brown, Louis Hudnell, Charles Gregory, Elias Dorsey, Jr., and Michael Williams—established Iota Phi Theta Fraternity, Inc., with the motto "Building A Tradition, Not Resting Upon One."

September 20

1984

The Cosby Show premiers on the NBC television network. *The Cosby Show* became one of the most successful television shows of all time; it ran for eight seasons, was broadcast throughout the world, and became one of the first programs to be recognized for consistently showing humane depictions of people of African descent.

For those who have managed to avoid seeing it, The Cosby Show *is a half-hour situation comedy about an upper middle class black family, the Huxtables. Cliff Huxtable (played by Bill Cosby) is a gynecologist and obstetrician, and his wife, Clair, is a lawyer. They have four daughters and a son; as the series has grown older, they have acquired in-laws and grandchildren. The Huxtables' attractive New York brownstone home is the setting for an endless series of comic domestic dramas. There is little in this description to distinguish this TV fiction from many others: we are used to a TV world populated by attractive professionals and their good-looking offspring. What makes the show unusual is its popularity, its critical acclaim, and the fact that all its leading characters are black.*

Source: From Sut Jhally and Justin Lewis. *Enlightened Racism: The Cosby Show, Audiences, and the Myth of the American Dream.* Boulder, CO: Westview Press, 1992, pp. 1–2.

Books

Bacote, Charles A. *The Cosby Show: Audiences, Impact, and Implications.* Santa Barbara, CA: Greenwood Press, 1992. Looks at the success of *The Cosby Show* as a sitcom that portrayed a mature image of African Americans.

MacDonald, J. Fred. *Blacks and White TV: Afro-Americans in Television Since 1948.* Chicago IL: Nelson-Hall, 1983. Looks at the advances made in portrayals of African Americans from *Julia* through to *The Cosby Show*.

Websites

THE COSBY SHOW—The Museum of Broadcast Communications. http://www.museum.tv/eotvsection.php?entrycode=cosbyshowt.

The Cosby Show Season 1 Episode 01—Pilot Presentation. http://www.youtube.com/watch?v=nFY0HBkUm8o.

Also Noteworthy

1830

First National Negro Convention of Free Men agrees to boycott slave-produced goods.

September 21

1926

John Coltrane is born in Hamlet, North Carolina. A tenor and soprano sax musician, Coltrane played with Dizzy Gillespie, Miles Davis, and Thelonious Monk in the 1950s. In the 1960s he led his own groups and changed the face of jazz with experimentation and improvisation, his later recordings reflecting his belief that music was a form of spiritual expression. Sometimes called simply 'Trane, his recordings include *Giant Steps, My Favorite Things* and *A Love Supreme.*

Heath describes Coltrane's practice regimen:
When I'd go to his apartment in the summertime, Trane would be stripped down to his boxer shorts. He'd be sweating and practicing all day . . . Anything that Trane grabbed, he would work on it until he got it. See, that was the thing about Coltrane. When he started to play tenor, he and [drummer] Philly Joe [Jones] and Percy [Heath] were on gigs around Philly. We were talking about the fact that the older tenor players like [Coleman] Hawkins and [Ben] Webster played in the key of D-flat because it was the heaviest key for the tenor—gets the best sound. "Body and Soul," all those tunes were in D-flat. Duke wrote a lot of tunes in D-flat. Trane said, "I'm going to practice in D-flat." Being who he was, he would zoom in and practice in D-flat for the next six months. And when he later [with Miles Davis] played a solo in D-flat on "Two Bass Hit," nobody ever played that much in D-flat on a blues in the history of the saxophone. . . .

Source: From Lewis Porter. *John Coltrane: His Life and Music.* Ann Arbor, MI: University of Michigan Press, 2000, p. 65.

Books

Nisenson, Eric. *Ascension: John Coltrane and His Quest.* Cambridge, MA: Da Capo Press, 1995. Biographical look at Coltrane traces his musical development as it paralleled his spiritual development.

Ratliff, Ben. *Coltrane: The Story of a Sound*. New York, NY: Macmillan, 2008. Looks at the musical development of Coltrane as an individual and the legacy of his sound on generations of musicians that followed.

Websites

John Coltrane—The official site. http://www .johncoltrane.com/.

John Coltrane live, 1965, playing "Naima." http://www.youtube.com/watch?v=q6Wwuxq XPOg.

Also Noteworthy

1815

General Andrew "Stonewall" Jackson honors the courage of the free Black troops who fought alongside him during the Battle of New Orleans, the last major battle against the British in the War of 1812.

1866

After the Civil War, the United States' 39th Congress passes an act to increase and fix the Military Peace Establishment of the United States; it creates the the 9th Cavalry Regiment, stationed in Greenville, Louisiana, and the 10th Cavalry Regiment, stationed in Fort Leavenworth, Kansas. The Ninth & Tenth Cavalries came to be known as the "Buffalo Soldiers."

1887

F. W. Leslie receives U.S. Patent No. 590,325 for his envelope seal.

1905

The largest African American-owned stockholder insurance company, the Atlanta Life Insurance Company, is founded by Alonzo Herndon.

1949

Artis Gilmore is born in Chipley, Florida. At 7 feet 2 inches and 240 pounds, Gilmore was a dominating center who played in both the American Basketball Association (ABA) and the National Basketball Association (NBA). Known as "The A-Train" and "The Gentle Giant," Gilmore was inducted into the Naismith Memorial Basketball Hall of Fame on August 12, 2011.

1967

Walter Washington is named mayor of Washington, DC.

September 22

1915

Xavier University, the first Black Catholic College in the United States, opens in New Orleans, Lousiana. Saint Katharine Drexel and the Sisters of the Blessed Sacrament originally established the college as a combined middle/high school and two-year Normal School for the education of African Americans and Native Americans.

Mother Katherine thought that the property was ideal for her education concept for black students and wanted to purchase it. Nonetheless, she realized that she had to avert problems in purchasing the property from the predominately white community because they would resist another black school in their neighborhood. As a result, Mother Katherine and the white lawyer representing the purchase thought it to be prudent to maintain Southern University in the purchase name. The headlines in the Morning Star *Newspaper regarding the opening of the school read, "Record Splendid Enrollment—Southern University, Under the Patronage of St. Francis Xavier, Will Open September 21 [1915] for Higher and Industrial Education for Males and Females of the Colored Race— Demand for Night Classes for Adults."*

Source: From Beverly Jacques Anderson, PhD. Cherished Memories: Snapshots of Life and

Lessons from a 1950s New Orleans Creole Village. Lincoln, NE: iUniverse, 2011, p. 207.

Books

Catholic University of America. *New Catholic Encyclopedia, Volume 3.* Farmington Hills, MI: Thomson/Gale, 2003. Contains an entry profiling Xavier University.

Smith, Norman R. *Footprints of Black Louisiana.* Bloomington, IN: Xlibris Corporation, 2011. Contains a look at how Katherin Drexel purchased the old Southern University for the establishment of Drexel.

Websites

Xavier University of Louisiana. http://www.xula .edu/about-xavier/index.php.

Xavier University's main administration building, original library, and convent are listed in the National Register of Historic Places in 2004. http://www.nps.gov/resources/site .htm?id=18248.

Also Noteworthy

1862

President Abraham Lincoln issues his preliminary Emancipation Proclamation, which declared that all enslaved Africans in rebel states should be freed as of January 1, 1863. Of course, this did not count the enslaved Africans in "non-rebel" states.

September 23

1932

Ray Charles Robinson (Ray Charles) is born to Bailey and Aretha Robinson in Albany, Georgia. Charles's family moved to Greenville, Florida, when he was a child, and as he gradually lost his sight while still young, they had him enrolled in the Florida School for the Deaf & the Blind in St. Augustine,

Florida. As an adult, Ray Charles became known as a talented pianist who could perform in nearly every musical genre.

> . . . *His growth was obvious. The musical elements he had come to know well—big band jazz, deep blues, and fervid gospel—were merging. The sound was distinctly Ray Charles.*
>
> *He later explained the lyrics to his songs to Joe Goldberg, author of* Jazz Masters of the Fifties:
>
> *The things I write and sing about concern the general Joe and his general problems. There are four basic things: love, somebody runnin' his mouth too much, having fun, and jobs are hard to get . . . When I put myself in the place of the . . . general Joe I'm singing about . . . I sing with all the feeling I can put into it, so that I can feel it myself.*
>
> *Source:* From Janet Hubbard-Brown. *Ray Charles: Musician.* New York, NY: Infobase Publishing, 2008, p. 40.

Books

Charles, Ray and David Ritz. *Brother Ray: Ray Charles' Own Story.* Cambridge, MA: Da Capo Press, 2003. Charles's autobiography is a look at his musical career and life.

Lydon, Michael. *Ray Charles: Man and Music.* London, UK: Psychology Press, 2004. Biographical profile of Ray Charles.

Websites

Ray Charles. http://raycharles.com/.

Ray Charles Foundation. http://www.theray charlesfoundation.org/.

Also Noteworthy

1907

Boogie woogie piano legend Albert Ammons is born in Chicago, Illinois, into a family of musicians. Ammons learned to play piano and the drums and is best remembered for his hit songs like "Boogie Woogie Stomp" and "Shout for Joy."

September 24

1893

Texas country blues singer and guitarist "Blind" Lemon Jefferson is one of seven children born to Alec and Clarissy Banks Jefferson, who were both sharecroppers on a farm in Couchman, Texas. His distinctive style of guitar playing and singing made Jefferson famous. He is best remembered for his classic blues songs "See That My Grave Is Kept Clean," "Jack of Diamonds," and "Matchbox Blues." The Blues Foundation Hall of Fame inducted "Blind" Lemon Jefferson in 1980.

> In 1925 Blind Lemon was invited to Dallas to make "race" records for Paramount Records. The following year he recorded his first hit record, "Got the Blues," followed in May with "Long Lonesome Blues." For the next two years Jefferson was considered the most successful country blues singer in the U.S. . . . With his popularity rising, Jefferson's travels took him from Dallas to Chicago, Georgia, Mississippi, and all points in between. At one point he had two cars, a chauffeur, and $1,500 in the bank—unheard of for a black man in postwar America.
>
> Source: From Scott Stanton. The Tombstone Tourist: Musicians. Jefferson, NC: McFarland, 2004), p. 122.

Books

Oliphant, Dave. *Texan Jazz*. Austin, TX: University of Texas Press, 1996. Author recalls the lasting impact of Blind Lemon Jefferson on the art of the Blues.

Uzzel, Robert L. *Blind Lemon Jefferson: His Life, His Death, and His Legacy*. Waco, TX: Eakin Press, 2002. Biography of Blind Lemon Jefferson also talks about his lasting influence on future guitarists.

Websites

Blind Lemon Jefferson singing "See That My Grave Is Kept Clean" is available on YouTube. http://www.youtube.com/watch?v=5S8Rjwwo2g4.

The Texas State Historical Association has an entry in memory of Blind Lemon Jefferson. http://www.tshaonline.org/handbook/online/articles/fje01.

Also Noteworthy

1894

The sociologist E. Franklin Frazier is born to James H. and Mary Clark Frazier in Baltimore, Maryland. Frazier became famous for his writings examining how people of African descent are incorporated into societies where their ancestors were formerly held as slaves.

1923

BeBop jazz trumpeter Theodore "Fats" Navarro is born in Key West, Florida.

1957

President Eisenhower orders Federal troops to enforce court-ordered desegregation as nine children integrate into Central High School in Little Rock, Arkansas.

September 25

1861

Secretary of the Navy Gideon Welles authorizes the enlistment of enslaved Africans as Union sailors.

> While the Army and Congress debated endlessly on whether to allow Negroes to fight, the Secretary of the Navy, Gideon Wells moved at once to utilize Negroes and newly freed slaves. Stivers tells us that:
>
> "As early as September, 1861, Gideon Wells adopted a policy of adding many of these Negroes to the National Naval Reserve force. Wells said, "The Department finds it necessary to adopt a regulation with respect to large and increasing

numbers of persons of color, commonly known as contraband, now subsisted at the navy yards and on board ships of war. They can neither be expelled from the service to which they have resorted, nor can they be maintained unemployed; and it is not proper that they should be compelled to render necessary and regular services without stated compensation. You are therefore author- ized, when their services can be made useful, to enlist them in the Naval Service, under the same forms and regulations as apply to other enlisted personnel. They will be allowed, however, no higher rating than boys at a compensation of $10 per month and one ration per day."

Source: From Chester A. Wright. *Black Men and Blue Water.* Bloomington, IN: AuthorHouse, 2009, p. 115.

Books

Niven, John. *Gideon Welles; Lincoln's Secretary of the Navy.* New York, NY: Oxford University Press, 1973. Biography of Welles and his anti slavery ideals.

Welles, Gideon. *Diary of Gideon Welles, Secretary of the Navy under Lincoln and Johnson, Volume 2.* Victoria, BC: AbeBooks/Houghton Mif- flin Company, 1911. Welles's diary includes his thoughts about hiring forming enslaved Africans to fight on the Union side.

Websites

Naval Secretary Orders Wages for Former Slaves. http://www.7score10years.com/index.php/ north/82-north/452-25-september-1861 -naval-secretary-orders-wages-for-former- slaves.

Witness to History: Lincoln's Trusted Friend Gideon Welles. http://www.hartfordinfo.org/ issues/documents/history/htfd_courant_020 809.asp.

Also Noteworthy

1974

Barbara Hancock becomes the first African American woman to be named a White House Fellow.

September 26

1968

The Studio Museum in Harlem opens in a rented loft at 2033 Fifth Avenue just off 125th Street in New York City. Co- founded by Frank Donnelly—a psycho- therapist and social worker—and Carter Burden, the Studio Museum was established to show the art of African Americans and people of African descent. The current museum is located on 125th Street between Adam Clayton Powell, Jr., Boulevard and Lenox Avenue and has a permanent collec- tion of more than 1,600 works. Included in that collection are works by Romare Bearden, Richard Hunt, Jacob Lawrence, Betye Saar, and an extensive archive of the work of photographer James VanDerZee.

..[I]n 1968 The Studio Museum in Harlem was founded. At the time, the work of many black artists was still excluded from mainstream gal- leries and museums. The mission of the new museum was to supply studio space for and sup- port the careers of African American artists, to pre- serve and exhibit art of Black Amerrica and of the African Diaspora, and to illuminate the impact of these on American culture. The museum closely adheres to this mission.

Source: From Suzanne Loebl. *America's Art Museums: A Traveler's Guide to Great Collections Large and Small.* New York, NY: W. W. Norton & Company, 2002, p. 309.

Books

Diamonstein, Barbaralee. *Inside the Art World: Conversations with Barbaralee Diamonstein.* New York, NY: Rizzoli, 1994. Includes interview with Kinshasha Holman Conwill, director of the Studio Museum of Harlem, regarding the founding of the museum.

Frye, Daniel J. *African American Visual Artists: An Annotated Bibliography of Educational Resource Materials.* Lanham, MD: Scarecrow Press, 2001. Looks at how art criticism of Black artisis helped define the mission of the Studio Museum of Harlem.

Websites

The Studio Museum in Harlem. http://www.studiomuseum.org/.

Studio Museum logo. http://vimeo.com/429081.

Also Noteworthy

1867

Maggie Lena Walker is born in Richmond, Virginia. Walker became the first female bank president in the United States when she took control of the St. Luke Penny Savings Bank.

1899

William Levi Dawson is born in Anniston, Alabama. A composer, professor, and choir director, Dawson famously wrote the "Negro Folk Symphony" of 1934.

1907

The People's Savings Bank is incorporated in Philadelphia, Pennsylvania, by one of the nation's early African American members of Congress, George H. White. After White was himself forced out of Congress due to the disenfranchisement of Black voters after Reconstruction, White pushed for Black economic advancement with his bank, which helped thousands of African Americans purchase homes.

1929

Ida Stephens Owens is born in Newark, New Jersey. Owens became the nation's first African American female biochemist when she received her PhD in biology and physiology from Duke University in 1967.

1937

Blues great Bessie Smith dies of injuries sustained in an automobile accident near Clarksdale, Mississippi.

1962

Sonny Liston knocks out Floyd Patterson in 2 minutes, 10 seconds of the first round to win the World Heavyweight boxing championship.

1981

Serena Jameka Williams is born in Saginaw, Michigan. Serena, alongside her sister, Venus, became one of the top-ranked female professional tennis players in the world.

September 27

1912

William Christopher Handy publishes the sheet music to his "Memphis Blues." The self-declared "father of the blues," W. C. Handy was originally from rural Florence, Alabama, and became a cornet soloist and bandmaster with minstrel shows against the wishes of his father, who was a Calvinist minister. With the publication of his blues songs, W. C. Handy became a nationally known celebrity and his father forgave him for becoming a musician.

...Handy...allowed that the original lyrics of his "Memphis Blues" were inspired by topical verses heard throughout black Memphis, as they were "sung, impromptu," during the 1909 mayoral campaign: "Mister Crump don't allow no east ridershere." Although his original 1912 sheet music edution of "The Memphis Blues" informed that it was "better known as 'Mister Crump,'" Handy did not combine the "Mister Crump" refrain with "The Memphis Blues" in print until A Treasury of Blues came out in 1949.

The earliest and most straightforward account of the historical relationship between Handy's

> *"Memphis Blues" and the folk song "Mister Crump" may be the one given in a 1923 press release heralding the Handy Orchestra's commercial recordings of that year: "One of the most recent issues by Handy's orchestra on Okeh records is 'Memphis Blues.' ... 'Memphis Blues' was known for two years prior to its publication as 'Mr. Crump,' and is well known to all Colored folks in the South. A little song that the Southerners used to sing about, 'Mr. Crump don't 'low no easy riders, but we don't care what Mr. Crump don't 'low, we're gonnta Barrel House anyhow,' furnished the theme for its composition by Mr. Hardy."*
>
> Source: From David Evans, ed. *Ramblin' on My Mind: New Perspectives on the Blues.* Champaign, IL: University of Illinois Press, 2008, pp. 84–85.

Books

Handy, William Christopher. *Father of the Blues: An Autobiography.* Cambridge, MA: Da Capo Press, 1991. Handy's autobiography recalls his life as a struggling Black musician in the beginning of the twentieth century; the book also looks at how he earned his first $100 for publishing "Memphis Blues."

Robertson, David. *W.C. Handy: The Life and Times of the Man Who Made the Blues.* New York, NY: Random House Digital, Inc., 2009. Biography of Handy looks at his iconic songs like "Memphis Blues" and "Beale Street Blues" and notes his rise from rural Florence, Alabama, childhood to internationally acclaimed songwriter and musician.

Websites

William Christopher "W.C." Handy—Memphis School. http://www.nps.gov/history/delta/blues/people/wc_handy.htm.

W. C. Handy's Orchestra of Memphis—A Bunch O Blues (1917). http://www.youtube.com/watch?v=OVxaYk25il4.

Also Noteworthy

1862

Frank F. Barclay begins publication of the bi- and tri-weekly African American newspaper, *L'Union.* The first Black newspaper in the South, *L'Union* was mostly published in French with occasional printings in English; it was designed to raise the concerns of New Orleans creoles while also focusing some attention on the lives of enslaved Blacks. Because of lack of funds, the newspaper ceased publication on July 19, 1864.

1827

Hiram Rhodes Revels is born a free Black in Fayetteville, North Carolina. Revels was the first African American to serve as member of the U.S. Senate when he served from February 25, 1870, to March 4, 1871. After the Senate, Revels served as the president of Alcorn Agricultural and Mechanical College (later "Alcorn State University"), the first state-supported institution for the higher education of African Americans in the United States.

1876

Edward Mitchell Bannister wins a bronze medal for a painting he displayed at the American Centennial Exposition in Philadelphia.

1950

Gwendolyn Brooks is awarded the Pulitzer Prize for her book of poetry, *Annie Allen.* She was the first African American so honored.

1950

Ralph J. Bunch is awarded the Nobel Peace Prize for his work in mediating a conflict between Palestinians and the newly established Jewish state of Israel. Arabs had gone to war arguing the Jewish state had been established on land that rightfully belonged to the Palestinians.

September 28

1785

David Walker is born in Wilmington, North Carolina; his mother was free but his father was enslaved. Walker grew up free and was educated and able to travel throughout the country. He became a leading advocate for the abolition of slavery and a noted writer and publisher. Walker famously wrote his *Appeal to the Coloured Citizens of the World*, a pamphlet that urged enslaved Africans to take up arms and fight against their continued slavery.

> Too militant for moderate black and white abolitionists, he created his own mandate and manifesto David Walker's Appeal in Four Articles; Together with a Preamble, to the Coloured Citizens of the World, but in Particular, and Very Expressly, to Those of the United States of America.
>
> The controversial four-part tract began as a lecture in Boston, the autumn of 1828, when Walker stirred an audience of the General Coloured Association of Massachusetts. His new anti-slavery challenge reached a wider public that December 20 in the black abolitionist weekly, Freedom's Journal, for which he was Boston agent and editorial contributor. By September 1829, he had written and combined four articles into a pamphlet, printed and distributed at his own expense. With two more editions in quick succession—each more incendiary than the previous—his final Appeal was seventy-eight pages. Working as if his days were numbered, he was prescient that they were. After his text began circulating in the South to the anger of slaveholders and politicians, who wrote Boston's mayor to suppress it, rumors were rampant of a high financial reward for David Walker, dead or alive. He had violated no Massachusetts law, and his work could not legally be stifled. But for Southerners who resented Denmark Vesey's attempted 1822 slave revolt and Gabriel's bloody rebellion in 1800, Walker was considered seditious for challenging slaves to rise against oppressors. Shortly after the third edition of his Appeal, the fourty-four-year-old author was found dead of uncertain causes in Boston on June 28, 1830, his mysterious death later attributed to poisoning.
>
> Source: From Faith Berry. *From Bondage to Liberation: Writings by and about Afro-Americans from 1700 to 1918.* New York, NY: Continuum International Publishing Group, 2006, p. 87.

Books

Burrow, Rufus. *God and Human Responsibility: David Walker and Ethical Prophecy.* Macon, GA: Mercer University Press, 2003. Looks at David Walker's deep religious understanding and how this affected his idea of social activism and the need to take up arms against African slavery.

Walker, David. *David Walker's Appeal to the Coloured Citizens of the World.* University Park, PA: Penn State Press, 2000. Full text of Walker's political call for African American freedom.

Websites

The North Carolina History Project has a biography of David Walker. http://www.northcarolinahistory.org/commentary/349/entry.

David Walker (1785–1830). http://college.cengage.com/english/lauter/heath/4e/students/author_pages/early_nineteenth/walker_da.html.

Also Noteworthy

1868

The Opelousas Massacre occurs. Racist whites launch a terror campaign in St. Landry Parrish, Louisiana, resulting in the deaths of at least 200 African Americans.

1895

National Baptist Convention (NBC) is organized in Atlanta, Georgia, by the joining of the Baptist Foreign Mission Convention, the American National Baptist Convention, and the National Baptist Educational Convention. Elias Camp Morris was elected the NBC's first president.

1898

Arthur James Riggs and Benjamin Franklin Howard are granted a copyright for the creation of The Improved Benevolent and Protective Order of Elks of the World. The Black Elks, as it is more commonly known, is established in Cincinnati, Ohio, where the first Lodge, Alpha Lodge No. 1, is also created. The Black Elks is the largest predominately African American fraternal organization in the world.

September 29

1975

WGPR-TV, the first African American–owned television station in the United States, begins broadcasting in Detroit, Michigan. Dr. William V. Banks, who served as the supreme grand master of the International Free and Accepted Modern Masons and order of the Eastern Star, owned WGPR (an acronym for "Where God's Presence Radiates"), which broadcast on UHF channel 62.

> . . . The first Black-owned television station in the United States was WGPR-TV (UHF channel 62) in Detroit (Grosse Pointe), Michigan. WPGR, which to owner William V. Banks seemed a logical extension of a successful FM radio station, began broadcasting on September 29, 1975. In practice, however, Dr. Banks quickly learned that programming Black-appeal television was much more difficult than programming Black-appeal radio. Johnson's case study of the first three years of WGPR revealed that the station was overly ambitious and its audience became dismayed with what was offered. "WGPR-TV fell victim to its own enthusiasm and inexperience. Its unreal programming goals set up levels of expectation within its audience that could only mean disillusionment with anything less." The station "promised innovated programming produced by Blacks for Blacks. It delivered old movies, westerns, and cartoons now in syndication from decades gone by." WGPR was more successful at realizing its goal of serving as a training ground for minorities, though

> not as much as if it had more revenues. Still, the station survived, and ultimately thrived. It stayed in Black control until 1995 when it was sold to CBS for $24 million.

> Source: From Donald G. Godfrey. *Methods of Historical Analysis in Electronic Media*. New York, NY: Psychology Press/ Routledge, 2006, p. 256.

Books

Johnson, Mary H. *A Case History of the Evolution of WGPR-TV, Detroit: First Black-Owned Television Station in the U.S., 1972–1979*. Victoria, BC: AbeBooks/University of North Carolina at Chapel Hill, 1979. Examines the reasons behind the creation of WGPR-TV.

Kiska, Tim and Ed Golick. *Detroit Television*. Mount Pleasant, SC: Arcadia Publishing, 2010. Book looks at this history of television broadcasting in Detroit and profiles WGPR-TV.

Websites

WGPR-TV African American History by Gary Gray. http://www.gibbsmagazine.com/WGPR-TV%20African%20American%20History.htm.

WGPR-TV Channel 62. http://www.thescenedetroit.com/262800.html.

Also Noteworthy

1784

First African American Masonic lodge is established by Prince Hall. Hall headed lodge number 459 and was referred to as the "Worshipful Master." He would also become a leading figure in the struggle for African Americans rights during this early period in U.S. history.

1940

First U.S. merchant ship commanded by an African American captain—Hugh Mulzac—is launched in Wilmington, Delaware. The ship is named the *Booker T. Washington*.

1962

President John F. Kennedy authorizes the use of federal troops to force the integration of the University of Mississippi.

1979

William Arthur Lewis, an economics professor at Princeton University, becomes the first African American to receive a Nobel Prize in Economics.

September 30

1928

Juan Pedro Montanez Tomás is born to Dolores Montanez Thomas in Spanish Harlem (El Barrio), New York. As an Afro-Latino of Puerto Rican and Cuban descent, he was celebrated as the writer and poet Piri Thomas. Thomas authored the best-selling autobiography *Down These Mean Streets* (1967) and was an important voice for the Nuyorican cultural movement.

> Down These Mean Streets . . . *is the autobiography of Piri Thomas, a dark-skinned child of Puerto Ricans who grew up in the 1930s and 1940s in the streets of East Harlem, an ethnically mixed New York City neighborhood of Blacks, Puerto Ricans, and Italians. The memoir chronicles Thomas's search for a sense of identity and his descent into drugs and street crime. It ends with his release from prison and his first steps toward rehabilitation.*
>
> *Thomas's story reveals the interconnectiness of race and ethnicity in American society. Wanting to be accepted as an American of Puerto Rican heritage, Thomas finds that people around him see nothing but his color. In one episode after another, a sometimes subtle, sometimes brutal racism meets him at every step. From a beating administered by a neighborhood Italian gang, to the racism of a high school classmate, to*

> *discrimination when he and a white friend search for jons, Thomas cannot escape the consequences of his color. Color differences among members of his family leave him questioning who he is and his own worth. He begins to accept the judgment that denies his worth in the broader society. His story is a moving tale of the pain and suffering inflicted by a racism that stymies his repeated attempts to assimilate into the broader American society. It reminds readers of the persisting barriers that American society has erected for immigrants of color and their descendants.*
>
> Source: From Thomas Dublin. *Immigrant Voices: New Lives in America, 1773–1986.* Champaign, IL: University of Illinois Press, 1993, p. 260.

Books

Thomas, Piri. *Down These Mean Streets.* New York, NY: Vintage Books, 1997. Piri Thomas's memoir about growing up in Spanish Harlem during the 1940s and 1950s.

Turner, Faythe Elaine. *Puerto Rican Writers at Home in the USA: An Anthology.* Seattle, WA: Open Hand Pub., 1991. Book includes a profile of Piri Thomas.

Websites

The Official Piri Thomas Website. http://www.cheverote.com/.

Race Matters: Piri Thomas. http://vimeo.com/10728880.

Also Noteworthy

1962

Under the protection of federal marshals, James Meredith enrolls as the first African American student at University of Mississippi.

1975

Boxing greats Muhammad Ali and Joe Frazier fight for the third and final time in the famed "Thrilla in Manila" boxing match. Muhammad Ali wins the match.

October

October 1

1951

The 24th Infantry Regiment, the last all–African American unit in the U.S. Army, is officially deactivated at Pusan, Korea. Members of the 24th Infantry Regiment who helped the U.S. Army displace indigenous Americans from parts of Texas and New Mexico, were popularly known as "Buffalo Soldiers."

> One of two all—African American regiments in the U.S. Army during the second half of the nineteenth century, the 24th spent most of its early career in the American West before fighting in the Spanish-American War and World War II. The regiment is best remembered for its role in the Korean War, however, where its controversial performance fueled the debate over desegregation of the armed forces.
>
> On July 28, 1866, the federal government passed the Army Reorganization Act, which provided a framework for the army following the massive changes the institution underwent during the Civil War. The act also specifically called for the formation of six all-African American regiments to be permanently established within the army: two cavalry units (9th and 10th) and four infantry units (38th, 39th, 40th, and 41st). In March 1869, Congress again ordered a reorganization of the army, mandating among other things that these four infantry units should be amalgamated into just two regiments. The 24th was created by combining the 38th and the 41st.
>
> *Source*: From Jonathan Sutherland. *African Americans at War: An Encyclopedia*. Santa Barbara, CA: ABC-CLIO, 2004, p. 413.

Books

Bowers, William T., William M. Hammond, and George L. MacGarrigle. *Black Soldier, White Army: The 24th Infantry Regiment in Korea.* Darby, PA: DIANE Publishing, 1997. Book looks at the performance of the 24th Infantry during the Korean Conflict, at a time when the troops faced segregation.

Scipio, Louis Albert. *Last of the Black Regulars: A History of the 24th Infantry Regiment (1869–1951).* Houston, TX: Roman Publications, 1983. Book looks at the storied history of the 24th Infantry Regiment.

Websites

Korean War: Forgotten 24th and 34th Infantry Regiments. http://www.historynet.com/korean-war-forgotten-24th-and-34th-infantry-regiments.htm.

The 24th Infantry Regiment. http://www.buffalosoldiers-lawtonftsill.org/24-inf.htm.

Also Noteworthy

1872

Morgan State College is founded in Baltimore, Maryland. Originally known as the Centenary Biblical Institute, the school was designed to train African American men to become ministers.

1940

Charles Drew is named supervisor of the "Plasma for Great Britain" project, which was an attempt to collect, test, and deliver large quantities of blood plasma for distribution in Britain during World War II.

1945

Donny Edward Hathaway is born in Chicago, Illinois. As a soul singer, Donny Hathaway is famed for soul staples like "This Christmas," "A Song for You," "Where Is the Love" (with Roberta Flack), and "Someday We'll All Be Free."

1962

James Meredith becomes the first African American student at University of Mississippi, after 3,000 federal troops quelled the riots by white students and their family members who were protesting his admission.

October 2

1935

Robert Henry Lawrence, Jr., is born in Chicago, Illinois. As a major in the U.S. Air Force, Lawrence became the first astronaut of African descent. Lawrence was scheduled to be the first African American in outer space, but he was killed in 1967 while flying as a co-pilot in an F-104 aboard a Manned Orbital Laboratory (MOL) mission.

> ... Robert Lawrence would have been the first African American in space, but he was killed in 1967 whilst flying in the backseat of an F104 on an ARPS mission to practise X-15-type landing approaches. The pilot of the aircraft, Major Harvey Royer, misjudged his approach and hit the runway hard, the undercarriage collapsing and launching the aircraft back into the air, now ablaze at its rear. It landed 2,000 ft further down the runway and disintegrated as it bounced once more. Both pilots ejected successfully, but Lawrence's parachute failed to deploy, and he was killed—Major Royer survived the accident.
>
> Source: From Philip Baker. *The Story of Manned Space Stations: An Introduction*. New York, NY: Springer, 2007, p. 13.

Books

Phelps, J. Alfred. *They Had a Dream: The Story of African-American Astronauts*. New York, NY: Presidio/Random House, 1994. Book looks at the first astronauts of African descent and the trials they went through to become part of the nation's space program.

Smith, Jessie Carney. *Black Firsts: 4,000 Ground-Breaking and Pioneering Historical Events.* Canton, MI: Visible Ink Press, 2003. Book includes a profile of Robert Lawrence and his contributions to the U.S. space program.

Websites

The Astronauts Memorial Foundation profiles Robert H. Lawrence, Jr. http://www.amfcse.org/honor/lawrence.htm.

Maj. Robert H. Lawrence. http://www.af.mil/information/heritage/spotlight.asp?id=123087647.

Also Noteworthy

1800

Nat Turner is born in Southampton County, Virginia. From August 21 to 22, 1831, Turner led a failed rebellion against African slavery that included some 75 Blacks and led to the death of 55 whites.

1967

Thurgood Marshall is sworn in as an associate justice of the U.S. Supreme Court, becoming the first African American to serve on the nation's highest court.

1986

President Ronald Reagan appoints Edward J. Perkins ambassador to South Africa.

October 3

1904

Bethune-Cookman College opens in Daytona Beach, Florida—it was originally named the Daytona Educational and Industrial Training School for Negro Girls. Bethune-Cookman was partly named after African American educator Mary McLeod Bethune, who was the founder of the National Council for Negro Women and an unofficial advisor on African American issues to Presidents Franklin D. Roosevelt and Harry S. Truman.

Bethune had founded Florida's Daytona Normal and Industrial Institute for Girls, which merged with the Cookman Institute for Men in 1923, becoming Bethune-Cookman College.

> At her peak, Bethune harnessed a considerable amount of moral authority as black American's "First Lady." She used her skills as a consensus builder to push an agenda for racial and gender inclusion. Having forsaken conventional family life—although she espoused it for race uplift—Bethune contented herself with being the symbolic "Mother Bethune" to a whole race. Except for her son, Albert (and even he felt neglected by his mother's frequent travels and preoccupation with work), her own family life was mostly nonexistent. She was, however, quite supportive of a large, extended family, some of whom she helped to educate at her school. She said that Albert was her first child and Bethune-Cookman College her second.
>
> Source: From Mary McLeod Bethune, edited by Audrey Thomas McCluskey and Elaine M. Smith. *Mary McLeod Bethune: Building a Better World: Essays and Selected Documents*. Bloomington, IN: Indiana University Press, 2001, p. 31.

Books

Flemming, Sheila Y. *Bethune-Cookman College, 1904–1994: The Answered Prayer to a Dream.* New York: Donning Co., 1995. Traces the history of the founding and mission behind Bethune-Cookman College.

Hanson, Joyce Ann. *Mary McLeod Bethune and Black Women's Political Activism.* Columbia, MO: University of Missouri Press, 2003. Book looks at McLeod Bethune's political activism and how it benefited African Americans and places like Bethune-Cookman College.

Websites

Bethune-Cookman University. http://www.cookman.edu/.

Dr. Mary McLeod Bethune's last will and testament. http://www.cookman.edu/about_BCU/history/lastwill_testament.html.

Also Noteworthy

1949

WERD, the first African American-owned radio station, opens in Atlanta, Georgia.

October 4

1864

From October 4th through 7th, the National Convention of Colored Citizens of the United States meet at the Wesleyan Methodist Church in Syracuse, New York. Some 140 participants attended, among them Frederick Douglass, who was elected president of the convention and wrote the official "Address to the People of the United States" on the part of the participants. Conference attendees demanded "the elective franchise" for African Americans and closed the gathering with the creation of the National Equal Rights League (NERL).

> . . . [N]orthern blacks overwhelmingly applauded the actions of the Syracuse Convention, including the creation of a national rights organization. For example, the Christian Recorder *viewed the convention as a harbinger of progress for African Americans, exulting, "The ball has been set in motion." In a similar vein, a meeting in Bridgeport, Connecticut, pledged to fully support all of the measures adopted by the convention. While the* Weekly Anglo-African *reminded its readers that "we have a half repentant nation to deal with, implacable and deep-seated prejudices to overcome, all the vices and sins engendered by two centuries of slavery to contend with," it nevertheless urged its readers to join the equal rights movement.*
>
> Source: From Hugh Davis. *We Will Be Satisfied with Nothing Less: The African American Struggle for Equal Rights in the North During Reconstruction.* Ithaca, NY: Cornell University Press, 2011, p. 26.

Books

Jenkins, Earnestine. *A Question of Manhood: A Reader in U.S. Black Men's History and*

Masculinity. Bloomington, IN: Indiana University Press, 1999. Book looks at how National Convention of Colored Men created the National Equal Rights League.

Litwack, Leon F. and August Meier. *Black Leaders of the Nineteenth Century*. Bloomington, IN: Indiana University Press, 1991. Book includes a profile of the National Equal Rights League.

Websites

National Equal Rights League (1864–1915). http://www.blackpast.org/?q=aah/national -equal-rights-league-1864-1915.

John Mercer Langston served as the first leader of the NERL. http://www.robinsonlibrary.com/ america/unitedstates/afroamericans/langston .htm.

Also Noteworthy

1864

First daily newspaper geared toward African Americans, *The New Orleans Tribune* (*Tribune de la Nouvelle Orleans*), is founded.

1913

Carrie Allen McCray is born in Lynchburg, Virginia. An African American writer, she is known for her works *Ajös Means Goodbye* (1966) and *The Black Woman and Family Roles* (1980), and for her memoir, *Freedom's Child: The Life of a Confederate General's Black Daughter* (1998).

October 5

1929

Autherine Juanita Lucy Foster is born to Hosea and Milton Lucy in Shiloh, Alabama. In 1952, Autherine Lucy Foster became the first African American to be enrolled at the University of Alabama (UA) in Tuscaloosa. After three days of violent demonstrations by white students who wanted to keep "'Bama white," Autherine Lucy was suspended and later expelled from the school.

> After her first class, as Lucy was whisked out a back door, the eggs came at her. They splattered the car she ducked into. A brick shattered the rear window. Ten or fifteen men charged the car. As Lucy ran inside Graves Hall for her next class, an egg hit her back. "Let's kill her, let's kill her," the crowd yelled. Gun barrels flashed. A mob of around a thousand shouted, "Hey, hey, ho, ho, where in the hell did that nigger go?" For three hours she remained locked in Graves Hall, praying for the courage to face death. Finally she was bundled by the state highway patrol onto the floor of a car and taken to the armed sanctuary of a black barbershop.
>
> ......
>
> Autherine Lucy was the first black student in the history of desegregation to be greeted with organized violence. More than a thousand Negroes had already entered southern colleges and universities uneventfully. But the University of Alabama decided to settle the crisis on the mob's terms: That very Monday night, the trustees suspended Lucy until further notice, "for her protection and for the protection of other students and staff members."
>
> Source: From Diane McWhorter. *Carry Me Home: Birmingham, Alabama—The Climactic Battle of the Civil Rights Revolution*. New York, NY: Simon & Schuster, 2001, pp. 98–99.

Books

Clark, E. Culpepper. *The Schoolhouse Door: Segregation's Last Stand at the University of Alabama*. New York, NY: Oxford University Press, 1995. Book looks at Alabama's tradition of white resistance to the Civil Rights Movement, including the violence against and suspension of Autherine Lucy from the University of Alabama.

Layton, Azza Salama. *International Politics and Civil Rights Policies in the United States, 1941–1960*. Cambridge, England: Cambridge University Press, 2000. Book includes information about how the results of the Autherine Lucy case impacted the image of the United States internationally.

Websites

National Women's History Museum profiles Autherine Juanita Lucy. http://www.nwhm.org/education-resources/biography/biographies/autherine-juanita-lucy/.

University of Alabama remembers the violence against Autherine Lucy Foster's enrollment. http://malonehoodplaza.ua.edu/autherine-lucy-foster/.

Also Noteworthy

1872

Booker T. Washington enters Hampton Institute in Virginia. Washington was 16 years old and had a total of 50 cents in his pocket.

1932

Perle Yvonne Watson is born in Los Angeles, California. As Yvonne Braithwaite Burke, she was elected to the California State Legislature from the 63rd Assembly District in 1966, and she became the first women of African descent to serve as a member of the U.S. House of Representatives from the West Coast. Braithwaite Burke was in office from January 3, 1973 through January 3, 1979, representing the 28th and 37nd districts.

October 6

1917

Fannie Lou Hamer is born Fannie Lou Townsend in Montgomery County, Mississippi. Hamer was the last of 20 children born to parents who were sharecroppers. Fannie Lou was herself tricked into working as a sharecropper when she was only 6 and, by age 13, she was a hired cotton picker. Hamer worked until as a sharecropper until she was fired, in 1962, because she had registered to vote. As a civil rights activist, Hamer worked with the Student Nonviolent Coordinating Committee (SNCC) and helped create the Mississippi Freedom Democratic Party (MFDP, an organization that famously challenged the seating of all-white Democratic Party representatives at the 1968 Democratic Party convention.

The following week Fannie Lou Jamer was part of a group of eighteen people who tried to register. The youngest of twenty children in a family of sharecroppers, Mrs. Hamer had lived all but two of her forty-four years in Sunflower County. For eighteen years she and her husband "Pap" had worked on the B.D. Marlowe plantation, where they had sharecropped and she was timekeeper. At the courthouse only Mrs. Hamer and one other Ruleville resident were permitted to take the registration test. That night Marlowe came down to the Hamer's house and demanded that she withdraw her application. When Mrs. Hamer responded that "I didn't go down there to register for you, I went down there to register for myself," Marlowe threw her off his plantation.

Source: From John Dittmer. *Local People: The Struggle for Civil Rights in Mississippi.* Champaign, IL: University of Illinois Press, 1995, p. 137.

Books

Jordan, June. *Fannie Lou Hamer.* New York, NY: Crowell, 1972. Short biography on the life of Fannie Lou Hamer.

Mills, Kay. *This Little Light of Mine: The Life of Fannie Lou Hamer.* Lexington, KY: University Press of Kentucky, 2007. Biography of Fannie Lou Hamer, looking at her activism and impact on U.S. political history.

Websites

Hamer's "Testimony before the Credentials Committee, Democratic National Convention." http://americanradioworks.publicradio.org/features/sayitplain/flhamer.html.

Fannie Lou Hamer: Speech to the DNC 1964 is on YouTube. www.youtube.com/watch?v=G-RoVzAqhYk.

Also Noteworthy

1921

Joseph Lowery is born in Huntsville, Alabama. The Reverend Joseph Lowery served as a minister of the United Methodist Church and helped Dr. Martin Luther King, Jr., organize the Southern Christian Leadership Conference (SCLC). Lowery was the chairman in charge of coordinating the 1965 Selma to Montgomery March and on January 20, 2009, he delivered the benediction during inauguration of Barack Obama as the 44th—and first African American—president of the United States.

October 7

1934

Playwright-poet Amiri Baraka is born under the name LeRoi Jones in Newark, New Jersey. As LeRoi Jones, Baraka became a well-known beat poet working out of New York's Greenwich Village neighborhood. But as he became part of Harlem's Black Arts Movement, Baraka started promoting a Black Nationalist literature. He returned to his roots after the 1967 rebellion in Newark, New Jersey, and created the NewArk Community Movement.

The Harlem Black Arts experiment inspired the development of a national Black Arts Movement and the establishment of some 800 black theaters and culture centers in the United States. Writers and artists in dozens of cities began to assemble to build alternative institutions modeled after the Harlem Black Arts Repertory Theater/School, blending the Black Arts and Black Power. Between 1966 and 1967, the Black Arts Movement spread quickly through a number of important black arts festivals and conventions. In 1966, Baraka organized a black arts festival in Newark, New Jersey, featuring Stokely Carmichael, the leading proponent of Black Power, and Harold Cruse, the foremost theorist of cultural nationalism; that event was important to the development of

Baraka's own cultural troupe, the Spirit House Movers and Players in Newark. The development of Black Arts West in San Francisco drew together Ed Bullins, Jayne Cortez, Marvin X, and Amiri Barake as well as Eldridge Cleaver of the Black Panther Party. Meanwhile two black arts conventions in Detroit mobilized artists and writers in the Midwest. Dudley Randall reported that perhaps 300 people attended the first Blacks Arts Convention in Detroit, held June 24–26, 1966, at the Central United Church of Christ. He explained that the scope of the convention "went beyond the arts, for in addition to workshops on literature, music, art, and . . . drama, there were workshops on education, religion, [black] history, and politics." This convention had national influence because people came "from most of the major cities across the nation."

Source: From Komozi Woodard. *A Nation Within a Nation: Amiri Baraka (LeRoi Jones) and Black Power Politics.* Chapel Hill, NC: University of North Carolina Press, 1999, p. 66.

Books

Baraka, Amiri. *The Autobiography of Leroi Jones.* Chicago, IL: Lawrence Hill Books, 1997. Baraka's autobiography looks at his youth in Newark and his transformation into a leader of the Black Arts Movement.

Jones, LeRoi. *Dutchman and the Slave: Two Plays.* New York, NY: Harper Perennial, 1971. Book contains the texts of two of Baraka's most famous plays.

Websites

Amiri Baraka's official Website. http://www .amiribaraka.com/.

Modern American Poetry has a page dedicated to Amiri Baraka. http://www.english.illinois.edu/ maps/poets/a_f/baraka/baraka.htm.

Also Noteworthy

1897

Elijah Muhammad is born Robert Poole in Sandersville, Georgia. Muhammad served as the leader of the Nation of Islam (the so-called Black Muslims) from 1934 until his death in 1975.

1967

Olympic Project for Human Rights (OPHR) was an organization established by Black athletes, including the Black Power Olympians Tommie Smith and John Carlos, alongside sociologist Harry Edwards. OPHR aimed to protest racial segregation and to support the African American struggle for human rights.

October 8

1941

Jesse Louis Jackson, Sr., is born on October 8, in Greenville, South Carolina, to Helen Burns. Helen was only 16 years old when she gave birth to Jesse, who was given the name Jesse Louis Burns. Jesse's biological father, Noah Louis Robinson, a former boxer, was married to a different woman when Jesse was born and he never took part in his son's life. When Jesse's grandmother married Charles Henry Jackson in 1943, they adopted Jesse and he took on their surname. Jesse Jackson went on to become an important civil rights activist and Baptist minister and later ran campaigns for the Democratic presidential nomination in 1984 and 1988. Jackson served as "shadow senator" for the District of Columbia from 1991 to 1997 and founded and later merged two organizations that became known as Rainbow/Operation PUSH (People United to Save Humanity).

Jackson began to revive and invigorate a Rainbow Coalition based on common economic interests of poor, low- and middle-income Americans by appealing directly to workers and farmers and articulating their fears and concerns. Because the economy of 1988 was still clinging precariously to the edges of the artificial credit-card prosperity of the Reagan era, it was difficult for Jackson to break through all the barriers of race and age. However, he came a long way toward overcoming white voters' fear of an African American as president of the United States. His success with them bodes well for the success of a long-term progressive strategy.

Source: From Jesse Jackson and Frank Clemente. Keep Hope Alive: Jesse Jackson's 1988 Presidential Campaign. Brooklyn, NY: South End Press, 1989, pp. 3–4.

Books

Jackson, Jesse with Roger D. Hatch and Frank E. Watkins. *Straight from the Heart.* Minneapolis, MN: Fortress Press, 1987. Book looks at Jesse Jackson's views on human rights, presidential politics, and religion.

Stone, Eddie. *Jesse Jackson.* Los Angeles, CA: Holloway House Publishing, 1988. Biography of Jesse Jackson includes a look at his role in the Civil Rights Movement and his later move toward being a presidential candidate.

Websites

Jesse Jackson and the Democratic Party. http://www.ellabakercenter.org/blog/2011/07/jesse-jackson-and-the-democratic-party/.

Rainbow PUSH Coalition. http://www.rainbowpush.org/.

Also Noteworthy

1930

Faith Ringgold is born in Harlem, New York. As an artist and writer, Ringgold is best known for her narrative quilts that depict the lives of African Americans, particularly those living in the traditionally Black neighborhood of Harlem, New York.

October 9

1894

The first African American military pilot, Eugene Jacques Bullard is born in Columbus, Georgia. When Bullard hopped a freighter to Europe, he ended up in France, where he joined the Foreign Legion, rose to the rank of corporal, and received the Croix de Guerre for his bravery. In World War I, he requested to join the French Air Force and became the first-ever Black fighter pilot, shooting down many enemy German fighters. Bullard's exploits were closely following by the Black press in the United States, and he became an inspiration for other young Blacks who wanted to be able to fly in airplanes.

Bullard was discharged from the French Army on Oct. 24, 1919. His World War I decorations included the Legion of Honor, Chevalier, Medal Militaire, Croix de Guerre, Croix de Combattant 1914–1918, Medaille Commemoration Francaise 1914–1918, and Medaille Verdun.

Source: From Anne Cipriano Venzon and Paul L. Miles. The United States in the First World War: An Encyclopedia. London, England: Taylor & Francis, 1999, p. 110.

Books

Carisella, P. J. and James W. Ryan. *The Black Swallow of Death: The Incredible Story of Eugene Jacques Bullard, the World's First Black Combat Aviator.* New York: Marlborough, 1972.
Lloyd, Craig. *Eugene Bullard: Black Expatriate in Jazz-Age Paris.* Atlanta: Univeristy of Georgia Press, 2006.

Websites

The National Museum of the U.S. Air Force has a bio of Eugene Bullard. http://www.nationalmuseum.af.mil/factsheets/factsheet.asp?id=705.
A digitized version of The Freedmen's Record, April, 1865, 49–56 and 61–65. http://mac110.assumption.edu/aas/reports/fr4-65.html.

Also Noteworthy

1888

O.B. Clare receives U.S. Patent No. 390,753 for his trestle.

1974

Frank Robinson becomes the first African American to manage a Major League Baseball team when he is named coach of the Cleveland Indians. 1974

October 10

1964

Clarence 13X founds the Five-Percent Nation of Gods and Earths (NGE) among the youth of Harlem, New York. Clarence 13X was born in Danville, Virginia, under the name Clarence Jowars Smith but was given the name Clarence 13X when he joined the Nation of Islam (NOI). Clarence 13X learned the "Supreme Wisdom Lessons" of the NOI. Part of the NGE's name comes from the NOI belief that 85 percent of Black people are docile and 10 percent have sold their souls, but there remain 5 percent of African Americans who can see past the lies they face daily, and they have a duty to teach knowledge to the rest of the population. After separating from the NOI, Clarence 13X spread an understanding of the Supreme Wisdom that became NGE teachings—that the Black man is God and that Black people were the earth's original inheritors.

The Nation of Gods and Earths (N.G.E.) could be considered a 'child' or yet another faction of the Nation of Islam, but the prevalence of this organization has made it more of a phenomenon than just an isolated party. The N.G.E. started with a man by the name of Clarence 13X, also known as "The Father" or "Allah," who took the supreme wisdom of Master Fard out of the confines of the Nation of Islamd and put it in the hands of the masses of youth throughout Harlem. The Father took the very same lessons that he had learned within the Nation for four years and put them in the hands of the 'babies' so that they too could learn the truth of their past. According to the Nation of Islam, Clarence 13x was expelled from the temple due to the fact that he did not follow the restrictive laws of The Nation of Islam. Persons within the Nation of Gods and Earths say that

> *"Allah" worked diligently to achieve the position of Lieutenant within the Nation and was expelled for his fiery teachings.*
>
> Source: From Abdul Noor. *The Supreme Understanding: The Teachings of Islam in North America*. Lincoln, NE: iUniverse, 2002, p. 165.

Books

Allah, Wakeel. *In the Name of Allah: A History of Clarence 13X and the Five Percenters*. New York, NY: Printing Systems, 2007. A definitive history of the founding and establishing principles of the Five-Percent Nation.

C'BS Alife Allah and Lord Jamar of Brand Nubian (FRW). *Knowledge of Self: A Collection of Wisdom on the Science of Everything in Life*. New York, NY: Supreme Design, 2009. Includes information on the studies and beliefs of Five Percenters.

Websites

AN provides information about the Five-Percent Nation. http://www.allahsnation.net.

NGE Links (Nation of Gods and Earths). http://www.g-linenationwear.com/nation_of_gods_and_earths_links.htm.

The Federal Bureau of Investigation maintained a file, "Clarence Smith (AKA 13x)." http://vault.fbi.gov/Clarence%20Smith%20%28aka%2013x%29.

Also Noteworthy

1899

Isaac R. Johnson receives U.S. Patent No. 634,823 for his bicycle frame.

1917

The Jazz pianist Thelonious Sphere Monk is born in Rocky Mount, North Carolina. After his mother moved the family to Harlem, New York, Monk studied the piano and became one of the most acclaimed jazz pianists.

1961

Otis Milton Smith is appointed to serve on the Michigan Supreme Court.

October 11

1911

The National Urban League (NUL) is founded in New York City, New York. The NUL consisted of the merger of three groups, the Committee on Urban Conditions, the Committee for Improving the Industrial Conditions of Negroes in New York, and the National League for the Protection of Colored Women. George Edmund Haynes (a Fisk University graduate and the first African American to earn a PhD from Columbia University) served as the NUL's first executive secretary, from 1910 through 1917.

> *By October 1911 three key groups had come together to work on the urban conditions of African Americans: Francis Kellor's National League for the Protection of Colored Women (NLPCW); the Committee for Improving the Industrial Conditions for Negroes (CIIN), and George Edmund Haynes and Ruth Standish-Baldwin's Committee on Urban Conditions Amongst Negroes (CUCAN). The newly formed organization was known as the National League on Urban Conditions Among Negroes (NLUCAN); later the name would be shortened to the National Urban League. With Haynes leading the charge, the racially integrated organization challenged the urban White elite to help alleviate the plight of urban African Americans by working with and supporting African American-based organizations. The prevailing ideology was that Whites were to work with Blacks for their mutual advantage and advancement rather than view them as a problem. Additionally, this urban White elite began to fund the educational activities of individuals entering into the social work profession. Upon graduation these individuals were placed in jobs within the Black community in which they provided direct services.*
>
> Source: From Karin L. Stanford. *Black Political Organizations in the Post-Civil Rights Era*. New

Brunswick, NJ: Rutgers University Press, 2002, p. 42.

Books

National Urban League. *Records of the National Office of the National Urban League for the Period 1910–60*. Washington, DC: Library of Congress, 1976. Fifty years of documents from the offices of the National Urban League.

Weiss, Nancy Joan. *The National Urban League, 1910–1940*. New York, NY: Oxford University Press, 1974. Profiles the founding and growth of the National Urban League.

Websites

National Urban League. http://www.nul.org/.

National Urban League entry in Encyclopedia Brittanica. http://www.britannica.com/EBchecked/topic/405560/National-Urban-League.

Also Noteworthy

1887

Alexander Miles receives U.S. Patent No. 371,207 for his improvements to the opening and closing of electric elevator doors.

1887

Granville T. Woods receives U.S. Patent No. 371,241 for his telephone system and apparatus.

1939

The National Association for the Advancement of Colored People organizes the Legal Defense and Education Fund.

October 12

1904

William Montague Cobb is born to Alexizne Montague and William Elmer Cobb in Washington, DC. Cobb was the first African American to earn a PhD in anthropology, and through his work as a physical anthropologist and anatomist, he studied the concept of race and showed how racism in the science of physical anthropology quickly became racist ideas that were later propagated in the wider society. Cobb's studies helped push the NAACP forward in its efforts to gain civil rights for African Americans, and he would serve as president of the organization from 1976 to 1982.

> According to Cobb, it was clear that the social processes which make racial categories have physical and biomedical implications. To confront these issues he had the NAACP National Health Committee employ the same strategy that the LDEF was developing. Following in the LDEF's footsteps, the National Health Committee marshaled the prevailing scientific and social scientific evidence to prove that segregated hospitals and restricted access to health care must be eradicated. The National Health Committee took a legislative approach, however.
>
> Cobb was the architect of the annual Imhotep National Conferences on Hospital Integration, which he began in 1957. The conferences were jointly sponsored by the NAACP and the National Medical Association, and they attracted many of the top biomedical scientists, anthropologists, sociologists, public health officials, and legislators. President Lyndon B. Johnson even attended. The group convened for seven years until its goal, passage of the Civil Rights Act of 1964, was met. Cobb prophetically outlined a plan for national health insurance and assisted in drafting the 1965 Medicare Bill.
>
> Source: From Lee D. Baker. *From Savage to Negro: Anthropology and the Construction of Race, 1896–1954*. Berkeley, CA: University of California Press, 1998, p. 186.

Books

Bass, Amy. *Not the Triumph but the Struggle: The 1968 Olympics and the Making of the Black Athlete*. Minneapolis, MN: University of Minnesota Press, 2004. Book looks at the strong influence of Dr. Cobb's anthropological studies on the ideas of difference and similarity among athletes of African descent and white athletes.

Montague Cobb, William with Lewis E. Week. *W. Montague Cobb, in First Person: An Oral History*. Victoria, BC: AbeBooks/L.E. Weeks, 1983. Cobb looks back at his anthropological studies and their larger meaning.

Websites

W. Montague Cobb/NMA Health Institute. http://cobb.nmanet.org/.

Looks at Dr. Cobb's role in creating a graduate chapter of the Omega Psi Phi fraternity, which was dedicated to professional men studying at Howard University. http://www.dcques.com/?page_id=36.

Also Noteworthy

1932

Richard Claxton "Dick" Gregory is born in St. Louis, Missouri. Initially famed as a political conscious comedian and civil rights activist, Dick Gregory is also known as a knowledgeable vegetarian and nutritional consultant. Gregory ran against Richard J. Daley for the mayoralty of Chicago, Illinois, in 1967, and in 1968 he was the Freedom and Peace Party candidate for president of the United States.

October 13

1902

Arnaud "Arna" Wendell Bontemps is born in Alexandria, Louisiana, to Paul Bismark, a brick mason, jazz musician, and minister, and Maria Carolina Pembroke Bontemps, a schoolteacher. The Bontemps moved to California and Arna was raised in the Watts section of Los Angeles. As a poet and writer, Bontemps became a leading figure in the Harlem Renaissance after moving to the famed Black neighborhood in 1926. Bontemps was celebrated for writing or co-writing some

22 books, including *God Sends Sunday* (1931); *Black Thunder* (1936); *Father of the Blues: An Autobiography* (W. C. Handy, edited by Bontemps, 1941); *Story of the Negro* (1948) and *One Hundred Years of Negro Freedom* (1961, reprint in 1980), among others. After living in Harlem, Bontemps served as the librarian of Fisk University in Nashville, Tennessee, from 1943 to 1965, taught at the University of Illinois from 1966 through 1969, and curated Yale University's James Weldon Johnson Memorial Collection of Negro Arts and Letters.

ARNA WENDELL BONTEMPS (1902–1973). Although Arna Bontemps was physically removed from Louisiana at an early age, and in spite of his parent's desire to rid him of the implications of southern African American tradition, he maintained a lasting appreciation for his ethnic heritage. This admiration formed the basis for all that Bontemps wrote, and for his recurring themes: the return; race and protest; alienation and exile; religion and meditation; escape and revolt; the African American folk tradition; and the lonesome boy. His academic career placed him in the South, where he produced the bulk of his literary efforts; but his best artistic achievements were the result of his affiliation with the New Negro Renaissance.

Source: From Joseph M. Flora, Amber Vogel, and Bryan Albin Giemza. *Southern Writers: A New Biographical Dictionary*. Baton Rouge, LA: LSU Press, 2006, p. 35.

Books

Bontemps, Arna Wendell. *God Sends Sunday: A Novel*. New York, NY: Simon & Schuster, 2005. Bontemps's first novel to look at African American life in the Southern United States.

Bontemps, Arna Wendell, Langston Hughes, edited by Charles Harold Nichols. *Arna Bontemps-Langston Hughes Letters, 1925–1967*. Saint Paul, MN: Paragon House, 1990. Collection of letters between Langston Hughes and Arna Bontemps, who were both great friends and leaders in the Harlem Renaissance.

Websites

Arna Bontemps African American Museum is based in his hometown of Alexandria, Louisiana. http://www.arnabontempsmuseum.org.

Arna Bontemps, Faith Weaver. http://harlem renaissancepoets.wikispaces.com/Arna+W %C2%A0Bontemps.

ARNAUD WENDELL BONTEMPS (1902–1973). http://ww2.tnstate.edu/library/digital/Bontemp.htm.

1909

Arthur "Art" Tatum, Jr., is born to Arthur Tatum and Mildred Hoskins in Toledo, Ohio. Both of Tatum's parents were musicians and, although he was blind in one eye, Tatum became a virtuoso jazz pianist.

> *Tatum was a sort of deity to his fellow musicians —not just to pianists, but to players of any instrument. No practitioner of the music called jazz had (or has) such perfect technical command, in the traditional sense, as did Art Tatum. But it wasn't just his astonishing facility that inspired awe in his colleagues. It was his phenomenal harmonic sense, his equally uncanny rhythmic gift, and his boundless imagination. Technique was merely the vehicle through which he expressed himself. What others could imagine, Tatum could execute, and what he could imagine went beyond the wildest dreams of mere musical mortals.*
>
> *Source*: From Dan Morgenster and Sheldon Meyer. *Living with Jazz*. New York, NY: Random House Digital, Inc., 2004, p. 34.

Books

Lester, James. *Too Marvelous for Words: The Life and Genius of Art Tatum.* New York, NY: Oxford University Press, 1995. Biography of Tatum looks at his initiation into music and his wide influence.

Scivales, Riccardo. *The Right Hand According to Tatum: A Guide to Tatum's Improvisational Techniques Plus 10 Transcribed Piano Solos.* Holmes, PA: MusicBooksNow/Shacor, Inc., 1998. Book looks at Tatum's skilled use of right-hand techniques while playing stride piano.

Websites

Art Tatum playing Jules Massenet's "Élégie." http://www.youtube.com/watch?v=aNAJlq n0nO4.

Art Tatum playing "All the Things You Are." http://www.youtube.com/watch?v=_bPgf_ol XeE&feature=related.

Also Noteworthy

1876

Meharry Medical College is established as the Medical Department of Central Tennessee College of Nashville, Tennessee. Meharry became one of only a few African American medical colleges in the United States.

1901

Edith Spurlock Sampson is born in Pittsburgh, Pennsylvania. Sampson became an attorney and later served as a judge. In 1950, President Harry Truman appointed Sampson to serve as an alternate U.S. delegate to the United Nations. Sampson became the first African American to officially represent the United States at the United Nations.

1914

Garrett A. Morgan receives U.S. Patent No. 1,113,675 for his invention of the gas mask.

October 14

1896

Oscar McKinley Charleston is born in Indianapolis, Indiana. The seventh of 11 children, Charleston's father, Tom, was of the Sioux nation and his mother, the former Mary Jeannette Thomas, was African American. Known as "the Hoosier Comet," Charleston was 6 feet tall and 190 pounds and played center field. He even served 10 years as a player-manager in baseball's Negro National League from 1915 to 1945. Charleston had a lifetime batting average of .353 during his 27-year career.

> Although I only saw him play that one time back in 1936, from what everybody told us the best outfielder ever was Oscar Charleston. All-around. Field, run, throw, hit, Oscar could do it all. He managed for a long time and for several different clubs when his playing days were up. Oscar Charleston was as hard-nosed a manager as he was a player. He especially didn't like to hear a ballplayer complain. If the umpire called a bad strike or something like that (and you know how ballplayers usually do), well, you'd get no sympathy from Oscar Charleston. I saw him one time when he was managing Philadelphia, and they had a pitcher in there by the name of Bill Ricks. Ricks complained about a couple balls that he thought should have been called strikes. And he was out there kicking and carrying on, and Charleston went out there and talked to him. Charleston was pretty short-tempered, and you could tell he was getting hot. Then he snatched the ball out of Rick's hand, turned his back towards home plate, and threw the ball to his catcher as if to say he could beat him pitching backwards. And I'll tell you, the catcher didn't have to shift too much to catch that ball. He was just that way. Can you imagine Cito Gaston or Tommy Lasorda doing that today? The players wouldn't stand for it. Once Charleston felt that you were overdoing it and complaining too much, he just told them, "This is a game that you're supposed to play and play it rough and you ain't got no business complaining." He just figured you weren't supposed to be no baby out there. He wanted to know, was you a crybaby or was you a man. He was that type of manager. He was nice to talk to, he just didn't back down from nobody. He knew baseball.
>
> *Source*: From Frazier Robinson, Paul Bauer, John O'Neil, and Gerald Early. *Catching Dreams: My Life in the Negro Baseball League*. Syracuse, NY: Syracuse University Press, 2000, p. 144.

Books

Bak, Richard. *Cobb Would Have Caught It: The Golden Age of Baseball in Detroit*. Detroit, MI: Wayne State University Press, 1991. Includes a look at how Oscar Charleston almost single-handedly defeated the Detroit Tigers—of Ty Cobb fame—when he played with the St. Loius Giants.

Holway, John. *Black Diamonds: Life in the Negro Leagues from the Men Who Lived It*. Westport, CT: Meckler, 1989. Includes a biographical look at Charleston and his impact on baseball.

Websites

Oscar Charleston is profiled on "The Forgotten Leagues." http://www.theforgottenleagues.com/oscar_charleston_pp.htm.

Negro Leagues Baseball eMuseum looks at Oscar Charleston. http://coe.ksu.edu/nlbemuseum/history/players/charleston.html.

Also Noteworthy

1834

Harry Blair receives U.S. Patent No. X8447 for his corn-planting machine. Blair, who was born in Montgomery County, Maryland in 1807, was the second African American to receive a U.S. patent—and the first to be recorded as a person of African descent in the records of the U.S. Patent Office.

1964

At age 35, Martin Luther King, Jr., becomes the youngest man ever to win the Nobel Peace Prize.

2001

Ruth Jean Simmons takes office as the 18th president of Brown University; she is the first person of African descent named to serve as president of an Ivy League institution. Simmons had previously served as president of Smith College from 1994 through 2001, as a professor at Princeton University, and as provost at Spelman College from 1990 to 1992.

Thousand Oaks, CA: SAGE Publications USA, 2008, p. 40.

October 15

1837

Fannie Muriel Jackson Coppin is born enslaved. But when her aunt, Sarah Clark, saw how intelligent Fannie was, she earned money and saved the $175 needed to purchase Fannie's freedom. Fanny was later paid to work as a servant and used that income to study. She went on to attend Ohio's Oberlin College in 1860, and even while a student there, she spent her evenings teaching free reading and writing courses to other African Americans. After graduating in 1865, Fanny taught Greek, Latin, and Mathematics at the Ladies Department at Philadelphia's Institute for Colored Youth (which later became Cheyney University of Pennsylvania) before being named the school's principal. Fannie Jackson Coppin was the first African American woman to become a school principal. She would marry Reverend Levi Jenkins Coppin, a minister at Bethel A.M.E. Church in Baltimore, MD and, together, they founded a missionary school called the Bethel Institute in South Africa. Although Fanny Jackson Coppin died on January 21, 1913, the Baltimore, MD-based Fanny Jackson Coppin Normal School for the training of teachers was named in her honor in 1926; the school is now known as Coppin State University.

> ...At Oberlin, she studied Latin, Greek, French, and mathematics, and during her junior year was appointed a pupil-teacher in the college preparatory department. Although some fears were expressed about how students would respond to having a Black teacher, Fannie Jackson was so successful that she had to add classes and ultimately turn away some students.
>
> Source: From Linda C. Tillman, ed. The SAGE Handbook of African American Education.

Books

Jackson Coppin, Fanny. *Reminiscences of School Life and Hints on Teaching (African-American Women Writers, 1910–1940)*. New York, NY: G.K. Hall & Company, January 1995. As an educator, journalist, and activist for social and educational reform, Fanny Jackson Coppin writes about her work in the United States and in South Africa.

McDonnell, Peter. *Helping Others: The Story of Fanny Jackson Coppin*. Columbus, OH: Zaner-Bloser, Incorporated, 2005. This young-adult book looks at the life and work of Fannie Jackson Coppin.

Perkins, Linda M. *Fanny Jackson Coppin and the Institute for Colored Youth, 1865–1902 (Educated Women)*. New York, NY: Garland, 1987. This book looks at the history of the Philadelphia, Pennsylvania-based Institute for Colored Youth and the integral role Fanny Jackson Coppin played in promoting it.

Websites

Coppin State University features a biography of Fannie Jackson Coppin. http://www.coppin.edu/welcome/fjcoppin.asp.

The non-profit BlackPast.org has a write-up about the Oakland, California-based Fannie Jackson Coppin Club, an all-women's church group devoted to community service, which was named in honor of Coppin and her work. http://www.blackpast.org/?q=aaw/fannie-jackson-coppin-club.

"Fanny Jackson-Coppin, A Priceless Gift to Humanity," an article on Suite101.com by Maisah B. Robinson, PhD, is an homage to Coppin's life and work. http://www.suite101.com/article.cfm/african_american_history/40498.

1966

Huey Newton and Bobby Seale form the Black Panther Party (originally called the Black Panther Party for Self Defense) in

Oakland, California. Wearing guns, cameras, and law books, members were assigned with defending African American community residents of Oakland and San Francisco from police harassment, brutality, and murder. The group was founded on the principles of its "Ten-Point Program," a document that called for "Land, Bread, Housing, Education, Clothing, Justice and Peace," as well as exemption from military service that would use African Americans to "fight and kill other people of color in the world who, like Black people, are being victimized by the White racist government of America."

> It was mid-October 1966 when Huey and Bobby met up at the Oakland War on Poverty office, around the corner from the North Oakland Services Center, where Bobby worked and not far from where he lived. Huey and Bobby's organization and "political party" was about to be officially unveiled. Unlike any other association, this would be an organization founded on action, not merely talk and debate. The two young men were eager to construct a first draft of a document that would eventually define their new organizations goals and demands. A specific ten-point program would soon emerge, reading like a bill of rights, with its political and economic agenda, partly constitutional, and partly inspired by the Declaration of Independence.
>
> Source: From David Hilliard. Huey: Spirit of the Panther. New York, NY: Basic Books, 2006, p. 28.

Books

Hilliard, David, ed. The Black Panther. New York, NY: Atria Books, 2007. Book includes original articles and documentation about the rise and legacy of the Black Panther Party.

Hilliard, David and Lewis Cole. This Side of Glory: The Autobiography of David Hilliard and the Story of the Black Panther Party. Reminiscences of Hilliard about the foundations of the Black Panther Party; Hilliard was one of the first members of the Black Panther Party (BPP) and served as its chief of staff.

Websites

The Black Panther Party for Self-Defense. http://libcom.org/library/the-black-panther-party-for-self-defense.

BlackPanther.org features information, documentation, biographies, video, and more about the Black Panther Party. http://www.blackpanther.org/.

Also Noteworthy

1949

William Henry Hastie, Jr., is named a judge on the U.S. Circuit Court of Appeals for the Third Circuit.

1991

Clarence Thomas is confirmed as an associate justice of the U.S. Supreme Court, the second African American to serve on the nation's highest court.

2005

The Millions More Movement holds a march in Washington, D.C.

October 16

1968

U.S. Olympic team 200-meter race runners Tommie Smith and John Carlos go shoeless and wear black socks as they come up to the victory medal podiums. After winning first and third place in the 200 meter race at the Summer Olympics in Mexico City, the two dropped their heads and raised black-gloved fists to the sky in a Black Power salute during the medal ceremony when the "Star Spangled Banner" was played. Ostracized and often jobless upon their return to the United States, the two were not celebrated until 2009 when ESPN: The Magazine awarded them the Arthur Ashe Courage ESPY Award.

> *It was there that Smith decoded the symbols of protest. "The right glove that wore on my right hand signified the power within black America. The left glove my teammate John Carlos wore on his left hand made an arc with my right hand and his left hand, also to signify black unity. The scarf that was worn around my neck signified blackness. John Carlos and me wore socks, black socks, without shoes, to also signify our poverty."*
>
> *Source: From Richard Hoffer. Something in the Air: American Passion and Defiance in the 1968 Mexico City Olympics. New York, NY: Simon & Schuster, 2009, p. 177.*

Books

Hartmann, Douglas. *Race, Culture and the Revolt of the Black Athlete: The 1968 Olympic Protests and Their Aftermath*. Chicago, IL: University of Chicago Press, 2004. Book includes a look at Carlos and Smith and the reactions to their stance at the '68 Olympics.

Smith, Tommie and David Steele. *Silent Gesture: The Autobiography of Tommie Smith*. Philadelphia, PA: Temple University Press, 2007. Smith's autobiography contends that his gesture was a protest in favor of the human rights of all Olympic athletes.

Websites

Mexico 1968 contains a look at the Tommy Smith and John Carlos protest. http://www.historylearningsite.co.uk/Mexico_1968.htm.

From the Vault: black power shocks the Olympics. http://www.guardian.co.uk/sport/blog/2008/oct/14/olympicsandthemedia-athletics.

Also Noteworthy

1859

The radical African slavery abolitionist John Brown leads an attack on the U.S. federal arsenal at Harpers Ferry, Virginia (now West Virginia), that lasts from October 16 through 17. Brown led a group of some 21 men on the raid: their aim was to acquire weapons that they could take to enslaved Africans in the South. With weapons in hand, Brown planned to help enslaved Africans fight for their freedom. The raid resulted in two Blacks killed, two captured, and one escaped. John Copeland and Shields Green were hanged at Charlestown, Virginia, Dec 16.

1922

Leon Howard Sullivan, the pastor who would become the author of the Sullivan Principles, is born in Charlestown, West Virginia.

1973

Maynard Holbrook Jackson, Jr., is elected the 54th mayor of Atlanta, Georgia. He is the city's first-ever mayor of African descent.

1995

The Million Man March—which brings Black men together to share time in fellowship and unity—takes place on the Mall in Washington D.C. Organized by the Honorable Min. Louis Farrakhan, an estimated 1.5 million African Americans attended the event.

October 17

1711

Jupiter Hammon, who later becomes the United States' first published African American poet, is born. Hammon's father, whose name was Opium, knew how to read and made certain his son could read as well. Both were enslaved their entire lives, yet Jupiter was able to have one of his poems published in 1760.

> *The first published African American poet, Jupiter Hammon was a slave who belonged to the Lloyed Family of Queens Village, Long Island (now in Queens, New York City). His poetry celebrates his deep Christian faith, which, given his status as a slave owned by Christians, is perplexing to many*

modern readers. The issue of slavery rarely surfaces in his verse, except as background. In 1786, however, he treated the topic in his Address to the Negroes of the State of New York, in which he shows a willingness to bear slavery meekly (for now) but expresses his disapproval and calls for eventual emancipation.

Source: From James G. Basker. Amazing Grace: An Anthology of Poems about Alavery, 1660–1810. New Haven, CT: Yale University Press, 2002, p. 137.

three home runs on the first three pitches he saw during the final game of the 1977 World Series against the Los Angeles Dodgers. Reggie Jackson was born to Martinez and Clara Jackson in Wyncote, Pennsylvania, on May 18, 1946. Jackson played in Major League Baseball with the Kansas City/Oakland Athletics, Baltimore Orioles, New York Yankees, and California Angels. He maintained a career batting average of .262 and amassed some 563 career home runs.

Books

Hammon, Jupiter and Stanley Austin Ransom. *America's First Negro Poet: The Complete Works of Jupiter Hammon of Long Island.* Port Washington, NY: Associated Faculty Press, 1983. Edited selection of Jupiter Hammon's poetry.

O'Neale, Sondra Ann. *Jupiter Hammon and the Biblical Beginnings of African-American Literature.* Lanham, MD: Scarecrow Press, 1993. Critical examination of Hammon's poetry and religious leanings.

Websites

FamousPoetsAndPoems.com/Poets/Jupiter Hammon. http://famouspoetsandpoems.com/poets/jupiter_hammon.

University of Houston has posted selections from Hammon's "An Evening Thought: Salvation by Christ, with Penitential Cries." http://coursesite.uhcl.edu/HSH/Whitec/texts/AfAm/afampoetry/hammonevethot.htm.

Also Noteworthy

1888

Capital Savings Bank of Washington, DC, one of the first banks created to serve African Americans, is organized.

October 18

1977

As a member of the New York Yankees, Reginald Martinez "Reggie" Jackson hits

There is no finer example than Reggie Jackson, who on a single day in 1977 assured himself of the kind of notoriety reserved for special hitters. The fact that the feat occurred in a World Series at Yankee Stadium made it all the more prominent.

Three pitches, three different pitchers, three swings, and three home runs. An unimaginable feat, which rocketed the New York Yankees to the Series championship in the sixth game.

Jackson, of course, was a home run hitter of considerable note long before he earned himself the name Mr. October for his heavy hitting in the World Seres. In 10 previous seasons—one in a late-season callup in the last year of the Kansas City A's, eight with the Oakland A's, and one with the Baltimore Orioles—the sturdy Jackson had reached double figures in home runs nine times, once winning and once trying for the home run title in the American League.

Source: From Rich Westcott. Great Home Runs of the 20th Century. Philadelphia, PA: Temple University Press, 2001, p. 121.

Books

Macht, Norman Lee. *Reggie Jackson.* New York, NY: Chelsea House Publishers, 1994. Looks at the Hall of Fame career of Reggie Jackson.

Perry, Dayn. *Reggie Jackson: The Life and Thunderous Career of Baseball's Mr. October.* New York, NY: HarperCollinss, 2010. In-depth biography of Reggie Jackson looks at his popularity, skill, and the controversies around his character.

Websites

Reggie Jackson's (MONSTER) 3rd homer Gm. 6 1977 World Series (Oct 18 1977). http://www.youtube.com/watch?v=1hNJLVQNhhE.

The 44 Store—Authentic Premium Baseball Memorabilia. http://www.reggiejackson.com.

Also Noteworthy

1926

Charles Edward Anderson "Chuck" Berry is born in St. Louis, Missouri. As a musician, Chuck Berry is widely considered a central figure in the popularization of a form of rhythm and blues that came to be known as rock and roll. Berry gained fame for his hits "Johnny B. Goode," "Roll Over, Beethoven!," "Maybellene," and "Riding Along In My Automobile," among others.

1948

Playwright Ntozake Shange, author of *For Colored Girls Who Have Considered Suicide When the Rainbow is Enuf*, is born.

October 19

1859

Byrd Prillerman is the last of 17 children born to John Franklyn and Charlotte Prillerman in Shady Grove, Virginia. Prillerman was enslaved at birth, but went on to become a co-founder of the West Virginia Colored Institute (which was renamed the West Virginia Collegiate Institute in 1915 and the West Virginia State College in 1929; and, in 2004, it became West Virginia State University) and served as the institution's president from 1909 to 1919.

But through the efforts of Prof. Byrd Prillerman, A.M., and Rev. C.H. Payne, D.D., the Legislature established the West Virginia Colored Institute in Kanawha county, in 1891. This school was established to meet the requirements of the Morrill act of congress providing for the establishment of Agricultural and Mechanical Colleges.

Source: From West Virginia State Department of Education and Thomas C. Miller. *History of Education in West Virginia*. Victoria, BC: AbeBooks/ The Tribune Printing Company, 1904, p. 295.

Books

Johnson, Mordecai Wyatt, edited by Richard Ishmael McKinney. *Mordecai, the Man and His Message: The Story of Mordecai Wyatt Johnson*. Washington, DC: Howard University Press, 1997. Biography/autobiography of Howard University former president Mordecai Johnson includes a profile of Prillerman's influence in educating African Americans.

Shawkey, Morris Purdy. *West Virginia, in History, Life, Literature and Industry, Volume 2*. Victoria, BC: AbeBooks/The Lewis publishing company, 1928. Includes a look at Prillerman's efforts to establish an institution of higher learning for African Americans and a summer school for teachers in the city of Charleston.

Websites

Byrd Prillerman is profiled by the West Virginia Division of Culture and History. http://www.wvculture.org/history/histamne/prillerm.html.

West Virginia State University. http://www.wvstateu.edu.

Also Noteworthy

1900

The painter Henry Ossawa Tanner is awarded a silver medal at the Universal Exposition in Paris, France, for his 1895 painting "Daniel in the Lion's Den."

1943

Paul Robeson opens in *Othello* at New York City's Shubert Theater. The show runs for 296 consecutive performances.

1944

The U.S. Navy is opened to African American women.

October 20

1890

Jelly Roll Morton is born Ferdinand Joseph LaMothe to F. P. Lamothe and Louise Monette in New Orleans, Louisiana. As a jazz pianist, Morton became a seminal figure in jazz and a widely celebrated pianist and composer.

> *If any man ever lived who knew how to produce the sweet out of the bitters, it was Jelly Roll Morton. During these lonely years in Chicago when he was trying to scrape together "that second thousand" so that he could send for Anita, he set down in notes the flower of his companions, realizing at last the musical plans that had taken form in his mind in Storyville, and Jelly Roll Morton and his Red Hot Peppers produced the finest recordings of New Orleans music ever made. There may be more deeply emotional and moving jazz records than Black Bottom Stomp, Doctor Jazz, Sidewalk Blues, Grandpa's Spells, Shreveport, Turtle Twist, but none more subtly designed and brilliantly executed, none with such a rich rhythmic and harmonic texture, none touched with such true fire. Here Jelly Roll, an equally remarkable composer, orchestral leader and pianist, purifies and extends New Orleans hot tradition, while strictly abiding by its canons. His records outnumber his published compositions almost two to one, but, with a half dozen exceptions, all are his own tunes, a recording career topped by no one in jazz except the redoubtable Ellington. From the very first session these discs exhibit a harmonic finesse and a rhythmic variety which outshines those of other leaders.*
>
> *Source:* From Alan Lomax. *Mister Jelly Roll: The Fortunes of Jelly Roll Morton, New Orleans Creole and Inventor of Jazz.* Berkeley, CA: University of California Press, 1973, p. 193.

Books

Pastras, Philip. *Dead Man Blues: Jelly Roll Morton Way Out West.* Berkeley, CA: University of California Press, 2003. Fresh look at the biography of Jelly Roll Morton with new scholarly accounts and eyewitness narratives.

Reich, Howard and William Gaines. *Jelly's Blues: The Life, Music, and Redemption of Jelly Roll Morton.* Cambridge, MA: Da Capo Press, 2004. In-depth biography of the virtuoso pianist Jelly Roll Morton.

Websites

Jelly Roll Morton. http://www.wright.edu/~martin.maner/morton.html.

Jelly Roll Morton's "King Porter Stomp." http://www.youtube.com/watch?v=h8_2ISGOIjU.

Also Noteworthy

1898

The first African American–owned insurance company, North Carolina Mutual Life Insurance Company, is founded. In 1906, the NC Mutual Life Insurance Company famously moved to Durham, North Carolina's Parrish Street (which was known as Black Wall Street), where it became the largest African American–owned insurance company in the world.

1937

Juan Antonio Marichal Sánchez is born in Laguna Verde, Dominican Republic. Marichal played for Major League Baseball's San Francisco Giants, Boston Red Sox, and Los Angeles Dodgers. He won more games than any other pitcher during the 1960s, and was inducted into the Baseball Hall of Fame in 1983.

October 21

1917

John Birks "Dizzy" Gillespie is born in Cheraw, South Carolina. As a jazz trumpeter, Dizzy Gillespie is recognized as a pioneer of bebop and a major promoter of Latin jazz in the United States. Gillespie died on January 6, 1993, in Englewood, New Jersey.

> "Mr. Minton, who was the first black delegate of Local 802, wanted to head this club, and he put Teddy Hill in charge," recalled Dizzy in 1976. "He had Monk and Kenny Clarke (I think Kenny was the leader) and Kermit Scott and Joe Guy. Joe had worked in Teddy's band before. Then Charlie Christian used to come down every night and all of us used to congregate in Minton's and then after hours at the Uptown House. Those two places were the spawning grounds of our music."
>
> Source: From Alyn Shipton. *Groovin' High: The Life of Dizzy Gillespie*. New York, NY: Oxford University Press, 2001, p. 87.

Books

Gillespie, Dizzy with Al Fraser. *To Be, or Not . . . to Bop*. Minneapolis, MN: University of Minnesota Press, 2009. Biography of Dizzy Gillespie, with excerpts of interviews from Gillespie and other musicians.

Vail, Ken. *Dizzy Gillespie: The Bebop Years, 1937–1952*. Lanham, MD: Scarecrow Press, 2003. Illustrated biography of Dizzy Gillespie, featuring newspaper clippings, photographs, posters, and record reviews.

Websites

Nostalgia Cubana—Dizzy Gillespie en Cuba. http://www.youtube.com/watch?feature=player_embedded&v=mBCy7te9MF4#at=27.

Charlie Parker & Dizzy Gillespie—Hot House (1952). http://www.youtube.com/watch?v=Clp9AeBdgL0&feature=player_embedded#!.

Also Noteworthy

1872

John H. Conyers is the first African American admitted to the U.S. Naval Academy.

1912

Jazz tenor saxophonist Carlos Wesley "Don" Byas is born in Muskogee, Oklahoma. Don Byas is known as an innovator in both bebop and swing jazz styles.

1944

George Junius Stinney Jr., is executed in Columbia, South Carolina, for the murder of 11-year-old Betty June Binnicker and 8-year-old Mary Emma Thames, two white girls, of Alcolu, South Carolina. Stinney was convicted by an all-white jury for the crime; the jury deliberated a total of 10 minutes before reaching their decision. Only 14 years old at the time of his execution, Stinney was the youngest person executed in the United States in the twentieth century.

1948

Radio station WDLA in Memphis, Tennessee, airs *The Town Jamboree*, an R&B show and the first all-Black programming.

1979

The Black Fashion Museum opens in Harlem, New York.

1986

George Alcorn receives U.S. Patent No. 4,618,380 for his spectrometer.

October 22

1906

Three thousand African Americans demonstrate and nearly riot in front of the Walnut Street Theatre in Philadelphia, Pennsylvania, to protest a theatrical presentation of Thomas Dixon's *The Clansman*, a novel that glorified the Ku Klux Klan. While attending a performance of the play earlier that day, African

Americans seated in the segregated balcony had hurled eggs at the actors on the stage. By nighttime, protestors were out shouting against the play. Local clergy members took the lead in the protest, claiming that *The Clansman* depicted people of African descent as "beast[s] of the jungle" and that the play encouraged whites to lynch African Americans. After the clergy demanded a meeting with Mayor John Weaver, they were able to have the remaining scheduled performances of the play cancelled—at least until the following year. *The Clansman* book later became the basis for D.W. Griffith's racist film, *Birth of a Nation*.

Philadelphia Mayor John Weaver closed the play, and was sued by the Walnut Street Theatre for doing so:

No evidence has been produced showing or tending to show that the Mayor acted with any purpose other than the preservation of the public peace. A number of citizens complained to him that a play, called "The Clansman," was to be enacted, and that the probable result of the exhibition was to arouse a strong and hateful antagonism between two large groups of citizens assembled in and about a limited space, a great part of them in one building. Moreover, leaders of one group had issued a paper which could not be otherwise interpreted than as a call to lawlessness and violence.

. . . . . .

From all the evidence, we are satisfied that the play is a malicious libel upon a class of citizens, and in effect advocates their enslavement or destruction, despite of constitutions and laws and common humanity.

Source: From Pennsylvania Courts, Henry C. Titus, Robert Jones Monaghan, Theophilus Baker Stork, Martin V. Bergen, Meredith Hanna, John Cromwell Bell, American Bar Association. *The District Reports, Containing Cases Decided in the Various Judicial Districts of the State of Pennsylvania. v. 1–30: 1892–1921, Volume 15*. Victoria, BC: AbeBooks/E. P. Allinson, 1906, pp. 795–796.

Books

Davis, Andrew. *America's Longest Run: A History of the Walnut Street Theatre*. University Park, PA: Penn State Press, 2010. Includes a look at the controversial run of *The Clansman* at the Walnut Theatre.

Mayer, David. *Stagestruck Filmmaker: D.W. Griffith & the American Theatre*. Minneapolis, MN: University of Minnesota Press, 2009. Biography of D. W. Griffith includes a look at the Philadelphia protest against *The Clansman*.

Websites

The Clansman: a historical romance of the Ku Klux Klan (1906). http://www.archive.org/details/clansmanhistoric00dixorich.

Thomas Dixon, Jr.: Conflicts in History and Literature. http://docsouth.unc.edu/southlit/dixon_intro.html.

Also Noteworthy

1854

James "Jimmy" Allen Bland is born to free parents in Flushing, Long Island, New York. An accomplished composer, Bland was performing professionally by the age of 14 and soon become known as "the world's greatest minstrel man." He is known to have worked with several African American minstrel groups and written hundreds of songs, but Bland is most famous for composing "Carry Me Back to Old Virginny" in 1878. That song soon became the Virginia state song.

1936

Bobby Seale is born in Dallas, Texas. In 1966, Seale and Dr. Huey P. Newton co-founded the Black Panther Party for Self Defense and wrote the Black Panther Party Platform and 10-Point Program.

1953

Clarence S. Green, MD, becomes the first African American certified in neurological surgery in the United States.

1963

More than 200,000 students boycotted Chicago public schools to protest *de facto* segregation.

October 23

1947

The National Association for the Advancement of Colored People (NAACP) petitions the United Nations at Lake Success regarding racial conditions in the United States. W. E. B. DuBois, who served as the organization's director of special research, spearheaded the NAACP's 155-page petition entitled, "An Appeal to the World: A Statement on the Denial of Human Rights to Minorities in the Case of Citizens of Negro Descent in the United States of America and an Appeal to the United Nations for Redress." The document linked the history of racism in the United States to the treatment of people of color under colonial imperialism. It was delivered to the United Nations Division on Human Rights and debated by the Drafting Committee as they looked at how to design the United Nations.

The first petition to the United Nations was submitted by the National Negro Congress (NNC) in 1946. And it was not the only nongovernmental organization to submit one: by January 1946, the UN had received about a thousand petitions or appeals from such organizations around the world. A collection of scholarly articles, the petition described the social, economic, and political injustices faced by Black Americans and appealed for aid. Passed at the NNC's annual convention in Detroit, it was sent across town to UN Secretary General Trygve Lee, who happened to be in Detroit for the auto industry's Golden Jubilee. There was concern by some members of the NNC, particularly William L. Patterson, that the petition had been hastily created. Five years later, as executive secretary of the Civil Rights Congress, Patterson submitted We Charge Genocide, a petition that detailed the enormity of American racial

violence and exposed the complicity of local, state, and federal officials.

In 1947 W.E.B. Du Bois supervised An Appeal to the World, a petition submitted to the United Nations by the NAACP. In the introduction, he presented an overview of African American history stressing that slavery, disfranchisement, mob violence, and peonage had undermined democracy in the United States. "The disfranchisement of the American Negro makes the functioning of all democracy in the nation difficult," DuBois maintained, because it allowed the conservative south to rule the nation—"and as democracy fails to function in the leading democracy in the world, it fails to function in the world." DuBois warned that as the host nation for the diverse national representatives of the United Nations, (many of whom may be "mistaken for a Negro"), and as a world leader, the first obligation of the United States was to end the racial caste system. As the United States quickly moved into a position of control at the UN, however, it blocked any consideration of the domestic status of U.S. racial minorities.

Source: From Martha Biondi. *To Stand and Fight: The Struggle for Civil Rights in Postwar New York City.* Cambridge, MA: Harvard University Press, 2006, p. 58.

Books

Anderson, Carol Elaine. *Eyes Off the Prize: The United Nations and the African American Struggle for Human Rights, 1944–1955.* Cambridge, England: Cambridge University Press, 2003. Looks at how the NAACP took the opportunity to fight for the human rights of African Americans as the United Nations was being formed.

Plummer, Brenda Gayle. *Window on Freedom: Race, Civil Rights, and Foreign Affairs, 1945–1988.* Chapel Hill, NC: UNC Press Books, 2003. Includes a look at W.E.B. DuBois' writing of "An Appeal to the World" and his push to get it heard internationally.

Websites

Library of Congress has an online version of an original copy of "An Appeal to the World."

http://myloc.gov/Exhibitions/naacp/world warii/ExhibitObjects/AppealToTheWorld.aspx.
University of Amherst contains the DuBois' collection that has a copy of "An Appeal to the World." http://www.library.umass.edu/spcoll/ead/mums312_9.html.

October 24

1948

Kweisi Mfume (which means, "conquering son of kings") is born under the name Frizzell Gerald Gray to Mary Elizabeth Willis Gray and Rufus Tate in Turners Station, Maryland. Mfume was elected to serve as the Democratic congressman from Maryland's Seventh Congressional District in 1986, and he served for five terms—from the 100th through the 104th Congress. Mfume was the chairman of the Congressional Black Caucus from 1992 to 1994 and became president and CEO of the National Association for the Advancement of Colored People (NAACP) in 1996, where he served until 2004.

> A former member of a street gang, the African American Kweisi Mfume changed his life when he decided to complete school and, as he put it, make something of himself. He then became a radio announcer, city councilman, congressman, and president of the National Association for the Advancement of Colored People (NAACP). Mfume was born Frizzell Gray on October 24, 1948, in Turners Station, Maryland near Baltimore, to Mary Elizabeth Willis Gray and Rufus Tate. He was given the last name Gray, however, because he was raised by his stepfather, Clifton Gray.
>
> Source: From Neil A. Hamilton. *American Social Leaders and Activists*. New York, NY: Infobase Publishing, 2002, p. 265.

Books

Mfume, Kweisi with Ron Stodghill. *No Free Ride: From the Mean Streets to the Mainstream*. New York, NY: Random House/One World,

1996. Mfume's autobiography traces the troubles he had as a teenager and his decision to make something of his life.
Paterra, M. Elizabeth. *Kweisi Mfume: Congressman and NAACP Leader*. Berkeley Heights, NJ: Enslow, 2001. Biography of Kweisi Mfume looks at his work in Congress and with the NAACP.

Websites

Rep. Kweisi Mfume's answer to a question about the impact of race on a primary he was running. http://www.youtube.com/watch?v=sIKtFb56V3M.
Kweisi Mfume biography. http://www.biography.com/people/kweisi-mfume-12782299.

Also Noteworthy

1980

U.S. District Judge Patrick Higginbotham rules that Republic National is guilty of discrimination against African Americans and women.

2005

Civil rights activist Rosa Parks dies at the age of 92. Parks's body lay in state in Washington, DC's Capitol Rotunda before she was buried.

October 25

1992

Toronto Blue Jays manager Clarence Edwin "Cito" Gaston becomes the first African American to manage a team to the World Series of Major League Baseball.

> Cito Gaston belongs on a short list of baseball managers: he is one of only 21 who won multiple World Series. . . . After Toronto fired him in 1997, major league baseball took a collective pass on him for over a decade, until the Blue Jays tabbed him once more. Gaston is the only winner of multiple World Series titles unable to manage for as

long as he wanted. Why did the lords of baseball continually pass on a man who had as many world championships as Earl Weaver, Leo Durocher, Al Lopez, and Wilbert Robinson combined?

There is an obvious elephant in the room—race. Baseball does not have a particularly good track record hiring managers who, like Gaston, were too dark to play before 1947. It took over 25 years before the hiring of Frank Robinson broke that color barrier. By 1987, only he and Larry Doby had run a squad—and Doby lasted only 87 games. That year Dodgers GM Al Campanis said on television news show Nightline that blacks lacked the capabilities to be manager. Major league baseball responded to the furor Campanis created by setting up a program to aid the hiring of minority managers. Gaston was the first black manager hired after that incident.

Source: From Chris Jaffe. *Evaluating Baseball's Managers: A History and Analysis of Performance in the Major Leagues, 1876–2008*. Jefferson, NC: McFarland, 2010, pp. 212–213.

Books

Lapchick, Richard Edward. *100 Pioneers: African-Americans Who Broke Color Barriers in Sport.* Morgantown, WV: Fitness Information Technology, 2008. Includes a look at the quietly confident leadership Cito Gaston brought to the Toronto Blue Jays.

Staples, Billy and Rich Herschlag. *Billyball 2009: The Road to the Phillies-Yankees World Series.* Bloomington, IN: iUniverse, 2010. Contains a look at how Gaston helped turn the Toronto Blue Jays team around, after having thought that he was personally finished with baseball.

Websites

Cito Gaston Managerial Record—Baseball-Reference.com. http://www.baseball-reference.com/managers/gastoci01.shtml.

Cito Gaston Baseball Stats by Baseball Almanac. http://www.baseball-almanac.com/players/player.php?p=gastoci01.

Also Noteworthy

1892

L.F. Brown receives U.S. Patent No. 484,994 for his bridle bit.

1925

Emmett W. Chappelle is born in Phoenix, Arizona. After working as a biochemist, an exobiologist, and as an astrochemist, ultimately Chappelle worked as a remote sensing scientist with the Goddard Space Flight Center.

1940

Benjamin O. Davis, Jr., becomes the U.S. Army's first African American general.

1997

More than 2.1 million respond to the call for a Million Women March held in Philadelphia, Pennsylvania. This march galvanized sisterhood all over the world.

October 26

1900

La Unión Martí-Maceo is established by Tampa, Florida-based Afro-Cuban cigar workers under the name Los Libres Pensadores Martí-Maceo (The Martí-Maceo Freethinkers). The group was named in honor of Cuban War of Independence leaders Jose Martí and General Antonio Maceo Grajales. Los Libres Pensadores Martí-Maceo held their first official meeting at the home of Cuban immigrants Ruperto and Paulina Pedroso. They later merged with the Afro-Cuban group, La Unión, and adopted the name La Sociedad la Unión Martí-Maceo.

On October 26, 1900, Los Libres Pensadores Martí y Maceo was founded as an all-black Cuban organization. White Cubans retained control of the club they had previously shared, from which blacks were subsequently excluded. There is a curious silence that shrouds the details of how and why this split occurred. The minutes of Martí-Maceo do not record the reasons for its founding; Círculo Cubano's minutes of this period are lost; and the principals involved passed little lore about it on to their children. The only account was written by José Rivero Muñiz, who may have witnessed it firsthand but wrote about it more than fifty years later. His rendition blames Jim Crow, emphasized pragmatic consensus among those involved, and exonerates white Cubans of any suggestions of malice or cowardice. More contemporary authors, including ourselves, have questioned the honesty of this interpretation. If they really believed in Martí's ideals about Cuban solidarity, one reasons, they should have defied Jim Crow and stayed together.

Source: From Andrea O'Reilly Herrera. *Cuba: Idea of a Nation Displaced*. Albany, NY: SUNY Press, 2008, p. 134.

Books

Ervantes-Rodriguez, Ana Margarita and Alejandro (FRW) Portes. *International Migration in Cuba: Accumulation, Imperial Designs, and Transnational Social Fields*. University Park, PA: Penn State Press, 2011. Includes a look at the reasons behind the founding of the Libres Pensadores Martí-Maceo.

Lastra, Frank Trebín and Richard Mathews. *Ybor City: The Making of a Landmark Town*. Tampa, FL: University of Tampa Press, 2006. Book looks at the history of Ybor City and includes a look at the role played by mutual aid societies, like the Libres Pensadores Martí-Maceo.

Websites

Sociedad La Union Marti-Maceo. http://marti maceo.org/default.aspx.

The University of South Florida remains a digital archive of the Sociedad la Unión Martí-Maceo Records. http://www.lib.usf.edu/ aeon/eads/index.html?eadrequest=true&ead _id=U29-00053-M17.

Also Noteworthy

1899

William Julius Johnson is born in Snow Hill, Maryland. Johnson was known as Judy Johnson and "Mr. Sunshine" as he played third base with the Negro Leagues Baseball's Pittsburgh Crawfords.

1911

Famed gospel singer Mahalia Jackson is born in New Orleans, Louisiana. Jackson's recordings of songs like "His Eye Is on the Sparrow" and "Nobody Knows the Trouble I've Seen" gained her a broad audience. Mahalia Jackson was inducted into the Rock and Roll Hall of Fame in 1997.

1919

Edward William Brooke, III, is born in Washington, DC. In 1967, Brooke took office as a senator from the state of Massachusetts—he became the first African American elected to the U.S. Senate since the nineteenth century. Brooke served two terms in office, from 1967 to 1979, alongside Massachusetts Senator Ted Kennedy. Edward W. Brooke is born on October 26, 1919. In 1966, he won election as the U.S. senator from Massachusetts and became the first African American elected and re-elected to the U.S. Senate since Reconstruction. He served two terms.

October 27

1951

The National Negro Labor Council (NNLC) is founded in Cincinnati, Ohio. Some 900 African American labor delegates had met in Chicago the year before to attend the National Labor Conference for Negro Rights. The labor leaders had come together to denounce conservative-leaning elements in the country's labor movement who were so busy promoting anti-Communism that they started accepting racism and a lack of progress on civil rights. By October of 1951, the NNLC had 23 chapters across the country and initiated a campaign to have a Fair Employment Practices Committee (FEPC) clause included into all union contracts. The NNLC's "model FEPC clause" was modeled on a policy created under President Franklin Delano Roosevelt that ensured that contractors who won federal contracts did not own businesses that practiced discrimination in hiring, promotion, or wages.

The purge of communists and radicals from organized labor in 1947–50 was the principal reason for the decline in the AFL-CIO's commitment to the struggle against racial segregation. In the wake of the NAACP's stampede to the right, a left of center space on the political spectrum was open, and militant black workers took advantage of the opportunity. In June 1950, nearly 1,000 delegates met in Chicago at the National Labor Conference for Negro Rights. Robeson gave a moving plenary address which condemned the Cold War and supported détente with the Soviet bloc countries. . . . In 1950 and 1951, the committee helped to develop 23 Negro Labor Councils, each fighting to end segregated facilities at the workplace, expanding black job opportunities, and attacking racism in the unions. The militant Detroit Council, led by Hood, inspired the call for the creation of a new black progressive labor organization. In October 1951, the National Negro Labor Council was formed in Cincinnati, Ohio. The delegates at the convention represented unions expelled from the CIO for retaining communists, as well as members of both the AFL and CIO. Hood emerged as the president, and Young was elected executive secretary. Almost immediately, the National Negro Labor Council came under activists as the "tool(s) of the Soviet Union." Lester Granger of the National Urban League criticized the council as "subversive." In its brief history, the organization pressured to desegregate jobs in major U.S. firms; organized campaigns to increase

black workers' salaries and to upgrade their job ranks; led pickets against hotels and companies practicing Jim Crow; and challenged the unions to advance more black workers into leadership positions. The pressure against the Congress's pickets and protest activities was enormous. By December 1954, HUAC denounced the "pro-communist ideology" of the organization. It is true that communists participated in the National Negro Labor Council, but it no way were the desegregationist programs it carried out dictated or even directly influenced by the Party. By 1956, however, due to political pressures from the U.S. government, corporations and white labor leaders, the National Negro Labor Council had disappeared.

Source: From Manning Marable. *Race, Reform, and Rebellion: The Second Reconstruction in Black America, 1945–1990*. Jackson, MS: University Press of Mississippi, 1991, pp. 30–31.

Books

Foner, Philip Sheldon. *Organized Labor and the Black Worker, 1619–1981*. New York, NY: International Publishers, 1982. Book includes a look at the importance of the National Negro Labor Council.

Fullilove, Mindy Thompson. *The National Negro Labor Council: A History*. Victoria, BC: Abe-Books/AIMS, 1978. Comprehensive look at the founding and functioning of the National Negro Labor Council.

Websites

"The Role of the National Negro Labor Council in the Struggle for Civil Rights." http://www.politicalaffairs.net/the-role-of-the-national-negro-labor-council-in-the-struggle-for-civil-rights/.

Intro to Afro-American Studies includes a look at the National Negro Labor Council. http://www.eblackstudies.org/intro/chapter7.htm.

Also Noteworthy

1891

P. B. Downing receives U.S. Patent Nos. 462,043 and 462,096 for the letter box and street letter box.

1966

The "Freedom Budget for All Americans" designed by Bayard Rustin and A. Philip Randolph is introduced to the public at New York's Salem Methodist Church. A copy of the budget is available as a pdf: www.prrac.org/pdf/FreedomBudget.pdf.

1927

Ruby Ann Wallace is born to Gladys Hightower and Marshall Edward Nathaniel Wallace in Cleveland, Ohio. Her father and her stepmother, Emma Amelia Benson, raised Ruby in Harlem, New York. As the actress Ruby Dee, she worked in some of the most important African American films of the 1950s and 1960s. She was married to the actor Ossie Davis for 56 years, and the couple were well respected as producers, writers, and activists. They were close friends of both Martin Luther King, Jr., and Malcolm X and advocated for the dignity of Black people.

October 28

1937

Leonard Randolph "Lenny" Wilkens is born in Brooklyn, New York. Wilkens played for the National Basketball Association's (NBA) St. Louis Hawks and various other teams; he was a nine-time NBA All-Star during his 15-season career. After playing, Wilkens became a coach in the NBA for some 35 years: he famously served as the coach of the 1996 Atlanta Olympic Champion Men's Basketball team. Wilkens was inducted into the Naismith Memorial Basketball Hall of Fame as a player in 1989 and as a coach in 1998. In 1996, the NBA named Wilkens one of its 50 Greatest Players and one of the 10 Greatest Coaches in the league's history; he is the only person named to both lists.

Throughout a National Basketball Association (NBA) career spanning over four decades, Lenny Wilkens distinguished himself as a successful player, coach, and administrator. Wilkens began in the NBA as a first-round draft pick out of Providence College in 1960. He played a combined fifteen years for the St. Louis Hawks, Seattle SuperSonics, Cleveland Cavaliers, and Portland Trail Blazers. Wilkens became one of the first three African American player-coaches in the NBA in the 1960s era. He became head coach of the Seattle Supersonics in 1977 and the next year (1978–79) led that team to its only championship. Included among his numerous awards and accolades are an All-Star Game MVP trophy (1971), a Coach of the Year award (1994), and two Olympic gold medals (as assistant coach and head coach for the 1992 and 1996 games, respectively). In 1995, he surpassed the legendary Red Auerbach as the winningest coach in NBA history. His outstanding success as both a player and coach is reflected in his election as one of the Ten Greatest Coaches in NBA History, as well as one of the league's Fifty Greatest Players, on the NBA's fiftieth anniversary. He is the first African American to be inducted into the Basketball Hall of Fame as both a player (1989) and as a coach (1998). Most recently, he served as vice chairman for the Seattle SuperSonics, a position from which he resigned in July of 2007.

Source: From John C. Walter and Malina Iida. *Better Than the Best: Black Athletes Speak, 1920–2007.* Seattle, WA: University of Washington Press, 2010, p. 79.

Books

Klemash, Christian. *How to Succeed in the Game of Life: 34 Interviews with the World's Greatest Coaches.* Riverside, NJ: Andrews McMeel Publishing, 2010. Book includes an interview with and a profile of Lenny Wilkens.

Wilkens, Lenny with Terry Pluto. *Unguarded: My Forty Years Surviving in the NBA.* New York, NY: Simon & Schuster, 2001. Wilkens' autobiography looks at how he has shaped his life via playing—and winning—at basketball.

Websites

Lenny Wilkens Foundation. http://www.lenny wilkensfoundation.org.

Lenny Wilkens career highlights are featured on NBA.com. http://www.nba.com/video/channels/nba_tv/2011/10/20/20111020_lenny_wilkens_broll.nba/index.html.

Also Noteworthy

1798

Levi Coffin is born in Guilford County, North Carolina. Coffin was a respected Quaker and businessman but also used his home, located at 113 U.S. 27 North in Newport (Fountain City), Indiana, as a "Grand Central Station" for the Underground Railroad. Thousands of formerly enslaved African Americans stayed at Coffin's eight-room Federal style brick home before journeying on to Canada.

1920

Arthur Lee "Artie" Wilson is born in Springfield, Alabama. His mother, Martha Wilson, raised him in Birmingham, Alabama. Wilson played with the Negro Leagues' Birmingham Black Barons in 1948 and with the San Diego Padres of the Pacific Coast League (PCL) before playing with Major League Baseball. He was a professional baseball player for more than twenty years.

1981

Edward M. McIntyre is elected the first African American mayor of Augusta, Georgia.

October 29

1902

The Philadelphia, Pennsylvania-based Victor Talking Machine Company records three songs sung by the Dinwiddie Quartet. The Dinwiddie Quartet consisted of Sterling C. Rex (lead and first tenor), J. Clarence Meredith (second tenor), Harry B. Cruder (first bass) and James Mantel Thomas (second bass); their recording is the first of African American voices on a flat phonograph disc.

> Throughout the period of Reconstruction, financially strapped black institutions often formed vocal ensembles, the most famous of which was the Fisk Jubilee Singers, an eleven-member ensemble established in 1871, five years after Fisk University welcomed its first students. During the 1890s, many university jubilee ensembles began to shrink in size, performing and recording both sacred and secular material in four-part harmony. Recording for Columbia in 1895 and Victor in 1902, respectively, the Standard Negro Quartette from Chicago and the Dinwiddie Colored Quartet, comprised of students from the John A. Dix Industrial School in Dinwiddie, Virginia, made the earliest known recordings by African Americans quartets.
>
> Source: From W. K. McNeil. *Encyclopedia of American Gospel Music.* New York, NY: Psychology Press, 2005, p. 156.

Books

Brooks, Tim and Richard Keith Spottswood. *Lost Sounds: Blacks and the Birth of the Recording Industry, 1890–1919.* Champaign, IL: University of Illinois Press, 2004. Book includes a look at how the Dinwiddie Quartet came to record, after playing part in a traveling play called *The Smart Set.*

Lornell, Kip. *Virginia's Blues, Country & Gospel Records, 1902–1943: An Annotated Discography.* Lexington, KY: University Press of Kentucky, 1989. Includes a look at how the Dinwiddie Colored Quartet brought the sounds of Virginia's African Americans to a wider audience.

Websites

Dinwiddie Colored Quartet—Steal Away 1902. http://www.archive.org/details/DinwiddieColoredQuartet-StealAway1902.

The Dinwiddie Quartet—First Black Vocal Group to Make a Record. http://www.classicurbanharmony.net/dinwiddie_quartet.htm.

Also Noteworthy

1889

John Standard receives U.S. Patent No. 413,689 for his invention of an oil stove.

1924

Andrew Sturgeon Young is born in Dunbrooke, Virginia. Known for his sportswriting, A.S. "Doc" Young regularly published with the *Chicago Defender*, *Ebony Magazine*, and the *Los Angeles Sentinel*.

1947

The President's Committee on Civil Rights condemns the numerous racial injustices in the United States in a formal report entitled "To Secure These Rights."

1949

Alonzo G. Moron becomes the first African American president of Hampton Institute in Virginia.

1969

U.S. Supreme Court orders an end to all school segregation "at once."

October 30

1989

Frank L. Mingo dies of heart failure at the young age of 49. A famed advertising executive, Mingo was born on December 13, 1939, in McComb, Mississippi. Mingo and Caroline Jones co-founded the Mingo-Jones Advertising company in 1977, which in 1986 was renamed The Mingo Group. At the time of his death, The Mingo Group, Inc., was one of the United States' largest African American-owned and operated advertising agencies with billings of

$62 million a year. The Mingo Group was renamed the Chisholm-Mingo Group in 1996.

> *Originally founded in 1977 as Mingo, Jones, Guilemenot, the agency had at its inception three principals: Frank Mingo, Caroline Jones, and Richard Guilemenot. Each of them brought impressive industry experience from years of work at the executive levels of mainstream agencies. Mingo left a position as a vice president and management supervisor at McCann-Erickson, where he had recently overseen the product launch of Miller Lite beer. This was Mingo's second foray into agency ownership. He had originally partnered with Tom Burrell and Emmet McBain, but at the last minute had chosen the financial security of being an employee over the risk of ownership. Jones had served as a vice president at BBDO, where she had been the first black woman to hold that position at any mainstream agency. She had also been on the staff of the recently defunct Zebra Advertising and had briefly partnered with Kelvin Wall to set up the Black Consulting Group to guide companies on advertising and marketing campaigns to African Americans. For his part, Guilemenot had been an executive at Ted Bates and Company. But Guilemenot remained part of the new firm only for a few years, and when he left the firm shortened the name to Mingo-Jones.*
>
> *Source*: From Jason Chambers. *Madison Avenue and the Color Line: African Americans in the Advertising Industry*. Philadelphia, PA: University of Pennsylvania Press, 2008, p. 260.

Books

Biagi, Shirley and Marilyn Kern-Foxworth. *Facing Difference: Race, Gender, and Mass Media*. Thousand Oaks, CA: Pine Forge Press, 1997. Includes a look at how Mingo-Jones Advertising influenced the larger communities' understanding of ways to market to African Americans.

Strasser, Susan, Charles McGovern, and Matthias Judt. *Getting and Spending: European and American Consumer Societies in the Twentieth Century*. New York, NY: Cambridge University Press, 1998. Book includes a look at

Mingo-Jones Advertising and its impact on advertising to African Americans.

Websites

Funding Universe profiles the Chisholm-Mingo Group, Inc. http://www.fundinguniverse .com/company-histories/ChisholmMingo -Group-Inc-Company-History.html.

Advertising Hall of Fame profiles Former Chairman & CEO, The Mingo. Group and Muse Cordero Chen Frank L. Mingo. http://www .advertisinghalloffame.org/members/member _bio.php?memid=720.

Also Noteworthy

1895

Ossian H. Sweet is born in Orlando, Florida. Sweet received a medical degree from Howard University and moved to Detroit, Michigan. While working at Dunbar, Detroit's first African American hospital, Sweet purchased a home in an all-white neighborhood and famously fought off white attackers who tried to drive him and his family away. Today, the former Ossian H. Sweet House located at 2905 Garland Street in Detroit, Michigan, is a registered national historical site.

1916

Leon Day is born in Alexandria, Virginia. At 5 feet 9 inches and 170 pounds, Day became a top strikeout pitcher with the Baltimore Black Sox, Brooklyn/Newark Eagles, and the Baltimore Elite Giants of the Negro Baseball Leagues. Day appeared in a total of seven East-West All-Star games. On July 23, 1942, Leon Day pitched for the Newark Eagles and struck out 18 Baltimore Elite Giants to set a Negro National League record.

1922

Marie Van Britton Brown is born in Jamaica Queens, New York. Brown received U.S. Patent No. 3,482,037 on December 2, 1969, for a closed circuit television security system.

1933

Wallace Delaney Muhammad (Warith Deen Mohammed) is born in Hamtramck, Michigan. Muhammad became a minister in the Nation of Islam following his father, Elijah Muhammed.

1979

Richard Arrington is elected first African American mayor of Birmingham, Alabama.

October 31

1938

"Sister Rosetta" Tharpe records with Decca Records. Tharpe was born Rosetta Nubin in Cotton Plant, Arkansas on March 20, 1915. She was the daughter of Willis Atkins, who worked as a cotton picker and Madame Katie Bell Nubin, an evangelist singer with the Church of God in Christ (COGIC). Sister Rosetta began singing alongside her mother at a young age, and by the time she began recording, she had begun mixing church music sounds with the rhythms of jazz. Although her Gospel style was initially decried, it eventually became highly influential. Sister Rosetta Tharpe became the first Gospel singer to perform at both New York City's Apollo Theater and Carnegie Hall.

> *In the fall of 1938, Sister Rosetta Tharpe, accompanying herself on guitar, sang this modified version of "Hide Me in Thy Bosom." Some music reviewers referred to the song as a spiritual, but it was actually part of a new form of sacred music— known as "gospel"—that emerged in African American communities over the course of the twentieth century. Tharpe, a Pentecostal evangelist, began using gospel to reach the unregenerate as a young child in churches and at revivals, as well as on city streets. By October 1938, however,*

Tharpe had found new terrain on which to save souls. As her performance at New York's Cotton Club attested, this Pentecostal evangelist had turned to nightclubs and theaters. One black newspaper reported that Tharpe explained her decision this way: "She sings in a night club because she feels there are more souls in the nighteries that need saving than there are in the church." Moving from churches and revivals to nightclubs and theaters, Tharpe helped to secure a place for gospel in the commercial arena.

Source: From Beth Barton Schweiger and Donald G. Mathews. *Religion in the American South: Protestants and Others in History and Culture.* Chapel Hill, NC: UNC Press Books, 2004, p. 219.

Books

Jackson, Jerma A. *Singing in My Soul: Black Gospel Music in a Secular Age.* Chapel Hill, NC: University of North Carolina Press, 2004. Book looks at Sister Rosetta Tharpe's role in Gospel music and her impact on popular culture.

Wald, Gayle F. *Shout, Sister, Shout!: The Untold Story of Rock-and-Roll Trailblazer Sister Rosetta Tharpe.* Boston, MA: Beacon Press, 2007. Biography of the life and career of Sister Rosetta Tharpe.

Websites

Sister Rosetta Tharpe's "Didn't It Rain." http://www.youtube.com/watch?v=T0tnh0xeDzw.

Sister Rosetta Tharpe singing "Up above My Head." http://www.youtube.com/watch?NR=1&v=UNq8DejQRN8.

Also Noteworthy

1919

Marcus Garvey's Black Star Steamship Corporation—the Black Star Line—launches its first ship, the *S.S. Frederick Douglass*. Purchased with money received from donations from Universal Negro Improvement Association members, who received shares in the corporation, the *S.S. Frederick Douglass* sailed from Harlem's 125th Street Pier.

November

November 1

1969

"Black Solidarity Day" is first observed. "Black Solidarity Day" is the day prior to U.S. general elections in which people of African descent throughout the United States abstain from participation in the social, political, and economic affairs of the nation. By their absence Blacks and others peacefully oppose racism, social, and civil injustices. The day can fall at any time during the first week of November. Its founder—the former professor, playwright, author, and community activist Dr. Carlos E. Russell, founded the day based on the play *A Day of Absence* by Douglas Turner Ward.

...Carlos Russell, the holiday's founder, used another barometer of measuring Black Solidarity Day's success: the spirit of a growing closing ranks philosophy associated with the Black Power Movement:

Black people don't need the approval of the white community to celebrate our holidays, be they Dr. King's or Malcolm X's. Black Solidarity Day was our day, and even if those black people who did not participate this time will think long and hard about not participating on future days. Black people have tremendous power when we act in unison, and we hope that the momentum and the spirit of Black Solidarity Day will continue during the many days of solidarity we must plan for the future.

Russell was right. Black Solidarity Day did not need the support of whites. It continued to grow through the 1970s, spreading to other cities like Boston and Philadelphia. Like New York, the Boston Black Solidarity Day was held on the first Monday in November. Sometimes black Boston merged their Black Solidarity Day with Malcolm X Day on May 19—Malcolm X's birthday. It was befitting, many in the Boston black community thought, to sometimes merge the new Black Solidarity Day with the memory of a man whose service to African-Americans and blacks in the diaspora often focused on the concept of solidarity. In support of Malcolm X Day on May 19, 1970, a Black Solidarity Day parade in the South End section of Boston was organized by local community activist Calvin Hicks and the Boston Black United Front. The parade route traveled up Warren Avenue to Blue Hill Avenue, proceeding across Seaver Street and terminating at Franklin Park. The parade procession played some of Malcolm's famous speeches that underscored the theme of solidarity. Whether on the first Monday in November or on Malcolm X's birthday, the Black Solidarity Day remained a fixture of the northeast black protest calendar, giving African-Americans a chance to be heard, if not on Election Day with their vote, then certainly with their voice a day before.

Source: From Keith A. Mayes. *Kwanzaa: Black Power and the Making of the African-American Holiday Tradition*. New York, NY: Taylor & Francis, 2009, pp. 37–38.

Books

Brager, George, Harry Specht, and James L. Torczyner. *Community Organizing*. New York, NY: Columbia University Press, 1987. Book includes a look at the impact of absenteeism in making Black Solidarity Day a powerful tool in organizing.

Jackson, Gerald G. *We're Not Going to Take It Anymore*. Silver Spring, MD: Beckham Publications Group, Inc., 2005. Book includes a look at the impact of Black Solidarity Day on Africana and Black Studies departments at universities across the nation.

Websites

How much do you know about Black Solidarity Day? http://www.highbeam.com/doc/1P1-23 20712.html.

Black Solidarity Day 1972. http://openvault .wgbh.org/catalog/sbro-mla000944-black -solidarity-day-1972.

Also Noteworthy

1777

The African Free School of New York City is opened.

1872

Three African Americans are elected to major offices in Louisiana elections: C.C Antoine, lieutenant governor; P.G. Deslonde, secretary of state; W.B. Brown, superintendent of public education.

1887

Thirty-seven striking Louisiana sugar workers are murdered when Louisiana militia, aided by bands of "prominent citizens," shoot unarmed African American workers trying to get a dollar-per-day wage. Two of the leaders of the strike are lynched.

1898

C. W. Allen receives U.S. Patent No. 613,436 for a self leveling table.

1910

W.E.B. DuBois begins publication of the NAACP's monthly magazine, *The Crisis*.

1915

James Milton Turner, who was appointed by President Ulysses S. Grant to serve as Consul to Liberia in 1871, died.

1917

Margaret Taylor-Burroughs (nee Margaret Taylor) is born in St. Rose, Louisiana. An artist and activist, Taylor-Burroughs is credited with co-founding the Ebony Museum of Negro History and Art. The Ebony Museum was later renamed the DuSable Museum of African American History in Chicago, Illinois.

1945

John H. Johnson publishes the first issue of *Ebony* magazine, which eventually sold 25,000 copies. *Ebony* became a monthly publication that focused on the lives of successful African Americans. The magazine became the first to feature models of African descent posing in advertisements that showcased them driving cars and drinking soft drinks.

1951

Jet magazine is founded by the publisher of *Ebony* magazine, John H. Johnson.

1991

Judge Clarence Thomas is formally seated as the 106th associate justice of the U.S. Supreme Court.

November 2

1903

After she was elected to head the African American benevolent society, the Independent Order of St. Luke, in 1899, Maggie Lena Walker reorganizes many of the group's programs. Walker pushed the Richmond, Virginia-based Order to open the St. Luke Penny Savings Bank in Richmond, Virginia. It established the weekly newspaper, the *St. Luke Herald*, and a department store called the St. Luke Emporium.

When the St. Luke Penny Savings Bank came into existence, Maggie Lena Walker became, most historians agree, the first woman bank president in America. Later, because of new regulatory laws, the bank was separated from the order. At that point, St. Luke's became primarily an insurance company. The St. Luke Bank and Trust Company, as it was now called, merged with other black banks to become the Consolidated Bank and Trust Company, with Maggie Walker as chairman of the board. The bank still thrives today.

Source: From Darlene Clark Hine and Kathleen Thompson. *A Shining Thread of Hope: The History of Black Women in America.* New York, NY: Random House Digital, Inc., 1999.

Books

Daniel, Sadie Iola and Hallie Quinn Brown. *Women Builders.* Boston, MA: G.K. Hall, 1997. Book includes a look at Walker's founding of the St. Luke Penny Savings Bank.

Hoffman, Steven J. *Race, Class and Power in the Building of Richmond, 1870–1920.* Jefferson, NC: McFarland, 2004. Book looks at how St Luke's Penny Savings bank became one of the strongest symbols of African American economic independence in Richmond.

Websites

The Federal Reserve System profiles the St. Luke Penny Savings Bank. http://www.fedpartnership.gov/minority-banking-timeline/st-luke.cfm.

"Maggie Walker: A Rich Legacy for the Black Woman Entrepreneur." http://www.businessweek.com/smallbiz/news/coladvice/reallife/rl990706r.htm.

Also Noteworthy

1920

Five African Americans and two whites are killed in Ocoee, Florida, after whites riot to protest that fact that African Americans are registering to vote. Ocoee's African American community consisted of some 495 people, and months earlier, Mose Norman and Julius "July" Perry—two local Black landowners—spearheaded Black voter registration. When Norman and Perry tried to vote on November 2, they find their names not listed and after protesting were pistol-whipped. The Klan ultimately gathered to try to lynch both

men and ended up burning down some African American homes, two churches, and a Masonic Lodge. Klan members lynched Julius Perry, and Mose Norman fled to New York City, where he lived until 1949. After all of the land owned by African Americans, the lots were sold off to other whites for $1.50 an acre.

1954

Charles C. Diggs is elected Michigan's first African American congressman.

1953

Hulan Jack becomes the first African American to serve as the borough president of Manhattan, New York. Jack was sworn into office on December 31, 1953.

1954

Charles C. Diggs, Jr., is elected to serve as the state of Michigan's first congressman of African descent.

1958

World-renowned opera singer, Shirley Verrett, makes her debut in New York City.

1969

Howard N. Lee and Charles Evers are elected the first African American mayors of Chapel Hill, North Carolina, and Fayette, Mississippi respectively.

1982

The Pan-Africanist Rayford Whittingham Logan dies and joins his ancestors in Washington, DC. He was an educator, historian, and author of numerous books on African Americans, including the *Dictionary of American Negro Biography.* Among his honors was a 1980 NAACP Spingarn Medal.

1988

The Martin L. King, Jr., Federal Building is dedicated in Atlanta, Georgia. It is the first federal building in the nation to bear the name of the slain civil rights leader.

1999

Daisy Bates, who is best known for counseling the "Little Rock Nine," joins the ancestors at the age of 84. Bates had been an activist and helped her husband publish the African American-oriented Arkansas State Press before serving as president of the Arkansas Conference of NAACP. Bates' work with the Little Rock Nine propelled her activism to the national level. The Little Rock Nine were the students who broke the color barrier at all-white Central High School in Little Rock, Arkansas, in 1957.

November 3

1883

Danville Riot takes place when whites in the conservative Democratic Party of Danville, Virginia, take over the racially integrated local government by force. Even though the integrated government had been popularly elected, some whites believed that Blacks would terrorize whites, and when a group of armed white men stalked the streets, four African-Americans were killed and the local Black community was disenfranchised.

Danville Democrats responded first with the pen. They printed and distributed statewide the Danville Circular, which detailed the alleged abuses they suffered from local government and appealed for deliverance. "We cry out to you in our affliction," the document pleaded to white Virginians, "to help us throttle this viper of negroism [sic] that is stinging us to madness and death." The circular defined deliverance as a vote against Mahoneites in the statewide elections of 1883. One of the authors was tobacconist William

P. Graves, a scout for Jefferson Davis in 1865 and president of the trustees of Roanoke Female College in 1883. His close friend, John T. Averett, was a keen supporter of this appeal.

According to Readjusters, the Democratic sword was mightier than the Democratic pen. As the November elections in 1883 approached, emotions in Danville ran at fever pitch. On Saturday, November 3, three days before the election, white Democrats and black Mahoneites tangled with fisticuffs and gunfire on Main Street. Four blacks were killed, and two whites and three blacks were wounded. Republican newspapers across the nation dubbed the confrontation the "Danville Riot" and the "Danville Massacre." By contrast, Democratic newspapers in Virginia reported the affair as proof that Mahoneism inevitably led to black domination and attendant corruption and violence. In the end, these accounts frightened white Mahoneites in Virginia into voting Democratic, thus ending Mahone's political supremacy.

Source: From J. I. Hayes. *The Lamp and the Cross: A History of Averett College, 1859–2001.* Macon, GA: Mercer University Press, 2004, pp. 34–35.

Books

Bailey, Frankie and Alice Green. *Wicked Danville.* Charleston, SC: The History Press, 2011. Book includes a look at the 1883 "Danville Fracas."

U.S. Congress. *Congressional Edition, Volume 2178.* Victoria, BC: AbeBooks/U.S. G.P.O., 1884. Contains testimony regarding the riot in Danville and the disenfranchisement of the town's Blacks.

Websites

Danville Riot. http://www.historyengine.richmond.edu/episodes/view/506.

Register of the William Mahone Papers, 1853–1895. http://www.library.duke.edu/digitalcollections/rbmscl/mahone/inv/.

Also Noteworthy

1896

John W. Hunter receives U.S. Patent No. 570,553 for his portable weighing scales.

1942

William Dawson is elected to the U.S. Congress.

1949

Larry Holmes is born in Cuthbert, Georgia. Hall of Fame boxer and entrepreneur, Holmes started boxing at the age of 19 and had an amateur record of 19 wins and 3 losses. He had his first professional fight in 1973 and won the World Heavyweight Boxing Championship in 1978. Holmes successfully defended his title 20 times, second only to Joe Lewis, who had 25 successful defenses before he lost the title in 1985. After several comebacks, Holmes fought his last professional fight in 2002 and retired with a record of 69 wins and 6 losses. He was inducted into the International Boxing Hall of Fame in June of 2008. Holmes published his autobiography, *Larry Holmes: Against the Odds*, in 1998. He has extensive real estate holdings in Easton, Pennsylvania.

1981

Thirman L. Milner is elected mayor of Hartford, Connecticut, becoming the first Black mayor in all of New England.

1983

The Rev. Jesse Jackson announces his candidacy to become the president of the United States.

1992

Carol Moseley Braun is elected as the first African American woman to win election in the U.S. Senate. Braun served as the Democratic senator from Illinois from 1993 to 1999.

November 4

1988

Drs. William (Bill) and Camille Cosby announce a $20 million gift to Spelman College. This is the largest donation ever made by an African American family to any college. In his remarks to newly inaugurated President Johnetta B. Cole, Cosby stated, "I want Johnetta Cole to understand the love that Camille and I have for this college, the love we have for women who, in spite of odds against them, come to this school to challenge themselves, to challenge the school, then to challenge what we call 'the outside world.'" Less than three months after this donation, the Cosbys donated another $1.5 million to Meharry Medical College in Nashville, Tennessee—which received $800,000—and Bethune Cookman College in Daytona Beach, Florida—which received $750,000.

> Within a year, Camille and Bill Cosby announced a gift of $20 million to build the Camille Olivia Hanks Cosby Academic Center and to endow three faculty chairs at the college. This was by far the largest single private gift ever made to a black college, and the largest by a black American family or individual to any college, and the largest by a black American family or individual to any college. It became the centerpiece in a capital fund drive that eventually raised $113.8 million.
>
> *Source*: From Henry N. Drewry, Humphrey Doermann, and Susan H. Anderson. *Stand and Prosper: Private Black Colleges and Their Students*. Princeton, NJ: Princeton University Press, 2001, p. 171.

Books

Cole, Johnetta B. *Conversations: Straight Talk with America's Sister President*. Victoria, BC: AbeBooks/U.S. G.P.O., 1984. Cole recalls the gift of $20 million from the Cosbys to Spelman College and looks at how it affected her administration of the school.

Gregory, Dick and Shelia P. Moses. *Callus on My Soul: A Memoir*. New York, NY: Kensington Books, 2003. Gregory includes a look at Bill and Camille Cosby's donation to Spelman College, and the power of their contributions to historically black colleges.

Websites

"Spelman College: Facts" includes notation of the Cosby gift to the school. http://www.spelman.edu/about_us/facts/.

History of Spelman College in Atlanta: A Private College for Women. http://www.sparkplugpeople.com/spelman-college-in-atlanta-a-private-college-for-women/.

Also Noteworthy

1879

Thomas Elkins receives U.S. Patent No. 221,222 for his improved refrigerating-apparatus design.

2008

U.S. Senator Barack H. Obama II becomes the first African American to be elected president of the United States. President-elect Obama will be the 44th president.

November 5

1956

Nat King Cole becomes the first African American performer to host his own television variety show. Born Nathaniel Adams Coles in Montgomery, Alabama, Cole was a celebrated siger and jazz pianist who had hits with songs like "Straighten Up and Fly Right," "The Christmas Song," "Unforgettable," and "Mona Lisa." The Nat King Cole show appeared on NBC (National Broadcasting Company) on Tuesday nights and, although popular, the show went off the air after only 13 months because no national sponsors would support a program that upset the sensibilities of white racists.

People were talking about the impact of television on the entertainment business, some even calling it "the evil eye" that emptied the clubs and the theaters and the nightspots as people elected to sit at home staring at a small screen. Nat, realizing the power of the medium, wanted his own television show. Nobody seemed interested by Carlos Gastel kept trying, and finally NBC whoed real interest with the result that Nat was set to star in his own fifteen minute show on Monday nights at 7:30 p.m. It opened on November 5, 1956, and the reviews were fabulous. Since there were no sponsors, NBC picked up the bill for a start, hoping that sponsor would be attracted shortly.

Source: From Marianne Ruuth. Nat King Cole. Los Angeles, CA: Holloway House Publishing, 1992, pp. 139–140.

Books

Epstein, Daniel Mark. *Nat King Cole.* New York, NY: Farrar, Straus and Giroux, 1999. Biography of Nat King Cole written with the co-operation of Cole's family.

Gourse, Leslie. *Unforgettable: The Life and Mystique of Nat King Cole.* New York: St. Martin's, 1991. Biography of Nat King Cole delves into his storied musical career and life.

Websites

Nat King Cole. http://www.nat-king-cole.org/.

Nat King Cole. "When I Fall in Love." http://www.dailymotion.com/video/xxh7y_nat-king-cole-when-i-fall-in-love_music.

THE NAT "KING" COLE SHOW—The Museum of Broadcast. http://www.museum.tv/eotvsection.php?entrycode=natkingcole.

Also Noteworthy

1836

Theo Wright becomes the first African American to obtain a theology degree.

1926

Negro History Week is inaugurated by Carter G. Woodson.

1968

Shirley Chisholm becomes the first African American woman elected to congress, representing Bedford-Stuyvesant, Brooklyn, NY

1968

Adam Clayton Powell, Jr., is reelected to serve as the representative of Harlem, New York, even after having been previously suspended by his congressional colleagues.

1974

George Brown becomes the first Black Lt. Governor in the United States (Colorado).

November 6

1816

William Wells Brown is born to an enslaved woman named Elizabeth and a local white plantation owner named George Higgins. Brown escaped to the North, where he became a prolific abolitionist lecturer, novelist, playwright, and historian. Brown's *Narrative of William W. Brown, a Fugitive Slave, Written by Himself* became a bestseller, second only to the narrative of Frederick Douglass. He also wrote *The Black Man: His Antecedents, His Genius, and His Achievements*, a book that named great Black people in history who defied the negative stereotypes about uneducated and uninspiring people of African descent. On January 30, 1858, Brown published the first African American drama, *The Escape; or, A Leap for Freedom*. He wrote the book *Clotel or, The President's Daughter: a Narrative of Slave Life in the United States*, a fictionalized account of a white enslaver raping an enslaved African woman. The book is based on stories about how Thomas Jefferson carried on a master–slave romantic affair with the enslaved, Sally Hemmings.

William Wells Brown, traditionally regarded as the first African American man of letter and the founder of African American literature in Misssouri, has always stood in the shadow of his more famous contemporary, Frederick Douglass. Two years after Brown's first autobiography, Narrative of William W. Brown, A Fugitive Slave, was published with considerable fanfare in 1847, a newspaper reporter characterized the author as "a good-natured fellow, of respectable talents, and one whose lectures are more calculated to do good than those of almost any other man"— any man except, the reporter went on to add, Frederick Douglass. In 1849 the first review of the most widely read slave narratives of the era, including those of Douglass and Brown, was published in the Christian Examiner, a popular liberal-minded journal. To Ephraim Peabody, the Examiner's reviewer, Brown's experience was the more representative, and therefore the more informative to those who knew little of the realities of slavery, did not seem to occur to Peabody....

Source: From William Wells Brown, edited by William L. Andrews. *From Fugitive Slave to Free Man: The Autobiographies of William Wells Brown.* Columbia, MO: University of Missouri Press, 1993, p. 1.

Books

Brown, William Wells. *The Black Man: His Antecedents, His Genius, and His Achievements.* Victoria, BC: AbeBooks /J. Redpath, 1863. Brown's look at the achievements made by people of African descent throughout history.

Brown, William Wells. *Clotel.* New York, NY: Lightning Source Inc., 2008. Brown's look at the impact of slavery at the personal level, in particular through the lives of Sally Hemmings and Thomas Jefferson.

Websites

William Wells Brown—1814–1884. http://www.nsm.buffalo.edu/~sww/0history/wwb0.html.

William Wells Brown, First African American novelist, 1814–1884. http://www.nbhistoricalsociety.org/williamwellsbrown.html.

Also Noteworthy

1880

George Coleman Poage is born in Hannibal, Missouri. Poage was the first African American athlete to win a medal in the 1904

Olympic Games; he won two bronze medals for placing third in the 200-meter and 400-meter hurdles, which took place in St. Louis, Missouri.

1858

Samuel Eli Cornish, the social activist, journalist, and co-editor of *Freedom's Journal*, the nation's first African American newspaper, dies.

1900

James Weldon Johnson and John Rosamond Johnson compose "Lift Ev'ry Voice and Sing," a song generally known as the "Black national anthem."

1930

Derrick Albert Bell, Jr., is born in the Hill District of Pittsburgh, Pennsylvania. Bell attended the University of Pittsburgh law school and later went to work with the U.S. Justice Department in the Civil Rights Division. Bell became the first tenured professor of African descent at Harvard University's Law School.

1962

Augustus F. Hawkins is elected to serve in the U.S. Congress as a representative of California.

1963

Edward W. Brooke is elected to serve as attorney general of the state of Massachusetts.

1968

Election results show that some 97 African Americans are elected to state legislatures, 7 are elected to mayoralties, and 400 are elected to local governments in the former Confederate states.

1990

Sharon Pratt Dixon (now Kelly) is elected as the first female of any race to serve mayor of Washington, DC.

November 7

1967

Carl Burton Stokes is elected to serve as the 51st mayor of Cleveland, Ohio, becoming the first person of African descent to be elected to serve as mayor of a major U.S. city. Stokes was born in Cleveland to Charles and Louise (Stone) Stokes on June 21, 1927. In 1962, Stokes became the first person of African descent to serve in the Ohio House of Representatives for the Democratic Party. Stokes lost a campaign to become mayor of Cleveland in 1965 but won it in 1967.

> On the afternoon following his election Stokes gave a victory address at the annual Future of Cleveland luncheon. His central theme was that the citizens of Cleveland had to work together to revitalize the city. Stokes asked the attendees to forget about the election and look forward to the future. He closed by stating prophetically: "I promise you a lot of interesting things will be happening in our town in the next few years."
>
> Stokes later acknowledged that, having campaigned so hard to get elected, he had no idea what to do when he took office. "We went into those sessions with wild-eyed dreams of the reforms we would wreak on this corrupt machine, only to discover that we didn't even know where the buttons were." He was also overwhelmed by the widespread publicity his election generated. "The first days of our administration were awkward, to say the least. My unprecedented victory had made me an international celebrity, and reporters from all over the country were descending on our office asking for interviews." Black residents also flooded city hall. "Everybody wanted to talk to me," Stokes recalled, "to see me, to touch me. So many people

who had spent their lives feeling disenfranchised by the system now felt that I was their mayor."

Source: From Leonard N. Moore. *Carl B. Stokes and the Rise of Black Political Power*. Champaign, IL: University of Illinois Press, 2003, p. 61.

Books

Johannesen, Richard L. *Contemporary American Speeches*. Dubuque, IA: Kendall Hunt, 2000. Stokes's speech "A Black President: When?" is presented along with a biography of Stokes.

Stokes, Carl B. *Promises of Power: A Political Autobiography*. New York, NY: Simon & Schuster, 1973. Stokes autobiography looks at the expectations he confronted as the first African American to serve as mayor of a major U.S. city.

Zannes, Estelle. *Checkmate in Cleveland: The Rhetoric of Confrontation During the Stokes Years*. Cleveland, OH: Press of Case Western Reserve University, 1972. Looks at the controversies that arose during the mayoralty of Carl B. Stokes.

Websites

STOKES, CARL B.—The Encyclopedia of Cleveland History. http://ech.cwru.edu/ech -cgi/article.pl?id=SCB2.

Carl B Stokes—A Black Suite. http://www.you tube.com/watch?v=XUZ8GwFKzIg.

Also Noteworthy

1841

Africans revolt on board the slave trader *Creole*, which was en route from Hampton, Virgina, to New Orleans, Louisiana. The Africans overpowered the *Creole* crew and sailed the ship to the Bahamas, where they were granted asylum and their freedom.

1967

Richard Gordon Hatcher is elected mayor of Gary, Indiana. Hatcher was born in Michigan City, Indiana, the son of Carlton and Catherine Hatcher—he was the youngest of 13 children. Hatcher served as mayor of Gary from 1967 to 1987.

1989

L. Douglas Wilder is elected governor of Virginia, becoming the nation's first Black governor since the Reconstruction. David Dinkins was elected mayor of New York City, the first person of African descent to govern this major U.S. city.

November 8

1904

Horace Mann Bond is born in Nashville, Tennessee. A noted historian and social science researcher, Bond earned a PhD in education from the University of Chicago and taught at Langston, Fisk, and Dillard Universities before becoming the first president of Fort Valley State College in 1939 and later the first African American president of Lincoln University. In 1953, Bond famously provided research to support the NAACP's court brief for the 1954 U.S. Supreme Court *Brown v. Board of Education* decision.

Horace Mann Bond was born in 1904. In 1923 he received a bachelor's degree from Lincoln University. The noted educator took his M.A. and Ph.D. from the University of Chicago. Early in his academica career, Bond served as a key teacher and administrator at Fisk University and Dillard University. Between 1939 and 1957 Bond served as university president at Fort Valley State College, and Lincoln University. In 1957 Bond became dean of the School of Education at Atlanta University. Throughout his tenure in academia, Bond worked to abolish segregation while continually trying to improve the education of African American students. His influence as an educator and renowned sociologis is still seen in his articles, addresses, and his innovative critiques of intelligence and aptitude testing.

Source: From Davis W. Houck and David E. Dixon, eds. *Rhetoric, Religion and the Civil Rights Movement, 1954–1965*. Waco, TX: Baylor University Press, 2006, p. 178.

Books

Bond, Horace Mann. *Negro Education in Alabama: A Study in Cotton and Steel*. Tuscaloosa, AL: University of Alabama Press, 1969. Publication of Bond's dissertation on education among people of African Americans in mid-twentieth century Alabama.

Urban, Wayne J. *Black Scholar: Horace Mann Bond, 1904–1972*. Athens, GA: University of Georgia Press, 2008. Biography of Bond looks at his life and his educational pursuits, including his concerns for the ways people of African descent were educated.

Websites

Horace Mann Bond (1904–1972)—Career, Publications and Scholarly Pursuits, Family Life. http://education.stateuniversity.com/pages/1796/Bond-Horace-Mann-1904-1972.html#ixzz1dXDi8Lid.

Horace Mann Bond Papers, 1830–1979. http://asteria.fivecolleges.edu/findaids/umass/mums411_bioghist.html.

Also Noteworthy

1898

Whites riot in Greenwood County, South Carolina, lynching many African Americans and followed by a riot for two days in Wilmington, North Carolina. A mob of whites, led by some of Wilmington's most respected and influential citizens, destroyed the offices of the state's only daily African American newspaper. Coroner reports confirm nine Blacks were killed; some estimate hundreds died. Scores of others were driven from their homes.

1920

Esther Rolle is born in Pompano Beach, Florida. As a stage, film, and television actress, Rolle became famous for her role as Florida Evans on the television show *Good Times* (1974–979).

1938

Crystal Bird Fauset is elected to the Pennsylvania House of Representatives, becoming the first African American woman to sit in a state legislature.

1947

Minnie Julia Riperton is born in Chicago, Illinois. A singer and songwriter, Minnie Riperton is famed for the song "Lovin' You."

1953

Emmy, Screen Actors Guild, and Golden Globe award-winning actress Alfre Ette Woodard is born to Marion and Constance Woodard in Tulsa, Oklahoma.

1966

Edward W. Brooke III, a Republican Party member, is elected to serve as the U.S. Senator from Massachusetts, making Brooke the first person of African descent to serve in the Senate in some 85 years.

1983

W. Wilson Goode is elected the first mayor of African descent of Philadelphia, Pennsylvania.

1989

Basketball star Earvin "Magic" Johnson of the Los Angeles Lakers retires after being diagnosed with the AIDS virus.

1992

President-elect Bill Clinton appoints Vernon Jordan head of his presidential transition team, the first African American to have such a position.

November 9

1731

Benjamin Banneker is born to Robert and Mary Banneker in Ellicott's Mills in Baltimore County, Maryland. A descendant of free grandparents (who may have been from the Dogon people of present-day Mali) and parents who were farmers, Banneker—who was mostly self-taught—became a well-known mathematician. His work as an amateur astronomer led to his publishing *Benjamin Banneker's Pennsylvania, Delaware, Maryland and Virginia Almanack and Ephemeris, for the Year of Our Lord 1792*, a highly successful almanac. Banneker famously sent a copy of his almanac to Thomas Jefferson when he served as secretary of state, along with a letter repudiating Jefferson's racism and proslavery views. Banneker also worked as a surveyor helping to plan the area that would become Washington's District of Columbia.

Three things made 1791 the defining year of Banneker's life—the survey of Washington, the publication of his first almanac, and his letter to Jefferson—and it is arguable that the last was what made it truly an annus mirabilis, his miracle year. Launching a verbal attack on the country's founders and putting himself in the potential line of fire from many vicious pro-slavery adherents went against his inherited traits andhis upbringing. His Dogon ancestors and his own parents and grandparents were stouthearted people whos disciplined courage told them to keep a low profile. Knowing how small they were in numbers, how easily overpowered by the hordes around them, they used their intelligence to survive, avoiding confrontation. That was not only Banneker's heritage; it was his personality. For such a person to write to Jefferson as he did was like a deer turning to attack a lion. Astonishingly, this quiet-living man whom some have criticized for hiss long apparent indifference to social injustice suddenly challenged the system and its leaders with blazing words.

Source: From Charles Cerami. *Benjamin Banneker: Surveyor, Astronomer, Publisher, Patriot.* Jackson, MS: University Press of Mississippi, 1997, pp. 155–156.

Books

Bedini, Silvio A. *The Life of Benjamin Banneker.* Rancho Cordova, CA: Landmark Enterprises, 1984. Book looks at the life and historical impact of Benjamin Banneker.

Litwin, Laura Baskes. *Benjamin Banneker: Astronomer and Mathematician.* Berkeley Heights, NJ: Enslow Publishers, 1999. Biography of the eighteenth-century African American who helped survey Washington and was a famed astronomer.

Websites

The Mathematics Department of the State University of New York at Buffalo profiles Benjamin Banneker. http://www.math.buffalo.edu/mad/special/banneker-benjamin.html.

Inventionware.com provides a profile of Benjamin Banneker. http://www.inventionware.com/benjamin-banneker/.

Also Noteworthy

1799

Telemanque, who is known to history as Denmark Vesey, wins $1,500 in the Charleston, South Carolina, city lottery. He uses his winnings to purchase his freedom from enslavement.

1868

Medical School at Howard University opens with a total of eight students.

1946

Members of the Philadelphia Club establish The Links, Inc., in Philadelphia, Pennsylvania. The Links is an exclusive non-profit organization based upon the ideals of combining friendship and community service. Though founded in 1946, it was not formally incorporated until 1951.

November 10

1898

Race riot occurs in Wilmington, North Carolina, when Colonel Alfred Moore Waddell leads a violent mob of anti-African American Democratic Party whites through the town to force Wilmington's white Republican mayor and his Black and white city officials out of office. Local elections had led to a fusion ticket of African American and white Republicans who had been able to take office in Wilmington, a predominately Black city. Waddell is a white supremacist and former Confederate officer who was so proud of his actions that he later wrote a memoir about his leadership during the riot, which was published in a national magazine. Following the riot, some 22 African Americans lay dead. U.S. President McKinley and the state's governor each refused to do anything to stop the race-based coup. In 2007, the North Carolina Democratic Party officially issued an apology for the Wilmington Race Riots.

> *The extremists left no room for ambiguity. In speech after speech they proclaimed their harsh, violent, nasty views. God had placed blacks only a little higher that the apes—and there was apparently some doubt about that. Intending them for servility, He had marked them with His curse. Anything that might raise blacks from their naturally inferior status they denounced and, when in office, vetoed. Anything the white man might do (including lynching in cases of suspected rape) to defend his supremacy and especially the purity of his women was fully justified.*
>
> *There can surely be no quarrel with Woodward's thesis that the violent, abusive, inflammatory language of politicians was a powerfully destructive force in its own right. On occasion its dangerous potential bothered even the politicians themselves. "It is a glorious victory we have won,"*

> *Charles Aycock wrote in November 1898, just after a campaign during which Furnifold Simmon's Red Shirts had been unusually imaginative in devising methods of intimidating black voters in the eastern part of the state, "and the extent of it frightens me." A few days later a white mob shot up the black districts of the seaport of Wilmington, ran a black newspaper editor out of town, and drove the lawfully elected municipal government from office. A future state supreme court judge reflected that "the politicians have stirred the minds of the people more than they intended." The state government in Raleigh did nothing, the leader of the insurrection was widely hailed as a hero, and his revolutionary regime remained in control.*
>
> *Source: From John Whitson Cell. The Highest Stage of White Supremacy: The Origins of Segregation in South Africa and the American South. Cambridge, England: Cambridge University Press, 1982, p. 178.*

Books

Cecelski, David S. and Timothy B. Tyson. *Democracy Betrayed: The Wilmington Race Riot of 1898 and Its Legacy*. Chapel Hill, NC: UNC Press Books, 1998. Book looks at the violent overthrow of Wilmington, N.C.'s interracial government, its legacy on the politics of the post-Civil War South, and how it influenced other efforts to disfranchise African Americans in nearby Southern states.

Waldrep, Christopher and Michael A. Bellesiles. *Documenting American Violence: A Sourcebook*. New York, NY: Oxford University Press, 2006. Book contains Colonel Alfred M. Waddell's justification for the Wilmington Race Riot.

Websites

The Wilmington Race riot—1898. http://ncpedia.org/history/cw-1900/wilmington-race-riot.

1898 Wilmington Race Riot Report—Final Report, May 31, 2006. http://www.history.ncdcr.gov/1898-wrrc/default.htm.

1898 Wilmington Race Riot Commission. http://www.history.ncdcr.gov/1898-wrrc/.

Also Noteworthy

1891

Granville T. Woods receives U.S. Patent No 463,020 for his electric railway system.

1983

Wilson Goode is elected Philadelphia, Pennsylvania's first African American mayor.

November 11

1896

Shirley Graham Du Bois is born Lola Shirley Graham to Rev. David A. Graham and Elizabeth Etta (Bell) Graham in Evansville, Indiana. Rev. Graham was a minister in the African Methodist Episcopal (A.M.E.) and at one point served as president of Monrovia College in Monrovia, Liberia. Graham Du Bois grew up to study and teach music—she wrote the musical drama *Tom-Tom* to celebrate African-based rhythms—and worked for African American human rights alongside her famous husband, W.E.B. DuBois. In addition, she authored numerous plays, books, and articles about major figures in African American history.

Tom-Tom, she said later, was "an attempt to show the development of music from the most primitive drum beats to the highly complicated tonalities of today. This thread is traced through . . . the particular medium of the Negro." This exhaustive work was conceived by a woman without the formal training of many of her peers. While working at Howard she had also taken classes in music and had studied music in New York City in the summer of 1929 at the Institute of Musical Arts. But this was a far cry from the finished conservatory training of many with whom she was competing for funding and attention.

However, what she lacked in formal training she made up for in ideas: her gravitation to things African was inspired and provocative. Deftly she "took three pairs of timpani and wrote the

overture just for the timpani"; this, she recalled later, "had never been done before so I understand." She continued, "if you take three pairs—that is actually six drums—and pitch them and you just pitch them by the chain that is purely the timpani, it is a copy of the African drum."

This creativity was in the service of a theme of "premature Afrocentrism," for she described her opera as "the voice of Africa calling her children to a better understanding and a deeper appreciation for the gifts which she has showered upon them." Thus, this work placed her decisively on one side of a looming divide about the role of a Africa in African American life. The philosopher Alain Locke had counseled African Americans to look to Africa for inspiration, while other, more powerful forces sought to deny this tie. The New York Times, for example, boldly proclaimed, "American Jazz Is Not African." Graham's contemporary, the black painter Allan Randall Freelon, agreed with the paper of record and worried that African American artists would be "misled into attempting to create an African art in America. The American Negro," he asserted, "has no more actual knowledge of his 'tribal background' and 'jungle ways' than has the Anglo-American of ancient Druid Rites." Graham dissented, feeling that her work would help to reestablish transAtlantic ties long frayed, while reflecting ties that had not disappeared. Still, a dismissive, if not negative, attitude toward Africa was all too common at that time, particularly in the theater; Graham's work countered this trend.

Source: From Gerald Horne. Race Woman: The Lives of Shirley Graham Du Bois. New York, NY: NYU Press, 2002, p. 59.

Books

Du Bois, Shirley Graham. *His Day Is Marching on: A Memoir of W. E. B. Du Bois.* Indianapolis, IN: Bobbs-Merrill Co, 1971. Du Bois's memoir of her famous husband, W. E. B. Dubois.

Du Bois, Shirley Graham, edited by Esther Cooper Jackson and Constance Pohl. "Negroes in the American Revolution, No. 2, 1961" in *Freedomways Reader: Prophets in Their Own Country.* New York, NY: Basic Books, 2000. Graham's look at the role people of African descent played in the creation of the United States.

Websites

Du Bois, Shirley Graham, 1896–1977. Papers, 1865–1998 (inclusive), 1905–1975 (bulk). http://oasis.lib.harvard.edu/oasis/deliver/deepLink?_collection=oasis&uniqueId=sch00211.

Photos of Shirley Graham Du Bois are available in W. E. B. Du Bois Library UMass Amherst Special Collections & University Archives. http://www.library.umass.edu/spcoll/dubois/?cat=22.

Also Noteworthy

1890

D. McCree receives U.S. Patent No. 440,322 for his portable fire escape.

1831

Nat Turner, the leader of the Southampton Virginia revolt against African slavery, is hanged. Following his execution, Turner's body was skinned and his captors chopped up and sold portions of his body as souvenirs.

1917

Margaret Taylor-Burroughs is born in St. Rose, Louisiana, to Alexander and Octavia Taylor. She was an African American artist and writer and a co-founder of Chicago's DuSable Museum of African American History.

1969

George R. Carruthers receives U.S. Patent No. 3,478,216 for the Image Converter for Detecting Electromagnetic Radiation specially in Short Wave Lengths.

1983

Barrington Antonio Irving, Jr., is born in Kingston, Jamaica. but then raised in Miami,

Florida. After learning to "fly" using Microsoft Flight Simulator software while in high school, Irving majored in Aeronautical Science at Broward Community College; he ultimately earned his private, commercial pilot, and certified flight instructor licenses. On March 23rd, 2007, Barrington took off in his Cessna 400 named *Inspiration* on a historic solo flight around the world, becoming the first person of African descent to achieve that feat.

1989

The Southern Poverty Law Center (SPLC) inaugurates a civil rights memorial in Montgomery, Alabama, established in memory of the thousands who died trying to promote African American civil rights in the United States.

November 12

1941

National Negro Opera Company (NNOC) is founded in Pittsburgh, Pennsylvania. The NNOC was headquartered out of the William A. "Woogie" Harris House at 7101 Apple Street in the Homewood section of Pittsburgh. NNOC founder Mary Lucinda Cardwell Dawson ran her music school out of the 21-room Woogie House; one of her most famous students was Ahmad Jamal. The NNOC lasted until 1962.

Efforts of African Americans to produce grand opera date back to the late nineteenth century, as we have seen, with the productions of Theodore Drury. In later years there were sporadic attempts made to organize black opera companies, but it was not until 1941 that the first permanent one came into existence. Mary Cardwell Dawson (1894–1962), who founded the National Negro Opera Company in 1941 at Pittsburgh, Pennsylvania, prepared for a career in music with studies at the New England Conservatory and Chicago Musical College. In 1927 she set up the Caldwell School of Music in Pittsburgh and thereafter toured frequently with its resident Cardwell-Dawson Chorus.

Source: From Eileen Southern. *The Music of Black Americans: A History.* New York, NY: W. W. Norton & Company, 1997, p. 414.

Books

Bird, Christiane. *Da Capo Jazz and Blues Lover's Guide to the U.S.: With More Than 900 Hot Clubs, Cool Joints, Landmarks, and Legends, From Boogie-Woogie to Bop and Beyond.* Cambridge, MA: Da Capo Press, 2001. Book includes a short profile of the Cardwell-Dawson School of Music.

Eliza Smith Brown, Daniel Holland, and Pennsylvania Historical and Museum Commission. *African American Historic Sites Survey of Allegheny County.* Darby, PA: DIANE Publishing Inc., 1994. Book shows photos and provides information about 7101 Apple Street in Pittsburgh's Homewood section, the first headquarters of the NNOC.

Websites

National Opera House. http://www.national operahouse.org/.

Library of Congress maintains an archive of the National Negro Opera Company Collection. http://lcweb2.loc.gov/diglib/ihas/loc.natlib .scdb.200033821/default.html.

November 13

1930

Benny Andrews is born in Plainview, Georgia. One of 10 children born to sharecroppers, Andrews became the first in his family to graduate from high school and after serving in the U.S. Air Force, he was able to attend the Chicago Art Institute. Famed as a print-maker and painter, Andrews also gained notice for his activism, particularly in his role as a co-founder and co-chair of the Black Emergency Cultural Coalition (BECC) in 1969. BECC was created to protest the New York's Metropolitan Museum of Art "Harlem on my Mind" exhibit, which had been created without the input of Black curators. Andrews taught art for 29 years at New York City's Queens College and founded the Benny Andrews Foundation, Inc.

During the years from 1954 to 1966, he watched the evolution of the American Civil Rights movement from his perspective in the North. Though he did not participate in the marches and demonstrations of this period, he recognized the importance of these events and realized the significant changes taking place in his native South. In his fifth period, beginning in 1966, he entered a level of social and cultural activism which focused on his efforts to open museums and art galleries to a more diverse range of art and artists.

Source: From J. Richard Gruber, Benny Andrews, and Morris Museum of Art (Augusta, GA). *American Icons: From Madison to Manhattan, the Art of Benny Andrews, 1948–1997.* Jackson, MS: University Press of Mississippi, 1997, p. iv.

Books

Andrews, Benny and High Museum of Art. *Benny Andrews: The Bicentennial Series: ... Exhibition ... Organized by the High Museum of Art, Atlanta.* Atlanta, GA: High Museum of Art, 1975. Book looks at the life and artistic pursuits of Benny Andrews.

Pomegranate Communications, Inc. *Benny Andrews.* Petaluma, CA: Pomegranate Communications, Inc., 2003. Book uses excerpts from Andrews's 90-piece *Music* series to create a calendar featuring his work.

Websites

The April 12, 1971, *Time* magazine article, "Art: in a Black Bind" depicts the reasons behind the creation of BECC. http://www.time.com/ time/magazine/article/0,9171,904984,00.html.

artnet—The art world online has a Benny Andrews page, including his artist's statement. http://www.artnet.com/awc/benny-andrews .html.

Also Noteworthy

1894

With U.S. Patent No. 529,311, Albert C. Richardson copyrights his version of a casket-lowering device.

1951

Janet Collins, who was born in New Orleans, Louisiana, on March 2, 1917, becomes the prima ballerina with New York's Metropolitan Opera Co. when she appeared in Verdi's *Aida*.

November 14

1832

Mathilda (also Matelda) Taylor Beasley is born in New Orleans, Louisiana. Her enslaved mother was named Caroline and her father is believed to have been Native American. Mathilda famously opened a secret school and taught black children to read at a time when doing so was a crime. She married a free Black man named Abraham Beasley who owned a restaurant called the "Railway House" in Savannah, Georgia, along with land and property. After Abraham died in 1878, Mathilda became a nun; founded the Third Order of St. Francis, the state of Georgia's first order of African American nuns; and donated Abraham's land and properties to the Roman Catholic Church in return for support for her creation of the St. Francis Home for Colored Orphans. The Mother Mathilda Beasley Society in Savannah, Georgia, continues Mother Mathilda's work.

When Abraham Beasley died in 1877, he left his entire fortune to his wife, Mathilda. She gave her inheritance to the Catholic Church, with the request that part of the money be used to provide a home for African American orphans. Mathilda Beasley later traveled to York, England to become a Franciscan Nun. She returned to Savannah and provided a home for about "twenty children and spared no pains to teach these little folks." (Bishop Thomas J. Becher) In 1887, Mother Beasley founded the Colored Orphan Asylum and located it on the corner of 32nd and Habersham Streets, the site of the first Sacred Heart Catholic Church.

In 1889, Mother Beasley founded the Third Order of Saint Francis, the first order of African American nuns in Georgia. By 1896, the order had grown to five nuns. She wrote a letter to Jame Cardinal Gibbons asking for help for the orphanage, now called Saint Francis Home. However, no help was forthcoming. The girls living at the orphanage set several fires, which did not help the financial situation. The orphanage was later moved when Saint Benedicts Church was built on East Broad Street in the late 1890s. The orphanage operated until the early 1940's.

Source: From Pamela Howard-Oglesby and Brenda L. Roberts. Savannah's Black First Ladies, Vol. I: The Past, Present, and Future, Volume 1. Savannah, GA: Brenda L. Roberts, 2010, pp. 3–4.

Books

Brown, Camille Lewis. *African Saints, African Stories: 40 Holy Men and Women*. Cincinnati, OH: St. Anthony Messenger Press, 2008. Book includes a biographical profile of Mathilda Tayler Beasley.

Sheehy, Barry, Cindy Wallace, and Vaughnette Goode-Walker. *Savannah, Immortal City*. Austin, TX: Greenleaf Book Group, 2011. Book includes a profile of the life and work of Mathilda Taylor Beasley.

Websites

Mother Mathilda Beasley, O.S.F.—Georgia's First Black Nun. http://www.hmdb.org/marker.asp?marker=6009.

Matilda Taylor—Educator of Slave Children. http://www.georgiahistory.com/containers/221.

Also Noteworthy

1915

Tuskegee Institute educator and famed African American leader Booker T. Washington dies.

1916

Mabel Fairbanks, the first African American woman to be inducted into the Figure Skating Hall of Fame, is born. Fairbanks was denied entry into the predominately white world of skating, but as she got older she famously coached Olympic quality skaters Tai Babilonia and Randy Gardner, Kristi Yamaguchi, Rudy Galindo, and Tiffany Chin.

November 15

1979

Dr. William Arthur Lewis, a professor at Princeton University, is awarded the Nobel Memorial Prize in Economics for his publications about the economic problems faced by underdeveloped nations. Lewis's winning of a Nobel Prize in Economics made him the first person of African descent to win a Nobel in a category other than Peace. Lewis was born in St. Lucia and was the first person of African descent to teach in a British University or at Princeton University.

The Nobel Award that was presented to W. Arthur Lewis in 1979 cited the Princeton economist for his luminous article "Economic Development with Unlimited Supplies of Labour," which the journal Manchester School had published in its 1954 issue. It was unquestionably his outstanding scholarly achievment. A few individuals, perhaps resentful critiss, would go even further, contending that only this publication was worthy of the Nobel award. This would be unjust since such a comment ignores Lewis's many important contributions in economic analysis and economic history. But it is true that the article galvanized the new field of development economics, providing it with a legitimacy that it had not previously enjoyed. Moreover, nearly all of his later studies in economic history bore the imprint of the article.

Source: From Robert L. Tignor. W. Arthur Lewis and the Birth of Development Economics. Princeton, NJ: Princeton University Press, 2006, p. 79.

Books

Lewis, William Arthur. *Principles of Economic Planning, Volume 5.* New York, NY: Taylor & Francis, 2003. Lewis's description of how underdeveloped economies can mix state planning and laissez faire features to sure their economies.

Lewis, William Arthur, edited by T. E. Barker, A. S. Downes, J. A. Sackey. *Perspectives On Economic Development: Essays in the Honour of W. Arthur Lewis.* Victoria, BC: AbeBooks/University Press of America, 1982. Book profiles W. Arthur Lewis's work and looks at his influence on the economic theory of development.

Websites

Sir William Arthur Lewis, 1915—1991. http://www.stlucianobellaureates.org/arthur_lewis.htm.

Sir Arthur Lewis—Autobiography is available on the NobelPrize.org Website. http://www.nobelprize.org/nobel_prizes/economics/laureates/1979/lewis-autobio.html.

Also Noteworthy

1881

Payton Johnson receives U.S. Patent No. 249,530 for his swinging chair.

1887

Granville T. Woods receives U.S. Patent No. 373,383 for his synchronous multiplier railway telegraph.

1897

Langston University and Voorhees College are founded in Langston, Oklahoma, and Denmark, South Carolina, respectively.

1898

Lyda D. Newman receives U.S. Patent No. 614,335 for her synthetic brush with synthetic bristles.

1969

The Amistad Research Center is incorporated. Formerly related to the Congregational Church, the Center becomes independent and eventually moves to the campus of Tulane University in New Orleans, LA. Amistad collects African American books and manuscripts and will emerge as one of the great resources for studying Black history and culture.

November 16

1931

Charismatic religious leader Father Divine is arrested on charges of disturbing the peace in his hometown of Sayville, Long Island. He will become nationally known when the case's presiding judge dies suddenly of a heart attack. Father Divine was born George Baker, Jr., in the home of his parents, George and Nancy Baker, in 1879. Baker, Jr., was raised in a log cabin on Middle Lane in Rockville, Maryland. After moving to New York, Baker changed his name to Reverend Major Jealous Divine, or Father Divine. Under his Peace Mission Movement, Father Divine established racially integrated communal living centers and social welfare programs that featured model farms and hotels to help people survive the Great Depression.

> *Worship at Father Divine's Peace Missions centered on huge banquets. Hundreds of followers attended these banquets and feasted on elaborate, multicourse meals. All of the food first passed through Father Divine's hands before it made its way around the table. At the banquets, followers would testify on his behalf, explaining how he had improved their lives. During the Depression, Father Divine and his Peace Mission also provided thousands of meals to residents of Harlem.*
>
> *Father Divine encouraged his followers to make amends for wrongs they had committed in the past. Newspapers across the country carried stories of Father Divine's followers who paid off decades-old debts. Also, his followers took an active role in improving themselves and the communities in which they lived. For example, they enrolled en masse in New York City's night schools; and he urged members of the Peace Mission to intimidate drug dealers in Harlem.*
>
> *Political activism was an integral part of the Peace Mission. Father Divine sponsored voter-registration drives and supported other organizations in protests and boycotts. This activism culminated in the Righteous Government Convention, held at the Rockland Palace in Harlem in 1936. With thousands in attendance, Father Divine and his followers passed a series of planks in support of antilynching laws, the abolition of capital punishment, and destruction of weapons of war. An antilynching bill writtern by the Peace Mission was introduced in the U.S. Congress but was defeated. Members of the "black bourgeoisie" generally criticized Father Divine's religious movement, but they did take note of the impact his political and philanthropic activities had on Harlem.*
>
> *Source*: From Cary D. Wintz and Paul Finkelman. *Encyclopedia of the Harlem Renaissance, Volume 1*. New York, NY: Taylor & Francis, 2004, p. 361.

Books

Streissguth, Thomas. *Charismatic Cult Leaders.* Minneapolis, MN: The Oliver Press, Inc., 1995. Includes a long profile of Father Divine and describes how his followers worshipped at his Peace Missions.

Watts, Jill. *God, Harlem U.S.A.: The Father Divine Story.* Berkely, CA: University of California Press, 1995. Watts' biography of Father Divine looks at his growth from an itinerant preacher to a world-renowned religious leader.

Websites

The Truth about Father Divine, His Work and Mission. http://www.libertynet.org/fdipmm/.

Father Divine visits Hope Farm, 1938, Part 1. http://www.youtube.com/watch?v=l8PRY8NR2FE.

Also Noteworthy

1780

Paul Cuffee and other Black taxpayers of Massachusetts protest to the state legislature against taxation without representation, demanding the right to vote.

1873

William C. Handy, the self-declared "father of the blues," is born in rural Florence, Alabama. Handy became a cornet soloist and bandmaster with minstrel shows, against the wishes of his father, who was a Calvinist minister.

1873

Blacks win three state offices in Mississippi election: Alexander K. Davis, lieutenant governor; James Hill, secretary of state; T.W. Cardozo, superintendent of education. Blacks won 55 of the 115 seats in the house and 9 out of 37 seats in the senate, 42 percent of the total number.

1899

Lorenzo Johnston Greene is born in Ansonia, Connecticut. Greene became the assistant for Carter G. Woodson, and from 1965 to 1966 he served as president of Woodson's Association for the Study of Negro Life and History

1964

Dwight Gooden is born on this day in Tampa, Florida. Gooden went on to become the youngest player selected as Major League Baseball's National League Rookie of the Year in 1984. He was the youngest player to be chosen to play in the All-Star Game, and the youngest to win the Cy Young Award.

1981

Pam Johnson is named publisher of the *Ithaca Journal* in Ithaca, New York. This made Johnson the first African American woman to serve as the head of a daily newspaper.

November 17

1961

Local and national activists convene in the Albany, Georgia, home of local dentist, Dr. E.D. Hamilton, to form the Albany Movement.

> On September 22, 1961, the Interstate Commerce Commission published and order that prohibited segregated facilities for interstate travel effective November 1, 1961. In Albany, Georgia, a group of black ministers decided that they would assist in the implementation of that ruling. They wrote a letter to Albany's city officials requesting a biracial meeting to discuss how Albany could comply with the ICC ruling and desegregate the bus station. The response of the Albany officials was rude and violent. James Gray, owner of the Albany Herald published an editorial condemning the ministers for making such a proposal and the home of one of the ministers was bombed. The ministers were not cowed. They organized the "Albany Movement"- with the goal of desegregating the bus station.
>
> Source: From Frederic O. Sargent. *The Civil Rights Revolution: Events and Leaders, 1955–1968*. Jefferson, NC: McFarland, 2004, pp. 61–62.

Books

Morris, Aldon D. *The Origins of the Civil Rights Movement: Black Communities Organizing for Change*. Detroit, MI: Free Press, 1984. Author examines the people and events that were important to the Civil Rights Movement.

Nasstrom, Kathryn L. *Everybody's Grandmother and Nobody's Fool: Frances Freeborn Pauley and the Struggle for Social Justice*. Ithaca, NY: Cornell University Press/Sage House, 2000.

Author interviews Frances Freeborn Pauley, a white woman who helped campaign for Black civil rights.

Sargent, Frederic O. *The Civil Rights Revolution: Events and Leaders, 1955–1968*. Jefferson NC: McFarland, 2004. Book looks at the events and leaders of the Civil Rights Movement and how they affected U.S. history.

Websites

The Albany Civil Rights Institute (ACRI) museum tells the story of how local organizers kept the Albany Movement focused. http://www.albanycivilrightsinstitute.org/index.php?option=com_content&view=article&id=1&Itemid=1.

The Civil Rights Digital Library has an entry on the Albany Movement. http://crdl.usg.edu/events/albany_movement/?Welcome.

Civil Rights Movement Timeline gives a history of the Albany Movement. http://www.crmvet.org/tim/timhis61.htm#1961albany.

Also Noteworthy

1911

African American fraternal organization Omega Psi Phi is founded on the campus of Howard University.

1980

WHHM, the first African American–operated radio station, goes on the air at Howard University.

November 18

1978

More than 900 people, the majority of them African Americans, die in a mass murder–suicide pact in Jonestown, Guyana. The tragedy took place after California Congressman Leo Ryan came to Guyana to check out Jonestown and interview the people who had followed religious leader Jim Jones and his People's Temple to the South American country. James Warren "Jim" Jones originally founded the People's Temple in 1955 in Indianapolis, Indiana. The temple's principles were based on a combination of religious and socialist philosophies.

Who were the People's Temple members who left American to move to Jonestown, Guyana? The demographics paint a portrait of a religious movement attempting to break down the barriers of age, race, and class. . . . Weightman represents the more liberal estimate of black population with 80 percent, whereas Reiterman estimates that 70 percent of Jonestwon residents were black, 25 percent white, with the rest "a smattering of mulatto, Hispanic, American Indian and Asian". . . . .

In fact, a great deal of utopian desire motivated the urban blacks to follow Peoples Temple to the "Promise Land." Several months after the suicides, a black woman member who had not gone to Jonestown noted that Peoples Temple"-provided the atmosphere of love, trust and social concern that she found lacking in other black institutions" (Chidester 1988b, 44). The journalist Lawrence Wright suggested that it was more the belief in the "promise of racial equality" than in food, shelter, and economic security that motivated the black senior citizens to join Peoples Temple and then move to Jonestown. These were people who had internalized Marcus Garvey's Back to Africa movement during the 1920s; almost half of the elderly residents of Jonestown had already migrated once from the American South to California in search of a more just society.

The foundation of his [Jones's] ministry was a promise of racial equality. His followers had grown up in a racist society and suffered economic injustice, and, whether they came from a tenant farm in Mississippi or a cotton mill in Georgia, they had not found redemption in California. Jones made them believe that they could create it themselves—that they could make their own Paradise. (Wright 1993, 69)

Source: From Mary McCormick Maaga. *Hearing the Voices of Jonestown*. Syracuse, NY: Syracuse University Press, 1998, pp. 9–11.

Books

Chidester, David. *Salvation and Suicide: An Interpretation of Jim Jones, the Peoples Temple, and Jonestown*. Bloomington, IN: Indiana University Press, 1988. Biography of Jim Jones looks at his founding of the Peoples Temple and the mass suicide in Jonestown.

Moore, Rebecca, Anthony B. Pinn, and Mary R. Sawye. *Peoples Temple and Black Religion in America*. Bloomington, IN: Indiana University Press, 2004. Book reprints 10 essays that look at the convergence of the African American religious experience and the Peoples Temple.

Websites

The Jonestown Massacre—The Ministry of Terror. http://www.infoplease.com/spot/jonestown1.html.

Making Sense of the Nonsensical: An Analysis of Jonestown. http://www.guyana.org/features/jonestown.html.

Also Noteworthy

1797

The preacher, abolitionist, and women's rights activist Sojourner Truth is born with the name Isabella Baumfree on the Colonel Johannes Hardenbergh estate in Swartekill, in New York's Ulster County. In 1843, she gave herself the name Sojourner Truth.

1900

Theologian Howard Thurman is born in Daytona Beach, Florida. A minister, professor, and chaplain, Thurman became a pacifist and visited Mohandas Gandhi in India. There he learned about nonviolent resistance to oppression, a tactic later adopted by the Civil Rights Movement. Under the influence of Quakerism, Thurman developed a mystical, spiritual life, and his religious writings continue to be popular inspirational literature.

1941

Jack Benjamin Wilson wins the National Boxing Association's World Featherweight Championship in a decision against Richie Lemos.

1955

Roy Wilkins is named executive secretary of the National Association for the Advancement of Colored People.

1977

Ku Klux Klan member Robert Chambliss is convicted of the 1963 bombing of the Sixteenth Street Baptist Church in Birmingham, Alabama. Chambliss' terrorist act killed four young Black girls—Addie Mae Collins, Cynthia Wesley, Carole Robertson and Denise McNair—who were attending Sunday School at the time.

1978

NAACP Spingarn Medal is presented to Ambassador Andrew J. Young "in recognition of the deftness with which he has handled relations between this nation and other countries" and "for his major role in raising the consciousness of American citizens to the significance in world affairs of the massive African continent."

November 19

1921

The Major League Baseball star Roy Campanella is born in Philadelphia, Pennsylvania. On his birthday in 1953 he is named the Most Valuable Player in Major League Baseball's National League and he would be selected the MVP at least two more times during his career. Campanella played catcher for the Brooklyn Dodgers during a time when the team won five National League pennants and the 1955 World Series. Campanella's baseball career was tragically cut short after a car accident left him partially paralyzed.

> *In an era when baseball was still the unquestioned king of all sports, winning the MVP meant celebrity status in America. Roy was now a national figure, his name as recognizable as Liberace, Brando, and Doris Day. But exactly what, some wondered, made this half-Negro/half-Italian fellow so special? What set him apart from the pack?*
>
> . . . .
>
> *Watching Campy hit was almost worth the price of admission. Up to the plate he would plod, big bat (as heavy as 37 ounces by 1955) loaded with "grippy beeswax" in hand furiously chomping his gum or tobacco. Once settled in his usual foot-in-the-bucket stance, he would hack away, like "a kid in gang fights wielding a sock full of sand," wrote Milton Gross. "I never saw a guy who could swing like he could," recalled his teammate Glenn Mickens. "He ended up on that back leg . . . his knee catching the ground." But he usually managed to whack the ball hard somewhere, though he was very much a guess hitter. He ran surprisingly well for a catcher and could even steal an occasional base (as many as eight one year). "He always scored from second on a base hit," Carl Erskine insists. "He just had good instincts."*
>
> *Source: From Neil Lanctot. Campy: The Two Lives of Roy Campanella. New York, NY: Simon & Schuster, 2011, p. 270.*

Books

Campanella, Roy. *It's Good to Be Alive*. Lincoln, NE: University of Nebraska Press, 1959. Campanella's autobiography explores his joys in being an athlete, at having conquered racial barriers, and at being able to survive a terrible accident and enjoy life.

Young, Dick. *Roy Campanella*. Victoria, BC: AbeBooks/A.S. Barnes, 1952. Biography of Campanella and how he conquered the many challenges he faced.

Websites

The Official Site of Roy Campanella. http://www.roycampanella.com/.

What's my line?—Roy Campanella. http://www.youtube.com/watch?v=3_suJ_EXImk&NR=1.

Also Noteworthy

1901

Granville T. Woods receives U.S. Patent No. 687,098 for his electric railway third rail power distribution system.

1911

Omega Psi Phi is organized as an African American fraternity at Howard University. Omega Psi Phi Fraternity, Inc. was created by Professor Ernest E. Just, Edgar A. Love, Oscar J. Cooper, and Frank Coleman and designed to focus on issues manhood, scholarship, perseverance, and African American uplift.

November 20

1977

Walter Payton sets a (since broken) National Football League single-game rushing record with 275 yards while playing running back for the Chicago Bears in a game against the Minnesota Vikings. Born Walter Jerry Payton to Edward and Alyne Payton on July 25, 1954 in Columbia, Mississippi, Payton grew to be 5 feet, 10 inches, 200 pounds, and attended college at Jackson State University, where he rushed for 3,563 yards and broke the NCAA's scoring record. Payton was the first-round draft pick of the Chicago Bears in 1975 NFL Draft and played 13 seasons with that organization. Payton contracted bile duct cancer and died at age 46.

> *Walter Payton was given the nickname "Sweetness" due to his affable nature and there has never been a more fitting moniker for an NFL player. He was a fun-loving member of the Bears from 1975 to 1987 and a valued member of the Chicago locker room. He played the game with class, acted as a perfect role model away from*

the field, and was the poster child for how the NFL would love its players to act.

Those who played with Payton adored him. Those who battled against him every Sunday begrudged the yards he gained but respected him as a person and as one of the very best in NFL history.

Source: From Neil Reynolds. *Pain Gang: Pro Football's Fifty Toughest Players.* Dulles, VA: Potomac Books, Inc., 2006.

Books

Payton, Walter with Don Yaeger. *Never Die Easy: The Autobiography of Walter Payton.* New York, NY: Villard, 2000. Payton looks back at the highs and lows of his life in and outside of football.

Pearlman, Jeff. *Sweetness: The Enigmatic Life of Walter Payton.* New York, NY: Penguin, 2011. Biography on the life and tragic early death of Walter Payton.

Websites

The Pro Football Hall of Fame features an entry on Walter Payton. http://www.profootball hof.com/hof/member.aspx?PLAYER_ID=174.

The Walter & Connie Payton Foundation, which is designed to help "abused, neglected & underprivileged children in the state of Illinois" continues Payton's charitable work. http://www.payton34.com/foundation.asp.

Walter Payton #34 Sweetness Highlights. http://www.youtube.com/watch?v=-qCqtjIuIR0.

Also Noteworthy

1866

Howard University is founded in Washington, DC; the school was originally named Howard Normal and Theological Institute for the Education of Preachers and Teachers. The school was named after Major General Oliver Otis Howard, who served as a general for the Union Army during the U.S. Civil War and as the Commissioner of the Freedmen's Bureau from 1865 to 1872. Howard

served as the school's third president from 1869 to 1874.

1878

Actor Charles Sidney Gilpin is born in Richmond, Virginia. Gilpin's performance as Brutus Jones in Eugene O'Neill's play *Emperor Jones* was widely applauded.

1900

Granville T. Woods receives U.S. Patent No. 662,049 for his automatic circuit-breaking apparatus.

1910

Pauli Murray is born Anna Pauline Murray to Agnes Fitzgerald and William Henry Murray in Baltimore, Maryland. Murray became an author, the first African American female deputy attorney general of California, and the first woman of African descent to serve as an Episcopal priest in the United States.

1923

Garrett Morgan receives U.S. Patent No. 1,475,024 for his automatic three-way traffic signal. Morgan later sold his device to General Electric for $40,000.

1962

President John F. Kennedy signs an executive order barring racial and religious discrimination in federally financed housing.

November 21

1865

Kennell A. Jackson Jr., a professor of East African and African American history and director of Stanford University's African and African American Studies Program, dies at age 64 of pulmonary fibrosis. Jackson is known for his 1996 book *America is Me: The Most Asked and Least Understood Questions about Black American History*. Jackson was born on March 19, 1941, in Farmville, Virginia, to Kennell and Lottie Jackson.

> In the year 2019, Blacks will have been in America for four hundred years. In less than twenty-five years, we—as a nation—will reach this landmark. Being so focused on the end of the millennium, hardly anyone has mentioned that we are fast approaching this watershed in American history.
>
> Four hundred years confers a permanence, an aura of true and lasting quality, on the Black American past. Many nations in today's world are younger than four hundred years. Empires have been swept away during this time. Revolutionary movements have come and gone. Whole systems of thought have risen and disintegrated during these years. Through all of this, Black Americans have continued, winding their way toward the future. They are an enduring part of American and world history. The year 2019 will simply highlight this fact.
>
> Source: From Kennell Jackson. *America Is Me.* New York, NY: HarperCollins, 2009.

Books

Clough, Marshall S. and Kennell A. Jackson. *Mau Mau Syllabus, Volume 1.* Victoria, BC: AbeBooks/Clough, 1975. Book looks at the impact of the Mau Mau rebellion in Kenya.

Elam, Harry Justin and Kennell A. Jackson. *Black Cultural Traffic: Crossroads in Global Performance and Popular Culture.* Ann Arbor, MI: University of Michigan, 2005. Jackson and Elam look at the diasporic influence of African-based cultures.

Websites

Kennell Jackson, historian of Africa and longtime resident Fellow at Stanford University, dead at 64. http://news.stanford.edu/news/2005/november30/jackson-113005.html.

Memorial site for Kennel Ardoway Jackson. http://kennell-jackson.memory-of.com/About.aspx.

Also Noteworthy

1886

Samuel Shinkle Taylor is born to the Reverend Marshall W. Taylor and Catherine Hester Taylor in Cincinnati, Ohio. Taylor served as a minister and professor, wrote, and compiled the Works Projects Administration's Federal Writers' Project entitled *Survey of Negroes in Little Rock and North Little Rock*. Taylor was also an associate editor with the *Arkansas State Press* from 1949 to 1956.

1893

Granville T. Woods receives U.S. Patent No. 509,065 for his electric railway conduit.

1934

Ella Fitzgerald makes her singing debut at age 17 at the Apollo Theater in Harlem, New York. Fitzgerald was awarded first prize, a total of $25.

1962

George Branham, III, is born in Detroit, Michigan. Branham became a professional bowler at age 23 by becoming part of the Professional Bowlers Association tour. When he won the Brunswick Memorial World Open in 1986, Branham became the first African American to win a PBA championship.

November 22

1930

Elijah Muhammad founds the Lost-Found Nation of Islam in Detroit, Michigan. By July 31, 1960, Muhammad began calling for the establishment an all–Black state. By this time, membership in Nation of Islam had reached some 100,000 people.

The Nation of Islam teaches that God is a black man and not an invisible spirit. The African American is not the inferior, so-called Negro but the original man, god of the universe. The primeval black civilization was a divine culture from which originated all science, wisdom, and institutions for human progress. Due to reasons that will be explained later, the black nation of gods lost world supremacy to the white race. The white man differs from the original species in that he is not a creation of God. His is a man-made race, grafted by the dissatisfied black scientist Mr. Yacub approximately 6,000 years ago. Bent on producing a race evil and powerful enough to transform the original harmony into its opposite, Mr. Yacub set out systematically to drain a number of the original people of divine essence. In intervals, the brown, red, and yellow races appeared before his goal was reached: to create a race absolutely bereft of divinity. This was a race whose members were evil by nature, incapable of acting or thinking decently, or submitting to the law of Islam: the blond, blue-eyed white devils. In his omniscience, God gave the Devil 6,000 years to rule the earth. White world supremacy is equated with the evil era of the Devil and explains the experiences of the darker people in late world history: colonialism, slavery, racist oppression, and poverty. The gospel is that the era of the Devil now has expired. God descended in Detroit to reconnect with his lost-found Nation and raise from among them a Messenger. When the mentally "dead" blacks have united in Knowledge of Self and God, white supremacy will fall. God will himself exterminate the devils from the face of the earth in a global apocalyptic fire. Thereafter—in the hereafter—the world will be transformed into the black paradise it is predestined to become, where freedom, justice, and equality (that is, Islam) will be the conditions for eternal times to come.

Source: From Mattias Gardell. In the Name of Elijah Muhammad: Louis Farrakhan and the Nation of Islam. Durham, NC: Duke University Press, 1996, p. 59.

Books

Lee, Martha Frances. *The Nation of Islam, an American Millenarian Movement.* Victoria, BC: AbeBooks/Edwin Mellen Press, 1988. Book looks at the impact of the Nation of Islam on African American society.

Muhammad, Elijah. *History of the Nation of Islam.* Phoenix, AZ: MEMPS (Messenger Elijah Muhammad Propagation Society), 2008. Elijah Muhammad's look at the founding and propagation of the Nation of Islam.

Websites

The Supreme Wisdom—Nation of Islam. http://www.thenationofislam.org/supremewisdom.html.

Lost-Found Nation of Islam. http://www.lfnoi.com/.

Also Noteworthy

1884

Timothy Thomas Fortune begins publication of the *New York Freeman* (which was published until October 8, 1887) and later became the *New York Age* (which published from October 15, 1887 to February 27, 1960).

1986

George Branham, at age 24, becomes the first African American to win a Professional Bowlers' Association title, the Brunswick Memorial World Open, at Glendale Heights, Florida.

November 23

1921

Mamie Elizabeth Till Mobley, the mother of Emmett Louis Till, a 14-year-old boy who was lynched in Money, Mississippi, on August 28, 1955, is born Mamie Carthan on November 23. Born the only child of John and Alma Carthan in a small town near Webb, Mississippi, Mamie was raised in Illinois, because her father wanted to get his family away from the racism still prevalent in their native state. Mamie's insistence that her son's casket remain open for viewing during his funeral helped spur the Civil Rights Movement. Mamie Carthan Till Mobley lived until age 81; she died on January 6, 2003.

> Hardly a moment goes by when I don't think about Emmett and the promise of a lifetime. There are constant reminders. But, then, a mother really doesn't need reminders. Just as you always remember the agony of childbirth, you can never forget the anguish of losing a child.
>
> Source: From Mamie Till Mobley. *Death of Innocence: The Story of Hate Crime That Changed America.*

Books

Clarke, John Henrik. *Harlem Voices from the Soul of Black America,* 2nd edition. Brooklyn, NY: A & B Book Distributors Inc., September 1993.

Clarke, John Henrik. *My Life in Search of Africa.* New Jersey: Third World Press. February 1, 1999.

Till Mobley, Mamie. *Death of Innocence: The Story of Hate Crime That Changed America.* An autobiography written with Christoper Benson. New York: Random House, October 7, 2003. Mamie Till Mobley died the same year this autobiography was published.

Websites

The Website for the documentary program the *American Experience* provides a brief biography of the life of Mamie Till Mobley. http://www.pbs.org/wgbh/amex/till/peopleevents/p_parents.html.

Boston, Massachusetts's WGBH featured an interview with Mamie Till Mobley on June 24, 1988, showing how Till remained active as community activist with Chicago-area youth. http://openvault.wgbh.org/ton/MLA000589/index.html.

Trade and Environment Database (TED) Case Studies: Abolition of the Atlantic Slave Trade in the United States. This case study on United States involvement in the Atlantic Slave Trade examines the moral and legal arguments that were made in the U.S. Congress for both maintaining and criminalizing the slave trade. http://www.american.edu/TED/slave.htm.

Also Noteworthy

1897

Andrew Jackson Beard receives U.S. Patent No. 594,059 for his invention of the jerry coupler, a device that is still used today to connect railroad cars.

1897

John L. Love receives U.S. Patent No. 595,114 for his pencil sharpener.

1926

R. L. Burnside is born Robert Lee Burnside. A North Mississippi hill country blues singer, songwriter, and guitarist who lived much of his life in and around Holly Springs, Mississippi. He played music for much of his life, but did not receive much attention until the early 1990s. In the latter half of the 1990s, Burnside repeatedly recorded with Jon Spencer, garnering crossover appeal and introducing his music to a new fanbase within the underground garage rock scene.

1946

Bobby Lee Rush is born in Albany, Georgia, but raised in Chicago, Illinois. In 1968, Rush was a co-founder and served as the first defense minister of the Illinois chapter of the Black Panthers. After leaving the Panthers and working in various other political and non-political spheres, Rush became a Chicago city councilman. He moved on to the national level in 1993 when he was elected to serve as the U.S. Congressional Representative for Illinois's 1st district.

November 24

1868

Scott Joplin is born near Linden, Texas. Joplin became known as the "father of ragtime" with the publication of his composition "Maple Leaf Rag." Joplin introduced the United States—and eventually the world—to the post-Civil War music of African Americans, which provided a jaunty, celebratory look at the world.

> Joplin finished the first draft of "Maple Leaf Rag" in 1897 or 1898 and took it to several publishers in Kansas City and Sedalia, including A.W. Perry & Son. He knew it was special, for he said to Marshall, "Arthur, the Maple Leaf will make me king of ragtime composers." To his great disappointment, the piece was continually turned down. He kept on playing it in various clubs and saloons, however, polishing it with every performance. Other ragtime pianists also began to play it, and the piece soon started to become popular in the area. "Maple Leaf Rag" was much more sophisticated and melodious than "Original Rags."
>
> Finally, John Stark accepted it, and history was made. Many felt that Stark struck one of the bargains of the century, since sales of "Maple Leaf Rag" eventually made him a relatively wealthy man. The music business was not like it is today, however, when a new hit song can sell millions within months; but for the time, "Maple Leaf Rage" did well. The first year, it sold around 400 copies. By 1909, it had sold a half-million copies. Many orders came from the F.W. Woolworth chain of stores around the country. By 1909, Joplin's royalties amounted to $600 a year.
>
> Source: From Janet Hubbard-Brown. Scott Joplin: Composer. New York, NY: Infobase Publishing, 2006, p. 30.

Books

Berlin, Edward A. *King of Ragtime: Scott Joplin and His Era*. New York, NY: Oxford University Press, 1996. Biography of Scott Joplin looks at him as a major composer of post-Civil War African American music.

Curtis, Susan. *Dancing to a Black Man's Tune: A Life of Scott Joplin*. Columbia, MO: University of Missouri Press, 2004. Biography of Scott Joplin looks at his musical impact on the United States of the early twentieth century.

Websites

The Scott Joplin International Ragtime Foundation provides "A Biography of Scott Joplin (c.1867–1917)." http://www.scottjoplin.org/biography.htm.

Maple Leaf Rag Played by Scott Joplin. http://www.youtube.com/watch?v=pMAtL7n_-rc.

Also Noteworthy

1935

Ronald Vernie "Ron" Dellums is born in Oakland, California. He served as Oakland, California's forty-fifth (and third African American) mayor and as the U.S. Congressional Representative from California in the Ninth District.

1865

Mississippi legislature enacts Black Codes that restrict the rights and freedom of movement of African American freedmen. The Black Codes enacted in Mississippi and other Southern states virtually re-enslaved freedmen. In some states any white could arrest any person of African descent for being a "vagrant" and force them to work on roads and levees without pay. "Servants" in South Carolina were required to work from sunrise to sunset, to be quiet and orderly, and go to bed at "reasonable hours." It was a crime in Mississippi for people of African descent to own farm land; in South Carolina Blacks had to get a special license to work outside the domestic and farm laborer categories. In South Carolina, Blacks protested during a convention at the Zion Church of Charleston. The protesters composed a "Memorial to the Senate and House of Representatives" to list their complaints against the unjust system they were forced to live under.

1920

Percy Ellis Sutton is born in San Antonio, Texas, as the last of 15 children. Sutton became the famed attorney for Malcolm X and a borough president of Manhattan, New York. Sutton was also a major force in African American politics and business and was instrumental in saving New York's legendary Apollo Theatre in Harlem from the wrecking ball.

November 25

1897

Jazz pianist Willie "The Lion" Smith is born William Henry Joseph Bonaparte Bertholoff Smith to Frank Bertholoff and Ida Oliver in Goshen, NY. A stride piano player, Willie "The Lion" was a jazz icon usually seen with a cigar in his mouth and a derby hat on his head.

Willie the Lion Smith was almost alone in having hands and mind nimble enough to play with stride, as well as to play it. In the '20s, Smith was generally acknowledged to be the second-best player (after James P. Johnson), but during stride's heyday he wrote very little, and he recorded no piano solos. When Smith finally came into his own, it was too late for the acclaim that should have come to him. Most pianists and piano fans of the time were into boogie-woogie. It looked harder than it was to play, and it was fast and hot.

Smith was middle-aged before his talents as player and composer were recognized beyond Harlem. But once his music was heard, there was no mistaking it for anyone else's. His unparalleled sense of harmony gave his work textures that were unique. In fact, his nearly forty works for piano constitute the most harmonically sophisticated body of popular piano music by an American composer. His pieces are hybrids, as evocative of Debussy as of 133rd Street. He made a sort of Harlem impressionism that influenced those looking forward (Duke Ellington, Billy Strayhorn, Joes Bushkin, and Mel Powell) as well as those looking back (the ragtime revivalists Ralph Sutton, Dick Wellstood, and Mike Lipskin). Smith

never had a hit record, never wrote a hit song, and never composed for the theater. He earned his living as a piano player, and in his life as in his music, he went his own way. There was no personality, player, or composer quite like him.

Source: From David A. Jasen and Gordon Gene Jones. *Black Bottom Stomp: Eight Masters of Ragtime and Early Jazz*. New York, NY: Psychology Press, 2002, pp. 83–84.

Books

Doerschuk, Bob. *88: The Giants of Jazz Piano, Volume 1*. Milwaukee, WI: Hal Leonard Corporation, 2001. Includes a biographical chapter on Willie "The Lion" Smith.

Smith, Willie the Lion with George Hoefer. *Music on My Mind, the Memoirs of an American Pianist*. New York City: Doubleday & Company Inc., 1964. Autobiography of Willie "The Lion" Smith.

Websites

Willie "The Lion" Smith playing "Ain't Misbehavin'" in 1966. http://www.youtube.com/watch?v=4F0rd-ZbAiY.

Willie "The Lion" Smith—Fingerbuster. http://www.youtube.com/watch?v=KDMOkgSdy3E&feature=related.

Also Noteworthy

1884

The Philadelphia Tribune is founded by Christopher James Perry, Jr., to cover business policies and their affects on African Americans in Philadelphia, Pennsylvania. *The Philadelphia Tribune* is the oldest continually published African American newspaper in the nation.

1942

Guion Stewart "Guy" Bluford, Jr., is born in Philadelphia, Pennsylvania. On August 30, 1983, at 2 a.m., Colonel, USAF Bluford became the first African American astronaut in space when the National Aeronautics and Space Administration (NASA) launched the spacecraft *Challenger* with Bluford on board.

1955

The U.S. Interstate Commerce Commission bans segregation in buses and waiting-room terminals that feature interstate travel.

1958

Carol Taylor becomes the first Black flight attendant in the United States.

November 26

1878

Marshall Walter "Major" Taylor is born to Gilbert Taylor and Saphronia Kelter in Indianapolis, Indiana. Taylor would win fame as a world champion cyclist by winning the world 1-mile (1.6 km) track cycling championship in Montreal, Canada, in 1899.

Eighteen-year-old Marshall Walter Taylor and manager Birdie Munger stepped haltingly into the Garden spotlight. They had no natural constituency, of course—a black racer and a white trainer, after all! The Garden crowd reacted as promoters had known they would: nudging one another, whispering, titillated by the delicious possibilities of a black racer in a rare sanctioned competition against white rivals. The newly installed electrical lights hung down from the high girders and bathed the tiny wooden track in celestial light, looming over the Irishman's heavy brow, the German's stiff jaw line, and in Taylor's case his oil-black skin. He never got back "his old blackness," Munger used to say when he discussed their experiments with black-skin remover, but you wouldn't have known there was even the slightest diminishment next to a cavalry of Caucasian faces. Taylor was clearly a boy, not a man: blade-thin shoulders, an anxious look of uncertainty as he gazed straight ahead. He stood five foot six and weighed little more than 130 pounds for his first professional race.

He was virtually unknown in New York, but in a half-mile curtain-raising exhibition on Saturday night at the Garden he had whipped the reigning American sprint champion, Eddie "Cannon" Bald. "Round and round the track whirled the colored rider, pedaling away like a steam engine," described a reporter. "Once or twice he looked back, and although he was going on the bunch he kept on going like a scared rabbit. Eddie Bald was straining every nerve to catch the runaway African." The majority of newspaper reporters were disinclined to give Taylor much credit, saying that Bald was "quite lame" after a crash earlier in the evening, but the capacity crowd enjoyed the upset, especially the South Brooklyn contingent, which referred to Taylor as their "dark secret from Gowanus."....

Source: From Todd Balf. *Major: A Black Athlete, a White Era, and the Fight to Be the World's Fastest Human Being.* New York, NY: Random House Digital, Inc., 2008.

Books

Brill, Marlene Targ. *Marshall "Major" Taylor: World Champion Bicyclist, 1899–1901.* Breckenridge, CO: Twenty-First Century Books, 2007. Biography of Marshall Walter Taylor looks at his plight as one of the first internationally known Black athletes at the turn of the twentieth century.

Taylor, Marshall W. *The Fastest Bicycle Rider in the World: The Story of a Colored Boy's Indomitable Courage and Success Against Great Odds.* Freeport, NY: Books for Libraries Press, 1928. Taylor's autobiography looks at how he came to the sport of bicycle racing.

Websites

The Major Taylor Society. http://www.majortaylor.com/.

Major Taylor—Biography at a Glance. http://www.majortaylorassociation.org/biography.htm.

Also Noteworthy

1842

The largest of three servant uprisings in the Indian Territory begins in early November when 33 fugitive slaves from the Creek, Cherokee, and Choctaw Nations attempt to escape to Mexico. On November 26, the Cherokee mounted militia captured 31 of the fugitives about five miles north of the Red River.

1883

The itinerant preacher, abolitionist, and women's rights activist, Sojourner Truth, dies in Battle Creek, Michigan.

1895

National Negro Medical Association (NMA) is founded by Dr. Daniel Hale Williams. The NMA was founded because people of African descent were denied membership in the American Medical Association.

1911

William Henry Lewis is appointed to serve as assistant attorney general of the United States by President William Howard Taft. Lewis was the first person of African descent to be appointed to a sub-cabinet presidential post.

1970

Charles Gordone becomes the first African American playwright to receive the Pulitzer Prize (for *No Place to Be Somebody*).

November 27

1942

James Marshall "Jimi" Hendrix is born Johnny Allen Hendrix in Seattle, Washington. A famed rock musician, Jimi Hendrix had his first Top Ten hit with the song "Hey Joe." Hendrix also scored hits with "Purple Haze," "Foxy Lady," "Voodoo Child," "All Along The Watchtower," "Are You Experienced?" and numerous other songs. Hendrix's third

and final album, *Electric Ladyland*, was a double album released on October 25, 1968. Hendrix, who is widely considered the greatest rock and roll guitarist of all time, had a mere four-year career as a headlining rock star; he died in 1970 at the age of 27.

> *His extraordinary guitar playing and sensational public image have tended to obscure Jimi's excellent song-writing capabilities. Many of his songs operated on at least two levels or had more than one message to impart—he later said to close friends that he had to wrap up his metaphysical and spiritual intent in simplified language or through commonplace metaphors in order to get the material accepted by the record companies, and probably by most of his audience as well.*
>
> *Source*: From Harry Shapiro and Caesar Glebbeek. *Jimi Hendrix, Electric Gypsy*. New York, NY: Macmillan, 1995, p. 124.

Books

Lawrence, Sharon. *Jimi Hendrix: The Man, the Magic, the Truth*. New York, NY: HarperCollins, 2005. Lawrence's biography of Hendrix looks at his worldwide fame and the impact of his music.

Roby, Steven. *Black Gold: The Lost Archives of Jimi Hendrix*. New York, NY: Billboard Books, 2002. Biography of Jimi Hendrix looks at his attempts to expand his musical work into jazz and blues and to work groups like The Last Poets.

Websites

Jimi Hendrix performing "Hey Joe" on YouTube. http://www.youtube.com/watch?v=y_n_P40sEaM.

Jimi Hendrix | The Official Jimi Hendrix Site. http://www.jimihendrix.com/.

Also Noteworthy

1841

Thirty-five of the captured Africans who took part in a revolt on the Spanish slave-trading ship *Amistad* are returned to Africa.

1923

Jesse Ernest Wilkins, Jr., is born to Lucile B. Wilkins (nee Robinson) and J. Ernest Wilkins, Sr. in Chicago, Illinois. Wilkins entered the University of Chicago at age 13, becoming the school's youngest-ever student. At age 19, he became the seventh African American to obtain a Ph.D. in Mathematics. A famed physicist, mathematician, and chemical/nuclear engineer, Wilkins worked on the Manhattan Project during World War II.

1957

Dorothy Irene Height is elected president of the National Council of Negro Women, a post she would hold for some 40 years. Height was born in Richmond, Virginia, but her family raised her in Rankin, Pennsylvania. Height attended NYU and became a social worker before becoming active in civil rights and working with the National Council of Negro Women.

1989

Jennifer Karen Lawson becomes the first female chief programming executive for the Public Broadcasting Service (PBS).

1990

Charles Johnson is awarded the National Book Award for fiction for *Middle Passage*.

November 28

1929

Berry Gordy, Jr., is born in Detroit, Michigan's Harper Hospital to Bertha Fuller and Berry Gordy, Sr. Gordy's father had moved to Detroit from Sandersvill, Georgia, looking for work in the Ford Motor Company; his mother was originally from Milledgeville, Georgia. Berry Gordy was the couple's seventh child; in total, they would have eight. Berry Gordy, Sr., established a middle-class existence for his family by opening the Booker T. Washington Grocery and Meat Market. As a 29-year-old record producer, Gordy borrowed $800 from his family and became the founder of Motown Records, the label now known as the major vehicle for soul music. Gordy was able to assemble and maintain a roster of talented soul music musicians at Motown, including Smokey Robinson, Diana Ross, The Jackson 5, and Stevie Wonder.

> By 1965, as Motown accumulated more hits on the charts and its stars were recognized almost everywhere, Gordy was called "starmaker" or sometimes "magic man." He received the Small Businessman of the Year Award from Detroit's mayor. The company, which had $4.5 million in sales in 1963, had grown to $10 million the following year, and reached $15 million by 1965. There were now more than 100 employees and 175 artists.
>
> *Source*: From Gerald Posner. *Motown: Music, Money, Sex, and Power*. New York, NY: Random House Digital, Inc., 2005, p. 150.

Books

Gordy, Berry. *Movin' Up: Pop Gordy Tells His Story*. New York, NY: Harper & Row, 1979. The father of the creator of Motown Records recounts his life story.

Gordy, Berry. *To Be Loved: The Music, the Magic, the Memories of Motown: An Autobiography*. New York, NY: Warner Books, 1994. Gordy's personal account of the creation and building of Detroit, Michigan's famous Motown Records.

Websites

"Berry Gordy's Motown Records" recalls Gordy's life and legacy. http://www.history-of-rock.com/motown_records.htm.

Soulwalking has an in-depth biography of Berry Gordy. http://www.soulwalking.co.uk/berry%20gordy.html.

Also Noteworthy

1960

Richard Wright, the novelist and famous author of *Native Son*, dies.

November 29

1925

Saturnino Orestes Armas "Minnie" Miñoso Arrieta is born in Havana, Cuba. Miñoso played left field with several Major League Baseball (MLB) teams. Known as the "Cuban Comet," Miñoso made his MLB debut on April 19, 1949, with the Cleveland Indians. When he played for the Chicago White Sox on May 1, 1951, in Cominskey Park, Miñoso became the first baseball player of African descent to wear a White Sox uniform.

> ...It's fitting that he was the first black player to wear a Sox uniform. Because of race, Minnie didn't get to play regularly until he was 28 and he still hit for a .298 lifetime average and made All-Star teams seven times. He led the A.L. three times in stolen bases. He was a three-time Gold Glove winner.
>
> And you gotta love that he was given the honor of presenting the Sox lineup card at the final game in Cominskey on September 30, 1990.
>
> Source: From John Mullin. *The Best Chicago Sports Arguments: The 100 Most Controversial, Debatable Questions for Die-Hard Chicago Fans.* Naperville, IL: Sourcebooks, Inc., 2006, p. 174.

Books

Miñoso, Minnie, Fernando Fernández, and Robert Kleinfelder. *Extra Innings: My Life in Baseball.* Lake Bluff, IL: Regnery Gateway, 1983. Miñoso describes his career with the Chicago White Sox.

Miñoso, Minnie with Herb Fagen. *Just Call Me Minnie: My Six Decades in Baseball.* New York, NY: Sports Publishing LLC, 1994. Miñoso recounts his childhood in Cuba and looks at what it was like to be the first person of African descent to play for the Chicago White Sox.

Websites

Minoso. http://www.minoso.com/.
Minnie Minoso: What Can I Say, I'm Black. http://bleacherreport.com/articles/658053 -minnie-minoso-what-can-i-say-im-black.

Also Noteworthy

1915

William "Billy" Strayhorn is born in Dayton, Ohio. As an arranger for Duke Ellington, Strayhorn was responsible for such modern jazz classics as "Take the A Train."

1997

Civil rights activist and former Detroit, Michigan mayor Coleman Alexander Young dies. Young was a long-term activist who fought with the Tuskegee Airmen during World War II and in 1951 helped found the National Negro Labor Council, an organization that fought for Black labor rights.

November 30

1924

Shirley Anita St. Hill Chisholm is the oldest of four girls born to Charles Christopher St. Hill and Ruby Seale in Brooklyn, New York. Chisholm was sent at age 3 to live with her grandmother in Barbados and did not return to New York until she was 10. After graduating from Brooklyn College, Shirley married Conrad Chisholm and the two became active in their community, playing a major role in helping to form the Bedford-Stuyvesant Political League (BSPL). As a politician, Chisholm won a

New York state assembly seat in 1964 and in 1968 defeated Republican Party candidate James Farmer (the founder of CORE) in a race for the U.S. House: Chisholm became the first African American woman to serve in Congress when she was elected to represent New York's 12th Congressional District—she would serve as a congresswoman for seven terms, until 1983. On January 25, 1972, Chisholm famously announced, "I stand before you today as a candidate for the Democratic nomination for the Presidency of the United States. I am not the candidate of Black America, although I am Black and proud. I am not the candidate of the women's movement of this country, although I am a woman, and I am equally proud of that. I am not the candidate of any political bosses or special interests. I am the candidate of the people." After surviving three attempts on her life, Chisholm received 152 of the delegates' votes before withdrawing from the race.

> When Chisholm ran for president in 1972, she campaigned neither as the black not the female candidate—though she was proud to be both black and female—but the candidate of the people. Senator George McGovern easily defeated Chisholm and other contenders for the Democratic nomination, then lost to incumbent Republican president Richard Nixon in the general election. Chisholm's campaign was viewed, then as now, as largely symbolic. But she shrugged off the dismissive treatment her candidacy often got, predicting that future political campaigns by women and minorities would find a smoother path "because I helped pave it." She also helped create institutions that would pry apart the gates of political exclusion, including the Congressional Black Caucus and the National Women's Political Caucus.
>
> Source: From Catherine Ellis and Stephen Drury Smith, ed. *Say It Loud: Great Speeches on Civil Rights and African American Identity.* New York, NY: The New Press, 2010, pp. 102–103.

Books

Chisholm, Shirley. *Unbought and Unbossed: Expanded 40th Anniversary Edition.* Washington, DC: Take Root Media, 2010. Chisholm's own story of her political life and her understanding of Black life in the United States.

Neal, Mark Anthony, edited by Beverly Guy-Sheftall and Johnnetta B. Cole. "What Would Shirley Chisholm Say?" in *Who Should Be First?: Feminists Speak Out on the 2008 Presidential Campaign.* Albany, NY: SUNY Press, 2010. Looks at the bravado and integrity Shirley Chisholm brought to national politics.

Websites

Life and Career of Shirley Chisholm—C-SPAN Video Library. http://www.c-spanvideo.org/program/38274-1.

Women and political action profiles Shirley Chisholm. http://www.wloe.org/WLOE-en/action/shirleychisholm.html.

Shirley Chisholm's 1972 Presidential Campaign. http://www.jofreeman.com/polhistory/chisholm.htm.

Also Noteworthy

1897

J.A. Sweeting receives U.S. Patent No. 594,501 for his cigarette-rolling device.

1912

Gordon Roger Alexander Buchanan Parks is born to Andrew Jackson Parks and Sarah Ross in Fort Scott, Kansas. Gordon Parks became an internationally renowned photographer when he joined the staff of *Life* magazine. Parks worked with *Life* from 1948 through 1972 and he also famously directed the Hollywood films, *The Learning Tree* (1969), *Shaft* (1971), and *Shaft's Big Score!* (1972).

1918

Marcus Garvey publishes the editorial "Advice of the Negro to Peace Conference" in *The Negro World*. The editorial urges European and U.S. leaders to remember to respect Africa and its descendants. "We trust that the delegates to the Peace Conference will not continue to believe that Negroes have no ambition, no aspiration," Garvey wrote. "There are no more timid, cringing Negroes; let us say that those Negroes have now been relegated to the limbo of the past, to the region of forgetfulness, and that the new Negro is on the stage, and he is going to play his part good and well. He, like the other heretofore oppressed peoples of the world, is determined to get restored to him his ancestral rights."

1953

June Antoinette Pointer is born in Oakland, California, to Sarah and the Reverend Elton Pointer. June was the youngest member of the Grammy-winning soul/R&B group the Pointer Sisters, which consisted of Ruth, June, Anita, and later Bonnie. The Pointer Singers sang hit songs like "Jump (For My Love)," "Automatic," "Slow Hand," "He's So Shy," and "Baby Come and Get It."

1982

Michael Jackson's sixth studio album *Thriller* is released. *Thriller* became the best-selling album of all time and sold more than 45 million copies worldwide.

1988

The rapper L.L. Cool J performs in the first-ever rap concert by an African American on the continent of Africa—it takes place in Abidjan, the capital of Côte d'Ivoire. L.L. Cool J was born James Todd Smith on January 14, 1968, in St. Alban's, Queens, New York. After he donated some of the income from his 1987 album *Bigger and Deffer* to fund the building of a new hospital in the Côte d'Ivoire, L.L. Cool J was given the title Chief Kwasi Achi-Brou by the village elders of Grand Bassan.

December

December 1

1865

Shaw University, the first historically black college (HBCU) of the South, is founded in Raleigh, North Carolina. Rev. Henry Martin Tupper of Massachusetts, who had served as a chaplain in the Union Army, established Shaw under the auspices of the American Baptist Home Mission Society; Tupper also served as the University's first president. Initially named the Raleigh Institute, the school was renamed Shaw Collegiate Institute in 1872 in honor of Elijah Shaw, a philanthropist from New England. In 1991, Shaw University alumni Willie E. Gary, who had become a successful civil litigation attorney, presented his alma mater with a $10 million gift check.

The aim of the society at first was mainly to provide schools for the training of ministers and young men as Christian workers. But Dr. Tupper early perceived that the education of young women was of equal importance and in 1870 he received a few coming from different parts of the State, obtaining rooms and board for them in private families. When he first proposed educating young women the idea did not meet with much favor. It was looked upon as a doubtful if not an unwise step. In the meantime the number applying for admission continued to increase until in the spring of 1872 he determined again to appeal to Northern friends for aid, and for two months held a daily prayer meeting with the students, asking the Lord to open the way that suitable accommodations might be furnished for a female department. The following summer he went North and was so far successful in obtaining the necessary funds that upon his return in the fall he commenced a dormitory for girls, which was afterward named Estey Hall in honor of Deacon Jacob Estey and sons of Brattleboro, Vermont, who gave $8,000 toward its erection.

This was the first effort of the denomination in gathering colored girls into a boarding school,

and the Estey building was the first school edifice of any considerable size in the South erected solely for the accommodation of colored women for their Christian development and education.

Source: From J. A. Whitted, ed. *A History of the Negro Baptists of North Carolina*. Victoria, BC: AbeBooks/Edwards & Broughton Print. Co., 1908, pp. 151–152.

Books

Drew, Mary E. C. *Divine Will, Restless Heart.* Bloomington, IN: Xlibris Corporation, 2010. Biography of Dr. John Jefferson Smallwood, the grandson of freedom-fighter Nat Turner, who attended Shaw University and tried to create another school—the Temperance, Industrial and Collegiate Institute in Surry, Virginia—in Shaw's likeness.

Fitts, Leroy. *A History of Black Baptists.* Nashville, TN: Broadman Press, 1985. Looks at the establishment of Shaw University under the auspices of the American Baptist Home Mission Society.

Websites

History—Shaw University. http://www.shaw university.edu/Archives/history.htm.

A Brief History of Shaw University New Raleigh. http://www.newraleigh.com/articles/.../ a-brief-history-of-shaw-university/.

Also Noteworthy

1955

Rosa Parks refuses to change seats on a Montgomery, Alabama, bus and is arrested. On December 5 Blacks began a boycott of the bus system that continued until shortly after December 13, 1956, when the U.S. Supreme Court outlawed bus segregation in the city. Martin Luther King, Jr., organizes Birmingham bus boycott, marking the beginning of the Civil Rights Movement

1987

Carrie Saxon Perry begins her term as the mayor of Hartford, Connecticut, becoming the first African American female to serve as mayor of a major U.S. city.

December 2

1922

Charles Coles Diggs, Jr., is born the only child of Mayne Jones and Charles Coles Diggs in Detroit, Michigan. Diggs, Sr., was a mortician and real estate developer, the owner of the House of Diggs; in 1936 he was elected by a write-in campaign to serve as the first African American state senator in Michigan. In 1951, Diggs became the youngest member of the Michigan State Senate and in 1954 became the first African American elected to serve in the U.S. Congress from the state of Michigan, he served from January 3, 1955, to June 3, 1980. In 1969, Diggs proposed the creation of a Democratic Select Committee (DSC), composed of African American members of Congress and he was named the first chairman of the Congressional Black Caucus (CBC), which was founded during the 92nd Congress of 1971 through 1973. Rep. Diggs famously attended the trial of the two men who murdered 14-year-old Emmett Till. When the congressman traveled to Mississippi to sit in on the proceedings in September of 1955 he received the same Jim Crow treatment as any person of African descent: he was forced to sit at a segregated table assigned mainly to Black reporters. In Congress, Diggs helped pushed for the Home Rule Charter that allowed DC residents partial self-government. He also chaired the African Affairs Subcommittee and advocated for the elimination of South Africa's apartheid system. Diggs commitment to African issues was so deep that the think tank Trans Africa was founded in his congressional office.

...Charles C. Diggs (D-Michigan) was first elected to Congress in 1954 and made apartheid one of his top policy concerns from the outset. He was the founding chairman of the Congressional Black Caucus, and became the first black chairman of the House Subcommittee on Africa in 1969. Diggs and the CBC led many congressional inquiries into U.S. policy on southern Africa that gave anti-apartheid activists the opportunity to address Congress on the issue. He served on the Foreign Relations Committee for over twenty years, became the committee's expert on Africa, and established relations with the leaders of newly independent African stats. Nicknamed "Mr. Africa" by colleagues, Diggs became apartheid's most powerful opponent in the U.S. Congress. Reuters correspondent Raymond Hearst wrote that Diggs had turned his position in the Foreign Relations Committee into the main channel for anti-apartheid pressures.

Source: From Francis Njubi Nesbitt. *Race for Sanctions: African Americans Against Apartheid, 1946–1994.* Bloomington, IN: Indiana University Press, 2004, p. 74.

Books

Parker, Pearl T. *A Political Activist: Charles Coles Diggs, Jr., Michigan's First Black Congressman.* Victoria, BC: AbeBooks/Tennessee State University, 1984. A look at the progressive policies pushed by Rep. Charles Coles Diggs, Jr.

Ragsdale, Bruce A. and Joel D. Treese. *Black Americans in Congress, 1870–1989.* Darby, PA: DIANE Publishing, 1996. Book profiles Digg's congressional career as Michigan's representative.

Websites

DIGGS, Charles Coles, Jr.—Biographical Information. http://bioguide.congress.gov/scripts/biodisplay.pl?index=d000344.

Our History | The Congressional Black Caucus. http://thecongressionalblackcaucus.com/about/our-history/.

Also Noteworthy

1884

Granville T. Woods receives U.S. Patent No. 308,876 for his telephone transmitter.

1891

Charles Harris Wesley is born to Matilda and Charles Snowden Wesley in Louisville, Kentucky. A noted historian of African American culture, Wesley served as a minister of the African Methodist Episcopal Church, was the director of Research and Publications for the Association for the Study of Negro Life and History, and wrote *The History of Alpha Phi Alpha*, about the Black Greek-letter fraternity he was a member of.

December 3

1847

Frederick Douglass and Martin R. Delaney publish the first issue of the *North Star* in Rochester, New York. The *North Star*'s slogan was "Right is of no Sex—Truth is of no Color—God is the Father of us all, and we are all brethren." The newspaper was partly funded with £500 Douglass had raised while lecturing in England; it became a major force in the antislavery movement but also advocated for women's suffrage and education. Although the paper was renamed *Frederick Douglass's Paper* in 1851 it remained in publication for some 17 years. Named for the singular star that heads the Big Dipper and which so many enslaved Africans followed to reach the North and freedom, the *North Star* became the first publication to give voice to the central concerns of the nation's people of African descent.

> *Another important African-American paper, the North Star, was founded in 1847 and edited by Frederick Douglass, an escaped slave and probably the best-known African-American at the time. It had the following prospectus:*
>
> Frederick Douglass proposes to publish in Rochester, New York, a weekly antislavery paper with the above title. The objective of the North Star will be to attack slavery in all its forms and aspects; advocate universal emancipation; exact the standard of public morality; promote the moral and intellectual improvement of the colored people; and . . . hasten the day of freedom to our three million enslaved fellow-countrymen.
>
> *He called it the North Star because slaves escaping at night used the North Star as their guide. Along with others, Douglass helped push what abolitionists called "the War to Free the Slaves"—the U.S. Civil War.*
>
> Source: From Joseph Straubhaar, Robert Larose, and Lucinda Davenport. *Media Now: Understanding Media, Culture, and Technology*. Independence, KY: Cengage Learning, 2011, p. 74.

Books

Garrison, William Lloyd. *The Letters of William Lloyd Garrison: No Union with Slaveholders, 1841–1849*. Cambridge, MA: Harvard University Press, 1974. Book includes excerpts from a letter detailing Garrison's initial shock that Douglass had pushed forward to create the *North Star*, when he had been advised that it might not be advisable.

Willis, Jim. *100 Media Moments That Changed America*. Santa Barbara, CA: ABC-CLIO, 2010. Book includes a profile of Frederick Douglass and a look at why he helped found the *North Star*.

Websites

"Our Paper and Its Prospects" The North Star, December 3, 1847. http://docsouth.unc.edu/neh/douglass/support15.html.

The Library of Congress has a downloadable image of a *North Star* cover. http://www.loc.gov/exhibits/treasures/trr085.html.

Also Noteworthy

1922

Ralph Alexander Gardner-Chavis is born to Vivian Hicks Gardner and Clarence Chavous Gardner in Cleveland, Ohio. His work as a chemist led to the development of hard plastics, which helped advance the petrochemical and pharmaceutical industries.

1982

The 6 foot 1 inch Thomas "The Hit Man" Hearns defeats Wilfredo Benitez at the New Orleans, Louisiana, "Superdome" to win the WBC Junior Middleweight boxing title. Hearns, who was born on October 18, 1958, in Grand Junction, Tennessee, but raised in Detroit, Michigan, became the first person ever to win boxing titles in five different weight class divisions.

December 4

1969

Chicago chapter Black Panther Party (BPP) leader Fred Hampton and 18-year-old Mark Clark are shot to death by members of the Chicago Police Department (CPD) while seven others are maimed as they slept. The attack took place at 4 a.m. at the 2337 West Monroe apartment that served as the BPP headquarters. The CPD and the FBI's powerful counter-intelligence program (COINTELPRO) had decided to conduct a weapons raid on the BPP; Hampton's bodyguard, William O'Neill (an FBI informant) slipped secobarbital into Fred's drink to drug him before the raid started. Authorities initially claimed that BPP members had shot first during the raid, but evidence mounted to prove that both men were, in effect, assassinated. Hampton's body was discovered with a bullet hole in the head.

... Fred's efforts to work with and organize gang members caused fear throughout the police and FBI. After the meeting at Ranger headquarters, Chicago police, following an FBI trip, arrested a carload of armed Panthers driving away. This resulted in criminal charges against the Panthers and set off speculation that the Rangers had snitched on them. Years later we would learn that an FBI informant in the Panthers had tipped off his FBI control, who then notified the police.

On January 24, 1969, the Chicago police arrested Fred following an FBI tip that he was appearing on a local TV station. In front of the live cameras he was led away on an old traffic warrant. Later, Fred told people that when he got to the police car, he noticed he hadn't been cuffed. When placed in the back seat he saw there was a gun resting there. "I spotted a set-up," he said. "I put my wrists outside the car and started screaming, 'There's a gun in the car that somebody left.'" His quick thinking worked. That day he avoided police bullets.

Source: From Jeffrey Haas. *The Assassination of Fred Hampton: How the FBI and the Chicago Police Murdered a Black Panther.* Chicago, IL: Chicago Review Press, 2011, p. 44.

Books

Goodman, Mitchell. *The Movement Toward a New America: The Beginnings of a Long Revolution; (a Collage)—A What?. . . .* Victoria, BC: AbeBooks/Pilgrim Press, 1971. Includes a look at the impact of the murder of Fred Hampton and Mark Clark on the left-leaning movements of the 1960s.

Kirkpatrick, Rob. *1969: The Year Everything Changed.* New York, NY: Skyhorse Publishing Inc., 2011. Kirkpatrick explains the FBI attempts to discredit Fred Hampton, prior to his murder.

Websites

Fred Hampton: Black Libertarian—In His Own Words. http://vimeo.com/20302934.

The Last Hours of William O'Neal. http://www.chicagoreader.com/chicago/the-last-hours-of-william-oneal/Content?oid=875101.

Fred Hampton. http://www.thetalkingdrum.com/fred.html.

Also Noteworthy

1807

Prince Hall, the organizer of the nation's first African American Masonic lodge, dies in Boston, Massachusetts.

1906

Alpha Phi Alpha, Inc. (AΦA) is founded at Cornell University in Ithaca, New York as the first African American Greek-Letter fraternity. Seven young men who were isolated and felt it best to bond to ensure their survival founded Alpha Phi Alpha. Today, these men—Henry Arthur Callis, Charles Henry Chapman, Eugene Kinckle Jones, George Biddle Kelley, Nathaniel Allison Murray, Robert Harold Ogle, and Vertner Woodson Tandy—are known as the seven jewels of Alpha Phi Alpha.

1909

James A. Anderson founds the *New York Amsterdam News*, a Harlem, New York-based newspaper that covers the African American community. The *New York Amsterdam News* is still being published.

1973

Tyra Lynne Banks is born in Inglewood, California. Banks worked as a supermodel, gracing the covers of numerous high fashion magazines. She was the first person of African descent to grace the covers of *GQ* and the *Sports Illustrated Swimsuit Issue*. After modeling, Banks developed and became the CEO of her own television production company, which produced *The Tyra Banks Show* and *America's Next Top Model*.

December 5

1870

Willie M. "Bill" Pickett, the inventor of bulldogging, or steer wrestling, is born to Thomas Jefferson Pickett and Mary Virginia Elizabeth Gilbert Pickett in the Jenks-Branch community of Travis County, Texas. The second of some 13 children, Bill only attended school up to the fifth grade, after which he began working as a cow hand. With his brothers, Bill created the Pickett Brothers Bronco Busters and Rough Riders Association. In addition to working as cowboys, the young men gave demonstrations

on their bulldogging techniques. Bill was eventually hired to join the 101 Ranch Wild West Show where he performed alongside other cowboy greats like Buffalo Bill, Tom Mix, Will Rogers, Milt Hinkle, and Lucille Mulhall. Bill Pickett was the first African American enshrined in the National Cowboy Hall of Fame in 1971, and he was inducted into the ProRodeo Hall of Fame in 1989. In 1993, Pickett was honored with a "Legends of the West" U.S. postage stamp.

The story of Bill Pickett's legendary feat of biting down on the lower lip of an angry longhorn who was not behaving goes back to Rockdale, Texas, in 1903. Pickett subdued a longhorn by jumping on its back from his horse and wrestling the steer down by its horns. In the struggle, he bit down on the lower lip of the animal and jerked the animal flat. Soon people paid to see Pickett "bulldog" steers. There is a sculpture of Bill Pickett, who died in 1932, biting the lower lip of a steer in Fort Worth at the Cowtown Coliseum.

Source: From Edward M. Walters. *Finding Anything about Everything in Texas: 100 Credible Books and 100 Reliable Websites*. Lanham, MD: Rowman & Littlefield Publishing Group/Taylor Trade Publications, 2005, p. 13.

Books

Hanes, Bailey C. *Bill Pickett, Bulldogger: The Biography of a Black Cowboy*. Norman, OK: University of Oklahoma Press, 1989. Biography of Bill Pickett looks at the role he and other African Americans played in the United States's development of its western states.

Pinkney, Andrea Davis J. and Brian Pinkney. *Bill Pickett, Rodeo Ridin' Cowboy*. New York, NY: Harcourt Brace & Co., 1996. Biography of Pickett written for young adults.

Websites

National Cowboy & Western Heritage Museum has a biography of Pickett and information on a photo collection regarding Bill's work. http://www.nationalcowboymuseum.org/

research/cms/FindingAids/PACKARD/ tabid/322/Default.aspx.

Cowboy Bob's Campfire Conversations discusses the history of bulldogging and how Pickett brought it back to fame. http://www .lemen.com/stbull.html.

Also Noteworthy

1775

A memorial is dedicated in Cambridge, Massachusetts, to commemorate the fighting spirit of Salem Poor. Poor was an enslaved African who had bought his own freedom and later went on to fight at Bunker Hill with the Revolutionaries against England.

1870

Joseph Hayne Rainey of South Carolina is sworn in as a member of the House of Representatives; he is the second African American to serve in the U.S. Congress.

1932

The "king of gospel," the Reverend Dr. James Cleveland, is born in Chicago, Illinois. Rev. Cleveland was the founder of the Gospel Music Workshop of America (GMWA); he wrote some 400 songs, had 16 gold albums, and won four Grammys.

1932

Richard Wayne Penniman, a.k.a. "Little Richard," is born and raised in Macon, Georgia. As a singer-performer, Little Richard was one of the founding fathers of rock and roll, recording major hits like "Tutti Frutti," "Good Golly Miss Molly," "Long Tall Sally."

1935

The National Council of Negro Women is founded by Mary McLeod Bethune.

1955

Montgomery Bus Boycott begins, led by Martin Luther King, Jr. The boycott would last a little over a year, as it led to a November 13, 1956, Supreme Court decision banning segregation on Montgomery, Alabama, city buses. The Bus Boycott was officially ended on December 21, 1956.

December 6

1836

Thomas Downing helps found the all-Black United Anti-Slavery Society of the City of New York. Downing was New York City's first famous African American restaurateur; he was the owner of the Downing Oyster House, which opened in 1825 at 5 Broad Street and became a favored location for local politicians, stockbrokers, lawyers, and businesspeople. When Downing died on April 10, 1866, the New York Chamber of Commerce closed for the day to show its respect. Even while serving the city's wealthy, Downing—who was a free Black man and had never been enslaved—worked with local abolitionists as part of the Underground Railroad and worked to found educational opportunities for people of African descent.

The public record of Thomas Downing's involvement in the abolitionist movement began on December 6, 1836, when he helped found the all-black United Anti-Slavery Society of the City of New York. The American Anti-Slavery Society had been formed in Philadelphia in 1833, but Downing and others felt the need to establish their own group, which a local, rather than a national, emphasis and which would hold abolitionist meetings and conduct other activities in the black community. Downing served on the executive committee of the organization until 1839, when it evidently merged with the New York Anti-Slavery Society.

Source: From John H. Hewitt. *Protest and Progress: New York's First Black Episcopal Church Fights Racism.* New York, NY: Taylor & Francis, 2000, p. 85.

Books

Harris, Jessica B. *High on the Hog: A Culinary Journey from Africa to America.* New York, NY: Bloomsbury Publishing USA, 2011. Book includes a look at the success of Thomas Downing's oyster restaurant.

Kurlansky, Mark. *The Big Oyster: History on the Half Shell.* New York, NY: Random House, Inc., 2007. History of oysters and of the tradition of oyster restaurants includes a large segment on Thomas Downing and his famous restaurant.

Washington, Booker T. *The Story of the Negro; the Rise of the Race from Slavery, Vol II.* New York, NY: Doubleday/General Books LLC, 2010. The famous African American leader writes about Black people.

Websites

The Downing Street Playground is reportedly named to honor Thomas Downing. http://www.nycgovparks.org/parks/M027/highlights/8714.

The Negro in the Organization of Abolition looks at the role Blacks like Thomas Dowing played in the abolition of slavery. http://www.jstor.org/pss/271940.

1864

The Thirteenth Amendment to the U.S. Constitution, passed by the Senate on April 8, 1864, by the House on January 31, 1865, and ratified on December 6, 1865, abolishes slavery as a legal institution. With ratification of the Thirteenth Amendment in 1865, the United States had officially ended African enslavement. And with the subsequent ratifications of the Fourteenth (1868; which overturned the Supreme Court's Dred Scott decision and gave Blacks national citizenship) and Fifteenth (1870) Amendments to the constitution, African Americans were purported to have officially joined the body politic: they were guaranteed U.S. citizenship and the due process of law; and Black males were guaranteed the right to vote. The Civil War amendments granted Congress the power to enforce citizenship rights for some 4 million newly emancipated African Americans. Congress was empowered to use "appropriate legislation" to complete this task, but by the early 1870s, such legislation was rarely being implemented.

> [U]ntil the House voted on January 31, 1865, no one could predict which way it would go. As a few Democrats early in the roll call voted Aye, Republican faces brightened. Sixteen of the eighty Democrats finally voted for the Amendment; fourteen of them were lame ducks. Eight other Democrats had absented themselves. This enabled the Amendment to pass with two votes to spare, 119 to 56. When the result was announced, Republicans on the floor and spectators in the gallery broke into prolonged—and unprecedented—cheering, while in the streets of Washington cannons boomed a hundred-gun salute.
>
> Source: From James M. McPherson. *Battle Cry of Freedom: The Civil War Era.* New York, NY: Oxford University Press, 2003, p. 839.

Books

Remini, Robert Vincent. *The House: The History of the House of Representatives.* New York, NY: Smithsonian Books/Library of Congress/HarperCollins, 2006. Book details how the vote on the Thirteenth Amendment progressed and the notable legislatures who were on site to witness its passage.

Vorenberg, Michael. *Final Freedom: The Civil War, the Abolition of Slavery, and the Thirteenth Amendment.* New York, NY: Cambridge University Press, 2001. Author looks at the political parties and social movements that pushed for passage of the Thirteenth Amendment.

Websites

The National Archives has an image of the original Thirteenth Amendment online. http://www.archives.gov/historical-docs/document.html?doc=9&title.raw=13th%20Amendment%20to%20the%20U.S.%20Constitution%3A%20Abolition%20of%20Slavery.

The Website for *Harper's Monthly* has an article on "The End of Slavery: The Creation of the Thirteenth Amendment," which details the creation of the Thirteenth Amendment. http://13thamendment.harpweek.com/.

Also Noteworthy

1869

The Colored National Labor Union (CNLU) holds the first Black labor convention in history at Union League Hall in Washington, DC, from December 6 to 10, 1869. The 159 delegates to the convention designed the CNLU to help African American workers battle for collective bargaining rights. The CNLU even published a weekly newspaper called the *New National Era* and had Frederick Douglass as its editor.

1932

Richard B. Spikes of San Francisco, California receives U.S. Patent No. 1,889,814 for an automatic gearshift for cars; he licensed his patent for $100,000. Spikes also created improvements to the automobile directional signals and invented the beer keg tap.

1936

Richard Francis Jones becomes first African American certified in urology.

1961

Detroit, Michigan-based WGPR-FM goes on air as a pioneer African American-owned broadcaster.

1961

The writer/psychiatrist/social philosopher Frantz Omar Fanon dies at the National Institutes of Health in Bethesda, Maryland, just outside Washington, DC. Fanon had traveled to Washington for medical treatment after being diagnosed with leukemia. Famed for his books *Black Skin, White Masks* (1952), and *The Wretched of the Earth* (1961), Fanon's focus on the psychological problems created by internalized racism and oppression helped many of his followers formulate ways to work towards Black liberation.

December 7

1942

Reginald F. Lewis is born in Baltimore, Maryland. Lewis became a partner in Wallace, Murphy, Thorpe & Lewis, the first African American law firm on Wall Street. He later became the owner of TLC Beatrice International Holdings Inc., the largest black-owned business in the nation and the first to make more than $1 billion in annual sales. At one point in the 1980s, because of his legal and entrepreneurial work, Reginald Lewis was the richest African American in the United States.

> Building a successful law practice calls for something not taught in law school: The ability to hustle and self-promote. No one beats a path to an unheralded lawyer's door. The phone is usually quiet and when it does ring, chances are a bill collector is on the other end.
>
> Lewis realized all this when he left Paul, Weiss in 1970. As always, he had a plan. He joined Wallace and a handful of other attorneys in starting a black-run law firm geared toward business matters affecting New York City's black community. The firm has the distinction of being one of the first black law firms on Wall Street—if not the first. Its name was Wallace, Murphy, Thorpe and Lewis, but in time only Lewis would remain.
>
> Source: From Reginald F. Lewis with Blair S. Walker. *Why Should White Guys Have All the Fun?: How Reginald Lewis Created a Billion-Dollar Business Empire.* Baltimore, MD: Black Classic Press, 2005, p. 76.

Books

Dingle, Derek T. *Black Enterprise Titans of the B.E. 100s: Black CEOs Who Redefined and Conquered American Business.* Hoboken, NJ: John Wiley & Sons, 1999. Author looks at successful Black entrepreneurs and references the successes of Reginald Lewis.

Wiley, Elliott. *RFL, Reginald F. Lewis: A Tribute.* New York: Bookmark Publishing Corp., 1994. A look at Lewis's life and accomplishments.

Websites

"Remembering Reggie" by Clarence Davis gives a personal portrait of Lewis's young life and striving for success. http://www.nathanielturner.com/rememberingreggie.htm.

The Website for The Reginald F. Lewis Museum provides information about Lewis's life and legacy. http://www.reginaldflewis.com/biography.php.

Also Noteworthy

1931

Comer Cottrell, the founder of the Pro-Line hair care products company, is born in Mobile, Alabama. With his part in the 1989 purchase of the Texas Rangers, Cottrell became the first African American to own part of a Major League Baseball franchise.

1941

Doris "Dorie" Miller, a cook, Third Class on the U.S. Navy's *USS Arizona*, shoots down four Japanese warplanes during the surprise attack on Pearl Harbor. Miller was commended for his actions by the Secretary of the Navy Frank Knox received the Navy Cross May 27, 1942.

December 8

1925

Samuel George "Sammy" Davis, Jr., is born in Harlem, New York to Sammy Davis, Sr., and Elvera "Baby" Sanchez. With his father being a vaudeville actor and his mother a dancer, Davis grew up near the theater and became a renowned singer-dancer-actor who was widely referred to as "greatest living entertainer in the world." Davis performed in his first film at the age of six and was famously the only African American member of "The Rat Pack," a self-styled group of Hollywood-esque entertainers, including Humphrey Bogart, Frank Sinatra, Dean Martin, Joey Bishop, and Peter Lawford. While he was a vocal supporter of the Civil Rights Movement, Davis was also a supporter of the Republican Party's Richard Nixon—a fact that incurred him some animosity in the African American community. In 1972, Davis had a No. 1 hit with his recording of "The Candy Man."

> . . . a curious bond emerged between Sammy and Nixon. In some respects, the two men had vastly different personalities. The entertainer was harsh, exuberant, and such an extrovert he couldn't stand to be alone for a minute. By contrast, the president was something of a loner, an introvert, and more comfortable with ideas than with people. But they had both known impoverished youths, were unusually sensitive to criticism, and were more than a little controversial. Perhaps for these reasons, they felt like kindred spirits. In any event, Brown asserted, "Nixon like Sammy Davis, Jr., very much. He really admired and respected Sammy, and he wanted Sammy to know that. So much so that Sammy could call and get through to Nixon. I mean, there weren't a lot of people who could do that."
>
> Source: From Gary Fishgall. *Gonna Do Great Things: The Life of Sammy Davis, Jr.* New York, NY: Simon & Schuster, 2003, pp. 267–268.

Books

Davis, Sammy, Jane Boyar, and Burt Boyar. *Sammy: An Autobiography with Material Newly Revised from Yes I Can and Why Me?* New York: Macmillan, 2000. Davis's autobiography details his life and entertainment career.

Haygood, Wil. *In Black and White: The Life of Sammy Davis, Jr.* New York: A.A. Knopf, 2003. Biography examines Davis's personal life and character and looks at how they characterized his entertainment career.

Websites

Sammy Davis Jr.—The Candy Man. http://www.youtube.com/watch?v=AYihDAhVPko.
The Official Sammy Davis, Jr. Website. www.sammydavis-jr.com.

Also Noteworthy

1850

After studying in a two-year ladies' course, Lucy Ann Stanton graduates from Ohio State's Oberlin College with a bachelor of literature degree. Stanton is believed to be the first African American female to graduate from any college in the United States. After Oberlin, Stanton went on to become a teacher in the South during Reconstruction.

1936

The decision is rendered in the *Gibbs v. Board of Education in Montgomery County, Md.* case. The Gibbs case, which the NAACP filed against the state of Maryland, eliminated the practice of paying white teachers more than African American teachers.

1987

Kurt Lidell Schmoke becomes the first African American and the 46th official mayor of Baltimore, Maryland. Schmoke served in office from 1987 to 1999.

1976

U.S. federal government designates the Sweet Auburn District of Atlanta, Georgia a National Historic Landmark. Auburn Avenue is famous as the street where notable African American leaders lived at one time, among them Martin Luther King, Jr., NAACP leader Walter White and Maynard Jackson, Jr., who served as Atlanta's first African American mayor. The historic district was also home to the Rucker Building the city's first Black-owned office building, as well as to the *Atlanta Daily World*, the first African American-owned daily newspaper which was founded in 1928.

December 9

1925

John Elroy Sanford, who also answered to the stage name of "Red Foxx," is born to Fred Glen Sanford and Mary Alma Hughes Sanford in St Louis, Missouri. As a comedian, Foxx performed a stand-up act in Harlem, New York, for years before finding success with the release of comedy albums and later starring with Demond Wilson in the television sitcom *Sanford and Son*, which ran from 1972 through 1977.

The comedian was working at the Stadium Club on Los Angeles in 1954 when he met Dootsie Williams, owner of Dootones Records, a label specializing in doo-wop music and that had released the Penguins' 1954 hit "Earth Angel." Williams approached Foxx and suggested that his act be recorded. Foxx agreed and the result was The Laff of the Party, a live performance comedy album that became the first "party record," that is, a recording especially designed for party hosts to play for their guests after the children had gone to bed. The album earned a gold record, and over the next decade Dootones released 35 more Foxx albums, including One on Me (1960), The Sidesplitter (1961), He's Funny that Way (1961), The New Fugg (1962), and Hearty Laffs (1962)—not to mention eight other installments of The Laff of the Party. Even though other, better-known comedians like Shelley Berman, Bob Newhart, Dick Gregory, Bill Cosby, and Moms Mabely began to release live performance albums around this time, what distinguished Foxx and his work were his tone and his subject matter. While Cosby created a world that, although set in the inner city, involved middle-class values, idealized relationships, and nonthreatening street urchins such as his characters Fat Albets and Good Ol' Weird Harold, while Gregory increasingly sacrificed his punch lines for political diatribes, and Mabley never discussed sexual activity in much detail, Foxx spoke about the seedier side of life directly, aggressively, and unapologetically. He talked about sex, poverty, racism, and he treated each subject as an expected part of everyday life. He opened his shows with lines like, "To those of you who applauded, I want you to know I appreciate it. To those of you who didn't, I hope your dog dies" or "You gonna enjoy me if you never seen me before. Even if you seen me before, you gonna enjoy me again—'cause I'm good. That's true, sir. I swear to God and the three other white men, you're gonna enjoy me. Or someone will follow you home and burn it. It's like, you know, soft-sell militancy."

Source: From Eddie M. Tafoya. Icons of African American Comedy. Santa Barbara, CA: ABC-CLIO, 2011, p. 38.

Books

Rodriguez, Robert. *The 1950s' Most Wanted: The Top 10 Book of Rock & Roll Rebels, Cold War Crises, and All-American Oddities.* Dulles, VA: Potomac Books, Inc., 2006. Book includes a short biography of Redd Foxx and looks at his life as a comedian.

Starr, Michael Seth. *Black and Blue: The Redd Foxx Story.* Milwaukee, WI: Hal Leonard Books/Applause Theatre & Cinema, 2011. Biography of the comedian Red Foxx, who worked for years as a stand-up comedian and became a national name at the age of 49.

Websites

Official Site of Redd Foxx. http://www.cmgww .com/stars/foxx/foxx.html.

Redd Foxx shares a civil rights story. http:// www.youtube.com/watch?v=9Tdzbs7sWPI &feature=related.

Also Noteworthy

1872

Pinckney Benton Stewart (P.B.S.) Pinchback becomes the first person of African descent to serve as governor of a state when he takes over the reins as governor of Louisiana during Reconstruction. Pinchback had been serving as the lieutenant governor, but was named governor during the impeachment proceedings against the elected governor, Henry Clay Warmoth. Pinchback served as Louisiana's 24th governor for 35 days, from December 9, 1872, to January 13, 1873—a little more than a month.

December 10

1967

Stax-Volt recording artist Otis Redding and four members of the Bar-Kays (Otis's Memphis, Tennessee-based back-up band) are killed when the private twin-engine Beechcraft airplane they are traveling in crashes into frozen lake Monono, near Madison, Wisconsin. The group had been on its way to Madison for a performance at a club called The Factory near the University of Wisconsin, but when their plane crashed everyone on board died, except for Bar-Kays' trumpeter Ben Cauley. Otis Ray Redding, Jr.—who was 26 years old when he died—was born to Fannie and Otis Redding, Sr., on September 9, 1941, in Macon, Georgia. Redding's father was a Baptist minister and gospel, blues, and R&B heavily influenced Otis, Jr.'s musical inclinations. Redding's most famous song, "(Sittin' On) The Dock of the Bay," had been recorded just three days before he died and was his only million-selling song. But Redding is also known for the songs, "These Arms of Mine," "I've Been Loving You Too Long," and "Try A Little Tenderness." Redding also wrote the song "Respect," which became the signature song for the "queen of soul," Aretha Franklin.

A soul music giant, the gritty-voiced Otis Redding was born into poverty at a housing project in the musically right community of Macon, Georgia. After forming his own gospel choir at his preacher father's small Mount Ivy Baptist Church, Redding mastered the drums, piano and guitar by playing along with his records. Inspired by the success of fellow Macon resident Little Richard, Redding formed an R&B band against the wishes of his deeply religious father. Dropping out of school to support his family after his father fell ill, Redding spent his weekends entering talent contests with his Little Richard-like delivery. Beginning in 1958, Redding occasionally joined guitarist Johnny Jenkins' group The Pinetoppers; after hiring an unlikely 18-year-old, white, R&B fan Phil Walden as their manager, The Pinetoppers secured bookings throughout the South. Recording two solo singles, Redding landed scattered airplay with the upbeat 'Shout Bamalama'. After accompanying Johnny Jenkins and The Pinetoppers to the Stax-Volt studio in Memphis in 1952, Redding recorded two unscheduled solo tracks at the end of a Pinetoppers session. Backed by the house band, Booker T & The MGs, Redding recorded two songs for what would become his first single, 'Hey, Hey Baby' and the gospel-tinged, slow-climbing, B-side hit, 'These Arms of Mine.' Recording at the Stax-Volt studios but signed by Atlantic-Atco, Redding developed a fruitful writing relationship with MG's guitarist Steve Cropper. Recorded in 24 hours, the album Otis Blue (1965) spawned the hits 'I've Been Loving You Too Long' and a Redding composition that Aretha Franklin redefined two years later, 'Respect.'. . .

Source: From Nick Talevski. *Knocking on Heaven's Door: Rock Obituaries.* London, England: Omnibus Press, 2006, p. 540.

Books

Brown, Geoff. *Otis Redding: Try a Little Tenderness.* New York, NY: Canongate U.S., 2003. Biography of Otis Redding looks at his distinct voice and the southern influences on his music and career.

Freeman, Scott. *Otis!: The Otis Redding Story.* New York: St. Martin's Press, 2001. This biography of Otis Redding contains many of the recollections others have about Redding and his influence on soul music.

Websites

Celebrating 70 years of Otis Redding. www.otisredding.com/.

Otis Redding—Try a Little Tenderness. http://www.youtube.com/watch?v=KjoMSfPQUCA&feature=related.

Also Noteworthy

1950

Dr. Ralph J. Bunche becomes first African American awarded the Nobel Peace Prize. Bunche won the award for his work as a diplomat, having negotiated the 1949 armistice between one-year-old Israel and its Arab neighbors.

1964

Dr. Martin Luther King, Jr., is awarded the Nobel Peace Prize in Oslo, Norway. King is the youngest person to have won the Nobel as of this date and the third African American awarded the prize.

2009

The Nobel Peace Prize 2009 is awarded to Barack H. Obama "for his extraordinary efforts to strengthen international diplomacy and cooperation between peoples." Obama was the fourth U.S. President to be awarded the Nobel Peace Prize and the first U.S. president to receive the award during his first year in office.

December 11

1926

Willie Mae "Big Mama" Thornton is born in Montgomery, Alabama. Thornton's father was a minister and she started out singing Gospel music, but when she was 14 and her mother died, Thornton ran away from home and in 1941 joined Sammy Green's Atlanta, Georgia-based Hot Harlem Revue. Thornton grew to be 6 foot, 350 pounds, and took on the name "Big Mama." She became famous for her 1956 song "Hound Dog" (which was recorded two years later by Elvis Presley), and another song she wrote, "Ball and Chain," was covered and made famous by Janis Joplin.

> *A nearly perfect vehicle for Thornton, "Hound Dog" was released in 1953 and hit number one on the rhythm and blues charts in 1955. Author Ian Whitcomb described a Thornton performance of "Hound Dog" in Repercussions: "When Big Mama sings 'Hound Dog' she's slow and easy and also menacing, smiling like a sabre-tooth tiger, her black diamond eyes glinting fiercely. Then, with the band in full roar, she leaves her chair to ambulate off in a swaying promenade that has a certain military regality, and the whole house cheers like royal subjects." "Hound Dog" was Thornton's biggest studio success, selling over 500,000 copies. Still, Thornton often expressed bitterness over the credit Presley received for his recording. "That song [Presley's version] sold over two million records. I got one check for $500 and never saw another," the August 13, 1984, issue of Jet magazine quoted her as once stating.*
>
> *Source: From Jessie Carney Smith. Notable Black American Women. Bonn, Germany: VNR AG, 1996, p. 642.*

Books

Govenar, Alan B. *Texas Blues: The Rise of a Contemporary Sound*. College Station, TX: Texas A&M University Press, 2008. Book includes a profile of "Big Mama" Thornton.

Pendle, Karin. *Women and Music*. Bloomington, IN: Indiana University Press, 2001. Book includes a tribute/profile of Willie Mae "Big Mama" Thornton.

Websites

"Big Mama" Thornton performing "Hound Dog." http://www.dailymotion.com/video/x137v2_big-mama-thornton-hound-dog_music.

Big Mama" Thornton's biography is on All Music. http://www.allmusic.com/artist/big-mama-thornton-p553.

Also Noteworthy

1917

Death sentences are carried out against 13 African American soldiers stationed at Camp Logan's army training camp in Houston, Texas—they are hanged for reportedly participating in a riot. The soldiers were part of the third battalion of the all-Black 24th Infantry Regiment, they had gotten tired of the Jim Crow laws and racist insults they faced in Houston—particularly when they were training to go and defend democracy abroad, in France. Some 100 soldiers marched on downtown Houston with their rifles and in the space of two hours they killed 15 whites, 4 of them police officers. Sixty-four of the soldiers were tried for murder and mutiny; 13 received death sentences and the rest got life imprisonment.

December 12

1900

The National Negro Anthem, "Lift Every Voice and Sing," is composed by two brothers from the state of Florida, James Weldon and James Rosamond Johnson. James Weldon was 28 and his brother was 26 at the time. James Weldon had been the first African American elected to the Florida bar just two years previously, but he and his brother had decided to try their hand at a songwriting career.

> *"Lift Every Voice and Sing" is fittingly provocative. Yet its message, ingeniously crafted, does not fuel the fires of racial hatred. Sociologist E. Franklin Frazier pointed out that in "Lift Every Voice and Sing," James Weldon Johnson endowed the African American enslavement and struggle for freedom with a certain nobility. Frazier further noted that Johnson expressed an acceptance of the past and confidence in the future. It is likely that Johnson was attempting to cultivate a sense of history among his race. On the one hand, the lyrics reveal how African Americans were estranged from their cultural past by the impact of racial oppression and that they manifested the psychological and physical scars inflicted by that injustice. On the other hand, the song is irrefutably one of the most stalwart and inspiring symbols in American civil*

rights history. Not wanting African Americans to lose hope, James Weldon Johnson included in the lyrics none of his pragmatic reservations regarding justice for his race. His enriching directive is assuredly one of the mainstays of the song's mastery and endurance. Notwithstanding, he tells us in "Lift Every Voice and Sing" that we must persist—we must remain vigilant until victory is won.

Source: From Julian Bond. Lift Every Voice and Sing: A Celebration of the Negro National Anthem. New York, NY: Random House Digital, Inc., 2000, p. ii.

Books

Johnson, James Weldon and Debbie Egan-Chin. *Lift Every Voice and Sing: A Pictorial Tribute to the Negro National Anthem.* New York, NY: Jum at the Sun/Hyperion Books for Children, 2000. Centennial celebration of "Lift Every Voice and Sing" includes photographs and remembrances about the song's importance.

Peretti, Burton William. *Lift Every Voice: The History of African American Music.* Lanham, MD: Rowman & Littlefield, 2009. Places "Lift Every Voice and Sing" within the context of African American music—particularly as music has helped to define the Black American identity.

Websites

Kim Weston singing "Lift Every Voice and Sing." http://www.youtube.com/watch?v=lwyHil6pD7o&feature=related.

"Lift Every Voice and Sing" by James Weldon Johnson. http://www.poets.org/viewmedia.php/prmMID/15588.

Also Noteworthy

1870

Joseph Hayne Rainey of South Carolina is sworn in as a member of the House of Representatives; he is the first African American to serve in the U.S. Congress.

1899

George F. Grant receives U.S. Patent No. 638,920 for a golf tee.

1961

Martin Luther King, Jr., and some 700 demonstrators are arrested for demonstrating for civil rights in Albany, Georgia, between December 12 and 16th.

December 13

1903

Ella Jo Baker is born in Norfolk, Virginia. A life-long activist, Baker was the first national director of the Young Negroes Cooperative League in the 1930s and began working as a field secretary and later as head of several different branches of the National Association for Advancement of Colored People (NAACP) in the 1940s. In 1956 Baker co-founded the group In Friendship, along with Bayard Rustin and Stanley Levison. In Friendship sent financial support to the growing Civil Rights Movement in the South. In 1957, Baker joined the Martin Luther King Jr.—led Southern Christian Leadership Conference (SCLC) and ran the groups' "Crusade for Citizenship" voter registration campaign. In April 1960, Baker was the central adult figure in the formation of the Student Nonviolent Coordinating Committee (SNCC), a Black student-led nonviolent protest group.

The family wasn't poor, but it also wasn't one of means—particularly in the late twenties, just before the Great Depression broke. In 1927, Baker moved to New York City where she had relatives. There she became active in a consumers' rights movement. She also joined and worked for the National Association for the Advancement of Colored People (NAACP). She traveled around the South, talking about pressing issues—police brutality, unequal salaries between blacks and whites. She urged people to join the NAACP. She solicited money. *In 1942, the NAACP leadership made Baker national director of all the organization's local branches. Later, she served as president of the NAACP's New York chapter and worked on school desegregation.*

From 1958 to 1960, Baker worked for the Southern Christian Leadership Conference (SCLC). In 1960, she helped found the Student Nonviolent Coordinating Committee (SNCC, pronounced "Snick"). It was an organization established to coordinate the thousands of black southern students who had begun sitting in at lunch counters and other public places, and who had begun conducting mass, peaceful demonstrations to break the back of southern segregation. In 1964, Baker helped found the Mississippi Freedom Democratic Party, which would challenge the racism of the mainstream party at the 1964 Democratic convention. In the sixties, she was also on the staff of the Southern Conference Educational Fund (SCEF). . . .

Source: From Ellen Cantarow, Susan Gushee O'Malley, Sharon Hartman Strom, Florence Luscomb, Ella Baker, and Jessie Lopez De La Cruz. *Moving the Mountain: Women Working for Social Change.* New York, NY: Feminist Press, 1980, pp. 55–56.

Books

Charles, Joan E. The University of Oklahoma. Department of Instructional Leadership and Academic Curriculum. *Ella Baker and the SNCC: Grassroots Leadership and Political Activism in a Nonhierarchical Organization.* Norman, OK: University of Oklahoma/ProQuest, 2007. Biography of Ella Baker and her work in the Civil Rights Movement.

Dallard, Shyrlee and Andrew Young. *Ella Baker: A Leader Behind the Scenes.* Morristown, NJ: Silver Burdett Press, 1990. Book looks at Ella Baker's organizing skills and particularly her work with the Student Non-Violent Coordinating Committee.

Websites

Ella Baker Center: Who Was Ella Baker? www.ellabakercenter.org/ella/.

Ella Baker profiled on YouTube. http://www.youtube.com/watch?v=GRl6h-Cn4W0&feature=related.

Also Noteworthy

1913

Archie Moore is born Archibald Lee White in Benoit, Mississippi. The 5 feet 11 inch, 39-year-old Moore became the light heavyweight world-boxing champion in 1952.

1981

Dewey "Pigmeat" Markham dies of a stroke in the Bronx, New York. "Pigmeat" Markham was a famed stand-up comedian mainly known as a major draw on the African American chitlin' circuit. Also known as "Sweet Poppa Pigmeat," Markhan was only nationally known for performing his "Here comes the judge" routine on the *Rowan & Martin's Laugh-In* television show.

December 14

1829

John Mercer Langston is born in Louisa County, Virginia, to the white owner of the plantation, Captain Ralph Quarles, and Lucy Langston a mixed-race African Indian. Langston was elected township clerk of Brownhelm, Ohio, on September 10, 1855, becoming first African American to hold elective office in Ohio. Though born enslaved, Langston had been an activist in the antislavery movement. He attended and graduated from Oberlin College and when denied entry to law schools in Ohio studied under an attorney and passed the exams for the Ohio bar on his own in 1854. Langston became the first Black lawyer in Ohio and the first Black Congressman elected from Virginia. Langston served as president of the National Equal Rights League, an organization that fought for Black voting rights, and after the Union victory in the Civil War, he was named inspector general of the Freedmen's Bureau. John Mercer Langston was the founder of Howard University Law School and authored the 1894 autobiography, *From the Virginia Plantation to the National Capitol: or, The First and Only Negro Representative in Congress from the Old Dominion.*

> At the National Convention of colored man held at Syracuse in 1864, he was chosen head of the Equal Rights League, the plan for which had been adopted by that body. Mr. Langston entered upon the work of organizing the league with enthusiasm and energy, contributing very largely to the success of this first movement among colored man, which embraced the South as well as the North. Upon the undertaking by the Freemen's Bureau of the work of assisting in the maintenance of colored schools in the South, Langston was, at the suggestion of Chief Justice Chase, appointed its Inspector-General, with the duty of visiting the schools under its control for the colored youth of the South, and reporting their condition from time to time to General O.O. Howard, the head of the Bureau.
>
> *Source*: From John Wesley Cromwell. *The Negro in American History: Men and Women Eminent in the Evolution of the American of African Descent.* Washington, DC: The American Negro Academy, 1914, pp. 156–157.

Books

Cheek, William F. and Aimee Lee Cheek. *John Mercer Langston and the Fight for Black Freedom, 1829–65.* Champaign, IL: University of Illinois Press, 1996. Biography of Langston examines his political career in light of the social positions African Americans held in the North during the mid-1800s.

Langston, John Mercer. *From the Virginia Plantation to the National Capitol; or, the First and Only Negro Representative in Congress from the Old Dominion.* Edina, MN: American Publishing Company, 1894. Autobiography of John Mercer Langston.

Websites

Oberlin College profiles its school alumnus "John Mercer Langston." http://www.oberlin .edu/external/EOG/OYTT-images/JM Langston.html.

Black Americans in Congress profiles John Mercer Langston. http://baic.house.gov/ member-profiles/profile.html?intID=18.

Also Noteworthy

1939

Ernie Davis is born in New Salem, Pennsylvania, and raised for a while by his grandparents in Pittsburgh, Pennsylvania. He moved to Elmira, New York at age 12 with his mother and stepfather and became such a revered three-sport athlete at the Elmira Free Academy high school that more than 50 colleges—including Notre Dame and UCLA—offered him scholarships. But Davis went local and played for upstate New York's Syracuse University. As a football running back, Davis rushed for 2,386 yards and scored 220 points for the Syracuse University "Orangemen" and became the first African American player to win the Heisman Trophy. Davis was the No. 1 pick in the NFL draft and was chosen to play professionally with the Washington Redskins and later traded to the Cleveland Browns, but after developing leukemia in 1962, Davis died on May 18, 1963 at the age of 23.

1945

The *Las Vegas Review Journal* announces the opening of "Westside Park," a subdivision of 155 tract houses designed by famed Southern California-based architect Paul Revere Williams. Westside Park became a historic, predominantly African American, area in Las Vegas, Nevada.

December 15

1883

William Augustus Hinton is born to Augustus Hinton and Marie Clark in Chicago,

Illinois, both of his parents were formerly enslaved. Dr. Hinton was the first African American to teach at Harvard Medical School (he was initially a part-time faculty member, teaching bacteriology and immunology for more than 30 years before being promoted to a clinical professor in 1949); he was the first Black person to publish a textbook (*Syphilis and Its Treatment*, 1936); and is famous for developing the "Hinton Test" a flocculation method for diagnosing syphilis.

> *Scientists knew that the spinal fluid of patients with syphilis was chemically different from that of disease-free individuals; however, it was known how this fact could be put to use as a diagnostic tool. What Dr. Hinton sought was a test that was quick and sensitive and gave a diagnosis that could be read with complete certainty. He found the solution to the problem when he combined pure forms of beef protein, cholesterol, common table salt, and water. When a small sample of spinal fluid from a diseased person was added to this mixture at just the right temperature, the cholesterol in the mixture came out of suspension, and the murky looking liquid turned perfectly clear.*
>
>   . . . .
>
> *In 1936, all Hinton's research, and the findings of others as well, were put together in a medical textbook called Syphilis and Its Treatment, written by Dr. William Augustus Hinton.*
>
> *Source*: From James H. Kessler. *Distinguished African American Scientists of the 20th Century*. Santa Barbara, CA: Greenwood Publishing Group, 1996, p. 174.

Books

Brodie, James Michael. *Created Equal: The Lives and Ideas of Black American Innovators*. New York, NY: W. Morrow, 1993. Book includes a profile of Hinton and the importance of his syphilis test.

Hinton, William Augustus. *Syphilis and Its Treatment*. Victoria, BC: AbeBooks/The Macmillan Company, 1936. Hinton's original medical textbook, first published in 1936, was the first major text on syphilis.

Websites

Public Health Museum in Massachusetts profiles William Hinton. www.publichealthmuseum .org/William%20Hinton%20Exhibit.htm.

The Faces of Science: African Americans in the Sciences "William Augustus Hinton: Medical." https://webfiles.uci.edu/mcbrown/ display/hinton.html.

Also Noteworthy

1864

The Union Army's 13th U.S. Colored Troops (U.S.T.C.) defeats the Confederate Army of Tennessee at the Battle of Nashville. The U.S.T.C.'s victory was a decisive defeat and helped bring the Civil War to an end by the end of the next year.

1913

Harlem's Apollo Theater first opens as a burlesque theatre and later as a movie house. Later, on January 26, 1934, the theater began showing stage shows.

December 16

1859

The Clotilda—the last known schooner designed to transport enslaved Africans—lands in Mobile, Alabama, with between 110 and 160 Africans; it had come from Ghana, West Africa. The importation of enslaved Africans had been outlawed since 1808 but Timothy Meaher, a steamboat builder based in the North and owner of the *Clotilda*, was trying to skirt the laws. When he thought federal authorities might find out about his recently arrived cargo, Meaher had the *Clotilda* burned and tried to hide the enslaved Africans in various locations. Some of the Africans escaped and went on to establish the village of "AfricaTown," just outside of Mobile. AfricaTown's last known survivor was Cudjo Lewis (whose

African name was Kossula); Kossula lived into the twentieth century.

> After more than 300 years of slavery ended, there was one man remaining who had actually been born in the motherland of Africa. Before his death in 1935, Cudjo Lewsi described his capture:
>
> The tribes of Africa were engaged in civil war, and the prevailing tribes sold the members of the conquered tribes into slavery. The village of the Tarkbar tribe near the city of Tamale was raided by Dahomey warriors, and the survivors of the raid were taken to Whydah, now the People's Republic of Benin, and put up for sale. The captured tribesmen were sold for $100 each at Whydah. They were taken to the United States on board the schooner Clotilde, under the command of Maine Capt. William Foster. Foster had been hired by Capt. Timothy Meaher, a wealthy Mobile shipper and shipyard owner, who had built the schooner Clotilde in Mobile in 1856.
>
> Source: From Honor Books, Niral R. Burnett. *God Has Soul: Celebrating the Indomitable Spirit of African Americans*. Colorado Springs, CO: David C. Cook, 2004, p. 64.

Books

Diouf, Sylviane A. *Dreams of Africa in Alabama: The Slave Ship* Clotilda *and the Story of the Last Africans Brought to America*. New York, NY: Oxford University Press, 2007. Book looks at the lives of the Africans who survived the *Clotilda* voyage and how they established new lives—based on African traditions—in AfricaTown.

Robertson, Natalie S. *The Slave Ship* Clotilda *and the Making of AfricaTown, USA: Spirit of Our Ancestors*. New York, NY: Praeger, 2008. Book recounts the voyage of the *Clotilda* and looks at the lives that were forever changed by the enslaving of Africans.

Websites

The Library of Congress has a profile of "Africa-Town, USA." http://lcweb2.loc.gov/diglib/legacies/AL/200002671.html.

The Jim Crow Museum of Racist Memorabilia maintains the page "Question of the Month:

Cudjo Lewis: Last African Slave in the U.S.?" http://www.ferris.edu/jimcrow/question/july05/.

Also Noteworthy

1890

The Negro Methodist Episcopal Church is founded in Jackson, Tennessee.

1976

Civil rights activist Andrew Young is named Ambassador and Chief U.S. Delegate to the United Nations by President Jimmy Carter.

December 17

1951

Activists Paul Robeson and William Lorenzo Patterson petition the United Nations, charging the United States with race-based genocide. Robeson brought the petition to the U.S. Secretariat in New York while Patterson delivered it to the United Nations in Paris, where the fifth session of the General Assembly was in session.

> In 1951, in the midst of heightened Cold War tensions between the United States and the Soviet Union, a document presenting evidence of lynching, economic oppression, political disfranchisement, and racial segregation of Blacks was presented to the United Nations. Activist and artist Paul Robeson accompanied William L. Patterson of the Civil Rights Congress. The petition delivered to the U.N. office in New York is titled We Charge Genocide: The Crime of Government against the Negro People. With it, the issue of lynching finally reached the world stage.
>
> Source: From Gloria J. Browne-Marshall. *Race, Law, and American Society: 1607 to Present*. Boca Raton, FL: Taylor & Francis Group, LLC/CRC Press, 2007, p. 45.

Books

Dagbovie, Pero Gaglo. *African American History Reconsidered*. Champaign, IL: University of

Illinois Press, 2010. Book includes a long look at the *We Charge Genocide* petition.

Jones, Adam. *Genocide: A Comprehensive Introduction*. Boca Raton, FL: Taylor & Francis, 2010. Includes a look at the genocide petition and its presentation only 11 months after the Genocide Convention was established.

Websites

We Charge Genocide: The Historic Petition to the United Nations for Relief from a Crime of the U.S. Government against the Negro People. http://www.questia.com/PM.qst?a=o&d=9685712.

The Seattle Civil Rights and Labor History Project profiles W Patterson's organization, Civil Rights Congress. http://depts.washing-ton.edu/civilr/CivilRightsCongress.htm.

Also Noteworthy

1760

Deborah Sampson Gannett is believed to be born on this date in Plymouth, VA. Gannett famously fought as a soldier in the American Revolution under the name "Robert Shurtliff"—she served with the 4th Massachusetts Regiment.

1910

Melvin "Sy" Oliver is born in Battle Creek, Michigan. A jazz arranger and composer, Sy Oliver arranged songs for major jazz artists like Ella Fitzgerald.

1939

Eddie James Kendrick, the Temptations' co-lead singer and occasional songwriter, is born in Union Springs, Alabama.

1802

Henry Adams is born in Franklin County, Georgia. As a teacher and minister, Adams led his congregation to form the First African Baptist Church in 1842.

1939

James Carroll Booker III is born in New Orleans, Louisiana. As a jazz, R&B, and soul musician, Booker was famed as a piano wizard who worked with some of the most celebrated musicians of his time, including Fats Domino, Aretha Franklin, The Doobie Brothers, Rickie Lee Jones, Ringo Starr, Little Richard, Dr. John, Junior Parker, Wilson Pickett, and B.B. King.

1992

The author/activist/poet Audre Lorde dies in St. Croix.

December 18

1912

Benjamin Oliver Davis, Jr., is born in Washington, DC, the son of Elnora and Gen. B.O. Davis, Sr., the U.S. Army's first African American general. After graduating from West Point in 1936 (the first African American to graduate from West Point in the twentieth century), Davis Jr., served as a World War II commander of the Tuskegee Airmen's 99th Fighter Squadron and the 332nd Fighter Group. On April 16, 1965, Davis Jr., was named lieutenant general of the U.S. Air Force, at that time the highest rank ever attained by an African American in the armed services. Davis, Jr., was advanced to a four-star general on December 9, 1998.

Davis, along with the 99th Pursuit Squadron, served in North African and Sicily during World War II. After four months of active service in the Mediterranean, he returned to America in October 1943 to take command of the 332nd Fighter Group, a larger African American unit, based at Selfridge Field, Michigan. The unit was deployed to Italy in January 1944 and proved to be a highly efficient and effective force. On June 9 the unit, flying P-47 Thunderbolts and escorting B-24 bombers, flew to Munich, Germany, led by Davis.

During this mission the unit successfully destroyed several Me-109s. For his leadership skills and bravery on this mission, Davis was awarded the Distinguished Flying Cross—the first of many such awards. The medal was presented to Davis at the Ramitelli Air Base in Italy and was pinned on his chest by his father, Brig. Gen. Benjamin O. Davis Sr.

Source: From Jonathan Sutherland. *African Americans at War: An Encyclopedia.* Santa Barbara, CA: ABC-CLIO, 2004, p. 122.

Books

Davis, Benjamin Oliver. *Benjamin O. Davis, Jr., American: An Autobiography.* New York, NY: Plume, 1992. This autobiography examines his life in the U.S. military.

Earl, Sari. *Benjamin O. Davis Jr.: Air Force General & Tuskegee Airmen Leader.* Edina, MN: ABDO, 2010. Biography of Benjamin Oliver Davis, Jr., looks at his leadership in the military.

Websites

The Department of Defense profiles "General Benjamin O. Davis Jr." http://www.defense.gov/specials/africanam2003/jr.html.

Arlington Cemetery, where Gen. Davis, Jr., is buried, has information on his life. http://www.arlingtoncemetery.net/bodavisjr.htm.

Also Noteworthy

1852

George Henry White is born in Rosindale, North Carolina. White was elected to the U.S. Congress in 1896 as a representative of North Carolina. He served from 1897 to 1901.

1865

Congress passes the Thirteenth Amendment to the U.S. Constitution. The Thirteenth Amendment outlawed slavery, by stating that "Neither slavery nor involuntary servitude, except as a punishment for crime whereof the party shall have been duly convicted, shall exist within the United States, or any place subject to their jurisdiction." Most enslaved African Americans lived in states where freedom had been granted prior to the enactment of this Amendment. Thus the Thirteenth Amendment ended up freeing enslaved Africans in the states of Delaware and Kentucky.

1917

The actor/director/social activist Ossie Davis is born in Cogdell, Georgia. Born with the name Raiford Chatman Davis, as a child he was nicknamed R.C. Because his neighbors thought they were hearing "Ossie," that soon became his nickname. Davis became an inspiring actor/director who demanded respect for himself and for the African American characters he portrayed.

1971

Rev. Jesse Jackson founds Operation PUSH (People United to Save Humanity).

December 19

1875

Carter Godwin Woodson is born at New Canton, Virginia. Because his parents were enslaved, Woodson was mostly self-taught and did not enter Douglas High School in Huntington, West Virginia, until he turned 20 years old. Following that, Woodson earned a teaching diploma, a BA and an MA from the University of Chicago, and he became the second African American to receive a degree from Harvard when he received his PhD in history there. Dr. Woodson founded the Association for the Study of Negro Life and History and authored the famous book *The Mis-Education of the Negro*, which critically examines the unequal social status of Blacks in the United States. In 1916, Dr. Woodson began publishing the *Journal of Negro History*, and in 1926 he established "Negro History Week."

> Although he had studied the history of black education for more than twenty years, Woodson did not make critical public statements about contemporary black education until 1931. During the spring and summer of that year, he gave a series of speeches on the topic, among them, the commencement speech at Fisk University. He reported in the October issue of the Journal that after "looking over the recent college catalogues of the leading Negro colleges," he was convinced that these institutions did not "teach Negroes who they are, what they have done, and what they have to do." Two months earlier he had published an article, "The Mis-education of the Negro," in the Crisis' August issue, which annually was devoted to black education. The thesis of this and subsequent articles in the black press was that black institutions of higher education were educating the black bourgeoisie for roles they would be unable to assume in white society. "The so-called education of Negro college graduates," Woodson said, "leads them to throw away opportunities which they have and go in quest of those which they do not find."
>
> *Source*: From Jacqueline Anne Goggin. *Carter G. Woodson: A Life in Black History*. Santa Barbara, CA: LSU Press, 1997, p. 157.

Books

Woodson, Carter Godwin. *The Mis-Education of the Negro*. Scotts Valley, CA: ReadaClassic .com/CreateSpace, 1972. Woodson's classic critique of what education has meant and should mean to people of African descent.

Woodson, Carter Godwin and James L. Conyers. *Carter G. Woodson: A Historical Reader*. New York, NY: Garland Pub., 2000. Woodson's writings, explaining his understanding of Pan-Africanism and Black History.

Websites

Association for the Study of African American Life and History (ASALH) Website continues

Woodson's legacy. http://www.asalh.org/ index.html.

The Encyclopedia Virgina profiles Carter G. Woodson. http://www.encyclopediavirginia .org/Woodson_Carter_G_1875-1950.

West Virginia Archives and History notes the marker memorializing Woodson. http://www .wvculture.org/history/africanamericans/wood sonmarker.html.

December 20

1956

The 381-day Montgomery, Alabama, bus boycott ends when municipal bus service is finally desegregated. The Montgomery bus boycott—which lasted from December 1, 1955, to December 20, 1956—was the first of several civil rights protests against race-based segregation led by Martin Luther King, Jr.

> The cruelty of the Montgomery bus drivers was common knowledge, and it fueled racial tensions in the black community like gasoline on a fire. Many drivers would drive past a bus stop where blacks were waiting or drive off after the bus fare was paid in the front while the patron returned outside to reboard at the black entrance in the back. Some drivers would slam on their brakes to knock the standing passengers off balance or use guns to order black passengers off the bus for not having the correct change for the fare. Windows were opened on cold days to make riders uncomfortable. Once a driver closed the back door on a black woman and drove off with her arm stuck in the door. She was drug to next stop before she could get on. These types of cruelties aimed at black bus clientele contributed to the rising tension in Montgomery.
>
> *Source*: From Cheryl Fisher Phibbs. *The Montgomery Bus Boycott: A History and Reference Guide*. Santa Barbara, CA: ABC-CLIO, 2009, p. 4.

Books

Gray, Fred D. and Willy Siegel Leventhal. *The Children Coming on: A Retrospective of the*

Montgomery Bus Boycott. Montgomery, AL: Black Belt Press, 1998. Book looks at the lesser-known participants in the Montgomery Bus Boycott, who played as important a role as Rosa Parks and Martin Luther King, Jr.

Hare, Kenneth M. *They Walked to Freedom 1955–1956*. Willowbrook, IL: Sports Publishing LLC, 2005. Images and stories from the *Montgomery Advertiser* newspaper look at the incidents and people who played a major role in the Montgomery Bus Boycott.

Websites

The *Montgomery Advertiser* newspaper memorializes the Bus Boycott online. at http://www.montgomeryboycott.com/.

The Alabama Department of Archives and History provides an 11th-grade level course study about the Montgomery Bus Boycott. http://www.alabamamoments.state.al.us/sec55.html.

December 21

1911

Negro Leagues Baseball legend Josh Gibson is born in Buena Vista, Georgia. Gibson is known as the "home-run king" because many baseball historians estimate that during his 22-year baseball career, Gibson hit some 823 home runs.

> *The papers labeled him "Samson" after the famed Biblical strongman. Gibson's huge appetite for food, especially vanilla ice cream and hot dogs, was well known. Although he gained more and more attention, he always remained focused on the game. During his first season with the Grays, Gibson hit a home run in Yankee Stadium in the season-ending series against a good team, the New York Lincoln Giants. The home run reportedly traveled 500 feet into the bullpen in left field—a drive fans would claim for years was one of the longest home runs ever hit there, even longer than any by Babe Ruth or Mickey Mantle. Some people contend that the shot traveled out of the stadium, a feat no one had ever accomplished.*
>
> *Source: From Nick Twemlow. Josh Gibson. New York, NY: The Rosen Publishing Group, 2002, pp. 50–51.*

Books

Golus, Carrie. *Josh Gibson*. Breckenridge, CO: Twenty-First Century Books, 2010. Josh Gibson biography recalls him as one of the best baseball players of all time.

Ribowsky, Mark. *Josh Gibson: The Power and the Darkness*. Champaign, IL: University of Illinois Press, 2004. Biography of Gibson shows his role in the Negro Leagues and his legacy.

Websites

Josh Gibson Foundation. www.joshgibson.org/.
Josh Gibson—BR Bullpen. www.baseball-reference.com.

Also Noteworthy

1815

The Henry Highland Garnet is born to George and Henrietta in New Markey, Maryland. Both of Garnet's parents were enslaved when he was born but the family would use the Underground Railroad to escape from slavery and re-settle in New York City. Henry Highland Garnet became a famous abolitionist.

1943

W. E. B. DuBois becomes the first African American elected to the National Institute of Arts and Letters.

1959

Berry Gordy, Jr., establishes the Motown Record Corporation in Detroit, Michigan.

December 22

1960

Jean-Michel Basquiat is born in Brooklyn, New York. Basquiat dropped out of high school and started expressing himself as a graffiti artist. He was part of the Neo-expressionist movement and is known to have featured his heritage in works like "Irony of Negro Policeman" (1981) and "Untitled (History of the Black People)."

Jean-Michel Basquiat's life and career as a painter are nearly paradigmatic for the riddles of the art world in the 1980s. His rise to prominence was without parallel. The graffiti sprayer, who left mysterious and witty statements on the walls of SoHo and the East Village using the pseudonym SAMO, became a celebrated star, holding court in the explosive art scene of Zurich, New York, Tokyo and Los Angeles. He was courted and in the end worn down by an art market that saw prices shoot up to previously unimaginable heights as its mechanisms followed increasingly cutthroat and purely economic laws. Driven by an insatiable hunger for recognition, fame and money, wavering between megalomania and an insurmountable shyness, plagued by self-doubt and self-destructive impulses, Jean-Michel Basquiat died of an overdose on August 12, 1988, aged just 27. He had flashed through the creative heavens, his works sold by such prominent art dealers as Mary Boone, Larry Gagosian and Bruno Bischofberger, and he flickered out suddenly, before his artistic star could reach its full brilliance.

Source: From Leonhard Emmerling. Jean-Michel Basquiat: 1960–1988. Los Angeles, CA: Taschen, 2003, p. 7.

Books

Basquiat, Jean Michel and Rudy Chiappini. *Jean-Michel Basquiat*. New York, NY: Skira, 2005. Book looks at the legend of Basquiat and provides a look at some of his work.

Basquiat, Jean Michel and Tony Shafrazi. *Jean-Michel Basquiat*. New York, NY: Tony Shafrazi Gallery, 1999. Retrospective of Basquiat's work includes detailed look at his paintings.

Websites

Jean-Mich Basquiat Website. http://basquiat.com/.
Andy Warhol and Jean-Michel Basquiat, filmed in 1986. http://www.youtube.com/watch?v=foerFJqupYM.

Also Noteworthy

1995

Thelma "Butterfly" McQueen dies in Augusta, Georgia. Born January 7, 1911, in Tampa, Florida, McQueen legally took on the name "Butterfly" after performing the "Butterfly Ballet" during a performance of *A Midsummer Night's Dream*. Butterfly McQueen is most widely recognized, and often reviled, for her role as Prissy in the 1939 Hollywood film *Gone with the Wind*.

December 23

1815

Henry Highland Garnet, orator and abolitionist, is born enslaved near New Market, Maryland. He and his family all escaped to freedom in Philadelphia and next moved to New York. Garnet became a minister and worked with the American Anti-Slavery Society as an abolitionist. In 1843, Garnett told delegates to the National Negro Convention in Buffalo, New York, that fighting for Black liberation would be more worthy than asking for it. Garnet urged enslaved Africans to take up arms and fight for their freedom: "Brethren, arise, arise! Strike for your lives and liberties. Now is the day and the hour. Let every slave throughout the land do this, and the days of slavery are numbered. You cannot be more oppressed than you have been—you cannot suffer greater cruelties than you have already. Rather die freemen than live to be slaves. Remember that you are *four millions!*"

Henry Highland Garnet (1815–1881) was born in slavery in Maryland, escaped with his parents in 1824 and settled in New York City. Garnet was educated in the African Free School No. 1 and at Oneida Institute. A brief stay at the Canaan Academy in Canaan, New Hampshire, in 1835 was interrupted when the academy was destroyed by an infuriated mob opposed to the education of black students. Garnet prepared for the ministry, and in 1842 was licensed to preach. He became pastor of the Liberty Street Presbyterian Church in Troy, New York, and later of the Shiloh Presbyterian Church in New York City, a pastorate he held for more than forty years, during which time he became the foremost African American clergyman in the city.

Source: From Philip Sheldon Foner and Robert J. Branham. *Lift Every Voice: African American Oratory, 1787–1900*. Tuscaloosa, AL: University of Alabama Press, 1998, p. 198.

Books

Leeman, Richard W. *African-American Orators: A Bio-Critical Sourcebook*. Santa Barbara, CA: Greenwood Publishing Group, 1996. Contains a long biographical sketch of Henry Highland Garnet.

Litwack, Leon F. and August Meier. *Black Leaders of the Nineteenth Century*. Champaign, IL: University of Illinois Press, 1991. Article on Garnet looks at his political influence and his call for a violent overthrow of African slavery.

Websites

Garnet Congressional Address February 12, 1865. http://www.englishandwhite.com/id58.html.

Henry Highland Garnet, by Douglass. http://www.theliberatorfiles.com/henry-highland-garnet-by-douglass/.

Also Noteworthy

1832

Charter is granted to the Georgia Infirmary, the first African American hospital.

1869

Sarah Breedlove (Madam C. J. Walker) is born to Owen and Minerva Breedlove in Delta, Louisiana. Walker developed a hair-straightening method that made her the first African American woman millionaire.

1919

Alice H. Parker of Morristown, New Jersey, receives U.S. Patent No. 1,325,905 for her invention of a gas-heating furnace that could provide central heating.

1939

Guadalupe Victoria Yolí Raymond is born in the San Pedrito neighborhood of Santiago de Cuba. Guadalupe—who would become famous as La Lupe, La Yiyiyi, and La Reina de la Canción Latina—was raised in a poor family where her father, Tito Yoli, was an employee for the Bacardi Corporation. Tito Yoli wanted Lupe to become a schoolteacher, but ultimately, she became a Latin music and salsa singer. Throughout the 1970s, La Lupe was a salsa music diva: she became the first Latin singer to sell out a concert at Madison Square Garden.

December 24

1881

The Order of True Reformers—a fraternal organization of African Americans in the South—is founded by William Washington Browne in Richmond, Virginia.

The history of this organization, which appeared shortly after the Civil War, is intricately tied to its founding body, the International Order of Good Templars. The Good Templars created affiliated orders for blacks as a way to keep their own orders segregated. William Wells Brown, a black author and abolitionist, established a number of orders in southern states. However, he became convinced that the prevailing racism of the Good Templars did not work in the interest of its black members, so he left the international order and affiliated with a different group. Fahey reports that the Grand Lodge of Kentucky published a ritual and named a new order for blacks in 1871: the United Order of True Reformers. The headquarters of the Grand United Order was ultimately in Richmond, Virginia. Despite its origins, the True Reformers reflected the needs and interests of its black

membership. In addition to the rituals and traditional structure of a fraternal order, the True
Reformers offered its members death benefits
through insurance policies. Further, the order
reflected the desire of many blacks to become eco-
nomically self-sufficient. Its cooperative economic
programs included a bank, hotel, major insurance
company, regalia factory, funeral home, and real
estate interests. Its roster reportedly surpassed
40,000 members during its peak at the turn of
the twentieth century.

Source: From Clarenda M. Phillips. African
American Fraternities and Sororities: The Legacy
and the Vision. Lexington, KY: University Press of
Kentucky, 2005, pp. 85–86.

and her husband was disguised as her servant.
The two ended up in Boston's Beacon Hill
neighborhood, where they established a furniture business and were soon regularly featured on the abolitionist lecture circuit. The
Crafts left the U.S. for England in 1850—
after passage of the Fugitive Slave Law—
and published the book, *Running a Thousand
Miles for Freedom*. They only returned to the
United States after the Civil War and went
straight back to Georgia where they bought
some 1,800 acres of land and established the
Woodville Co-operative Farm School to
educate formerly enslaved people of African
descent.

Books

Du Bois, William Edward Burghardt. *Some Notes
on Negro Crime, Particularly in Georgia: Report of
a Social Study Made under the Direction of Atlanta
University; Together with the Proceedings of the
Ninth Conference for the Study of the Negro Problems, Held at Atlanta University.* Victoria, BC:
AbeBooks/Atlanta University Press, 1904.
DuBois's book includes a profile of the Order
and its members.

Edward Franklin Frazier. *Black Bourgeoisie*. New
York, NY: Simon & Schuster, 1997. Book
looks at how the Order held funds for its
members in case of death or sickness—and
particularly, in case of a lynching.

Websites

The Founder of the Order of True Reformers:
The Story of William Washington Browney.
http://www.aagsnc.org/columns/feb99col.htm.

Linking to Our Past—Grand Fountain, United
Order of True Reformers. www.vahistorical
.org/tah/truereformers.htm.

December 25

1848

Ellen Craft and her husband, William, arrive
in Philadelphia, Pennsylvania, as they escape
from slavery in Georgia. Ellen had dressed
herself to look like a white male slaveholder

. . . Gentleman of the Jury, you know the story of
William and Ellen Craft. They were slaves in Georgia; their master was said to be a "very pious
man," "an excellent Christian." Ellen had a little
baby,—it was sick and ready to die. But one day
her "owner"—for this wife and mother was only
a piece of property—had a dinner party at his
house. Ellen must leave her dying child and wait
upon the table. She was not permitted to catch
the last sighing of her only child with her own lips;
other and ruder hands must attend to the
mother's sad privilege. But the groans and moanings of the dying child came to her ear and
mingled with the joy and merriment of the guests
whom the mother must wait upon. At length the
moanings all were still—for Death took a Northside view of the little boy, and the born-slave had
gone where the servant is free from his master
and the weary is at rest—for there the wicked
cease from troubling. Ellen and William resolved
to flee North. They cherished the plan for years;
he was a joiner, and hired himself of his owner
for about two hundred dollars a year. They saved
a little money, and stealthily, piece by piece, they
bought a suit of gentleman's clothes to fit the
wife; no two garments were obtained of the same
dealer. Ellen disguised herself as a man, William
attending as her servant, and so they fled off and
came to Boston. No doubt these Hon. Judges think
it was a very "immoral" thing. Mr. Curtis knows no
morality here but "legality." Nay, it was a wicked
thing—for Mr. Everett, a most accomplished
scholar and once a Unitarian minister, makes

St. Paul command "Slaves, obey your masters!" Nay, Hon. Judge Sprague says it is a "precept" of our "Divine Master!"

Source: From Theodore Parker. *The Trial of Theodore Parker: With the Defence*. Manchester, NH: Ayer Publishing, 1855, p. 147.

Books

Craft, William and Ellen Craft. *The American Negro: Running a Thousand Miles for Freedom or, the Escape of William and Ellen Craft from Slavery*. Fairford, Gloucestershire, England: Echo Library, 2007. The Crafts's own recounting of their escape from slavery.

Moore, Cathy. *The Daring Escape of Ellen Craft*. Minneapolis. MN: First Avenue Editions, 2002. Young reader's book about the flight to freedom of Ellen and William Craft.

Websites

Digitized version of "Running a Thousand Miles for Freedom; or, the Escape of William and Ellen Craft from Slavery" by William and Ellen Craft. http://docsouth.unc.edu/neh/craft/menu.html.

The Smithsonian recounts the Craft tale "The Great Escape from Slavery of Ellen and William Craft." http://www.smithsonianmag.com/history-archaeology/The-Great-Escape-From-Slavery-of-Ellen-and-William-Craft.html#ixzz1ZxyNgsnX.

Also Noteworthy

1760

Jupiter Hammon becomes the first published Black poet with his poem, "An Evening Thought."

1907

Cabell "Cab" Calloway III is born to Cabell and Martha Calloway in Rochester, New York. "Cab" is the second of six children. After growing up in Baltimore, Maryland, Calloway attended law school but then quit to try to make it as a singer. He became a jazz scatter and singer, known for his talent and character.

1951

Florida NAACP official Harry T. Moore is killed by a bomb blast in Mims, Florida.

1956

Civil Rights leader the Reverend Fred Shuttlesworth is almost killed after terrorists placed dynamite sticks near his bedroom window. Shuttlesworth was a co-founder of the Alabama Christian Movement for Human Rights (ACMHR) and had declared that the ACMHR would challenge Birmingham's segregation laws on December 26, 1956. The dynamite under Shuttlesworth's window damaged his home, but he escaped with his life.

1971

Operation PUSH (People United to Save Humanity) is organized by Rev Jesse Jackson.

December 26

1894

Jean Toomer, author of *Cane* one of the most important books published during the Harlem Renaissance, is born in Washington, DC. Toomer was born with the name Nathan Pinchback Toomer: his father, Nathan Toomer, was a planter who had once been enslaved in the state of Georgia while his mother, Nina Pinchback, was the daughter of Pinckney Benton Stewart (P.B.S.) Pinchback, who was the first person of African descent to serve as governor of a state, when he governed Louisiana during Reconstruction.

Toomer's sojourn in Georgia produced an emotional intensity not unlike that of a summer romance. He despaired at the tenuousness of his visit, yet it had given him unparaelled exhilaration. Toomer grieved over the demise of an era marked by the folk spirit, but his grief may well have been for his having lost touch with that same spirit: "The folk-spirit was walking in to die on the modern desert. That spirit was so beautiful. Its death was so tragic. Just this seemed to sum life for me. And this was the feeling I put into 'Cane.' "Cane" was a swan-song. It was a song of an end.

Source: From Cynthia Earl Kerman and Richard Eldridge. *The Lives of Jean Toomer: A Hunger for Wholeness.* Baton Rouge, LA: LSU Press, 1989, p. 85.

Books

Jones, Robert B. *Jean Toomer and the Prison-House of Thought: A Phenomenology of the Spirit.* Anherst, MA: University of Massachusetts Press, 1993. Looks at Toomer's philosophical and psychological underpinnings, and how these affected his work.

Scruggs, Charles and Lee VanDemarr. *Jean Toomer and the Terrors of American History.* Philadelphia, PA: University of Pennsylvania Press, 1998. Book looks at the history of race relations in the United States and how the stigma of an African heritage and what that meant in society affected Toomer's life.

Websites

Modern American Poetry has a biography of Jean Toomer. http://www.english.illinois.edu/Maps/poets/s_z/toomer/toomer.htm.

A Jean Toomer Biography is presented on the University of Buffalo site. http://www.nsm.buffalo.edu/~sww/toomer/toomerbio.html.

Also Noteworthy

1966

Kwanzaa—the seven-day celebration of the Nguzo Saba (the seven guiding principles of traditional African values)—begins annually on this date. Kwanzaa lasts until January 1st; Dr. Maulana Karenga originated this African American holiday.

December 27

1807

Omar Ibn Sayyid, the Muslim African who was enslaved in the southern United States yet wrote the *Autobiography of Omar ibn Said* in 1831, arrives at the Charleston, South Carolina harbor.

In 1831, Omar ibn Sayyid, a North Carolina slave who may or may not have converted to Christianity, penned a short memoir in Arabic. In addition to recounting the details of his life in the United States, the manuscript contained a prologue excerpting a long passage from the qur'anic chapter entitled al-Mulk, or Power. This chapter of the Qur'an juxtaposes God's dominion over all things with the feeble attempts of human beings to control their own destinies. By including this passage, perhaps Omar ibn Sayyid was reminding himself that he was not master of the fate that had befallen him, and that while an earthly master claimed to own him, he truly belonged to God.

Source: From Edward E. Curtis. *Muslims in America: A Short History.* New York, NY: Oxford University Press, 2009, p. 23.

Books

Nyang, Sulayman Sheih. *Islam in the United States of America.* Chicago, IL: ABC International Group, 1999. Book includes a look at Omar Ibn Said as an example of someone who remained devoted to Islam, even though in a foreign land.

Said, Omar Ibn, translated by Ala Alryyes. *A Muslim American Slave: The Life of Omar Ibn Said.* Madison, WI: University of Wisconsin Press, 2011. Translation of Ibn Said's book about his enslavement in the United States.

Websites

Saudi Aramco World: The Life of Omar ibn Said. . . .www.saudiaramcoworld.com/issue/. . ./the.life.of.omar.ibn.said.htm.

Omar Ibn Sayyid | Archives Special Collections. http://forum.davidson.edu/archives/encyclopedia/omar-ibn-sayyid/.

December 28

1903

Earl Kenneth Hines, a.k.a. Earl "Fatha" Hines, the "father of modern jazz piano" is born in Dusquesne, Pennsylvania. Hines grew up in a middle-class family—both his parents were musicians, his father played the cornet and his mother played the organ.

> The twenty-four-year-old Hines had come to Chicago at the close of his teens. A native of Duquesne, Pennsylvania, where he was born on December 28, 1903, Earl Kenneth Hines grew up in a middle-class black family where, as he later described it, "I was just surrounded by music." Years later, critics would characterize his distinctive approach to the piano as the "trumpet style," linking it to the melody lines of Armstrong, yet the roots of this technique can perhaps be traced back to his childhood, when he began his musical studies learning trumpet from his father, who worked days as a foreman on the coal docks, and piano from his mother. But Hines's stylistic breakthrough went far beyond the use of trumpet-like lines on the piano. As part of his development, he also studied and assimilated elements of the classical repertoire as well as a wide range of popular styles, including the blues, ragtime, and early stride piano. Hines's ability to integrate these sources of inspiration seamlessly into his own vision of keyboard performance remains a crucial part of his legacy. For more than any other musician, Hines stands out as responsible for pushing jazz piano beyond the limiting horizontal structures of ragtime and into a more versatile and linear approach, one that continues to hold sway to this day.
>
> Source: From Ted Gioia. The History of Jazz. New York, NY: Oxford University Press, 2011, p. 11.

Books

Hines, Earl. *Selected Piano Solos: 1928–1941, Volume 56.* Middleton, WI: A-R Editions, Inc., 2006. The best piano solos of Earl "Fatha" Hines.

Shipton, Alyn. *Jazz Makers: Vanguards of Sound.* New York, NY: Oxford University Press, 2002. Contains a short biography of Earl "Fatha" Hines.

Websites

Earl Hines explains his influences and technique. http://www.youtube.com/watch?v=hgWvggDY2qA.
Earl Hines is profiled on RedHotJazz. http://www.redhotjazz.com/hines.html.

Also Noteworthy

1897

C. V. Richey receives U.S. Patent No. 596,427 for a fire escape bracket.

1914

Roebuck Staples is born in Winona, Mississippi. As a gospel and R&B songwriter and musician, he used the stage name "Pops" Staples and was the pivotal figure in the group The Staple Singers, which featured his children, daughters Mavis, Yvonne, and Cleotha and son Pervis, who all sang the vocals.

1932

The actress/singer Nichelle Nichols is born Grace Nichols in Robbins, Illinois. Nichols is famed for her television role as communications officer Lieutenant Uhura on the *USS Enterprise* in the television program *Star Trek*.

1954

Award-winning actor Denzel Hayes Washington, Jr., is born in Mount Vernon, New York. Denzel Washington is widely considered to be the best actor of his generation; he won the Academy Award for Best Supporting Actor for his role in the 1989 film, *Glory*, and the Academy Award for Best

Actor for his role in the film *Training Day* (2001).

December 29

1907

Robert Clifton Weaver is born in Washington, DC. Weaver served as the first U.S. Secretary of Housing and Urban Development (HUD) from 1966 to 1968 in the administration of President Lyndon B. Johnson; he was also the first African American to hold a cabinet-level position in the United States.

> ... as the civil rights movement gained momentum in the postwar years, Weaver was increasingly drawn into the struggle, where his experience, knowledge, and connections made him an invaluable member of the growing effort to fight racial discrimination in northern cities. Though the battle against segregation in education has received the most attention from historians, Weaver joined other activists in the equally important and hard-fought struggle against residential segregation. Through his work at the Whitney Foundation and his leadership of the National Committee against Discrimination in Housing, Weaver engaged the nation's political, business, and philanthropic elite in this effort. Although Weaver was already a well-known expert on housing issues, during this period he would develop a national reputation that would enable him to move into the high echelons of government, first in New York State and then in Washington.
>
> *Source*: From Wendell E. Pritchett. *Robert Clifton Weaver and the American City: The Life and Times of an Urban Reformer*. Chicago, IL: University of Chicago Press, 2008, p. 152.

Books

Weaver, Robert Clifton. *Negro Labor; a National Problem*. Victoria, BC: AbeBooks/Kennikat Press, 1969. Weaver looked at rates of employment among African Americans following World War II and how that affected society.

Weaver, Robert Clifton and William E. Zisch. *The Urban Environment: How It Can Be Improved*. Victoria, BC: AbeBooks/New York University Press, 1969. Weaver examines the progress of U.S. cities and how people live in them.

Websites

Robert C. Weaver Federal Building. http://www .gsa.gov/portal/ext/html/site/hb/category/ 25431/actionParameter/exploreByBuilding/ buildingId/1225.
The University of Illinois at Chicago maintains the "Robert C. Weaver Collection." http:// www.uic.edu/depts/lib/specialcoll/services/ rjd/findingaids/RWeaverf.html.

December 30

1892

Dr. Miles Vandahurst Lynk—the son of John Henry Lynk and Mary Louise Yancy, both of whom had been enslaved—publishes *The Medical and Surgical Observer*, the nation's first African American medical journal. Lynk was also the co-founder of the National Medical Association for African American Physicians and in 1900 he founded founded the University of West Tennessee.

> ... Most of Memphis's early physicians graduated from Meharry Medical College, but, in 1907, Dr. Miles V. Lynk relocated to Memphis the University of West Tennessee, which he had founded in Jackson, Tennessee in 1900. The university trained legal and medical professionals from several states and six countries; it also educated many Black Memphis physicians, including Benjamin F. McCleave, William O. Speight, and Ransom Q. Venson. Dr. Lynk also published the first medical journal in the country, co-founded the National Medical Association, published a magazine, founded a publishing house, and wrote three books, including an autobiography, Sixty Years of Medicine or the Life and Times of Dr. Miles V. Lynk *(1930)*.
>
> *Source*: From Miriam DeCosta-Willis. *Notable Black Memphians*. Amherst, NY: Cambria Press, 2008, p. 11.

Books

Lynk, Miles V. *Sixty Years of Medicine, or the Life and Times of Dr. Miles V. Lynk: An Autobiography*. Memphis, TN: Twentieth Century Press, 1951. Dr. Link recounts his life and the highpoints of his career.

Watson, Wilbur H. *Against the Odds: Blacks in the Profession of Medicine in the United States*. Piscataway, NJ: Transaction Publishers, 1999. Contains references to the importance of the work Dr. Miles Lynk contributed in the field of medicine.

Websites

The Tennessee History Classroom has a biography of Dr. Lynk. http://www.tennessee history.com/class/Lynk.htm.

The Tennessee Encyclopedia of History and Culture has an entry on Dr. Lynk. http://ten nesseeencyclopedia.net/entry.php?rec=818.

Also Noteworthy

1819

George Thomas Downing is born to Thomas and Rebecca West Downing in New York City. George's famous father was one of the founders of the all-Black United Anti-Slavery Society of the City of New York as well as the owner of the Downing Oyster House. George Thomas Downing opened his own Oyster House in Newport, Rhode Island, as an adult and took part in antislavery activities.

1842

Josiah Thomas Walls is born in Winchester, Frederick County, Virginia. As a congressman representing the state of Florida, Walls served for three terms—from 1871 to 1876. He was the first African American congressman to represent the state of Florida.

1952

The Tuskegee Institute reports that 1952 was the first year in the 71 years since the institution began keeping records that there were no lynchings of people of African descent.

December 31

1930

Odetta Holmes is born to Reuben Holmes and Flora Sanders in Birmingham, Alabama. Known by her first name only, as the blues and folk singer Odetta, she became famous for singing songs like "I'm on My Way," and "Oh Freedom"; she was known as "the voice of the Civil Rights Movement."

On the original liner notes to Odetta Sings Ballads and Blues, *producer Dean Gitter calls her "electrifying"—a curious and noteworthy word to describe the sound of a woman with an acoustic guitar. Gitter, of couse, is referring not to any technology per se but to the accumulated effect of Odetta's performance: her powerful contralto, her rhythmic guitar playing, which made the instrument into a second voice, so that she often needed no accompaniment but her own, and, not least, her regal bearing. The fact that she was perceived as "as tall as a man," like a twentieth-century Sojourner Truth, has always been a subject of fascination and, perhaps, fear. No wonder, then, that to Gitter she evoked African-American legends of yore—Ma Rainer, Bessie Smith, the young Leadbelly, Blind Lemon Jefferson—even as, at twenty-five years old, she embodied to him the "future" of folk music: "A magnificent new voice is here," he announced, "to sing the old songs."*

Source: From Colleen Josephine Sheehy and Thomas Swiss. *Highway 61 Revisited: Bob Dylan's Road from Minnesota to the World*. Minneapolis, MN: University of Minnesota Press, 2009, p. 176.

Books

Alcorn, Stephen and Samantha Thornhill. *Odetta*. New York, NY: Scholastic Inc., 2010. Young reader's biography of Odetta, including photos.

Barnett, LaShonda K. *I Got Thunder: Black Women Songwriters on Their Craft*. New York,

NY: Basic Books, 2007. Contains a chapter on Odetta's work and her life.

Websites

Odetta Live in concert 2005, "House of the Rising Sun" is on YouTube. http://www.youtube.com/watch?v=Aaya8jYZBO8.

The National Visionary Leadership Project features an interview, videos, and biography of Odetta. http://www.visionaryproject.com/gordonodetta/.

Also Noteworthy

1918

Dr. Yosef Alfredo Antonio ben-Jochannan is born. His mother was Puerto Rican and his father was originally from the Falasha Hebrew community of Gondar, Ethiopia. Dr. Ben, as he came to be known, spent a good portion of his youth in Puerto Rico and also attended college there. He worked as an adjunct professor at Cornell University's Africana Studies Department from 1976 through 1987. He began leading Afrocentric study tours to Egypt in 1946 and has written extensively about the true history of the Nile Valley and the origins of civilization.

Bibliography

Abbott, Lynn and Doug Seroff. *Out of Sight: The Rise of African American Popular Music, 1889–1895*. Jackson: University Press of Mississippi, 2003.

Abdul-Jabbar, Kareem and Alan Steinberg. *Black Profiles in Courage: A Legacy of African American Achievement*. New York, NY: HarperCollins, 2000.

African Holocaust Society. Features scholarly articles that try to present a balanced study of the African experience, past and present, http://www.africanholocaust.net/.

African Methodist Episcopal Zion Church. *The A.M.E. Zion Hymnal: Official Hymnal of the African Methodist Episcopal Zion Church*. Charlotte, NC: A.M.E. Zion Publishing House, 1996.

Alexander, Estrelda Y. *Black Fire: One Hundred Years of African American Pentecostalism*. Downers Grove, IL: InterVarsity Press, 2011.

Allah, Wakeel. *In The Name of Allah: A History of Clarence 13X and the Five Percenters*. New York, NY: Printing Systems, 2007.

Allen, Carole H. *Dare to Dream: Biography of Dr. Bernard A. Harris, Jr*. Bloomington, IN: Xlibris Corporation, 2007.

Anderson, Alan B. and George W. Pickering. *Confronting the Color Line: The Broken Promise of the Civil Rights Movement in Chicago*. Athens, GA: University of Georgia Press, 2008.

Anderson, Carol Elaine. *Eyes Off the Prize: The United Nations and the African American Struggle for Human Rights, 1944–1955*. New York, NY: Cambridge University Press, 2003.

Anderson, Reuben and Charles C. Bolton. *An Oral History with Reuben V. Anderson; Volume 320, Part 2 of Mississippi Oral History Program of the University of Southern Mississippi*. Charlottesville, VA: AbeBooks, 2008.

Anderson, Walter "Big Walt." *Sweet Nupe: An Unauthorized History of Kappa Alpha Psi*. Arlington, TX: Milk & Honey Pub., 2002.

Anderson, Wayne. *Plessy v. Ferguson: Legalizing Segregation*. Santa Monica, CA: The Rosen Publishing Group, 2003.

Andrews, Benny and High Museum of Art. *Benny Andrews: The Bicentennial Series: . . . Exhibition . . . Organized by the High Museum of Art, Atlanta*. Atlanta, Ga: High Museum of Art, 1975.

Angelou, Maya. *I Know Why the Caged Bird Sings*. New York: Random House Digital, Inc., 2009.

Anobile, Richard J. *The Wiz - The Super Soul Musical: Original Cast Album (1975 Broadway Cast) [Cast Recording]*. New York, NY: Atlantic Records Group/WEA International Inc., 1975.

Arsenault, Raymond. *The Sound of Freedom: Marian Anderson, the Lincoln Memorial, and the Concert That Awakened America*. New York, NY: Bloomsbury Publishing USA, 2010.

Aschenbrenner, Joyce. *Katherine Dunham: Dancing a Life*. Champaign, IL: University of Illinois Press, 2002.

Aswell, Tom. *Louisiana Rocks!: The True Genesis of Rock & Roll*. Gretna, LA: Pelican Publishing, 2009.

Axelrod, Alan. *Minority Rights in America*. Washington, DC: CQ Press, 2002.

Bacote, Charles A. *The Cosby Show: Audiences, Impact, and Implications*. Santa Barbara, CA: Greenwood Press, 1992.

Bailey, Richard. *They Too Call Alabama Home: African American Profiles, 1800–1999*. Victoria, BC: AbeBooks/Pyramid Pub., 1999.

Bak, Richard. *Turkey Stearnes and the Detroit Stars: The Negro Leagues in Detroit, 1919–1933*. Detroit, MI: Wayne State University Press, 1995.

Baker, Donald P. *Wilder: Hold Fast To Dreams: A Biography of L. Douglas Wilder*. Santa Ana, CA: Seven Locks Press, 1989.

Baker, Jean-Claude and Chris Chase. *Josephine: The Hungry Heart*. New York, NY: Cooper Square Press, 2001.

Baker, William J. *Jesse Owens: An American Life*. Champaign, IL: University of Illinois Press, 2006.

Banfield, Susan. *The Fifteenth Amendment: African-American Men's Right to Vote*. Berkeley Heights, NJ: Enslow Publishers, 1998.

Barnett, LaShonda K. *I Got Thunder: Black Women Songwriters on Their Craft*. New York, NY: Basic Books, 2007.

Basquiat, Jean Michel and Rudy Chiappini. *Jean-Michel Basquiat*. New York, NY: Skira, 2005.

Bass, Amy. *Not the Triumph But the Struggle: The 1968 Olympics and the Making of the Black Athlete*. Minneapolis, MN: U of Minnesota Press, 2004.

Bearden, Romare, and Harry Brinton Henderson. *A History of African-American Artists: From 1792 to the Present*. New York, NY: Pantheon Books, 1993.

Bearden, Romare, Ruth Fine, Mary Lee Corlett, National Gallery of Art (U.S.). *The Art of Romare Bearden*. Washington, DC: National Gallery of Art in association with Harry H. Abrams, New York, 2003.

Behnken, Brian D. *Fighting Their Own Battles: Mexican Americans, African Americans, and the Struggle for Civil Rights in Texas*. Chapel Hill, NC: UNC Press Books, 2011.

Bell, Bernard W. *The Contemporary African American Novel: Its Folk Roots and Modern Literary Branches*. Amherst, MA: Univ of Massachusetts Press, 2004

Benedetto, Robert, Jane Donovan and Kathleen Du Vall. *Historical Dictionary of Washington, Part 3*. Lanham, MD: Scarecrow Press, 2003.

Benson, George and Wolf Marshall. *Best of George Benson: A Step-By-Step Breakdown of His Guitar Styles and Techniques*. Milwaukee, WI: H. Leonard Corp., 2001.

Berlin, Edward A. *King of Ragtime: Scott Joplin and His Era*. New York, NY: Oxford University Press, 1996.

Berlin, Ira and Leslie Maria Harris. *Slavery in New York*. New York, NY: New Press, 2005.

Berry, Faith. *From Bondage to Liberation: Writings by and about Afro-Americans from 1700 to 1918*. London, England: Continuum International Publishing Group, 2006.

Beschloss, Michael R. *Reaching for Glory: Lyndon Johnson's Secret White House Tapes, 1964–1965*. New York, NY: Simon & Schuster, 2002.

Bey, Sharif. *Aaron Douglas and Hale Woodruff*. Saarbrücken, Germany: VDM Verlag, 2008.

Biagi, Shirley and Marilyn Kern-Foxworth. *Facing Difference: Race, Gender, and Mass Media*. Thousand Oaks, CA: Pine Forge Press, 1997.

The Biographical Directory of the United States Congress. Biography of Dawson's political life http://bioguide.congress.gov/scripts/biodisplay.pl?index=d000158.

Biography.com. William Lloyd Garrison biography http://www.biography.com/search/article.do?id=9307251.

Bird, Christiane. *Da Capo Jazz and Blues Lover's Guide to the U.S.: With more than 900 Hot Clubs, Cool Joints, Landmarks, and Legends, from Boogie-Woogie to Bop and Beyond*. Cambridge, MA: Da Capo Press, 2001.

Bird, Larry, Earvin Johnson, with Jackie MacMullan. *When the Game Was Ours*. New York, NY: Houghton Mifflin Harcourt, 2009.

Bishop, Dr. Rudine Sims. *Bishop Daniel A. Payne: Great Black Leader*. East Orange, NJ: Just Us Books, Inc., 2009.

Blair, Montgomery. *The Marvelous Musical Prodigy, Blind Tom, the Negro Boy Pianist*. Ithaca, NY: Cornell University Library, 1867.

Blaustein, Albert P., and Robert L. Zangrando. *Civil Rights and African Americans: A Documentary History* by Evanston, IL: Northwestern University Press, 1991.

Bloom, Ken. *Broadway: Its History, People, and Places: An Encyclopedia*. New York, NY: Taylor & Francis, 2004.

Bond, Horace Mann. *Negro education in Alabama: A Study in Cotton and Steel*. Tuscaloosa, AL: University of Alabama Press, 1969.

Boney, F. N. and Michael Adams. *A Pictorial History of the University of Georgia*. Athens, GA: University of Georgia Press, 2000.

Bontemps, Arna Wendell, Langston Hughes, edited by Charles Harold Nichols. *Arna Bontemps-Langston Hughes Letters, 1925–1967*. Saint Paul, MN: Paragon House, 1990.

Bourne, Stephen. *Ethel Waters: Stormy Weather*. Lanham, MD: Scarecrow Press, 2007.

Bowers, William T., William M. Hammond, and George L. MacGarrigle. *Black Soldier, White Army: The 24th Infantry Regiment in Korea*. Darby, PA: DIANE Publishing, 1997.

Boyd, Valerie. *Wrapped in Rainbows: The Life of Zora Neale Hurston*. New York, NY: Simon & Schuster, 2003.

Bradley, Stefan. *Harlem vs. Columbia University: Black Student Power in the Late 1960s*. Champaign, IL: University of Illinois Press, 2009.

Brager, George, Harry Specht, and James L. Torczyner. *Community Organizing*. New York, NY: Columbia University Press, 1987.

Brawley, Benjamin Griffith. *The Negro in Literature and Art: In the United States*. Whitefish, MT: Kessinger Publishing, 2006.

Breaking the Silence–Learning about the Transatlantic Slave Trade http://www.antislavery.org/breakingthesilence/index.shtml.

Breuer, William B. *War and American Women: Heroism, Deeds, and Controversy*. Westport, Ct: Greenwood Publishing Group, 1997.

Brill, Marlene Targ. *Marshall "Major" Taylor: World Champion Bicyclist, 1899–1901*. Breckenridge, CO: Twenty-First Century Books, 2007.

Brodie, James Michael. *Created Equal: The Lives and Ideas of Black American Innovators*. New York, NY: W. Morrow, 1993.

Brooks, Erik F, and Glenn L. Starks. *Historically Black Colleges and Universities*. Santa Barbara, CA: ABC-CLIO, 2011.

Brooks, Gwendolyn and Gloria Jean Wade Gayles. *Conversations with Gwendolyn Brooks*. Jackson, MS: Univ. Press of Mississippi, 2003.

Brooks, Tim and Richard Keith Spottswood. *Lost Sounds: Blacks and the Birth of the Recording Industry, 1890–1919*. Champaign, IL: University of Illinois Press, 2004.

Brown, Camille Lewis. *African Saints, African stories: 40 Holy Men and Women*. Cincinnati, OH: St. Anthony Messenger Press, 2008.

Brown, Cynthia Stokes, editor. *Ready from Within: A First Person Narrative: Septima Clark and the Civil Rights Movement*. Lawrenceville, NJ: Africa World Press, 1990.

Brown, Geoff. *Otis Redding: Try a Little Tenderness*. New York, NY: Canongate U.S., 2003.

Brown, Geoff and Chris Charlesworth. *James Brown: Doin' it to Death: A Biography*. London: Omnibus Press, 1996.

Brown, Hallie Quinn. *Homespun Heroines and Other Women of Distinction*. New York, NY: Oxford University Press, 1926.

Brown, James with Marc Eliot. *I Feel Good: A Memoir of a Life of Soul*. New York: New American Library, 2005.

Brown, Leslie. *Upbuilding Black Durham: Gender, Class, and Black Community Development in the Jim Crow South*. Chapel Hill, NC: UNC Press Books, 2008.

Brown, William Wells. *The Black Man: His Antecedents, His Genius, and His Achievements.* Victoria, BC: AbeBooks /J. Redpath, 1863.

Brown, William Wells. *Clotel.* New York, NY: Lightning Source Inc, 2008.

Browne-Marshall, Gloria J. *Race, Law, and American Society: 1607 to Present.* Cambridge, MA: Da Capo Press, 1995.

Bruns, Roger, editor. *Am I Not a Man and a Brother: The Antislavery Crusade of Revolutionary America, 1688–1788.* New York, NY: Chelsea House, 1977.

Bryant, Nicholas Andrew. *The Bystander: John F. Kennedy and the Struggle for Black Equality.* New York, NY: Basic Books, 2006.

Bryce, Robert M. *A Negro Explorer at the North Pole.* New York, NY: Cooper Square Press, 2001.

Buick, Kirsten Pai. *Child of the Fire: Mary Edmonia Lewis and the Problem of Art History's Black and Indian Subject.* Durham, NC: Duke University Press, 2010.

Burman, Stephen. *The Black Progress Question: Explaining the African-American Predicament.* Thousand Oaks, CA: Sage Publications, 1995.

Burrows, Edwin G. and Mike Wallace. *Gotham: A History of New York City to 1898.* New York, NY: Oxford University Press, 2000.

Byrd, W. Michael and Linda A. Clayton. *An American Health Dilemma: A Medical History of African Americans and the Problem of Race, Beginnings to 1900.* New York, NY: Routledge, 2000.

Campanella, Roy. *It's Good to Be Alive.* Lincoln, NE: University of Nebraska Press, 1959.

Cannon, Lou. *Official Negligence: How Rodney King and the Riots Changed Los Angeles and the LAPD.* Boulder, CO: Westview Press, 1999.

Carey, Charles W. *African-American Political Leaders.* New York, NY: Infobase Publishing, 2004.

Carisella, P. J. and James W. Ryan. *The Black Swallow of Death: The Incredible Story of Eugene Jacques Bullard, The World's First Black Combat Aviator.* New York: Marlborough, 1972.

Carmichael, Stokely. *Stokely Speaks: From Black Power to Pan-Africanism.* Chicago IL: Lawrence Hill Books, 2007.

Carmichael, Stokely with Michael Thelwell. *Ready for Revolution: The Life and Struggles of Stokely Carmichael (Kwame Ture).* New York, NY: Simon & Schuster, 2003.

Carroll, Diahann with Bob Morris. *The Legs Are the Last to Go: Aging, Acting, Marrying, and Other Things I Learned the Hard Way.* New York, NY: HarperCollins, 2009.

Carson, Clayborne. *In Struggle: SNCC and the Black Awakening of the 1960s.* Cambridge, MA: Harvard University Press, 1995.

Carter, Dan T. *Scottsboro: A Tragedy of the American South.* Baton Rouge, LA: LSU Press, 2007.

Carter, Patrick. *American History.* Toronto, Canada: Emond Montgomery Publication, 2007.

Carter, Patrick. *But for Birmingham: The Local and National Movements in the Civil Rights Struggle.* Chapel Hill, NC: UNC Press, 1997.

Cavendish, Marshall. *America in the 20th Century, Volume 12.* Tarrytown, NY: Marshall Cavendish, 2003.

C'BS Alife Allah and Lord Jamar of Brand Nubian (FRW). *Knowledge of Self: A Collection of Wisdom on the Science of Everything in Life.* New York, NY: Supreme Design, 2009.

Cecelski, David S. and Timothy B. Tyson. *Democracy Betrayed: The Wilmington Race Riot of 1898 and Its Legacy.* Chapel Hill, NC: UNC Press Books, 1998.

Chafe, William Henry. *Civilities and Civil Rights: Greensboro, North Carolina, and the Black Struggle for Freedom.* New York, NY: Oxford University Press, 1981.

Chang, Jeff. *Can't Stop, Won't Stop: A History of the Hip-Hop Generation.* New York, NY: Macmillan, 2006.

Chapman, Charles H. *Mel Bay Presents Interviews with the Jazz Greats— and More.* Pacific, MO: Mel Bay Publications, 2001.

Charles, Joan E. The University of Oklahoma. Department of Instructional Leadership and Academic Curriculum. *Ella Baker and the SNCC: Grassroots Leadership and Political Activism in a Nonhierarchical Organization.* Norman, OK: University of Oklahoma/ProQuest, 2007.

Charles, Ray and David Ritz. *Brother Ray: Ray Charles' Own Story*. Cambridge, MA: Da Capo Press, 2003.

Chase-Riboud, Barbara. *Hottentot Venus: A Novel*. New York, NY: Random House Digital, Inc., 2004.

Chase-Riboud, Barbara. *Sally Hemings: A Novel*. Chicago, IL: Chicago Review Press, 2009.

Cheek, William F. and Aimee Lee Cheek. *John Mercer Langston and the Fight for Black Freedom, 1829–65*. Champaign, IL: University of Illinois Press, 1996.

Cherry, Robert Allen. *Wilt: Larger Than Life*. Chicago, Il: Triumph Books, 2004.

Chisholm, Shirley. *Unbought and Unbossed: Expanded 40th Anniversary Edition*. Washington, DC: Take Root Media, 2010.

Church Terrell, Mary. Colored Woman in a White World. Waco, TX: Eakin Press, 2002.

Clark, E. Culpepper. *The Schoolhouse Door: Segregation's Last Stand at the University of Alabama*. New York, NY: Oxford University Press, 1995.

Clarke, John Henrik. *Africans at the Crossroads: Notes for an African World Revolution*. Lawrenceville, NJ: Africa World Press, Inc. & The Red Sea Press, Inc, 1992.

Clarke, John Henrik. *Harlem Voices from the Soul of Black America*, 2nd edition. Brooklyn, NY: A & B Book. Distributors Inc. September 1993.

Clarke, John Henrik. *My Life in Search of Africa*. Lawrenceville, NJ: Third World Press. February 1, 1999.

Clay, William L. and Malaika Adero. *Just Permanent Interests: Black Americans in Congress, 1870–1992*.

Cleaver, Eldridge. *Soul on Ice*. Miami, FL: San Val, Incorporated, 2003.

Cleaver, Eldridge, Kathleen Cleaver, and Cecil Brown. *Target Zero: A Life in Writing*. New York, NY: Macmillan, 2007.

Clegg, Claude Andrew. *The Price of Liberty: African Americans and the Making of Liberia*. New York, NY: University of North Carolina Press, 2003.

Cohen, Rodney T. *Fisk University*. Mount Pleasant, SC: Arcadia Publishing, 2001.

Coleman, Rick. *Blue Monday: Fats Domino and the Lost Dawn of Rock 'n' Roll*. Cambridge, NY: Da Capo Press, 2006.

Collier-Thomas, Bettye. *Jesus, Jobs, and Justice: African American Women and Religion*. New York, NY: Random House Digital, Inc., 2010.

Collings, Mark and Lennox Lewis, eds. *Muhammad Ali: Through the Eyes of the World*. New York, NY: Skyhorse Publishing Inc., 2007.

Congressional Black Caucus-History & Agenda http://thecongressionalblackcaucus.lee.house.gov/history_details.html.

The Congressional Black Caucus Foundation http://www.cbcfinc.org.

Conyers, James L. *Engines of the Black Power Movement: Essays on the Influence of Civil Rights Actions, Arts, and Islam*. Jefferson, NC: McFarland & Co., 2007.

Cooke, Sam. *Portrait of a Legend 1951–1964: Piano/Vocal/Chords*. New York, NY: Warner Bros. in association with Abkco Music, 2004.

Copson, Raymond W. *The Congressional Black Caucus and Foreign Policy*. Hauppauge, NY: Nova Publishers, 2003.

Cornell University. The John Henrik Clarke Africana Library http://www.library.cornell.edu/africana/clarke/.

Cort, John C. *Dreadful Conversions: The Making of a Catholic Socialist*. Bronx, NY: Fordham University Press, 2003.

Cothran, John C. *A Search of African American Life, Achievement and Culture: First Search*. Carrollton, TX: Stardate Publishing, 2006.

Cottrell, Robert Charles. *The Best Pitcher in Baseball: The Life of Rube Foster, Negro League Giant*. New York, NY: NYU Press, 2004.

Cox, Graham. *What Irony! Herbert C. Pell, Crimes Against Humanity, and the Negro Problem*. Houston, TX: University of Houston/ProQuest, 2008.

Cox, Joseph. *Great Black Men of Masonry*. Bloomington, IN: Universe, 2002.

Craft, William and Ellen Craft. *The American Negro: Running a Thousand Miles for Freedom or the Escape of William and Ellen Craft from Slavery*. Fairford, Gloucestershire, England: Echo Library, 2007.

Cramer, Alfred W. *Musicians and Composers of the 20th Century- Volume 2*. Ipswich, MA: Salem Press, 2009.

Crump, William L. *The Story of Kappa Alpha Psi: A History of the Beginning and Development of a College Greek Letter Organization, 1911–1991*. Philadelphia, PA: Kappa Alpha Psi Fraternity, 4th edition, 1991.

C-Span's "Book-TV." Interview with Franklin, available at http://www.c-spanvideo.org/program/194400-1.

Cullen, Frank, Florence Hackman, and Donald McNeilly. *Vaudeville Old & New: An Encyclopedia of Variety Performances in America, Volume 1*. Boca Raton, FL: Routledge, Taylor & Francis Group/Psychology Press, 2004.

Culp, Daniel Wallace. *Twentieth Century Negro Literature: Or, A Cyclopedia of Thought on the Vital Topics Relating to the American Negro*. Ann Arbor, MI: J. L. Nichols & Co./ University of Michigan, 1902.

Curtis, Susan. *Dancing to a Black Man's Tune: A Life of Scott Joplin*. Columbia, MO: University of Missouri Press, 2004.

Dagbovie, Pero Gaglo. *African American History Reconsidered*. Champaign, Ill: University of Illinois Press, 2010.

Dahl, Linda. *Stormy Weather: The Music and Lives of a Century of Jazzwomen*. Milwaukee, WI: Hal Leonard Corporation, 1996.

Dallard, Shyrlee and Andrew Young. *Ella Baker: A Leader Behind the Scenes*. Morristown, N.J.: Silver Burdett Press, 1990.

Dance, Stanley. *The World of Swing: An Oral History of Big Band Jazz*. Cambridge, MA: Da Capo Press, 2001.

Darden, Robert and Bob Darden. *People Get Ready!: A New History of Black Gospel Music*. New York, NY: Rizzoli, 2000.

Darraj, Susan Muaddi and Rob Maaddi. *Roberto Clemente*. New York, NY: Infobase Publishing, 2008. Davidson, Basil. *The African Slave Trade*. Boston: Little, Brown/Back Bay Books, 1988.

Davis, Andrew. *America's Longest Run: A History of the Walnut Street Theatre*. University Park, PA: Penn State Press, 2010.

Davis, Angela Y. *Angela Davis—An Autobiography*. New York, NY: Random House, 1974.

Davis, Angela Y. *Women, Race, & Class*. New York, NY: Random House Digital, Inc., 2011.

DeAngelis, Gina. *The Massachusetts 54th: African American Soldiers of the Union*. Mankato, MN: Capstone Press, 2002.

Delany, Martin Robison. *The Origin of Races and Color*. Mobile, Alabama: Black Classic Press, 1879.

Detroit, Michigan Recorder's Court. *Ossian Sweet Collection*. Victoria, BC: AbeBooks, 1925.

Diamonstein, Barbaralee. *Inside the Art World: Conversations with Barbaralee Diamonstein*. New York, NY: Rizzoli, 1994.

Dickerson, Dennis C. *Militant Mediator: Whitney M. Young Jr*. Lexington, KY: University Press of Kentucky, 2004.

Dickstein, Morris. *Dancing in the Dark: A Cultural History of the Great Depression*. New York, NY: W. W. Norton & Company, 2010.

Dingle, Derek T. *Black Enterprise Titans of the B.E. 100s: Black CEOs Who Redefined and Conquered American Business*. Hoboken, NJ: John Wiley & Sons, 1999.

Diouf, Sylviane A. *Dreams of Africa in Alabama: The Slave Ship Clotilda and the Story of the Last Africans Brought to America*. New York, NY: Oxford University Press, 2007.

Dixon, Phil S. *Andrew "Rube" Foster, a Harvest on Freedom's Fields*. Bloomington, IN: Xlibris Corporation, 2010.

Doerschuk, Bob. *88: The Giants of Jazz Piano, Volume 1*. Milwaukee, WI: Hal Leonard Corporation, 2001.

Dollee.com. The Playwrights Database. http://www.doollee.com/PlaywrightsH/hansberry -lorraine.html.

Dorsey, Brian. *Spirituality, Sensuality, Literality: Blues, Jazz, and Rap as Music and Poetry*. Vienna: Braumüller, 2000.

Drachman, Virginia G. and National Heritage Museum (Lexington, MA). *Enterprising Women: 250 Years of American Business*. Chapel Hill, NC: UNC Press Books, 2002.

Drape, Joe. *Black Maestro: The Epic Life of an American Legend*. New York: Morrow, 2006.

Dray, Philip. *Capitol Men: The Epic Story of Reconstruction Through the Lives of the First Black Congressmen*. New York, NY: Houghton Mifflin Harcourt, 2008.

Drew, Mary E. C. *Divine Will, Restless Heart*. Bloomington, IN: Xlibris Corporation, 2010.

Du Bois, Shirley Graham. *His Day Is Marching On: A Memoir of W. E. B. Du Bois*. Indianapolis, Indiana: Bobbs-Merrill Co, 1971.

Du Bois, Shirley Graham. "Negroes in the American Revolution, No. 2, 1961" in *Freedomways Reader: Prophets in Their Own Country* edited by Esther Cooper Jackson and Constance Pohl. New York, NY: Basic Books, 2000.

Du Bois, William Edward Burghardt. *Some Notes on Negro Crime, Particularly in Georgia: Report of a Social Study Made Under the Direction of Atlanta University; Together with the Proceedings of the Ninth Conference for the Study of the Negro Problems, Held at Atlanta University, May 24, 1904*. Atlanta, GA: Atlanta University Press, 1904.

Dunbar, Paul Laurence and Lida Keck Wiggins. *The Life and Works of Paul Laurence Dunbar: Containing His Complete Poetical Works, His Best Short Stories, Numerous Anecdotes and a Complete Biography of The Famous Poet*. Kila, MT: Kessinger Publishing, 2006.

Dunbar, Paul Laurence and William Andrew. *The Sport of the Gods*. New York, NY: Penguin, 2011.

Duncan, Joyce. *Ahead of Their Time: A Biographical Dictionary of Risk-Taking Women*. Santa Barbara, CA: Greenwood Publishing Group, 2002.

Durbin Christian, James. *Newspapers and the Orangeburg Massacre: Framing a Deadly Encounter*. Columbia, S.C.: University of South Carolina, 2004.

Durocher, Kristina. *Raising Racists: The Socialization of White Children in the Jim Crow South*. Lexington, KY: University Press of Kentucky, 2011.

Dyja, Thomas. *Walter White: The Dilemma of Black Identity in America*. Lanham, MD: Ivan R. Dee Publisher, 2010.

Earl, Sari. *Benjamin O. Davis Jr.: Air Force General & Tuskegee Airmen Leader*. Edina, MN: ABDO, 2010.

Edds, Margaret. *Claiming the Dream: The Victorious Campaign of Douglas Wilder of Virginia*. Chapel Hill, NC: Algonquin Books, 1990.

Edward Franklin Frazier. *Black Bourgeoisie*. New York, NY: Simon & Schuster, 1997.

Egerton, Douglas R. *Death Or Liberty: African Americans and Revolutionary America*. New York, NY: Oxford University Press, 2009.

Elam, Harry Justin and Kennell A. Jackson. *Black Cultural Traffic: Crossroads in Global Performance and Popular Culture*. Ann Arbor, MI: University of Michigan, 2005.

Eliza Smith Brown, Daniel Holland, Pennsylvania Historical and Museum Commission. *African American Historic Sites Survey of Allegheny County*. Darby, PA: DIANE Publishing Inc., 1994.

Ellis, Mark. *Race, War, and Surveillance: African Americans and the United States Government During World War I*. Bloomington, IN: Indiana University Press, 2001.

Emilio, Luis Fenollosa. *A Brave Black Regiment: The History of the Fifty-Fourth Regiment of Massachusetts Volunteer Infantry, 1863–1865*. Cambridge, MA: Da Capo Press, 1995.

Estes, Carol Ann. *The Death of Vernon Dahmer: Klan Violence and Mississippi Justice in the 1960s*. University of Southern Mississippi, 1988.

Evans, Janet Lynn. *"We'll Take Care of the Counting*": A Cultural, Rhetorical and Critical Analysis of Electronic Voting Technology*. Boulder, CO: University of Colorado at Boulder, 2007.

Ezra, Michael. *Muhammad Ali: The Making of an Icon*. Chicago, IL: Temple University Press, 2009.

Fairclough, Adam. *To Redeem the Soul of America: The Southern Christian Leadership Conference and Martin Luther King, Jr.* Athens, GA: University of Georgia Press, 1987.

Farner, James. *Lay Bare the Heart: An Autobiography of the Civil Rights Movement*. Fort Worth, TX: TCU Press, 1998.

Feather, Leonard G. *Inside Jazz, Roots of Jazz*. Cambridge, MA: Da Capo Press, 1977.

Ferguson, Carroy U. *Transitions in Consciousness from an African American Perspective: Original Essays in Psycho-Historical Context*. Lanham, MD: University Press of America/ Rowman & Littlefield Publishing Group, 2004.

Fireside, Harvey and Marc H. Morial. *Separate and Unequal: Homer Plessy and the Supreme Court Decision that Legalized Racism*. New York, NY: Basic Books, 2005.

Fisher, Ada Lois Sipuel, and Danney Goble. *A Matter of Black and White: The Autobiography of Ada Lois Sipuel Fisher*. Fort Worth, TX: TCU Press, 1998.

Fitts, Leroy. *A History of Black Baptists*. Nashville, TN: Broadman Press, 1985.

Flipper, Henry Ossian. *The Colored Cadet at West Point. Autobiography of Lieut. Henry Ossian Flipper, U. S. A., First Graduate of Color from the U. S. Military Academy*. New York, NY: Cherry Lane Music, 2003.

Flucker, Turry, and Phoenix Savage. *African Americans of Jackson*. Mount Pleasant, SC: Arcadia Publishing, 2008.

Foner, Philip Sheldon. *Organized Labor and the Black Worker, 1619–1981*. New York, NY: International Publishers, 1982.

Foote, Thelma Wills. *Black and White Manhattan: The History of Racial Formation in Colonial New York City*. New York, NY: Oxford University Press, 2004.

Ford, Lacy K. *Deliver Us from Evil: The Slavery Question in the Old South*. New York, NY: Oxford University Press US, 2009.

Ford, Roderick O. *The Evasion of African American Workers*. Bloomington, IN: Xlibris Corporation, 2008.

Fradin, Dennis B. and Judith Bloom Fradin. Fight On!: Mary Church Terrell's Battle for Integration. New York, NY: Houghton Mifflin Harcourt, 2003.

Franchino, Vicky. *Compass Point Early Biographies: George Washington Carver*. Mankato, MN: Compass Point Books, 2001.

Franklin, Buck Colbert, John Hope Franklin and John Whittington Franklin. *My Life and an Era: The Autobiography of Buck Colbert Franklin*. Baton Rouge: Louisiana State University Press, 1997.

Franklin, John Hope. *Mirror to America: The Autobiography of John Hope Franklin*. New York: Farrar, Straus and Giroux, 2005.

French, Scot. *The Rebellious Slave: Nat Turner in American Memory*. New York, NY: Houghton Mifflin Harcourt, 2004.

Fritts, Ron and Ken Vail. *Ella Fitzgerald: The Chick Webb Years & Beyond*. Lanham, MD: Scarecrow Press, 2003.

Frost, Karolyn Smardz. *I've Got a Home in Glory Land: A Lost Tale of the Underground Railroad*. New York, NY: Macmillan, 2008.

Frye, Daniel J. *African American Visual Artists: An Annotated Bibliography of Educational Resource Materials*. Lanham, MD: Scarecrow Press, 2001.

Fullilove, Mindy Thompson. *The National Negro Labor Council: A History*. Victoria, BC: AbeBooks/ AIMS, 1978.

Gaillard, Frye. *The Greensboro Four: Civil Rights Pioneers: A Profile*. Charlotte, NC: Main Street Rag Pub. Co., 2001.

Garner, Erroll and Sy Johnson. *The Erroll Garner Anthology: The First Anthology of Erroll Garner's Compositions*. New York, NY: Cherry Lane Music, 2003.

Garrison, William Lloyd. *The Letters of William Lloyd Garrison: No Union with Slaveholders, 1841–1849*. Cambridge, MA: Harvard University Press, 1974.

Garrison, William Lloyd; edited by William E. Cain. *William Lloyd Garrison and the Fight Against Slavery: Selections from The Liberator*. New York: Bedford Books of St. Martin's Press, 1994.

Garrow, David J. *Bearing the cross: Martin Luther King, Jr., and the Southern Christian Leadership Conference*. New York, NY: HarperCollins, 2004.

Gaye, Frankie and Fred E. Basten. *Marvin Gaye, My Brother*. Milwaukee, WI: Hal Leonard Corporation, 2003.

Gellman, David Nathaniel. *Emancipating New York: The Politics of Slavery and Freedom, 1777–1827*. Baton Rouge, LA: LSU Press, 2006.

George, Luvenia A. *The Early Piano Rags (1899–1916) of James Hubert ("Eubie") Blake: A Stylistic Study and Annotated Edition*. Ph.D. diss., Baltimore, MD: University of Maryland Baltimore County, 1995.

Giddings, Paula J. *In Search of Sisterhood: Delta Sigma Theta and the Challenge of the Black Sorority Movement*. New York, NY: HarperCollins Publishers, 2007.

Gillespie, Dizzy with Al Fraser. *To Be, Or Not . . . to Bop*. Minneapolis, MN: University of Minnesota Press, 2009.

Gilyard, Keith. *Liberation Memories: The Rhetoric and Poetics of John Oliver Killens* Detroit, MI: Wayne State University Press, 2003.

Giovanni, Nikki and Bryan Collier. *Rosa*. New York, NY: Simon & Schuster, 2003.

Glasco, Laurence Admiral and Federal Writers' Project (Pa.). *The WPA history of the Negro in Pittsburgh*. Pittsburgh, PA: University of Pittsburgh Pre, 2004.

Glasrud, Bruce A. *Blacks in East Texas History: Selections from the East Texas Historical Journal*. College Station, TX: Texas A&M University Press, 2008.

Goldfield, David R. *Black, White, and Southern: Race Relations and Southern Culture, 1940 to the Present*. Baton Rouge, LA: LSU Press. 1991.

Gourse, Leslie. *Unforgettable: The Life and Mystique of Nat King Cole*. New York: St. Martin's, 1991.

Gordy, Berry. *Movin' Up: Pop Gordy Tells His Story*. New York, NY: Harper & Row, 1979.

Gordy, Berry. *To Be Loved: The Music, the Magic, the Memories of Motown: An Autobiography*. New York, NY: Warner Books, 1994.

Govenar, Alan B. *Texas Blues: The Rise of a Contemporary Sound*. College Station, TX: Texas A&M University Press, 2008.

Graber, Mark A. *Dred Scott and the Problem of Constitutional Evil*. New York, NY: Cambridge University Press, 2006.

Grady-Willis, Winston A. *Challenging U.S. Apartheid: Atlanta and Black Struggles for Human Rights, 1960–1977*. Durham, NC: Duke University Press, 2006.

Grant, Donald Lee. *The Way It Was in the South: The Black Experience in Georgia*. Athens, GA: University of Georgia Press, 2001.

Green, Al and Davin Seay. *Take Me to the River: An Autobiography*. Chicago, IL: Chicago Review Press, 2009.

Greenberg, Kenneth S. *Nat Turner: A Slave Rebellion in History and Memory*. New York, NY: Oxford University Press, 2004.

Greene, Erik. *Our Uncle Sam: The Sam Cooke Story from His Family's Perspective*. Bloomington, IN: Trafford Publishing, 2005.

Gregory, Dick and Shelia P. Moses. *Callus on My Soul: A Memoir*. New York, NY: Kensington Books, 2003.

Griffith, Benjamin E. *America Votes!: A Guide to Modern Election Law and Voting Rights*. Chicago, IL: American Bar Association, 2008.

Grimké, Archibald. "A Madonna of the South" in *The Southern Workman*. Victoria, BC: AbeBooks/ Hampton Institute Press, 1900.

Guelzo, Allen C. *Lincoln's Emancipation Proclamation: The End of Slavery in America*.

Gunderson, Gary. *Boundary Leaders: Leadership Skills for People of Faith*. Minneapolis, MN: Fortress Press, 2004.

Haber, Louis. *Black Pioneers of Science and Invention*. New York, NY: Houghton Mifflin Harcourt, 1992.

Haley, Alex. *Roots: The Saga of an American Family*. Boulder, CO: Westview Press, 2007.

Hall, Gwendolyn Midlo. "The Franco-African Peoples of Haiti and Louisiana: Population, Language, Culture, Religion, and Revolution." In *Revolutionary Freedoms: A History of Survival, Strength and Imagination in Haiti* by Cécile Accilien, Jessica Adams, Elmide Méléance, Ulrick Jean-Pierre. Coconut Creek, FL: Educa Vision Inc. 2006.

Hammon, Jupiter and Stanley Austin Ransom. *America's First Negro Poet: The Complete Works of Jupiter Hammon of Long Island*. Port Washington, N.Y.: Associated Faculty Press, 1983.

Handleman, Philip and Craig Kodera. *A Dream of Pilots*. Gretna, LA: Pelican Publishing Company, 2009.

Handy, William Christopher. *Father of the Blues: An Autobiography*. Cambridge, MA: Da Capo Press, 1991.

Handyside, Chris. *Folk*. Chicago, IL: Heinemann-Raintree, 2006.

Hanes, Bailey C. *Bill Pickett, Bulldogger: The Biography of a Black Cowboy*. Norman, OK: University of Oklahoma Press, 1989.

Hanson, Joyce Ann. *Mary McLeod Bethune and Black Women's Political Activism*. Columbia, MO: University of Missouri Press, 2003.

Hare, Kenneth M. *They Walked to Freedom 1955–1956*. Willowbrook, IL: Sports Publishing LLC, 2005.

Harris, Leonard and Charles Molesworth. *Alain L. Locke: Biography of a Philosopher*. Chicago, Il: University of Chicago Press, 2008.

Harris, Leslie M. *In the Shadow of Slavery: African Americans in New York City, 1626–186*. Chicago, Ill: University of Chicago Press, 2004.

Harris, Middleton A., Morris Levitt, Ernest Smith, and Toni Morrison. *The Black Book: 35th Anniversary Edition*. New York, NY: Random House Digital, Inc., 2009.

Hartmann, Douglas. *Race, Culture and the Revolt of the Black Athlete: The 1968 Olympic Protests and Their Aftermath*. Chicago, IL: University of Chicago Press, 2004.

Haugen, Brenda. *Thurgood Marshall: Civil Rights Lawyer and Supreme Court Justice*. Mankato, MN: Compass Point Books, 2007.

Hayden, Tom. *Rebellion in Newark: Official Violence and Ghetto Response*. New York, NY: Vintage Books, 1967.

Haygood, Wil. *In Black and White: The Life of Sammy Davis, Jr*. New York: A.A. Knopf, 2003.

Heath, David. *Elections in the United States*. Mankato, MN: Capstone Press, 1999.

Heard, Alex. *The Eyes of Willie McGee: A Tragedy of Race, Sex, and Secrets in the Jim Crow South*. New York: Harper, 2010.

Hein, David and Gardiner H. Shattuck, Jr. *The Episcopalians*. Harrisburg, PA: Church Publishing, Inc., 2005.

Henry, Charles P. *Ralph Bunche: Model Negro Or American Other?* New York, NY: NYU Press, 2005.

Hill, Errol, and James Vernon Hatch. *A History of African American Theatre*. New York, NY: Cambridge University Press, 2003January, Brendan. *The Emancipation Proclamation*. Danbury, CT: Scholastic Inc: Children's Press, 1998.

Hill, Pauline Anderson Simmons. *Too Young To Be Old: The Story of Bertha Pitts Campbell, a Founder of Delta Sigma Theta Sorority, Inc*. Bloomington, IN: AuthorHouse/Peanut Butter Pub., 1981.

Hilliard, David, editor. *The Black Panther*. New York, NY: Atria Books, 2007.

Hinnant, Denise Ellaine. *Sculptor Augusta Savage: Her Art, Progressive Influences, and African-American Representation*. Crestwood, KY: University of Louisville, 2003.

Hinton, William Augustus. *Syphilis and Its Treatment*. Victoria, BC: AbeBooks/The Macmillan company, 1936.

Hirsch, James S. *Riot and Remembrance: America's Worst Race Riot and Its Legacy*. Ba New York, NY: Mariner Books, 2003.

Hoffman, Steven J. *Race, Class and Power in the Building of Richmond, 1870–1920*. Jefferson, NC: McFarland, 2004.

Holiday, Billie with William Dufty. *Lady Sings the Blues*. New York, NY: Random House Digital, Inc., 2006.

Holway, John. *Black Diamonds: Life in the Negro Leagues from the Men Who Lived It*. Westport, CT: Meckler, 1989.

Honey, Maureen. *Shadowed Dreams: Women's Poetry of the Harlem Renaissance*. Piscataway, NJ: Rutgers University Press, 2006.

Horton, James Oliver and Lois E. Horton. *Slavery and the Making of America*. New York, NY: Oxford University Press, 2005.

Hotaling, Edward. *The Great Black Jockeys: The Lives and Times of the Men Who Dominated America's First National Sport*. New York: Forum, 1999.

Hughes, Langston. *Not Without Laughter*. New York, NY: Simon & Schuster, 1995.

Hurston, Zora Neale. *Their Eyes Were Watching God*. Saint Paul, MN: EMC/Paradigm Pub., 2004.

Hutton, Frankie. *The Early Black Press in America, 1827 to 1860*. Santa Barbara, CA: Greenwood Publishing Group, 1993.

Ikenson, Ben. *Patents: Ingenious Inventions: How They Work and How They Came To Be*. New York, NY: Black Dog & Leventhal Publishers, 2004.

Jackson Coppin, Fanny. *Reminiscences of School Life and Hints on Teaching (African-American Women Writers, 1910–1940)*. New York, NY: G.K. Hall & Company, Jan 1995.

Jackson, Gerald G. *We're Not Going to Take It Anymore*. Silver Spring, MD: Beckham Publications Group, Inc., 2005.

Jackson, Jerma A. *Singing In My Soul: Black Gospel Music in a Secular Age*. Chapel Hill, NC: University of North Carolina Press, 2004.

Jackson, Michael. *My World: The Official Photobook, Volume 1*. New York, NY: Mj Licensing Llc, 2006.

Jakoubek, Robert E. *James Farmer and the Freedom Rides*. Minneapolis, MN: Millbrook Press, 1994.

Jeffries, Judson L. *Huey P. Newton: The Radical Theorist*. Jackson, MS: Univ. Press of Mississippi, 2006.

Jeffries, Judson L. *Virginia's Native Son: The Election and Administration of Governor L. Douglas Wilder*. West Lafayette, IN: Purdue University Press, 2000.

Jenkins, Earnestine. *A Question of Manhood: A Reader in U.S. Black Men's History and Masculinity*. Bloomington, IN: Indiana University Press, 1999.

Jerome, Fred and Rodger Taylor. *Einstein on Race and Racism*. Piscataway, NJ: Rutgers University Press, 2006.

John Henrik Clarke: A Great and Mighty Walk. DVD, directed by St. Claire Bourne, 1996. 90 minutes.

Johnson, Hannibal B. *Acres of Aspiration: The All-black Towns In Oklahoma*. Waco, TX: Eakin Press, 2002.

Johnson, James Weldon. *The Autobiography of an Ex-Colored Man*. Minneapolis, Minnesota: Filiquarian Publishing, LLC., 2007.

Johnson, James Weldon and Debbie Egan-Chin. *Lift Every Voice and Sing: A Pictorial Tribute to the Negro National Anthem*. New York, NY: Jum at the Sun/Hyperion Books for Children, 2000.

Johnson, Mary H. *A Case History of the Evolution of WGPR-TV, Detroit: First Black-Owned Television Station in the U.S., 1972–1979*. Victoria, BC: AbeBooks/University of North Carolina at Chapel Hill, 1979.

Johnson, Mat. *The Great Negro Plot: A Tale of Conspiracy and Murder in Eighteenth-Century New York*. New York, NY: Bloomsbury Publishing USA, 2007.

Johnson, Mordecai Wyatt, edited by Richard Ishmael McKinney. *Mordecai, the Man and His Message: The Story of Mordecai Wyatt Johnson*. Washington, DC: Howard University Press, 1997.

Jones, LeRoi. *Dutchman and The Slave: Two Plays*. New York, NY: Harper Perennial, 1971.

Jones, Martha S. *All Bound Up Together: The Woman Question in African American Public Culture, 1830–1900*. Sydney, Australia: ReadHowYouWant.com, 2009.

Jordan, Steve Tom Scanlan. *Rhythm Man: Fifty Years in Jazz*. Ann Arbor, MI: University of Michigan Press, 1993.

Joseph, Peniel E. *The Black Power Movement: Rethinking the Civil Rights-Black Power Era*. New York, NY: CRC Press, 2006.

Joseph, Peniel E. *Waiting 'Til the Midnight Hour: A Narrative History of Black Power in America*. New York, NY: Macmillan, 2007.

Jules-Rosette, Bennetta. *Josephine Baker in Art and Life: The Icon and the Image*. Champaign, IL: University of Illinois Press, 2007.

Just, Ernest Everett. *Studies of Fertilization in Platynereis Megalops*. Chicago, Il: University of Chicago, 1915.

Kappes, Serena. *Hank Aaron*. Breckenridge, CO: Twenty-First Century Books, 2005.

Katz, Jonathan. *Resistance at Christiana: The Fugitive Slave Rebellion, Christiana, Pennsylvania, September 11, 1851: A Documentary Account*. Ed. Darlene Clark Hine and Earnestine Jenkins. New York, NY: Crowell, 1974.

Kersten, Andrew Edmund. *Race, Jobs, and the War: The FEPC in the Midwest, 1941–46*. Champaign, IL: University of Illinois Press, 2000.

Kessler, James H. *Distinguished African American Scientists of the 20th Century*. Santa Barbara, CA: Greenwood Publishing Group, 1996.

King, Martin Luther, Jr. *Why We Can't Wait*. New York, NY: Penguin Group/Signet Classic, 2000.

King, Jr. Martin Luther; Edited by Clayborne Carson, Ralph E. Luker, and Penny A. Russell. *The Papers of Martin Luther King, Jr. Volume I: Called to Serve, January 1929–June 1951*. Berkeley, CA: University of California Press, 1992.

King, Jr. Martin Luther; Edited by James Melvin Washington. *A Testament of Hope: The Essential Writings and Speeches of Martin Luther King, Jr.* New York, NY: HarperCollins, 1991.

Kirschke, Amy Helene and Aaron Douglas. *Aaron Douglas: Art, Race, and the Harlem Renaissance*. Jackson, MS: Univ. Press of Mississippi, 1995.

Kiska, Tim and Ed Golick. *Detroit Television*. Mount Pleasant, SC: Arcadia Publishing, 2010.

Konchar Farr, Cecilia. *Reading Oprah: How Oprah's Book Club Changed the Way America Reads*. Albany, NY: SUNY Press, 2005.

Kremer, Gary R., Ed. *George Washington Carver In His Own Words*. Columbia, MO: University of Missouri Press, 1991

Kryder, Daniel. *Divided Arsenal: Race and the American State During World War II*. New York, NY: Cambridge University Press, 2001.

Lanctot, Neil. *Negro League Baseball: The Rise and Ruin of a Black Institution*. Philadelphia, Pennsylvania: University of Pennsylvania Press, 2004.

Langston, John Mercer. *From the Virginia Plantation to the National Capitol; or, The First and Only Negro Representative in Congress from the Old Dominion*. Edina, MN: American Publishing Company, 1894.

Laney, Garrine P. *The Voting Rights Act of 1965: Historical Background and Current Issues*. Hauppauge, NY: Nova Publishers, 2003.

Lanning, Michael Lee. *The American Revolution 100: The People, Battles, and Events of the American War for Independence, Ranked by Their Significance*. Naperville, IL: Sourcebooks, Inc., 2009.

Lapchick, Richard Edward. *100 Pioneers: African-Americans Who Broke Color Barriers in Sport*. Morgantown, WV: Fitness Information Technology, 2008.

Lawrence, Beverly Hall. *Reviving the Spirit: A Generation of African Americans Goes Home to Church*. Jackson, TN: Grove Press, 1997.

Lawrence, Jacob. *The Great Migration: An American Story*. New York, NY: HarperCollins, 1995.

Lawrence, Sharon. *Jimi Hendrix: The Man, the Magic, the Truth*. New York, N.Y.: HarperCollins, 2005.

Layton, Azza Salama. *International Politics and Civil Rights Policies in the United States, 1941–1960*. Cambridge, England: Cambridge University Press, 2000.

"Lecture on Haiti: The Haitian Pavilion Dedication Ceremonies." http://haitiforever.com/window sonhaiti/fdouglass1.shtml

Lee, Martha Frances. *The Nation of Islam, an American Millenarian Movement*. Victoria, BC: AbeBooks/Edwin Mellen Press, 1988.

Lehman, Paul Robert. *The Development of the Black Psyche in the Writings of John Oliver Killens, 1916–1987*. Lewiston, NY: Edwin Mellen Press, 2003.

Leonard, Richard D. *Call to Selma: Eighteen Days of Witness*. Boston, MA: Unitarian Universalist Association of Congregations, 2002.

Lester, James. *Too Marvelous for Words: The Life and Genius of Art Tatum*. New York, NY: Oxford University Press, 1995.

Lewis, David Levering. *W. E. B. DuBois—The Fight for Equality and the American Century, 1919–1963*. New York, NY: Macmillan, 2001.

Lewis, P.H. *Selma: The Other Side of 1965*. Victoria, BC: AbeBooks/Factor Press, 2001.

Lewis, William H. "Abraham Lincoln" in *Masterpieces of Negro Eloquence, 1818–1913* edited by Alice Moore Dunbar-Nelson. Mineola, NY: Courier Dover Publications, 2000.

Library of Congress http://memory.loc.gov/cgi-bin/query/P?mfd:8:./temp/~ammem_3RrF. Facsimilie of Douglass' handwritten speech at the Haitian Pavilion dedication ceremonies.

Lincoln Charles Eric and Lawrence H. Mamiya. *The Black Church in the African-American Experience*. Durham, NC: Duke University Press, 1990.

Lindfors, Bernth. *Ira Aldridge: The African Roscius*. Rochester, NY: Boydell & Brewer Inc, 2010.

Litwack, Leon F. and August Meier. *Black Leaders of the Nineteenth Century*. Bloomington, IN: Indiana University Press, 1991.

Litwin, Laura Baskes. *Benjamin Banneker: Astronomer and Mathematician*. Berkeley Heights, NJ: Enslow Publishers, 1999.

Lloyd, Craig. *Eugene Bullard: Black Expatriate in Jazz-Age Paris*. Atlanta: Univeristy of Georgia Press, 2006.

Loewen, James W. *Lies Across America: What Our Historic Sites Get Wrong*. New York, NY: Simon & Schuster, 2007.

Logan, Rayford W. *Howard University: The First Hundred Years 1867–1967*. New York: NYU Press, August 2004.

Lorde, Audre and Cheryl Clarke. *Sister Outsider: Essays and Speeches*. New York, NY: Random House, Inc., 2007.

Lornell, Kip. *Virginia's Blues, Country & Gospel Records, 1902–1943: An Annotated Discography*. Lexington, KY: University Press of Kentucky, 1989.

Lowry, Beverly. *Harriet Tubman: Imagining a Life*. New York NY: Random House, Inc., 2008.

Lydon, Michael. *Ray Charles: Man and Music*. London, UK: Psychology Press, 2004.

Lynk, Miles V. *Sixty Years of Medicine, or The Life and Times of Dr. Miles V. Lynk: An Autobiography*. Memphis: Twentieth Century Press, 1951.

Mabee, Carleton and Susan Mabee Newhouse. *Sojourner Truth: Slave, Prophet, Legend*. New York, NY: NYU Press, 1995.

MacDonald, J. Fred. *Blacks and White TV: Afro-Americans in Television Since 1948*. Chicago IL: Nelson-Hall, 1983.

Macmillan Library Reference USA. *Black Women in America*. New York: Macmillan Library Reference USA, 1999.

Malone, Ross. *Tales from Missouri and the Heartland*. Bloomington, IN: AuthorHouse, 2010.

Manning, Christopher. *William L. Dawson and the Limits of Black Electoral Leadership*. DeKalb, IL: Northern Illinois University Press, 2009.

Marable, Manning, and Leith Mullings, editors. *Let Nobody Turn Us Around: Voices of Resistance, Reform, and Renewal: An African American Anthology*. Lanham, MD: Rowman & Littlefield, 2000.

Marable, Manning. *Race, Reform, and Rebellion: The Second Reconstruction and Beyond in Black America, 1945–2006*. Jackson, MS: Univ. Press of Mississippi, 2007.

Maraniss, David. *Clemente: The Passion and Grace of Baseball's Last Hero*. New York, NY: Simon & Schuster, 2007.

Markowitz, Gerald E and David Rosner. *Children, Race, and Power: Kenneth and Mamie Clark's Northside Center*. Charlottesville, VA: University Press of Virginia, 1996.

Marshall, Alice Jefferson, et al. *A Life of Quiet Dignity: Naomi Sewell Richardson*. New York, NY: Red Elephant Publishers, 1995.

Martin, Henry and Keith Waters. *Jazz: The First 100 Years*. Florence, KY: Cengage Learning, 2005.

Martin, Tony. *Literary Garveyism: Garvey, Black Arts, and the Harlem Renaissance*. Bloomington, IN: Majority Press, 1983.

Mathieson, Kenny. *Giant Steps: Bebop and the Creators of Modern Jazz 1945–65*. New York, NY: Canongate U.S., 1999.

Mattocks, Carolyn Regennia Mpa. *I Can Do Anything*. Bloomington, IN: Xlibris Corporation, 2009.

Mayer, Henry. *All on Fire: William Lloyd Garrison and the Abolition of American Slavery*. New York: W.W. Norton, 2008.

May, Vivian M. *Anna Julia Cooper, Visionary Black Feminist: A Critical Introduction*. Boca Raton, FL: CRC Press/Taylor & Francis Group, LLC, 2007.

Mayer, David. *Stagestruck filmmaker: D.W. Griffith & the American Theatre*. Minneapolis, MN: University of Minnesota Press, 2009.

Mays, Benjamin Elijah, edited by Orville Vernon Burton. *Born to Rebel: An Autobiography*. Victoria, BC: University of Georgia Press, 2003.

Mays, Benjamin Elijah. *The Relevance of Mordecai Wyatt Johnson for Our Times: The Inaugural Address in the Mordecai Wyatt Johnson Lecture Series*. Washington, DC: Howard University, 1978.

McCann Posey, Josephine. *Alcorn State University and the National Alumni Association*. Mount Pleasant, SC: Arcadia Publishing, 2000.

McCants, Clyde T. *American Opera Singers and Their Recordings: Critical Commentaries and Discographies*. Jefferson NC: McFarland, 2004.

McClellan, Lawrence. *The Later Swing Era, 1942 to 1955*. Santa Barbara, CA: Greenwood Publishing Group, 2004.

McFeely, William S. *Frederick Douglass*. New York: W. W. Norton & Company, 1995.

McKinney, Richard I. *Mordecai, the Man and His Message: The Story of Mordecai Wyatt Johnson*. Washington, DC: Howard University Press, 1997.

McKinstry, Carolyn Maull and Denise George. *While the World Watched: A Birmingham Bombing Survivor Comes of Age During the Civil Rights Movement*. Bloomington, IN: Xlibris Corporation, 2010.

McKissack, Pat and Fredrick McKissack. *African-American Inventors: A Proud Heritage*. Brookfield, CT: Millbrook Press, 1994.

McKiven, Henry M. *Iron and Steel: Class, Race, and Community in Birmingham, Alabama, 1875–1920*. New York, NY: UNC Press, 1995.

McLaren, Joseph. *Langston Hughes, Folk Dramatist in the Protest Tradition, 1921–1943*. Santa Barbara, CA: Greenwood Publishing Group, 1997.

McMillan, Felicia Piggott. *The North Carolina Black Repertory Company: 25 Marvtastic Years*. Greensboro, NC: Open Hand Publishing, LLC, 2005.

McMurray, Linda O. *George Washington Carver: Scientist and Symbol*. New York: Oxford University Press, 1981.

McNeil, Genna Rae. *Groundwork: Charles Hamilton Houston and the Struggle for Civil Rights*. Philadelphia, PA: University of Pennsylvania Press, 1984.

McPherson, James M. *Battle Cry of Freedom: The Civil War Era. Volume 6 of Oxford History of the United States*. New York, NY: Oxford University Press US, 2003.

Mead, Chris. *Joe Louis: Black Champion in White America*. Mineola, NY: Dover Publications, 2010.

Megginson, W. J. *African American Life in South Carolina's Upper Piedmont, 1780–1900*. Columbia, SC: Univ of South Carolina Press, 2006.

Mfume, Kweisi with Ron Stodghill. *No Free Ride: From the Mean Streets to the Mainstream*. New York, NY: Random House/One World, 1996.

Miller, Frederic P., Agnes F Vandome, and John McBrewster. *Gabriel Prosser*. Mauritius: VDM Publishing House Ltd., 2010.

Miller, James A. *Remembering Scottsboro: The Legacy of an Infamous Trial*. Princeton, NJ: Princeton University Press, 2009.

Mills, Kay. *This Little Light of Mine: The Life of Fannie Lou Hamer*. Lexington, KY: University Press of Kentucky, 2007.

Minoso, Minnie with Herb Fagen. *Just Call Me Minnie: My Six Decades in Baseball*. New York, NY: Sports Publishing LLC, 1994.

Mirror to America: The Autobiography of John Hope Franklin. New York: Farrar, Straus and Giroux, 2006.

Moffi, Larry and Jonathan Kronstadt. *Crossing the Line: Black Major Leaguers, 1947–1959*. Lincoln NE: U of Nebraska Press, 2006.

Monson, Ingrid Tolia. *Freedom Sounds: Civil Rights Call Out to Jazz and Africa*. New York, NY: Oxford University Press, 2007.

Montague Cobb, William with Lewis E. Week. *W. Montague Cobb, in First Person: An Oral History*. Victoria, BC: AbeBooks/L.E. Weeks, 1983.

Moore, Rebecca, Anthony B. Pinn, and Mary R. Sawye. *Peoples Temple and Black Religion in America*. Bloomington, IN: Indiana University Press, 2004.

Moreland, Laurence W., Robert P. Steed, and Todd A. Baker. *Blacks in Southern Politics*. New York, NY: Praeger Publishers, 1987

Morin Isobel V. *Women Chosen for Public Office*. Minneapolis, MN: The Oliver Press, Inc., 1995.

Morris, Aldon D. *The Origins of the Civil Rights Movement: Black Communities Organizing for Change*. Detroit Michigan: Free Press, 1984.

Moses, Shelia P. and Bonnie Christensen. *I, Dred Scott: A Fictional Slave Narrative Based on the Life and Legal Precedent of Dred Scott*. New York, NY: Simon & Schuster, 2005.

Muhammad, Elijah. *History of the Nation of Islam*. Phoenix, AZ: MEMPS (Messenger Elijah Muhammad Propagation Society), 2008.

Murphy, Patricia J. *Garrett Morgan: Inventor of the Traffic Light and Gas Mask*. Berkeley Heights, NJ: Enslow Publishers, 2004.

Murrin, John M., Paul E. Johnson, James M. McPherson, and Gary Gerstle. *Liberty, Equality, Power: A History of the American People, Compact*. Independence, KY: Cengage Learning, 2007.

Nadell, Martha Jane. *Enter the New Negroes: Images of Race in American Culture*. Cambridge, MA: Harvard University Press, 2004.

Naden, Corinne J. *Ronald McNair*. New York, NY: Chelsea House, 1990.

Nagle, Jeanne M. *Oprah Winfrey: Profile of a Media Mogul*. New York, NY: The Rosen Publishing Group, 2007.

The National Archives. Digitized version of the original Emancipation Proclamation www .archives.gov/exhibits/featured_documents/emancipation_proclamation/transcript.html.

National Association for the Advancement of Colored People. *NAACP: Celebrating a Century: 100 Years in Pictures*. Layton, Utah: Gibbs Smith, 2009.

The National Black United Front. "The John Henrik Clarke Virtual Museum" Website http:// www.nbufront.org/MastersMuseums/JHClarke/JHCvmuseum.html.

National Equal Rights League. *Proceedings of the First Annual Meeting of the National Equal Rights League Held in Cleveland, Ohio, October 19, 20, and 21, 1865*. Charleston, SC: Nabu Press, 2010.

National Urban League. *Records of the National Office of the National Urban League for the period 1910–60*. Washington, DC: Library of Congress, 1976.

Neal, Mark Anthony. "What Would Shirley Chisholm Say?" in *Who Should Be First?: Feminists Speak Out on the 2008 Presidential Campaign* edited by Beverly Guy-Sheftall, Johnnetta B. Cole. Albany, NY: SUNY Press, 2010.

Nemec, David. *Players of Cooperstown: Baseball's Hall of Fame*. Lincolnwood, IL: Publications International, 1995.

Nemiroff, Robert. *To Be Young, Gifted and Black: An Informal Autobiography*. New York: Signet, 1970.

Nettles, Darryl Glenn. *African American Concert Singers Before 1950*. Jefferson, NC: McFarland, 2003.

Newman, Mark. *Divine Agitators: The Delta Ministry and Civil Rights in Mississippi*. Athens, Georgia: University of Georgia Press, 2004.

Newman, Richard S. *Freedom's Prophet: Bishop Richard Allen, the AME Church, and the Black Founding Fathers*. New York: NYU Press, 2008.

Nisenson, Eric. *Ascension: John Coltrane and His Quest*. Cambridge, MA: Da Capo Press, 1995.

Norrell, Robert Jefferson. *Up from History*. Cambridge, MA: Harvard University Press, 2009.

Nyang, Sulayman Sheih. *Islam in the United States of America*. Chicago, IL: ABC International Group, 1999.

Obama, Barack. *Barack Obama: What He Believes in from His Own Works*. Rockville, MD: Arc Manor LLC, 2008.

Obama, Barack edited by Tim Davidson. *The Essential Obama: The Speeches of Barack Obama*. Chicago, IL: Aquitaine Media Corp, 2009.

Ogletree, Charles J. *All Deliberate Speed: Reflections on the First Half-Century of Brown v. Board of Education*. New York: W. W. Norton & Company, 2004Richardson, Julieanna L. *An Evening with Harry Belafonte & Danny Glover / a History Makers Production*. New York: Carousel Film & Video, 2003.

Oliver, Paul. *The Story of the Blues*. Lebanon, NH: UPNE/ Northeastern University Press, 1998.

Oliver, Paul, Max Harrison and William Bolcom. *The New Grove Gospel, Blues and Jazz: With Spirituals and Ragtime*. New York, NY: Dafina Books/ Kensington Publishing Corp, 2002.

Oluonye, Mary N. *Garrett Augustus Morgan: Businessman, Inventor, Good Citizen*. Bloomington, In: AuthorHouse, 2008.

O'Neale, Sondra Ann. *Jupiter Hammon and the Biblical Beginnings of African-American Literature*. Lanham, MD: Scarecrow Press, 1993.

Osagie, Iyunolu Folayan. *The Amistad Revolt: Memory, Slavery, and the Politics of Identity in the United States and Sierra Leone*. Athens, Georgia: University of Georgia Press, 2003.

Otfinoski, Steven. *African Americans in the Performing Arts*. New York, NY: Infobase Publishing, 2003.

Owens, L. L. *The Great Chicago Fire*. Edina, MN: ABDO, 2007.

Paradis, Wilfrid H. *Black August: Origins, History, and Significance*. Victoria, BC: AbeBooks/Books 4 Prisoners Crew, 2004.

Parker, Marjorie H. *Alpha Kappa Alpha Through the Years, 1908–1988*. Chicago Mobium Press, 1990.

Parker, Pearl T. *A Political Activist: Charles Coles Diggs, Jr., Michigan's First Black Congressman*. Victoria, BC: AbeBooks/Tennessee State University., 1984.

Parks, Rosa with James Haskins. *Rosa Parks: My Story*. Newton, KS: Paw Prints, 2009.

Pastras, Philip. *Dead Man Blues: Jelly Roll Morton Way Out West*. Berkeley, CA: University of California Press, 2003.

Paterra, M. Elizabeth. *Kweisi Mfume: Congressman and NAACP Leader*. Berkeley Heights, NJ: Enslow, 2001.

Patrick, John J. *Founding the Republic: A Documentary History*. Santa Anna, CA: Greenwood Publishing Group, 1995.

Partridge, Elizabeth. *Marching for Freedom: Walk Together, Children, and Don't You Grow Weary*. New York, NY: Penguin, 2009.

Patterson, Tiffany Ruby. *Zora Neale Hurston and a History of Southern Life*. Philadelphia, PA: Temple University Press, 2005.

Pearlman, Jeff. *Sweetness: The Enigmatic Life of Walter Payton*. New York, NY: Penguin, 2011.

Pearson, Edward A. *Designs Against Charleston: The Trial Record of the Denmark Vesey Slave Conspiracy of 1822*. Chapel Hill, NC: University of North Carolina Press, 1999.

Peretti, Burton William. *Lift Every Voice: The History of African American Music*. Lanham, MD: Rowman & Littlefield, 2009.

Perry, Dayn. *Reggie Jackson: The Life and Thunderous Career of Baseball's Mr. October*. New York, N.Y.: HarperCollinss, 2010.

Persons, Georgia Anne. *Dilemmas of Black Politics: Issues of Leadership and Strategy*. New York, NY: HarperCollins, 1993.

Peterson, Oscar with Richard Palmer. *Jazz Odyssey: My Life in Jazz*. New York, NY: Continuum Intl Pub Group, 2006.

Peterson, Oscar. *Oscar Peterson-Jazz Exercises, Minuets, Etudes and Pieces for Piano*. Milwaukee, WI: Hal Leonard, 2005.

Pfeffer, Paula F. *A. Philip Randolph, Pioneer of the Civil Rights Movement*. Baton Rouge, LA: Louisiana State University Press, 1996.

Phelps, J. Alfred. *They Had a Dream: The Story of African-American Astronauts*. New York, NY: Presidio/Random House, 1994.

Phillips, Clarenda M. *African American Fraternities and Sororities: The Legacy and the Vision*. Lexington, KY: University Press of Kentucky, 2005.

Pinkney, Alphonso. *Red, Black, and Green: Black Nationalism in the United States*. New York, NY: Cambridge University Press, 1979.

Plummer, Brenda Gayle. *Window On Freedom: Race, Civil Rights, and Foreign Affairs, 1945–1988*. Chapel Hill, NC: UNC Press Books, 2003.

Pohlmann, Marcus D. and Linda Vallar Whisenhunt. *Student's Guide to Landmark Congressional Laws on Civil Rights*. Santa Barbara, CA: Greenwood Publishing Group, 2002.

Poitier, Sidney. *Life Beyond Measure: Letters to My Great-Granddaughter*. New York, NY: Harper Collins, 2009.

Potter, Joan. *African American Firsts: Famous Little-Known and Unsung Triumphs of Blacks*. New York, NY: Dafina Books/ Kensington Publishing Corp, 2002.

Preszler, June. *Juneteenth: Jubilee for Freedom*. Mankato, MN: Capstone Press, 2006.

Pursell, Carroll W., editor. *A Hammer in Their Hands: A Documentary History of Technology and the African-American Experience*. Cambridge MA: MIT Press, 2005.

Quarles, Benjamin. *Allies for Freedom: Blacks and John Brown*. Cambridge, MA: Da Capo Press, 2001.

Quarles, Benjamin. *The Negro in the Making of America*. New York NY: Simon & Schuster, 1996.

Ragsdale, Bruce A. and Joel D. Treese. *Black Americans in Congress, 1870–1989*. Darby, PA: DIANE Publishing, 1996.

Ratliff, Ben. *Coltrane: The Story of a Sound*. New York, NY: Macmillan, 2008.

Reef, Catherine. *African Americans in the Military*. New York, NY: Infobase Publishing, 2009.

Reich, Howard and William Gaines. *Jelly's Blues: The Life, Music, and Redemption of Jelly Roll Morton*. Cambridge, MA: Da Capo Press, 2004.

Remini, Robert Vincent. *The House: The History of the House of Representatives*. New York, NY: Smithsonian Books/Library of Congress/HarperCollins, 2006.

Resnick, Abraham. *They Too Influenced a Nation's History: The Unique Contributions of 105 Lesser-Known Americans*. Lincoln, NE: iUniverse, 2003.

Reverby, Susan M. *Examining Tuskegee: The Infamous Syphilis Study and its Legacy*. Chapel Hill, NC: UNC Press Books, 2009.

Richardson, Joe Martin. *A History of Fisk University, 1865–1946*. Tuscaloosa, AL: University of Alabama Press, 1980.

Rivers, Larry E. and Canter Brown. *Laborers in the Vineyard of the Lord: The Beginnings of the AME Church in Florida, 1865–1895*. Gainesville, FL: University Press of Florida, 2001.

Robertson, David. *W.C. Handy: The Life and Times of the Man Who Made the Blues*. New York, NY: Random House Digital, Inc., 2009.

Robertson, Natalie S. *The Slave Ship Clotilda and the Making of AfricaTown, USA: Spirit of Our Ances-tors*. New York, NY: Praeger, 2008.

Robeson Jr., Paul. *The Undiscovered Paul Robeson, An Artist's Journey, 1898–1939*. Hoboken, NJ: John Wiley & Sons, 1 edition. March 2, 2001.

Robinson, Harry G., and Hazel Ruth Edwards. *The Long Walk: The Placemaking Legacy of Howard University*. Washington, DC: Moorland-Spingarn Research Center, Howard University, 1996.

Robinson, Jackie, edited by Michael G. Long. *First Class Citizenship: The Civil Rights Letters of Jackie Robinson*. New York, NY: Macmillan, 2007.

Robinson, Tiny and John Reynolds. *Lead Belly: A Life in Pictures*. Santa Ana, CA: Seven Locks Press, 1989.

Roby, Steven. *Black Gold: The Lost Archives of Jimi Hendrix*. New York, N.Y.: Billboard Books, 2002.

Rodriguez, Junius P. *Slavery in the United States: A Social, Political, and Historical Encyclopedia, Volume 2*. Santa Barbara, CA: ABC-CLIO, 2007.

Rodriguez, Robert. *The 1950s' Most Wanted: The Top 10 Book of Rock & Roll Rebels, Cold War Crises, and All-American Oddities*. Dulles, VA: Potomac Books, Inc., 2006.

Rogers, Joel Augustus. *From "Superman" to Man*. Ann Arbor, MI: AbeBooks/Helga M. Rogers, 1957.

Rogers, Joel Augustus. *World's Great Men of Color, Volume 2*. New York, NY: Simon & Schuster, 1996.

Roskill, Andrew. *Althea Gibson: Breaking the Color Barrier in Tennis*. New York, NY: Webster's Digital Services, 2010.

Ross, Lawrence C. Jr., *The Divine Nine: The History of African American Fraternities and Sororities* New York: Kensington Publishing Corporation, 2002.

Rummel, Jack. *African-American Social Leaders and Activists*. New York, NY: Infobase Publishing, 2003.

Russell, Dick and Alvin F. Poussaint. *Black Genius: Inspirational Portraits of America's Black Leaders*. New York: Skyhorse Publishing Inc., 2009.

Rustin, Bayard, Devon W. Carbado and Donald Weise. *Time on Two Crosses: The Collected Writings of Bayard Rustin*. Berkeley, CA: Cleis Press, 2003.

Rutkoff, Peter M. and Alvin L. Hall, editors. *The Cooperstown Symposium on Baseball and American cul-ture, 1997 (Jackie Robinson)*. Jefferson, NC: McFarland, 2000.

Said, Omar Ibn, translated by Ala Alryyes. *A Muslim American Slave: The Life of Omar Ibn Said*. Madison, WI: Univ of Wisconsin Press, 2011.

Santoro, Gene. *Myself When I Am Real: The Life and Music of Charles Mingus*. New York, NY: Oxford University Press, 2001.

Sargent, Frederic O. *The Civil Rights Revolution: Events and Leaders, 1955–1968*. Jefferson NC: McFarland, 2004.

Schecter, Barnet. *The Devil's Own Work: The Civil War Draft Riots and the Fight to Reconstruct America*. London, England: Bloomsbury Publishing USA, 2007.

Schmoke, Kurt L., Seth M. Kronemer, Jacqueline C. Young. *A Legacy of Defending the Constitution: Howard University School of Law: 1869–2009*. Washington, DC: Howard University School of Law, 2009.

The Schomburg Center for Research in Black Culture. "Legacy Exhibition: John Henrik Clarke Section" available online http://www.nypl.org/research/sc/WEBEXHIB/legacy/imgins15.htm.

Schneider, Mark. *Boston Confronts Jim Crow, 1890–1920*. Lebanon, NH: University Press of New England (UPNE), 1997.

Schroeder, Alan. *In Her Hands: The Story of Sculptor Augusta Savage*. New York, NY: Lee & Low Books, 2009.

Scipio, Louis Albert. *Last of the Black regulars: A History of the 24th Infantry Regiment (1869–1951)*. Houston, TX: Roman Publications, 1983.

Scott, Rebecca Jarvis. *Degrees of Freedom: Louisiana and Cuba After Slavery*. Cambridge, MA: Harvard University Press, 2005.

Sernett, Milton C. *African American Religious History: A Documentary Witness*. Durham, NC: Duke University Press, 1999.

Sethi, S. Prakash and Oliver F. Williams. *Economic Imperatives and Ethical Values in Global Business: The South African Experience and International Codes Today*. New York, NY: Springer, 2000.

Shawkey, Morris Purdy. *West Virginia, in History, Life, Literature and Industry, Volume 2*. Victoria, BC: AbeBooks/The Lewis publishing company, 1928.

Shea, Therese. *John Lee Hooker: Master of Boogie and Blues*. New York, NY: Gareth Stevens, 2010.

Sheehy, Barry, Cindy Wallace, and Vaughnette Goode-Walker. *Savannah, Immortal City*. Austin, TX: Greenleaf Book Group, 2011.

Sherrow, Victoria. *Uniquely South Carolina*. Chicago, IL: Heinemann-Raintree Library, 2004.

Shipton, Alyn. *Jazz makers: Vanguards of Sound*. New York, NY: Oxford University Press, 2002.

Sikora, Frank. *Until Justice Rolls Down: The Birmingham Church Bombing Case*. Tuscaloosa, AL: University of Alabama Press, 1991.

Silver, Christopher and John V. Moeser. *The Separate City: Black Communities in the Urban South, 1940–1968*. Lexington, KY: University Press of Kentucky, 1995.

Simone, Nina. *The Nina Simone Piano Songbook*. London, England: Faber Music, 2008.

Singh, Nikhil Pal. *Black is a Country: Race and the Unfinished Struggle for Democracy*. Cambridge, MA: Harvard University Press, 2004.

Sluby, Patricia Carter. *The Inventive Spirit of African Americans: Patented Ingenuity* Westport, Ct: Greenwood Publishing Group, 2004.

Smalls, Charlie, Lyman Frank Baum and William Ferdinand Brown. *The Wiz: Adapted from "The Wonderful Wizard of Oz" by L. Frank Baum*. New York: Samuel French, Inc., 1979.

Smith, Jessie Carney. *Black Firsts: 4,000 Ground-Breaking and Pioneering Historical Events*. Canton, MI: Visible Ink Press, 2003.

Smith, Jessie Carney. *Powerful Black Women*. Canton, MI: Visible Ink Press, 1996.

Smith, Jr., J. Clay. *Rebels in Law: Voices in History of Black Women Lawyers*. Ann Arbor, MI: J. L. Nichols & Co./ University of Michigan, 1902.

Smith, Jr., J. Clay and Thurgood Marshall. *Emancipation: The Making of the Black Lawyer, 1844–1944*. Baton Rouge, LA: LSU Press, 2007.

Smith, Judith E. *Visions of Belonging: Family Stories, Popular Culture, and Postwar Democracy, 1940–1960*. New York, NY: Columbia University Press, 2004.

Smith, Mark Michael. *Stono: Documenting and Interpreting a Southern Slave Revolt*. Columbia, SC: University of South Carolina Press, 2005.

Smith, Norman R. *Footprints of Black Louisiana*. Bloomington, IN: Xlibris Corporation, 2011

Smith, Susan Lynn. *Sick and Tired of Being Sick and Tired: Black Women's Health Activism in America, 1890–1950*. Philadelphia, PA: University of Pennsylvania Press, 1995.

Smith, Tommie and David Steele. *Silent Gesture: The Autobiography of Tommie Smith*. Philadelphia, PA: Temple University Press, 2007.

Smith, Willie the Lion with George Hoefer. *Music on My Mind, The Memoirs of an American Pianist*. New York City: Doubleday & Company Inc., 1964.

Solomon, Mark I. *The Cry was Unity: Communists and African Americans, 1917–36*. Jackson, MS: Univ. Press of Mississippi, 1998.

Southall, Geneva Handy. *Blind Tom, the Black Pianist-Composer: Continually Enslaved*. Lanham, MD: Scarecrow Press, 2002.

Southern Women's Institute. *Golden Days: Reminiscences of Alumnae, Mississippi State College for Women*. Jackson, MS: Univ. Press of Mississippi, 2008.

Spann, Edward K. *Gotham at War: New York City, 1860–1865*. Lanham MD: Rowman & Littlefield, 2002.

Spartacus Educational. William Lloyd Garrison biography http://www.spartacus.schoolnet.co.uk/USASgarrison.htm.

Spencer, Frederick J. *Jazz and Death: Medical Profiles of Jazz Greats*. Washington, DC: Univ. Press of Mississippi, 2002.

Stanton, Mary. *Freedom Walk: Mississippi or Bust*. Jackson, MS: Univ. Press of Mississippi, 2003.

Starr, Kevin. *The Dream Endures: California Enters the 1940s*. New York, NY: Oxford University Press, 1926.

Starr, Michael Seth. *Black and Blue: The Redd Foxx Story*. Milwaukee, WI: Hal Leonard Books/Applause Theatre & Cinema, 2011.

Stephenson, D. Grier. *The Right to Vote: Rights and Liberties Under the Law*. Santa Barbara, CA: ABC-CLIO, 2004.

Stockley, Grif. *Blood in Their Eyes: The Elaine Race Massacres of 1919*. Fayetteville, AR: University of Arkansas Press, 2004.

Stokes, Carl B. *Promises of Power: A Political Autobiography*. New York, NY: Simon & Schuster, 1973.

Stone, Eddie. *Jesse Jackson*. Los Angeles, Ca: Holloway House Publishing, 1988.

Stowell, Jay S. *Methodist Adventures in Negro Education*. Ann Arbor, MI: The Methodist book concern/University of Michigan, 2007.

Sugrue, Thomas J. *Sweet Land of Liberty: The Forgotten Struggle for Civil Rights in the North*. New York, NY: Random House, Inc., 2009.

Sullivan, Otha Richard and James Haskins. *African American Inventors*. Hoboken, NJ: John Wiley & Sons, 1998.

Swain, Carol M. *Black Faces, Black Interests: The Representation of African Americans in Congress*. Lanham, MD: Rowman & Littlefield, 2006.

Sweeney, Fionnghuala. *Frederick Douglass and the Atlantic World*. Chicago: University of Chicago Press, 2007.

Szwed, John. *So What: The Life of Miles Davis*. New York, NY: Simon & Schuster, 2004.

Taylor, Charles A. *Juneteenth: A Celebration of Freedom*. Greensboro, NC: Open Hand Publishing, LLC, 2002.

Taylor, Marshall W. *The Fastest Bicycle Rider in the World: The Story of a Colored Boy's Indomitable Courage and Success Against Great Odds*. Freeport, N.Y.: Books for Libraries Press, 1928.

Taylor, Quintard. *In Search of the Racial Frontier: African Americans in the American West, 1528–1990*. New York, NY: W. W. Norton & Company, 1999.

Taylor, Quintard and Shirley Ann Wilson Moore, editors. *African American Women Confront the West, 1600–2000*.

Taylor, Stephen. *Fats Waller on the Air: The Radio Broadcasts and Discography*. Lanham, MD: Scarecrow Press, 2006.

Terrill, Robert. *Malcolm X: Inventing Radical Judgment*. East Lansing, MI: MSU Press, 2004.

Thomas, Brook. *Plessy v. Ferguson: A Brief History with Documents*. New York, NY: Bedford Books, 1997.

Thomas, Hugh. *The Slave Trade: The Story of the Atlantic Slave Trade, 1440–1870*. New York: Simon & Schuster, 1999.

Thomas, Piri. *Down These Mean Streets*. New York, NY: Vintage Books, 1997.

Thomas, Ron. *They Cleared the Lane: The NBA's Black Pioneers*. Lincoln, NE: University of Nebraska Press, 2004.

Thornton, John K. "African Dimensions of the Stono Rebellion." In *A Question of Manhood: A Reader in U.S. Black Men's History and Masculinity, vol. 1*. Ed. Darlene Clark Hine and Earnestine Jenkins. Bloomington, IN: Indiana University Press, 1999.

Till Mobley, Mamie. *Death of Innocence: The Story of Hate Crime that Changed America*, an autobiography written with Christoper Benson. New York: Random House, October 7, 2003.

Tindall, George Brown. *South Carolina Negroes, 1877–1900*. New York, NY: University of South Carolina Press, 2003.

Tolson, Melvin Beaunorus, edited by Raymond Nelson. *"Harlem Gallery", and Other Poems of Melvin B. Tolson.* Charlottesville, VA: University Press of Virginia, 1999.

Towle, Wendy. *The Real Mccoy: The Life of an African-American Inventor.* Logan, IA: Perfection Learning Corporation, 1995.

Tripp, L. O. *African-American Astronauts: Guion S. Bluford, Jr., Charles F. Bolden, Jr., Frederick D. Gregory, Bernard A. Harris, Jr., Mae C. Jemison.* Mankato, MN: Capstone Pr Inc, 2000.

Truth, Sojourner with Olive Gilbert and Nell Irvin Painter. *Narrative of Sojourner Truth: A Bondswoman of Olden Time, with a History of Her Labors and Correspondence Drawn from Her Book of Life.* New York, NY: Penguin Classics, 1998.

Tuck, Stephen G. N. *We Ain't What We Ought to Be: The Black Freedom Struggle from Emancipation to Obama.* Cambridge, MA: Harvard University Press, 2010.

Tucker, Phillip Thomas. *Cathy Williams: From Slave to Buffalo Soldier.* Mechanicsburg, PA: Stackpole Books, 2002.

Tuttle, Brad R. *How Newark Became Newark: The Rise, Fall, and Rebirth of an American City.* Piscataway, NJ: Rutgers University Press, 2009.

The University of Southern Mississippi—McCain Library and Archives. *Dahmer (Vernon F.) Collection.* Hattiesburg, MS: University of Southern Mississippi Libraries Special Collections, 1999.

Urban, Wayne J. *Black Scholar: Horace Mann Bond, 1904–1972.* Athens, GA: University of Georgia Press, 2008.

Urquhart, Brian. *Ralph Bunche: An American Odyssey.* New York, NY: W. W. Norton & Company, 1998.

Uzzel, Robert L. *Blind Lemon Jefferson: His Life, His Death, and His Legacy.* Waco, TX: Eakin Press, 2002.

Vail, Ken. *Dizzy Gillespie: The Bebop Years, 1937–1952.* Lanham, MD: Scarecrow Press, 2003.

Ventura, Varla. *Sheroes: Bold, Brash, and Absolutely Unabashed Superwomen from Susan B. Anthony to Xena.* San Francisco, CA: Conari Press, 1998.

Vine, Phyllis. *One Man's Castle: Clarence Darrow in Defense of the American Dream.* New York, NY: HarperCollins, 2005.

Vorenberg, Michael. *Final Freedom: The Civil War, the Abolition of Slavery, and the Thirteenth Amendment.* New York, NY: Cambridge University Press, 2001.

Vose, Clement. *Caucasians Only: The Supreme Court, the NAACP, and the Restrictive Covenant Cases.* New York: University of California Press, 1992.

Wald, Gayle F. *Shout, Sister, Shout!: The Untold Story of Rock-and-Roll Trailblazer Sister Rosetta Tharpe.* Boston, MA: Beacon Press, 2007.

Waldrep, Christopher. *Racial Violence on Trial: A Handbook with Cases, Laws, and Documents.* Santa Barbara, CA: ABC-CLIO, 2001.

Walker, David. *David Walker's Appeal to the Coloured Citizens of the World.* University Park, PA: Penn State Press, 2000.

Ward, Andrew. *The Slaves' War: The Civil War in the Words of Former Slaves.* Orlando, FL: Houghton Mifflin Harcourt, 2008.

Ware, Susan. *Modern American Women: A Documentary History.* New York, NY: McGraw-Hill, 2001.

Washington, Booker T. *The Story of the Negro; The Rise of the Race from Slavery, Vol II.* New York, NY: Doubleday/General Books LLC, 2010.

Washington, Booker T. *Up from Slavery: An Autobiography, an African American Heritage Book.* Radford, VA: A&D Publishing/Wilder Publications, 2008.

Watson, Wilbur H. *Against the Odds: Blacks in the Profession of Medicine in the United States.* Piscataway, NJ: Transaction Publishers, 1999.

Weaver, Robert Clifton. *Negro Labor; A National Problem.* Victoria, BC: AbeBooks/Kennikat Press, 1969.

Weaver, Robert Clifton and William E. Zisch. *The Urban Environment: How it Can Be Improved.* Victoria, BC: AbeBooks/New York University Press, 1969.

Webster, Laura Josephine. *The Operation of the Freedmen's Bureau in South Carolina, Volume 1, Issue 2.* Northampton, MA: Department of History of Smith College, 1916.

Weiss, Nancy Joan. *The National Urban League, 1910–1940.* New York, NY: Oxford University Press, 1974.

Weiss, Stuart L. *The Curt Flood Story: The Man Behind the Myth.* Columbia, MO: University of Missouri Press, 2007.

Wells Brown, William. *The Black Man: His Antecedents, His Genius, and His Achievements.* Boston, MA: J. Redpath, 1863.

West, Michael Oliver, William G. Martin, and Fanon Che Wilkins. *From Toussaint to Tupac: The Black International Since the Age of Revolution.* Chapel Hill, NC: UNC Press Books, 2009.

Wilkens, Lenny with Terry Pluto. *Unguarded: My Forty Years Surviving in the NBA.* New York, NY: Simon & Schuster, 2001.

Williams, David Salter. *From Mounds to Megachurches: Georgia's Religious Heritage.* Athens, Georgia: University of Georgia Press, 2008.

Williams, Elsie A. *The Humor of Jackie "Moms" Mabley: An African American Comedic Tradition.* New York, NY: Garland Publishing, 1995.

Williams, Paul R. *The Small Home of Tomorrow.* Santa Monica, CA: Hennessey & Ingalls, 2006.

Wilson, August, with an introduction by Toni Morrison. *The Piano Lesson.* New York, NY: Theatre Communications Group, 2007.

Wilson, Donald, and Jane Wilson. *The Pride of African American History.* Bloomington, IN: 1st Books Library, 2003.

Willson, Joseph, edited by Julie Winch. *The Elite of Our People: Joseph Willson's Sketches of Black Upper-Class Life in Antebellum Philadelphia.* University Park, PA: Penn State Press, 2000.

Wimbush, Vincent L. and Rosamond C. Rodman. *African Americans and the Bible: Sacred Texts and Social Textures.* Harrisburg, PA: Continuum International Publishing Group, 2001.

Wolper, David L. with David Fisher. *Producer: A Memoir.* New York, NY: Simon & Schuster, 2003.

Women of color/Women of Words http://www.scils.rutgers.edu/~cybers/hansberry2.html.

Wolf, Naomi. *Give Me Liberty: A Handbook for American Revolutionaries.* New York, NY: Simon & Schuster, 2008.

Woods, Tricia. *Complete Blues Keyboard Method: Beginning Blues Keyboard, Book & CD.* Van Nuys, CA: Alfred Publishing, 1999.

Woodson, Carter Godwin. *The Mis-Education of the Negro.* Scotts Valley, CA: ReadaClassic.com/CreateSpace, 1972.

Woodstra, Chris, Gerald Brennan and Allen Schrott. *All Music Guide to Classical Music: The Definitive Guide to Classical Music.* Milwaukee, WI: Hal Leonard Corporation, 2005.

Wright, Stephen Caldwell. *On Gwendolyn Brooks: Reliant Contemplation.* Ann Arbor, MI: University of Michigan Press, 2001.

X, Malcolm with Alex Haley. *Autobiography of Malcolm X.* New York, NY: Penguin Popular Classics, 2007.

Young, Andrew. *An Easy Burden: The Civil Rights Movement and the Transformation of America.* Waco, TX: Baylor University Press, 2008.

Young, Andrew and Kabir Sehgal. *Walk in My Shoes: Conversations Between a Civil Rights Legend and His Godson on the Journey Ahead.* New York, NY: Macmillan, 2010.

Zannes, Estelle. *Checkmate in Cleveland: The Rhetoric of Confrontation During the Stokes Years.* Cleveland, OH: Press of Case Western Reserve University, 1972.

Zinn, Howard. *SNCC: The New Abolitionists.* Cambridge, MA: South End Press, 2002.

Zinn, Howard. *A People's History of the United States, 1492-present.* New York, NY: HarperCollins, 2003.

Zolten, Jerry. *Great God A'Mighty! the Dixie Hummingbirds: Celebrating the Rise of Soul Gospel Music.* Santa Monica, CA: Oxford University Press, USA, 2003.

Zuczek, Richard. *Encyclopedia of the Reconstruction Era: A-L.* Albany, NY: SUNY Press, 2005.

Index

About the Author

KAREN JUANITA CARRILLO is a Brooklyn, New York-based writer and photographer. She specializes in covering African American and Afro-Latino history, literature, and politics.

In 2002, she was awarded the National Newspapers Publishers Association's "Perspective Reporting Award: For human-interest coverage of the impact of September 11th, highlighting diverse perspectives in African American communities." In 2003, she was a New California Media Awards winner in the "Civil Liberties" reporting category. In 2005, she received the New York Association of Black Journalists' first prize award for "General/Spot News" reporting, and in 2008, she won the NYABJ's second place prize award for "International News" reporting.

Karen Juanita Carrillo is a co-founder of the non-profit organization, Afropresencia.com. Carrillo is the author of *The View from Chocó: The Afro-Colombian Past, Their Lives in the Present, and Their Hopes for the Future* (2010). Carrillo has lectured and published articles and photographs in numerous publications in the United States, South America, and Europe.